D1626502

**GEARRFAR FÍNEÁIL AR DHAOINE A BHFUIL
LEABHAIR THAR TÉARMA ACU**

FINES WILL BE CHARGED ON OVERDUE BOOKS

AR AIS FAOIN DÁTA DATE DUE	AR AIS FAOIN DÁTA DATE DUE

A History of the Conservative Party

Volume One
The Foundation of the Conservative Party
1830–1867
Robert Stewart

Volume Two
The Rise of the Tory Democracy 1867–1902
Paul Addison

Volume Three
The Age of Balfour and Baldwin 1902–1940
John Ramsden

Volume Four
From Affluence to Disillusion 1940–1974
John Barnes

A History of the Conservative Party

The Foundation
of the Conservative Party
1830–1867

Robert Stewart

Longman
London and New York

Longman Group Limited London

*Associated companies, branches and representatives
throughout the world*

*Published in the United States of America
by Longman Inc., New York*

© Robert Stewart 1978

First published 1978

ISBN 0 582 50712 X

Library of Congress Cataloging in Publication Data

Stewart, Robert MacKenzie.
  A history of the Conservative Party.

  Bibliography: p.
  Includes index.
  CONTENTS: Stewart, R The foundation of the Conservative Party, 1830–1867.
  1. Conservative Party (GT. Brit.)—History.
I. Title.
JN1129. C7S85   329.9'41   77–3280
ISBN 0-582-50712-X (v. 1)

Set in 11 point Bembo by Woolaston Parker Ltd, Leicester
and printed in Great Britain by Richard Clay (The Chaucer Press) Ltd, Bungay, Suffolk

Contents

Part I   The Tory ancestry: The age of Liverpool and Wellington

Part II   The age of Peel

Part III The age of Derby

List of illustrations

Acknowledgements

I wish to thank the British Academy and the Twenty-Seven Foundation for the research grants which they awarded to me while this book was being written. I wish also to thank Lord Blake for allowing me to use at length the Derby Papers, which are in his keeping. John Vincent, with characteristic generosity, lent to me his photocopies of the Stanley diaries; the Earl of Derby has very kindly given permission to quote from them. Sir Phillip Rose allowed me to use the election notebooks of his namesake and ancestor. I am grateful to him and also to Bernard Gill, who transcribed for me two very long and important letters of Rose in Sir Phillip's possession. Hugh Cameron brought to my attention certain letters in the Hardinge Papers and allowed me to use his transcriptions of them. Hugh Hanley directed me to the Archdeacon MSS, deposited at the Buckinghamshire Record Office, and Timothy McCann guided me to relevant portions of the Goodwood MSS, deposited at the Sussex Record Office. The Broadlands MSS have been used with the permission of the trustees of the Broadland Archives.

We are grateful to the following for permission to reproduce copyright material:
Author's Agent for an extract from *Journals of Mrs. Arbuthnot* by Francis Bamford and the Duke of Wellington, published by Macmillan; Ernest Benn Ltd. for extracts from *Three Early 19th Century Diaries* (1952) by A. Aspinall, published by Williams & Norgate; The Controller of Her Majesty's Stationery Office for extracts from the *Prime Ministers' Papers: Gladstone Volumes*; The author for extracts from his unpublished D.Phil. thesis 1968 by T. J. Nossiter; Royal Historical Society for extracts from *Correspondence of Arbuthnot* by A. Aspinall 1941 and *Formation of Canning's Ministry* by A. Aspinall.

We regret that we have been unable to trace the authors of two unpublished M.A. Theses by L. Jones and G. B. Kent and would appreciate any information that would enable us to do so.

Abbreviations used in references

Add.MSS	British Museum Additional Manuscripts
Blackwood's	*Blackwood's Magazine*
Econ.HR	*Economic History Review*
EHR	*English Historical Review*
Eng.Hist.Docs	*English Historical Documents*
Hist J	*Historical Journal*
J Brit.Stud.	*Journal of British Studies*
J Eccles.Hist.	*Journal of Ecclesiastical History*
J. Econ. Hist.	*Journal of Economic History*
JMH	*Journal of Modern History*
Proc.Brit.Acad.	*Proceedings of the British Academy*
Trans.Roy.Hist.Soc.	*Transactions of the Royal Historical Society*

For Hilda Neatby.   In memoriam.

Introduction

It is sometimes said that Conservatives suffer from the want of a permanent ideology and a doctrinal literature. They are supposed to be ruled by their appetites, not their minds. 'Men are conservatives', Emerson held, 'when they are least vigorous, or when they are most luxurious. They are conservatives after dinner.'[1]* The Conservative party has always been, although far from exclusively, the party of the well fed. But a man's brain is not judged by the contents of his stomach. Conservatives themselves, at any rate, have seldom been embarrassed by their distaste for doctrine and their distrust of ideology. Radical ideology, arising from a conviction of what is right, employs the language of ethics and inhabits the future. Conservative theory, arising from events, employs the language of experience and dwells in the present. Conservatives do not renounce ideology because they scorn the intellect. Nor because they place a high value on order and stability are they careless of liberty, although Macaulay believed that they were.

> If, rejecting all that is merely accidental, we look at the essential characteristics of the Whig and the Tory, we may consider each of them as the representative of a great principle, essential to the welfare of nations. One is, in an especial manner, the guardian of liberty, and the other of order. One is the moving power, and the other the steadying power of the State. One is the sail, without which society would make no progress; the other the ballast, without which there would be no safety in a tempest.[2]

It flattered Macaulay's Whiggery to make devotion to liberty the preserve of his party. The Whigs were, indeed, descended from the champions of freedom of conscience and parliamentary government against religious uniformity and royal absolutism. But the English party system has never resolved itself into the simple opposition of order and liberty. Prescription, Disraeli told the House of Commons in 1852, was 'the most important element of order, of liberty, and of progress'; its violation was 'an element of disturbance', leading to discontent and offering a premium to extravagant projects.[3]

---

* References and notes at the end of this Preface and the end of each chapter.

For most of the nineteenth century the chief object of the Conservative party was to defend the weight in society and government of the monarchy, the landed interest, and the Church of England. As late as the 1880s, Lord Randolph Churchill, in reply to the question how far in the direction of liberalism a Tory democrat might go, said 'to any extent' provided that he did not abandon the monarchy, the House of Lords, the union of Great Britain and Ireland, and the connection between Church and State. Political quarrels within the Conservative party reflected differences of judgement about how, not whether, to safeguard these institutions when they were under siege from the advancing forces of industrialism, democracy, Irish nationalism, and religious Dissent. It was impossible to ignore certain facts: that the proportion of adult males employed in agriculture declined from one-third in 1831 to one-fifth in 1851, that by 1851, for the first time in English history, more than half the population lived in towns, or that by the same date Anglican worshippers were a majority in only three of the twenty-nine towns which that year's census returns listed as lying within the chief manufacturing districts of the nation. Rapid and visible changes in society gave rise to a succession of demands for legislative reform. To those demands there were, broadly speaking, three kinds of Conservative response.

There were, first, those Conservatives, known as the Ultras, who would resist to the last ditch and, if defeated, fight to regain the lost ground. There was no more virulent last-ditcher than the fourth Duke of Newcastle, who in 1829 made a frenzied, impractical effort to secure a Protestant government to replace Wellington's administration when Wellington conceded the necessity of Catholic emancipation. In 1832, when Wellington had once more offended Newcastle's sensibilities by toying with the idea of forming a government to carry a moderate parliamentary reform Bill, Gladstone, who was seeking to enter parliament at Newcastle's 'pocket' borough of Newark, recorded a conversation with his patron.

N. He [Wellington] is a calculating man, and indeed Mr Gladstone (I speak this privately) he is not a safe man. He would upon occasion yield anything from motives of expediency.

G. I suppose your Grace thinks, that he would resist manfully up to a certain point, and then make the best terms he could, and that he would deal with all questions alike upon this principle, and that there is nothing which he would not give up under sufficiently urgent circumstances.

N. I do think so . . . But this kind of conduct will not save the country. In my mind this is what a man should do – he should make up his mind, with as much moderation as he chooses, to the objects on behalf of which he deems it essential to make a stand; and when he has done this, no extremities should induce him to swerve. People must get into their right positions, and act upon their own principles, and rigidly adhere to them – nothing else will do for us, and I believe the time is not far distant when this will be the case.[4]

The mark of the Ultra was his elevation of consistency into the primary moral criterion by which a politician was to be judged. Fifteen years later, the heirs of Newcastle and the Ultras were Lord George Bentinck and those protectionists who refused to accept the decision of parliament to abolish the Corn Laws.

Then there were those Conservatives whom Huskisson called the 'sulkers', backbenchers who held 'that the Treasury bench should never take a step towards improvement, without the apology and discredit of compulsion, and without sustaining a previous defeat in an unavailing attempt to oppose it'.[5] They would not raise a finger to prosper reform. They resented the actions of government which introduced it. But they accepted the accomplished deed. Theirs was the central viewpoint of nineteenth-century Conservatism, adopted by Peel in 1831–32 and by Salisbury in 1867. It included the argument (a kind of 'domino theory') that the granting of one reform stimulated the demand for another. Concession was not entirely a conservative action, as Lord Grey claimed in 1831 and Peel in 1846. It contained a revolutionary implication. Conservatives ought, therefore, to hold out as long as possible. But once change had occurred, then it had to be accepted, since to attempt to reverse it would inflict upon the nation the very suffering and conflict which it was the duty of Conservatives to prevent. 'All that I hope for', Wellington confessed in 1836, 'is, that the change in the position of the country may be gradual, that it may be effected without civil war, and may occasion as little sudden destruction of individual interests and property as possible. We may all by degrees take our respective stations in the new order of things, and go on until further changes take place *ad infinitum*.'[6] When the Conservative government introduced its Reform Bill in 1867, Salisbury, eager to do everything in his power to prevent its passing, resigned from the cabinet. Once the Bill had become law, he advised Conservatives to recognize their duty 'to accept a political defeat cordially, and to lend their best endeavours to secure the success, or to neutralize the evil, of the principles to which they have been forced to succumb'.[7]

Of the third type of Conservative the most illustrious representative was Peel. He not only would have agreed with Mr Gresham, the Conservative leader in Trollope's *The Prime Minister*, that 'as the glorious institutions of the country are made to perish, it is better that they should receive the *coup de grâce* tenderly from loving hands than be roughly throttled by Radicals',[8] he carried the argument forward. Before the Reform Act of 1832 Peel recognized that a government could not last in defiance of public opinion. The intellectual task of a Conservative statesman was to judge the moment when public opinion was ripe and then act upon it. It was the point of view put by J. R. Ward in 1810.

> J[effrey] also says [in the *Edinburgh Review*, January 1818] that there ought to be a reform in Parliament, because the people wish for it. If the two propositions contained in this sentence form part of the Whig creed, all I can say is that I am a Tory. . . . I am by no means persuaded that the people's wishing for reform is a reason for *immediately* granting it to them. A *long continued* and *strongly expressed* wish

of the people of every country ought, no doubt, to be gratified; but it is the part of a wise and strong Government to resist popular clamour, to choose the proper season for granting requests, and to wait till it has had time to distinguish between the real permanent will of the country and a mere transitory cry.[9]

The Conservative ought not to ignore the movement of public opinion; it was not his role to foster it. Once persuaded that change was necessary, and therefore desirable, Peel was willing, as in 1829 and 1846, to make the Conservative party its agent.

Peel's attitude differed from Salisbury's only by degree, but the degree mattered. Peel's view had much to recommend it. Conservatives need not resist a change which they recognize to be an advance. On the other hand, their need to be convinced helps to force the reformers to do their homework. In that way Conservative resistance serves the nation's interest. The difficulty is to make coincide the moment when public opinion is ripe and the moment when the party is ready to act upon it. Salisbury's course was the safer, Peel's the more exciting. Neither had room for the Ultras and the last-ditchers. Yet the Conservative party accommodated all three strands of opinion. Their interaction, and the conflicts to which it gave rise, underlie the history of the party between 1815 and 1867.

All stories have to start somewhere. This book begins by tracing the ancestry of the Conservative party to the year 1794, the year in which events in revolutionary France and their repercussions in England led Englishmen, members of parliament and those outside who cared about such things, to align themselves with the forces of 'progress' or 'reaction'. To choose that date is to find the origin of the Conservative party, not yet called by that name, inside parliament. In 1951 the Research Department of the Labour party said of the Conservative party that it

> has always been primarily a *parliamentary party* . . . organized round a parliamentary leader, and owing no allegiance to any party organization in the country. The local Tory associations and their national federations are mere adjuncts to this parliamentary machine. . . . The Tory party is a grouping of Tory politicians round a parliamentary leader.[10]

That description, however true of the party now, is broadly accurate of the party before 1867. In that regard the Conservative party was no different from the Whigs and Liberals. Mid-Victorian political parties were, as H. J. Hanham has described them, 'the instruments through which the politicians at Westminster worked upon the constituencies'.[11] Party organization and constituency organization were not exactly the same thing. Nor are they today. In June 1974 the political correpondent of the *Daily Telegraph* pointed out that, although the Conservative leadership had not recommended Conservative–Liberal pacts in certain constituencies to defeat Labour candidates, 'Conservative constituency organizations are practically autonomous, and the party's central organization could do nothing to prevent them from making such local arrangements as they thought fit'.[12] But whereas the exercise of constituency independence is now rare, in mid-Victorian England it was the rule. The spread of the Conservative organization outward from Westminster was cautious and uneven. As late as 1867 there were many constituencies without any official Conservative organization.

The function of the central party managers in the years between 1832 and 1867 was not so much to construct a regular pattern of constituency organizations throughout the country as it was to use the various forms of local politics for the benefit of Conservative candidates. Conservative politicians were not much interested in narrowing the gap between parliamentary politics and local politics. They abhorred the radical notion that members of parliament ought to behave as delegates. In a way, the party managers at Westminister were interested in making the electors vote Conservative, not in making them Conservatives. That was a realistic assessment of the limits of organization in a political system in which voting reflected many things besides opinion, above all the influence of landed property. Opinion often worked upon the electorate, especially in the counties and small boroughs, in an indirect fashion. In the village of Rattery, in Devonshire South, twenty of the twenty-one electors were tenants of Sir Walter Carew. At the 1832 elections Carew voted for the Whig candidate and his tenants followed suit. At the by-election of 1835 Carew went over to the Conservatives. So did his tenants.[13]

Landlord authority, however, was not complete. It depended less on the landlords' power over the material conditions of their tenants' lives, and more on the electors' genuine deference to their superiors. It is clear from the frequency with which they made the point that most landlords found coercive means of compelling a tenant's vote repugnant and that, given the choice, they preferred an efficient farmer to a politically docile one. Issues like parliamentary reform and agricultural protection could disrupt the even tenor of deferential polities. The gap between Westminster and the constituencies was not unbridgeable. Constituency pressure was often exerted upon members of parliament. The 'papal aggression' fever which infected the country in 1851 led to the Whig government's introduction of a Bill to make the assumption of territorial titles by Catholic divines illegal. It was a storm in a teapot, but many members of parliament were unwilling to offend Protestant sensibilities in their constituencies. Sir James Graham was one of the few members to speak against the Bill, and Edward Stanley, the son of the Conservative leader, observed that Graham's speech pleased the House of Commons

> because though his sentiments were opposed to those prevalent out of doors, and to the votes of an immense majority of M.P.'s, yet most of these votes were given in compliance with the wishes of constituents and nothing could contrast more strongly with the tone of bigotry assumed in debate, than the private conversation heard in the lobbies night after night.[14]

The passionate Protestant outburst of 1851 was an extraordinary display of public feeling. The flow of power from the constituencies was neither regular nor insistent. The electoral correspondence of the party managers was taken up, not with the opinions of the electorate, but with the intentions and power, both of money and influence, of the important individuals, landowners and ironmasters, in the constituencies. That is why, in the years before 1867, the centre of party remained inside parliament. No government, between 1832 and 1867, resigned as the result of a general election, even when it appeared obvious that a majority had been returned against it. Peel in 1835, Melbourne in 1841, and Derby in 1852 and 1859 all remained in office until they were defeated in the House of Commons. In 1852 Derby, the Prime Minister of a minority government, promised Queen Victoria that he would not ask for a dissolution until he had exhausted the attempt to turn the Conservative minority into a majority. It might not be possible to make a government party in the House of Commons; it was not impossible and it was worth a try.

It might be said that nowadays, although politicians pay lip service to local concerns, elections are fought on national issues, whereas a century ago, although politicians paid lip service to national issues, elections were decided by local matters. Things are not so simple. That national party organizations were still, in mid-Victorian England, embryonic ought not to obscure the fact that Conservative candidates stood for the same things in all parts of the country. Their election addresses and their speeches on the hustings did not vary greatly from one constituency to another. How deeply the national issue raised, or more often alluded to, by candidates cut into the politics of influence and local affairs is a question to which a satisfactory answer may be difficult to find. But in the years after 1830 the Conservative party, while it remained principally a parliamentary party, took its first strides beyond the confines of Westminster.

This book is about the Conservative party, not Conservatism. It places rather more emphasis on the ways in which the Conservative party operated, rather less on the ideas which it propagated. Of course, form and content are as inseparable in the life of a political party as they are in the life of a novel. Yet for the purpose of analysis they may be separated and this book is more about form than content. It may be hoped, nevertheless, that readers will find its significance to extend beyond the Conservative party. The history of a single party, although it looks at events from one side, necessarily sheds light on the broader development of the party system itself. Readers will find, however, that this book contains less than is fashionable of what passes for erudition under the name of psephology. As Henry Fairlie has written, the voters carry with them on polling day 'a secret whose character not even they know'.[15] When a social group, or class, or economic interest self-consciously adopts a political argument and strives to make it prevail, it is possible to link class, ideas and voting. There is little dispute about the connection (although there may be about its extent) between free trade, Dissent, and the urban bias of mid-nineteenth-century Liberalism. But when a group is mute, tables of voting statistics culled from poll books tell the historian very little. That more publicans voted Conservative than Liberal does not say why they did, and no theory of merely statistical probability is able to suggest that they did so because they were publicans. Where the past is silent, ignorance is better than guesswork.

Robert Stewart
Chelsea,
February 1977

Notes and References

1 R. W. Emerson, *The Essays of Ralph Waldo Emerson*, San Francisco, 1934, 256.
2 T. B. Macaulay, 'The Earl of Chatham', in *Critical and Historical Essays* (Everyman's Library), London, 1966, i, 404–5.
3 27 April 1852, *Hansard*, Third Series, cxx, 1218–22.
4 Gladstone memorandum, 9 October 1832: Gladstone, *The Prime Ministers' Papers*, ii, 24–5.
5 Huskisson to Lord Granville, 9 March 1826, quoted in Aspinall, *Lord Brougham and the Whig Party*, 280.
6 Wellington to Croker, 26 October 1836; Croker, *Correspondence and Diaries*, ii, 284.
7 'The Conservative surrender', *Quarterly Review*, Oct. 1867, 535.
8 Anthony Trollope, *The Prime Minister*, 1876, Ch. 34.
9 Ward to 'Ivy', 22 [February], 1810: Dudley, *Letters to 'Ivy'*. 92–4. By the time of the reform crisis of 1831–32, Ward had become Lord Dudley. Illness prevented him from voting on Lord Lyndhurst's wrecking amendment to postpone the reform bill's disfranchising on 7 May 1832, but if Aspinall was right in saying that he would probably have voted for the amendment (A. Aspinall, 'The Last of the Canningites', *EHR*, 1935, 669), then Ward's criteria for judging the strength of public opinion were exacting.
10 McKenzie, *British Political Parties*, 2nd edn, 11.
11 *The Reformed Electoral System in Great Britain, 1832–1914* (Historical Association Pamphlet), 5.
12 *Daily Telegraph*, 22 June 1974.
13 Gash, *Politics in the Age of Peel*, 177–8.
14 Stanley MSS, Diary, 20 March 1851.
15 Fairlie, *The Life of Politics*, 112.

The Duke of Wellington and Sir Robert Peel, from a painting by F. X. Winterhalter.

Part I

The Tory ancestry:
The age of Liverpool
and Wellington

Chapter 1

Tory origins

Toryism and the party system

When George III came to the throne in 1760 the word 'Tory' had fallen into practical disuse and the word 'party' was in disgrace. By the end of the century the idea of party had asserted itself and Toryism, although it scarcely dared speak its name, had been reborn. Yet the phrase 'Tory party' was still almost impossible; it jarred, like an oxymoron, on eighteenth-century ears.

Although the Tories in 1688 had been forced by James II to choose the Church and abandon the king (and so deal the death-blow to divine hereditary monarchy), eighteenth-century Toryism retained its attachment to the prerogatives of the Crown. In constitutional theory and in law the Crown and the Church were the supremely national institutions, the highest expressions of the homogeneity of the nation. Party, on the other hand, was regarded by everyone of importance (with the notable exception, in the last part of the century, of the Rockingham Whigs) as an instrument of faction, a malign growth on the body politic. Indeed, for so long as the Crown remained the centre of the political activity, that view was bound to be held by defenders of the mixed constitution, since the object of party was to divest the king of his prerogative powers, above all the power to make and unmake ministries. In the pursuit of power a party in opposition must attack the executive. Systematic party opposition in the eighteenth century was therefore tainted with disloyalty and remained so until the Crown ceased to exercise real, independent executive authority. One of the great difficulties, or at least sorrows, of the Tories in the reform struggle of 1831–32 was that in resisting reform they placed themselves in opposition to the king. As late as 1846, Sidney Herbert answered the protectionists who accused Peel of betraying his party by repealing the Corn Laws with the claim that party was 'contrary to the whole spirit of our constitution'.[1] Peel knew better. By the mid-nineteenth century Herbert's argument was distinctly old-fashioned. Peel explained his resignation in June 1846 in these words: 'A Government ought to have a natural support. A Conservative Government should be supported by a Conservative party.'[2] Governments, which in the eighteenth century had depended on the Crown for their parliamentary majority, had now to look to the bonds of party.

The 1832 Reform Act merely accelerated the shift in the balance of the constitution from the Crown to the House of Commons. Despite the appearance of strength which the Crown gained from its alliance with the younger Pitt, the powers of the monarchy gradually waned in the half-century before the reform crisis, not simply because its mechanical instruments of power, which went by the name of 'influence', were gradually whittled away by 'economical' reforms,[3] but also because opinions and principles, stimulated by the French Revolution and the increased pressure for legislative reforms which accompanied the industrial revolution, began to make their claims more forcibly upon politicians. One of George III's objections to party was that 'the king had the right to the services of all his subjects, and that therefore politicians ought not to make conditions, before accepting office, about the measures to be pursued or the men with whom they would or would not serve'.[4] Personal opinions on public matters only rarely interfered with the eighteenth-century politician's service to the Crown, because governments were not ordinarily held responsible for more than the administration of justice and the revenue and the conduct of foreign and colonial business. The major part of a parliamentry session was devoted to the raising of supplies, and even outspoken opponents of a ministry shrank from denying the king's ministry its lifeblood.

By 1827 the issue was blurred. Canning's appointment as Prime Minister was a major crisis, both for the Crown and for the party of 'Church and king'. Amid the wrangling of jealous personalities in March and April 1826 there is audible a faint echo of 1688. By siding with the 'Catholic' Canning, George IV seemed to be offering the Tories a choice between the Church and the Crown and, as in 1688, the high Tories, or the great part of them, chose the Church. John Croker warned the Ultra-Tory, Viscount Lowther, that by refusing to serve under Canning he would place himself in a false position, since 'an opposition to the Crown can hardly be kept distinct from an opposition to Ministers'; and when the Duke of Clarence, heir to the throne, was made Lord High Admiral in Canning's government, Croker was unable to understand how any 'true Tory' could commit himself to opposition for two reigns.[5] Nevertheless, six members of Liverpool's cabinet put their objections to Canning above their loyalty to the Crown and resigned. Theirs was a shortsighted decision, and an unfortunate one for Toryism, but it was a mark both of the diminished stature of the Crown and of the extent to which the party spirit had infected Toryism. The decline of royal power made parties necessary, since the bond of party had, eventually, to replace Treasury patronage as the link between the government and the House of Commons. But the effect was partly the cause. The rise of parties eroded the constitutional position of the monarchy.

There is little agreement among historians about the stage of their development which parties had reached before the 1832 Reform Act. Despite the fact that the Whigs had, in the early 1790s, a central party fund and central agents to assist in the electoral work of the constituencies,[6] nationally organized parties of a modern kind did not exist until the last third of the nineteenth century. But the absence of national party organization does not make it anachronistic to speak of parliamentary parties in the early part of the century. In the electoral conditions before 1832 the history of party is naturally to be found principally inside parliament. It was there that the fate of governments was decided. Nowadays party affiliation, in ordinary circumstances, determines a member of parliament's behaviour. In the early nineteenth century parties were defined by the behaviour of members. Parties were made in the House of Commons.

Party distinctions, moreoever, even though parties were not nationally organized, existed in the constituencies and often represented different interests and opinions. 'Whig' and 'Tory' meant something in Scotland, where in the fifty years before the Reform Act, the highly successful control of a tiny electorate by Tory governments and by self-perpetuating Tory burgh councils led reformers naturally to adopt the Whig label. At Liverpool, where the two seats were habitually shared by an anti-government independent candidate and a pro-government nominee of the town corporation, in a kind of urban version of the court–country polarity of eighteenth-century politics, the issues raised by the French wars and the evangelical campaign against slavery divided the leaders of the independents into Pittites and Foxites. At the 1812 election there appeared, in addition to the corporation's candidate, General Gascoyne, George Canning for the Tories and Henry Brougham and Thomas Creevey for the Whigs. And the challenge from Brougham and Creevey was so strong that Canning was forced into an electoral pact with Gascoyne.[7] In large towns especially, such as Nottingham,[8] where there was a large Dissenter population, the issues of the repeal of the Test and Corporation Acts, the abolition of Church rates, and the emancipation of the Catholics gave substance to distinctions of Whig and Tory. Political and religious liberalism drew Dissent and Whiggery together and separated them from the Tories. The relationship between political behaviour and social and economic status is more difficult to determine. At Nottingham elections between 1803 and 1818 the framework knitters supported the Whigs by about two to one, but the hosiers shared their votes equally between the two parties. The compilers of the Nottingham poll books may have been right to divide the electorate into burgesses and freeholders. Disagreement over the local issue of enclosure, the most prominent issue in the town's politics in those years, exposed the clear rivalry between the predominantly Anglican and Tory freeholders and the dissenting and Whig burgesses. Allegiances formed in local politics were apt to be transferred to parliamentary contests, even though the basis of them was not a matter of direct parliamentary concern.[9]

The view that it is misleading to speak of parties, even parliamentary parties, before 1832, is usually advanced by one of three arguments or by a mixture of them: the argument that even within parliament there was not the degree of organization which would justify the use of the word 'party'; the argument that what may appear to be a party is merely a temporary combination of smaller units, proprietary groups of persons clustered around important individuals; and the argument that there was no real division of opinion between Whigs and Tories. Occasionally the very language in which the absence of party is described is the language of party.

> In spite of party loyalties there were no real political parties in the late eighteenth and early nineteenth centuries. There were political groups held together more or less closely and for long or short terms by identity of interest, by personalities, by common enmity, or by principle.[10]

To deny the name of party to a group of men united by interest, principle, friendship, and common enmity, because one ingredient, bureaucratic organization, is missing, is to give to party a narrow, mechanical interpretation. The question whether informal methods of organization were more suited to the requirements of the age is not raised. Sometimes the argument takes the narrower ground that no Tory party existed.

> The existence of a formed Whig opposition was an exception, not a contradiction, to the characteristic shapelessness of politics . . . The Whigs, in fact, were in the anomalous position of forming a party in a non-party political system.[11]

Yet, in a non-party system, what is the explanation for the Tories' fierce resentment at what they mistakenly believed to be Canning's habitual flirtation with the Whigs, for the widespread expression of distaste for the 'unprincipled' coalition of Whigs and Canningite Tories in 1827, or even for the frequency with which, in the 1820s, politicians prematurely declared parties to be at an end?

It would be wrong to conclude from the fact that parties were not the exclusive, nor even perhaps the most important, factors in the political battle that they counted for nothing at all. The history of the pre-1832 Tory party is not easy to trace. Being the party of government, it had for its use the office of the Treasury and the patronage which office provided. Because they were attached to the Crown and because they were in office, the Tories found it unpalatable and unnecessary to build a formal party organization. But organization is the consequence of men's decision to act together, an outward sign of party, not the fact of it. As Herbert Butterfield warned those people who wished to judge later periods by the criteria which Namier applied to the special circumstances at the accession of George III, 'a purely positivist attempt to describe party in the nude – to anatomise the material thing – is bound to have its pitfalls for the historian; for a great proportion of the existence of party lies in the realm of human thought'.[12] That party meetings were infrequently held in the days of Lord Liverpool's administration, that almost half of the members of the House of Commons remained outside the confines of party,[13] and that the desire for 'broad-bottom', non-party governments moved many hearts up to 1830 and beyond, are evidence that a rigid, comprehensive two-party system was still a thing of the future. The tendency in the half-century after the start of the French wars was nevertheless towards a two-party system.

In 1805 Charles James Fox estimated the number of the 'King's friends', those members of the House of Commons who would support any ministry of King's choice, to be 180, larger than the opposition's 150 and larger than the combined Pitt–Addington party of 120.[14] Thereafter the party of the Crown swiftly declined. The only estimate of their number which Pares found in the reign of George IV was thirty-seven.[15] Party waxed while the monarchy waned. When the Duke of Wellington joined Liverpool's government in 1818 he did so on the condition that, should the government fall, he retained the freedom to come to any arrangement with the succeeding administration without being bound to enter into 'factious opposition' with the outgoing cabinet, and Liverpool concurred unreservedly in the Duke's constitutional scruples.[16] But the days when prime ministers resigned without taking their colleagues with them were over. Three years later, when Liverpool informed his colleagues that if he resigned in consequence of the King's proscription of Canning's entry into the government, his decision ought not to prevent their carrying on, he was told by Lord Bathurst that he deceived himself if he believed that his resignation would not entail a complete change.[17] In the end Canning was forced on the King by the strength of the cabinet's resolve. Liverpool learned the lesson well. He came more and more to rely on cabinet solidarity as a weapon to use against the King and thereby assisted the development of party, since the mark of party, in its early stages, was the continued cooperation in opposition of men who had acted together in the support of government.

The reduced power of the Crown to control the House of Commons and appoint and dismiss ministers was not the sole condition of the growth of parties. The storm of the French Revolution broke upon the placid waters of eighteenth-century political debate and brought to the country a division of opinion on fundamental questions of social order and constitutional structure, a division which was not new, but which was sharper than had been experienced since the seventeenth century. It divided the Whig opposition to Pitt into 'pro-French' and 'anti-French' sections and, in 1794, took the Duke of Portland and the conservative Whigs out of the party of Fox and into the government of Pitt. The immediate force of the French Revolution was to debilitate the Whig opposition and to provoke a rally of public approval for royal government. Its lasting effect was to insinuate into the English ruling class divisions of principle which formed the basis of enduring political attitudes, by the adoption of which a man confessed himself to be either a Whig or a Tory, though he might not use the names.

Pares located the origin of the modern British party system in the year 1794.

> The relation of parties to classes and ideas was, to some extent, sorted out between 1792 and 1794. . . . The younger Pitt was George III's Prime Minister: but his political theory was at least as progressive as Fox's and his political economy much more so. Both of them began by thinking Burke's crusade for the old order a piece of romantic nonsense. But the period of the 1790s brought about a different alignment. Portland, Loughborough, and Malmesbury [Whigs] did not join a reactionary Government; they rather made it reactionary by joining it. About parliamentary reform, the abolition of the slave trade, and the repeal of the Test Act they had differed not only from Pitt but still more from Fox, and they tried to turn the negotiations for a coalition between the two into an opportunity for exacting guarantees against reforms from both of them. The Portland Whigs, rather than Pitt's circle of professional administrators, were the real nucleus of the tory party. . . . In spite of the renewed confusion of parties between 1801 and 1812 . . . the effects of this new alignment were never wholly lost. At least the Conservative party of today can trace its ancestry back to it, and it must have been the social and national and class solidarity so created, which carried the once discredited remnant of the Pittites through their disagreements over Catholic Emancipation and the gratuitous troubles caused by Canning's personal ambition, to the triumphs of 1814 and the long, unquestioned ascendancy of Lord Liverpool.[18]

Whether the realignment had the same basis in class as it had in the realm of ideas is doubtful. There was little class difference between the Whigs and the Tories until well into the nineteenth century, and Pares himself was aware that the attempt to explain the development of the two-party system by 'the formula of increasing tension between classes' had to be made cautiously.[19] English Dissenters were tarred, unfairly, with the brush of French republicanism and atheism – Burke, one of the Whigs turned Pittite, turned round on his former opinions and voted against Beaufoy's motion to repeal to the Test and Corporation Acts in 1789 – and at the elections of 1790 Dissent, which flourished in the expanding urban environment, 'once so strong for Pitt, turned generally against him'.[20] In the provinces in 1791–92 Tory clubs were formed to combat the Dissenters. But only after 1815, when the end of the war allowed reform questions once again to come to the fore, did class divisions begin to play a part in separating Whigs and Tories. Within parliament, nevertheless, a decisive shift in party loyalties occurred. A more recent historian has endorsed Pares's argument that that realignment was of lasting influence.

> The admission of Portland and other opposition Whigs to the Ministry in 1794 was to prove far from the triumph of royal government which it appeared at the time. Once in office the Portland Whigs did not forget the principles of party solidarity which had been built up laboriously over three decades. They entered the king's government, but in doing so they did much to transform the government party into the image of the Rockingham party. After Pitt's death, Portland's leadership held the Pittites together out of office and led them back into government together as it had once led Rockingham's following in 1782–3. And

despite the rivalries among the Pittites after Portland's retirement 1809 they continued to possess some party traits hardly less marked than those of their opponents, especially in their dealings with the monarchy; by the time of the Regency they were capable of being almost as careless of the ruler's wishes as were the opposition Whigs.

The developments of the 1780s and 1790s moved both the Pittites and the Foxites closer to a recognizable modern stance. Even during the partial relapse into factional politics which followed the death of Pitt and Fox in 1806 the two sides continued to have over 150 members each. Soon after Waterloo an acquiescence in the name Tory by most of those to whom it was applied, a development made possible by the new respectability cast upon the term owing to its association with conservative opinions in resistance to revolutionary France, speeded the acceptance of party assumptions. At the same time a powerful, if delayed, tide of opinion in favour of reforms of all kinds favoured a continuance of the party divisions between the government and the opposition sides.[21]

After a long period in which every politician had signified his adherence to the Hanoverian settlement by calling himself a Whig, Toryism had been reborn, fathered not by Jacobitism but by conservatism, and reared, paradoxically no doubt, by the younger Pitt.

Although his wartime government brought into conjunction those elements which were to comprise the Tory party, Pitt was not himself the founder of a party. He always thought of himself as a revolution Whig and he never attempted to build a party in the House of Commons: his personal following in 1788 was reckoned at only fifty-two, more than a hundred fewer than the Fox–North group,[22] and in 1805 at only sixty, the same as Addington's and ninety fewer than the Whig opposition.[23] His long ascendancy was based on the confidence placed in him by George III and the independents in parliament. His eminence rested on his character, on his reputation for administrative efficiency, and on his budgets. Pitt proved wrong those of his friends who complained that a government could not be built on 'such a narrow system as public virtue',[24] but the system was too narrow to support a party. Pitt's resignation in 1801, over George III's refusal to allow the cabinet to discuss Catholic emancipation, split his government into two sections, those who went into opposition with him and those who remained in Addington's government. The Pittites included Grenville and Dundas, the two leading Whigs, Windham and Spencer, and Castlereagh and Canning. In the Addington government were the lesser lights, Portland, Westmorland, and Liverpool. They, with Chatham, formed the 'Protestant' nucleus of Addington's ministry, which drew into it the additional 'Protestants', Spencer Perceval, Hawkesbury (Liverpool's son, the future Prime Minister), and Hobart. There was the origin of the division which marked every Tory government between 1807 and 1830 into 'Catholic' supporters of Catholic emancipation and 'Protestant' opponents of it.

Despite a brief trial of reunion when Pitt formed his second administration in 1804, the separation continued after Pitt's death in January, 1806. Pitt's death and the formation of the first really Whig government since 1784 were the making of the Tory party. The administration of the 'Talents' brought together Windham, Spencer, the Grenvilles, and Foxites, in a reunion of the Whig party of 1789. Since Addington, now sitting in the Lords as Viscount Sidmouth, also joined the government, the Pittites, numbering no more than fifty or sixty, stood alone in opposition. Sidmouth remarked that 'a standard is raised under the firm of Castlereagh, Hawkesbury, and Canning',[25] and if to those three are added Eldon and Perceval, there was the nucleus of a new Tory party. The name 'Tory' was still not much used; only Canning called himself one.[26] Nevertheless, in July 1806 the Pittite leaders met and compacted together to behave as a party. Grenville's offer of a cabinet post to Canning later that month met with the answer that he was 'bound by engagements which prevented him from acting otherwise than in concurrence with the body of the Opposition' and that his associates were bound by the same engagement to each other.[27] Grenville would not take in the Pittites as a body and the negotiations ended before they had really begun. Canning had not been making convenient excuses. He told Lord Lowther that had it not been for 'other considerations' than his sentiments towards Lord Grenville, he would gladly have joined the Talents.[28]

The cohesion among the Pittites was strengthened by the fall of the Talents in 1807 and the formation of a government led by the Duke of Portland. Nearly all the members of that government – Perceval, Eldon, Canning, Castlereagh, Hawkesbury, Huskisson, Wellington – owed their inspiration and their political training to Pitt. Portland's ministry included all the major figures in the Tory party before 1830 except Peel and Goderich. It also included the leading Pittites of the past: Dundas, Camden, Bathurst, and Westmorland. In 1809 Canning's quarrel with Castlereagh broke up the party once again. Portland resigned and Spencer Perceval formed a government which excluded Castlereagh and Canning. But, even though that left the government dependent, in Perceval's words, on 'the public sentiment of loyalty and attachment to the King' and on the votes of the country gentlemen,[29] it was a purely Pittite government and the fragmentation of the party was temporary. In 1812 the effort to form a Whig–Tory government after the assassination of Perceval broke down in circumstances that showed clearly that there were two main parties in parliament, neither of which was prepared to compromise its opinions. The Whigs rejected the Marquess of Wellesley's offer of four or five cabinet places in a coalition government: they would take office as a party, in control of the government, or not at all.[30] The very fragility of party rallied its defenders. Just before his death, Perceval called coalition a 'hopeless idea' and Eldon gave his opinion that coalitions were 'frauds upon the people' and that the differences between Tories and Whigs over Spain, America, Catholic emancipation, and the state of the currency were 'too deep to be skimmed over'.[31] However much politicians paid lip service to the ideal of a 'broad-bottom' government in the years between 1806 and 1830, differences between the parties prevented its translation into practice. Canning's government was not an exception: it was an avowed coalition of two parties, not a 'broad-bottom' government.

The failure to install a Whig–Tory government in 1812 left it in the hands of Lord Liverpool to reconstruct Perceval's government. Sidmouth and Castlereagh returned to the fold. In 1814 Canning accepted the embassy at Lisbon and in 1816 he returned to the cabinet as President of the Board of Control. In the next few years alarm at Whig sympathy with radical unrest in the north drove the Grenvilles back into the government lobbies, and with the entry into the cabinet of their representative, Charles Wynn, in 1821, the reunion of the Pittite party was complete. G. H. Guttridge, in *English Whiggism and the American Revolution*, put the argument against the existence of a two-party system in the reign of George III.

> In effect, one party enjoyed a long reign of supreme power, declined, and was succeeded by a new, arising partly from its own ranks, and partly from elements hitherto unrepresented. This new party . . . eventually yielded to yet a third, similarly constituted, and not to be mistaken for its predecessor in opposition.[32]

That was not the pattern of governments from 1807 to 1828. On the contrary, they exhibited a remarkable continuity of personnel, a continuity unknown in the eighteenth century. In 1822 the Prime Minister, the Lord Chancellor, the three Secretaries of State, the Chancellor of the Exchequer, and the First Lord of the Admiralty were men who had held their posts unbroken from the formation of Liverpool's government in 1812. Despite the internal quarrels of the Pittites, the party of Portland and of Perceval and of Liverpool was, at least in its leadership, one party with a tradition dating from the days of Pitt.

Parties were still identified above all by their leadership. Qualities of personal leadership were important because the members of the House of Commons were drawn almost exclusively from one class. Both parties had, in Matthew Arnold's phrase, 'the bond of a common culture'; and 'what they said and did had the stamp and style imparted by this culture, and by a common and elevated social condition'.[33] Austin Mitchell's analysis of the House of Commons elected in 1820 shows that, despite the high claims which the Whigs sometimes made, their party was no more aristocratic than the government party, which, although it contained fewer elder sons, had more sons and brothers of peers in its ranks. Both parties drew about equal support from the gentry and the legal profession. The government had a majority of men with a military or naval background, though they were perhaps drawn more by the government's control of honours and promotions than by its Toryism, and also a majority of the men connected with the West and East Indian interests.[34] One group, however, was noticeably pro-Whig: bankers, merchants, and manufacturers. W. R. Brock listed ninety-six members of the 1820 parliament who could be described as the 'commercial interest'. Not all of them, of course, could be strictly separated from the landed interest, but apart from the two Whitmores, the representatives for Bridgnorth, whose family had been established in Shropshire for more than two hundred years, none of them had a landed ancestry going back more than a generation and all of them were currently engaged in banking, trade, or manufactures.[35] By their votes in divisions of 1822–23, ninety-four of them can be classified as either 'Tory and Tory-inclined' or 'Whig and Whig-inclined'. The Whigs had a majority of the bankers, manufacturers, and brewers; the merchants and men of unspecified commercial connections were evenly shared. The totals are fifty-four 'Whig and Whig-inclined' and forty 'Tory and Tory-inclined'.[36] Such calculations are necessarily imprecise, but the tendency to Whiggism of the commercial men was a portent of one of the distinguishing marks between Liberals and Conservatives in mid-Victorian England.

Under the impact of industrialism, the language of class, with its implication of a society cross-sected horizontally, was just beginning to replace the traditional language of a society which thought of itself as cross-sected vertically into interests. Lord Holland's summary of the political situation in 1826 included the word 'class', but it was based on the clash of interests and religion:

> Political parties are no more. Whig and Tory, Foxite and Pittite, Minister and Opposition have ceased to be distinctions, but the divisions of classes and great interests are arrayed against each other, – grower and consumer, lands and funds, Irish and English, Catholick and Protestant.[37]

It is true that by the end of Lord Liverpool's government in 1827 parties, especially the Tory party, were as divided within themselves as parliament was into parties. Mitchell's study of the 1820 parliament, however, provides statistical evidence of two important facts for the history of party: that there was a hardening of lines which produced a House with 'a two-party system modified by the existence of unreliable groups on the fringes of both sides' and that the large majority of members from the important counties and the large boroughs where Whigs, who therefore had 'a clear claim to be the most popular party'.[38] Neither of these facts would make sense in a political world which could be adequately described in the language of Namier. It is not surprising that the Whigs, imprisoned in opposition by George IV's ban on their leader, Lord Grey, should seek in the support of the people a counterweight against the Crown. Whig and Tory came to represent a general divergence into liberal and conservative attitudes and in the process those adjectives eased their way into the vocabulary of party politics by 1830.

It is unusual, in a stable parliamentary system, for the party conflict to reveal itself in the extreme expression of opposing views on specific political issues. When Richard Hart Davis said from the backbenches in 1819 that 'the only difference he knew of between a good old Whig and Tory was that the Whig apprehended the more immediate danger to the Constitution from the undue influence of the Crown, whereas the Tory conceived that it was as likely to arise from the encroaching and overbearing licence of the people', he was not, despite the additional remark that 'both would be found fighting under the same banner whenever a real attack was made upon the Constitution', denying the significance of party distinctions. He was explaining why he was 'not ashamed of avowing himself a Tory'.[39] So, too, the Duke of Wellington confessed that he did not have a clear idea of any distinctive principles of Whigs, Tories, and Canningites; nevertheless, his 'great anxiety in politics was to *keep the Whigs out*'.[40] The essence of his Toryism, as it was to be of Peel's and Derby's, was the defence of the constitution and the preservation of social stability.

> I am for maintaining the prerogatives of the Crown, the rights and privileges of the Church and its union with the State; and these principles are not inconsistent with a determination to do everything in my power to secure the liberty and promote the happiness of the people.[41]

A Whig would not have blushed to say that. But the Whigs voted against the Tory government's Bill to suspend Habeas Corpus in 1817 and against the 'Six Acts' of 1819, in consequence of which the Grenvilles moved over to the government side of the House. The Whigs were proud of their version of their history, that they were the champions of freedom and the enemies of arbitrary government, the party which had defended the balanced constitution against the attacks made on it by George III. They were proud, too, to have been kept to the paths of liberty by Fox and his small band of followers in the 1790s, while faint hearts applauded Pitt's legislation against the radical societies. By the 1820s the *Edinburgh Review* and Lord John Russell had succeeded in identifying the Whig party with the cause of parliamentary reform. Richard Hart Davis's instinct to side with the Tories was right; it was his prediction that was wrong. When the assault on the constitution came, Whig and Tory did not fight under the same banner. It was Wellington who, discerning no differences between Whig and Tory principles, correctly foresaw that Whig practice, born of numerical weakness, would be to yield to the Radicals and, as he believed, ruin the constitution of the country.[42]

Constitutional questions tested whether a man were a Tory, as the Duke of Montrose explained to Wellington in justification of his opposition to the repeal of the Test and Corporation Acts in 1828.

> As to measures on foreign policy, on corn, and Bills of such nature, I think it right to give up my own opinions to a government in which I have full confidence; but on reform of Parliament, on the Catholic question, and the repeal of the Corporation and Test Acts, I consider them so materially affecting the constitution of the country, that till I am convinced of the propriety of changing the present system, I cannot agree to the Bill now in the House, or to change the present state of things as relating to the two other points.[43]

Tory 'constitutionalism' contained within itself a major difficulty: how to save the constitution by means of party. In 1810 Spencer Perceval appealed for the reunion of Sidmouth, Castlereagh, and Canning with his government because he believed that only a united Pittite party would have the strength to uphold the existing system.[44] Since, however, party itself was as great a danger as any other to the monarchical constitution, that amounted to saying that the Tory party had to retain power permanently in order to protect the prerogative of the Crown against party. It was because that was impossible, as well as meaningless, that the Tories, though they did not put it that way, were forced, in the years from 1827 to 1835, to choose party and desert the prerogative.

The parliamentary party, 1812–1827

The persistent tendency in modern English politics towards a two-party system has meant that political parties have always contained within themselves conflicts of interest and opinion. Party unity depends upon the success with which those differences are reconciled by the party leadership and subsumed by agreement on the fundamental objects of the party. It is not to be measured by the extent to which those differences, and the separate groupings of party members which they produce, are obliterated. Too much significance has been accorded to the existence of 'proprietary groups' within Lord Liverpool's party. Historians have occasionally been misled by the language in which contemporaries referred to those groups. There was, for example, talk of a 'Peel party' after Peel's resignation of the Irish Secretaryship in 1818, based on Peel's failure to give the government a regular support in the sessions of 1819 and 1820 and on the frequency with which he entertained his friends to dinner. But Charles Arbuthnot, a government Whip and a friend of Peel, saw no signs that Peel was collecting adherents, although he was attracting a following, and would 'never suspect him of any dishonest deals'.[45] Peel's six years at the Irish Office had established him as a leader of the 'Protestant' Tories in the House of Commons, and contemporary references to his 'party' meant simply that there were Tories who looked to him as the standard bearer of Protestantism in the party. His infrequent attendance in the House in 1819 gave substance to his statement that he had no wish to take a course hostile to the government, but merely one 'unfettered by any official connection' with it.[46] Peel was making a considerable name for himself; he had established a claim as Canning's rival for the future leadership of the party; but he neither was, nor ever wished to be, the head of a faction whose votes and opinions he commanded.

The Grenvilles are a different matter. They were a throwback to the politics of the eighteenth century, a 'connection' held together by ties of family loyalty, consisting of the six members who owed their seats to the electoral influence of the titular head of their group, the waspish Marquis of Buckingham, and about five others.[47] With the exception of their genuine and consistent attachment to the cause of Catholic emancipation, their ruling passion was to gain honours and offices and their distinguishing mark the notion that no government ought to stand which did not include one of their representatives. They were, in Castlereagh's words, 'an intriguing, grasping set, rating their pretensions ridiculously high'.[48] Their bubble was pricked in the years 1820–21. Liverpool's government was just then out of favour with George IV for its handling of his divorce from Queen Caroline, and the King would happily have replaced it with a Whig ministry. Isolated in the grandeur of Stowe, Buckingham fussed himself with dreams that rumours of a ministry headed by Lord Grenville might come true, until Grenville informed him that the King 'had only the alternative of putting himself fairly and fully into the hands of one or other of the two great parties'.[49] Reluctantly, George IV admitted that the Whigs were too weak in the House of Commons to be charged with forming a government (though the difficulty was compounded by his determination that Grey should not be Prime Minister) and in doing so he moved the constitution one more step away from the days when a government gathered a party around itself *after* taking office. Liverpool remained in office and the Grenvilles were drawn firmly into the Tory orbit. From the beginning of the Queen Caroline affair Grenville had decided that 'the manner in which the Opposition have of late years, most unfortunately for themselves and for the country, been drawn on to mix themselves up with the countenance and defence of reformers of the wildest description, seems to me, I regret to say it, to throw the balance at this time wholly on the side of their opponents'.[50] In December 1821, at the price of promoting Buckingham to a dukedom, Liverpool brought Charles Wynn into the cabinet in order, as he said, to forestall the formation of 'a sort of middle party that might, with the aid of Mr Canning, have embarrassed the government'.[51] So was the last of the independent aristocratic connections seduced, by ambition, by the weight of opinion, and by the deliberate intention of a Tory Prime Minister to restrict the King's choice of ministers,[52] into the steadily broadening two-party system.

The importance of the Grenvilles, in Liverpool's eyes, derived from the possibility that they might ally themselves with the Canningites. The Canningites are often described as a 'party', but the name is barely justified by their behaviour from 1801 to 1827. The Canningites were not a connection bound by kinship or by obligations to an aristocratic patron, although the inner core of the group had its origins in friendships formed at Eton and Christ Church. At no time was Canning's following larger than fifteen members, and they were never bound to him. In 1806, when Canning compacted to act together with the main body of the Pittites, two of his closest colleagues, Lord Morpeth and Sturges Bourne, joined Grenville's government. Four Canningites followed him out of office in 1809, but two did not, and two others, out of office, attached themselves to Perceval. At the elections of 1812 Canningite candidates were still considered sufficiently separated from the rest of the Pittites to be opposed by government candidates,[53] but a year later, when Wellesley Pole asked to be released from connection with the Canningites, Canning took the opportunity to make 'the declaration, which otherwise need not have been made till towards the meeting of Parlt., of perfect freedom to all who had been enlisted under the same banners'. His ally, the Marquess of Wellesley, concurred in the decision, which 'amounted to a dissolution of party connection'.[54] Charles Ellis, a schoolboy friend of Canning and one of the inner Canningite circle, thought that the declaration was superfluous.

> I said that we had never been of sufficient importance to deserve the name of a Party, and that I was not aware that there was any reason, in anything which had happened, why we should not be, all of us, as great friends as ever. And that, for anything I knew to the contrary, we were so.[55]

By 1816 Canning was back in the cabinet and thereafter there was no such thing as a Canningite party, only a recognizable element of Canning's supporters (advocates, for one thing, of Catholic emancipation) within the Tory party. Canning's decision to resign in 1820, in consequence of his long friendship with Queen Caroline, was taken without consulting any of the Canningites, for reasons which he explained to Lord Binning.

> No purpose is more fixed in my mind than that of not getting again into the difficulties and responsibilities which attended my last retirement from office. I will have no connexion or confederacy. I will bind myself to nobody, and will on no account allow anyone to bind themselves, avowedly or implicitly, to me. With respect to all with whom I had any such communion, *liberavi animam meam*. And I do not deny that 1812 (to which you refer) sickened me of *a Party* for ever.[56]

There remained members of parliament who considered themselves Canningites down to Canning's death and beyond, men who looked to Canning for guidance and who wished to see him become Prime Minister; but there is little sense to Aspinall's statement that the Canningites 'ceased to exist as an organized Party after January 1828 when Wellington succeeded Goderich'.[57] They never had been an organized party.

Groups like the Canningites and the Grenvilles received as much attention as they did because of the limited control which the government was able to exercise over its supporters in the House of Commons. The government had a precarious dependence on a shifting majority. For that there were two principal reasons. In the eighteenth century the patronage of the Crown was a glue which held the executive and the House of Commons together. By the last quarter of the nineteenth century that adhesive was provided by the extra-parliamentary organizations of the political parties. The intervening period was marked by the failure of party organization to expand rapidly enough to fill the gap left by the Crown's withdrawal from active politics.

Secondly, the convention that a government ought to resign after a defeat in the House of Commons was not yet fully worked out. As late as 1848 Lord John Russell reminded those critics who chastised his government for its failure to carry its Bills that it was a very recent notion that the government should initiate and be held responsible for every alteration in the country's laws, and that 'Ministers of the Crown are chiefly appointed to administer the affairs of the Empire'.[58] The transfer of legislative responsibility from the House of Commons to the government was a slow process evolved over the course of the nineteenth century.[59] Liverpool's government was always assured of a majority on a direct vote of confidence; on other questions members felt free to vote against the government without thereby implying a loss of confidence in it. Even Bills of major importance, like the Corn Law of 1815, were not ministerial measures.[60] Right down to 1830 Lord Grey maintained that parliamentary reform could not be made a party question and the most important issue of all in the post-Waterloo years, Catholic emancipation, remained an 'open question'. Ministers were at liberty to take whatever line they pleased on the issue, with the result that, throughout Liverpool's prime ministership, the Tory cabinet and the parliamentary party were openly divided into 'Catholic' and 'Protestant' wings.

Neither Liverpool nor Castlereagh, the leader of the House of Commons, acknowledged the right of the government to *expect* support from their party. Castlereagh found it painful, on one occasion in 1815, simply to feel himself 'obliged by a sense of duty to the Prince Regent's service to represent to the Official Friends of the Government. . . the indispensable necessity under the present circumstances of the session, of giving their constant attendance throughout the Evening',[61] and Liverpool would 'never attempt to interfere with the individual member's right to vote as he may think consistent with his duty upon any particular question'.[62] Political realities made toleration of private members' independence a necessary virtue. Between 1812 and 1826 the government party in the Commons was never larger than 260 members. Party division in the lobbies could not have produced a majority. It might, on the other hand, as Canning believed, drive members away from the government, since *avowed* party affiliation was still rare.[63]

The government possessed no extra-parliamentary means to punish a recalcitrant supporter, since there was no central machinery able to deprive him of the party's support at the next elections. What little management of the elections existed was directed by the government whips, Arbuthnot and William Holmes, the latter described by one Tory as 'our great calculator upon relative numbers'.[64] The Whips (Holmes was an exception) derived their function as electoral 'managers' from their being at the Treasury, the source of patronage. But patronage was a diminishing electoral asset. According to Canning, Liverpool had only ten seats at his disposal at the elections of 1826, and the number of placemen and pensioners in the Commons had fallen from about 200 in 1760 to fewer than fifty in 1821.[65] Secret service money, freely spent on elections by eighteenth-century ministers, was untouched by Liverpool,[66] who was inhibited from spending what little money was available by Curwen's Bill of 1809, which prohibited the purchase of parliamentary seats. Private persons disregarded the Act with impunity, but Liverpool was unwilling to risk exposing the government.[67] Liverpool's rectitude, in an age of vanishing sinecures and a reduced pension fund, made the management of the Commons more difficult than it might have been under a less scrupulous Prime Minister. In the early 1820s appointments to the Treasury and to the higher posts in the Customs Department were removed from the political sphere by reforms which he initiated. Nor was he willing to continue the habit of using the Church as an aid to party management; he was able to say, in truth, that 'no minister ever made so little use of the patronage of the Church for political or family purposes'.[68]

Liverpool's reluctance to use the old methods of government influence was not balanced by an interest in building a purely party organization. There is a reference by Canning in 1825 to an electoral 'committee of management', apparently consisting of members of parliament, and in 1826 Henry Hobhouse wrote in his diary that at that year's elections 'by better management on the part of the Govt., greater advantage might have been gained'.[69] But indications of the absence of management are the fact that at Cambridge, in 1826, Palmerston, the 'Catholic' Secretary at War, was opposed by three 'Protestants', two of them his colleagues in government, and the remark by a Tory in 1820 that ministerialist losses at the elections of that year were 'owing, in some instances, to their friends retiring from Parliament without giving notice'.[70] Liverpool and Castlereagh had therefore to conduct the business of the government in parliament within the limitations imposed on them. Men whose electoral expenses were paid by themselves, by a patron, or by a subscription raised among their friends, were not beholden to the government. It is true that during Liverpool's administration public business and the votes in the House of Commons became more and more party matters,[71] and that was a noteworthy change from eighteenth-century practice. But early nineteenth-century members of parliament remained free of obligation to party. Mitchell's analysis of the House of Commons from 1812 to 1826 divided members into government supporters (ranging from 250 to 261) and government fringe (78 to 99), opposition supporters (149 to 171) and opposition fringe (16 to 83), and waverers in the middle (48 to 102).[72] Even the regular supporters of the government, however, could not always be counted upon. The 1818 elections, for example, were believed to have returned 71 ministerialists out of 100 Irish members, but Castlereagh complained that their discipline was 'very relaxed' and an analysis of thirty-six divisions in 1821–22 shows only 45 Irish members voting regularly with the government.[73]

The Whips had great difficulty in persuading members to attend debates and to stay there, even on major questions, long into the night, until the division of the House. Trying to raise a majority night after night taxed Arbuthnot's patience, as he complained to Castlereagh in 1819.

> For the first two days of the week . . . we were sitting till very late at night with nearly empty benches on our side of the House, & with benches crammed up to the very corners on the Opposition side. We fortunately escaped the disgrace of dividing in a minority. . . . Of official men we had very few indeed. Those who staid, complained, as I have heard, that I don't keep good Houses – those who went away equally complain that I require attendance needlessly. Worn out with bodily fatigue & vexation I twice during the week wrote at night to Lord Liverpool that our office men wd. not attend, & that the independent members declared to me that they would not try to support those in office who wd. not take the trouble of trying to support themselves. . . . the evil of non-attendance was thought so serious that Long & Huskisson went with me to Fife House [Liverpool's residence], and joined with me in declaring that the Govt. would be broken down in a fortnight's time unless those in office wd., throughout the evening, *without pairing off*, devote themselves to the House. Lord L. talked a great deal of what was expected from official men in his early years, but he wd. not have been moved to take the proper step if it had not been suggested that you & he together shd. call a meeting. To this he has agreed; & I trust that the language of the meeting to the official men will be so decided and peremptory as to leave them no alternative. They must be told that it is expected of them all to be there during the whole course of every evening, & that the coming down merely to get a pair will not do. I am as adverse as anyone to the task imposed upon me unless I am supported. . . . I find from wellwishers & friends of mine that at the clubs the country gentlemen talk loudly of my presuming to ask them to stay when the office men are not there; & here it is to be remembered that with all our sweeping reductions of patronage, I have not the tie I once had upon the independent members,[74]

Liverpool rarely called meetings of the kind to which he agreed here, but then party meetings, whether of official men only or attended by the country gentlemen, were usually ineffective. One famous occasion, the meeting called by Lord Liverpool one morning in April 1818, at which the members present were told that the government message asking for increased grants to the royal dukes would be sent to the Commons that afternoon, was described by Bootle Wilbraham, the Tory member for Dover.

> In consequence of a circular letter from Lord Liverpool, nearly seventy M.P.s, chiefly of the country gentlemen, met at Fife House on Monday, when he explained that the death of the Princess Charlotte had rendered it desirable to have a direct heir to the throne, and that the Prince had encouraged his brothers to marry. It was therefore proposed that the Duke of Clarence (as the one through whom an heir may be expected) should have his income, now £25,000, made up to £40,000. . . . When Lord Liverpool had explained this, nobody said a word, but everybody rose up and went away; and I never saw disapprobation more strongly marked than by that silence. Some few mentioned their opinion privately to the Minister; but this seemed to have no effect, till the message was given to the House of Commons, and various county members got up one after another, and gave their opinions.[75]

The increase was beaten down to only £10,000.

That a member's classification was not necessariy determined by his behaviour in the division lobbies is illustrated by the description of Sir John Astley, the member for Wiltshire, in the *Black Book* of 1823: 'voted for reducing two Lords of Admiralty, one Postmaster General, and repeal of Salt Tax: otherwise a ministerialist, rarely voting for reducing Estimates or Establishments.'[76] Astley is called a ministerialist despite having voted against the government on precisely those questions to which, in 1822, the government attached great importance: Arbuthnot's circular at the beginning of the session had called attention to the special need for the friends of the government to vote against the reduction of offices, in order to preserve the influence of the Crown. The session of 1822 was the most difficult in all Liverpool's years as Prime Minister. Falling agricultural prices and hard credit terms had put the country gentlemen and the Tory gentry in a quarrelsome temper. The government defeated the motion to repeal the salt tax by only four votes and failed to save the offices of the two Lords of the Admiralty and one Postmaster General. Henry Bankes, the member for Corfe Castle, was thoroughly anti-Whig, but he voted to abolish the office of the Postmaster General because he knew that 'these occasional defeats neither shake nor endanger the Ministers, who are much more popular than their fixed opponents, both in the House, and among the better sort of people'.[77]

The constitutional habits of the age thus make it impossible to measure the real strength of the Tory party by government totals in the division lobbies. Thomas Grenville called the country gentlemen 'blockheads', who, discontented because the price of corn did not remain high enough to sustain their rent rolls, vented their spleen by thwarting and opposing a government which they did not wish to see removed from office.[78] Wellington, too, spoke sharply of their 'acting in concert, and as a party independent of, and without consultation with, the Government, which they profess to support but really oppose'. But he recognized that parliamentary organization and constitutional practice had not kept pace with the increasing demands placed upon the executive when he rejected Buckingham's suggestion that the government ought to resign after its defeat on the lords of the admiralty. 'It wd not do', Wellington wrote, 'to refuse to carry on the business when our general line of policy was approved merely because an office or two had been objected to.'[79] The country gentlemen had not yet been brought within the bounds of party. The day was not far off. When the government did threaten to resign if beaten, as it did on Henry Brougham's motion for a reduction in taxation in February 1822, and on motions objecting to Henry Wynne's appointment to the Swiss embassy, it received majorities of over 100. Antipathy to the Whigs secured a majority for the government whenever a vote was made a test of confidence.[80] The question was how often that should be done. In 1816 Liverpool told a deputation of Tories that the property tax, introduced as a wartime expedient in 1797, was still 'of essential importance to the country'. The government would bear none of the responsibility if the House of Commons repealed it.[81] The Commons did so, but defeat on a major financial matter did not provoke the government to resign. By the early 1820s Peel was becoming concerned about the weakness of the executive and its habitual submission to the wishes of the House of Commons.

> I agree entirely with what you say in your letter to Phillimore [Charles Wynn wrote to Buckingham in May 1822] as to the absurdity of the distinction of vital and indifferent points. All ought to be vital. This is the course which Peel every day recommends. He has lately taken a much bolder and decided tone both in Parliament and Cabinet.[82]

Liverpool did not go so far as Wynn suggested, but he used the threat of resignation often enough to advance the idea of the legislative responsibility of the executive and the practice of government control of the House of Commons. Not until Peel's government of 1841–46, however, was the issue squarely faced.

A far greater threat to Liverpool's government and the Tory party than a fractious House of Commons lay, at any rate, in the festering dispute, after 1822, between the 'liberal' and 'Ultra' wings of the party. Liverpool was fortunate that the Catholic issue did not come to the boil during his premiership. By treating the subject of Catholic emancipation as an 'open question', he enabled 'Catholics' and 'Protestants' to co-habit the party and the cabinet. Because he commanded the trust and the loyalty of the 'Ultras', he was able to support the Canningites' liberal foreign and commercial policies without wrecking the government. But as early as 1824 it was recognized that Liverpool's retirement would produce a crisis in the Tory party. As one of the Grenvilles, William Fremantle, put it in 1824, 'the seeds of dissolution are so thick that no one can say how they will be scattered or mixed up'.[83]

Notes and References

Toryism and the party system

1 Asa Briggs, *The Age of Improvement*, London, 1959, 343.
2 Memorandum for the cabinet, 21 June 1846: Parker, *Sir Robert Peel from his Private Papers*, iii, 364.
3 See Foord, 'The waning of the influence of the Crown', *EHR* Oct. 1947, 484–507.
4 Memorandum of George III, [November–December, 1765]: *Eng. Hist. Docs, 1714–1783*, 82.
5 Croker to Lowther, 17 April 1827: Aspinall, ed., *The Formation of Canning's Ministry, February to August, 1827*, 106–7; Feiling, *The Second Tory Party*, 352.
6 O'Gorman, *The Whig Party and the French Revolution*, 13–21. It is not clear from O'Gorman's study that what he calls a 'nascent party organization' survived the defection of the Portland Whigs to Pitt's government in 1794.
7 B. Whittingham-Jones, 'Liverpool's political clubs, 1812–1830', *Trans. Hist. Soc. Lancashire and Cheshire*, 1958, 118.
8 See Thomas, *Politics and Society in Nottingham, 1785–1835*, 114–68.
9 I think that that process was less direct than Thomis implies by his statement that 'even in Parliamentary elections the issue of real importance to people . . . was the friction between the burgess and his supposed enemy, the freeholder, over the question of enclosure' (*ibid*, 168).
10 Rolo, *George Canning*, 59.
11 Gash, *Mr Secretary Peel*, 9.
12 Butterfield, *George III and the Historians*, 220.
13 It is a curious fact that in his *Parliaments of England*, published in 1844, Henry Stooks Smith designates every member returned for the elections from 1794 to 1832 a Whig or a Tory. His certainty is remarkable, but at least it demonstrates that the discussion of pre-reform politics in the language of party is not merely a modern habit.
14 Fox to Lord Lauderdale, 12 July 1805: *Eng. Hist. Docs, 1783–1832*, 255.
15 Pares, *King George III and the Politicians*, 189.
16 Wellington to Liverpool, 1 Nov. 1818; Liverpool to Wellington, 9 Nov. 1818; *Eng. Hist. Docs, 1783–1832*, 115.
17 Liverpool to Bathurst, 27 June 1821; Bathurst to Liverpool, 28 June 1821: *ibid*, 150.
18 Pares, *George III and the Politicians*, 194–5.
19 *Ibid*, 192.
20 Feiling, *Second Tory Party*, 183.
21 B. W. Hill, 'Executive monarchy and the challenge of parties, 1689–1832: two concepts of government and two historiographical interpretations', *Hist. J.*, xii, 3 (1970), 396–7.

22 L. B. Namier, 'Monarchy and the party system', in his *Crossroads of Power*, 229.
23 *Eng. Hist. Docs, 1783–1832*, 255.
24 Feiling, *Second Tory Party*, 165.
25 Ziegler, *Addington*, 254.
26 Namier, 'Monarchy and the party system', 221.
27 Grenville to Lord Wellesley, 16 Oct. 1806: *Wellesley Papers*, i, 225–9.
28 Canning to Lowther, 26 Sept. 1806: *ibid*, i, 210–14.
29 Namier, 'Monarchy and the party system', 231. Namier commented justly that Perceval's description of his government was 'the basic structure of eighteenth-century politics'.
30 See the correspondence in *Wellesley Papers*, ii, 87–116.
31 Feiling, *Second Tory Party*, 269.
32 Guttridge, *English Whiggism and the American Revolution*, 138.
33 Matthew Arnold, 'Democracy', in *Mixed Essays, Irish Essays and Others*, New York edn, 1896, 3.
34 Mitchell, *The Whigs in Opposition, 1815–1830*, 66–71.
35 Brock, *Lord Liverpool and Liberal Toryism*, 287–9
36 The members in Brock's list have been tested against the tabulation of votes in *Analysis of the British House of Commons as at Present Constituted*, London, 1823. For two of Brock's ninety-six members, no votes were recorded. The table below is a breakdown of the total figures.

	Tory and Tory-inclined	Whig and Whig-inclined
Bankers and financiers	11	25
Merchants and men of unspecified connections	14	14
East India interest	6	4
West India interest	6	2
Brewers	1	5
Manufacturers	2	4
	40	54

37 Feiling, *Second Tory Party*, 401–2.
38 Mitchell, *Whigs in Opposition*, 66, 72. Mitchell's conclusions are confirmed by Beales's examination of divisions in 1821 and 1822, in which 546 members voted consistently for either the government or the opposition and only 23 members split both ways, and of those in 1823, for which the corresponding figures were 500 and 98 (Beales, 'Parliamentary parties and the "Independent" member, 1810–1860', in Robson, *Ideas and Institutions of Victorian Britain*, 15).
39 Foord, *His Majesty's Opposition*, 444.
40 Memorandum upon Mr Huskisson's Retirement from Office, 20 May 1828: Wellington, *Despatches, Correspondence, and Memoranda*, iv, 451–3; Mrs Arbuthnot, *Journal*, 4 Nov. 1821, i, 123–4.
41 Memorandum of 20 May 1828.
42 Mrs Arbuthnot, *Journal*, 4 Nov. 1821, i, 123–4; C. Arbuthnot, *Correspondence*, 24n; Wellington to Bathurst, 24 June 1821: *Despatches*, i, 176.
43 Montrose to Wellington, 28 April 1828; *ibid*, iv, 410.
44 Perceval to Castlereagh, 22 Aug. 1810 (draft): *Wellesley Papers*, ii, 22–33.

The Parliamentary party 1812–1827

45 Arbuthnot to Castlereagh, 14 March, [1819]. C. Arbuthnot, *Correspondence*, 13–18; Mrs Arbuthnot, *Journal* 13 Nov. 1820, i, 52–3.

46 Gash, *Secretary Peel*, 285.

47 Austin Mitchell found it 'possible to identify' in the House of Commons elected in 1812 fourteen Canningites, eleven Grenvilles, and four Wellesleyites (*Whigs in Opposition*, 76).

48 Mrs Arbuthnot, *Journal* 5 Jan. 1822, i, 133.

49 Grenville to Buckingham, 11 June 1820: Buckingham and Chandos, *Memoirs of the Court of George IV*, i, 32–4.

50 *Ibid.*

51 Mrs Arbuthnot, *Journal*, 5 Jan. 1822, i, 133. Mrs Arbuthnot bristled at this 'prostituting the honours of the peerage most shamefully' (*ibid*, 22 Dec. 1821, i, 130).

52 See Charles Arbuthnot to Robert Williams, 17 June 1821 (draft): 'It was felt by those of Lord Liverpool's colleagues who met yesterday at Lord Londonderry's, that the touchstone of the King's sincerity [that is, his confidence in Liverpool's government] will be his refusal or his consent to make an offer to the Grenvilles . . . for the union with this powerful family would not only add strength and respectability to ourselves, but it must necessarily deprive his Majesty of one of the chief elements to which he would look when he undertook the formation of a new Government.' (*Correspondence*, 23–4.)

53 L. Huskisson, *The Huskisson Papers*, 1931, 87–9; Aspinall, 'The Canningite party', *Trans. Roy. Hist. Soc.*, 4th series, 1934, 192; Feiling, *Second Tory Party*, 275.

54 Canning to Huskisson, 24 July 1813: *Huskisson Papers*, 91–2.

55 Aspinall, 'Canningite Party', 193.

56 Canning to Binning, 28 Dec. 1820: *ibid*, 203.

57 *Ibid*, 219.

58 Walpole, *The Life of Lord John Russell*, ii, 96.

59 A summary of that process is given in Cromwell, 'The losing of the Initiative by the House of Commons, 1780–1914', *Trans. Roy. Hist. Soc.*, 5th series, 1968, 1–23.

60 Vansittart to Huskisson, 1815 (*Huskisson Papers*, 97–8): 'The question [Corn Laws] will certainly be agitated with great warmth, and Government ought to be prepared with an opinion upon it, if not as a *Ministerial* measure, certainly as one in which the members of Government cannot avoid taking a part individually.' See also Lord Ellenborough's diary for 17 July 1830: 'The East Retford [disfranchisement] question. . . . The Duke *thinks* it will be thrown out, and I *hope* it will. . . . The interfering with the existing franchise was never made a Cabinet question. The giving the franchise to Bassetlaw rather than to Birmingham was, and it was because after an agreement that we should all vote for Bassetlaw, Huskisson voted for Birmingham and then resigned, that the separation [of Huskisson and other Canningites from the government in 1828] took place. These questions were never made Government questions before, and it is much better they should not be.' (*A Political Diary, 1828–1830*, ii, 315.)

61 Briggs, *Age of Improvement*, 188n.

62 Brock, *Liverpool and Liberal Toryism*, 101.

63 Canning to Wellesley, 12 Dec. 1812: *Wellesley Papers*, ii, 128–30.

64 Henry Bankes to Lord Colchester, 6 May 1819: Colchester, *Diary and Correspondence*, iii, 75–6.

65 *Wellesley Papers*, ii, 161; Kemp, *King and Commons, 1660–1832*, 97; Bartlett, *Castlereagh*, 169. The Duke of Wellington discovered the dwindling returns from patronage when he became Prime Minister in 1828: 'The whole system of the patronage of the Government is in my opinion erroneous. Certain members claim

a right to dispose of everything that falls vacant within the town or country which they represent; and this is so much a matter of right that they now claim the patronage whether they support upon every occasion, or now and then, or when not required, or entirely oppose.' (Wellington to Peel, 1829: Parker, *Peel*, ii, 140–1.)

66 'In the winter of 1833, Donald Home told me that when the Tories quitted office in 1830, they left some £300,000 of accumulated secret service money' (Gladstone memorandum, October 1834: *Memoranda*, 39).

67 Brock, *Liverpool and Liberal Toryism*, 100.

68 *Ibid*, 88–93.

69 Canning to Liverpool, 5 Sept. 1825; Canning, *Some Official Correspondence*, i, 289–91; Hobhouse, *Diary*, 121.

70 Mr Hatsell to Lord Colchester, 10 April 1820: Colchester, *Diary*, iii, 125.

71 Mitchell, *Whigs in Opposition*, 66. It may be significant that the number of government supporters reached its peak and that of opposition supporters and waverers its trough in the short parliament of 1818 to 1820, the years when the renewed radical challenge to the existing political system sharpened the difference between Whig and Tory.

72 See Fraser, 'The conduct of public business in the House of Commons, 1812–1827' (unpublished Ph.D. thesis).

73 Bartlett, *Castlereagh*, 172.

74 Arbuthnot to Castlereagh, 14 March, [1819]: C. Arbuthnot, *Correspondence*, 13–18.

75 Wilbraham to Lord Colchester, 15 April 1818: Colchester, *Diary*, iii, 43–4.

76 *Supplement to the Black Book; or Corruption Unmasked!!*, London, 1823, 136.

77 Bankes to Lord Colchester, 6 May 1822: Colchester, *Diary*, iii, 253. A selection of seventy divisions in 1822–23 records Bankes as voting ten times for the government and twice against it (*Analysis of the British House of Commons*, London, 1823).

78 Grenville to Buckingham, 4 March 1822: Buckingham, *Memoirs of George IV*, i, 291–2.

79 Wellington to Buckingham, 6 March 1822: *ibid*, i, 292–3; Mrs Arbuthnot, *Journal*, 14 March 1822, i, 150.

80 W. H. Fremantle to Buckingham, 11 March 1822: 'You may depend upon it nothing can be more precarious than the situation of the Government at the present moment . . . the difficulties are great, and we shall only be extricated from them by the fear of the country gentlemen bringing in the Opposition. The defence of the Post Office will be most arduous; it can only be taken on the ground of influence, which must be maintained. If it is lost, which seems to be apprehended, it cannot alone form a sufficient ground for the breaking-up of the Government. It is undoubtedly (coupled with other measures which have taken place) a good ground for Government to hold the language of retirement, but they must rest such a step on some important proof of want of confidence – I mean the loss of any taxes – as, indeed, a small division against the repeal of a tax, which would be almost as discreditable to them as the repeal itself.' (Buckingham, *Memoirs of . . . George IV*, i, 295–8).

81 Brock, *Liverpool and Liberal Toryism*, 178.

82 Buckingham, *Memoirs of . . . George IV*, i, 326–7. In 1835, when Peel resigned after his government had suffered a series of defeats in the Commons, he explained to William IV that 'there is a great public evil in permitting the House of Commons

to exhibit itself to the country free from any control on the part of the Executive Government, and usurping, in consequence of the absence of that control, many of the functions of the Government' (Peel to William IV, 29 March 1835: Peel, *Memoirs*, ii, 91–3).

83 Fremantle to Buckingham, 19 June 1824 Buckingham, *Memoirs of . . . George IV*, ii, 91.

Chapter 2

Toryism divided

Ultras and liberals

Parties in the reign of George IV extended little beyond the House of Commons and the dining clubs of Westminster. Like top-heavy houses which stand on no foundation, they were vulnerable to a storm. In 1821 the Duke of Wellington, whom the experience of military command had made uneasy and occasionally petulant in the face of disagreement, said that 'ours is not, nor ever has been, a controversial cabinet upon any subject'.[1] Six years later the storm broke. Lord Liverpool, the victim of a stroke in February 1827, resigned the premiership, and the Tory cabinet, rendered less complacent, and therefore less harmonious, by the infusion of new blood in 1822 and 1823, fell apart.

To replace Liverpool, George IV sent for George Canning, the Foreign Secretary and Tory leader in the House of Commons. Canning was the most brilliant and the least trusted member of the cabinet. He was also the reputed leader of the progressive, reforming wing of the government. His elevation to the premiership aroused the suspicions and offended the manners of those Tories who, from loyalty to Lord Liverpool, had suffered his ascendancy in the government during five acrimonious years. Men who like each other can tolerate disagreements; in 1827 many Tories were not fond of Canning. Personality always counts for a great deal in politics. But parties fell apart more easily in the early nineteenth century than now, for the reason that, there being no bureaucratic organization, there was no question of either party to a divorce losing the custody of it. When Canning succeeded Liverpool, six cabinet ministers – Peel and the Duke of Wellington, Eldon, Westmorland, Bathurst, and Melville – and thirty-five junior officers left the government.

The root of the conflict lay far back, in the origins of Pitt's party, when Burke changed his mind and Pitt his policy. That party was a coalition whose cement was the fear of revolution, and the character of a coalition it never quite lost. For so long as the threat of Napoleon and, once that had been removed, the threat of disorder at home, gave Tory governments enough to do in simply resisting parliamentary reform, the emancipation of the Catholics, and schemes for raising the standard of living of the poor, the coalition held together. The government which Liverpool formed in 1812 was a singularly homogeneous body. Only one of its leading members had been born in the industrial counties north of the Trent, and he was Lord Eldon, the Chancellor, who was the archetype of Tory rigidity. There was little reason for the government to question the landed aristocracy's stranglehold on political life when only seventy-eight members of the House of Commons cast their votes against the 1815 Corn Law, which sought to protect the economic basis of the agriculturalists' power by prohibiting the import of foreign wheat when the home price fell below 80s a quarter. Already, nevertheless, there were signs of the nascent power of industry and commerce. In 1812 Lord Brougham's successful campaign against the government's orders-in-council, which were intended to counteract Napoleon's Berlin and Milan decrees, but which crippled British trade and caused large unemployment, was described by Lord Castlereagh as the first triumph of the new industrial interests over the landed aristocracy.[2] Then, in 1819, under Peel's lead, the government itself, by reverting to the prewar policy of tying the issue of paper money to the amount of gold in reserve, the effect of which was to restrict circulation and lower prices, espoused the views of financiers and brought hardship to the farmers, who were forced to honour in an appreciated currency fixed rents and long-term contracts which had been negotiated in a depreciated one.

The resumption of cash payments in 1819 was not an isolated aberration from Tory policy, but a foretaste of that leavening of the government's attitudes in the 1820s which earned for Liverpool's administration in its last years the name of liberal Toryism and which has ever been attributed to the yeast which entered the cabinet in the years from 1821 to 1823: Canning (who had entered the cabinet in 1816 but had resigned in 1820 when he sided with Queen Caroline in George IV's divorce proceedings), Peel, William Huskisson, and Frederick Robinson. The importance of the new men in changing the face of Toryism should not be exaggerated. The surgery did not cut very deeply into the backbenches. Their predecessors, moreover, had begun the operation. When Robinson brought down the first of his trade-freeing budgets in 1824, the Whig Earl of Minto told him that he 'should have liked to see the faces of your clerks, who had imbibed their liquors of wisdom in the school of George Rose & Vansittart, when you first ventured to broach your abominable heresies'.[3] Robinson denied, however, that he had departed from the spirit of Vansittart's finance; the principles of the 1824 budget had been agreed to by Vansittart before he left the Exchequer. The gradual transition to free trade, which marks the economic policy of nineteenth-century governments, had begun as early as 1813, with the ending of the East India Company's monopoly of trade between England and India. Canning's liberal departures in foreign policy drove Wellington into intriguing against him, behind his back, with the King. But it was Canning's predecessor, Lord **Castlereagh** (whose tradition the Ultra-Tories taunted Canning with defiling), who instructed Wellington not to support the Holy Alliance's proposal to invade Spain against the Spanish 'constitutionalists' at the Congress of Verona in 1822. Castlereagh would have broken with the despotic northern powers and recognized the new South American republics as surely as Canning did. On the other great question of the day, Catholic emancipation, the issue which more than any other threatened the unity of the Tory party, Castlereagh was as convinced an emancipationist as Canning, while Canning was no more eager than Castlereagh to force the reform on the King. Nor was Canning in advance of his party on parliamentary reform. Like Peel and like Wellington, like the whole party, he was content to 'guard with pious gratitude the flame of genuine liberty, that fire from heaven, of which our Constitution is the holy depository'. [4]

For all that, the public at the time, and historians later, were right to notice a change after 1822. Castlereagh's suicide in August of that year gave Liverpool the opportunity to reconstruct his government and opened the way for Canning and his friends to dominate the cabinet. The trust which the Ultras placed in Liverpool while Castlereagh was his adjutant gave way to suspicion and jealousy when, as they believed, Liverpool came under the sway of Canning. Charles Wynn, the Grenvillite, was struck with 'the manner in which Canning has assumed to himself, even in the presence of Lord Liverpool, the tone and authority of Premier',[5] and Peel found 'Ld Liverpool's meanness & subjection to Canning . . . beyond expression contemptible & disgusting . . . for that even on matters of his own business, with which Mr. Canning cd have no concern, Ld L. always answered him by saying, "I'll speak to Canning about it" '.[6] Huskisson's entry into the cabinet in October 1823 as President of the Board of Trade (replacing Wellington's Ultra friend, Lord Maryborough) was taken as evidence of Canning's hold on Liverpool.[7] And the Ultras' misgivings deepened when, in 1824, Liverpool threatened to resign if Canning's decision to recognize the independence of the newly proclaimed South American republics were blocked. During the prolonged struggle in the cabinet over that policy, Robert Plumer Ward advised the Duke of Buckingham that Canning's greatest ally was Lord Liverpool, 'who, to use the expression used to me, is "Ultra against the Ultras" '.[8]

Canning's enemies were happy to use any instrument against him. In October 1823 Charles Arbuthnot, the Secretary to the Treasury, sent to Liverpool a long letter, which the Duke of Wellington had approved, warning him that the King would dismiss him if he continued to surrender to Canning.

> [The King] hates what he calls the *sarcastic* ways of Canning . . . he is wild with the idea, & you may call it insanity if you please, that Canning never leaves you for a moment at rest, & that by assiduity, by perseverance, by insinuation, & by every tool & weapon he can use, he continues to pervert yr. better judgement & to turn you in all things to his own purposes . . . I know those of your colleagues who are

devotedly attached to you, & who, I am grieved to say, do share this feeling of the King.[9]

Such an offensive letter to a man of Liverpool's experience and authority was bound to defeat its object. Liverpool replied to Arbuthnot's insult by reminding him that it was not the practice of the country for the Prime Minister and the leader of the House of Commons 'to look at each other with jealousy & suspicion'. The notion, furthermore, that Canning had ever *assumed* authority or influence beyond his competence 'must be grounded upon the notion that Canning & I happen to have agreed more nearly than some of our other colleagues'.[10]

The new ministers changed the style of Tory government. Scepticism gave way to enthusiasm; industry replaced lethargy. Canning, beaten to the premiership by Liverpool in 1812, was at the height of his powers, eager to press his claim to the succession. Peel and Robinson were men whose careers lay before them and who were eager to make their mark. To older men with smaller appetites their energetic behaviour seemed to imply a judgement. One of the reasons that Robinson's budgets raised eyebrows was that, unlike Vansittart, he could talk. It was noticeable, too, that whereas Castlereagh's disengagement from the Holy Alliance had been apologetic, Canning's was ostentatious. Even Peel, the darling of the 'Protestants' for his resolute opposition to Catholic emancipation, came to the Home Office persuaded that the tone of the country was, 'to use an odious, but intelligible phrase', more liberal than the policy of the government, and that there was a feeling, 'becoming daily more general and more confirmed', in favour of 'some undefined change in the mode of governing the country'.[11] After 1822 the Foreign Office, the Home Office, the Exchequer, and the Board of Trade were in the keeping of politicians eager, not simply to govern the country, but to change it. By those Tories who had little liking for the broadening responsibilities of government, for the dawning importance of expertise and analysis, the new men were rebuked as 'political theorists without a foot of land of their own'.[12]

The new ministers' aspirations were the more readily fulfilled because, as Wellington lamented, 'the present Cabinet was one in which each individual acted according to his own judgement & without any party views'[13] and because every liberal innovation, except Catholic emancipation, was supported by Lord Liverpool. For the last four years of Liverpool's administration the cabinet was a battleground, where an uneasy peace was maintained between the Ultras, Wellington, Eldon, Bathurst, and Westmorland, and the liberals, Liverpool, Canning, Robinson, and Huskisson. Peel, busy at the Home Office bringing order and humanity to an outworn legal tanglewood,[14] was placed somewhat uncomfortably in the middle.

Swords were drawn first over Canning's systematic attempt to withdraw England from cooperation with the repressive regimes of Europe and attach her to the causes of nationalism and constitutionalism. Canning turned down the King of Portugal's request for troops to help defeat his rebellious army, declined the Spanish invitation to attend a congress to settle the question of the rebellious Spanish colonies in the new world, and in the end, along with the United States, recognized their independence without consulting the European powers. The famous speech in which he explained that it was to England's commercial advantage to be on a recognized footing with those countries and in which he congratulated himself for having called in the new world to redress the balance of the old, was loudly cheered by the Whig opposition. His own backbenchers received it in silence. Most important were the effects of all this on the Duke, the saviour of Europe from Napoleon. In 1821 Wellington had acknowledged the necessity of Canning; despite misgivings, he knew that the lead in the House of Commons and the Foreign Office required a man of Canning's ability.[15] Two years later he was violently abusive of Canning, pouring out a stream of anger to his confidante, the Ultra-Tory Mrs Arbuthnot. When Canning refused to send troops to Portugal, the Duke 'exclaimed with the utmost bitterness that every day shewed more & more the irreparable loss we had sustained in Lord Londonderry [Castlereagh] & what a misfortune it was to have Mr. Canning, who was for yielding every point to the Revolutionists & who, every day, sunk us lower & lower in the political scale'.[16] Twelve months later, although the target was Lord Liverpool, the villain was still Canning.

> 'He said [Mrs Arbuthnot recorded] . . . that Ld Liverpool had *changed his politics*, that he had treated all the Cabinet & his colleagues shamefully, for that he had abandoned all the Powers of Europe in order to league himself with the revolutionary rascals and blackguards of Europe and America, that this might be right or wrong, it was a matter of opinion, but it was not Lord Liverpool's line until he became the slave of Mr. Canning, & it was at direct variance with the principles upon which his Government was originally formed.[17]

In its economic policies, too, the government paid regard to changing circumstances. Tory economic practice had for some time been firmly *laissez-faire*. In 1816 Lord Sidmouth allowed that distress in the country was widespread and severe, but he 'saw no reason for believing that it would or could be alleviated by any proceedings at a public meeting, or by parliament itself'.[18] Castlereagh's answer to the demand that the government provide relief for the hungry in 1819 was just as forthright.

> When the hon. member said, 'give the people food and employment', did he think that it was possible for the legislature to do that? Was it possible for any fund to be established that would secure employment, amidst all the fluctuations of commerce and manufactures? Upon what principles could government act, if in seasons of difficulty they were to recognise the policy to take from one class merely for the purpose of giving to another? Such a practice was equally inconsistent with all the rules of sound policy, and with the very nature of property in general.[19]

To that non-interventionist policy there was, of course, one outstanding exception: the high tariff wall which, from a mixture of motives, nationalist and aristocratic, was maintained to protect British industry and agriculture. In the early 1820s the farmers were suffering a considerable letdown after the boom years of the war. Encouraged by the prospective high prices which the Corn Law of 1815 held out, they had produced an abundance of grain and, except for the year 1817, grain prices had moved downwards. By 1822 the most vociferous critics of the Corn Law were not the townsmen, but the farmers, who had waited in vain for the onset of parity prices. In that year the government yielded to the agriculturalists and replaced the 80s fixed limit on the import of wheat with a sliding scale of tariffs which began with a 1s duty when the home price was 85s a quarter. The 1822 Act, however, marked the last time that a Tory or Conservative government pandered to the exclusive interest of the wheat-growers. It was passed because the disastrously wet harvest of 1821 had so spoiled the corn as to make it scarcely edible and because the price of livestock, especially in the western counties, was so low that farmers could not pay their rents. Intelligent landlords knew that agriculture's difficulties were not simply seasonal. The Earl of Redesdale complained in the autumn of 1822 that his rents were reduced to the level of a century earlier, even though inflation had doubled prices since then; and he attributed the change to the competition from industry.

> The prevalence of the mercantile and moneyed interest over the agricultural, makes arable land of much less competitive value than belonged to it 100 years ago . . . in the course of another century, population increasing so rapidly as it has increased in the last 100 years, a large importation of grain will take place, in consequence of the establishment of what is called free trade. I look, therefore, to a comparative diminution of the profits of arable land *as such*; and that it is, therefore, important to consider how land may be made valuable when not cultivated with the plough.[20]

Agriculture continued to hold a special place in the national economy because of the social and political power of the landed class and because the food which it provided was the indispensable foundation of industry until reduced transport costs in the mid-century made large-scale importation of foreign corn worthwhile. Even so, agriculture no longer dominated the economy. By 1800 it employed only about one-third of the population and produced the same proportion of the national income.[21] The landlords and farmers could not, therefore, claim the whole attention of ministers. While at the Board of Trade, Robinson had given his opinion in the Commons that 'the restrictive system of commerce in this country was founded in error and calculated to defeat the object for which it was adopted'.[22] In 1822 he turned down pleas for higher duties on imported butter, hides and tallow.

In the years 1824 to 1826 Robinson brought down three free-trade budgets. 'Free trade' then meant the old Pittite policy of ending prohibition, not abolishing tariffs altogether. The major changes in the first two years were the reduction of the duty on coal, iron, wine and hemp, the replacement of the prohibition on silk imports by a 30 per cent *ad valorem* duty, and the abolition of the tariff on foreign wool. The last of those represented a significant change of mind by the government. The quality of British short staple wool had so deteriorated that by 1820, it was estimated, the Yorkshire woollen industry depended upon imports for two-thirds of its supply. The sixpenny tax on imported wool which had been imposed in 1819 to help the English sheep-grazers therefore hit the industry hard.[23] Its repeal after only five years showed the sensitivity of Liverpool's reconstructed ministry to industrial opinion. In a small way it gives point to W. R. Brock's exaggerated statement that 'the most striking feature of this period is the virtual abandonment of the agriculturalists by the Government and its conscious seeking after commercial support'.[24] The same tendency was implicit in Huskisson's repeal of the Spitalfields Acts, which allowed the wages of weavers and details of manufacture to be fixed by magistrates. Masters could not employ weavers from other districts nor employ their capital outside their own. The result was a high standard of living for the Spitalfields workers. Huskisson guided the repeal of the Acts through the Commons in 1823, but the Lords, led by his cabinet colleagues Eldon and Harrowby, who harked back to an older, more paternal, economic outlook, as the Tory Radicals of the 1830s and 1840s were to do, blocked it. Huskisson's answer to the argument that repeal would impoverish the weavers was that without it there would soon be no manufacture to employ them, and in 1824 the Lords gave way.[25]

In 1825 over-speculation brought on one of the most severe financial crises of the century. Panic in the financial world meant stagnation and bankruptcy in trade and industry and, for the workers, wage cuts and unemployment. Rioting spilled over the north country in 1826 and petitions for the repeal of the Corn Laws flooded parliament. In May the government introduced two measures: the first allowed the corn which was sitting in bonded warehouses to come on to the market at the small duty of 10*s* a quarter; the second gave the government the discretionary power during the summer recess to admit foreign corn as it deemed necessary. Canning rejoiced in the government's victory, by the astonishing margins of three to one in the Commons and five to two in the Lords, and explained to Lord Granville that the opposition's hope of overturning the government was dashed because 'many pledges, given in the heat of rural anger, were broken'.[26] The diarist, Thomas Creevey, believed those Acts to be a milestone in Tory and English history.

> It certainly is the boldest thing that ever was attempted by a government – after deprecating any discussion on the corn laws during the present session, to try at the end of it to carry a corn law of their own by a *coup de main*, and to hold out the landed grandees as the enemies of the manufacturing population if they oppose it – the charm of the power of the landed interest is gone; and in a new parliament Canning and Huskisson may effect whatever revolution they like in the corn laws.[27]

Creevey's burial sentences for the dead were premature. But Liverpool's coalition was disintegrating. The large majorities for the Corn Bill were filled with opposition names, and many of the Prime Minister's oldest political friends, men like the Duke of Newcastle, the Duke of Northumberland, Lord Hertford, and Lord St Germans, either voted against the government or stayed away. The government's antidote to over-speculation, a Bill to prohibit country bankers from issuing notes below the value of £5, angered the agricultural inflationists who wanted Peel's 1819 currency measure revoked and provoked the same pattern of voting. Mrs Arbuthnot unloosed her rage on her journal: 'Our party, as a party, is entirely broke up, and it remains to be seen how long the Whigs will give us *support* without *places*. Messrs. Canning & Huskisson have certainly most completely destroyed the confidence which the country had in Liverpool's adminis-tration.'[28] Liverpool's majority in the House of Commons had come to rest almost as much on the votes of the opposition as upon the sufferance of his traditional supporters, not, it is true, a remarkable development in those days, but neither, as Huskisson remarked, 'a very comfortable or a very secure state of things'.[29]

Perhaps, then, what the Whig maverick, Lord Brougham, called the Ultras' 'very unusual fit of resignation'[30] in 1827 was to be expected. Yet a large part of the responsibility for breaking up the Tory party rests with Peel and Wellington. Had they agreed to remain and serve under Canning, the ministers who resigned with them would almost certainly have followed suit. Canning would not then have had ranged against him the bulk of the Tory aristocracy. Peel and Wellington each offered a somewhat sheepish defence of his action. Neither of them took lightly the decision to abandon the Crown. But they found refuge from their consciences in the rickety shelter of Protestant exclusion. Canning had been, throughout his career, the bearer of Pitt's unredeemed pledge to emancipate the Catholics, especially in Ireland, by opening up to them civil offices and parliamentary seats. Liverpool was an opponent of the Catholic claims, in the language of the day a 'Protestant', but he had kept his government together by making Catholic emancipation an 'open question' on which ministers were free to vote as they wished. On three occasions in the 1820s the House of Commons voted in favour of emancipation, only to be thwarted each time by the Lords. Peel and Wellington justified their resignations in 1827 by arguing that the change to a 'Catholic' Prime Minister would so shift the balance in favour of the Catholics that resistance would become fruitless. Peel, who remained on friendly terms with Canning, allowed of his late colleagues 'that on all matters of domestic and general policy (with the exception of the Catholic question) my opinions are in accordance with theirs'.[31]

Fears of Canning's 'Catholic' zeal, if they were genuine, were exaggerated. Canning was an emancipationist because, like Pitt, he believed an estranged Irish population to be a source of weakness in the empire. His

'Catholic' sentiments did not prevent him from persistently opposing the repeal of the Test and Corporation Acts, which placed similar disabilities on Protestant dissenters. Like Liverpool, he formed his government on the understanding that emancipation would be an 'open question'. Wellington himself had already reached the conclusion that emancipation could not be much longer postponed, and there was nothing in Canning's past behaviour to suggest that he would force the issue.[32] If concern for the Anglican constitution were the true motive of Peel and Wellington, then it was imprudent to drive Canning into the hands of the Lansdowne Whigs, the most pro-Catholic party in parliament. The Anglican constitution was safer in the hands of a mixed Tory government than it was in the hands of a Whig–Canningite coalition.

Wellington had come to dislike Canning.[33] He explained to Lord Jersey in April 1827 that he resigned 'not on account of any political differences with Mr. Canning. . . but that to Mr. Canning he had personal objections, and they could not be overruled'.[34] As Mrs Arbuthnot put it in 1825, 'they might as well try to amalgamate oil & vinegar as the Duke & Mr. Canning'.[35] Much of the misfortune Canning brought upon himself. The Tory party had not forgotten his display of untempered ambition in 1812 when, too arrogant to accept Castlereagh's sacrifice of the Foreign Office, he demanded the leadership of the House of Commons with it and lost both. He was short with his colleagues, reserved in his communication with them, and slow to consult them. He was also given to fits of temper so violent that they could be met only by silence. Wellington was not mean. He knew that Canning's 'talents were astonishing, his compositions admirable . . . his fertility and resources inexhaustible';[36] but he also shared the prevalent opinion that Canning was devious, the pronounced flaw which even the Canningite journalist and member of parliament, John Wilson Croker, lamented in Canning.

> Poor Canning's greatest defect was the jealous ingenuity of his mind. . . . His acuteness discovered so many tortuous byroads on the map of human life, that he believed they were much more travelled than the broad highway. . . . He could hardly take tea without a stratagem. I said of him that his *mind's eye* squinted; but this was altogether a mode of his *mind* . . . for his heart and spirit were open, generous, and sincere.[37]

There was no truth to the charge that since 1820 Canning had been flirting with the Whigs and that in 1827 he began negotiations with them before the Tory ministers handed in their resignations; but the rumour, given false substance by a determined press campaign for a Whig–Canningite coalition, was widely believed.

Canning was flamboyant. His Tory opponents resented the success with which, by making public speeches, publishing despatches, and coddling the press, he courted public favour. 'Running a race of popularity' Mrs Arbuthnot called it.[38] Canning was an innovator (Lord Liverpool never made a public speech outside parliament)[39] and his openness to the public smacked of democracy. Wellington was understandably disturbed by 'the facility with which he [Canning] espoused the most extravagant doctrines of the Reformers and Radicals, although himself the great champion of Anti-Reform'.[40] Wellington's dislike of Canning was not fleshless. It fed on his antagonism to the Canningites' liberalism. A wide range of issues had called into play 'those deep-lying differences of temperament and opinion on which the more superficial differences of party are based'.[41] Nevertheless it would be wrong to say that Wellington's estrangement from Canning was merely a symptom of his Toryism. Had that been so, he would not have tried, once the break had been accomplished, to reunite the Canningites and the Ultras in 1828.

A few weeks after he had become Prime Minister, Canning talked of his disappointment at the Ultra Tories' rejection of his leadership, signified by the Lords' opposition to the 1827 Corn Bill.

> It is a great misfortune that the Lords take so narrow a view of their present situation, that they cannot see that we are on the brink of a great struggle between property and population; that such a struggle is only to be averted by the mildest and most liberal legislation. Mark my words, that struggle will some day come, when probably I may be removed from the scene; but if the policy of the Newcastles and Northumberlands is to prevail, that struggle cannot be staved off much longer.[42]

Canning's recipe for the survival of Toryism was simple. To avert radical reform, fomented by social divisions, the confidence of the commercial men and the manufacturers had to be won. And aristocratic government at home must put on a liberal face abroad. But what Canning conceived as Tory strategy, the Ultras condemned as vulgar ambition. Charles Greville, no radical, called the Ultras 'idiots' for failing to see that Canning was the one man capable of arresting the torrent for reform.[43]

What alternative had Peel and Wellington to offer? They knew that the Duke of Newcastle's scheme for a purely 'Protestant' government was hopeless;[44] sloughing off the Canningites would not save the Tory party. They knew, too, that they were dealing a blow to the royal prerogative. And if they believed that they were standing guard over the Church, they lacked foresight. Their Ultra followers might have believed that Canning weakened, not strengthened, the cause of Toryism. So old Sidmouth, who had saved George III against Pitt in 1801, argued that 'by declining to form such a connection . . . which they must have known was liable and likely to be soon dissolved' the Ultras acted in the Crown's defence.[45] But the Ultras, at least, went on to fight a last-ditch battle against Catholic emanicipation. Peel and Wellington did not.

At the beginning of 1828 Wellington attempted to reconstruct the old Liverpool administration. By then the damage was done. The reunion lasted four months. Then, having lost the Canningites, Wellington took up their policy. In 1829 Catholic emancipation came much worse from a 'Protestant' government than it would have from a 'mixed' one. By 1830 the government, alienated from Tories on both the left and the right, was too weak, too remote from public feeling, to handle the reform crisis and Toryism reaped the whirlwind.

'Catholics' and 'Protestants'

After decades of dominating the political scene, the old Tories found themselves, in March 1827, isolated from power and in danger of becoming an obsolete faction in politics. Canning was able to form a government drawn chiefly from his own band of followers and the section of the Whig party led by Lord Lansdowne. The time had come, one of those Whigs recommended, for all party distinctions 'other than those which divide the friends from the enemies of sound and liberal principles' to be forgotten.[46] Francis Burdett, the radical member for Westminster, rejoiced at the prospect which lay before the country.

> A greedy, bigoted, narrow-minded faction has like a nightmare oppressed the country ever since the commencement of the reign of George III to the present time, and so exhausted it, or possessed themselves of its strength, that it had lost the power, and almost the will, to shake it off. This their strength, however, probably produced their overthrow, for presuming too far, thinking they could not be got rid of, when no one else could, they unseated themselves; having done so, are we to endeavour to set them up again?[47]

Yet within less than a year they were set up again and the experiment in Whig–Canningite government was over: by January 1828 the Tory party was back in power, faced with the task of patching up its recent quarrel.

In August, after just four months as Prime Minister, Canning succumbed to inflammation of the liver, a cruel fate for a man whom one of his biographers has described as remarkable as a personality 'chiefly because his energies were so consciously and uncompromisingly dedicated to the gratification of political ambition'.[48] Canning's death left his small group of about thirty followers leaderless.[49] Huskisson, his natural successor, had incurred all the odium of his dead master among the Tories without winning the affection of the public to counterbalance it. It was only because the King was too deeply offended by the Ultra–Tories' attempt to dictate to him the choice of Liverpool's successor to invite them back that Robinson, elevated to the peerage as Viscount Goderich, was entrusted with the duty of carrying on Canning's government. It was a charge beyond the skill and the courage of a born junior minister.[50] Goderich resigned before facing the ordeal of meeting parliament in January 1828, leaving behind him the most undistinguished ministry in English history.

There are no grounds (other than the unpredictability of the future) for believing that Canning's death destroyed the chance that his hastily accomplished coalition might have led to a permanent realignment of the party structure. Canning accepted the coalition only as an unwelcome necessity. He had always believed that the Whigs' interest in parliamentary reform stood in the way of real union. That was part of the ground on which the Whigs who looked to Lord Grey as their leader refused to have any part of the coalition. Canning stipulated that, since Catholic emancipation was to be an 'open question', the cabinet must be united in its opposition to parliamentary reform and the repeal of the Test and Corporation Acts.

The size of Whig support for the coalition cannot be gauged. Certainly it extended well beyond the thirty or forty Whig members at the Brook's club meeting in April which decided that the Lansdownites should enter the government. But the only important division in the House of Commons during Canning's ministry took place on a Bill to disfranchise the corrupt borough of Penryn and it was defeated by the Whigs because it proposed to sink Penryn in the adjacent hundreds, thus retaining its rural character, rather than to transfer the representation to Manchester or some other large town. Only three Whigs took ministerial posts in the government, which gave some point to the jaundiced remark of the Ultra–Tory, Lord Londonderry, that 'two tails' had been brought together, 'the first instance of an amalgamation, where *nearly* everyone is secondary in name, character, and consideration'.[51] The strength of the coalition was that the adherence of Lansdowne and his friends debilitated the Whig opposition and that Lord Grey and the Duke of Wellington could not be brought to act together. Its weakness was that it stood on no principle; those Whigs who supported it did so primarily to keep out the Ultra–Tories, which even the Lansdownite, Lord Abercromby, thought 'confounding all notions of right & wrong in politics'.[52] The Whig members of the government continued to meet at Brooks' and to receive the whip from their own man, Viscount Duncannon, not from the Treasury. Once Canning had gone the coalition lost much of its charm for the Whigs. In October Londonderry reported that 'there will be as many Whigs coming to Opposition as there will be any trimmers to Lord Goderich'[53] and Lord Bexley, one of three 'Protestant' Tories who had been persuaded to remain in the government, advised his colleagues to bury their personal feelings and seek a reunion of the Tory party.[54]

The bitterness of the Tories against Canning and his government is not in doubt. When, for example, the *Courier*, the leading ministerialist newspaper in Liverpool's day, gave its support to Canning, it lost the patronage of a large section of the party and was thrown out of reading rooms all over the country.[55] Nevertheless, the Tory split bore the marks more of a separation than a divorce. William Holmes, an ultra–Tory 'Protestant' who was a Whip in Liverpool's government, retained that post under Canning and Goderich. Whether Peel was right in believing that Canning kept him on 'to obtain a majority in the House of Commons *against* the Roman Catholic question',[56]

Holmes acted unofficially as a link between the two sections of the Tory party, sending a list of Goderich's cabinet to the Arbuthnots before it was published and keeping them up to date throughout the autumn on the friction between the Whigs and the Canningites. While Holmes acted as a spy for the Ultra–Tories, both Peel and Wellington threw cold water on Ultra proposals to conduct an all-out opposition to the coalition. On 11 May Peel declared in the House of Commons that he was satisfied with Canning's statement of the government's policy and that he would not enter into factious opposition. Lord Londonderry was displeased to find Peel's adherents preaching neutrality,[57] but it made it easier to Wellington to invite the Canningites to join his government in January 1828.

Throughout his reign as Regent and King, George IV had effectively excluded the possibility of a Whig government by placing Lord Grey under interdict. When Goderich resigned he therefore found himself with no one to turn to but Wellington and Peel. Without hesitation they agreed that an Ultra government could not be formed. Peel, disposed by all his past behaviour to welcome the advice of his mentor, the Bishop of Oxford, that only a liberal government was consistent with the safety of the country's institutions, told the bishop that 'the wise and generous part is to leave nothing untried that can unite those who differed, at least who separated, on no other account than a question about Canning's claim to be Prime Minister'.[58] To his trusted Irish friend, William Gregory, Peel wrote a letter marked 'most private', in which he confessed that he cared nothing for the dissatisfaction of the Ultra–Tories. 'This country ought not, and cannot, be governed upon any other principles than those of firmness no doubt, but firmness combined with moderation.'[59] There was also the circumstance, which was to weaken the right wing of the party for the next generation, that the Ultras were weak in debating ability and averse to business. That, in Peel's view, made the fate of an Ultra government inevitable.

> Supported by very warm friends, no doubt, but those warm friends being prosperous country gentlemen, foxhunters, etc. etc., most excellent men, who will attend one night, but who will not leave their favourite pursuits to sit up till two or three o'clock fighting questions of detail, on which, however, a Government must have a majority, we could not have stood creditably a fortnight.[60]

Mixed Tory government was therefore resurrected. Four Canningites kept the offices which they had held in Goderich's government: Huskisson the Colonial office, Lord Dudley the Foreign Office, Lord Palmerston the War Office, and Charles Grant the Board of Trade. Of the four Ultras who had resigned with Peel and Wellington eight months before, only Lord Bathurst was invited to reclaim his place. The Ultras' pique at the exclusion of Bexley, Westmorland and even the seventy-seven-year-old Eldon, was only partially mollified by the appointment of the 'Protestant' leader of the country gentlemen, Sir Charles Wetherell, as the Attorney-General.

In the moral language which fell easily from the lips of the extreme Tories, the Duke of Newcastle described the inclusion of 'all the *rubbish* men' as a breach of honesty and a failure of courage.[61]

A period of quiet was needed to erase the mutual suspicions with which the recent antagonists could not help regarding each other. Unfortunately for the party, urgent questions of foreign policy, the Corn Laws, and parliamentary reform could not be postponed. From the start the cabinet fell into the old quarrels between Ultras and liberals, and when the government finally broke up in May 1828 it did so as much because of Wellington's belief that the Canningites had never intended cooperation as because of the disagreements themselves.

Foreign policy matters did not provoke an open clash between the two wings of the government. But in the attitudes taken towards the Greeks' fight for independence from Turkey lie the origins of a debate that was to occupy politicians of all parties for much of the nineteenth century. That debate has always gone by the name of the Eastern Question. At its centre was the threat of Russian expansion into the Balkans and Turkey-in-Europe. English interest in the area arose from the desire to protect the trade route to India. The issue was clouded, however, by the concern for the plight of those Christians in the Balkans who were subjected to the overlordship of the Muslim Turks. When, later in the century, the question became acute, English opinion was divided between those people who, on the whole, trusted Russia and were moved by Christian conscience to oppose Turkey's rule in Europe and those people who wished to prop up the 'sick man of Europe' as a buffer against a Russian advance to the Mediterranean.

In the 1820s the debate was still embryonic. It was important for the Tory party, nevertheless, because both arguments found their proponents inside the cabinet. Wellington believed that it was his duty to guard British interests from the danger of Russian aggrandisement. Palmerston, a Canningite, was, in the 1820s a defender of the other view.

> I confess I should not be sorry some day or other to see the Turk kicked out of Europe and compelled to go and sit cup-legged, smoke his pipe, chew his opium and cut off heads on the Asiatic side of the Bosphorus. We want civilisation, activity, trade and business in Europe, and your Mustaphas have no idea of any traffic beyond rhubarbs, figs and red slippers; what energy can be expected from a nation who have no heels to their shoes and pass their whole lives slip shod?[62]

When Canning came to the Foreign Office in the autumn of 1822, eight months after the Greek proclamation of independence from Turkey, he brought with him the suspicions of Russia which he had inherited from Pitt. He was concerned, not to assist the Greeks, but to prevent the outbreak of a Russo-Turkish war. His recognition of the Greek belligerents in 1823 was no more than a practical step taken to protect British commerce and it was accompanied by an avowal of strict British neutrality. In the next four years, however, Canning was led by his policy of cooperating with Russia to prevent war to the point, in July 1827, of signing the Treaty of London. That treaty bound France, Russia and Great Britain to secure Greek autonomy under Turkish suzerainty and to interfere to impose a settlement if Turkey did not accept an armistice within fourteen days. The terms of the treaty reached the admirals of the allied squadrons on 8 August, the day of Canning's death. Turkey had rejected an armistice and the result was the destruction of the Turkish and Egyptian fleets at the battle of Navarino.

British policy in the eastern Mediterranean had traditionally rested upon friendship with Turkey, and Wellington contemplated the independence of Greece and the disintegration of the Turkish empire with alarm. On his return to office he was eager to reverse the direction of Canning's policy. With Huskisson's consent he put in the speech from the throne a reference to the battle of Navarino as 'an untoward event' and to Turkey as an 'ancient ally'. For the next four months Wellington fought obstinately against the united opposition of the Canningite ministers to evade fulfilling the obligations undertaken in the Treaty of London, and although the quarrel never came to a head, it soured relations in the cabinet. 'The sentiment of Palmerston which gave mortal offence to the Duke,' Huskisson wrote to Lord Granville after the Canningites had resigned, 'was that the administration of the country would be deserving of support . . . exactly as it acted in all matters of foreign and domestic policy on the principles of Mr. C.'[63] Wellington seized the first opportunity to rid himself of the Canningites partly because he was weary of their unrelenting insistence upon cooperation with Russia.[64]

In March the cabinet took up another legacy from Canning's government, the alteration in the Corn Laws. Charles Grant drew up a Bill almost identical with the one which the Lords had thrown out in the previous year. He was supported by his three Canningite colleagues and also by Peel, Henry Goulburn and Lord Melville, while Wellington, Aberdeen, Bathurst and Ellenborough fought for a higher scale of duties than the 1827 Bill provided. In the end a compromise was reached, which was a concession to the agriculturalists. At the lower end of the scale the duties remained high and corn was to be admitted free only when the home price reached 74s, not the 70s level proposed in 1827. The dispute was settled only after a month's bitter wrangling and it had its effect on Wellington. Lord Ellenborough's diary contains an illuminating description of him early on in the cabinet struggle, a description which pinpoints several of Wellington's shortcomings as a party leader and Prime Minister.

> The Duke has been ill all the week. He is disappointed at not carrying his own plan at once. He feels he is looked up to by the great landed interest, and he is afraid of being reproached by his friends. He thought a strong Corn Bill would give us a weight in the House and the country and strengthen the Administration. He imagines Huskisson and the others will make no concessions and expect them from him. In fact they have made great concessions, and, I believe, really wish to

keep the Government together. They have behaved very fairly. If we break up, it will be the Duke's fault, and his agricultural friends will be furious. The new Government would force a worse Bill upon the country. The Duke thinks they could not; but he is mistaken, and overcalculates his strength. He has only been approached by those who think as he does upon the Corn question, and he mistakes their voice for that of the nation.[65]

A month later, after repeated offers of resignation from Grant and a prolonged effort to keep him and the other Canningites in the government, Ellenborough had come to agree with the Duke that the reunion was a mistake in the first place.

The end came in the middle of May, when a misunderstanding led to Huskisson's voting against the rest of the cabinet on a Bill to deprive the corrupt borough of East Retford of its representation and sink it in the surrounding hundreds. As a gesture of apology, Huskisson sent a letter of resignation to Wellington. To his surprise it was accepted; and Palmerston, Grant and Dudley went out with him. 'We joined as a party,' Palmerston wrote; 'as a party we retired.'[66] That was the Duke's unreasonable complaint. It was to be expected that the Canningites, who were a minority in the cabinet, should act together. Neither in foreign policy nor in the matter of the Corn Laws did their views prevail. But Wellington, irritated by the daily fighting in the cabinet and seeing no end to it, was happy to let them go. The poison which entered the party in 1827 was still at work.[67]

The departure of the Canningites delighted the Ultra-Tories. It also seriously weakened the government. In June 1828 the Speaker of the House of Commons listed twenty-one to twenty-five members in the rump of the Canningite party,[66] but they were not a solid voting block and not all of them went over to steady opposition. But without the Canningites the government lacked authority in the House of Commons and a link with liberal opinion in the country. The Peninsular veterans who replaced Huskisson and Palmerston, Sir George Murray and Sir Henry Hardinge, were loyal friends of Wellington and in time were to prove their worth to the party; but they were not men to excite the electorate. 'We have done more than any Govt ever did before in the time in reducing expenditure, putting down unnecessary offices, taking off taxes & pacifying Ireland,' Mrs Arbuthnot wrote after the government's disappointment at the 1830 elections, '. . . and yet we get no credit, because we have no speakers to puff our deeds.'[69]

The advent of what the Ultra-Tories called 'pure' Tory government was mistimed. Since the founding of the Catholic Association by the astute popular orator, Daniel O'Connell, in 1823, the campaign for Catholic emancipation had been making rapid headway in Ireland. O'Connell was able to play upon three main grievances of the Irish Catholics: that they were compelled to pay tithes for the support of an alien Church Establishment, that most of the profits from the land which they worked passed into the pockets of an absentee English aristocracy, and that the English government showed no interest in relieving the crushing pressure on the land which was the result of a rapid increase in population combined with industrial stagnation in the wake of English competition after the Union of 1800.

For the Irish Catholics representation at Westminster was the first step towards either more liberal legislation for Ireland or withdrawal from the Union. At the 1826 elections, which in Ireland were a test of strength between the influence of the Catholic Church and the influence of Protestant property over the minds and votes of the tenant farmers, the emancipationists made a net gain of only three seats. In three uncontested elections, however, anti-Catholics replaced pro-Catholics. What mattered was that in six popular contests the anti-Catholic candidates had been decisively beaten. The power of the Catholic tenantry in alliance with the Catholic Church was for the first time revealed. Then the Clare by-election in July 1828 gave 'Protestants' an even greater shock. Vesey Fitzgerald, Charles Grant's successor at the Board of Trade, was standing for re-election. He was an emancipationist and a popular member of parliament. His election seemed certain. The Catholic Association, however, flush with its successes in 1826, put up O'Connell against him. On the fifth day of polling, trailing by more than a thousand votes, Fitzgerald withdrew from the contest.

That result changed the ground of the emancipation debate. It was no longer merely a question of the number of votes in parliament. The Clare election raised the question whether government under the existing law could be much longer carried on. The government could never again appoint a member from a southern Irish constituency to the cabinet: he would simply not be re-elected. More important, at the next general election Ireland would probably return as many as sixty Catholic candidates unable to take their seats. (Catholics were not barred from standing for election; they were prevented from taking a seat in parliament by the requirement that members swear two oaths, one denying transubstantiation and the other pledging loyalty to the sovereign as governor of the Church of England.)

While the Clare election was in progress, Peel received reports of the Irish temper. Fitzgerald wrote that the Catholic organization was 'so complete and so formidable that no man can contemplate without alarm what is to follow in this wretched country'.[70] His opinion was confirmed by the Lord Lieutenant, the Marquess of Anglesey.

> Such is the extraordinary power of the Association, or rather of the agitators. . . that I am quite certain they could lead on the people to open rebellion at a moment's notice. . . . I believe their success inevitable – that no power under heaven can arrest its progress. There may be rebellion, you may put to death thousands, you may suppress it, but it will only be to put off the day of compromise; and in the meantime the country is still more impoverished, and the minds of the people are, if possible, still more alienated, and ruinous expense is entailed upon the empire.[71]

By 1825, although his supporters did not suspect it, Wellington had decided that Catholic emancipation ought soon to be conceded.[72] By 1828, to resist was more than impracticable; it was dangerous.

The official case for Catholic emancipation was almost unanswerable.[73] It was accepted by all the 'Protestant' ministers, including Henry Goulburn, J. C. Herries, and Lord Bathurst. To maintain the existing system, Peel argued, would leave the government with two courses: to remain inactive with respect to Irish affairs or to propose measures of restriction and control of the emancipation campaign. The first was impossible and the second fraught with difficulty. In 1828 the Commons had voted by a majority of six to settle the question; support for a policy of coercion was therefore improbable. In addition, a government formed on the principle of resistance could not find enough ministers of experience and ability to run the country's affairs. England already employed five-sixths of its infantry in keeping peace in Ireland; a rebellion there could not be defeated without calling home colonial troops. Finally, there was a consideration close to Peel's heart, the damage that was done to the aristocratic constitution by the prolonged division between the two branches of the legislature on the Catholic question.[74]

In 1829 the government successfully got its Emancipation Bill through parliament. In his comprehensive statement of the argument for the Bill on 5 March, Peel did not pretend that he now believed emancipation to be right. Nor did he repent of his long and staunch opposition to it.

> I do not think it was an unnatural or unreasonable struggle. I resign it, in consequence of the conviction that it can be no longer advantageously maintained; from believing that there are not adequate materials or sufficient instruments for its effective and permanent continuance. I yield therefore to a moral necessity which I cannot control, unwilling to push resistance to a point which may endanger the Establishment that I wish to defend.[75]

Twice in his career Peel discarded, on cogent grounds, a major part of his party's tradition. Anti-Catholicism and agricultural protection were the very core of the Tory party in the two generations after 1815. There was a third element, the mixed constitution of King, Lords and Commons. In 1829 and 1846, when his government introduced the repeal of the Corn Laws, Peel claimed, not unreasonably, to be acting as a true Conservative in the defence of the constitution. But constitutions are in themselves valueless. Their function is to protect values and interests. When defenders of a constitution see their values overthrown and their interests unprotected, they may begin to question the worth of the constitution. Throughout the 1820s the Tory 'Protestants' and agriculturalists were unable to persuade an unreformed House of Commons to inflate the currency, to arrest the trend towards free trade, or to repeal the malt tax. Catholic emancipation was the bitterest defeat of all. The Canningites seemed to have been harried out of the party in vain. The Emancipation Bill was opposed in the Commons by 173 supporters of the government on the second reading and 142 on the third reading. In the

Lords 109 Tory votes were cast against it. Resentful and angry at being abandoned, many of the dissidents went into opposition, and some of them turned their thoughts towards parliamentary reform.

Notes and References

Ultras and liberals

1 Buckingham, *Memoirs of . . . George IV*, i, 237.
2 Aspinall, *Lord Brougham and the Whig party*, 25. It was also, of course, a diplomatic yielding to the demands of President Madison.
3 Jones, *'Prosperity' Robinson*, 106.
4 Speaking in the debate in 1822 on Lord John Russell's motion for an inquiry into the state of the representation: quoted in Rolo, *Canning*, 162.
5 Wynn to Buckingham, 26 Sept, 1822: Buckingham, *Memoirs of . . . George IV*, ii, 125–32.
6 Mrs Arbuthnot, *Journal*, 3 Feb, 1824, i, 284–5.
7 William Fremantle, for one, called 'the whole arrangement' by which Huskisson and Robinson replaced Maryborough and Vansittart 'a complete victory for Canning' (Fremantle to Buckingham, 29 Sept, 1823: Buckingham, *Memoirs of . . . George IV*, ii, 7–9). But Liverpool informed Vansittart that Castlereagh had been 'most anxious' to place Huskisson in a more prominent position (Liverpool to Vansittart, 14 December, 1822: Yonge, *The Life and Administration of . . . 2nd Earl of Liverpool,* iii, 208–10); and Wellington told the Duke of Buckingham, who felt slighted at being passed over, that Canning 'certainly made no stipulation' for Huskisson (Wellington to Buckingham, 23 Sept, 1823: Buckingham, *Memoirs of . . . George IV*, ii, 6).
8 Ward to Buckingham, 28 Sept, 1824: *ibid*, ii, 125–32.
9 Arbuthnot to Liverpool, [*c.* 7 Oct, 1823]: C. Arbuthnot, *Correspondence*, 46–57.
10 Liverpool to Arbuthnot, 8 Oct, 1823: *ibid*, 57–8.
11 Peel to Croker, 23 March 1820: Croker, *Correspondence and Diaries*, i, 170.
12 The phrase is the Duke of Rutland's, quoted in Feiling, *Second Tory Party*, 345.
13 Mrs Arbuthnot, *Journal*, 26 Sept, 1823, i, 259.
14 His Gaols Act of 1823, with its uniform set of rules for prison government, its provision for monthly inspection, and its requirement of annual reports to the Home Secretary, was a foretaste of that invasion of rural administration by the central government which many Tories found an objectionable feature of Whig legislation in the 1830s.
15 See Canning, *Correspondence*, i, 22–3.
16 Mrs Arbuthnot, *Journal*, 1 Aug, 1823, i, 247–8.
17 *Ibid*, 24 Sept, 1824, i, 339.
18 Ziegler, *Addington*, 342.
19 Bartlett, *Castlereagh*, 184.
20 Lord Redesdale to Lord Colchester, 8 Sept, 1822 and 26 Sept, 1824: Colchester, *Diary*, iii, 256–8 and 342–3.

21 Hobsbawm, *Industry and Empire*, 77.

22 Jones, 'Prosperity' *Robinson*, 72.

23 See R. G. Wilson, *Gentlemen Merchants*, 113–14.

24 Brock *Liverpool and Liberal Toryism*, 182.

25 In 1825 the repeal of the Combination Acts, which had made it illegal for workers to combine for purposes of work, hours and wages, passed through parliament almost without debate.

26 Canning to Lord Granville, 12 May 1826: Canning, *Correspondence*, ii, 53–4.

27 Creevey to Miss Ord, 13 May 1826: *The Creevey Papers*, ii, 101.

28 Mrs Arbuthnot, *Journal*, 14 May 1826, ii, 25–6. Palmerston remarked in the same year that 'the real Opposition of the present day sit behind the Treasury bench; and it is by the stupid old Tory party, who bawl out the memory and praises of Pitt while they are opposing all the measures and principles which he held most important; and it is by these that the progress of the Government in every improvement which they are attempting is thwarted and impeded' (Aspinall, *Brougham and the Whig Party*, 138). Lord Rosslyn satisfied Creevey 'by facts that nothing can equal the rage of the old Tory Highflyers at the liberal jaw of Canning and Huskisson' (Creevey to Miss Ord, 14 April 1826: *Creevey Papers*, ii, 99).

29 Huskisson to Lord Grenville, 9 March 1826: Aspinall, *Brougham and the Whig Party*, 280.

30 Brougham to Lord Lansdown, [c. 16 April], 1827: Aspinall, *Formation of Canning's Ministry*, 96–7.

31 Peel to Lord Eldon, 9 April 1827: Parker, *Peel*, i, 460–2.

32 Charles Wynn found Canning's language on the question to be 'in such a tone as to lead me to doubt extremely whether he can be relied upon' and believed that 'when it comes to the point, you will find him on almost every subject make some excuse for siding with the Protestant party' (Wynn to Buckingham, [Dec.] 1822 and 28 August 1823. Buckingham, *Memoirs of George IV*, i, 397–9 and 490–2).

33 I do not share the apocalyptic view of Sir Keith Feiling expressed in this statement: 'On a small thing in the scale of history, the personal hatred of Wellington for Canning, a great and predestined thing had come to pass: the end of a party' (*Second Tory Party*, 352).

34 Sir Robert Wilson, *Canning's Administration*, 16.

35 Mrs Arbuthnot, *Journal*, 9 Feb, 1825, i, 375.

36 Greville, *Memoirs*, 10 Aug. 1827, i, 183–4.

37 Croker to Brougham, 14 March 1839: *Correspondence*, ii, 352. The remark about tea comes from 'Julia', one of the satires on women by the eighteenth-century poet, Edward Young: 'For her own breakfast she'll project a scheme,/Nor take her tea without a stratagem.'

38 Mrs Arbuthnot, *Journal*, 22 April 1824, i, 304.

39 A decade later Canning's example was being followed. Lord Althorp spoke at a public dinner in September 1831, and by the end of 1833 one newspaper could speak of 'the customary ministerial dinner circuit'. Brougham, Lord John Russell and Lord Stanley had all delivered public speeches. But they were all Whigs, and William IV reprimanded Lord Melbourne in 1834 for allowing the practice to continue (Jennings, *Party Politics: Appeal to the People*, 121).

40 Memorandum, 1827: Wellington, *Despatches*, iv, 179–80.

41 Lord Stanley to Disraeli, 27 Jan, 1857: Moneypenny and Buckle, *The Life of Benjamin Disraeli*, iv, 61–3.

42 Memorandum, 3 June 1827: Canning, *Correspondence*, ii, 321.
43 Greville, 11 Aug, 1831, *Memoirs*, ii, 181–3.
44 See Peel to Eldon, 9 April 1827: Parker, *Peel*, i, 462–3; Peel to the Bishop of Oxford, 15 Jan, 1828: *ibid*, ii, 30–1; Wellington to Canning, 7 May 1827: Colchester, *Diary*, iii, 505–7.
45 Sidmouth to Viscount Exmouth, 21 April 1827: Aspinall, *Formation of Canning's Ministry*, 150–1.

'Catholics' and 'Protestants'
46 Spring–Rice to Lansdown, 6 Sept, 1827: Aspinall, *Politics and the Press c. 1780–1850*, 220.
47 Burdett to Lansdown, 21 April 1827: Aspinall, *Formation of Canning's Ministry*, 146–7.
48 Rolo, *Canning*, 17.
49 Aspinall lists thirty-two Canningites in 1827 in an appendix to his article, 'The last of the Canningites'.
50 After listening to a debate in the Lords on Catholic emancipation in 1829, Mrs Arbuthnot described Goderich's performance in her journal: 'Lord Goderich was *beneath criticism*, he ranted and tore like a strolling player, and some one remarked to me that, if he had not been swamped before, he had now done it effectually for that he shewed he had not ballast enough to keep himself afloat on the stream of mediocrity.' (*Journal* 6 April 1829, ii, 263).
51 Londonderry to Wellington, 12 Aug, 1827: Wellington, *Despatches*, iv, 83–6. The three Whig ministers were Lansdowne, Home Secretary, Lord Carlisle, Commissioner of Woods and Forests, and the worn-out George Tierney, Master of the Mint. Of thirty-seven other government places, Whigs filled only six.
52 Abercromby to Lord Carlisle, [February 1827]: Aspinall, *Formation of Canning's Ministry*, 28.
53 Londonderry to Lord Burghesh, 20 Oct, 1827: Westmorland, *Correspondence of Lord Brughesh, afterwards Eleventh Earl of Westmorland*, 261–2. In July Arbuthnot sent this report to Peel: 'I have heard from both Holmes [the whip] and Herries [not in Canning's government, but in Goderich's] that the exactions of the Whigs drive Canning nearly out of his senses . . . Herries says that Canning and the Whigs are so far asunder as pole from pole, that Canning's time is spent in resisting their encroachments, that of these encroachments even Huskisson now complains bitterly . . . and that in short the two parties are so at variance that sooner or later they must split and break to pieces.' (Parker, *Peel*, i, 491–2).
54 Bexley to J. C. Herries, 1 Sept, 1827: E. Herries, *Memoir of the Public Life of . . . John Charles Herries*, i, 210–11.
55 Aspinall, *Politics and the Press*, 218.
56 Colchester, *Diary*, iii, 527.
57 Londonderry to Mrs Arbuthnot, 18 April 1827: Aspinall, *Formation of Canning's Ministry* 114–15.
58 Bishop of Oxford to Peel, 6 Jan, 1828: Peel MSS, Add. MSS 40343, ff. 101–3; Peel to the Bishop of Oxford, 15 Jan, 1828: Parker, *Peel*, ii, 30–1.
59 Peel to Gregory, 18 Jan, 1828: Peel, *Memoirs*, i, 15–17.
60 Peel to Gregory, 1 Feb, 1828: *ibid*, i, 17–18.
61 Newcastle to Lord Colchester, 15 Jan, 1828: Colchester, *Diary*, iii, 537–8.
62 Palmerston to E. Littleton, 16 Sept, 1829: Fay, *Huskisson and his Age*, 95.

63 Huskisson to Lord Granville, 3 June 1828: *ibid*, 93.
64 See the entries in Ellenborough's diary for 11 and 12 May 1828: 'Just as we were coming away [from a cabinet meeting] Huskisson began to talk about co-operation with Russia, a point settled long ago, and on which we are pledged to one line of conduct by solemn public declarations of our views . . . the never-ending return to the same point annoys the Duke very much'; 'I find Bathurst and the others very angry indeed at Huskisson's revival of the old proposal for acting with the Russians' (Ellenborough, *Political Diary*, i, 103–4).
65 *Ibid*, 14 March 1828, i, 56–7.
66 Ashley, *The Life of . . . Palmerston: 1846–1865*, i, 123.
67 See Ellenborough, *Political Diary*, 29 March and 2 May 1828, i, 73 and 96–8. Charles Arbuthnot, whose main source of information was the Duke, thought that Wellington's attitude was justified: 'Many had doubts whether the taking Canning's friends was wise or not. I knew that the Duke was so circumstanced as at that time to have no option left to him; and having reunited himself with that party, he was determined to act with them most cordially & fairly. It was very soon evident that the reunion on their part had been hollow & insincere, & that they were still in combination as a separate party, always on the look out to thwart the Duke, & ready to overthrow him if the means existed. It was therefore most fortunate for him that Huskisson (in his eagerness to be courted & to be intreated to remain) overshot his mark.' (Arbuthnot to Lord Cowley, 22 Nov, 1828: Arbuthnot, *Correspondence*, 109–11). Wellington told Lord Colchester early in February that he had been compelled to take in Huskisson because Peel had refused to lead in the Commons without him (Colchester, *Diary*, iii, 547).
68 *Ibid*, 2 June, 1828, iii, 567–8.
69 Mrs Arbuthnot, *Journal*, 26 Aug, 1830, ii, 382.
70 Fitzgerald to Peel, 5 July 1828: Peel *Memoirs*, i, 113–15.
71 Anglesey to Lord Francis Gower, 2 July 1828: *ibid*, i, 146–9. Lord Francis Gower, the Chief Secretary of Ireland, passed the letter on to Peel at Anglesey's request.
72 See Mrs Arbuthnot, *Journal*, 5 March 1825, i, 380.
73 It is concisely put in Peel's memorandum of 12 Jan, 1829 (Peel, *Memoirs*, i, 284–94).
74 One additional argument of Peel's, that the youth of the country, particularly the young members of parliament, favoured Catholic emancipation (Memorandum of 12 Jan.; Peel to the Bishop of Oxford, 8 Feb, 1829: *ibid*, i, 360–2) seems to have been wrong. Of the new members elected to the Commons in 1826, those born before 1780 split 13–11 in favour of emancipation, those born between 1780 and 1790 split 22–16 against, and those born after 1800 were 22–18 against (Machin, *The Catholic Question*, 195).
75 Quoted in Gash, *Secretry Peel*, 570.

Chapter 3

Toryism and reform I:
Inside parliament

The last Tory government

The passing of the Act of Catholic Emancipation completed the disruption of party alliances which had begun with the resignation of Lord Liverpool. Whiggery was divided in its loyalty between Lord Grey and Lord Lansdowne and Toryism was dissolved into its elements, the Canningites, the Ultra 'Protestants', and the followers of Wellington and Peel. Yet the instinct for party, Croker believed, remained the mainspring of English politics.

> I am one of those [he wrote in 1830] who have always thought that party attachments and consistency are in the *first* class of a statesman's duties, because without them he must be incapable of performing any useful service to the country. I think, moreover, that it is part of our well-understood, though unwritten, constitution, that a party which aspires to govern this country ought to have *within itself* the means of filling all the offices, and I therefore disapprove of making a *Subscription Ministry* to which every man may belong, without reference to his understood principles or practices.[1]

That was a severe construction of English constitutional history. Between 1828 and 1830 there were many politicians, Whig and Tory, who longed for a return to the 'broad-bottom' governments of the mid-eighteenth century. But despite Wellington's reputation for studied disinterest in party,[2] the notion did not appeal to him. From the time when he dismissed the Canningites from his government in the spring of 1828 to the day in November 1830 when his government fell, Wellington's strategy was to hold together his own following and to conciliate the Ultra opponents of Catholic emancipation. Of course Wellington's view of party was mixed with the idea of service to the Crown. He was careful, in 1830, to refer to his followers as 'the party of government'[3] and his behaviour rested on the negative judgement that the disparate forces of the opposition were incapable of combining to overthrow him. The strategy failed because Wellington was unable to regain the allegiance of the hard core of the Ultras and because he would not trim his policy to meet the resuscitated enthusiasm for parliamentary reform.

Palmerston believed that the origin of Wellington's strategy lay in the vote of the House of Commons on 12 May 1828 to consider the Catholic claims.

Wellington studied the list of absent members and decided that a majority of the whole House was pro-Catholic. A few days later the Canningites were out of the government, discarded, so Palmerston believed, as a sop to the Ultras from a Prime Minister who had decided that the time was ripe to settle the Catholic question.[4] If that was the Duke's reasoning, he miscalculated. The second reading of the Emancipation Bill was opposed by 173 Tory commoners and 109 Tory peers. For most of them, opposition to emancipation did not imply permanent opposition to the government. Nevertheless, one cabinet minister, Sir Henry Hardinge, estimated that the combined loss of Canningites and Ultras cost the government fifty seats, or a hundred votes in a division.[5]

Wellington treated the dissident Tories with forebearance. Of the three ministers who voted against emancipation, only Sir Charles Wetherell was expelled from office, and he was suspected of having leaked the news of the government's conversion.[6] Throughout the summer and autumn of 1829 Wellington resisted pressure to form a junction with the Grey Whigs. Lord Rosslyn was given the Privy Seal and Sir James Scarlett took Wetherell's place as Attorney-General, but the support of the body of the Whigs could not be bought so cheaply. Office for Grey himself was the required price, and Wellington would not share power with any Whig leader, least of all Lord Grey.[7]

The 1830 session of parliament therefore began with a potential majority of Whigs, Canningites and Ultras against the government. From the Whigs there was little apparent danger. The main body of them were content to follow the genial lead of Lord Althorp, who, although he found fault with the government's handling of foreign affairs, would not offer organized opposition to ministers who pursued conciliation and economy at home.[8] A small group of Ultras, however, led by the ambitious Sir Richard Vyvyan, only twenty-eight years old, made it their business to remove Peel and Wellington from office. In the summer of 1829 Vyvyan had counted thirty-five Tories 'strongly opposed to the present government' and eighty-nine doubtful Ultras 'who voted in favour of the third reading but whose sentiments are unknown'.[9] Wellington kept the allegiance of the doubtfuls. Vyvyan's energetic attempt to organize an alliance of Whigs and Ultras under the nominal leadership of the deeply unpopular Duke of Cumberland ended in failure.[10] By November he was writing to Lord Eldon of the gradual defection from their ranks.[11] He succeeded, nevertheless, in keeping an organized group of about thirty Ultras in existence throughout 1830.

The motives of the Ultras were mixed. All of them shared, to some degree, the anger which provoked the Duke of Newcastle to describe Wellington, in the extravagant language to which he was given, as 'the most unprincipled, most artful, most heartless, most ambitious and most dangerous man, not excepting Cromwell, that this country has seen for many a long year'.[12] It was difficult for ardent Protestants ever to place their trust in Wellington again. When a large number of Ultras, in defiance of their convictions and their past behaviour, declined to oppose a Jewish Relief Bill in April 1830, Wellington told Peel that they were 'pretending that they did not like to oppose a measure for which they should afterwards be called upon to vote, etc.'.[13] The Ultras' animosity was strengthened by the government's prosecution, in the autumn of 1829, of the Ultra-Protestant newspaper, the *Morning Journal*, for libellous attacks against ministers. (A number of Ultras subscribed money to help save the paper, but it went out of business in the following May.)[14] A handful of Ultras became converted to parliamentary reform, seduced by the argument that the Protestant sentiment of the country would have been properly represented in a House of Commons elected by popular constituencies. To attribute the success of the Catholic campaign to the irresponsibility of rotten borough members may have been false reasoning – in Buckinghamshire the borough members split evenly on the issue[15] – but there was a subtler argument for spiteful men. The Anglican Church was far more important to the constitution than the ramshackle electoral system. 'Upon what principle,' asked the Ultra Lord Falmouth, 'will you talk of preserving the tree of the constitution, when you have laid your axe to the root?'[16]

Wellington's difficulties were increased by the two great currents which gathered force as the year 1830 went on: an economic recession, particularly in agriculture, and a revival of interest in parliamentary reform. For three years wages had been falling and unemployment rising.[17] In the speech from the throne the government acknowledged the existence of distress, but avowed that it was partial and recommended caution in proposing remedies. That did not satisfy the farmers and tradesmen, who attended county meetings to petition for a reduction in taxation, the abolition of sinecures and pensions, and the paring of the military and naval establishments. The tide ran so strong that many county Tories were 'forced on account of their constituents to unite in the general cry of distress'.[18] The Ultra leader, Sir Edward Knatchbull, member for Kent, moved an amendment to the address censuring the government for not perceiving that the distress was general throughout the country, and the government was saved from defeat only by the votes of twenty-eight Whigs.[19]

Further evidence of the Ultras' hostility came when they stayed away from the vote on Lord John Russell's motion to give two members each to Manchester, Leeds and Birmingham, and when they joined with Canningites and Whigs to support a motion for a select committee to inquire into the state of the labouring classes and the effect of taxation on industrial production.[20] The government managed to defeat both motions, but the Ultras' behaviour prompted Lord Ellenborough to revive his campaign for an alliance between the government and the Grey section of the Whigs.[21] Wellington remained uninterested. The moment for such a junction had passed. Grey was roused from semi-retirement by the government's seeming blindness, both to the extent of hardship in the country and to the spirit of unrest which it was breeding. 'But what in the name of God,' he wrote to 'Ben' Ellis, 'can be meant by talking of increased . . . distress in *some parts* of the country? I should like to know what part is exempt.'[22] Grey's mind had been moved. He had begun to believe that the continuance in office of an inflexible Tory government threatened to provoke revolutionary feelings in the country capable of destroying the existing social structure. That change of mood coincided with the death of George IV. For Grey the accession of the mildly pro-Whig William, Duke of Clarence, opened the door to office. It also opened the door to cooperation with the Ultras, from whom the Whigs had shied away at the beginning of the 1830 session, largely because of their unwillingness to associate themselves with the Duke of Cumberland. Over the mind of George IV Cumberland had exercised a powerful influence, and the King's death, as Wellington observed, put an end to Cumberland's political power.[23]

At the dissolution of the 1826 parliament in July 1830 there were no symptoms of cooperation between the government and any of the groups in opposition. Events were moving in the other direction. In the last week of June Huskisson proposed to Grey an alliance to turn out the Duke. In the first week of July Palmerston turned down the offer of a cabinet place unless Grey and Huskisson came in with him. And the Whigs decided, at a meeting at Lord Althorp's, at last to conduct themselves as a systematic opposition. 'Here, then, I am,' Grey wrote, 'declared against the Ministers, and though without any formal union, supported by the favourable disposition of all the parties not connected with the Government.'[24] Wellington apprehended the forces which were gathering against him. He did not draw from that the inference that he needed to change his policy or bend himself to the reform breeze. That all four opposition groups had achieved some kind of common purpose was evidence to him that their motives were personal, not based on principle. There were, he wrote to Peel in June, varying degrees of interest in reform, but 'at the present moment there is very little difference of principle among public men in general'.

> I don't know that we should not be sufficiently strong in numbers to undertake to carry on the government, particularly after the return of a new Parliament, even though this opposition should be formed as I have supposed and reinforced, as it will most probably be, by some who now support the government. If we should not be sufficiently strong, I confess that I don't see the remedy.[25]

Before the elections of 1830 the Tory Whip, William Holmes, put the government's strength 'on any great question' in the House of Commons at 300.[26] For the first time since 1812 a Tory government was at risk on a vote of confidence. Its survival depended upon a clear expression of approval by the electorate. That was something difficult to gauge in an age when Lord Brougham laid himself open to criticism for publishing 'indecent and unconstitutional *tabular* details' of the votes and affiliations of private members.[27] Extensive and lavish bribery prevented returns from being an accurate reflection of electoral opinion. Although the government gained seats, most observers, even on the government side, interpreted the elections to have gone decisively against it. Joseph Planta, the chief election manager, gave the government 311 members and counted, in addition, thirty-seven 'doubtfuls' favourable to the government. There were also twenty-four 'very doubtful'.[28]

What mattered was how the doubtfuls judged the meaning of the election results. In pre-reform elections interest was focused on the popular constituencies, especially the large counties in England and Wales, where, despite the small number of contests (only nine in 1830) and the pervasion of 'legitimate' landlord influence, the 40s freeholders were deemed to express their free opinion. There, if anywhere, 'public opinion' was to be measured. At the 1830 elections, indeed, the much-vaunted power of landlord influence was overcome. 'Wherever the elections approached to the character of being popular,' the *Annual Register* recorded, 'no candidate found himself a gainer by announcing that he had been, or intended to be, an adherent of the existing government.'[29] It was that, despite the numerical gain in seats, which gave 'very little prospect of amendment in the character or power of the ministry.'[30] No election carried more significance than that for Yorkshire. Lord Brougham, the radical Whig and the leading advocate in parliament of electoral reform, modestly called his return for the largest county in the country 'the most extraordinary event in the history of party politics'.[31] Brougham's victory was all the more important because of Yorkshire's unrepresented industrial towns. William Ord, a Whig member of parliament, called him 'the member for Yorkshire, or rather one should say the member for Leeds, Huddersfield, and Sheffield'.[32] At Devonshire, according to Viscount Sandon the most Tory county in England,[33] the Whigs won a contested election. Middlesex returned the famous Radical leader, Joseph Hume, unopposed, apparently at the invitation of local Tories.[34] Not one cabinet minister was returned for a popular constituency. Of the 82 English and Welsh county seats, the government won only 28, and of the 28 members for the 13 most popular boroughs, it could claim only 3. The *Annual Register* counted 236 English and Welsh members returned by constituencies more or less popular and divided them into 78 ministerialists, 142 opposition, and 16 neutral.[35] Ministerialist strength rested on a few gains in Ireland, where the 40s freeholders had been disfranchised in 1829 in order to weaken the effect of Catholic emancipation, in the close boroughs, and in Scotland, where the Tories controlled every seat. The contraction of the Tories' electoral base since the days when they had been able to count upon the fair support of the independent country gentlemen was exposed by the vote on the first reading of the Whigs' Reform Bill in March 1831. Despite the shock which the Bill's extensive redistribution of seats gave to moderate opinion, the representatives of the 'open' constituencies which Peel had listed in 1829 voted in favour of it by sixty-nine votes to fifteen.

The elections in the counties were marked by an unexpected rift in the supposed solidarity of agricultural society. Denis le Marchant, Brougham's shrewd and knowledgeable private secretary, commented that one salient feature of the county elections was that the small gentlemen and independent farmers separated themselves from the aristocracy and opposed government candidates.[36] Another observer made the same point.

> The combined influence of small properties in the hands of the many has in several instances preponderated over the influence of great properties in the hands of the few. Yorkshire, Devonshire, Cambridgeshire, and Surrey have exhibited decisive examples that in the elections for counties which were formerly little more than close boroughs in the hands of a few great families, the middle classes are becoming too strong for the aristocracy.[37]

D. C. Moore has argued that this turn of events was the consequence of the lead which Ultra–Tories gave to reform agitation and that there was, really, no breakdown of rural solidarity.[38] There is some evidence for the view During the elections in Cornwall Vyvyan recommended an alliance between Ultras and Whigs, and in Derbyshire the old Tories lectured the government candidate on reform and retrenchment, leading the Duke of Devonshire to call it 'a Whig county now'.[39] Wellington's policies had turned almost the entire Tory press against him and *The Times* viewed the elections as a contest between the government and the Ultra–Tory or country party.[40] But the only modern study of a particular county, Buckinghamshire, a corn-growing county and seat of Lord Chandos, the Ultra Whip in 1830, throws doubt on Professor Moore's argument. At a great county protest meeting in February 1830 the chair was taken by a grocer, the resolutions were moved by a brewer, and the chief speakers were two farmers, a corn merchant and a surgeon. Neither Chandos nor any squires attended. 'Reforming sentiment in Bucks . . . far from being a product of the discontents of the landed classes, was rather largely a product of discontent with the landed classes, springing from an intense resentment against landed influence.'[41]

When traditionally Tory landlords changed their opinions or lost control over their inferiors, the Tory party had neither the power nor the authority to intervene. Party organizers did not presume to trespass on the ground of the independent country gentlemen. Planta lamented the failure of government candidates in Cambridgeshire, Suffolk, and Devonshire, but he defended himself to Peel against possible criticism of his electoral management. 'I must repeat that these matters are utterly unmanageable by anything that can be done from hence.' Upon the selection of candidates, the nature of a campaign, and even the decision whether to contest a seat, the party managers had no influence in the English counties. 'In such things as we can influence & in some degree controul, we have not been unsuccessful.'[42]

In one regard Planta was putting a bold face on defeat. The government used all the means it could muster against the Canningites, many of whom were vulnerable, since they had been returned for 'Treasury seats' in 1826. Still, the government made only a few gains and failed to keep the Canningite leaders out of parliament. The most striking Canningite successes were the returns of Charles and Robert Grant. They were both abolitionists and there was a close link between the abolition of slavery and reform, owing to the abolitionists' belief that a corrupt House of Commons would remain subservient to the pro-slavery West India interest. It has been suggested that the government's vigorous use of its influence against Canningite candidates, by revealing the coarseness of Treasury manipulation of the corrupt boroughs, turned the Canningites into reformers.[43] It may have pushed them harder in that direction, but by their votes in 1828 and 1829, the followers of Huskisson had already departed from Canning's immoveable adherence to the existing system. At Staffordshire, in 1830, E. J. Littleton was returned as a Whig, and John Denison stood (and was defeated) at Newcastle-under-Lyme as a moderate reformer.[44]

The elections gave prominence to a cluster of issues – reform, retrenchment, agricultural distress and anti-slavery sentiment – and however Planta and Charles Ross, his assistant, might coax a statistical majority for the government out of the returns, mere numbers could not disguise the truth in Sir Thomas Fremantle's observation that 'those candidates who stood on the Government interest found no advantage from it, but on the contrary were invariably obliged to abandon such ground for the ground of reform and economy, and are committed in almost every instance to conditional engagements on these points'.[45]

The lesson of the elections was that no government could now stand on the ground of outright resistance to reform. Yet there now occurred one of the signal events in the history of Toryism: the Duke of Wellington's comprehensive declaration against the reform of parliament. On 2 November Lord Brougham unexpectedly announced that he would bring forward his plan of reform in a fortnight. That announcement drew from Wellington the forthright statement that his government neither had, nor intended to produce, a measure of reform. He went further. He did not believe that the existing system of representation could be improved and he believed that it possessed the 'full and entire confidence of the country'.[46]

It was a remarkable statement, made in defiance of the election results and of the spreading agricultural revolt throughout the south and the south-east. Why did he make it? According to some historians it was a blunder, to be explained by the Duke's isolation and his naive political sense.[47] By others it is explained as the inevitable result of the recent turnabout on Catholic emancipation. The reputations of Peel and Wellington could not withstand another conversion on a major article of Tory faith.[48] It is also explained as an eleventh-hour grasp for the support of the Ultras. Those explanations tell part of the story. But they rest on two assumptions. They assume that accidental circumstances dictated Wellington's behaviour, thereby implying that in other circumstances, left to his own lights, he would have acted differently. And they assume that a small dose of Tory reform would have carried the party successfully through the crisis.

Of the second assumption Peel said all that is necessary.

> We are too apt to think that any great political event, or great popular excitement, is referable to some one cause. Whether the Duke had made his speech in November 1830 or not, we should never have been able to stem the tide that was setting in in favour of Radical Reform.[49]

The other raises more difficult questions of the meaning of party and the expectations which a party raises in the minds of its supporters. Robert Blake has written that there was nothing inevitable about the shipwreck and that 'the party's past did not preclude a compromise on this issue'.[50] It might then be asked whether there is ever an issue on which a party may not compromise. Two elements in the recent history of the Tory party stand out. The first is that Tory ascendancy rested heavily on those nomination boroughs which would be the first victims of the reformers' axe. In 1827 Croker sent to Canning a list of those boroughs which showed that Tory peers controlled 203 of them and Whig peers only 73.[51] Tories therefore had an immediate interest in preserving the electoral system. The second is that throughout the 1820s, while the Tory government was adjusting its views on economic and social questions, it had remained staunch against even the mildest schemes of piecemeal reform, the last being Lord John Russell's motion for a Bill to extend the representation to Manchester, Birmingham and Leeds.

Only in the more distant past did Toryism find room for parliamentary reform, in the days before the rebirth of the Tory party, when Burke was a Whig and Pitt a reformer. The Tory party which had grown up after 1793 had closed the door on reform. Burke allowed that the extent of the suffrage was a matter to be decided by prudence and experience, according to the circumstances of the age, but the basis of his political thought was his rejection of the Radicals' belief in the 'rights of man'. Tories were taught by Burke not to confuse, as the Radicals did, rights and desires. Toryism was rooted in the idea of justice, not rights. The need for reform had to be demonstrated by showing that it would produce better government. 'Government,' Burke wrote, 'is a contrivance of human wisdom to provide for human wants.' Wellington believed that, in the various reforms of the previous decade, Toryism had been providing for them. The mere desire of the people for reform could become a Tory argument for it only if it was believed that the failure to satisfy that desire would make government impossible. On that ground Peel and Wellington took up Catholic emancipation in 1828. That England was in a similar condition in the autumn of 1830 was less evident. Perhaps Wellington lacked prescience. But it robs the reform crisis of its significance for Toryism if the explanation of his behaviour rests solely on accidents. Conservatism necessarily suffers irreversible defeats. Yet if Conservatives always surrender to the enemy before the battle, they deny themselves the opportunity of victory. More important, they undermine their prospects for the future by inviting the taunt that theirs is a party which says what it does not mean and guards what it will not defend.

Two weeks after Wellington's speech his government was destroyed when the House of Commons voted by 233 votes to 204 for Henry Parnell's motion to refer the civil list to a committee. The majority included many previous supporters of Tory governments. After the 1830 elections, Planta drew up a list of twenty-three violent Ultras, whom he expected to be anti-ministerialist, and thirty-seven moderate Ultras, whom he expected to be friends.[52] They voted as follows:

Voting on Parnell's Civil list motion

	for	against	absent
37 moderate Ultras	15	7	15
23 violent Ultras	14	2	7

The new parliament contained eleven old Canningites, who met at Palmerston's house in the first week of November and decided 'to go all lengths, so far as respected turning out the Government'.[53] Eight of them voted with Parnell, only one with the government. 'Protestant' revenge, agricultural discontent, and the rising sentiment for reform in the English counties combined to defeat the government. The most significant aspect of the division on Parnell's motion was that only fifteen of the members for the English county seats – those country gentlemen who for so long had been the backbone of the 'party of government' – supported the ministry. That was the mark of how dependent on the rotten boroughs the Tory party had come to be.

The defeat of the government does not prove the indiscretion of Wellington's anti-reform declaration nor the futility of his solicitude for the Ultras. It is impossible to know whether a more hedged statement would have won Wellington more Ultra votes; and historians have been quick to censure him without paying enough regard to the subsequent history of the Ultras. When Lord John Russell introduced the Whigs' Reform Bill in March 1831 fifty-eight of Planta's Ultras were still in the House of Commons. They voted forty-seven to ten against the Bill. The eleven Canningites voted seven to three in its favour. Two years later, the first reformed parliament contained twenty-five of Planta's Ultras, twenty of them back within the Conservative party. Of the remaining six Canningites only one, Viscount Sandon, was a Conservative.[54]

If Peel was right, a moderate statement from the Duke would neither have saved his government nor forestalled radical reform. His unbending stance lost the party none of its parliamentary supporters in the long run. If reform was inescapable, it was better for the Tory party that it should come from the Whigs.

The 1832 Reform Bill

The contents of the Great Reform Bill, the debate on it, and the dramatic events which attended its passage have been too fully discussed to merit more attention.[55] To men living in 1831, if not to a modern school of historians, the Whigs' plan of reform was so sweeping in its destruction of ancient borough representation, so democratic in its extension of the suffrage to £10 householders, and therein so revolutionary in its implications for the future, that from the night that it was revealed to an astonished House of Commons, 1 March 1831, there was no question for the Tories but to oppose it. ('We have got the cholera at Sunderland,' wrote Mrs Arbuthnot. 'I think it a far inferior evil to the Reform Bill.'[56]) The only question was how, whether to oppose the Bill root and branch and take no further interest in it or to occupy a lower plane of resistance and, by amendments in committee and negotiations with the government, attempt to modify it.

What mattered, above all, was how Peel answered the question. Although the Tory party did not yet recognize officially any such position as leader of the opposition, Peel towered over his colleagues in intellect, in political experience, and in national influence. His part in the Catholic trauma and his condescending manner had cost him the affection of his followers, but he was indispensable to them. They could act neither contrary to, nor without, him.

Peel was not simply indulging in self-pity when he described his retirement from official life after eighteen years as a source of unmixed satisfaction.[57] For two years he had carried the difficult burden of sustaining Wellington's government in the Commons' debates almost alone. He had suffered a savage campaign of ridicule and abuse in the press for his betrayal of the Protestants. He retired to Drayton Manor to sulk, to brood and to consider his future course in politics. Retirement was, however, foreign to his nature. 'Peel was a man,' Professor Gash has written, 'who throve on power, responsibility and action. The sudden deprivation of all three brought him in the years 1831–32 to the lowest point of his political life.'[58] When his ex-cabinet colleague, J. C. Herries, visited him at Drayton in late January 1831, he found him 'acting very imperfectly the character of a country gentleman indifferent to office and politics'.[59]

Peel took no part in the daily activities of the party stalwarts who, from the moment that Wellington was defeated, busied themselves with the establishment of a new organization and the financing of the Tory press. At Drayton he came to two conclusions: that his future career must be founded on a realistic acceptance of the new political world which reform would create and that his close association with the Ultra–Tories, now broken, must not be renewed. The friction between the right wing of the Conservative party and Peel, which was to bedevil the party for the next twenty years, had its origin in the aftermath of Catholic emancipation and Wellington's fall. 'I would not abandon any one opinion I entertain,' Peel told Henry Goulburn, 'in order to conciliate Ultra-Tory support. I positively, as I told Sir R. Vyvyan, would not advance . . . on the currency question, for instance, one single yard, to gain a whole party.'[60] In January and February of 1831, as rumours of the breadth of the Whig proposals spread, some of the Ultras attempted to persuade Wellington to rally the fragments of the party under his and Peel's banner.[61] Wellington poured cold water on the suggestion.

> We are not at this moment on better terms with our former friends than we were. I firmly believe that the majority of them prefer the Whigs to us. The reason is this, their objection to us is without reason, and personal. They must see that we were right, and they wrong upon the R.C. question; but they are angry with us for that very reason.
>
> Then, I must add that there are difficulties in the way of an accommodation with that party, which appear to me to render it impossible under existing circumstances . . .
>
> Every day may produce an alteration. I certainly will not consent to any compromise of principle; I will oppose every measure which I may think revolutionary; but I cannot think it would be right to commence a regular factious opposition at the present moment.[62]

Once the publication of the Whig measure had driven back even the hard core of the Ultras into the ranks of the anti-reformers, Wellington began to move closer to them and to encourage reconciliation. But Peel's position, based on a longer-term strategy, did not change. By June 1831, the elections over and a fresh battle on the second Reform Bill to come in the autumn, Peel, although happy to vote with the Ultras against reform, remained uninterested in a formal party connection with them.[63] He was then at the nadir of his reputation within the party.

> As to Peel [wrote Mrs Arbuthnot], he appears to hate every body & every body hates him, but he shewed consummate ability & powers of speaking of the highest order during the late short session; & it is not possible for anyone to lead except him, but he is cross grained, timid, afraid of committing himself, afraid of having followers & a party for fear they shd be a clog upon him in any future arrangements; not that he has any projects of joining the enemy, but if called upon to form a Govt, he wd like to be in a position to choose who he pleased without anyone having claims on him. . . . He is supercilious, haughty & arrogant & a most bitter & determined hater. He has been down at his place in Staffordshire almost ever since the dissolution, & has scarcely had any communication with anyone.[64]

The Tory response to the reform crisis was therefore governed by Peel's determination to resist the reformers' arguments with all his powers, to record a direct negative against their proposals, but not to become closely involved in a resolute campaign against the details of the Reform Bill in committee. The result was that the Bill which became law in 1832 owed only two important provisions, although they were very important, to the Tories: the famous Chandos amendment enfranchising the £50 tenants-at-will in the counties and General Gascoyne's amendment to maintain the number of English seats in the House of Commons, which forced the dissolution of 1831 and was incorporated in the revised Bill presented to the new parliament after the 1831 elections. For the next thirty-five years the Conservative party, whose essential strength lay in the English counties, had reason to be grateful for those amendments.

Peel's attitude was reasonable, given the state of the Tory party in 1831–32. For a fractious party to mount a serious attack on the Bill in committee was impracticable, especially after the large Whig majority returned at the 1831 elections. The sources of Peel's intransigence, however, lay deeper. The House of Lords, with a Tory majority, faced a real practical choice between outright resistance and selective amendments, and when the revised Bill went to the Lords in 1832, those Tory peers known as the 'waverers', who had been negotiating with the cabinet for a compromise, in order to avoid pushing the government to create new peers by defeating the Bill outright, recommended that it be given its second reading and then altered in committee. Peel advised against such a course in a long letter written to the leading waverer, the Earl of Harrowby.[65] The gist of his argument was that the evils which would follow from 'the infusion of a popular and democratic spirit into the House of Lords' were preferable to those which would follow from the Lords' abdication of their constitutional responsibility. The Tories' chief objection to the Reform Bill was, after all, that it destroyed the constitutional balance of King, Lords and Commons and threatened to submerge the aristocracy in democracy. If the Whigs were allowed to achieve their purpose by the mere threat of creating peers, then they would gain the prize 'without incurring the odium and disgust of the crime'.

> Why have we been struggling against the Reform Bill in the House of Commons? Not in the hope of resisting its final success in that House, but because we look beyond the Bill, because we know the nature of popular concessions, their tendency to propagate the necessity for further and more extensive compliances. We want to make the 'descensus' as 'difficilis' as we can – to teach young inexperienced men charged with the trust of government that, though they may be backed by popular clamour, they shall not override on the first springtide of excitement every barrier and breakwater raised against popular impulses; that the carrying of extensive changes in the Constitution without previous deliberation shall not be a holiday. . . . Suppose that we had given way, that we had acquiesced in the Bill, and given no trouble to the Ministers. My firm belief is that the country, so far from being satisfied with our concessions, would have lost all reverence and care for remaining institutions, and would have had their appetite whetted for a further feast at the expense of the Church, or the monarchy. . . . Mine is a melancholy view, as it excludes the prospect of success. It excludes, however, participation in the crime.

The spirit of Peel's argument, that Toryism could not participate in a radical Reform Bill, underlay the party's conduct in 1831–32. It ensured the collapse of Wellington's hopeless attempt to answer the King's call to form an administration in May 1832. Of course, if Peel's advice had been followed to the letter, the result would have been disastrous for the party. As Professor Kitson Clark remarked, by yielding to the threat of a creation of peers, the Tories kept their majority in the upper house, 'and that was of more use to them than would have been courage in an unpopular cause'.[66] Nevertheless, by resisting reform to all practical limits, the Tory party had retained its character. Peel was shrewd enough to perceive the truth in the paradox that the appeal of Conservatism in the new world of politics would be all the stronger for having fought openly against its creation.

The bold sweep of the Reform Bill may have left the Tories no choice but to oppose it. It should not, even so, be overlooked that their very opposition was a step in the transformation of the Tory party from the party of government to the Conservative party and hence in the development of the modern party system. The support which William IV gave to reform – by giving ministers leave to introduce their Bill, by granting them a dissolution after the defeat on General Gascoyne's amendment in April 1831, and by promising to create peers – dismayed and angered the Tories.[67] Peel believed that once the King had 'so far sanctioned the measure as to allow it to be introduced', it became 'very difficult for any minister to prevent all change in the representation'.[68] Peel was being a trifle old-fashioned. The notion that the Crown gave its sanction to a measure in principle by allowing its introduction – or even, as when George III, in 1801, refused to allow Pitt to raise Catholic emancipation in cabinet, by allowing ministers to discuss it – belonged to a previous age of genuinely personal monarchy. But he was not being stupid. In the eighteenth century most questions of domestic legislation were introduced by private member; neither the Crown nor the government was constitutionally responsible for them. In the years from 1815 to 1830 there had been a great increase in the number of government Bills and therefore a rapid advance of the notion of ministerial responsibility for legislation. At the same time the Crown had not yet withdrawn from the sphere of active politics. It was, however, being forced out. William IV could not – had he wanted to – prevent Grey's government from bringing in its Reform Bill. He was powerless to influence its contents. Yet the Whig ministers made unsparing use of the King's name to attract support for it. Hence arose the Tories' difficulty: how could they support the Crown, which was now powerless to prevent governments from introducing legislation, but which was nevertheless believed still to give that legislation its blessing?[69]

The difficulty was emotional, not practical. The inevitable answer was to oppose the King. Even before the Reform Bill was introduced that decision had, in fact, been made when the Tories, out of office, sloughed off their past principles and set about transforming themselves into an opposition party with a permanent organization and the rudiments of an electoral machine.[70] The same difficulty presented itself to the bishops in the House of Lords and they, too, made the same decision. Historically, their place was above the party battle. Their function was to support, or at least not to oppose the Crown and its ministers, since it was their obligation and their interest to uphold lawful authority and the established institutions of the country. In fact the episcopal bench was deeply Tory, since from the time of the French Revolution reform had been associated with dissent and unbelief. During the long years of Tory rule they had been able to dress their Toryism in the garb of constitutional propriety. Whig rule raised the spectre of a Radical assault on the Church and brought the bishops' Toryism into the open. In 1834, when the bishops were lining up against the Irish Tithes Bill, Charles Greville wrote that 'to see the Bench of Bishops in direct and angry collision with the King's Prime Minister is a sorry sight',[71] but by that time the bishops had ceased to belong to the party of the Crown. On the second reading of the second Reform Bill, in October 1831, twenty-one bishops voted against the government, only one for it;[72] and, heedless of William IV's plea to the Archbishop of Canterbury to restrain the bishops from meddling in party politics, eight of them voted against the Irish Church Bill in 1833, again only one for it.

The bishops were a separate group in the House of Lords, but their appearance on the open ground of the party battle coincided with the disappearance of the party of the Crown in the Lords as a whole. Paley had assigned to the Lords, as their proper function, 'to fortify the power and secure the stability of regal government'. By the 1830s even the core of the King's party, the Scottish and Irish representative peers and the household peers, were being whipped. Like the bishops, they voted against the Reform Bill, and by the end of the decade Greville remarked truly that, for the first time, all the peers were 'either Whigs or Tories arrayed against each other and battling for power'.[73]

The disappearance of the party of the Crown, and of the principle which had sustained it, was a natural response to the rising temperature and widening scope of party debate. It denuded the Tory party of one of its two cardinal articles of faith. The change in the party's name in these years from Tory to Conservative did not signify a break in the party's continuity. But it acknowledged that the historical function of Toryism was too restricted to answer the requirements of the mid-nineteenth century. The Tory response to the reform crisis represented the final triumph of the idea of a loyal opposition, which has justly been described as 'the ultimate criterion of a democratic State' and 'the most important contribution which British political practice has made to the development of free government'.[74] As the Crown moved out of politics, the Tory party, under its new name, entered unabashedly into the party battle, where, in and out of office, its function was to oppose radicalism. Those men whom, as late as 1830, the Duke of Wellington had called the party of government became, in the space of three or four years, the 'great Conservative party'.

Notes and References

1 Croker, *Correspondence and Diaries*, ii, 82.
2 A. S. Turberville, for example, wrote that 'although he was a thorough Tory, none was ever less of a party man' (*The House of Lords in the Age of Reform, 1784–1837*, 227). Aspinall described him as a man 'who cared little for party, and who was never an ordinary party leader' (*Brougham and the Whig Party*, 183).
3 Wellington to the Duke of Northumberland, 16 March 1830: Wellington, *Despatches*, vi, 532–3.
4 The Earl of Donoughmore also believed that the Duke turned out the Canningites in order to bring in a Catholic settlement: see Machin, *Catholic Question*, 200.
5 Ellenborough, *Political Diary*, ii, 60
6 Mrs Arbuthnot wrote in her journal on 28 March 1829: 'I talked a great deal with the Duke about the arrangements to be made when the Catholic Bill has passed and how the different offices shd be filled. The question is what party he shd unite himself with. His anxious wish, I may say determination, is to draw the Tories round him again & his notion is, when the Bill has passed, to send for Ld Lowther, Mr Bankes & others who have resigned ... & say that the Bill is passed & the cause of difference at an end & that he hopes they approve the general measures of the Govt and that they will resume their offices.' (*Journal*, ii, 260).
7 When he was forming his government in January 1828 Wellington told Peel that offices were 'open to all mankind, except one person, Lord Grey' (Parker, *Peel*, ii, 27). In June 1829 he described Grey to Mrs Arbuthnot as 'a very arrogant & a very obstinate man. He has seen a good deal of him in the coal committee & says he is quite sure he wd be a very disagreeable person to do public business with' (Mrs Arbuthnot, *Journal*, 26 June 1829, ii, 291).
8 Althorp to T. F. Kennedy, 4 Feb, 1829: Cockburn, *Letters*, 205–6.
9 Machin, *Catholic Question*, 183–4.
10 See the correspondence between Vyvyan and the other leading ultra county member, Sir Edward Knatchbull, in Knatchbull–Hugessen, *Kentish Family*, 177–90. See also B. T. Bradfield, 'Sir Richard Vyvyan and the fall of Wellington's government', *University of Birmingham Historical Journal*, xi, 2 (1968), 141–56.
11 Machin, *Catholic Question*, 186.
12 Knatchbull–Hugessen, *Kentish Family*, 179.
13 Wellington to Peel, 6 April 1830: Parker, *Peel*, ii, 145–6.
14 Aspinall, *Politics and the Press*, 342–4.
15 Davis, *Political Change and Continuity*, 79.
16 Cannon, *Parliamentary Reform*, 191.
17 See the chart in Rostow, *British Economy of the Nineteenth Century*, 125.

18 Arbuthnot to Lord Cowley 11 April 1830: C. Arbuthnot, *Correspondence*, 125–8.
19 Broughton, *Recollections of a Long Life*, iv, 7–8.
20 Ellenborough, *Political Diary*, 24 Feb. and 18 March 1830, ii, 201 and 241–15.
21 'The Tories are most radical. Sir R. Vyvyan told Holmes or Planta his object was to reduce the Government majorities as much as possible . . . I took home Sir George Murray. He expressed his surprise the Duke should cling to the hope of reclaiming the Ultra–Tories, whom he would not get, and who were not worth having. I confess I think he carries it on too long, although I am not surprised he should have wished it at first.' (*ibid*, 7 Feb, 1830, ii, 185–7).
22 Brock, *The Great Reform Act*, 69.
23 Memorandum of a letter from Wellington to Peel, [June, 1830]: Wellington, *Despatches*, vii, 106–8.
24 Flick, 'The fall of Wellington's government', *JMH*, March 1965, 64.
25 Memorandum, [June, 1830]: Wellington, *Despatches*, vii, 106–8.
26 Ellenborough, *Political Diary*, 2 May 1830, ii, 233–4.
27 Anon, *Observations on Two Pamphlets . . . Attributed to Mr. Brougham*, 70.
28 Planta's total calculations were these: friends, 311; moderate ultras, 37; doubtfuls favourable, 37; very doubtful, 24; foes, 188; violent ultras, 23; doubtfuls unfavourable, 23; and Huskisson party, 11. (Fragment. Peel MSS, Add. MSS 40401, ff. 181–95).
29 *Annual Register*, 1830, 146.
30 W. H. Fremantle to the Duke of Buckingham, 26 Aug, 1830: Buckingham and Chandos, *Memoirs . . . of William IV and Victoria*, i, 43–5.
31 Brougham (attributed), 'The Ministry and the state of parties', *Edinburgh Review*, July 1830, 582.
32 Old to Kennedy, 23 Sept, 1830: Cockburn, *Letters*, 236–7.
33 Machin, *Catholic Question*, 188.
34 Brock, *Reform Act*, 94.
35 *Annual Register*, 1830, 147. These figures are identical with the ones given in *The Result of the General Election; or What Has the Duke of Wellington Gained by the Dissolution?*, 1830, whose author (anonymous) claimed to have seen the Treasury lists.
36 D. le Marchant to F. T. Baring, 14 Aug, 1830: Baring, *Journals and Correspondence* i, 66.
37 Anon, *Parties and Factions in England at the Accession of William IV* (pamphlet), 48.
38 Moore, 'The other face of reform', *Victorian Studies*, Sept, 1961, 7–34.
39 Brock, *Reform Act*, 104.
40 Aspinall, *Politics and the Press*, 101; *Times*, 14 July 1830.
41 Davis, *Political Change and Continuity*, 87.
42 Planta to Peel, 18 Aug, 1830: Peel MSS, Add, MSS 40401, ff. 103–3.
43 Brock, *Reform Act*, 87.
44 Wedgwood, *Staffordshire Parliamentary History from the Earliest Times to the Present Day*, 66.
45 Fremantle to Buckingham, 26 Aug, 1830: Buckingham, *Memoirs of . . . William IV and Victoria*, i, 43–5.
46 *Hansard*, 3rd series, i, 52. Wellington's attitude was not a disease of advancing years. In January 1830 the Oxford Union passed a motion against parliamentary reform by 73 votes to 3 (Gladstone to W. W. Farr, 4 Feb, 1830. *The Prime Minister's Papers: 2 Memoranda*, 212–14).
47 Brock, *Reform Act*, 69, 121–3.

48 Blake, *The Conservative Party*, 1970, 11.
49 Brock, *Reform Act*, 119–20.
50 Blake, *Conservative Party*, 11.
51 Croker to Canning, 6 April 1827: Croker, *Correspondence and Diaries*, i, 370–2.
52 Peel MSS, Add. MSS 40401, ff. 181–95.
53 Broughton, *Recollections*, iv, 60.
54 See Appendix 1.
55 The best modern account of the passing of the Bill is Brock's *Reform Act*. For the debate on the Bill, see the first chapter of Gash, *Politics in the Age of Peel*.
56 Mrs Arbuthnot, *Journal*, 6 Dec, 1831, i, 437. Mrs Arbuthnot died of cholera in 1834.
57 Peel to Henry Hobhouse, 24 Nov, 1830: Peel MSS, Add. MSS 40401, ff. 290–5. Mrs Arbuthnot described Peel as 'completely broke down by the fatigue & wear of mind consequent upon having no help' and 'delighted at having so good an opportunity for resigning' (*Journal*, 15 and 20 Nov, 1830, ii, 401–2).
58 Gash, *Sir Robert Peel*, xvii.
59 Aspinall, *Politics and the Press*, 334.
60 Peel to Goulburn, [November/December, 1830]: Parker, *Peel*, ii, 170–1.
61 See Lord Burghesh to Wellington, 27 Feb, 1831: Wellington, *Despatches*, vii, 408; Londonderry to Buckingham, 5 and 25 Jan, 1831: Buckingham, *Memoirs of . . . William IV and Victoria*, i, 189–90, 196–8.
62 Wellington to Buckingham, 26 Jan, 1831: Buckingham, *Memoirs of . . . William IV and Victoria*, i, 199–201.
63 Peel to Goulburn, 5 June 1831: Parker, *Peel*, ii, 187–8.
64 Mrs Arbuthnot, *Journal*, 8 June 1831, ii, 422–3.
65 Peel to Harrowby, 5 Feb, 1832: Parker, *Peel*, ii, 199–202.
66 Kitson Clark, *Peel and the Conservative Party*, 53.
67 Ellenborough recorded Wellington's feelings on the matter: 'There never has been a state of things like the present – mob, Ministers & King united against the property of the country. The King had by the Dissolution placed himself in the situation of C[harles] the 1st when he gave up the power of dissolving the Long Parl. He could not now dissolve this.' (Aspinall, ed., *Three Early Nineteenth Century Diaries*, 112.) See also Londonderry to Burghesh, 19 Nov, 1831: 'All feelings of public conduct and public spirit are become dead, and mortified by the imbecile apathy of the monarch, and the weakness which pervades his character, makes me feel we shall have no security or peace in England until the Almighty delivers us from his reign.' (Westmorland, *Correspondence of Burghesh*, 268–70.)
68 Mrs Arbuthnot, *Journal*, 29 March 1831, ii, 415–16.
69 The difficulty was not, of course, unprecedented. There had been occasions, such as the repeal of the Stamp Act by the Rockingham ministry when the King's friends, acting on the knowledge of the King's private disapproval, voted against ministers.
70 These matters are discussed in the next chapter.
71 Turberville, *The House of Lords in the Age of Reform*, p. 315.
72 The government was beaten by forty-one votes. 'I don't believe', wrote Mrs Arbuthnot, '. . . he [Grey] expected to be beat by nearly so many & had persuaded himself that the Bishops wd not dare to vote. The Ministers are furious with them, and all the venom of the Radical Press is let loose against them, & *disfranchising* the Bishops is now openly preached by the 'Times' &

petitioned for by the blackguards all over the country.' (*Journal*, 23 Oct, 1831, ii, 429–30.)

73 This paragraph is based on Large, 'The decline of "the Party of the Crown" and the rise of parties in the House of Lords, 1783–1837', *EHR*, Oct, 1963, 669–95.

74 T. D. Walden, quoted in Fairlie, *The Life of Politics*, 194–5. Precisely the same point was made by a contributor to the *Edinburgh Review* in 1855, when, it has been alleged, party was in disfavour: 'It is the legal and acknowledged existence of an organised opposition to the Government which is, in these times, the most salient characteristic of a free country and its principal distinction from despotisms . . . a political opposition, though it may be an institution highly distasteful to a reigning despot, is a necessary condition for freedom and political progress.' (Foord, *His Majesty's Opposition*, 4).

Chapter 4

Toryism and reform II: Outside parliament

The 'Charles Street Gang'

Politicians who prepared to return to London at the beginning of 1833 scarcely knew what to expect from the first parliament elected under the terms of the Reform Act. Against the hugh phalanx of Whigs, reformers and Radicals of many hues, stood about 150 Tories who had survived the elections of the previous December. Not since the days of Whig exclusion had the future of Toryism looked so bleak. 'I believe I ought to go & shut myself up,' Charles Arbuthnot wrote to the rising star of the Tory organization, Francis Bonham. 'I cannot bear to hear from morning till night the dreary forebodings of every person I meet, & I bear it the less as my own mind is dreary enough already. No smash given by Napoleon in the midst of his greatest successes was more complete & terrific than the overthrow wch. has struck our Party to the ground.' Arbuthnot agreed with Bonham that the Whig government was not immortal; but he was voicing the fears of many of his colleagues when he predicted that its heirs would be, not the Tories, but the extreme Radicals.[1] The Ultra leader, Sir Richard Vyvyan, suggested to the electors of Bristol that in order to avert Radical rule Whigs and Tories ought to come together.[2] The stimulus of the reform battle, however, had raised party temperatures. Constituencies which for a generation had 'kept the peace' (and avoided the expense of a contest) by returning one Whig and one Tory suddenly, in 1831, had been treated to the Bacchanalia of a contest and more often than not had responded by ousting the Tory and sending back to Westminster two reformers. 'Two parties are now generated,' Croker wrote to Peel, 'which never will die.'[3]

It was remarkable, indeed, with what speed and determination a group of influential Tories, immediately after the resignation of Wellington's government, had set about the organization of the Tory party. The initiative came from men who had long served the Crown in offices in which the distinction between professional administrators (the equivalent of the modern civil service) and party politicians had not yet been drawn – men like Joseph Planta, Secretary to the Treasury from 1827 to 1830, and William Holmes, Treasurer of the Ordnance and chief government Whip in the Commons from 1820 to 1830. Within just a week of the Duke's fall, they, J. C.

Herries, Lord Ellenborough, and the Duke's old friends, Arbuthnot and Sir Henry Hardinge, had formed a committee to direct the operations of the opposition. Men who had learned the arts of management necessary to uphold a government, who might have looked forward to ending their careers as they had begun them, in the pay of the Crown, now put their training at the service of a party.

The object of the committee was to defeat reform, by keeping compact the Tory party in parliament, by rebuilding the Tory press in order to rally opinion in the country, and by lending what assistance it could to Tory candidates at the next general election. From the outset the committee's view of its function went far beyond the mere whipping of votes in parliament, as an entry in Ellenborough's diary for 23 November 1830 indicates. 'Called on Arbuthnot. We are to have a little stock purse & to have printed notes, &c. He will see Croker & secure a Morning & evening newspaper & *John Bull.*'[4] In none of its purposes was the committee immediately successful. Its activities, nevertheless, in the years 1831 and 1832, laid the foundations of the organization of the Conservative party.

It was in those years that the word 'Conservative', which Daniel O'Connell called 'the fashionable term, the new-fangled phrase now used in polite society to designate the Tory ascendancy',[5] became accepted as the name of the party. First used, apparently, in the *Quarterly Review* in January 1830, it was quickly adopted. Early in 1831 Mrs Arbuthnot used the word in her journal for the first time; and by 1832 even the Ultra-Tory publication, *Blackwood's Magazine,* had accepted it.[6] The Whigs having taken up reform in earnest, backed by the Radicals who proclaimed their designs on the Established Church and the monarchical constitution, the principal duty of Tories was clearly to conserve the constitution in Church and State. The word 'Tory', although it appealed (as it still does) to men with a deep reverence for the past, smacked of high resistance to Whig constitutionalism and of the insensitive *hauteur* of Eldon, Sidmouth, and the Duke of Cumberland. 'Conservative' was a drier name, but one more appropriate to the party which had survived the reform crisis and which aspired, under Peel, to regain public confidence in its ability to govern the nation. 'Peel', Greville wrote in 1835, after the fall of Peel's first, short ministry, 'clearly does not intend that there shall be (as far as he is concerned as their leader) a *Tory* party, though of course there must be a Conservative party, the great force of which is the old Tory interest.'[7]

Greville had put his finger on the source of Peel's acute discomfort in opposition. Everyone knows Macaulay's description of Gladstone in the 1830s as 'the rising hope of those stern and unbending Tories'. Less well known are the words which came after: 'who follow, reluctantly and mutinously, a leader whose experience and eloquence are indispensable to them, but whose cautious and moderate opinions they abhor'.[8] Peel's character and manner have been the subject of grotesque caricature. With friends or a small company he could be amiable. Nevertheless he was almost universally regarded in the early 1830s as unsuited by temperament for the leadership of a party. The Scottish journalist, Archibald Alison, said that on a gathering his presence 'operated as a refrigerator' and Lord Bathurst found him 'to want that cordiality of manner, & that elevation of mind, one of which wins the affections, & the other commands the respect, of a popular assembly'.[9] The warmth of Peel's personality did not radiate beyond the circle of his close friends and associates. In 1837 Lord John Russell sent to Lord Melbourne a waspish letter which he had received from Peel. 'Peel's answer is cross and sarcastic,' Melbourne wrote in reply, 'but I take that to be the real nature of the man, and it is only prudence and calculation that ever make him otherwise.'[10] Peel recognized his shortcomings. 'I feel a want of many essential qualifications which are requisite in party leaders; among the rest, personal gratification in the game of politics and patience to listen to the sentiments of individuals whom it is equally imprudent to neglect and an intolerable bore to consult.'[11] Peel took pride in the qualities of reserve and shyness which his critics condemned. His strength as a minister, namely his abstention from the passions which act upon a party, was his weakness as a leader. Throughout his career, therefore, he did not seek to overcome what others, but not he, considered to be personal faults. The result was a series of incidents like one described by Lord Ellenborough in July 1831.

> Last night there was a division on the wine duties which left us in a minority of 157 to 258. . . . This is bad. The case was not a very strong one & not very well fought, but the worst of it was that Peel, having sat out the greatest part of the debate, went away without speaking or voting. This has made all the Party very indignant. It disheartens and disgusts. . . . No Party can be kept together unless they are well and gallantly led.[12]

Conservative fractiousness in 1831–32 did not, of course, stem wholly from defects in Peel's leadership. Constitutional pratice assigned no recognized place to party leaders in opposition. (From 1815 to 1830 the Whig leadership had been vacant, unexercised, or in dispute.) It was not to be expected, moreover, that the disagreements and distrusts which had characterized the party in the last years of Tory rule should be dispersed overnight by the shock of defeat. They remained. And there was one occasion, in the midst of the debate on the Reform Bill, when three Tory meetings took place simultaneously, one at Peel's, one at Sir Richard Vyvyan's, and the third at Charles Wetherell's. Throughout the session, the Ultras, even those who voted against the Reform Bill, sat on the crossbenches, distinct from the rest of the party. Numerous attempts were made to bring the two wings of the opposition together. Wellington effected a union of the Tory peers. But Peel, although he continued to play a leading part in planning the opposition's parliamentary operations, refused to be drawn into acting as leader of the party. The notes which Holmes, as Whip, sent to members soliciting their attendance at debates, did not go out in Peel's name. Peel showed no interest in the activities of the party committee. And he remained proof against suggestions that he patch up his quarrel with the Ultras.

Peel was looking ahead to the day when he might be asked to form a government. When it should come he did not want his prospects of success to be damaged by close alliance with the Ultras. He explained to Herries why he would not attend a party dinner in June 1831.

> So far as the dining implies a new party connection, it is a point on which everyone must be at liberty to decide for himself. I shall most certainly claim the privilege myself individually. I presume the Duke of Cumberland will be there – perhaps in the Chair. As I have not been on speaking terms with his Royal Highness since the Catholic question, I am not to be at once committed to a party connection with him such as, very possibly, attendance at that dinner would imply.[13]

Within months of the formation of Grey's government, speculation had begun about the possibility of detaching conservative Whigs – especially ex-Canningites like Lord Stanley and Palmerston – from the government and bringing them into a moderate Conservative party led by Peel. Peel was eager not to discourage such a move by open friendliness with the Ultras. His past association with them was largely accidental. Had he not, as a young man, been given the post of Irish Secretary, from which eminence he had uttered his party's conventional Protestant sentiments, he would never have become their 'darling'. Having broken with them, he meant never to be placed in that false position again. In a letter marked 'most private', he had confided to a close friend at the beginning of 1828 that the whinings of those Ultras who were dismayed by the inclusion of the Canningites in Wellington's government meant nothing to him. 'I care not for the dissatisfaction of Ultra-Tories. This country ought not, and cannot, be governed upon any other principles than those of firmness no doubt, but firmness combined with moderation.'[14] When the first reformed parliament met in 1833, Peel was his own man, not the acknowledged leader of the party,[15] free to chart his own course and leave others to decide whether they wished to follow him. Despite the extravagant, misleading emphasis which has been placed on Peel's contribution to the Conservative recovery after 1832 – briefly, that he united a new party behind a reformist policy – the original impulse to organize the party came from other men, whose motive was to do battle with the reformers. The careless language in Donald Southgate's statement that 'the party owed its *formation* to Peel's conviction that the conservative forces which could be mustered in a party . . . were wider than anyone else imagined'[16] arises from, and abets, the confusion implicit in the widely used phrase, 'Peel's Conservative party'. No leader, especially not Peel from 1832 to 1846, owns his party.

Peel's semi-retreat did not stop lesser men from reorganizing the party. The committee which had formed itself in November 1830 had, at first, no fixed residence. Meetings took place as matters dictated at several houses, principally Arbuthnot's, Herries', and Planta's in Charles Street, off St

James's Square. At Croker's suggestion the committee also met regularly for dinner at the Athenaeum. At one of those dinners, on 2 February 1831, it was decided to take premises near Jermyn Street 'for our reunions'.[17] For whatever reason that decision was abandoned and, since the approach of the parliamentary session made it urgent to have a permanent office, rooms in Planta's house were given over to the sole use of the committee. Planta refused to accept payment for the rooms, but an important step towards changing the informal committee into a semi-official secretariat was the hiring of Edward Fitzgerald as a paid secretary. From Charles Street notes were sent to members of parliament, parliamentary strategy was discussed, electoral matters were attended to, and the management of the press was conducted. It was soon apparent that so substantial an undertaking needed to be placed on a proper footing. On 16 June, two days after the assembling of the parliament elected in the spring of 1831, Planta's house was made the official headquarters of the committee. Planta had by then vacated the house. The fifteen Conservatives present at the meeting when that decision was made (including Wellington, but not Peel) agreed to pay £5 each towards the maintenance of the house, the cost of notes, and Fitzgerald's salary. Subscriptions from party members brought in some thousands of pounds more.

The committee's work was not entirely novel. Its routine business was done by men like Planta and Holmes who had been accustomed to supervising government affairs from the Treasury. *Ad hoc* committees of election had been appointed throughout the years of Tory rule, and they had usually a small 'General Fund' at their disposal. Governments, too, had always provided Treasury money and official information to those newspapers who agreed to tow the government line. But it was new for an *opposition* to conduct those operations in a professional and permanent fashion. There was something unrespectable about it, and the committee was derisively referred to by the Whigs as the 'Charles Street Gang'.

Charles Street soon proved unsatisfactory. By far the most important part of its business was relations with the press and there were many Conservatives who agreed with the Duke of Wellington that 'the gentlemen!!! of the Press are so demoralized that nobody can approach them without incurring the risk of loss of character'.[18] When, therefore, the Charles Street's press activities involved the committee in financial embarrassment and the risk of scandal, Conservatives began to look for a new party centre. There were other reasons. In December 1831 Holmes complained that Planta's house was too small and proposed that a larger house be taken and turned into a club.[19] Charles Street had neither the space nor the character to serve as the headquarters for the party as a whole. What was wanted was an establishment which, in addition to housing the Whips and the election managers, should act as a social centre for Conservative members of parliament, a fusion of Charles Street and the old Tory club,

White's, which had by then lost most of its political flavour. Peel and Wellington agreed to act as trustees of a new club and on 10 March 1832, at the Thatched House Tavern, the Marquess of Salisbury presided over a meeting called to consider the offer of Lord Kensington's house in Carlton Terrace. The offer was accepted and a week later the club was formally named the Carlton. The entrance fee and the annual subscription was fixed at £10. Before the end of the month, 500 Conservatives had agreed to join; by 1833 the membership was 800. Charles Street remained the centre until the new premises were ready, but by 1833 the Carlton had taken over its functions. After moving into new quarters on Pall Mall in 1835, the Carlton remained the party headquarters until the establishment of Central Office in 1868.

The foundation of the Carlton Club was the major achievement of the small committee from which it sprang. In their specific aim of spreading Conservative opinions through a revitalized Conservative press the committee was disappointed. They began their work at a time when the combined influence of the revived movement for parliamentary reform and Wellington's distaste for the world of journalism[20] was to make almost the entire London press Whig or Radical. The main support of Wellington's government, the evening *Courier,* went over to the Whigs in November 1830. So did the *Sun.* Professor Aspinall described the *Courier's* defection as 'characteristic shabbiness',[21] but the paper had suffered for being Canningite in 1827 and had seen four editors come and go under government pressure from 1828 to 1830. There was point, moreover, to the *Courier's* explanation in its first leader after the change that its new allegiance derived from the Duke's outright rejection of any electoral reform. The only papers left supporting the opposition were the *Morning Post,* two evening dailies, the *Standard* and the *Star,* and one Sunday, *John Bull.* The first of those had too small a circulation to rival the Whig *Times* and *Morning Chronicle,* while the high Toryism of both the *Standard* and *John Bull* restricted their popular appeal and made politicians wary of close connexion with them.

None of the Tory papers had a direct link with the party. On 23 November 1830 it was decided to secure a morning and an evening paper. Four days later Ellenborough recorded that Croker had promised 'to manage the *John Bull'.*[22] There were various methods of influence for the committee to consider: buying newspapers outright, securing them as reliable party organs with financial assistance, and writing regular articles for them to publish. Their first endeavours concerned the possibility of establishing a new Conservative morning paper and the improvement of the *Morning Post.* The proprietor of the *Standard,* Mr Baldwin, proposed to Lord Lowther that the party should begin its own paper, with him in charge, on the same scale as *The Times.* Baldwin asked for £10,000; Lord Lowther thought £30,000 would be nearer the mark. The 'press fund' at Charles Street was not nearly large enough to meet Baldwin's requirements, and the committee, which was undoubtedly relieved not to enter into the risky commercial business of newspaper ownership, abandoned the idea of running its own paper. At the same time Lowther, who accepted that a newspaper was 'not likely to succeed unless conducted as a matter of trade', noted the ambivalent attitude which was to remain with the Conservative party for years to come. 'When the proposal was made from the *Standard,* not the least encouragement was given by any of our friends to establish the morning paper. They all scold and grumble because a morning paper is not established but will not contribute to put one on its legs.'[23]

Once Baldwin's offer was rejected, the committee turned its attention to the *Morning Post* and the evening papers. In return for enlarging the paper (which was, as it turned out, not done) and improving its reports of parliamentary debates, the editor of the *Post* was promised information and articles. The evening *Star* printed only 150 copies daily and was therefore useless. For its evening paper the committee looked instead to the *Albion,* which had begun publication in the week that Wellington resigned. A former editor of the *Courier,* Mr McEntagart, was hired at £300 annually to be a liaison officer between the paper and the party and the paper was given an annual subsidy of £300. Subsidies, Herries hoped, would prove preferable to ownership. 'We shall not be bound to continue the aid longer than while we approve of the conduct of the paper, and we shall therefore hold the editor, and our own agent in the business, more completely under obligation to us.'[24] Herries was too sanguine. In the spring of 1831 Croker complained that the Conservative press was asleep[25] and Lowther confessed that the management of the *Morning Post* was a failure. 'Old Byrne [the editor] has a sale for his fashionable news, and *we* had authority to assist him with reporters and a Parisian correspondence, but he would neither delay his press nor give room for such intelligence. I conclude he knows his own trade better than we do, and that he would not risk the readers of his fashionable news for the prospect of making his paper a more decided political one.[26] The *Albion* was not much better. By the beginning of 1832 its circulation was only 1100 and it was heavily in debt.

Subsequent ventures yielded as little reward. The party suffered from the overwhelming support in the country for reform.

> One of the worst signs of the times [Lowther wrote] is that none of our old literary Tory supporters will risk any part of their capital in a Tory morning newspaper. They have no confidence in such a scheme, and think the Tories a declining party. . . . I have taken infinite trouble, and the result is, the Tories will not subscribe, and none of the printers or literary Tory supporters will embark their own capital in such a scheme.[27]

Provincial newspapers struggled against the tide of reform. The Tory *Dumfries Journal* was bought by Whig businessmen in 1832 for £500, the former editor having 'been ruined by the decrease of sale consequent to his zealous and fearless assertions of good, though unpopular, principles'.[28] In Kent there were newspapers published at Maidstone, Canterbury and Rochester, none of them Conservative.[29]

Attempts to buy the *Public Ledger and Guardian* and the *Morning Herald* in the summer of 1831 came to nothing. It was impossible to raise the money, especially so soon after the heavy expenses which Conservative candidates had incurred at the 1831 elections. Lord Mahon attempted to raise £10,000 by subscription in a circular asking Conservatives to give £50 to effect 'an object of great and pressing importance to the constitutional cause'. The circular did not, however, state that the object was the purchase of a newspaper. Mahon presumably knew that such an appeal would fall on deaf ears. An unspecific request, as Wellington pointed out, was also bound to fail.

> It calls upon 200 persons to spare £50 each at the disposal of Holmes and Mr Fitzgerald, without requiring explanations how the same shall be employed. Supposing that there are 200 gentn. able to part with such a sum without inconvenience, which I think doubtful, you would scarcely expect that they would not require an explanation of the objects of the subscription.[30]

There was as yet no rational structure of party finance. Parties were still little more than the sum of the individual members of parliament who composed them. Those individuals tended to their own business. They looked after their electoral arrangements and expenses for themselves. They might answer, spasmodic requests to contribute money for a limited, specified purpose, but they were, for the most part, unwilling to contribute to a fund for the general maintenance of a party organization which they believed to be of no direct personal advantage to them. The Charles Street committee was left with only meagre resources, which went to the distribution of anti-reform pamphlets and the assistance of William Praed, a member of parliament and a contributor to the *Morning Post* and the *Albion,* and Theodore Hook, editor of *John Bull*.[31]

Two further episodes confirmed the Conservatives in their distrust of newspaper men. The first concerned a Mr W. R. Jordan, a journalist who was introduced to Hardinge by the Rev. G. R. Gleig, the friend and biographer of Wellington. Gleig had taken a continuing interest in the press and he persuaded Hardinge to employ Jordan. Jordan was paid £1,000 out of Hardinge's pocket to 'organize a System of general Management of the Press' and to use his contacts to bring Conservative influence to bear on a number of newspapers, principally the *Morning Herald*. That was in August 1831. Within a month Hardinge and Gleig realized that they had been duped. The money had not been put to its proper purpose, nor would Jordan return it. And since Hardinge's initiative was highly irregular – it amounted to bribery – legal action would embarrass him and the Conservative party. 'It is quite clear,' Gleig wrote, 'that our thousand pounds are gone, unless we make up our minds to expose Mr Jordan and in so doing expose ourselves.' It was, he told Hardinge, 'an act of great forebearance – but a prudent act – in you to lie still'.[32]

The employment of McEntagart as a general press officer landed the party in a similar difficulty. By the spring of 1831 McEntagart was complaining that he needed money. He was given £200 from the committee's general fund. In September fresh complaints gained him another £200 from the same source. Still unsatisfied, despite having been hired at £300 a year, he extorted £75 from Herries in the spring of 1832. He was then informed that he could expect no more assistance. Herries went so far as to deny that he had ever been hired for money. McEntagart, whatever his faults, had a grievance and his language became threatening. At last, in August 1833, he started legal proceedings against Herries as the agent of the party. Fearful that the proceedings at Charles Street might become publicly known, the committee settled out of court. An arbitrator awarded McEntagart £333 and costs.[33]

Those somewhat shady affairs highlight the sensitivity of the Charles Street Gang to charges of tampering with the press. They also illustrate the undefined status of the Charles Street committee. There was no clear line drawn between the committee's fund and the personal money of the committee members. Hardinge's advance to Jordan was made on his own initiative with his own money. So was a further £350 which he loaned to William Praed, possibly for electioneering purposes, and which was repaid.[34] One of Hardinge's qualifications as a party manager may have been his wealth and his liberality. Nor was there a defined relationship between the committee and the Conservative party. When Wellington, one of the founding members of the committee, heard of McEntagart's demands, he dissociated himself from the dispute, insisting that neither he nor the Conservative party bore any legal or moral liability for Herries's indiscretions.

> I know nothing of writing for newspapers or any other transaction in which some of the less prudent of the members may have engaged themselves. . . . The question is whether a society such as we were at Charles Street (and I swear that I was not three times in the house) are bound by the acts of each other as a co-partnership. If we are, there can be no question, we should enquire into Mr. McIntagart's case; ascertain who he says employed him; get to the bottom of it, and give him reasonable compensation among us. But I am convinced that we were not to be considered as such a society. It would be in fact for the D. of Northumberland, the D. of Buccleugh, Baring and others to give men of nothing the command of their purses. . . . Happen what may, the affair will be very disagreeable to Herries. But it is better for him that it should stand upon the ground of his having employed McIntagart than that it should stand upon that of his being employed by the party.[35]

Arbuthnot, who had been at the centre of the committee's affairs, agreed, He declined to make himself 'a party to a transaction from which I have kept free'.[36]

Where the money to pay McEntagart's award was found is not known. Certainly there was no fund left at Charles Street. In the summer of 1833, before the award was made, the committee was already in debt to the amount of £960. A subscription had to be raised to supply the debt and the Duke's mournful remark was that 'we were all guilty of the sin of belonging to Charles Street, or rather, being subscribers to the expence of the institution'.[37] The party's first experiment in some kind of central organization was a notable failure. The unhappy experience left its mark on the Conservative party, which, for the next forty years remained suspicious of journalists and shied away from entanglements in the world of newspapers.

The reform elections

The elections of 1831 and 1832 were extraordinary events, in their concentration upon the single issue of reform quite unlike any other elections in the nineteenth century. At the first of them, the last held under the old electoral conditions, candidates in all parts of the country heard the cry 'the Bill, the whole Bill, and nothing but the Bill', though there were many places where candidates could afford to ignore it. The second election followed too closely in the wake of the reform excitement for passions to have subsided sufficiently to allow the Conservative revival to begin. In 1831 the Conservatives lost enough seats to ensure the Reform Bill of an easy passage through the Commons; in 1832 they suffered their worst defeat in history.

However badly it may have managed some of its affairs, the Charles Street committee was not responsible for the party's electoral failure. At both elections it acted as an electoral headquarters and, with the money left over from the 'general fund' of the last Tory government and some additional cash raised by subscription, it did what it could.[38] No complete picture of the committee's financial position can be drawn from the isolated clues which have survived, such as the entries in Lord Ellenborough's diaries.[39]

[23 April, 1831] Went to Hardinge's. He suggested one of my brothers standing for Wells & said many peers had subscribed. I said I would give £1000 towards the election of one of my brothers, & if neither stood, £500 as a subscription . . .

Lord Bute has given £1000 towards the subscription, & a man I did not know came in & gave a draft for the same sum while I was at the room.

The writs go out tonight. Endeavours are making to induce the gentlemen who signed the declaration against the Reform Bill to come forward and subscribe.

[25 April, 1831] Heard from Dudley & called upon him at 3. He rode with me to the c[ommittee] room. Gave a draft for £1000 & promised another £1000 . . .

The D. of Buccleuch has given £10,000 and promises, if it should be necessary, £10,000 more. Ld. Powis gives £2,000 and promises £4,000 if it should be required.

The electoral purse seems to have been well filled by the standards of the time. The 1831 elections were as critical for the Tories as any the party has ever fought. The Tories who sat for borough seats threatened with abolition by the Whigs' Reform Bill were fighting for their political lives. It is improbable, therefore, that the committee did not deploy its resources as effectively as possible. Yet when the election was over there was a surplus of funds large enough to supply £2,500 to the Tory candidate for a by-election at Dublin City and £11,000 to Lord Ashley, a leading party orgainizer, for one at Dorsetshire. Even sums as large as those, however, especially when applied only to a few selected constituencies, made little impression on an electoral system which was so expensive that Lord Northumberland could, according to Lord Grey, put up £100,000 at Northumberland only to see his candidate, Matthew Bell, forced to retire from the contest.[40] At the Orange stronghold of Liverpool, too, where General Gascoyne, the success of whose motion against the reduction in the number of English seats forced the dissolution, was defeated, the candidates spent £100,000.[41] Nor was it only in the boroughs, where bribery was especially prevalent, that costs soared. At the 1830 election at Leicestershire, the Duke of Rutland, without a canvas, spent £6,000 on re-electing his brother, Lord Robert Manners. At the next election, he predicted, 'if there should be a *premeditated* contest . . . £50,000 would not more than cover the expense'.[42]

There was, at any rate, more than a financial limit to the committee's scope of action. Many candidates did not want money or any other kind of interference from London, since they might, by accepting it, injure a reputation for independence and honesty. However wisely and efficiently the party managers directed their business, they could have but a slight effect on the election results as a whole.

In the constituencies, where the real management of the elections was located, Tories were less ready to part with their money in what they foresaw as a hopeless cause. Those men who contributed handsomely to the central fund, the committee members themselves and wealthy peers like the Duke of Buccleuch and Lord Bute, were professional politicians. The gentry in the countryside, on whom local candidates depended for assistance (or for nomination), were not caught up in Westminster politics. Political influence was just one facet of their local authority and standing, which might be dented by backing an unpopular candidate. From the tide of reform, which spurred Charles Street to great exertions, many Tories ran in fear.

> They [the Whigs] have so managed the elections [wrote Mrs Arbuthnot] that they will get anything they please; they have by the furious writing of their papers, excited the people into a perfect state of madness; the most dis-

graceful outrages have been in a manner sanctioned by the Govt, who take no pains to prevent or quell riots; the anti-reformers have not dared to appear out of their houses, candidates have been nearly beat to death who were anti-reformers . . . and all over the three Kingdoms the Govt have, in the most barefaced manner, informed all voters holding Govt situations, however small the value, that if they did not vote for the Govt candidates they wd be dismissed.[43]

Mrs Arbuthnot was seldom discreet in her language or restrained in her partisanship. On this occasion, nonetheless, the substance of her remarks was true.[44] One source of her information was her husband, who accounted a deeper reason for Tory lethargy.

> You know what a Tory Knightley is. He plainly owned to me that had he been in the House he shd. have supported the present Govt., & he told me that he had apologised to Ld. Althorp [the Whig cabinet minister] for not being at his election. The disturbing state of the country prevented him . . . he is dreading that their breaking down wd. give power to the Radicals, so *inveterate,* says he, *is the whole country against us!* . . . He says that our refusing to consent to a moderate reform has stirred up the whole population against us . . . He had been sure, he says, for a long time that we could not stand, & the change had pleased him because he thought these men wd. stand between us & the Radicals. What nonsense! But alas it is nonsense wch. has spread far and wide.[45]

Yorkshire returned four reformers unopposed, 'the Conservative party dreading either the expense or the tumult of the conflict'.[46] At Bath the anti-Tory feeling was so strong that no Conservative was nominated for the traditional Tory share of the borough's representation.[47] Even West-bury, the seat at the disposal of Sir Manasseh Lopes which had rescued Peel after his defeat at Oxford University in 1829, returned two reformers, one of them Sir Manasseh's nephew and heir, who 'thought popularity the better part of valour'.[48]

The elections were, as they continued to be for many years, spread over several weeks. The government won notable early victories which made it evident that they would gain a sufficient majority to pass their reform measures. That meant that new elections would follow shortly and Tory candidates, therefore, prudently declined to squander money and offend public feeling by continuing the battle. At Lincolnshire the Tory member, Colonel Chaplin, who had voted against reform, declined to stand for re-election. 'But when Chaplin and his fellow Tories declined a contest in 1831 they were thinking in terms of local as much as of national politics. They were already looking beyond the enactment of the Bill, and were husbanding their resources for the battles over the divided county that were to come.'[49]

Of the eighty-two English and Welsh county members, twenty-seven voted against the second reading of the Reform Bill and thirty-four for

General Gascoyne's wrecking amendment. The Tories won only six of those county seats in 1831. Yet the number of contested county elections rose from nine in 1830 to only eleven in 1831. The explanation of the apparent discrepancy in the two sets of figures was the widespread phenomenon of Tory withdrawal from the fight. As Ellenborough had lamented at the beginning of the elections, the party wanted candidates more than subscriptions.[50]

There was, of course, no pattern which stamped itself on all the elections. Three examples, the elections at Caernarvon boroughs, at Ashburton, and at Berkshire, are instructive of the variety of early nineteenth-century electoral behaviour. At Caernarvon the Paget family, with the Marquess of Anglesey at its head, exercised a declining but still preponderant influence. In 1830 its member, Sir Charles Paget, had retired from parliament because as a non-party man and a member of the royal household he would have been committed to support Wellington's government and he had decided that he could no longer do so. Rather than give up his household salary and go into opposition, he retired. In 1831, with the Whigs in power, he stood once more for election and was successful. It was hardly, however, a party victory, except in the most negative sense that Paget's anti-Toryism no longer prevented him from combining a parliamentary seat with a household office. John Sanderson, Paget's election agent, solicited the support of the local gentry on specifically non-party grounds, as in a letter to Colonel Edwards, a landowner of extensive property and influence. The occasion was the election of 1830, before Paget decided not to stand, but nothing happened to alter the nature of his candidacy in 1831. Paget had met with hostility by his vote for Catholic emancipation, but Sanderson believed that the question did not, and *ought* not to, interest the electors.

> It is, on the contrary, believed that the Burgesses of Carnarvon generally would be reluctant to desert a Family whose claims are admitted to be founded upon National Services; and an invariable attention, during a period of forty-six years, to the local interest of the Boroughs, and the personal interests of individuals, and families, both in and out of Parliament. Sir Charles always possessed the confidence of his constituents without diminution from the hour of his first Election until he retired from Parliament; and his name is now never mentioned amongst them without calling forth expressions of respect. The acknowledged integrity of his Character would, also, be likely to secure to him renewed support; and place both representative and constituent upon the footing which the Constitution recognizes; leaving to each the right of free communication of opinion, and free exercise of judgement.
>
> I am led to say this because it is not meant to be concealed that Sir Charles Paget's principles oppose anything like a pledge upon Questions of general and Public Interest, which are reserved for discussion in Parliament. . . . Now Sir, with respect to the expected Opposition. . . . There is no intention on the

part of Sir Charles Paget, or his friends, to dispute for a moment the weight of Mr. Smith's pretensions: he has great interest from property in Houses within the Boroughs, and of land in their several districts . . . but others will not wholly overlook the not unusual consequences of Elections Contests – the dissolution of long subsiding friendships – the disunion and various other evils which Political contests creates in families and neighbourhoods – and the wasteful expense that ensues. It is the Patronage that Mr. Smith seeks.[51]

Caernarvon remained in the hands of a government supporter. That government was now Whig. But it was only the accident of Sir Charles Paget's personal scruples which gave party any play in the matter. In the midst of the great excitement of the reform question, Caernarvon went its placid way, selecting its member on grounds quite foreign to national political issues.

Ashburton presents a different picture, a constituency in which a change of opinion mattered, but in which that change involved the electorate only indirectly. It is an example of the way in which, in mid-Victorian England as well as in 1831, the combination of a change of opinion and the weight of 'influence' could shift the party allegiance of a constituency. Lord Clinton had held the nomination of one of Ashburton's two members for twenty years and for all of that time he had excerised his control in the Tory interest. In November 1830 he went over to the side of the Whigs, partly for the same reason as Paget. He was a Lord of the Bedchamber. At Ashburton, however, there was the added complication that Lord Clinton's steward and election agent, Dr Tucker, was just then transferring the stewardship to his son Robert. Robert was an enthusiastic Radical. He canvassed the former Tory adherents to the Clinton interest in the Radical cause and successfully kept their votes. When Charles Arbuthnot retired from the representation in February 1831 the Clinton candidate, who was the Whig father-in-law of Lord Clinton, was returned unopposed. The 'peace of the borough' had been broken; the days of shared representation were over. And at the general election three months later, Ashburton returned two reformers against a single Tory candidate.[52] There can be little doubt that the bulk of the electors did not change their minds. What mattered was that the wielder of influence had changed his.

There were places, nevertheless, where the established patterns of electoral behaviour were upset, as they had been in 1830. Where that happened, as in Berkshire, the movement against the Tories in the counties, which had begun in 1830, continued. The great landowners of Berkshire remained united. Almost all of them signed a 'Berkshire Declaration' against the Reform Bill. That did not prevent the majority of farmers and freeholders in the county from sticking to the persuasion that agricultural distress, unemployment, and fluctuations in the price of grain were attributable to bad government and that bad government was the result of the unreformed House of Commons. They were bent on reform and they forced the sitting Tory member, Robert Palmer, to with-draw from the contest on nomination day. Two reformers were then returned without a poll.[53] The same welling up of anger and the same readiness to apply a party remedy occurred in Buckinghamshire.[54] Professor Gash warns that the Berkshire result was 'a notable triumph for reform', but not a triumph for the Whigs, and 'still less a triumph of one party over another'.[55] It is an odd judgement, based, presumably, on the prejudice that parties did not exist and sustained by the knowledge that Palmer won his seat back at a by-election in June, 1832. Yet it is doubtful whether the Charles Street managers, as the results slowly came in, saw things in that light. Of course, there was no guarantee that the farmers of Berkshire had made a permanent switch to the Whigs. But the Tories, in 1831, were the party of anti-reform. In Berkshire, and else-where, the farmers broke through the restraints of influence to cast their votes for reform. By doing so, and by electing Whig candidates, they were exercising their power to influence, through party, national decisions at the expense of traditional local loyalties. Party, whatever else it does, represents opinion. Those farmers who wished to make their voices heard on a great national issue did so, not by continuing to vote Tory and trusting to a Tory member's sensitivity to their desires, but in the only manner open to them, by voting for the candidate of the party which offered to grant their demand.

The Berkshire result amounted to a remarkable upheaval of tra-ditional voting habits, an upheaval which could not take place outside the 'popular' counties. Nevertheless, the Conservatives suffered as near to a landslide defeat as the closed electoral system was able to produce. Their maximum strength in the 1830 House of Commons was about 315. In the new House they were reduced to under 270.[56] Herries told Peel that the 'best news we have' was the election of thirteen Conservatives among the sixteen Scottish representative peers, a gain on the previous session.[57] Even the figure of 270 flattered the Conservative position, since many of the members who comprised it were returned for boroughs about to lose one or both of their representatives. The Tories had become what their enemies had long been wrong to call them, a 'borough faction'. Of the 111 borough seats doomed by the Reform Bill, the Tories won 82,[58] evidence less of Whig gerrymandering than of Tory strength in the unpopular boroughs. In the English nomination boroughs as a whole, the Tories won 164 seats and lost only 76; in the 'open' boroughs they won 34 and lost 162.[59] In the counties the Tories were decimated: of the 82 English and Welsh county members they claimed only six, both members for Shropshire and one for each of Buckinghamshire, Huntingdonshire, Westmorland, and Monmouthshire. Great Tory interests like the Lowther in Westmorland and Cumberland, the Newcastle in Nottinghamshire, and the Beaufort in Gloucestershire, were crushed. Even Scotland, whose tiny electorate had for years been in the pay of the Tory aristocracy, returned a slight majority of members in favour of reform. In the end, a recent historian has written, 'the Tories could do little save comfort themselves with the wry reflection that never had the old system shown itself more responsive to public opinion than when it stood on the brink of extinction'.[60]

Eighteen months later the first elections under the terms of the Reform Act took place. That the Conservatives were reduced to a party of fewer than 150 members in the House of Commons surprised no one. The Charles Street fund was exhausted and no more money was subscribed.[61] Even Holmes, unable to pay for a contest from his own pocket, was compelled to retire from parliament.[62] His place as chief election manager, although not as Chief Whip, was taken by Bonham, who in the summer of 1832 came forward as the leading expert at Charles Street, replying to futile appeals for money, dispatching candidates to constituencies unable to field their own, and in general keeping up to date with developments in all the constituencies.[63] Arbuthnot found incomprehensible 'the policy of letting the enemy take all possible measures for the next election', and chastised Peel and Wellington for sitting back as if nothing could be done.[64] Wellington confessed that he had nothing left, after two costly elections, to contribute and Peel, still out of spirits, gave only £50 at Staffordshire.[65] Lord Lowther, prominent at Charles Street for the previous two years and, before the débâcle of 1831, tenacious of his parliamentary interest in Westmorland and Cumberland, spent the autumn of 1832 abroad.[66]

> It was impossible not to be struck [a correspondent wrote to Lord Aberdeen], on the one hand with the great activity displayed in various parts of the country by the reforming Whig and revolutionary parties; and on the other with the torpor, listlessness, and Turkish waiting upon Providence displayed by the Conservative party.[67]

Those considerations, non-financial, which had inhibited Conservatives in 1831 continued to persuade possible candidates of the advantages of withdrawal over a salvage operation. Ralph Sneyd resisted Viscount Sandon's flattering invitation to stand at North Staffordshire.

> It is now some years since, in a manner that still enhanced the boon, you voluntarily made the offer reiterated in the letter I received yesterday. At that time I was very desirous of Parliament, and very ambitious of so honourable a seat. The old Influences of Family and Property were yet in the ascendant. . . . In 1823 one of the members for Staffordshire with the backing offered to me might have considered himself seated for life if he fulfilled the conditions of his Election diligently and conscientiously. In 1832 one of the candidates for the Department of the Upper Trent, entering the lists with my obsolete opinions, and disqualified (pro tanto) by the circumstances which I might formerly have pleaded as

recommendations, even in the doubtful event of his success, c'd only retain his seat by perpetual contests, and he would assuredly be dislodged by the first popular question on which he happened to be on the unpopular side.[68]

Had Sneyd foreseen the authority which property and influence were to maintain in mid-Victorian England he might have accepted Sandon's offer. As it was, like Croker, another crusty Tory, he decided never to taint himself by membership of the vulgar reformed House of Commons. In 1832 a political career was not an engaging prospect for a Tory of the old school. Even for ambitious Conservatives there were reasons to lie low, as James Lindsay, who decided not to go to the poll at Fifeshire, explained to Peel.

> Policy with reference to the future has dictated this course of not going to the Poll in order to prevent a large party of the £10 constituency registering their votes against me, votes hastily pledged during the Reform Jubilee, which they now regret, but will fulfil. Once polled it would have been a sort of enlistment with the opposite party, and I should find it much more difficult hereafter to detach them.[69]

Lindsay's cloud had a paste silver lining. He was beaten in 1835 and Fifeshire remained Whig or Liberal for the rest of the century.

The Conservatives' difficulty in making headway against a triumphant and confident party of reform was increased by the circumstance that, as the opposition party, they were also fighting the King, who had given no public indication of his doubts about the ability of the Whig ministers to control the Radicals. Conservatives believed that official royal support gave the government a great advantage.[70] It was not simply that there were a dozen or so seats, such as the naval and customs ports, in which government patronage was the decisive influence at elections. It was, Lord Londonderry said, that 'so long as royalty is bound up ostensibly with Whiggery, you cannot get the moderate men in the country to budge'.[71] For years, after all, the Tories had argued that reasonable and loyal men ought to eschew faction and uphold the king's government. The Conservatives needed a spell in office, which the short-lived ministry of 1834–35 was to provide, to dispel the Tory past and demonstrate that they were a party worthy of royal favour.

The Conservative party from 1832 to 1867 was predominantly, although never exclusively, the party of the land, the party of the Established Church, and the party of England. The elections of 1832 were, in those respects, a true indication of the future. Of the 147 members who may be classified as Conservatives at the beginning of the 1833 parliament,[72] 114 sat for English and Welsh seats, eight for Scottish, and twenty-five for Irish. The Conservatives had won 22.8 per cent of the 500 English seats, 14 per cent of the fifty-three Scottish seats, and 23.7 per cent of the 105 Irish seats. The low percentage in England was not of long-term importance. Unless the party were never to revive at all, it could depend upon restoring its position in the English counties, where the connection made between agricultural distress and parliamentary reform had worked so handsomely to the Whigs' advantage. Already, in 1832, Conservative candidates were making protection to agricultural products one of the chief items in their election addresses. Indeed, the one bright spot in the 1832 election results for the Conservatives was their recovery in the English counties, where their representation jumped from six to forty-three, helped, of course, by the sixty-five new county seats created by the Reform Act.

The important statistic was the Scottish. For fifty years Scottish seats had been virtually at the disposal of Tory governments. The electorate, overwhelmingly rural, was so tiny (just over 3,000 in 1831) that elections were easily controlled by a series of alliances with the Scottish nobility by which government patronage was extended in return for electoral services. The survival of feudal practice and the pressure of clan loyalty, particularly in the Highlands, assisted the process. In Scotland, therefore, the Reform Act effected a more startling break with the past even than in England. Tory control crumbled at the elections of 1832, for which the registered electorate were 65,000. Thereafter, to the long-established marriage of Whiggery and reform, symbolized by the founding of the *Edinburgh Review* in 1802, was added the desire for the reform of the Kirk. Presbyterianism, reinforced by the distinctively Scottish legal and educational institutions, forged an enduring link between Liberalism and the majority of the electorate, and provided the base of Liberal hegemony in mid-Victorian Scotland.

Ireland, too, except for the Protestant strongholds in the north, was to remain a Liberal and Irish radical constituency until 1922. (That was a permanent change from the days before 1830, when Ireland had ordinarily returned about seventy Tories and thirty Whigs.) So, in Wales, did 1832 bring the beginning of Conservative decline, although never so marked as in Scotland. In Monmouthshire the old Tory interest of the Beauforts and the Morgans was now represented solely by Lord Granville Somerset, one of the county members. In south-east Wales as a whole the relative strength of the parties changed from a Conservative majority of nine to three in 1831 to a Whig majority of seven to five. The mining and iron-manufacturing districts of Wales changed their political colour under the widened franchise of the Reform Act. Symptomatic of the industrial and urban bias of Whiggery was the result at Monmouth boroughs, where tanneries and shipbuilding were the most important of a variety of trades. Monmouth boroughs had been the seat of the Marquess of Worcester, heir to the Beaufort dukedom, since 1813. In 1832 the Marquess was defeated by Benjamin Hall, an industrialist and a champion of Welsh nonconformity.

From the newly enfranchised towns, the Conservatives were almost shut out: those towns returned sixty-four members, only two of them Conservatives, William Bolling, a cotton merchant, at Bolton and Aaron Chapman at Whitby. At the other end of the scale were those small boroughs in which the influence of a great landowner or an established family still prevailed, despite the Reform Act. Professor Gash has listed fifty-two such boroughs as 'proprietary' (although they could no longer simply be bought and sold) and thirteen as 'family'. In those constituencies the Conservatives nearly held their own: the 'proprietary' borough patrons returned seventy-three members, thirty-nine reformers and thirty-four Conservatives; the 'family' boroughs returned eight reformers and eleven Conservatives.[73] Even in those constituencies there were some notable Conservative setbacks. Scarborough, controlled since 1806 by the Tory interests of the Mulgrave family and the Duke of Rutland, fell to two reformers. Ripon, notorious for its electoral subservience to Miss Lawrence, the owner of Studleigh Park, with its burgage tenures, also returned two reformers, although by the 1835 elections Miss Lawrence's building of cowsheds and small tenements to create faggot £10 voters regained for her the absolute control of the borough.

It was, finally, noticeable that many Conservative candidates attributed their defeat to the hostility of the Dissenters.[74] John Walter, the victorious Whig candidate at Berkshire, drew most of his strength from the Newbury and Maidenhead districts, both noted for their high proportion of Dissenters. 'I owe little,' he told his electors after the poll, 'to that order which calls itself, or is considered, the aristocracy of Berkshire. The middle and industrious classes . . . are they to whom I feel myself most sensibly indebted.'[75] The support of nonconformity for the Whigs in 1832 owed something to the anti-slavery question, which, now that parliamentary reform was out of the way, became the most prominent Radical issue at the elections. The Agency Committee of the Anti-Slavery Society, which received financial support from the nonconformist organizations, pledged 150 candidates to abolition.[76] There was a host of other questions which, after the abolition of slavery in 1833, were to keep the Dissenters tied to the Whigs.

One other feature of the Conservative party did not, perhaps, escape Peel's notice amid the general gloom. The parliamentary party elected in 1832 contained seventy members, nearly half its total, who had not sat in the House of Commons before 1830. There was, at least, new material with which to build, in the age of reform, a Conservative party out of the ashes of Toryism.

Notes and References

The 'Charles Street Gang'

1 Arbuthnot to Bonham, 6 Jan, 1833: Peel MSS, Add. MSS 40617, ff. 9–10.
2 Bradfield, 'Sir Richard Vyvyan and the country gentlemen, 1830–1834', *EHR*, Oct, 1968, 737–8.
3 Croker to Peel, 10 April 1831: Parker, *Peel*, ii, 181.
4 Aspinall, *Three Diaries*, 22.
5 *Spectator*, 25 May 1832.
6 *Quarterly Review*, Jan, 1830, 276; Mrs Arbuthnot, *Journal*, 29 March 1831, ii, 415; *Blackwood's*, Jan, 1832, 115.
7 Greville, *Memoirs*, 14 June 1835, iii, 205–7.
8 Macaulay, 'Gladstone on Church and State', in *Critical and Historical Essays*, ii, 237.
9 Alison, *Some Account of My Life and Writings*, i, 366.
10 Prest, *Lord John Russell*, 123.
11 Peel to Goulburn, [1830]: Parker, *Peel*, ii, 170.
12 Ellenborough Diary, 12 July 1831: Aspinall, *Three Diaries*, 103–4.
13 Peel to Herries, 7 June 1831: *ibid*, xl.
14 Peel to Gregory, 18 January, 1828. *Peel Memoirs*, i, 15–17.
15 Ellenborough Diary, 12 March 1833 (*ibid*, 315–6): 'There has been no call yet made upon Peel to take the lead! The delay in doing all that is necessary is quite heart-breaking.'
16 Southgate, ed. *Conservative Leadership*, 2.
17 Ellenborough Diary, 2 Feb, 1831: *ibid*, 45.
18 Wellington to Viscount Mahon, 17 Sept, 1831 (copy): Aspinall, *Politics and the Press*, 468.
19 Aspinall, *Three Diaries*, lii–iii.
20 Aversion to the grubby work of the ungentlemanly press was a common trait of nineteenth-century politicians. Wellington's attitude was particularly venomous. In the days when his peninsular campaign had been severely criticized in the press, he was sickened by 'the statements of supposed facts, and the comments upon supposed transactions' and he learned to despise the 'blackguard editors of newspapers', their 'vulgar insinuations' and their 'ignorance and presumption and licentiousness' (Aspinall, *Politics and the Press*, 198).
21 *Ibid*, 241.
22 Ellenborough Diary, 27 Nov, 1830: Aspinall, *Three Diaries*, 27.
23 Lowther to Lord Lonsdale, 7 May, 1831: Aspinall, *Politics and the Press*, 330.
24 Herries to Mrs Arbuthnot, [Dec, 1830]: *ibid*, 332.

25 Croker to Mrs Arbuthnot, [4 April 1831]: C. Arbuthnot, *Correspondence*, 140.
26 Lowther to Lord Lonsdale, 7 May 1831: Aspinall, *Politics and the Press*, 332.
27 Lowther to Lord Lonsdale, 5 Jan, 1832: *ibid*, 334.
28 Sir John Malcolm to Wellington, 26 Dec, 1832: Wellington, *Despatches*, viii, 500.
29 Aspinall, *Three Diaries*, lx.
30 Mahon to Wellington, 25 Oct, 1831; Wellington to Mahon, 27 Oct, 1831 (copy): Aspinall, *Politics and the Press*, 471–3.
31 Ellenborough Diary, 16 April 1831: 'There has been a subscription for disseminating publications against the Bill. Hardinge, gave £35, the D. of Northumberland £100, Ld. Clive the same. R. Clive gave £50. I have given £50. Some of this is given to Theodore Hook who is very active indeed.' (Aspinall: *Three Diaries*, 79.)
32 This paragraph is based on Gleig's correspondence with Jordan and Hardinge in August and September 1831 (Hardinge MSS, McGill University Library). I am grateful to Mr Hugh Cameron for showing me this correspondence. Concern for secrecy guided all the party's publishing activities, even the seemingly innocent matter of raising money to help Praed with his literary work. In 1834, when Hardinge collected £300 for the purpose, he was careful not to send a list of subscribers to Mrs Arbuthnot through the post (Aspinall, *Politics and the Press*, 339).
33 Aspinall, *Three Diaries*, lxi–lxv.
34 W. M. Praed to Hardinge, 3 March and 2 April 1834: Hardinge MSS.
35 Wellington to Arbuthnot, 12 Nov, 1833: Aspinall, *Politics and the Press*, 459–60.
36 Arbuthnot to Wellington, 10 Nov, 1833: *ibid*, 480.
37 *Ibid*, 459–60.

The reform elections

38 Robert Blake was mistaken in saying that 'it is not clear that any such fund existed for the Conservative or Tory party before 1832' (*Conservative Party*, 1–2). The fund existed before 1830, was administered by Arbuthnot, and was kept with the banker, John Kirkland (Aspinall, *Three Diaries*, xlvii).
39 *Ibid*, 86–8.
40 *Ibid*, xlvii n.
41 Cowherd, *The Politics of English Dissent*, 78.
42 Rutland to Mrs Arbuthnot, 21 Sept, 1830: C. Arbuthnot, *Correspondence*, 130–1.
43 Mrs Arbuthnot, *Journal*, 16 May 1831, ii, 419.
44 Mrs Arbuthnot's report has been supported by Michael Brock (*Reform Act*, 197): 'The pattern of violence in 1831 was unusual . . . in being one-sided. Virtually all the intimidation was exercized by reformers. It is impossible to believe that fear of physical ill-treatment had no effect in deterring opponents of the bill.'
45 Arbuthnot to his wife, 13 Nov, 1831. C Arbuthnot, *Correspondence*, 135–6. Sir Charles Knightley lost his seat at the 1830 elections, but returned as Conservative member for Northamptonshire South at a by-election in November 1834.
46 *Annual Register*, 1831, 154.
47 Neale, *Class and Ideology in the Nineteenth Century*, 50.
48 Brock, *Reform Act*, 195.
49 Olney, *Lincolnshire Politics*, 94.
50 Ellenborough Diary, 23 April 1831: Aspinall, *Three Diaries*, 86–7.

51 Sanderson to Colonel Edwards, 6 June 1830. L. Jones, 'An edition of the correspondence of the First Marquis of Anglesey relative to the general elections of 1830, 1831, and 1832', unpublished thesis.

52 Hanham, 'Ashburton as a parliamentary borough, 1640–1868', *Trans. Devonshire Association*, 1966, 236–7.

53 Gash, *Politics in the Age of Peel*, 300–4.

54 Davis, *Political Change and Continuity*, 93–8

55 Gash, *Politics in the Age of Peel*, 302.

56 Mrs Arbuthnot put the figure at 270 (*Journal*, 8 June 1831, ii, 422). At the beginning of the new session Holmes sent out 266 notes to members and in September, after the division which sent the Reform Bill to the House of Lords, he still counted 266 Conservatives (C. Arbuthnot, *Correspondence*, 141, 145–6).

57 Herries to Peel, 5 June 1831: Peel MSS, Add. MSS 40402, ff. 89–91.

58 This figure is based on the party classification of members in Smith *Parliaments of England*.

59 *The Times*, 1 June 1831.

60 Cannon, *Parliamentary Reform*, 221.

61 Herries, *Memoir*, ii, 162–3.

62 Holmes to Peel, 17 Nov, 1832: Peel MSS, Add. MSS 40403, f. 100.

63 See, for example, Bonham to Peel, 13 Nov, 1832 (*ibid*, ff. 95–6), in which Bonham gave Peel details of progress at Devonshire South, Essex South, Gloucestershire, Bristol, and Oldham. The next day Bonham was writing to Peel about Honiton (Bonham to Peel, 14 Nov, 1832, *ibid*, ff. 93–4). The committee of elections formed in May was composed·of Holmes, Bonham, Charles Ross, Lowther, Praed, Herries, and Peach (England), George Clerk, Cumming Bruce, Lord Rosslyn, Lord Maitland, Viscount Stormont (Scotland), and Hardinge, George Dawson, Lord Fitzgerald, Lord Farnham, and the Earl of Roden (Ireland). (Ellenborough Diary, 20 May 1832: Aspinall, *Three Diaries*, 266.)

64 Arbuthnot to his wife, 17 June 1832, and to his son 25 June 1831: *Correspondence*, 161.

65 Wedgwood, *Staffordshire Parliamentary History*, 87.

66 Lord Londonderry to Lord Burghesh, 8 Oct, 1832: Westmorland [Burghesh], *Correspondence*, 270–2.

67 Herries, *Memoir*, ii, 162–3. Charles Wynn reported that Denbighshire boroughs was lost 'merely because none of the gentlemen of the neighbourhood will incur the expense' (Wynn to Peel, 27 Nov, 1832: Peel MSS, Add. MSS 40403, ff. 119–20).

68 Sneyd to Sandon, 7 Feb, 1832: Kent, 'Party politics in the county of Staffordshire during the years 1830 to 1847', unpublished thesis, Ch. 7, appendix F.

69 Lindsay to Peel, 14 Dec, 1832: Peel MSS, Add. MSS 40405, ff. 140–2.

70 Arbuthnot to his son, 5 July 1832: 'I hope they [the Whigs] will be out before the elections, for the next parlt. will depend much upon our party being in or out of office' (*Correspondence*, 161); Londonderry to Lord Burghesh, 8 October, 1832: 'Had the King given us a chance before the new Parliament, by dismissing Lord Grey, the game might have come into our hands' (Westmorland [Burghesh], *Correspondence*, 270–2).

71 *Ibid.*

72 Lord Mahon made a list of 150, but the list has not, apparently, survived (Mahon to Peel, 8 Jan, 1833: Peel MSS, Add. MSS 40403, ff. 167–9). I have calculated the

figure of 147 from the classifications given in Buckingham's *Parliamentary Review* and Dod's *Pocket Parliamentary Companion* for 1833. They agreed on 142 Conservative members. To that number I have added three more, whom Planta called Conservatives (Peel MSS, Add. MSS 40421, ff. 158–62), and also the two Pembroke members, Sir John Owen and Hugh Owen Owen, whom Buckingham called reformers. Dod was right to place them in the Conservative camp. At the 1831 elections constituency feeling had forced them to trim their Tory sails to the reform wind, but in the 1833 parliament they voted consistently with the Conservatives (see Williams, 'The Pembrokeshire elections of 1831', *Welsh History Review*, 1960, 37–64).

73 Gash, *Politics in the Age of Peel*, 438–9, 197. There is some overlap in the two lists, since Chippenham, Cirencester, and Westbury are placed in both categories, which cannot be sharply distinguished. A 'family' borough was not always secure, as Dod pointed out about Leominster: 'Influence. Chiefly possessed by Mr. John Arkwright of Hampton Court; but the electors are said to appreciate most highly a candidate with good pecuniary resources' (*Electoral Facts*, 181).

74 See, for example, George Clerk to Peel, 23 Dec, 1832: Peel MSS, Add. MSS 40403, ff. 150–1; also Kent, 'Party politics in Staffordshire', Ch. 2.

75 Gash, *Politics in the Age of Peel*, 306.

76 Cowherd, *Politics of Dissent*, 84. Gladstone made a list of the number of times he was asked questions about specific issues during his canvass of Newark. Slavery headed the list with 'about 60', followed by the ballot, eight, and other issues mentioned three times or less. (Gladstone memorandum, Sept.–Oct, 1832: Gladstone, *Memoranda*, 3–20.

Part II

The age of Peel

Chapter 5

The foundations of Conservatism

Peel and moderate Conservatism

In May 1841 William Gladstone surveyed the political landscape of England and saw, cutting through its hills and valleys, one prominent relief feature.

> The principle of party has long predominated in this country; it now has a sway almost unlimited; and this I think belongs to the nature of a system of what is termed real representation. If Members of Parliament be really *chosen* by the people and if the actual effective power over Government be there, they must be chosen upon grounds few, simple, comprehensive; minutiae and shades of creeds cannot be duly appreciated by constituencies: they cannot make policies the study of their lives individually: they must pin their faith upon some general and leading terms, and by these terms must be defined and determined the great parties which are to contend for mastery in the State.[1]

Ten years earlier that analysis would have been vitiated by its failure to mention the Crown. By 1841 the Crown had been effectively removed from the arena of party politics: in Gladstone's acute language, the role of Party had increased from predominance to sway. It has been the argument of this book that party occupies a rightful place in the history of pre-reform politics. Had it not, parties would not have acquired such a clear definition in the 1830s. It was in the 1830s that parties took on a recognizably modern appearance, characterized, as Professor Gash has written, by 'a body of politicians with coherent organization and a rudimentary philosophy of action, who provided the legislative foundations either for a Ministry or for an Opposition aiming at its replacement'.[2] A party majority came to replace the Crown as the rock on which a ministry stood.

Gladstone was right to ascribe the change to the action of 'real representation', although his language obscures the realities of electoral behaviour which qualified it and which prevented parties from developing into mass instruments of the modern kind. Nothing is more eloquent of the broad significance of the Reform Act than the manner of its accomplishment. In 1829 Peel and Wellington had carried Catholic emancipation by overriding public opinion (outside Ireland) by parliament; in 1831 Grey turned the tables and called in public opinion to override parliament. The Reform Act was not passed in a fit of constitutional abstraction. It was a response to the claims of some people hitherto unrepresented to make their voices heard, the starting-point of an argument, not its resolution. From the national point of view, the 1830s were remarkable for the severity with which two parties contended against each other. In 1836 Henry Bulwer spoke of 'times like the present, when two parties professing two perfectly distinct creeds, are struggling for power'.[3] The result was an expansion of the content of political debate, in G. M. Young's dry rhetoric, the transformation of the treatment of public business 'from Humbug to Humdrum'.[4] From the standpoint of the Conservative party, the 1830s were remarkable as a decade of recovery. Power did not pass, as many Tories had feared that it would, to Colonel Sibthorp's 'dregs of the community' or even to Croker's 'vulgar privileged pedlary';[5] in 1841 the Conservatives were rewarded for their continuous exertions with a large parliamentary majority and office. It took three elections for the Conservatives to whittle down the Whig majority and it was their good fortune that those elections took place in the short space of six years, in 1835, 1837, and 1841. The Conservative victory of 1841 was not the expression of a sudden change in the public mood; it was the culmination of a slow-maturing Conservative sentiment.

To illustrate what he meant by sociological laws analogous to those natural laws which take a negative form, Karl Popper gave this example: 'You cannot introduce a political reform without strengthening the opposing forces, to a degree roughly in ratio to the scope of the reform.'[6] On the morrow of the 1832 elections, the ground for Conservative optimism was even broader than that. Conservatives could look forward to a reassertion of Conservative sympathies among some of the reformers themselves. The 1832 Act was born partly of fear, by men of wealth for their property, by members of parliament for their seats. Whether England was actually close to revolutionary violence,[7] the apprehension of it drew men of widely different opinions together as reformers. There is no doubt that as parliamentary reformers they represented the majority of the nation. But for the principal reform issues which lay ahead, the Dissenters' grievances against the privileges of the Church of England and the Irish Radicals' grievances against the forms of English overlordship, their support was more narrow and sectional. On those issues they would be the representatives of minorities. Yet the strength of radicalism within the Whig party, or as an adjunct to it, was too large for the government to ignore. That was the root weakness of the Whig government and the source of potential benefit to the Conservative opposition.

The Conservative weakness was that, partly because the weight of Tory history hung albatrosslike about them and partly because they had conducted a root-and-branch opposition to the Reform Bill, they were, in the popular mind, the party of reaction. Thomas Arnold wrote that in the House of Commons in 1830 the parties had ranged themselves into 'the advocates of property on one side, and of general intelligence and numbers on the other'.[8]

Dr Arnold was adopting the conceit of those Whig reformers, like Brougham, who identified the 'people' as the middle class and called them the wealth and intelligence of the country. But, however unfairly, he was expressing a widely held opinion which the Conservatives needed to counteract.

It was, as Sir Ivor Jennings has put it, 'the historic function of the Liberal party . . . to reform the political institutions of the eighteenth century so as to adapt them to the conditions of the nineteenth century'.[9] It was the function of the Conservative party to defend those institutions, not indiscriminately from reform, but from annihilation. Peel's job, as he saw it, was to lead the party forward by taking it back to the days of liberal Toryism before the Canningites had been discarded. The experience of the 1820s may not have been encouraging; on the other hand, there was point to the argument that an exclusively landed party, if it learned nothing from events between 1828 and 1832, could look forward to permanent opposition. No one could forecast the precise effect of the Reform Act. By a number of its provisions – the addition to the number of county seats, the withdrawal of large towns from the county electorate, the transfer to the borough rolls of those 'independent' 40s freeholders who were also £10 occupiers, and the enfranchisement of the 'dependent' copyholders, leaseholders, and tenants-at-will – the power of the landowning gentry and aristocracy at county elections had been increased. Nor was it destroyed in the boroughs. The new popular electorate, nevertheless, posed difficulties for a genuinely Conservative party. Croker said, in 1836, that 'an Opposition which does not outbid the Ministry for popularity is a bubble'; yet he saw no purpose in keeping together an innovating Conservative party.[10] Croker's pessimism was unjustified. Conservatives in opposition have much to gain by attending events, by awaiting the day when their opponents fall out among themselves or exhaust their radical energy. In the 1830s they had to look, not only to the electorate, but to the House of Commons. Inside parliament there were moderate reformers to be charmed. The Conservative party had the opportunity to become the haven of the disenchanted. Peel's difficulty was to make his party acceptable and attractive to those Whigs who were not prepared to remain in a party of radicalism, but who were still reformers, without alienating the traditional Tory core of his own following.

It was a characteristic of Peel's career that he often found the former easier than the latter. Professor Gash has described him, at the beginning of 1833, as 'more unpopular and more estranged from his party than he had been even in November, 1830', yet having survived the reform years 'with his character uncompromised and his future policy uncommitted'.[11] Peel had carefully laid the ground of his future course in his speech against the Reform Bill on 5 March 1831. While stating that the Bill was too extensive to be altered in detail and that he would therefore oppose it outright, he made it plain that he was opposed to the particular measures which the Whigs had introduced, not to reform in principle. Once the Bill became law, therefore, he was in a position to set about reshaping Conservative policy in accordance with the new spirit of the age.

Before the 1833 session of parliament began, Peel outlined his view of Conservative strategy to Henry Goulburn. No good would come from combining with the Radicals to defeat the government: 'Our policy ought to be rather to conciliate the goodwill of the sober-minded and well-disposed portion of the community, and thus lay the foundation of future strength.[12] Eighteen months later, when the strains within the Whig–Radical majority were beginning to tell, Peel continued to preach patience.

> My opinion is decidedly against all manoeuvring, and coquetting with the Radicals, for the mere purpose of a temporary triumph over the Government. I attribute much of the present weakness of the Government, and still more of the present strength of the Conservative party, to the adherence to principle by that party and to their forbearance from the little devices and artifices by which perhaps in other days parties have been strengthened.
>
> How can the Conservative party, if again called to the Government, hope to maintain itself, except by conciliating the goodwill, at least by mitigating the hostility, of many of the more moderate and respectable supporters of the present Government? The surest way to prevent this is by finesse, and party tactics.
>
> If the present Government breaks up through its own difficulties and misunderstandings, there is ground for a forcible appeal to the country in behalf of their successors. If it breaks up, or avails itself of the pretext of breaking up, in consequence of a union between Radicals and Conservatives, in my opinion the Government which succeeds it will have a very short-lived triumph.[13]

Peel's position was given its fullest public expression in his address to the electors of Tamworth in December 1834, the famous Tamworth Manifesto.[14] Peel had just become Prime Minister, in precisely the circumstances which he had predicted, and as the head of a minority government was seeking to enlist the support of 'that class which is much less interested in the contentions of party, than in the maintenance of order and the cause of good government' by an 'appeal to the good sense and calm judgment of the people'. From various parts of the country he had received reports, in the first two weeks of December, that his chances at the coming elections were hampered by the public reaction against the unexpected dismissal of Lord Melbourne and the caretaker premiership of the Duke of Wellington, which had produced the impression that Peel's government would be beholden to the Ultra–Tories. Sir Thomas Lethbridge, himself a former Ultra, reported that 'the feelings & sentiments of that portion of the People with whom I am associated in the several Counties where my Property is' evinced 'a general and most extensive desire . . . among nearly all classes for an Entire Reform of abuses in Church and State'.[15] Sir Thomas and others[16] urged on Peel the necessity of making a public declaration of his moderate views before the elections. The result was the Tamworth Manifesto, addressed to Peel's local constituents, but approved by the cabinet and released in the national press. It was thus the nearest thing to a party manifesto before Gladstone's programme of 1874.[17]

The manifesto was the creed of moderate Conservatism. Its principal articles were the acceptance of the Reform Act as the irrevocable settlement of a great constitutional dispute – 'which no friend to the peace and welfare of this country would attempt to disturb' – and the willingness to act within the spirit of the Reform Act by conducting 'a careful review of institutions, Civil and ecclesiastical, undertaken in a friendly temper, combining, with the firm maintenance of established rights, the correction of proved abuses and the redress of real grievances'. Moderate, or Peelite, Conservatism took the view, propounded by Gladstone in 1852, that 'a liberal policy would be worked out with greater security to the country through the medium of the Conservative party'.[18] The strategy which Peel recommended in 1833 and 1834 remained the basis of the party's parliamentary behaviour for the rest of the decade. Its principle was the defence of the constitution, its tactic to wait for Radical assaults on the constitution to drive moderates into the Conservative fold.

The defence of the constitution meant, in Conservative rhetoric, the preservation of the prerogatives of the Crown, the upholding of the independence of the House of Lords, and the continuation of the union of the Established Church and the State. In almost every speech, every election address, from 1833 to 1841, Conservatives placed great emphasis on those principles. The rhetoric and the reality could hardly match. It was impossible to maintain anything but the shadow of the royal prerogatives of ministerial appointment and parliamentary dissolution. In 1834 William IV appointed a Conservative ministry (although not the individuals who composed it), but it was unable to stand against the House of Commons elected in January 1835. In 1831 William had no choice but to grant to the Whig government a dissolution (and no monarch has refused a Prime Minister's request for one since). The vaunted independence of the House of Lords, too, was gone. In 1835 Peel's minority government suffered a series of defeats in the House of Commons. Lord Kenyon, one of the most active of the Ultra peers in 1829, pleaded with Peel not to resign on that account.

> I would beg to urge that no resolutions nor bills passed by a factious Reformed House of Commons, and not consented to by you, can affect your honour.
>
> It is an occurrence which an independent House of Lords could guard the country against. No such House of Lords will exist if you resign. It may be swamped or not, but independent it will no longer be, but will pass every measure, however infamous, which the House of Commons sends up.[19]

Three weeks after receiving that letter, Peel, after more defeats, deferred to the Commons' majority and resigned. Throughout the 1830s the Conservative majority in the House of Lords was used sparingly. In the latter years of the decade, it is true, a series of amendments wrecked much of the government's Irish and Church legislation. But on those questions it was the Lords, not the government, who were speaking for the majority of the nation. They were passed, too, when the House of Commons, especially after the elections of 1837, was nearly equally divided between government and opposition supporters. In the earlier period the government had a much better record of legislative achievement. The lesson of the 1830s for the House of Lords was that independence was severely hedged and could be exercised only with great restraint. It was a hard lesson to learn and the major threat to the unity of the Conservative party in those years came from the Tory peers.

The claims which the Conservatives made for the monarchy and the House of Lords were not redeemable. They were not meant to be. The cry of 'the constitution in danger' was meant to strike chords resonant of things far deeper than details of constitutional procedure. The union of Church and State, for example, represented far more than mere legal erastianism, as Croker explained to Southey in 1824, in a letter describing what he meant by that union.

> I do not mean the mere *political* connection of Church and State; but that mixture of veneration and love, of enthusiasm and good taste, of public liberty and selfcontrol, of pride in our ancestors and hopes from our posterity, which affects every patient and Christian mind at the contemplation of that glorious system which unites in such beautiful association and such profitable combination, our civil and ecclesiastical constitution.[20]

The Church of England was the ark of the Conservatives' constitutional covenant. All his reflections, the high-Church Gladstone wrote in 1841, brought him 'more and more to the conclusion that if the principle of national religion (a principle, which is my bond to parliamentary life) is to be upheld, or saved from utter overthrow, it must be by the united action of the Conservative party'.[21] The evangelical Lord Ashley thought that there was 'no hope of Conservative government, none', unless it were 'founded on truth, Religion, the Welfare of Man, & the honour of God'.[22] The Established Church stood as a warranty that the nation was a Christian nation and its statesmen Christian statesmen. Its supreme status in the politics of the 1830s derived from the attacks on its establishment and its property by the Radicals and the Dissenters and, on their behalf, by occupants of the highest echelons of Whiggery.

Constitutional issues, of themselves, have little political weight. The attention of the political nation in 1641 would not have been wrapt in the actions of the Long Parliament, had not the constitutional questions at issue been the tip of an economic and social iceberg. So in the 1830s the defence of the constitution signified much more than a yearning for stability and continuity. The independence of the House of Lords represented the social and economic power of the landowners and, more widely, the place of agriculture in the national economy. That independence was declining, not simply because the Reform Act strengthened the will of the House of Commons, but because its economic base was contracting. Similarly, to maintain the Established Church in its integrity was to protect the rights of property. (Although the Church was a parliamentary creation, Peel made one of its three 'safe' attributes that it had an 'inalienable claim' to its property.)[23] It meant also preserving the union with Ireland, since the strongest link between Ireland and England, apart from the vast Irish estates in the possession of English landowners, was the Irish Church.

The most important question at issue between the parties in the years from 1832 to 1837 was whether revenues of the Church of England were to be diverted to secular purposes. Resistance to such an invasion of the Church's property was taken by Peel to be the touchstone of a Conservative.

> I suppose [he wrote to Goulburn at the beginning of 1833] the 140 [Conservative] members of whom you speak will agree as to the strict appropriation of Church property to purposes *bona fide* connected with the interests of the established religion . . . as to the resistance to all such schemes as excluding the Church the bishops from the House of Lords; as to the protection of agriculture, the maintenance of public faith to the public creditor.[24]

It was symptomatic of the main ground of the Conservative recovery in the 1830s that the demise of the first Whig government was heralded in May 1834, when Lord John Russell tied the Whig party to the policy of the lay appropriation of surplus Irish Church revenues. Four ministers resigned from Lord Grey's cabinet in protest against a policy which challenged both the religious purpose of the nation and the rights of property. Moreover, the policy attacked the Church precisely where its Protestant mission was most required, in Catholic Ireland. Russell's action was denounced by Conservatives as truckling to Daniel O'Connell and the Irish Radicals, a theme which was to gain frequency and urgency in the second half of the decade, when Lord Melbourne's government was at the mercy of the Irish Radicals in the House of Commons. Henceforth, in Conservative pronouncements, there was joined to the constitutional trinity of King, Lords, and Church, the House of Commons. Its freedom and independence, too, needed to be defended, 'enslaved, as it now is, under the domination of the Irish agitator and his satellites'.[25]

The demise of the Ultras

Peel's letter describing what he considered to be the essential attitudes of a Conservative was written in answer to one from Goulburn, urging upon him 'perfect union and complete concert with all who called themselves Conservatives, as the only hope of keeping the party together'. Peel's reply, recommending that the party occupy a neutral position as umpire between the Whigs and the Radicals, disappointed Goulburn, because its evinced Peel's continued reluctance to cooperate with the Ultras.[26] Peel's attitude was understandable. The party structure in the House of Commons at the beginning of 1833 was fluid. Nearly half the members had not sat in the last parliament. Opportunities therefore existed for the Conservative party to attract recruits from within the House of Commons. In his first speech to the reformed House, Peel raised the standard of moderation and pronounced that the enemy was radicalism, not the Whig government, which, when it promoted the cause of order, would receive his cordial support. In that spirit Peel wished to rally round him politicians of the centre in both parties.

In July 1833 he received fresh evidence of the injury which close association with the Ultras could do to his strategy. A local jurisdiction Bill to establish county courts for the recovery of small debts came before the House of Lords after an untrammeled passage through the Commons. The measure was approved by Wellington, who arranged that the Conservative peers should not oppose it on second reading. He was unable to enforce the arrangement; but, although Lord Eldon and Lord Lyndhurst divided the House, the Bill received a large majority. A few days later, Lord Brougham, the Chancellor, let slip the phrase that the Bill was a government measure. Immediately a large number of Conservative peers began to canvass against it and they succeeded in throwing it out on third reading. The victory was Lord Lyndhurst's, 'for nothing but his unceasing, indefatigable exhortations would have removed the Duke's objections or have collected the Tories in such numbers'.[27]

The crowing of the Tory peers over their minor victory was a reaction to their defeat on a major measure, the Irish Church Temporalities Bill, a few nights earlier. Pressure from Peel, exerted through Wellington, got the Bill through, but the angry storms which accompanied its passage exposed the deep dissatisfaction with which many Tory peers regarded Peel's leadership. It produced an open breach between Wellington and the Ultra peers. The Irish Church Bill abolished ten of the twenty-two bishoprics in Ireland; it imposed a tax on the remaining sees and ordinary benefices in place of the old Church cess for the repair of church buildings and the cost of services (thereby relieving Catholics from contributing to the upkeep of the Anglican Church); and it smuggled in the principle of lay appropriation by leasing episcopal estates on a new basis and placing the expected increase in revenue from the new scheme in the hands of the state for whatever purposes parliament should approve. The Bill provided an excellent opportunity for Peel to display his concern for protecting the rights of property and the constitution while acknowledging the need to rectify obvious abuses. Twenty-two bishoprics were excessive for the small Anglican population of Ireland and the abolition of the cess was a step towards relieving Catholics of supporting an alien Church without endangering the Church's financial position. Once the Conservatives in the Commons persuaded the government to abandon the appropriation clause, clause 147, they were content to let the Bill pass.

Peel was anxious that it should not be thrown out by the Lords. That would simply promote the unity of the government side to no purpose, since a Conservative government was impossible. It would give substance to Radical attacks on the House of Lords. Nor did Peel wish to place himself in opposition to the Archbishop of Canterbury, who approved the Bill.[28] Such considerations were lost on the Ultra peers. By trying to persuade them to accept the Bill, Wellington earned their disgust. The Ultra peers met at the house of the Duke of Cumberland and resolved to fight the Bill to the end. On second reading they mustered ninety-eight votes against it, a much stronger showing than the Earl of Rosslyn, Wellington's Whip, had anticipated. That was not enough to defeat the Bill, however, and Rosslyn reported the Ultras to be 'in mortal ill humour'.[29]

The Ultras' unsuccessful challenge to the government produced a schism in the Conservative ranks. Rosslyn heard that the Ultras were determined to offer the command of 'their mutinous little troop' to Lyndhurst and at a rancorous meeting after the Bill had received its third reading Wellington apparently told the Duke of Buckingham that he no longer considered himself to be the head of the party in the Lords. Rosslyn himself regretted that the party appeared to be broken up, but he was too experienced a politician to mistake an estrangement for a divorce, and predicted that even many of those who voted against the third reading would soon follow the Duke as steadily as ever.[30] A year later, after the whole Conservative party had, with Peel's blessing, united to defeat a Bill to admit Dissenters to the universities, a meeting took place at Apsley House, described by Lord Londonderry.

> Our meeting took place today at twelve, at the Duke's. It was merely an *omnium gatherum* of all the party. I should think fifty or sixty attended. There were no bishops; but *all wavers* . . . in short it was the whole party.
>
> The Duke said he had assembled us to know the course desired or wished by noble lords for the remainder of the session. . . . It was absolutely necessary . . . to keep together, if we meant to do anything, and to have peers to hold proxies . . .
>
> It seemed evident by this exordium that we were met to give pledges to remain in town to the end of the session. D. of Gloucester and Cumberland both declared their readiness to remain until they received his Grace's acquiescence to their departure. . . . The Duke then said he should be mainly guided [on the Irish Tithes bill] by the sentiments of the bishops. This seemed to satisfy even the *Ultras* of the meeting. D. of Cumberland said to me, he was privately sure *this assurance* was all that we need desire.[31]

That meeting did not end Peel's and Wellington's difficulty in restraining the Conservative peers. Whenever the leaders seemed to compromise a cardinal article of the Tory faith they encountered stubborn opposition. Beneath the quarrels over particular pieces of legislation lay the fundamental dispute about the role of the House of Lords as an independent arch of the mixed constitution. 'It is only making the H. of Lords – as the Radicals pronounce it – of *no use* to the country' was Londonderry's verdict on what he called Wellington's 'secession' from opposition.[32] Wellington bowed to Peel's judgement, but he reminded him that it was 'not easy to make men feel that they are of no consequence in the country, who had heretofore had so much weight'.[33]

The degree of party unity in the House of Commons is not easy to assess. It cannot be fairly gauged simply by testing the fidelity with which Conservatives followed Peel into the division lobbies, because Peel was reluctant to give them a clear lead. Goulburn and Herries wanted him to attend a series of party meetings, in order to weld the party together, but Peel disliked such meetings. They accentuated differences and their proceedings seldom remained secret.[34] For the 1833 parliament the difficulty is compounded by Peel's voting record. On forty-three selected divisions he voted against the government only three times.[35] Such subservience to the government dismayed his Conservative critics, but Lord Melville was annoyed by the language of '*soi-disant* Conservative Newspapers' and those members of both Houses who wished to turn the government out 'from no other apparent motive than hostility to present Ministers, & totally forgetting that all those doctrines & anti-*governmental* principles (I use the word advisedly as opposed to anti-*Administration*) are much more at variance with our sound principles than those of our Whig ministers'. By opposing for the sake of opposition, Melville feared, the Ultras would 'disgust all really loyal & well-intentioned conservatives who look only to the stability of the Monarchy & preservation of the Constitution'.[36]

The division lists are, however, helpful in determining the size and character of the section of the party which wished to tie the Conservative party to the repeal of the malt tax and a drastic alteration of the currency system. The malt tax repealers, led by the Marquis of Chandos, the 'Farmers' friend', were representative of those men whom Melville found wanting in the principles of sound government. Not much was to be gained by repealing the tax, and barley-growers were, at any rate, the most prosperous farmers in the country. [37] But its repeal would be a sign to the agricultural interest that it could still expect special favour. Peel would have nothing to do with it. He accepted the government's case that, since the malt tax produced an annual revenue of about £5 million, which was one-tenth of the national revenue, its repeal would entail the imposition of an income tax. Nor had he any sympathy with the currency reformers. He had been, after all, the minister responsible for the introduction of a 'tight money' policy by the deflationary return to the gold standard in 1819. From its inception that policy had been the object of attack by Matthew Attwood, the member for Birmingham, who in 1829 had been converted to parliamentary reform by the conviction, like that of the Ultra 'Protestant' converts, that only a corrupt, unreformed House of Commons could year after year uphold a currency system so inimical to the material welfare of the people. Attwood's support was drawn mostly from county members, landowners who came out of the Napoleonic wars heavily mortgaged and who suffered from the steady decline of agricultural prices in the following two decades.

There were four divisions in the 1833 parliament by which the strength of the malt and currency section in the Conservative party was tested, with the following result.

Motion	Conservative Ayes
Attwood's motion for relief of agricultural distress, 21 March 1833	24
Attwood's motion for an alteration of the currency, 24 April 1833	49
Chandos's motion for the repeal of the malt tax, 26 April 1833	40
Chandos's motion for the repeal of the malt tax, 27 February 1834	48

Of the forty-nine who voted for currency reform and the forty-eight who voted to repeal the malt tax there were thirty-two Conservatives in both lists. The outer limit of the group is therefore sixty-five, but the 'core' is only thirty-two. It is no surprise that twenty-one of the core sat for county seats and ten of the remaining eleven for 'proprietary' boroughs in which the influence of a landowner was paramount.[38] They are not to be equated with the Ultras of recent Tory history. For one thing, more than half of them had not sat in parliament before 1830. Of the fourteen who had, four had voted in favour of Catholic emancipation and six against. One noteworthy aspect of the divisions is that the split in the party occurred because the Conservative agriculturalists voted *against* the government. They were not country gentlemen proudly exercising their independence of party by supporting the Crown's ministers. They constituted a special interest group within the Conservative party, men who were not imbued with what their leaders called 'sound principles of government' and who could not be relied on to foreswear their opinions, or bury them, when a Conservative government should come into office.

The 1833 parliament contained forty-four Ultras who had voted either against Catholic emancipation or for Parnell's civil list motion which brought down Wellington's government. Only nine of them, however, had voted against Wellington on both occasions. The Ultras were neither a strong nor a closely knit group in the House of Commons and during the years 1833–34 they were reabsorbed into the Conservative party. The process had begun in 1831, when all nine of the Ultra 'core' had voted against the Reform Bill. At the start of the new parliament, nevertheless, Sir Richard Vyvyan had hopes of leading an Ultra party of about fifty members, and the party managers were concerned to thwart his ambitions. In February 1833 Herries, who in the previous four years had assiduously cultivated links with both wings of the party, was delegated to speak individually to the most prominent Ultras – Vyvyan, Sir Edward Knatchbull, Sir Robert Inglis, and Viscount Stormont – with a view to holding a meeting of all the party to elect Peel as leader.[39] Knatchbull and Vyvyan insisted upon the places in a future Conservative cabinet being fixed in advance. Vyvyan visited Peel and 'talked of making him *their Minister* if they succeeded in depreciating the currency!', at which Peel 'naturally fired'.[40] Neither the proposed meeting nor the election of Peel took place. But the annual party dinner at Greenwich in June was attended by Lord Lyndhurst and Sir Charles Wetherell and by other Ultras, Lord Mansfield, Lord Lincoln, Lord Stormont, Knatchbull, and Vyvyan, who had not attended the function before and whom Ellenborough called 'new fish'. 'Nothing,' he added, 'could be more united than the company.'[41]

The harmony proved to be more than temporary. Peel's government, formed in December 1834, included four Ultras, plus Lord Lyndhurst as Chancellor and Lord Lincoln, one of the agriculturalist core (whose acceptance of office almost certainly required the consent of his father, the Ultra Duke of Newcastle). Chandos refused office because Peel would not promise to repeal the malt tax and Vyvyan was out of the country when the ministry was being formed. But Knatchbull, Vyvyan's second-in-command, accepted the paymastership of the forces and a seat in the cabinet.[42] Vyvyan returned from Vienna, soured by Peel's success, to rail at Knatchbull's 'betrayal' and to find himself 'virtually shorn of my House of Commons influence. I could hardly reckon on half a dozen followers.'[43] Even the Duke of Marlborough, father of the Marquis of Blandford, who had begun the Ultras' desertion of Wellington in 1829, put the past behind him when Peel formed his government.

> My political Creed [he wrote to Peel] may be collected, principally from my never having taken my seat in the reformed Parliament. My inclination to serve the present Administration may be collected from the same source. . . . The attachment of myself & my son Charles, who is coming in for Woodstock, will be devoted to your Administration.[44]

Blandford himself, who gave up his Woodstock seat to his brother, asked to be removed to the House of Lords and assured Wellington 'of the sincerity with which I desired to support him, or any *Conservative* administration'.[45]

The separation of Vyvyan and Knatchbull signalled the end of Vyvyan's dream of organizing a cohesive Ultra party in the House of Commons.[46] His failure illustrates the peculiar difficulty which afflicts the right wing of conservative parties in a system which resolves itself into two main parties. Observers who have remarked that conservative parties are less subject to internal fissures than radical parties have sometimes found the explanation to be the conservative's inherent regard for order and authority.[47] There is more to it than that. Disagreements are naturally less apt to arise among men who are concerned to preserve the existing structure of a society than they are among men who have a desire to alter it. And when they do arise they are more dangerous. A radical wing can break away from a left-wing party in the reasonable belief that doing so attracts attention to its cause, protects it from adulteration, and enhances its future prospects. The radical can break up his party without sacrificing the world which he hopes to create. It remains to be created. The extreme Conservative has less scope. If he breaks up his party, he not only loses his immediate object, as happened with Catholic emancipation in 1829 and the Corn Laws in 1846, but he also weakens the force of Conservatism, hands power to his opponents, and thereby assists radical triumphs which are almost certain to be permanent. His action proclaims his attachment to honour more than his sense of politics and he sacrifices part of the world which he wishes to preserve. There are times when the sacrifice, by serving as an example which offers the promise of Conservative renewal, may not be in vain. Chandos thought that the issue of the malt tax called for such a sacrifice, but his eccentricity was not widely shared.[48] The Ultra Duke of Newcastle told Peel in March 1835 that his satisfaction at seeing Peel at the head of affair was 'not pure and unmixed', since he, Newcastle, was 'not a Reformer at all'. He would 'yield nothing to the spirit of reform, innovation, revolution, by whatever name it may be called . . . because in my view of the case, concession leads to revolution'. Newcastle was, nevertheless, eager that Peel should remain in office to keep out 'the enemies of order and good government, the friends of anarchy, spoliation, and revolution'.[49]

Instances of Ultra–Tory candidates' bucking the official party line at the 1837 elections are difficult to find.[50] From 1835 to 1841 no recognizable, distinct Ultra wing operated within the Conservative parliamentary party.

Notes and References

Peel and moderate Conservatism

1 Gladstone, *Memoranda*, 135–7.
2 Gash, *Reaction and Reconstruction*, 126.
3 *Ibid.*
4 Young, *Victorian England*. 2nd edn, 1953, 32. Edward Norman makes the point that the most comprehensive party and the most modern in the 1830s was O'Connell's Repeal party, with its elections managed by agents (usually priests), centralized control, election pledges demanded of candidates, and a permanent political fund raised on a mass basis. 'English observers were unable to comprehend the Repeal party,' he writes, 'because political organization on that scale was unknown to them. The main English parties, by comparison, were still mere connections.' (Norman, *A History of Modern Ireland*, 64–5.) But it ought to be remembered that O'Connell's was a very special kind of party. It was sectional and it was a 'one-issue' party. It did not aspire to government. In those ways it resembled a mass protest movement, not a political party.
5 *Hansard*, 3rd series, vi, 575; Croker, *Correspondence and Diaries*, ii, 115.
6 Popper, *The Poverty of Historicism*, 62.
7 It is a matter of controversy. Hobsbawm cites the years 1831–32 as the only period since the seventeenth century when there was 'something like a revolutionary situation' (*Industry and Empire*, 55) and Thompson believes that the country 'was within an ace of a revolution' (*The Making of the English Working Class*, 817). But George Rudé believes that the Radical leader, Francis Place, 'hoodwinked' the Whigs into believing that only reform could avert revolution in the large towns (quoted in Rowe, *London Radicalism*, xxv).
8 Watson, *The English Ideology: studies in the language of Victorian politics*, 180.
9 Jennings, *Party Politics*, 74.
10 Croker to Lord Hertford, 30 Sept, 1836: Croker, *Correspondence and Diaries*, ii, 282.
11 Gash, *Sir Robert Peel*, 39.
12 Peel to Goulburn, 3 Jan, 1833: Parker, *Peel*, ii, 212–14. Peel's advice was seconded by Lord Mahon, one of the Whips in the House of Commons. Mahon wanted the Conservatives to give up their places in the House opposite the Treasury bench to the Radicals and move below the gangway, as 'an outward and visible sign of what is now a most important truth, that the chief battle is to be between the Government and the Radicals' (Mahon to Peel, 8 Jan, 1833: Peel MSS, Add. MSS 40403, ff. 167–9). Mahon's advice was not taken.
13 Peel to Goulburn, 25 May 1834: Parker, *Peel*, ii, 243–4.
14 The Tamworth Manifesto is printed in Peel, *Memoirs*, ii, 58–67.

15 Lethbridge to Peel, 12 Dec, 1834: Peel MSS, Add MSS 40405, ff. 89–91. Lethbridge told Peel that unless he made his opinions known to the country 'the returns will be nearly *as they were before* – and there will be pledges, given more against Men, than Measures'.

16 John Walker, the reformer who was standing as a Liberal Conservative at Berkshire, believed that such a declaration could alone prevent 'the explosion of that unreasonably angry hostility to the Duke of Wellington' (Walter to Sir James [Scarlett], 10 Dec, 1834: *ibid*, ff. 24–5). Goulburn and Alexander Baring took the same view (Kitson Clark, *Peel and the Conservative Party*, 209).

17 See Morley, *Gladstone*, ii, 486. Not until 1892 did a Conservative leader issue an address to the electorate of the whole country. In 1838 Disraeli made the impertinent offer to Peel to draft anonymously 'a species of manifesto of the views and principles of the Conservative party'. It was not accepted (Bulmer-Thomas, *The Growth of the British Party System*, i, 82).

18 Morley, *The Life of William Ewart Gladstone*, i, 419.

19 Kenyon to Peel, 26 March 1835: Parker, *Peel*, ii, 295.

20 Kitson Clark, *Churchmen and the Condition of England*, 27.

21 Gladstone memorandum, 9 May 1841: Gladstone, *Memoranda*, 135–7.

22 Diary of the 7th Earl of Shaftesbury, 27 May 1834: Broadlands MSS, SHA/PD/1.

23 Peel, *Memoirs*, i, 77–80. The others were that it was a Church to which the monarch must conform and whose bishops had a right to sit in parliament.

24 Peel to Goulburn, 3 Jan,1833: Parker, *Peel*, ii, 212–4.

25 *Leicester Conservative Standard*.

26 Goulburn to Herries, 4 Jan, 1833: Herries, *Memoir*, ii, 163–4

27 Le Marchant diary, 21 July 1833: Aspinall, *Three Diaries*, 360–2.

28 Arbuthnot to his son, 22 July 1833. C. Arbuthnot, *Correspondence*, 171–2.

29 Rosslyn to Mrs Arbuthnot, 20 July 1833: *ibid*, 171.

30 Rosslyn to Mrs Arbuthnot, 27 July and 5 Aug, 1833: *ibid*, 173–4, 174–5.

31 Londonderry to the Duke of Buckingham, 2 Aug, 1834: Buckingham, *Memoirs of . . . William IV and Victoria*, ii, 115–16.

32 Londonderry to the Duke of Buckingham, 25 March 1833: *ibid*, ii, 370–.

33 Wellington to Peel, 23 July 1833: Parker, *Peel*, ii, 218.

34 Ellenborough diary, 12 March 1833: Aspinall, *Three Diaries*, 315–6.

35 Glynn, 'The private member of Parliament, 1833–1868', unpublished thesis, 166.

36 Melville to Peel, 20 May 1833: Peel MSS, Add. MSS 40403, ff. 249–52.

37 Spring, 'Lord Chandos and the farmers, 1818–1846', *Huntingdon Library Quarterly*, May 1970, 265.

38 The odd borough out was Shrewsbury, the seat of Sir John Hanmer, who was elected for the first time in 1832. One of the 'core' was the future Peelite free-trader, Lord Lincoln. He, too, was in parliament for the first time and dutifully followed the instructions of his father, the Ultra Duke of Newcastle.

39 Ellenborough diary, 27 Feb, 1833: Aspinall, *Three Diaries*, 308.

40 Ellenborough diary, 1 May 1833: *ibid*, 324.

41 Ellenborough diary, 22 June, 1833: *ibid*, 340–1.

42 The three other Ultra appointments were the Orange leader, the Earl of Roden (Household), Lord Lowther (Joint Treasury Secretary), and Lord Stormont (Lord of the Treasury).

43 Bradfield, 'Vyvyan and the country gentlemen', 742.

44 Malborough to Peel, 21 Dec, 1834: Peel MSS, Add. MSS 40407, ff. 28–9.

45 Blandford to Peel, 12 Dec, 1834: *ibid*, Add. MSS 40405, ff. 76–7. The Ultra peer, Lord Kenyon, urged Peel not to resign after a series of defeats in the Commons in the first weeks of the 1835 parliamentary session: 'I anxiously trust you will nail your colours to the mast, and not quit our Sailor – and now repentant – king' (Kenyon to Peel, 26 March 1835: Parker, *Peel*, ii, 295). Ultra acquiescence in the formation of a Peel government was also marked by Stanley Giffard's offer, which Peel declined, of the services of the high Tory *Standard*, in order 'to obviate the possibility that this power which I have been the means of erecting should operate to embarrass the formation of progress of a Conservative government in any degree' (Giffard to Peel, 8 Dec, 1834: *ibid*, Add. MSS 40404, ff. 304–6).

46 It also ended a friendship. 'I went to Peel's last night,' Knatchbull wrote to his wife in 1841. 'When I was coming away about the time other people did, on the stairs no one else being there I met Sir R. Vyvyan – we passed' (Knatchbull–Hugessen, *Kentish Family*, 234).

47 'The Conservative Party', Reginald Northam wrote, 'has been a better disciplined party than those of the Left ... because Conservatives ... place a high value on leadership as a factor in collective achievement' *Conservatism the Only Way*, 90). And in supremely silly vein, Glickman writes that 'Toryism ... grasps the necessity of power ... In a particularly difficult situation, involving many alternative courses of action, the Tory will not ask, "Shall we sit down and talk about it?".' Rather his first impulse is to blurt, "Who's in charge here?".' ('The Toryness of English Conservatism', *Brit. Stud.*, Nov, 1962, 133.)

48 Chandos's protege, Thomas Fremantle, refused Peel's offer of the Secretaryship of the Treasury, even though Peel was making arrangements for him to come in for a new seat and thus escape the strings attached to the Duke of Buckingham's borough patronage. But Fremantle acted from loyalty to Chandos and Buckingham, not from devotion to the repeal of the malt tax, and after the 1837 elections he became the party's Chief Whip in the House of Commons. (Peel to the Marquis of Exeter, 16 December, 1834: Peel MSS, Add. MSS 40405, ff. 289–90; Fremantle to Peel, 16 Dec, 1834: *ibid*, ff. 295–6.)

49 Newcastle to Peel, 29 March 1835: Parker, *Peel*, ii, 296–7.

50 Close, 'The elections of 1835 and 1837 in England and Wales', unpublished thesis, 356.

Chapter 6

The Conservative recovery I: Inside parliament

The desertions from Whiggery

Twentieth-century governments are made and lost at elections. In the eighteenth century governments were made and unmade in the House of Commons. Between the Reform Acts of 1832 and 1867 the balance, although it was tilting towards the twentieth century, wavered between the two practices. When the Carlton Club attempted to boycott Philip Pusey, the member for Berkshire, after his vote in favour of the Irish Church Bill in 1835, Croker asked Peel to restrain the 'madmen'. 'A *majority*', he wrote, 'might brand *deserters* – but, if there are to be no deserters, how are our Carltonians ever to be in a majority again?'[1] Croker's question, assuming, as it did, that elections did not by themselves turn a minority into a majority, was founded on the knowledge that there were many members, especially those who, like Pusey, sat for county seats, who might call themselves Whig or Conservative, but whose return was not dependent upon party organization and who were able to change parties with little risk to their seats. Sir Thomas Lethbridge did not 'anticipate any great alteration of Men' from the 1835 elections, but he did 'anticipate a vast alteration of *sentiment* among those returned'.[2] It was therefore in keeping with the habits of the age that the foundations of the Conservative recovery in the 1830s should have been laid inside the House of Commons, in the movement of reformers across the floor of the House into the Conservative party.

The process began in the midst of the reform struggle itself. By the time that the Bill had become law, popular enthusiasm had been so aroused that reform looked less like the gift of an obliging Whig *noblesse* and more like the ransom wrung by the 'people' from a frightened government. Men who at the start had looked upon the Reform Bill as the final settlement of a long-agitated question, by the end had doubts whether the Whigs would be able to resist future demands for a secret ballot, triennial parliaments and household suffrage, in short, for democracy. The only Ultra member of Grey's government, the Duke of Richmond, confided to Lord Wharncliffe his alarm that 'we have created the monster which will turn upon us';[3] and Sir James Graham, the most conservative member of the committee of four which drafted the original Bill, decided that although it was futile to resist the progress of radicalism, 'to steady its direction and check its velocity will be our task'.[4]

That kind of apprehension among conservative reformers (first revealed by the large majority, 232 votes to 148, given to Chandos's amendment to strengthen landlord influence at county elections by enfranchising the £50 tenants-at-will) produced the first group of seceders from the government benches. The 1832 elections returned ten Conservatives who had been reformers in the previous parliament.[5] All of them, except the ex-Canningite, Charles Wynne, who had resigned from Grey's government soon after the details of the Reform Bill had been published, had voted for reform. Some of them, of course – notably the two Owens and Robert Palmer – resumed what may be considered their natural places after a self-preserving submission to their constituents' opinions. Six of them had been accounted ministerialists during the Tory governments of the 1820s. What marked them most, as a group, was that eight of them sat for English (or Welsh) county divisions, the fertile ground of Conservative growth in the next nine years.

Those ten early converts, or penitents, were joined by many more in the next five years. Statistical precision on the matter is impossible. Various tests yield conflicting totals and some of the members themselves would have hedged about which party they belonged to before 1837. From a number of sources, however, the number of reformers who made their way into the Conservative party between 1833 and 1837 may be calculated as thirty-one, making a total since 1832 of forty-one.[6] That total may be too small. (It is almost certainly not too large. Every one of the forty-one members who was still in the Commons in 1839 paid his subscription to receive the Conservative Whips' circulars.[7]) The exact size of the group is not important. What mattered was the appeal which Peel's brand of Conservatism was making for moderate men, an appeal which carried beyond the House of Commons. At by-elections in 1833 and 1834 the Conservatives gained ten seats and lost none.[8] By the summer of 1834 *The Times*, a warm supporter of Lord Grey in 1830, had broken with the Whigs and was turning towards the Conservatives. Then, aspects of the 1835 elections, at which the Radicals increased their representation from about 140 members to nearly 200, gave pause to conservative Whigs. One of those was Lord Spencer, who, as Lord Althorp, had presided with bluff equanimity over the government party in the Commons from 1830 to 1834.

> I must admit [he wrote to Francis Baring in January 1835] that in the peculiar circumstances of this Dissolution the Whigs were quite justified in preferring Radicals to Tories if the Radicals were willing to prefer Whigs to Tories, but I think they ought to have gone no further. I think they ought not in Marylebone to have supported two Radicals and turned out a Whig; I think that in Finsbury they ought not to have withdrawn a Whig to give way to a Radical; and I think that the Whig newspapers expressing great triumph at the election of Whittle Harvey was going too far. The Whigs must remember that if they are again to form an Administration, they will find, as they did before, the Radicals their most bitter

opponents, and they ought not therefore to assist them against Whigs. I see, for instance, the *Globe* rejoicing that Lord Oxmanton has been driven from his county for some friend of O'Connell's. I presume the effect of all this will be that the next Administration must be purely Radical and that the power of a moderate, or if you please an ultra, Whig to do any good is at an end. I do not care for this myself, because I think that if the country chooses to be governed by a Radical Administration they ought to be so governed, and if they do not choose it they have the power of preventing it in their own hands. But if from private reasons of an imperative nature I felt myself justified in retiring from public life, this state of things increases greatly my desire to do so.[9]

Whether Peel would be the beneficiary of the movement of Whig opinion depended partly upon the fortunes of the 'Derby Dilly'. That was the name which O'Connell contemptuously gave to the small group of politicians who sought, in 1834–35, to form a centre party of moderate Whigs and Conservatives.[10] The Dilly's history began with the resignation of four cabinet ministers – Lord Stanley, Sir James Graham, the Duke of Richmond and Lord Ripon – from Grey's government in May 1834, in protest against the government's commitment to the principle of the secular appropriation of surplus revenues of the Irish Church. The break had long been foreseen. None of the four seceders was an impeccable Whig. Stanley, the leader of the Dilly, was the heir to the ancient Whig title and fortune of the house of Derby. He had entered parliament as a Whig in 1820, but in 1827–28 he held minor posts in the governments of Canning and Goderich (now Lord Ripon) and he was thereafter considered to be a Canningite. Graham, too, was of Whig background, but although nominally a Whig throughout the 1820s he had formed no strong attachment to that party and by the end of the decade was described, albeit extravagantly, by the *Carlisle Patriot* as 'a good sound Tory'.[11] Ripon was an ex-Canningite and Richmond an Ultra-Tory.

For some years Stanley and Graham had been at the centre of conversations about a realignment of parties which should bring Peel and the conservative Whigs together. Graham was one of the most frequently mentioned Whig go-betweens when the possibility of a Grey–Wellington junction was being mooted in 1829–30,[12] and he was already looking to Stanley as his leader.

I hope you will take the field in force [he wrote to Stanley in July 1828], and I think you will find a strong and respectable body willing to act under you... the aspect of affairs is so clouded by difficulties that the chances are some capital blunder may be committed; and then will arise the golden opportunity of forming a party in the House of Commons on some broad and intelligible principle . . .

You are the person on whom I rest my hopes. You contain all the great requisites; you may reunite a scattered force which it is the interest of the country to see consolidated, and by concert and judicious management I really am disposed to believe the road to power is open.[13]

Stanley had then been in parliament only eight years. His only official experience was as a Lord of the Treasury in Canning's administration and Under-Secretary for the Colonies in Goderich's. He showed no interest in the proposal and Graham did not again write to him on the subject until 1834.

By then the question of Stanley's future was a major political talking-point. In 1831 Stanley had become Irish Secretary and a member of the cabinet.[14] The Irish office led him into bitter clashes with O'Connell, on which occasions it was noticeable that Peel did his best to encourage the rift by praising Stanley and stressing his differences with the Radicals. When Stanley defended the government's Irish Coercion Bill against the Radicals' attacks in 1833, Peel 'complimented Stanley exceedingly, and without any air of vengeance threw his shield over him'.[15] After the debate Stanley wrote to Peel thanking him for his generosity. By that time the two men had spent many hours together on the select committee investigating the operation of the tithe in Ireland; in April 1832 Stanley had sent to Peel a confidential memorandum outlining the basis of his proposed report, with the covering phrase, 'there is no very great difference in the views which we entertain'.[16] Religious and Irish questions were drawing the two men together. A month after the Whig resignations of May 1834 Graham discussed the position of the Irish Church with Peel and reported to Stanley that 'Peel was very easy in his manner with me, quite communicative, and most anxious to impress me with the conviction that he desired to act on this occasion in the strictest union with you'.[17]

Two obstacles stood in the way of permanent union: Stanley's liberalism and his ambition to form a centre party. Stanley had presided over the consolidation of the Irish Board of Works in 1831, the two central features of which, the provision of state funds for industry and the extension of central government control over local administration, were heartily disliked by Conservatives. He had established the national schools in Ireland, which not only place, Irish primary education under the direction of the national government, but also made it non-sectarian. His liberalism was most strikingly shown by his attempt to reform the Irish grand juries by transferring the main burden of the county cess (the Irish equivalent of the county rate) from tenants to landlords, a proposal to which even O'Connell objected as an unwarranted increase in the landowners' tax bill. There were many Conservatives who looked with misgiving on Peel's endeavours to accommodate Stanley and the conservative Whigs. One of Peel's closest colleagues was Henry Goulburn. He was not an Ultra, but he was a staunch Churchman, and in 1833 he looked with disfavour on Peel's support for Stanley's Irish Church reforms. Peel acknowledged the gulf of opinion which separated Stanley and Goulburn, and then told Goulburn that it had to be bridged. 'The alternatives are, the reconcilement of such views and the adoption of a course which each can conscientiously take; or that each, and those who agree respectively with each, should take their own line, and risk the consequences to the Church of dissension among its friends.'[18]

Once Stanley and Graham had left the Whig government, the first obstacle to union with Peel had been largely removed: Stanley's liberalism stopped short at precisely the point, the secular appropriation of Church revenue, at which cooperation with the Conservatives became an attractive proposition. There remained the question of his ambition to lead a new centre party. Stanley had been encouraged by Grey and Melbourne to look upon the Whig leadership, and therefore ultimately the premiership, as his natural inheritance.[19] 'This is the main question,' Lord Londonderry wrote in 1833. 'Is Peel's star of power or Stanley's to have the ascendant?'[20] Stanley possessed two qualities for leadership which Peel noticeably lacked. He had the rare ability to rally the House of Commons by the sheer force of his oratory; and his high station and country habits made him personally congenial to the members who made up the backbone of the Conservative party. When, therefore, in November 1834 Lord Althorp was removed by his father's death to the House of Lords and William IV accepted the resignation of Melbourne's government rather than have Lord John Russell succeed Althorp as leader of the House of Commons, Stanley was powerfully placed to influence events.

William IV might have sent for Stanley, whose prospects, as a Whig, of finding a majority in the Commons were better than those of any Conservative. Instead he sent for the Duke of Wellington. Peel was in Italy. Wellington accepted the commission to form a government on the understanding that he would hand over to Peel on the latter's return. On 9 December Peel arrived back in London, 'not altogether satisfied' with the King's 'premature and impolitic' dismissal of Melbourne, but unable to 'reconcile it to my feelings, or indeed to my sense of duty, to subject the King and the Monarchy to the humiliation, through my refusal of office, of inviting his dismissed servants to resume their appointments'. That, at least, was the defence of his decision to govern with the backing of only about 160 Conservatives in the House of Commons which Peel gave to Stanley in a letter written on the evening of his return, inviting Stanley to join his government.[21] It was not, of course, the whole story. Peel was not inhibited by high-minded notions of constitutional propriety and service to the Crown from refusing to cooperate in the attempt to construct a reforming Tory ministry in May 1832. Then he calculated that the attempt would end in fiasco and compromise both him and the Tory party. In the autumn of 1834, although it is true that his freedom of action was restricted by Wellington's having already accepted the premiership for him in commission, he expected that taking office in an extremely fluid political situation would stimulate the growth of his party.

The fate of Peel's government hung on Stanley's decision. Two disenchanted reformers who were in transit to the Conservative party urged him to accept Peel's offer. One was Viscount Sandon.

> If you hold off, or give only a cold support, will not the moderate, the only real, Whigs all over the country, whether as Representatives or Electors, do the same? And if they do, can this Government stand? And if this Government does not

stand, what Government succeeds? A moderate Whig Government? No; at best the late Government returns: weak, unstable, intriguing; a prey to every influence but the right one, undermining any Institution which it did not desire or dare to assail; such it was before; but how will it return? Not by their own strength; that is nothing; but by the strength of the Radicals; and will that strength be lent to them, but upon terms either express or implied. . . . Perhaps you will say, how can I, a Reformer, without utter loss of character join the Duke or Peel, anti-Reformers, and is not character a pearl beyond all price to a public man? Now you are not a man to be led away by name: let us put things in another shape. How can I who supported a Reform in the Constitution of Parliament, which is carried out and which is over and irrevocable, and which I carried only for the purpose of preventing Reform in the same Body from being carried further, how can I join men who rejected that Reform and denounced it, but who have no notion of going back on it, but would assist me in . . . its original object, namely in preventing further Parliamentary Reform . . . as to Church reform, are you nearer to Peel or the late Government? . . . he supported the Irish Church Bill, modified as it passed the House of Commons; he has supported various schemes for settling the question of Tithes in Ireland; he has expressed himself favourable to a proper settlement of the same question in England. . . . The men of property and education all together are not too much; divided they must give way.[22]

From Belfast, James Emerson Tennent had two weeks earlier sent similar advice.

I have just returned to Belfast from the south of Ireland and I cannot refrain from acquainting you with the *extraordinary* anxiety which prevails in all quarters relative to your acceptance or rejection of office under the new Government. The Tories universally conceive that it would be utter madness for the Duke of Wellington to attempt a *rigid* Tory administration, and openly avow their conviction that his ministry cannot last a month unless it includes in its measures a salutary reform, civil, ecclesiastical and corporate [municipal corporations]. The Whigs, at the same time, consider that your acceptance of office would be a sufficient & satisfactory test of his intentions in this respect, & will at once give their confidence to him; and I assure you that at this instant all parties await with anxiety your determination as the settlement of the crisis.

   . . . *should you join him* you will at once bring along with you the entire of the moderate Whig party of the House of Commons, those for instance who supported the Coercion Bill.[23]

Tennent enclosed a list of eleven Irish Whig members who would support a Conservative government which included Stanley and Graham.

   Sandon's letter was a piece of shrewd political analysis and an accurate forecast of the future course of politics should Stanley not join Peel. Both he and Tennent based their argument on the assumption that Peel's government would fail if Stanley and Graham remained outside it. It was that aspect of the matter which interested Stanley's closes advisers, Graham and the Duke of Richmond. Despite Peel's apparent willingness to award cabinet places to all four of the ex-Whig cabinet ministers,[24] they were determined to play for higher stakes. Richmond passed on to Stanley Lord Grey's remark that if he held off and waited for the failure of Peel's government, he would be Prime

Minister within a year.[25] Graham, basing his opinion on reports that William IV already regretted having dismissed Melbourne, believed that Peel would be given only a 'limited commission to form a Coalition Government'. He and Stanley ought therefore to refuse to join it, giving as their reason that they objected to its high Tory elements. 'That would naturally lead His Majesty', Graham argued, 'to admit whom he, as well as we may desire, and to exclude those whom we could consider obnoxious. This would cause Peel joining us, not us him, which is the object to be kept in view.'[26]

Even before Peel had arrived back in England and made his offer to Stanley, the decision had been taken not to join him.[27] On 10 December Stanley wrote to Peel explaining that decision.[28] He allowed that recent events had narrowed the differences between them, especially on Church questions, and he praised Peel for his moderation and fairness in opposition. Yet there were two more important considerations which dictated his course. The first was the Ultra section of the Conservative party. Peel had successfully checked their intemperance, but 'while such an exercise of influence naturally lessens objections applying to yourself, the very circumstances of its having been required tends to increase the difficulty of my serving in your ranks'. When Grey had retired from the premiership in June, Wellington had made a bitter speech in the Lords attacking the whole of Grey's achievement, including the abolition of slavery, for which Stanley had been the responsible minister. The Duke's presence in the government 'must stamp upon the administration about to be formed the impress of his name and principles'.

The second consideration was the duty of public servants not to sacrifice their public character.

> The sudden conversion of long political opposition into the most intimate alliance, no general coincidence of principle, except upon one point, being proved to exist between us, would shock public opinion, would be ruinous to my own character, and injurious to the Government which you seek to form.
>
> The reputation of those who take part in public affairs is a matter of national importance; and confidence in public men has been more shaken by coalitions than by all the other acts of personal misconduct taken together. This consideration applies with peculiar force to the offer which you have now made to me. If any beneficial moral effect were produced by my separation from Lord Grey and my former colleagues, and my abandonment of office for the sake of conscience and principle, that effect would be wholly destroyed by my speedy return to office with their political opponents: the motives of my former conduct would be suspected, whereas now they cannot be impugned.

That argument may have been a cloak to shield Stanley's ambition. Yet he was to take the same line on future occasions – most notably when he resigned from Peel's government in 1845 in opposition to the repeal of the Corn Laws – when to do so seemed certain to damage his prospects. By conventional political standards Stanley's ambition was muted, partly, perhaps, because accidents of birth had relieved him of the need to prove his fitness for political leadership. It was not simply the accident of blue blood. Macaulay cited Stanley as the only example of a brilliant parliamentary debater who had not practised long hours and suffered failures to become one: 'With the exception of Mr. Stanley, whose knowledge of the science of parliamentary defence resembles an instinct, it would be difficult to name any eminent debater who has not made himself a master of his art at the expense of his audience.'[29] On hearing him speak in the Commons in 1832 Gladstone described him as the cleverest man he had seen, 'quicker than thought itself', though Brougham, agreeing, added that 'at sixty he would be the same – still by far the cleverest young man of the day'.[30] With such gifts, Stanley not surprisingly preferred the pleasures of a shooting party to the drudgery of departmental administration.[31] More important, the security of his position, socially and politically, encouraged him to indulge in the Ultras' passion for consistency. Like the Ultras (not, of course, only them), Stanley raised political consistency to the level of a moral imperative. It is not so very strange that by 1846 Stanley should find himself the leader of the right wing of the Conservative party.

In the letter in which he refused office Stanley promised Peel an independent support for a moderate Conservative government. By the end of December, however, he was writing to Graham that Peel was throwing away his chances by appointing Ultras like the Orange leader, the Earl of Roden, to the government.[32] At the elections in January the Derby tenants in Lancashire South were instructed to vote against the two Conservative candidates and for two Radicals,[33] while in the northern division of the county, Stanley's constituency, Stanley was cheered for his declaration of allegiance to the Whig party and his assertion that Peel's government did not have the confidence of liberal-minded men.[34] At the same time, the gains made by the Radicals at the elections worried many Whigs, and when it became known that the opposition intended to put up a Radical, James Abercromby, against the Conservative candidate for the speakership, Charles Manners Sutton, Stanley decided that the opportunity had arrived to test the amount of support for a centre party. On the eve of the 1835 session of parliament, two meetings were held at Stanley's house in Carlton Gardens. The result was disappointing. Among Stanley's papers is a 'List of Members of Parliament who gave in their adhesion on Wednesday, 23 Feby. 1835'. Including Stanley, the list contained only thirty-eight names, a far cry from Lord George Bentinck's estimate a month earlier of eighty-six supporters, a total which Stanley had rightly rejected.[35]

Within little more than a month the Derby Dilly collapsed. One of the reasons for its failure was its inability to attract Conservative supporters. A party of the moderate centre needed to detach members from both parties, but of the thirty-eight members on Stanley's list, not one was a Conservative; they were all either Whigs or reformers on the way to becoming Conservatives. That was a mark of the solidity of the Conservative party, which was the roadblock in the Dilly's way. The Dilly could have succeeded only if Stanley had been asked to form a government. Peel received the commission and reaped the benefit. He immediately dissolved parliament, cut the ground from under Stanley's feet by promising municipal reform and Church reform, and at the elections in January nearly doubled the Conservative representation in the Commons. William IV placed the leadership of the Conservative party firmly in Peel's grasp and left little scope for Stanley to compete with him. Peel, indeed, was at a loss, in January 1835, to understand how Stanley could have 'visions of the helm'.

> I envy not Stanley's *visions* of my place. I would not exchange my place for his.
> I should have thought that in such a crisis as that in which we are, almost unconsciously, living, a man might have made up his mind as to some definite course of action; that he might have ranged himself on one side or the other; that if he left his colleagues because they were *Destructives*, to use his own word . . . if he set the example to his Sovereign of withdrawing from them his confidence – I should have thought, having been one of the main causes of the King's embarrassment, he might, on the highest and most courageous principles, have assisted in the King's defence.
> Mind what I say. . . . If he really entertains the principles he professes, he *shall* not be able to maintain them and oppose me.[36]

Peel's prediction came true. When, in late March, a week before Lord John Russell was to bring forward a motion for the lay appropriation of Irish Church funds, the Whigs and the O'Connellites concluded a pact of alliance at Lichfield House, Stanley wrote to Peel that matters were placed on a new footing.[37] Cooperation with the Whigs was now beyond recall. When the vote came on, and Peel was defeated by ten votes, the Dilly divided six for Russell and twenty-three against. That vote ended Peel's first government. It also sealed the fate of the centre party. Graham's hope that Peel's failure would lead to a government of Whigs and Conservatives led by Stanley disappeared. Melbourne's government came back, tied to its Radical tail. The logic of the argument which Sandon and Emerson Tennent had put forward was now irresistible.

The absorption of Stanley and Graham into the Conservative party was a gradual process. Not until 1841 did they join the Carlton Club. But as early as May 1835 they were working with Bonham to secure the influence of the Duke of Portland, the father of the Dillyite, Lord George Bentinck, on the side of Conservative candidates at by-elections for Nottingham and Ayrshire.[38] Behind the scenes Graham worked closely with Peel from 1835 to 1837. Stanley was less easily accommodated; he and Peel rarely communicated directly and it was not until after the 1837 elections that the union could be said to be accomplished. At those elections Graham lost his Cumberland seat.[39] He was returned as a Conservative at a by-election for Pembroke boroughs in February 1838. Stanley in the meantime had announced at a meeting of Conservatives in December 1837, that 'with regard to every public question now pending – with regard to the quarter from which danger to our institutions is to be apprehended – and to the manner in which that danger is to be met – there subsists between us the most uniform and unqualified concurrence'.[40] By the beginning of 1838, Graham and Stanley were becoming what they were to be in the government of 1841–46, Peel's closest advisers.[41]

The Derby Dilly, instead of leading to a new party, had proved to be a coach carrying men from Whiggery to Conservatism. Of its thirty-nine identifiable members, twenty-eight sat for part or all of the parliament of 1837–41, nineteen of them as Conservatives, nine as Whigs.[42] A larger group can be identified from the division on the speakership election in 1835. Manners Sutton was supported by seventy-two non-Conservatives who were prepared to give Peel's government a fair trial. Of those twenty-six were Conservatives after 1837, fifteen Whigs. The calculation of Conservative gains inside the House of Commons made at the beginning of this chapter do not include seven of the Dillyites nor ten of the non-Conservatives in the speakership group. Those seventeen were not included in the earlier total of forty-one gains, either because they were first elected to the reformed parliament after 1832 or because they cannot be identified as Conservatives before the parliament of 1837–41. They bring the total number of members who crossed the floor of the House to the Conservative benches between 1832 and 1841 to fifty-eight.[43]

It is not possible to measure either the impact of the converts' behaviour on the country or the extent to which their behaviour was influenced by the movement of opinion in the constituencies. Certainly the two went hand in hand. At the elections of 1835 it was the Whig section of the Liberal party which was squeezed by the Conservative revival. The Conservatives made eighty-one net gains at those elections, only *one* of them at the expense of a Radical;[44] it seems probable, therefore, that in the country as in the House of Commons, some Whigs were drifting into Conservatism. At Haddingtonshire in 1837, to take one example, Lord Ramsay defeated the incumbent Whig, Robert Ferguson, and the decisive factor in his victory may have been Lord Elcho's transfer of allegiance from the Whigs to the Conservatives. Ramsay's campaign began with the circulation of a requisition asking him to come forward as the Conservative candidate. It received 260 signatures.

> And when, Elcho's name having headed the requisition, he himself walked into the market with me, and instantly began a vigorous canvass for me, they [the Whigs] saw at once the game was up; their faces fell to their feet. . . . Elcho's name was a tower of strength to us, for, as the son of so large a proprietor as Lord Wemyss, his influence of course was great, and he was at the same time from his character and manners and from his intercourse with the tenantry in the hunting field, certainly the most personally popular man in the County. But besides all this, he had been in the days of Reform a Reformer. He gradually cooled on that: but he had never declared his change of sentiments, he had never come forward in

public . . . he was always represented as a Reformer by my opponents and claimed as a supporter of Ferguson. His appearance therefore was a thunderbolt and was of essential service to me.[45]

The pull of party

In his short first premiership, Peel emerged from the shallows of the reform crisis as a major national figure, standing at the head of a revived party which, after the 1835 elections, was, if the Whigs and Radicals are considered separately, the largest single party in the House of Commons.

He has raised his reputation to such a height [Greville wrote] . . . he has established such a conviction of his great capacity, and of his liberal, enlarged, and at the same time safe views and opinions . . . he stands so proudly eminent, and there is such a general lack of talent, that he must be recalled by the voice of the nation and by the universal admission that he is indispensable to the country.[46]

From Gladstone came the highest praise that that Christian in politics could bestow.

The rare selfcommand, the quick and farsighted tact, the delicacy and purity of principle and temper by which the speeches of this great man have been distinguished in a period of extraordinary stress and trial, bear the marks, it may be fairly said, of a Providential governance.[47]

The one substantial achievement of the 1834–35 administration was the establishment of the Ecclesiastical Commission. Peel had tied Conservatism to the principle that the state had no authority to alienate the revenues of the Church. If that principle were to be upheld, the Church needed to reorganize the appalling state of its finances. The huge gap in incomes which separated the wealthy bishops from the lower clergy, the starkly inadequate provision for the cure of souls in the manufacturing towns, and the continued existence of clerical sinecures, non-residence, and pluralism were evils that the enemies of the Church would make the most of, if her friends did not remove them.[48] William Howley, the Archbishop of Canterbury, and Bishop Blomfield of London shared Peel's concern. With their enthusiastic advocacy the Ecclesiastical Commission was issued in February 1835. Its reference was not simply to catalogue abuses, but to find remedies for them. In that way, and also by giving clerical commissioners a majority over lay members, Peel ensured that the control of Church administration would remain in friendly hands. The Ecclesiastical Commission, by combining reform and institutional continuity, was a showpiece of Peel's blended Conservatism. In other ways, too, Peel had demonstrated his good faith as a liberal Conservative. His government had introduced a Bill to legalize civil marriages for Dissenters and had promised to reform the tithe in England and Ireland.

The spirit of moderation which marked Peel's first government was carried forward into opposition. Peel refused to take any responsibility for the Conservative peers' demolition of the Municipal Corporations Bill in August 1835, and the following year he blocked the suggestion of a Conservative amendment to the Address, because he doubted that 'Stanley & Co.' would support it.[49] Some Conservatives grumbled at 'the trimming course on all subjects that are brought forward with a view of securing the dilly passengers'.[50] but Peel's tempered Conservatism issued from deeper sources and embraced wider aspirations than the need to catch Stanley. Peel wished to stake his reputation and the future of the Conservative party on the fulfilment of the promise contained in the Tamworth manifesto and the few months of Conservative government. 'The recourse to faction,' he said, not for the first time, in 1837, 'or temporary alliances with extreme opinions for the purpose of faction, is not reconcilable with *Conservative* opposition.'[51]

For the most part the Conservative members of parliament came, not always gracefully, to accept Peel's position. In the Lords the Conservative majority was capable of throwing out any Whig measure it chose, and there were Orange peers, like Cumberland and Roden, who, with the fidgety Lyndhurst, were willing to exploit the rising sentiment of anti-Irish feeling in England and lead the Ultras down an independent path.[52] To restrain them Peel relied on Wellington, who agreed with Peel that wild Ultra defiance of the House of Commons would not only lose Stanley to the party, but would present the Radicals with a popular electoral cry against the House of Lords.[53] By the late 1830s Wellington had succumbed to the view, sensible in itself, that the Conservatives were better placed to check radicalism in opposition than in office. Lord Aberdeen took the point as far as it went, but he did not forget that the rank and file did not always understand 'these cool speculations', which placed the party 'in a false position, viz. that of an opposition without the desire of obtaining office'.[54] Peel was content to use the Conservative majority in the Lords as a brake on the government until the reaction in favour of Conservatism should reach its full tide. It was his achievement to win over to that view Lord Londonderry, the most influential of the Ultra peers. Londonderry was far from happy with Peel's seeming disregard of the reality 'that a body of men acting together must have the rewards of ambition, patronage, and place always before their eyes', but it was a measure of the growth of party consciousness that he reconciled himself to Peel's tactics.

> I feel there is but one man and one party for us now, and that is Peel; and bad as the Conservative chance may be, rely upon it that if that party is split into any section, the Whigs are in for ever. On this score, perhaps, it is well that our friend the K[ing] of H[anover] is out of the country, for it diminishes the possibility of an ultra party.[55]

Wellington used all his influence to keep the party in the Lords in line.[56] That the Whigs' Municipal Corporations Bill, which swept away the oligarchic and mainly Tory councils in 184 English and Welsh boroughs, was eventually passed in 1835 owed much to Wellington's close consultations with the party leaders in the Commons and to the series of meetings of Conservative peers over which he presided.[57] Peel and Wellington sat back while the Lords blocked the government's attempt to settle the Irish tithe question on the basis of appropriation in 1835 and 1836, but they persuaded them to accept the Irish Municipal Corporations Bill and the Union of the Canadas Bill in 1840.

In the House of Commons the unity of the party was hardly threatened. In the years of opposition from 1835 to 1841 there were only three occasions when, on a major party issue, Conservative backbenchers revolted against the party leadership, though in view of the difficulties which Irish questions were to present to Peel's second government, it is significant that the three revolts came on Irish issues: forty-two Conservatives voted against the Irish education grant in 1835, thirty-nine against the Irish Corporations Bill in 1839, and forty-two against the grant to the Catholic seminary at Maynooth in 1840.[58]

The cohesiveness of such a large party in opposition was a remarkable development, for which there are several possible explanations. For one thing, Peel, after a few years in semi-withdrawal, gave the party a continuing lead. The importance of that was shown in 1838, when there was some danger that a Radical motion of censure upon the Colonial Secretary, Lord Glenelg, might receive enough Conservative support to defeat the government. Peel was not yet prepared to take office. To meet the danger he decided that the Conservatives would draft their own motion. He called a meeting of the party to explain Conservative strategy and persuaded the backbenchers to adopt it. Despite the impatience of many of them to eject Melbourne's government, Peel achieved a signal success. When the night of the vote arrived, the opposition had no notion of the opposition's tactics. No Conservative voted out of line. The party's figures in the division were 287 votes cast, eleven paired, two tellers, and fourteen absent. Including three vacancies, it put Conservative strength at 317 members, exactly the number which Bonham had produced after the 1837 elections.[59] That demonstrated how tightly party lines had come to be drawn. A few years earlier such accuracy would have been impossible.

Party meetings, rare before 1835, were a regular occurrence in the second half of the decade. Their beneficial effect was supplemented by an improved system of whipping. After 1837 the Chief Whip was Sir Thomas Fremantle, who was appointed on Granville Somerset's recommendation. William Holmes, who had been Chief Whip from 1820 to 1832, wanted the job, but Granville Somerset advised Peel that although Holmes was 'very much looked up to by the Lowther *Set*, the great bulk of our Friends would not tolerate him'.[60] Fremantle was an ideal Whip, whose acceptance of the office put the lie to Peel's remark that the Secretaryship of the Treasury 'was a place which required a gentleman to fill it, and which no gentleman would take'.[61] Fremantle was a country gentleman from Buckinghamshire, the heart of agricultural England, and a close friend of the Duke of Buckingham and the Marquis of Chandos. The squires on the backbenches were more willing to gratify his requests that they come up early in the session and stay late than they had been to follow the advice of the 'official' men who had previously been Chief Whips. It was also to the party's advantage that Fremantle was a backbencher without ambitions of his own to infect his loyalty to the leadership. He was discreet, straightforward, and popular.

Under Fremantle pairing, which in the early nineteenth century had been largely a private matter, was rigorously supervised by the Whips. Fremantle's efficiency showed itself in the large number of pairs which he was able to arrange, 137, for example, on the Lords' amendment to the franchise clause of the Irish Corporations Bill in 1838, and in the low absentee rate of Conservative members in divisions.[62] One of his innovations was to establish, in 1837, a fund to pay for the circulars addressed to members asking them to attend debates and vote in divisions. The fund was administered by Fremantle and Lord Redesdale, the Chief Whip in the Lords, and supplied by a voluntary subscription of £2 collected from Conservatives in both Houses. Edward Fitzgerald, the former secretary of the Charles Street committee, was paid to look after the printing and distribution of the circulars. In 1837 the number of subscribers was 109 peers and 175 commoners, in 1838 it was 94 peers and 285 commoners, and in 1839 it was 69 peers and 251 commoners. Enough money was raised to pay Fitzgerald and the cost of sending out material: £384.9s.4d in 1837 for 46,000 circulars and 10,000 sheets for the Westminster election and £416.10s.7d in 1838 for 51,000 circulars and 65,000 'lithographed Enclosures'.[63]

The Carlton Club, which by the end of 1839 boasted 1,100 members,[64] also played its part, not only in fostering a spirit of camaraderie in the party, but also in providing a place where the pary managers could meet the backbenchers and keep an eye on the mood of the party. It may also have helped to unite the party in another way. A member of parliament who wished to be elected to the Carlton damaged his chances of election every time he divided against the Conservatives.

None of the organizational methods of holding the party together would have been so successful had not the Conservatives been sensible that, in what they believed was an age of crisis, their duty was to present a solid bulwark against the reformers. 'The grand object with every well-wisher to good government', Graham recommended, 'must be to soften down asperities, to reconcile differences, to stimulate the lukewarm, to moderate the impetuous and, as the One Thing on which the Salvation of the State depends, to keep *the Party together*.'[65] What struck contemporaries as quite unprecedented was the absence from the parliament of 1837 of the previously substantial contingent of neutrals and doubtfuls. The result of the sharp divide in opinion between the parties on the main issues was the virtual elimination of the independents from the House of Commons. The 1837 elections showed a marked advance in candidates' party consciousness. At the 1835 elections many candidates, including Peel, had not used the word 'Conservative' in their election addresses. Two years later, following Peel's declaration in his address that he acted 'in cordial concurrence with that powerful Conservative party with which I am proud to boast of my connexion', the label was commonly and prominently displayed.[66] Bonham located only five doubtfuls in the House of Commons at the end of 1839, and even them he described as '*now* rather Conservative'.[67] A study of the votes of the 567 members who sat in the 1837 parliament has shown that only seven of them failed to align themselves with one party or the other.[68] Fremantle's lists of fourteen divisions between 1838 and 1840 tell the same story. For eleven of those divisions he noted no doubtfuls at all. Whipping was not able to prevent some cross-voting: despite Fremantle's elimination of the doubtfuls, his totals for the Conservatives in those divisions, including pairs and absentees, vary between 311 and 324.[69] That margin was tiny in comparison with previous experience. For the first time skill in debate counted for little against the power of the whips and the pull of party. As the diarist, Thomas Raikes, put it, party influence was so pervasive that 'there are few, if any, floating voters who are sufficiently independent or unprejudiced to be gained by any sudden convictions; so decidedly are the minds of all made up on the subject, before the discussion takes place'.[70]

Notes and References

The desertions from Whiggery

1 Croker to Peel, 30 July 1835: Peel MSS, Add. MSS 40321, f. 156.
2 Gash, *Sir Robert Peel*, 94.
3 Brock, *Reform Act*, 315.
4 Johnson, 'Sir James Graham and the "Derby Dilly"', *University of Birmingham Hist. J.*, iv.1 (1953), 67.
5 See Appendix 2.
6 Dod's *Electoral Facts* gives twenty members returned as 'Liberals' at the 1832 elections and as Conservatives in 1835 or 1837. Dod published the *Electoral Facts* in 1853, however, and his judgement of whether a man had been a Conservative in 1832 was often influenced by later events. His *Pocket Parliamentary Companions*, compiled after each general election, are more reliable. In them he classified as Liberals in 1832 nearly two dozen members who appear in the *Electoral Facts* as Conservatives. An example of Dod's double standard is General O'Neill, the member for Antrim. The *Electoral Facts* makes him a Conservative at the 1832 elections, but both Buckingham, in his *Parliamentary Review*, and Dod, in the *Pocket Companion* for 1833, called him a Liberal. He had been considered a ministerialist in the 1820s, but voted for the Reform Bill. By 1836 the *Assembled Commons* said of him that he 'supported reform, but generally acts with the Tories'. In the *Pocket Companions* for 1833 and 1835 Dod defined Conservatives as 'gentlemen who take an opposite view of the Reform Act from that entertained by its promoters'. For the list of the thirty-one members, see Appendix B.
7 According to Fremantle's lists: Fremantle MSS, 80/3.
8 Berwickshire (Sir Hugh Hume-Campbell), Dover (J. Halcomb), Dudley (T. Hawkes), Gloucester (H. T. Hope), Gloucestershire E (C. W. Codrington), London (G. Lyall), Perthshire (Sir George Murray), Somerset E (W. Miles), Sudbury (E. Barnes), Sunderland (Alderman Thompson). I have included Alderman Thompson in the list of gains inside the House of Commons.
9 Spencer to Baring, 15 Jan, 1835: Baring, *Journals and Correspondence*, i, 112–13.
10 O'Connell took the name from an eighteenth-century poem, 'The Loves of the Triangles': see W. D. Jones, *Lord Derby and Victorian Conservatism*, 59n.
11 Ward, *Sir James Graham*, 81.
12 See Mrs Arbuthnot, *Journal*, 26 and 30 June 1830, ii, 290, 293.
13 Graham to Stanley, 15 July 1828: Parker, *Graham*, i, 71.
14 The post had not previously been of cabinet status, but Grey wanted the future leader of the Whig party, as everyone assumed Stanley to be, in the cabinet (Aspinall, 'The Cabinet Council, 1783–1835', *Proc. Brit. Acad.*, 1952, 160–2.)

15 Littleton diary, 7 Feb, 1833: Aspinall, *Three Diaries*, 296–7.

16 Gash, *Sir Robert Peel*, 50–1.

17 Graham to Stanley, 3 July 1834: Parker, *Graham*, i, 206–7. In 1833 Peel wrote to Goulburn that in considering whether to move an amendment to the Address and, if so, what to put in it, 'a material question would also be whether Lord Stanley and his friends would cordially concur' (Parker, *Peel*, ii, 224–5).

18 Peel to Goulburn, 25 May 1833: *ibid*, ii, 220–1. In 1821, when Goulburn was appointed Chief Secretary for Ireland, Mrs Arbuthnot described him as 'the most furious Protestant there ever was' (*Journal*, 6 Dec, 1821, i, 130). Lord Ashley was then only twenty years old.

19 When Disraeli remarked to Melbourne in 1834 that he wished to become Prime Minister, Melbourne replied that nobody could compete with Stanley. 'There is nothing like him. . . . You must put these foolish notions out of your head; they won't do at all. Stanley will be the next Prime Minister, you will see.' (Melbourne, *Memoirs*, 275).

20 Londonderry to Buckingham, 25 March 1833: Buckingham, *Memoirs of . . . William IV and Victoria*, ii, 37–8.

21 Peel to Stanley, 9 Dec, 1834: Peel, *Memoirs*, ii, 33–5.

22 Sandon to Stanley, 10 Dec, 1834: Derby MSS, 127/3.

23 Tennent to Stanley, 23 Nov, 1834: *ibid*, 131/7.

24 Bentinck to Richmond, 2 Dec, 1834; Richmond to Stanley, 7 Dec, 1834: *ibid*, 131/13.

25 Richmond to Stanley, 15 Nov, 1834: *ibid*, 131/13.

26 Johnson, 'Graham and the Derby Dilly', 72.

27 Richmond to Stanley, 7 Dec, 1834: 'They mean, it is said, to have a cabinet consisting of five of themselves, four Stanleys and two High Tories; is it possible that such a cabinet could last, could it be a united one, the more I reflect upon the course we have decided upon, the better satisfied I am that our decision is right' (Derby MSS, 131/13). Peel arrived back in London two days after this letter was written.

28 Peel, *Memoirs*, ii, 36–42.

29 Macaulay, 'William Pitt', *Essays*, i, 379.

30 Gladstone memoranda, 9 Oct, 1832, and 28 April 1838: Gladstone, *Memoranda*, 24–5, 102.

31 See, for example, Bootle Wilbraham to Lord Colchester, 14 Oct, 1827: 'I am glad of his appointment [as Lord of the Treasury] more on private grounds than public ones, because it will give Stanley habits of business, and break the habit of shooting, eternal shooting – the only pursuit, besides reading, that he can follow at a place [the Derby seat of Knowsley, Lancashire] where he is only third in command and in generation' (Colchester, *Diary*, iii, 526).

32 Stanley to Graham, 29 Dec, 1834: Parker, *Graham*, i, 223.

33 Whether Stanley had a hand in issuing these instructions is not clear, but it is unlikely. 'I *believe*', Francis Egerton wrote to Peel, 'Lord Stanley to be entirely innocent of any active participation in the determined opposition I have received from the house of Knowsley' (Peel MSS, Add. MSS 40412, ff. 17–18). Egerton was one of the Conservative candidates at Lancashire South.

34 Parker, *Peel*, ii, 266; Jones, *Derby and Victorian Conservatism*, 55. See also Arbuthnot to his son, 12 March 1835: 'Ld. Stanley & Sir Js. Graham have both declared on the hustings & elsewhere, that they have no confidence in the present ministers' (C. Arbuthnot, *Correspondence*, 190–1).

35 Derby MSS, 20/1. See Appendix 3. The names are in Stanley's hand on twelve loose sheets. Some may have been lost, but the list is probably complete. Ellenborough reported that 'at least 40 members met with Stanley' (Ellenborough diary, 24 Feb, 1835, PRO 12/28/5).

36 Peel to Croker, 10 Jan, 1835: Croker, *Correspondence and Diaries*, ii, 255–6.

37 Stanley to Peel, 29 March 1835: Peel MSS, Add. MSS 40418, f. 288.

38 Bonham to Peel, 6 May 1835: *ibid*, Add. MSS 40420, ff. 137–40. In April 1835 Gladstone recorded a conversation with Lord Aberdeen: 'Lord Aberdeen acquainted me that Graham speaking for himself and Lord Stanley declared their identification in principles and views with Peel the day before, April 12 – saw that an attempt would be made on the Corporation question to separate them – believed that they might certainly meet and agree upon a basis if each would agree the one to go as high the other as low as could be done with honour and consistency – declared the new cabinet [Melbourne's] would be one of Jacobins and infidels – and lamented that he had made two mistakes for which he did not know how he could ever atone – voting for the Roman Catholic claims – and for the Reform Bill. And a perfect readiness to combine in Administration was indicated. All this apparently intended to go to Peel.' (Gladstone memorandum, 15 April, [1835]: Gladstone, *Memoranda*, 49–51.)

39 He trailed badly behind the two Liberal candidates, winning 500 fewer votes than the second-placed candidate. He suffered from the turncoat's inability to please either side. He had the backing of the powerful Tory Lowther interest, but it had to be wielded secretly. 'The Yellows (the Lowther party),' Holmes informed Peel, 'will not vote for him if he comes under a blue flag, and the blues will desert him if he has a yellow one; the consequence is he can have no chance at all. The Lowthers cannot openly uphold him.' (Holmes to Peel, 1 Aug, 1837: Peel MSS, Add. MSS 40424, f. 1.)

40 Gladstone memorandum, 15 Dec, 1837. Gladstone, *Memoranda*, 84–6.

41 In February 1838 Sir Francis Egerton, disturbed that the 200 votes given to a motion for the secret ballot signified the *'commencement de la fin'*, was concerned to know what the Conservative party ought to do. 'Peel's opinion has not transpired . . . I think Peel will wait for the arrival of Graham and Stanley before he suffers an opinion to escape him.' (Egerton to Arbuthnot, 17 Feb, 1838: Parker, *Peel*, ii, 359–60.)

42 See Appendix 3. The figures here and immediately below are calculated on the basis of Fremantle's lists of party members, 1839–40.

43 See Appendix 4. This total is close to the fifty-one 'doubtfuls' whom the *Spectator* counted in the 1835 parliament, 'most of whom,' the journal commented, 'speedily hoisted Tory colours'. At the beginning of the 1837 parliament the *Spectator's* list of doubtfuls was down to fewer than a dozen (*Spectator*, 19 Aug, 1837).

44 Close, 'The elections of 1835 and 1837 in England and Wales', unpublished thesis, 368.

45 Lindsay, 'Electioneering in East Lothian, 1836–37', *Trans. East Lothian Antiquarian and Field Naturalists' Society*, 1960, 50. This article consists of extracts from Ramsay's private journal. The quotation given here is a later note to the entry of 31 Dec, 1836.

The pull of party
46 Greville, *Memoirs*, 3 April 1845, v, 212–13.

47 Gladstone memorandum, April, [1835]: *Memoranda*, 31–2. From the Chief Whip of the Whigs came similar praise in 1837: 'His [Peel's] retirement from the lead would be a great political event, & might induce many reflecting people to consider twice before they lent their assistance to the destruction of Ld. Melbourne's Govt. I should look upon it as one of the greatest evils that could befall the Country in the present circumstances. While he remains, he checks the violence of his party, & as they cannot quarrel with him they submit, altho' with the worst possible grace, to his sense of the danger of a mere factious opposition in Parliament.' (Edward Ellice to Lord Holland, 16 Sept, [1837]: Holland House MSS, Add. MSS 51587, ff. 110–13.)

48 See Peel to the Bishop of Exeter, 21 Jan, 1835, and Peel to the Bishop of Durham, 23 Feb, 1835: Peel, *Memoirs*, ii, 75–85.

49 Peel to Croker, 12 Jan, 1836: Croker, *Correspondence and Diaries*, ii, 301–4.

50 Londonderry to Buckingham, 9 March 1836: Buckingham, *Memoirs of . . . William IV and Victoria*, ii, 228–9.

51 Peel memorandum, 4 July 1837: Parker, *Peel*, ii, 336–8.

52 For details of the Conservative peers' behaviour and their relations with Peel and Wellington, see Kitson Clark, *Peel and the Conservative Party*, *passim*, and Large, 'The House of Lords and Ireland in the age of Peel, 1832–50', *Irish Historical Studies*, Sept, 1955, 367–99.

53 Wellington was at times as scathing as Peel in his outbursts against the ultra peers. 'They don't care a pin about our opinions. They will risk the public interests, or a general quarrel between the Houses . . . in order to enjoy a momentary triumph. . . . I cannot adequately express my disgust with such people.' (Wellington to Peel, 28 March 1839: Parker, *Peel*, ii, 385).

54 Aberdeen to Princess Lieven, 7 Feb, 1938: E. Jones Parry, ed. *The Correspondence of Lord Aberdeen and Princess Lieven, 1832–1854*, i, 98–9.

55 Londonderry to Buckingham, 1 Sept, 1837: Buckingham, *memoirs of . . . William IV and Victoria*, ii, 287–9. The Duke of Cumberland was the King of Hanover.

56 Graham to Bonham, 26 Nov, 1839: 'My fears have long been most anxious with regard to the [health of the] Duke; if we lose him, the Game is all but desperate; and how the H. of Lords is to be arranged, I have no idea' (Peel MSS, Add. MSS 40616, ff. 113–4).

57 Colchester, *Memoranda*, 55–6.

58 Close, 'The formation of a two-party alignment in the House of Commons between 1832 and 1841', *EHR*, April 1969, 269. Revolts on minor issues were sometimes less easy to contain. A Radical motion censuring the administration of the Marines in February 1838, was supported by eighty-six Conservatives, despite Peel's habitual warnings against combination with the Radicals (Peel to Wellington, [27] Feb, 1838: Parker *Peel*, ii, 367).

59 Gash, *Sir Robert Peel*, 204–5.

60 Granville Somerset to Peel, 9 Aug, 1837. Peel MSS, Add. MSS 40424, ff. 47–50. Holmes had played an ambiguous part in the sorry affair involving the Charles Street committee and the press agent, McEntagart. In the 1820s he had earned a reputation for leaking government information to the opposition. See, for example, Edward Ellice, the Liberal Whip, to Lord Holland, [1833]: 'Billy Holmes has not made, and will not make, his appearance in this part of the world. . . . His friend, the Speaker, is much less to be trusted, although no prudent man would confide many thoughts, *he did not wish to be published*, to either. But be assured, that our *liaison* has not been without its advantages.

Some of your friends can tell you that there is nothing of which the Tories are more jealous, or apprehensive.' (Holland House MSS, Add. MSS 51587, ff. 33–6.) Holmes kept his place at the periphery of the party's management throughout the 1830s, probably as a link with the Ultra-Tories, in particular the Lowther set.

61 Stanley MSS, Diary, 28 July 1852.
62 See Appendix 5.
63 For details of this fund, see the record books and the correspondence between Fremantle and Redesdale in the Fremantle MSS, 80/5.
64 Bonham to Peel, 25 Nov, 1839: Peel MSS, Add. MSS 40427, ff. 262–3.
65 Graham to Bonham, 16 Oct, 1838: *ibid*, 40616, ff. 17–20.
66 Close, 'Elections of 1835 and 1837', 354.
67 Bonham to Peel, Dec, 1839; Peel MSS, Add. MSS 40427, ff. 381–2.
68 Close, 'Formation of a two-party alignment', 275.
69 See Appendix 5.
70 Gash, *Reaction and Reconstruction*, 127. The growth of party solidarity in the 1830s was more noticeable among Conservatives than among the Whig, Liberal, Radical, and Irish nationalist sections of their opponents. Even so, William Thomas has presented a good argument for the view that a major cause of the Philosophic Radicals' disintegration after 1837 was their inability to reconcile their objection to party as 'faction' with the hardening of the Whig–Radical relationship into party (Thomas, 'The Philosophic Radicals', in *Pressure from Without in Early Victorian England*, ed. Hollis, 52–79).

Chapter 7

The Conservative recovery II: Outside parliament

The foundation of Conservative associations

The increased party solidarity in the House of Commons in the 1830s, a development which reflected the importance which politicians attached to the differences of opinion separating Liberals and Conservatives, had its parallel in the constituencies. There, too, the parties acquired a sharper definition from the improved methods of electoral organization which they adopted. The traditional structure of constituency politics was local in its scope and rested on social deference and various forms of bribery and corruption for its management. The exercise of the franchise was regarded primarily as a function of the voter's place in the social order or as a financial transaction, not as an act of political judgement. That system had superimposed upon it in the 1830s new forms of party organization: the permanent supervision of electoral affairs at the centre and the activities of registration societies and party associations in the constituencies. The new forms did not, nor were they intended to, replace the traditional electoral processes. But they gave the parties a physical presence beyond Westminster, thereby making them more national and adding a dimension to the political life of the country.

A model of the traditional structure of local politics emerges from the correspondence of the Marquess of Anglesey, the head of the Paget family, from 1830 to 1832.[1] Lord Anglesey was a Whig, but the representation of Caernarvonshire and Caernarvon boroughs was, for him, scarcely a matter of party politics. It was principally an extension of estate management and family influence. Anglesey's object was to have members of his family returned to Westminster with the least expense possible, therefore preferably without a contest. He took no direct part in electoral business himself, but left it in the hands of his estate agent, John Sanderson, whose job it was to enlist the support of the wielders of influence in the constituency and to prevent national issues from trespassing on Caernarvon politics. There was no interference from the Whig party managers in London. The chief element in electioneering was what Sir Charles Paget scornfully called 'the fawning, cringing system of personal canvass',[2] made by the candidate himself and organized by his own or his patron's staff of estate stewards, men who were well known to the voters. As Sanderson advised Sir Charles in 1831, 'anything like an open canvass by mere agents would be rather prejudicial to your interest than otherwise'.[3]

Already, nevertheless, the insulated politics of deference was being eroded by the spread of industrialism, as Richard Garnons, an elector for Caernarvon, an expanding town with a prosperous trade in shipbuilding and slate-quarrying, pointed out to Sir Charles Paget in 1830.

> It is clearly the interest of the Burgesses of Caernarvon to continue and secure the connexion, which has so long and so beneficially to that place, subsisted between your Family and the Borough; but the increased commerce of that town has made a corresponding increase of its population. Strangers from all parts have settled there, and the attachments and opinions of its present inhabitants are much altered since you first was elected there [1806] – and very lately the affairs of the Corporation have been managed with so much violence and turbulence, and party spirit, that I have ceased to attend the public meetings there.[4]

Political opinions could not be kept out of Caernarvon elections. Garnons, for years a Paget supporter, deserted to the Tory candidate in 1831, because the dangers to which the country was exposed by the reforming Whig ministry made it 'an imperious Duty in every man to sacrifice all private and personal considerations in defence of the General Good'.[5] Dissent, too, was making its voice heard. R. A. Poole, the solicitor who was Paget's agent in Caernarvon, informed Sanderson before the 1832 elections that the slavery question was exciting great interest among the Dissenters and 'may turn the scale with many a voter who (putting *that* question aside) may be disposed to submit to influence'.[6]

The threat which issues like parliamentary reform and the abolition of slavery posed to the smooth operation of deferential politics grew stronger as the years passed. The 1830s and 1840s were a time of unprecedented extra-parliamentary agitation by interest groups of various kinds; large-scale campaigns were conducted to secure civil rights for Dissenters, the abolition of the Corn Laws, a ten-hour day for factory hands, and the six points of the Charter. The awakened political enthusiasm was reflected in the provincial press. By the mid-1830s, according to the *Companion to the Newspaper*, every provincial newspaper in England, apart from a few commercial journals, 'now sustains a political character'.[7]

A more immediate spur to the development of party organization were certain provisions of the 1832 Reform Act. Every voter had to pay one shilling to be registered – in the counties once only, in the boroughs annually – on the electoral rolls. Registration was expensive, totalling £83,364 in 1832 and 1833.[8] It was also complicated. Not only was there a variety of qualifications for the franchise, but any individual could challenge the registration of an elector on a number of grounds – change of address, failure to pay rates, or simple ineligibility – and the objection was automatically upheld if the elector did not appear to defend his registration. The Reform Act thus expanded the market for election experts and widened the area for potential party organization. To pay for the registration of electors, to assemble a list of objections, and to counter opponents' objections became a full-time activity. In the boroughs the annual registration battles in the courts not only forced the pace of constituency organization, but also stimulated and sustained party feeling in the electorate. That effect was reinforced, too, by the Municipal Corporations Act of 1835, which replaced self-perpetuating oligarchies by elected councils in 184 incorporated boroughs in England. (Similar Acts were passed for Scotland and Ireland in 1833 and 1840.) The immediate beneficiaries of the Act were the Liberals. All over the country elected Liberal councils replaced the pre-form Tory oligarchies. The deeper effect of the Act was to give the voters in the incorporated boroughs a keener interest in politics. Like the annual registrations, the annual borough elections injected new life into the party system and imparted, as the remote activities of London politicians could not, a continuity to political affairs in the provinces.

It was against that background that the rapid growth of Conservative organization in the constituencies took place. In the years from 1832 to 1836 Conservative associations were established throughout the country. They had, it is true, their antecedents. At Liverpool, for instance, there existed, before the Reform Act, seven political clubs, four of them – the Backbone Club, the Canning Club, the Pitt Club, and the True Blue Club – Tory. They helped to organize election contests,[9] but it is significant that none of them bore a party label and that each of them was called a club. Their most important function was the annual dinner. The activities of the new associations were constant and almost entirely political. Lord Brougham affected to see in the associations a deep plot laid by the party managers at the Carlton to frustrate the free working of the reformed electoral system.[10] He was right to point out that the new associations were different from the previous kind of political union, such as Attwood's in Birmingham, which had been formed to achieve a specific object and, when the object was gained, had disbanded. But he was wrong to contend that the Conservative party, through the Carlton, established a centralized network of associations directed and controlled from London. The associations were the fruit of local enthusiasm and initiative.

Newark Conservatives were among the first to form a Conservative association, in 1831, in reaction to the collapse of the Duke of Newcastle's influence there at the election of that year. Branch clubs were formed and meeting to celebrate Newcastle's birthday in 1832 was attended by more than 300 members.[11] Neither the origins nor the subsequent operations of the association owed anything to the Carlton. Nor did the association set itself up as a rival to Newcastle for the control of Newark elections. The Duke was expected to continue to select his candidates and pay for their contests, as he did in 1832 when he nominated Gladstone for the seat and shared the expenses with Gladstone's father. The association then worked for Gladstone, who attributed his return to 'the work of the people themselves exclusively'.[12]

The first county association was founded in 1833 in Durham by the Ultra Lord Londonderry. It operated on the same basis as the Newark association: independence of the central party and dependence upon cooperation with the local Conservative aristocracy. When that cooperation broke down in the early 1840s, the Carlton did not interfere. Londonderry was crotchety and authoritarian, and although his insistence on retaining the unfettered right to nominate his own candidates was not at all exceptional, he antagonized members of the local association. Ill-feeling turned into open dispute in 1843 when, at the Durham borough by-election, Londonderry supported the Radical free-trader and the Anti-Corn Law League's candidate, John Bright, against a Conservative candidate whom he had not nominated. Durham Conservatives appealed to Peel to settle the dispute, but he refused to intervene.[13]

That unhappy episode was a particularly sharp example of the friction which could develop between an ambitious association and a jealous landowner. In a majority of the counties, where landlord influence prevailed, formal organization remained superfluous. As late as 1874 there were Conservative associations in only forty-four of the eighty-two English county divisions.[14] Dorset Conservatives, for example, remained without one until 1883. They felt no need of formal organization. From 1832 to 1841 the county returned two Conservatives and one Liberal, from 1841 to 1857, three Conservatives. The only contested election between 1832 and 1867 occurred in 1857, when the Liberals' regaining of a seat marked a return to the 'peace of the county' after Conservative domination in the protectionist era. An association would merely have cost Dorset Conservatives money and increased the risk of contested elections.[15]

It is not possible to discover the exact number of Conservative associations, but by the beginning of 1837 there were several hundred of them. Peel's brief premiership acted as a spur to their formation. The chairman of the Chatham association told Fremantle that Peel's rise had reawakened the Conservative spirit in the town and led to the founding of an association.

> This was a most difficult undertaking – indeed it seemed hopeless. Intimidation and the diffusion of false political principles had so well done their work that our enemies fearless defied us to proceed. However by taking every fair opportunity of addressing the Electors, by a constant attendance at Weekly and Monthly meetings . . . the number of our Association, at first only 43, now [1842] amounts to 270.[16]

Radical gains at the 1835 elections, the Lichfield compact between the Whigs and the Irish followers of O'Connell, and the resignation of Peel's government acted as further goads. In July 1835 *Blackwood's Magazine* called on Conservatives to form associations to disseminate anti-Radical literature and win the battle in the registration courts. It advised the associations to leave candidates to bear the costs of canvassing and elections, but to raise money themselves to pay for registration. Each association should have a central headquarters and branch societies, should charge a subscription fee, and should hire solicitors to supervise the registration.[17] Similar recommendations came from *The Conservative*, a monthly newspaper started in July 1836, with no official connection with the party, to spread news of Conservative meetings throughout the country and to encourage the proliferation of Conservative associations.[18]

What evidence exists suggests that the associations were energetic bodies. The history of the Staffordshire association has been studied in some detail,[19] and since Staffordshire combined entrenched landed political influence with an expanding industrial population in the Black Country, it may be taken as representative. Owing chiefly to the Liberals' content with their hold on seven of the county's ten seats in 1831, it was the Conservatives who first began to organize in Staffordshire. But despite a concerted assault on the register after 1832, the Conservatives won only six of the county's fourteen seats at the 1835 elections. All four county members were Liberals. Something more was needed, and a Conservative association was formed at Stafford in March 1835. Its first test came at the by-election for Staffordshire South in the following May, when the Conservative candidate, Sir Francis Goodricke, beat his Liberal opponent, George Anson, by 223 votes. Anson attributed his heavy defeat to the Liberals' failure to register the 40s freeholders efficiently and to 'the influence of the Landlords and Clergy and the Conservative Unions, who were too well organized, their secret canvass too long commenced, and their plans too well matured'.[20] Within a year the Staffordshire association had branches in every part of the southern division of the county, and John Smith, the secretary, sent a report of their progress to Viscount Sandon.

> I wish to acquaint your Lordship and the Conservative Noblemen of the situation in South Staffordshire at the moment. The constituency has increased from about 4,500 to about 7,300. We have reprinted the register in several townships, and copies have been sent to each branch committee (of which there are 17). They have been put in the hands of 3 or 4 friends in each parish, who have made their enquiries and afterwards met; they have consulted the poll books, showing who voted for and against us at the last election. They have had reference to the list showing who were put on the Register by the Conservatives, and who by the Destructives, and their returns show a decided available majority of from 800 to 1,100 in favour of the Conservatives.
>
> Canvass books and other necessaries are in the hands of our friends; they are on the alert and the County can be canvassed in 12 hours.[21]

In 1838 the association started a journal, the *Staffordshire Gazette*, but it made little impact and failed to survive the competition from the established county newspaper.

The extensive work of the association soon outstretched its means. By May

1837 the association was £1,000 in debt.[22] The heavy expenses of that summer's closely fought elections increased the debt and Staffordshire landowners began to question the worth of contested elections. In 1841 the leading gentry of both parties, unwilling to bear the cost of a contest, agreed to share the representation of the southern division. The association was not consulted about the arrangement. Abandoned by the gentry, it lost its usefulness and for the next two decades ceased to be a prominent part of Staffordshire politics.

That was a pattern repeated in many constituencies. At Cheltenham, which the Liberals won without a contest in 1832, the Conservatives formed an association and put up a candidate, Jonathan Peel, for the first time in 1837. He won only 31 per cent of the vote. Assiduous attention to the register by the local association reduced the Liberal majority at the next election from 334 to 109, but the effort was beyond the means or the willingness of Cheltenham Conservatives to pay. At the end of 1840 an officer of the association informed Lord Ellenborough that the expense of striking nearly 700 electors off the rolls that year had cost £200 and put the association £300 in debt.[23] The decline of an association's activities in the 1840s was not always for financial reasons. The Buckingham Conservative association was established in November 1837, and in its first two months attracted 242 members, whose subscriptions and donations totalled £81.2s.6d. Three years later the membership had risen to 270 and the credit balance at the end of the year was £16.16s.2d. The expenses of the association were small, entailed principally by the printing of handbills, since the association did not contribute to the cost of registration. It was disbanded in 1845, not because it was bankrupt, but because of the split in the party over the repeal of the Corn Laws. For the next seven years its place was taken by the local Agricultural Protection Society, formed in 1844,[24] which was, in effect, the old association under a new name. Henry Smith, the secretary of the Conservative association, became the secretary of the new society. The passing of the Conservative association did not, therefore, mean a decline in the party's local organization. And, as at Buckingham, so in many other constituencies, the apparent demise of Conservative associations is to be explained by their translation into protection societies in the mid-1840s.

Registration and canvassing were the principal activities of the Conservative associations, but occasionally circumstances permitted an association to participate in the selection of candidates and the financing of elections. Before the Newark by-election of 1840 the Conservative association in the borough met to discuss the nomination of a candidate. It was agreed that a Newark resident would be desirable, but when two local gentlemen declined the invitation to stand, and negotiations with Lord Lincoln, heir to the Duke of Newcastle, failed to produce a candidate, the association turned to the Carlton for assistance. The association offered to subscribe £800 towards the election if either Sir Frederick Thesiger or

Sergeant Goulburn would take the nomination and agree to put up the same amount. Two members of the association went up to London, where the search for a candidate ended with Thesiger's acceptance of the nomination.[25]

Such an exercise of authority by a local association was rare. More characteristic was the subdued role played by the East Cumberland association, which, in December 1839, discussed the question of candidates for the next election and 'put matters in hand, either for a good Battle, or for a compromise of one Seat', but left it to the president of the association, Sir James Graham, who agreed to pay the expenses of the canvass and the poll in his own district, to sound out the constituency's most influential landowner, Lord Lonsdale, on the nomination of a country gentleman.[26] Graham did not approach Lonsdale because he was president of the association; he was president of the association because he was in a position to negotiate with Lonsdale. The East Cumberland association did not change the personal nature of county politics; what it did was give a party face and a party name to the processes of electioneering which already existed. The associations were buttresses to, not encroachments on, deferential politics. But, as Professor Gash has written of the Berkshire association, they served 'not merely to increase the control of the landed gentry over the county electorate, but to harden that control into a party and parliamentary mould'.[27]

The ease with which Conservatives accepted the new associations was, therefore, another mark of the progress made by the idea of party in the 1830s. In an open letter to the secretary of the North Lancashire Conservative Association, Stanley put the case against formal constituency organization.

> Beware how you organise the whole country in such a manner that every man must be a partisan; and do not deceive yourselves by thinking that such an occurrence, forced on by you, would strengthen your influence or augment your proportionate numbers. Beware, above all things, how you array the landed gentry and their dependents, in our mixed population, against the inhabitants of the mercantile and manufacturing towns. You ask no change in your county representatives, but you feel the democratic influence in the manufacturing boroughs. If you wish to create, to foster, to envenom it, interfere in their elections by your Conservative associations; bring an extraneous influence to bear on their proceedings; and if their be a democratic spark in the town, you will kindle it into a flame. . . . It is a lamentable state of things when national good is sacrificed for the attainment of party triumph; but that party incurs a heavy responsibility which takes the first step towards provoking such a conflict . . . [and creating] a system which should establish throughout the country, for political objects, and for permanent and systematic exertions, two rival sets of political associations engaged in a deadly struggle with each other for the maintenance of extreme principles.[28]

It must be remembered that Stanley wrote that letter in the midst of his attempt to build a centre party. Even so, it is surprising that more Conservatives did not share, at least publicly, his apprehensions about the ultimately democratic implications of the electorate's participation in party organization. In 1833 a motion of the Ultra-Tory George Finch, to suppress political unions had been easily beaten and had attracted only ten Conservative votes.[29] In August 1835 Sir Samuel Whalley, the Liberal member for Marylebone, presented a petition to the House of Commons from the vestry of the parish, which complained of the 'inquisitorial and vexatious proceedings' of the Marylebone Conservative Association. Whalley attacked the Conservatives for sponsoring the very kind of union which they had denounced during the reform debates. The association had been established, he argued, 'for the sake of prolonging party feuds – for the sake of reviving religious hostility – for the sake of keeping alive the recollection of events which ought to sleep forgotten'. Such associations were 'fatal to the harmony and well-being of society'. In reply, W. A. Mackinnon, the chairman of the Marylebone association, contented himself with pointing out that in using the rate books of the parish to compile lists of electors, Conservative agents were doing no more than was allowed to any rate-payer by the Select Vestry Act.[30]

Whalley's protest against the associations was singular. No other parish filed a similar petition against them. Conservative members of both Houses took part in, or at least lent their names to, their formation – G. S. Harcourt and Lord Chandos in Buckinghamshire W. A. Mackinnon, H. J. Hope, and ten peers in Marylebone, and R. A. Spooner and the Earl of Dartmouth in Birmingham. The guests at the second annual meeting of the London Conservative Association included four leading party managers, Viscount Stormont, Viscount Mahon, Granville Somerset, and Sir George Clerk.[31] Present needs outweighed future contingencies: the explanation of the Conservatives' attitude is contained in Charles Wynne's letter to Peel, in which he defended his decision to become vice-president of the Denbighshire Conservative Society.

> I much dislike all Political Associations as I consider them always liable to be perverted from their original objects and tending to produce irritation & reaction, & usually to check the exercise of individual judgement and opinion. At the same time I see our friends promoting them all over the Country and there is frequently utility in acquiescing in what one cannot prevent. The circumstances of the present time also in some degree justify it.[32]

The extent of the associations' contribution to the Conservatives' electoral recovery in the 1830s is difficult to measure. In 1835 *Blackwood's* credited them with the Conservative victories at Devonshire, Lancashire South, Staffordshire South, Inverness-shire, Roxburghshire, and Stirlingshire.[33] In 1837 Bonham claimed that the Conservative gain at Brighton was achieved solely by the good management of the Conservative association,[34] and Edward Buller, the Liberal candidate at Staffordshire North, explained his defeat as the result of the Conservatives' 'large organized associations, having correspondents in all parts of the country by whom a canvass was simultaneously commenced'.[35]

Whatever their precise achievement in recruiting the Conservative vote, the associations attest to the fact that the Conservative reaction of the 1830s had a popular base. It was something more than the mere reassertion of influence by Conservative landowners and borough patrons.

Bonham and the Carlton

Early in May 1835, just after the resignation of Peel's first government, Francis Bonham wrote a letter to Peel drawing attention to a speech made by Lord John Russell in Devonshire, in which Russell had promised that the Whig government would dissolve parliament if its Bills were defeated. Bonham urged upon Peel the necessity to avoid the mischief of 1831, which might have been diminished but for 'our shutting our eyes against the impending danger'. What was needed was 'a very small and quiet and active Committee' to obtain information and prepare for a dissolution.

> For myself, I am ready to *devote my whole time* out of the H. of C. to this work and with a very small Committee hardly more than 7 composed of G. Somerset (*above all others*), Lord Lincoln, Clerk, Fremantle, and any others whom you might wish to recommend . . .
> I know what G.S. did at the late Election, by his almost single exertions, for some of our friends did us more harm than good. Then we had to find Candidates & organize friends in almost every place. *Now that work is done*, and a tenth part of the Exertion then applied would at least preserve if not increase our present strength.[36]

Bonham was saying that electoral management ought not to be left to *ad hoc* committees formed at the time of a dissolution, but ought to be placed on a regular, permanent footing. His advice was taken. Although he was given no title, Bonham became the first full-time agent of the Conservative party. Under his direction electoral management was supervised from the Carlton Club more regularly, more thoroughly, and more professionally than ever before. Bonham named Sir George Clerk, Chief Whip until his defeat at the 1837 elections, Granville Somerset and Fremantle as his principal assistants.[37] To them must be added Sir Henry Hardinge, Charles Ross, an assistant whip, Sir James Graham and Lord Rosslyn.

The election committee was not composed of experts, divorced from the daily concerns of the parliamentary party or isolated from decisions of high policy. Rosslyn, Hardinge, and Granville Somerset were cabinet ministers in the 1834–35 government, and Lincoln, Fremantle and Clerk were at the Treasury. They were therefore closely tied to the party leadership and owed their positions to their high social or political status. Bonham's correspondence with them, and with less well known men in the constituencies, furnished him with a rich store of details about the condition of the party in almost every constituency in the country. Graham, for example, who took special responsibility for Scotland, from 1838 to 1840 sent Bonham, during the recess, weekly reports on the selection of candidates, the views of influential landowners, the sources of money, the state of the registration, and the mood of the electorate.[38] Bonham himself went about the country, visiting constituencies and acquainting himself with local circumstances.[39]

The range of the Carlton committee's interests was almost unlimited; its powers were severely restricted. In none of the four chief departments of electoral management – the registration, the selection of candidates, the organization of the canvas and the payment of expenses – did the Carlton act as prime mover. Those functions remained, in the first instance, the preserve of the constituencies. There is, indeed, no reason to suppose that Bonham and the party leaders wished to overcome local jealousies and build up a wealthy, encompassing electoral machine in London. It would have been remarkable if they had, at the very time when Conservative backbenchers were expressing deep misgivings about the extension of central government administration and the diminution of parish authority which were part of such Whig legislation as the 1833 Factory Act and the 1834 poor law. There were obvious advantages in doing no more than working the existing system of electoral politics as efficiently as possible. In an age when elections were less 'general' elections and more a coincidence of local events, a wide range of personal contacts was the stuff of electioneering and the foundation of electoral success. It was logical to leave the management of individual elections in the hands of resident solicitors, who through their private and council business were versed in the details of community life. They had personal standing in the community, an extensive clientele among the gentry, and, often, a finger in local patronage. James Emerson Tennent's election agent in Belfast, 'an eminent solicitor . . . in rich practice' called Bates, is representative of the type, except for the singular circumstance that he was unpaid.

> If there is one man in Ireland, to whom, more than any other, *conservatism* is deeply indebted, it is . . . Mr Bates. *For ten years* he has drudged like a slave for us in Belfast, attended our registries, conducted our elections, fought our petitions in committee of the House, acted as secretary to all our societies, got up our public meetings, *subscribed largely to all our funds* and at the same time never accepted *one shilling* of a fee for all his long services![40]

Solicitors were the backbone of party organization in the constituencies. The system of objections to the register and the petitioning against members allegedly returned by corrupt or intimidating methods required men of legal skill who were intimately acquainted with local affairs. For representing candidates in legal cases solicitors were highly paid. It was not until the number of petitions dwindled later in the century that solicitors ceased to find electoral agency profitable and more central control of organization became necessary.

The Carlton office was valuable chiefly as a nerve-centre of information, collecting it and distributing it, both to the constituencies and to the party leaders.[41] By his up-to-date knowledge of the state of the registry and the need of the public, Bonham knew when to prod local Conservatives into activity. He was also able to furnish party leaders with facts to take into account when they were deciding upon parliamentary strategy.

> I am sorry [Graham wrote to Bonham in November 1839] that your more full and accurate Enquiry after the recent Municipal Elections and the completion of the new Register leads you to take a less sanguine view of our real Position. Anything, however, is better than false hopes: and accuracy of information is the only solid groundwork of safe conduct. Before our plan of campaign is fixed, the facts, on which a sound judgement is to be formed, should be brought before our leaders in the surest and clearest form.[42]

Bonham and his assistants did not interfere directly in registration, except as individuals in their own neighbourhoods. They did not raise a fund to subsidize registrations, nor did they hire solicitors as agents. They did not usually, that is to say, encroach uninvited upon what Professor Gash has called 'the almost complete political autonomy of the country gentry'.[43] When, as rarely happened, they did interfere, the reaction could be sharp. In 1841 Robert Christopher, a prominent agricultural backbencher, who in 1837 had shared the representation of Lincolnshire North uncontested with a Liberal, suddenly found himself in a contest 'forced on me by a knot of meddling politicians of the Carlton' who had sent down a second Conservative candidate. Christopher complained to Fremantle that 'the C.C. fomented my contest without consulting me', and although it is evident that his chief grievance was the expense to which a contest would subject him, he added that 'till certain persons who have no weight in the country will give over underhand work they will ruin the conservative cause'.[44]

The effectiveness of the Carlton office was restricted by the hostility of the country gentlemen to centralized authority, and, therefore, by a lack of funds. Country gentlemen contributed generously to local contests in which they had a personal stake, and naturally claimed, therefore, the right to manage their own electoral business without interference. They were seldom willing, or left with the resources, to contribute in addition to a central fund, over the appropriation of which they exercised no control. The ability to distribute money to those constituencies where it was most needed was thus denied to the party managers. They could not put up candidates in places where the local Conservatives declined to spend money. That the Conservative gentry of Staffordshire South should, without consulting either the party leaders or the local Conservative association, contract with the Whigs to share the representation of the constituency in 1841 angered Bonham and destroyed his hopes of winning both seats. But he did not attempt to dissuade them.[45] When he did intervene in a constituency's affairs, however mildly, he was discreet. In 1832 he asked Peel to suggest to Lord Villiers, the Conservative candidate at Honiton, that he might do more to assist the return of the second Conservative candidate at the election. Villiers's return was certain, and Bonham had learned that he looked solely to his own position. Conservative electors might therefore plump for him or cast their second vote for the Whig candidate. A gentle nudge might rouse Villiers to the danger. 'I do not absolutely know that it will be necessary,' Bonham told Peel, 'nor do I think in throwing out this hint it should be known to come from me.[46]

Delicate situations of that kind, involving members of parliament or important landowners, drew Peel, briefly, into electoral business. In 1835 he asked Charles Wynne to persuade his brother, Sir Watkin Wynne, the member for Denbighshire, to abandon his declared neutrality in the contest for the second Denbighshire seat and exert his influence on behalf of William Bagot against the sitting Whig member, Robert Biddulph. 'You know the best mode of doing it effectually,' Peel told Wynne, 'and therefore I write to you rather than to Sir Watkin. I wish that he could, considering the issues that are at stake on the issue of the general election, give a warm and decided support to a man of such Principles & Character as Mr. Bagot.'[47] Peel's entreaty was fruitless. In Denbighshire more than political issues were at stake.

> At the last election [Wynne replied] for the County of Denbigh between Mr. Biddulph and Mr. Kenyon, my brother declared that from Respect & Gratitude to the County of Denbigh he would take no part whatever in promoting the success of either candidate, but remain completely neutral.
>
> Notwithstanding the ties of relationship & long hereditary connexion with the Bagot family, he now feels himself bound to persevere in the same course. Many of his warmest friends support Mr. Biddulph and as they have during many years been zealous in promoting my Brother's interest when he was opposed to them in politics, he thinks they have still a right to claim from him real & complete neutrality, not by preventing his tenant-dependants from voting, but leaving them to follow their own wishes uncontrolled.[48]

Such were the ways of the political world, and his experience of them led Bonham to pour scorn on the scheme started by a few Conservatives to establish a central registration society in 1837.

> Perhaps [he wrote to Peel] you may have heard that some more zealous than wise friends of ours, Lds Strangford, Exmouth, Dr Link [?], Bob Scarlett, Disraeli cum multis alliis [*sic*], and two or three attorneys formed themselves into what they called a 'Registration Committee' to *manage* the Registrations of the Empire!!! and they collected a certain number of five pound Subscriptions. On writing to me at Brighton to join and aid them *personally*, I pointed out the inefficiency and utter absurdity of such a plan, and unless they collected a sum that would enable them to fee all the hungry Registration Attorneys and retainers, who would most certainly claim their assistance, the mischief that might result from the attempt. However they persisted, and as I *hear* that the Committee is dissolved, They probably have satisfied themselves that my advice was good.[49]

Despite the limitations imposed upon it, the Carlton office was something more than a research department. It had a small central fund at the elections of 1835 and 1837, despite Lord Rosslyn's avowal to Lord Melville that none existed.[50] The fund was administered by Rosslyn and Hardinge. In 1835 Rosslyn gave £500 to Disraeli and to George Henry Smyth.[51] And a memorandum in Hardinge's hand records that in 1835 'an agreement was made upon honor, that Sir J. Elley should undertake the Contest for Windsor & to incur thereby an Expenditure of £500. Beyond that amount the necessary aid (pecuniary) was to be afforded by the C[arlton] C[lub].' Elley fulfilled his part of the bargain; but it was a measure of the Carlton's scant resources that a year later he was still pressing Hardinge for the money promised to him.[52] Party leaders occasionally answered appeals for money individually. In 1837 Lord Lowther thanked Peel for sending £50 to help William Holmes at Berwick, especially since that earnest of the party's support would encourage local subscriptions, and in the same year the Birmingham election agent thanked him for his 'liberal contribution'.[53]

No doubt Disraeli and Holmes were glad of the money they received, but the amounts were tiny in an age when a contest rarely cost less than £2,500 and often more than £10,000.[54] It is impossible to know the size of the central fund or very much about the uses to which it was put. Because their assistance had to be highly selective, the Carlton managers kept the fund secret and often, as Rosslyn did to Melville, denied that it existed. Candidates, too, might suffer from the disclosure that they were obliged to the central party. C. O. S. Morgan of Tredegar, the Conservative candidate at the Monmouthshire by-election of 1840, resented (or, at least, thought it prudent to pretend that he did) the rumour that he was in the pay of the Carlton. 'The house of Tredegar,' he assured the electors, 'was not a beggar on the country. No such thing had been offered him, and if it had it would have been refused.'[55]

There was one exception to the primarily local nature of election subscriptions: the Spottiswoode fund. It was raised after the 1837 elections to subsidise petitions against successful Liberal candidates, especially in Ireland, by a group of Conservative supporters, led by A. Spottiswoode, the Queen's printer. Their national appeal was enthusiastically supported by the Conservative press, but the party leaders, while they privately supported it, avoided being publicly associated with it. On 21 December *The Times* reported that £13,000 had been subscribed, a modest amount, since legal proceedings concerning a single petition could cost as much as £5,000. Nevertheless, despite the fact that the Liberals responded by organizing a similar fund (theirs, indeed, was raised by the central party agent, James Coppock), Conservative objections outran Liberal ones by thirty-five to thirteen. That each party unseated seven opponents, however, suggests that Conservative suspicions of gross corruption by the Liberals were misplaced.[56]

The Carlton's role in the selection of candidates varied according to circumstances. There was a list of candidates ready to send down to the constituencies on request. Rosslyn informed Peel in 1835 that he had 'started Mr. Ferrand for Peterborough upon letters from Ld. Westmorland & the D. of Wellington'[57] and Sir George Clerk was afforded an early passage back to Westminster at the Stamford by-election of 1838, when Lord Exeter, the borough patron, agreed to have him as the Carlton's nominee, since there was no local man eager for the seat.[58] But Bonham and Peel could do little on their own initiative. Colonel Sibthorp's jealousy of a Conservative rival at Lincoln prevented the borough from returning two Conservatives and G. H. Ward's refusal to give up the nomination to a more popular Conservative cost the party the representation of the Isle of Wight in 1837.[59] Nor were the party managers able to prevent a contest which they believed might damage the party. In 1835 the zeal of Northumberland Conservatives to oppose Lord Howick ended Peel's hopes that Howick, the son of Lord Grey and a most influential Whig moderate, might follow Graham and Stanley out of the Whig party and give his government independent support.[60]

The list of candidates at the Carlton was not exhaustive; it was often difficult to find the right man, with a sufficiently large purse, for a particular constituency. Pressed by Falmouth Conservatives in the autumn of 1839 to find a candidate to send down to the by-election there, Bonham tried nine persons. The Falmouth party had stipulated that the candidate must be able to spend £3,000 of his own money. None of the men whom Bonham approached would risk, so late in the life of the 1837 parliament, '*such* a speculation', and Bonham abandoned his search.[61]

The principal link between Westminster and the constituencies remained what it had long been, patronage, although it did not render much service to a party out of office. In 1842 Herbert Vaughan, a leading Conservative at Cardigan, explained to Fremantle, who needed no instruction, the necessity of giving the patronage of the borough, vested chiefly in the post office and the customs, to J. S. Harford, the Conservative candidate at the 1841 elections, even though Harford had been defeated.

> I am sure from your well known high conservative principles, that you will be kind enough to support *our Association by every fair & proper means* in your power. *Great exertions* were made at the last election, by the Con. Gents. particularly in Cardigan, & the contributary Boroughs of Lampeter & Adpar, & I do not mean to except the Contributary Borough of Aberystwith, to return a conservative member . . . we have no doubt that on the next occasion we shall be successful & return a staunch conservative . . . it is always necessary to strengthen & keep up a certain influence in the breasts of the various voters of the Borough; and to accomplish that most desirable object, the Borough Patronage *ought* to be vested in the hands of the Borough Member, if a *ministerialist*, but if he be opposed to the administration, then I most humbly submit, it *ought* to be *placed* in the *hands* of the *ministerial candidate*, tho' perhaps a defeated one, to reward *his* supporters, as well as to *draw* over to *his side any waverers*, or in fact any voters of the opposite party; and we *all well know* the *loaves and fishes* will have a *wonderful influence*.[62]

Harford was given control of the patronage. Despite Peel's frequent outbursts against the tyranny of claimants for reward, he recognized that the party depended upon the work of office-seekers in the country.[63] Their merits were therefore assessed, their claims balanced one against another, and the meats doled out. It had to be done. Patronage, although it was in much smaller supply than twenty-five years earlier, still oiled the wheels of politics.

The effect of organization

After the 1832 elections the Conservatives had about 150 seats in the House of Commons. At the next three general elections – in 1835, 1837 and 1841 – their numbers rose to about 290, 313 and 370. How far are those gains to be explained by improved organization? Organization is often made the scapegoat for defeat; it flatters a party's *amour propre* to believe that its supporters did not get to the polls, not that they did not exist. Organization and opinion are, it is true, different things. Yet what one man calls organization is often simply another man's enthusiasm. The expansion of the Conservative party's organization, at the centre and in the constituencies, was the manifestation of Conservatives' willingness to make strenuous efforts, not simply to rescue the party from the unfamiliar regions of opposition, but to save the constitution and the social order from what they called the 'destructive' designs of the reformers.

It was, certainly, the view of their opponents that the Conservatives had more money. 'You will have observed the other day,' Lord Normanby wrote to Lord John Russell on the eve of the 1841 elections, 'that in almost all the speculations as to possible gains, the seats in question were those to be won by money. We know pretty well from past experience on which side this influence will preponderate.'[64] Edward Ellice, the Liberal Whip, made the same point in 1837: 'The other party have money. We are literally without a shilling; & many of our friends will be in great danger, for want of any trifling amount.'[65] In 1841 Denis le Marchant, a Liberal manager, reported that the Liberals had spent £25,000 out of their central fund,[66] not a lavish expenditure, but far from modest by the standards of the age. There is, unfortunately, no comparable Conservative figure, but the Conservative central fund is unlikely to have been much larger. Ellice and Normanby were probably referring to money spent by candidates individually and the best evidence that their laments had some truth to them may be that the Conservatives' correspondence contains no countervailing references to Liberal wealth.

The Conservative managers were well pleased with the state of their preparations before both the 1837 and the 1841 elections. Just before the first constituencies began polling in 1837, Granville Somerset was prevented by gout from 'settling the few places yet unprovided for', but he told Peel that Stroud was the only one of importance among them.

The Thing . . . which gives me the most confidence is the universality of exertion on our side & the only Cases of Candidates retiring being Elley for Windsor (*his stinginess* being the Cause), Goodricke from Bewdley, which we have long known by its connection with Stamford to be hopeless, & Sir J. Beresford from Chatham, which the influence of Government fully accounts for.[67]

In 1839, two years before the next elections (though they might have come at any time), Graham was satisfied that 'our general preparations for a dissolution are far advanced and well arranged'.[68]

One sign of improved organization, perhaps, was the increase in the number of Conservative candidates, from only 390 in 1835 to more than 450 in 1837.[69] In 1835 Granville Somerset complained that the want of candidates had cost the party from twenty to thirty seats.[70] There are indeed many seats which it appears, on the surface at least, that the Conservatives would have won had they contested them, since they fell to the party on the first occasions that they were contested. That is a plausible interpretation to place on the returns from the nine leading arable counties in England, constituencies which formed the backbone of the Conservative party from 1841 to 1867.

Conservative performance at nine counties, 1835–41

County	1835		1837		1841	
	Candi-dates	Seats won	Candi-dates	Seats won	Candi-dates	Seats won
Bedfordshire (2 members)	1	1	1	1	2	2
Cambridgeshire (3)	2	2	2	2	3	3
Essex (2)	2	2	2	2	2	2
Hertfordshire (3)	1	1	2	2	3	3
Huntingdonshire (2)	1	1	2	2	2	2
Lincolnshire N (2)	1	1	1	1	2	1
Lincolnshire S (2)	0	0	0	0	2	2
Norfolk E (2)	2	2	2	2	2	2
Norfolk W (2)	1	0	2	2	2	2
Rutlandshire (2)	1	1	1	1	1	1
Suffolk E (2)	2	2	2	2	2	2
Suffolk W (2)	2	1	2	2	2	2
Totals (26)	16	14	19	19	25	24

There is an almost exact correlation between the number of candidates and the number of seats won. And, since the pattern was repeated in other places,[71] the inference might be drawn, not only that improved organization lay behind the Conservative recovery in the late 1830s, but that better organization earlier might have brought the party to power in 1837, when the Liberal majority was only about thirty seats.

There is some ground for the argument. After the extraordinary Whig gains in the counties in 1831 and 1832, it was reasonable for Conservatives to expect that a return to uncontested sharing of county divisions would be to their advantage. At Norfolk East in 1835 the Whigs agreed: they rejected the Conservatives' offer of a compromise. The Conservatives, who believed that their position was weak, were therefore forced to put up two candidates.[72] In the event both sides were shown to have miscalculated. Two Conservatives were returned. Yet it is far from obvious that everywhere where no contest occurred the Conservatives had exhibited undue caution. For one thing, the want of candidates may have been considerably less than the statistics imply. The bare figures always understate the number of Victorian elections which were, in fact, contested, because many candidates withdrew after the canvass and did not go to the poll. They had contested the seat, found that they could not win, and cut their financial losses by retiring. For another, the central organization was unable to force the pace of county politics. Where the local gentry conceived it to be their interest to 'keep the peace' of a county, organization was impotent. There was always, especially in the counties, a time-lag between a shift in opinion and a corresponding change in the representation, precisely because the domestic interests of the country gentlemen often conflicted with their political opinions. The desire to avoid disturbing established relations in the neighbourhood and also to avoid the expense of electioneering worked to persuade even gentlemen of strong opinions to share the representation with their opponents. Issues of great moment could change the habit of years. That is what happened in the late 1830s, when to the concern for the constitution was added the fear of the Anti-Corn Law League. But it took three elections to break down the Liberal majority. The results at Norfolk West suggest that, before the protectionist issue became important, the full Conservative reaction had not set in. In 1835 the lone Conservative candidate was defeated. Two years later the Conservatives won both seats. By then the Conservative tide in the counties was rising quickly. As the number of Conservative candidates in the counties rose, the number of Liberal candidates fell away. Putting candidates in the field did not produce the Conservative revival, it attested to it.[72]

The same may be said of the registration. 'On the whole,' David Close has concluded, after a careful study of the elections, 'the Liberal election managers' record of achievement, between 1835 and 1837, compares favourably with that of their Conservative counterparts. Although they were probably less efficient in collecting information and providing candidates, they were more enterprising and energetic in promoting registration.[73] Yet the only conclusion to be drawn from the registration statistics is that the Liberals benefited marginally in the boroughs and the Conservatives in the counties.[74] Where opinion, class, and whatever other factors, favoured a party, there that party gained on the register. Registration would have had an influence on the elections only if one party had ignored it. By itself it could not overcome real disabilities, such as the bias which the tenant-at-will franchise, in a system of open voting, gave to the Conservatives in the counties. 'In those counties *we* have *best* registered,' Joesph Parkes wrote after the 1837 elections, 'the Tories beat us; their activity (excited by ours) having more *material* . . . to practise on.'[75]

The growth of the Conservative party's organization (and that of their opponents) in the 1830s appeared to fill a vacuum. That vacuum was created by the withdrawal of the Crown from political action, a withdrawal which was virtually completed, so far as elections were concerned, by 1832, and also by the abolition of the rotten boroughs in 1832. Those two changes combined to remove the element of *government* from the constituencies, provoking the Duke of Wellington to ask of the Whig reformers the famous question, how the King's government was to be carried on. Before 1832 an election always returned the government in power, which was, thanks to the power of the Crown, the government of the monarch's choice. After 1867 there was developed a new instrument of government, the modern, highly centralized party. And more important than that development, the yearly increasing extent of government responsibility for economic and social matters meant that the electorate became more interested in the kind of government which it was electing than in the individual members of parliament. As the influence of government decisions on the daily lives of the voters became more directly visible, so the voters came to expect members of parliament to be loyal to the party which they wished to see placed in office. That, far more than mechanics of party discipline, has produced the cohesive parliamentary parties of the twentieth century. The electorate came to understand that to send an independent to Westminster was very nearly (except for special purposes, such as Welsh or Scottish nationalism) to nullify the real power which the franchise gave to them.

In the intervening years, between 1832 and 1867, the authority of party, or of the element of government, was weak in the constituencies, because the electorate was still small enough to be controlled by men of influence in the community and because the voters' expectations of a government were far lower. Mid-Victorian elections were far from being contests between two parties giving the electorate the choice of alternative governments. The House of Commons still had a powerful say in the making of governments. Those reformers who turned Conservative between 1832 and 1837 did not, with the rare exception of Sir James Graham at Cumberland East (which

Graham described as 'essentially Radical'[76]), forfeit their seats. Without the influence of the Crown or the pocket boroughs at its disposal and without the weight of a solid party in the constituencies, a government could not *secure* a majority at an election. Dissolution was therefore not a threat which a government could effectively hold over members, despite members' dread of election expenses. Nor, since few members of parliament depended upon their party's money for their return, were they susceptible to the threat of expulsion from the party.

To be elected a mid-nineteenth-century candidate nearly always needed some money of his own and the backing of influential men in the constituency. He was not, as the modern candidate is, *primarily* the respresentative of a potential government. In those circumstances the Conservative associations were mostly a gloss on the structure of politics. They did not provide a link between the parliamentary party and the electorate. They did not, like modern parties, carry the element of government into the constituencies. Despite their existence, party, as an institution, remained a parliamentary creature. That is not to say that it is silly to speak of mid-Victorian parties. It is simply to recognize them for what they were. The Carlton Club and the local Conservative associations were important advances in the development of parties. They did not change them in the short space of a decade.

The reason that the independents were almost eliminated from the House of Commons in the 1830s is not that the institutions of party had suddenly been transformed. It is not that mechanical changes in the nature of party suddenly, after 1837, made independence more difficult. It is that changed conditions made it less desirable. The 1832 Reform Act brought a new class into the electorate, a class whose desires were different from those of the landed interest which had been overwhelmingly preponderant in the pre-reform electorate. And the changes in society which had forced the Reform Act also stimulated that expansion of government activity in social and economic fields which, although it began in the 1820s, was the special mark of the legislation of the 1830s. So long as a landed parliament was accountable to only one class and governments took a restricted view of their responsibilities, independence, far from reducing a member's influence, could enhance it. But in the 1830s politicians had a profound impression that great issues had arisen, upon the resolution of which depended the future course of the nation. On the Conservative side, the tightly-knit parliamentary party of 1837–41 was a reflection of the anxiety with which Conservatives observed the growing power of Radicalism. That sense of crisis, together with the practical necessity of working the registration clauses of the Reform Act, also produced the Conservative associations. They were an embodiment of the Conservative resolve that the Radicals should not prevail. They and the Carlton Club were not themselves the growth of the party. They were the evidence of it.

Notes and References

The foundation of Conservative Associations

1 Jones, 'Correspondence of the first Marquis of Anglesey', unpublished thesis, *passim*.

2 *Ibid*, 425–6.

3 *Ibid*, 223–5.

4 *Ibid*, 33–6.

5 *Ibid*, 217–8.

6 *Ibid*, 460–1.

7 The majority of the provincial newspapers were Liberal. None of the four largest, with a circulation of more than 3,000 (the *Leeds Mercury*, the *Stamford Mercury*, the *Liverpool Mercury* and the *Manchester Guardian*) was Conservative. Of the 175 newspapers outside London, 100 were Liberal and 75 Conservative; of the 60 newspapers with a weekly circulation of 1,000 or more, 37 were Liberal and 23 Conservative. The total Liberal circulation in 1836 was 72,000; the Conservative circulation was 31,000. (*Companion to the Newspaper*, Aug, 1836.)

8 *Chambers's Historical Newspaper*, Feb, 1835.

9 Whittingham-Jones, 'Liverpool's political clubs', *passim*.

10 Lord Brougham (attributed), 'Tory and Reform associations', *Edinburgh Review*, Oct, 1835, 167–84.

11 Golby, 'A great electioneer and his motives: the fourth Duke of Newcastle', *Hist. J*, viii, 2 (1965), 213–14.

12 Gladstone to W. W. Farr, 21 Dec. [1832]: Gladstone, *Autobiographica*, 218–19.

13 J. T. Nossiter, 'Elections and political behaviour in County Durham and Newcastle, 1832–74', unpublished thesis, 102–20.

14 *Elections and Party Management*, 20.

15 *Ibid*.

16 T. Hill to Fremantle, 29 Dec, 1842: Fremantle MSS, 80/21.

17 'Conservative associations', *Blackwood's Edinburgh Magazine*, July 1835, 1–16.

18 *The Conservative*, 1 July 1836.

19 See Kent, 'Party politics in Staffordshire', *passim*, and 'The Beginnings of party political organization in Staffordshire, 1832–41', *North Staffordshire Journal of Field Studies*, 1961, 86–100.

20 Kent, 'Party politics . . .', chapter 4.

21 Kent, 'Beginnings of party organization', 90.

22 A statement of the Staffordshire association's receipts and expenditure is given in Appendix 6.

23 H. L. Lawrence to Ellenborough, 13 Nov, 1840: Peel MSS, Add. MSS 40617, ff. 94–5.

24 Archdeacon MSS, D/AR/6/1–2 (two volumes listing the membership and subscriptions of the Buckingham association from 1837 to 1845); see also the volume of 'Minutes of Proceedings' of the association (*ibid*, D/AR/6/un-numbered).
25 T. Huddlestone to Peel, 24 Nov, 1839: Peel MSS, Add. MSS 40427, ff. 259–60.
26 Graham to Bonham, 15 Dec, 1839: *ibid*, Add. MSS 40616, ff. 133–4.
27 Gash, *Politics in the Age of Peel*, 314–15.
28 *Chambers's Historical Newspapers*, July 1835.
29 Buckingham, *Parliamentary Review*, 1833, iii, 104.
30 11 Aug, 1835, *Hansard*, 3rd series, xxx, 258–65.
31 *The Conservative*, 1 Aug, 1836.
32 Wynne to Peel, 25 April 1836: Peel MSS, Add. MSS 40420, ff. 74–5. The *Leicester Conservative Standard*, March 1835, offered a similar defence: '*Radical* – "You complain of political unions, and you establish a political union of your own." *Conservative* – "Yes! and I complain of a thief who brings a crow-bar to open up my door, and I put up an iron bar inside to defend it." '
33 *Blackwood's*, July 1835, 11.
34 Bonham to Peel, 23 Sept, 1837: Peel MSS, Add. MSS 40424, ff. 140–1.
35 Kent, 'Party Politics . . .', chapter 4.

Bonham and the Carlton

36 Bonham to Peel, 4 May 1835: Peel MSS, Add. MSS 40420, ff. 126–7.
37 Bonham to Peel, 20 Nov, 1839: *ibid*, Add. MSS 40428, f. 244.
38 *Ibid*, Add. MSS 40616, *passim*.
39 For example, Bonham to Peel, [6 May 1837]: 'I found the ground at Berwick too thoroughly occupied before I arrived there, to give me any hope of success, except by means that might (if I succeeded) have also sent me to Newgate, & I also felt I was a trustee for other people's money, & that I ought not to move unless I was quite certain of success' (*ibid*, Add. MSS 40420, ff. 141–3).
40 Emerson Tennent to Fremantle, Nov, 1841: Fremantle MSS, 110/10. Election agents were not always solicitors. They included, very occasionally, a country gentleman, like Mr Lawrence, at Gloucestershire East, whose application for a government office in 1841 was forwarded to Fremantle by Lord Redesdale: 'Our position in this division of the county is mainly owing to his exertions, & he has spent a good deal of money in the canvass. . . . He is known all over the division, far better than Codrington or Charteris, & both certainly in a great degree owe their seats to his efforts. He has some influence in Cheltenham & the late good fight there agt. Craven Berkeley . . . was greatly promoted by his exertions. He belongs to a class who are generally satisfied by a commission for a son or relation etc. – I mean that he is a country gentleman – but circumstances, it appears, render office of importance to him.' (Redesdale to Fremantle, 25 Nov, 1841; *ibid*.)
41 A letter from a Mr Sydney in 1839 illustrates the kind of information which Bonham received and was asked to provide: 'Can you tell me the politics of Sir Hy. Maud, & can he be got at in any way? He has taken the brewing interest of one Thompson at Rochester, which will give him gt. influence there, especially over the Public Houses in all that district, which heretofore have been used against us, and if it cd. be turned in our favour wd. make considerable difference in the County Election (they say 30 votes) & probably in the town

also: – Sir John R. Reid is Maud's partner, I believe, & perhaps he might be managed through him.' (Sydney to Bonham, 27 Nov, 1839. Peel MSS, Add. MSS 40617, ff. 75–6.) Sir John Rae Reid was the Conservative member for Dover.

42 Graham to Bonham, 10 Nov, 1839: *ibid*, Add. MSS 40616, ff. 109–12.

43 Gash, *Politics in the Age of Peel*, 257.

44 Christopher to Fremantle, 13 and 15 Sept, 1842: Fremantle MSS, 110/13.

45 Bonham to Peel, undated: Peel MSS, Add. MSS 40485, f. 2.

46 Bonham to Peel, 14 Nov, 1832: *ibid*, Add. MSS 40403, ff. 93–4.

47 Peel to C. Wynne, 1 Jan, 1835 (copy): *ibid*, Add. MSS 40409, ff. 59–60.

48 C. Wynne to Peel, [2 Jan, 1835]: *ibid*, ff. 61–2.

49 Bonham to Peel, 1 Jan, 1838. *ibid*, Add. MSS 40424, ff. 277–8.

50 Melville to Rosslyn, 7 Dec, 1834: 'When you state that there will be no fund for Electioneering expenses, I am sorry to hear it – not with reference to Leith [where Melville's son was standing] or even to Scotland generally – but to England, where I am quite sure it will be wanted.' (*Ibid*, Add. MSS, 40405, ff. 30–2.)

51 Rosslyn to Peel, 5 Jan, 1835: *ibid*, Add. MSS 40409, ff. 146–7.

52 Memorandum of 6 Feb, 1836: Hardinge MSS.

53 Lowther to Peel, 26 June and 10 July 1837; J. W. Whately to Peel, 19 July and [23 July], 1837: Peel MSS, Add. MSS, 40423, ff. 285, 310, 351–2, and 367–8.

54 A table of the election expenses at Staffordshire North in 1837 is given as an example in Appendix 7.

55 David, 'Political activity in south-east Wales', 149–50. At the Sunderland by-election of 1841, the Whigs thought it worth their while to denounce the Conservatives' attempt to 'invade the independence of the borough' by sending down a candidate as the nominee of the Carlton Club (Heesom, 'The Sunderland By-Election, September, 1841', *Northern History*, ix, 1974, 66–7).

56 This paragraph is based on Close, 'Elections of 1835 and 1837', unpublished thesis, 444–8.

57 Rosslyn to Peel, 5 Jan, 1835: Peel MSS, Add. MSS 40409, ff. 146–7.

58 Exeter to Peel, 1 April 1838: *ibid*, Add. MSS 40425, ff. 1–2.

59 Ripon to Peel, 4 Aug, 1837; W. B. Baring to Peel, 5 August 1837: *ibid*, Add. MSS 40424, ff. 8–9, 15–16.

60 Melville to Rosslyn, 10 Dec, 1834: 'I am sorry to find that Mr Liddell is to oppose Lord Howick in Northumberland; it has produced a great change of feeling at Howick where the tone previously was very moderate' (*ibid*, Add. MSS 40405, ff. 33–5).

61 Bonham to Peel, 5 Dec, 1839: *ibid*, Add. MSS 40427, ff. 278–9.

62 Vaughan to Fremantle, 31 Oct, 1842: Fremantle MSS, 81/2.

63 The process also worked in reverse. When the Earl of Sandwich asked Peel and Wellington to use their influence to persuade the Duke of Manchester to support a second Conservative candidate at Huntingdonshire in 1835, he was turned down because Manchester had not been offered a place in Peel's government. (Sandwich to Peel, [9 Jan, 1835]; Peel to Sandwich, 12 Jan, 1835 (copy): Peel MSS, Add. MSS 40409, ff. 314–5, 316).

The effect of organization

64 Normanby to Russell, 10 May 1841: Russell, *Later Correspondence*, i, 34–5.

65 Ellice to Lord Holland, [1837]: Holland House MSS, Add. MSS 51581, ff 8–9.

66 Close, 'Elections of 1835 and 1837', 176.

67 G. Somerset to Peel, 18 July 1837: Peel MSS, Add. MSS 40423, ff. 346–8.
68 Graham to Arbuthnot, 8 June 1839: C. Arbuthnot, *Correspondence*, 205–6.
69 G. Somerset to Peel, 18 July, 1837: Peel MSS, Add. MSS 40423, ff. 346–8.
70 Close, 'Elections of 1835 and 1837', 188; but it is worth noting that Joseph Parkes made the same claim for the Liberals (*ibid*, 183).
71 *The Times*, for instance, predicted on 8 July 1837 that the Conservatives would gain one seat at each of Devonshire North, Cumberland East, Northumberland North, Staffordshire North, and Worcestershire West. The party contested only two of those seats and gained them both. The others, except for Cumberland East, which was gained at a by-election in 1839, were gained in 1841.
72 Gash, *Politics in the Age of Peel*, 246–7.
73 Close, 'Elections of 1835 and 1837', 413.
74 *Ibid*, 460–1.
75 Nossiter, 'Elections in Durham and Newcastle', 415.
76 Graham to Bonham, 14 Sept, 1839: Peel MSS, Add. MSS 40616, ff. 84–5.

Chapter 8

The triumph of Conservatism

Opinion and the Conservative majority of 1841

Parties had little authority in the constituencies. They nevertheless had more meaning there than a strict description of the electorate as deferential, parochial and corrupt would suggest. Opinion played an important part in giving the Conservatives their handsome majority in 1841, just as it had brought them low in 1831–32. There was a logical connection between the opinions which Conservatives broadcast in the 1830s and the geography and sociology of their majority. Had there not been, it is hard to see how so many Conservatives, whether right or wrong in the particular interpretation which they placed on events, could have believed that Peel's government of 1841–46 betrayed those Conservatives whose interests he had been raised to power to defend and prosper.

The politicians of the 1830s, who understood the subtle modes of gaining votes, were in no doubt that elections often turned on questions of public policy. The reduction of the tax on newspapers in 1836 encouraged the spread of the provincial press, so that most towns came to have at least one Liberal paper and one Conservative paper. It was also in the 1830s that the practice of candidates' circulating printed addresses to their constituents, outlining their position on major issues, became general. There would have been no reason for them to do so, nor for Peel to publish the Tamworth Manifesto, if opinion had carried no electoral weight. But it did. John Walter found little evidence of party spirit in Berkshire's villages and rural districts in 1834; but he believed that 'much may undoubtedly be done in correcting wrong opinions and inculcating right ones'.[1] Colonel Sibthorp, according to his election agent, lost Lincoln in 1832 because of his opposition to the Reform Bill and the abolition of slavery and regained it in 1835 because he pledged himself to the spirit of the Tamworth Manifesto.[2]

One of the reasons for the larger role played by opinion after 1832 was the enfranchisement of the £10 householder in the boroughs and the addition to the representation of the manufacturing towns. For the most part, despite the retention of the vote by some working-class electors under the freeman franchise, the boroughs contained a predominantly pre-industrial electorate of shopkeepers, professional people, craftsmen and artisans, men who were not seriously exposed to external pressures and who were capable of forming political opinions. At the Berwick election of 1835 Alexander Pringle, the Conservative member for Selkirkshire, reported that the ten-pounders in the towns and villages demonstrated their freedom from landlord influence.

> In two villages in Berwickshire – Earlston and Redpath – situated apart from any large towns – on the lands of three beneficent, resident conservative proprietors – out of 34 electors, 30 went to a distance to vote for the *liberal* candidate, Sir Francis Blake, a stranger to the county, in a contest got up a few days before the election.[3]

But it was not only in the towns that opinion mattered. For some time historians have argued that until 1885 county elections were apolitical and reflected only the balance of landlord control, and that political conflict, properly called, took place only in the larger boroughs.[4] One of the factors which have led historians to believe this is the Conservative domination of the English county constituencies between 1841 and 1880. Yet it is improbable that the Conservatives would have maintained that hold had not their policies squared with county opinion. 'The farmers, of course, are all against us,' Charles Wood, the Whig minister, remarked after the 1841 elections.[5] Why 'of course'? Why 'all'? Not because of landlord control which was not, of course, all Conservative, but because of the farmers' misgivings about a number of Whig tendencies, not least that which was pulling the Whig party in the direction of free trade in grain.

There was, at any rate, nothing peculiarly Victorian about the fidelity of a large number of constituencies to one party. Only a small proportion of constituencies today are marginal. Yet it would be foolish to suggest that elections in the marginal constituencies are more 'political' than those in safe ones. A man does not have to change his opinion to prove that he has one. Nor is there any meaning to the frequently made statement that elections are won and lost in the marginal constituencies; the notion that they are may nevertheless have contributed to historians' emphasis on those boroughs in Victorian elections which frequently changed hands. The large boroughs and the north-east, which remained faithfully Liberal between the Reform Acts, and the English counties, which remained Conservative, were not, as Professor Vincent has written, 'mute in the business of moulding governments'.[6] They, too, sent members to parliament. Understanding why they did not change their votes is as important as understanding why others did. The Liberal governments of the mid-century owed a great deal to the restrictions which were placed on the Conservative party precisely because Conservatives were wary of offending opinion in the agricultural counties. It is true that the Reform Act, by removing urban voters from the county constituencies and adding the tenants-at-will, copyholders, and leaseholders to them, was calculated to extend the scope of landed influence, which continued to exercise great power after 1832. Charles Seymour, however, found that only 30 per cent of the reformed county electorate was composed of the new voters, the remaining 70 per cent consisting of those forty-shilling freeholders to whom, before 1832, politicians had looked for the free expression of the electorate's opinion.[7] And Close's analysis of the 1835 elections in England and Wales revealed that the Conservatives did not perform significantly better in those county constituencies in which the tenants-at-will formed at least one quarter of the electorate: 'coercion of tenants-at-will by landlords seems to have been only a minor factor in the Conservatives' English county strength'.[8] The county electorate was not immune from the contagion of political opinion. At Buckinghamshire, in 1835, three Conservatives were returned, and the poll books show that a large number of previously Liberal electors voted against a Liberal candidate who advocated the repeal of the Corn Laws. They were not following a shift in landed influence. The only important shift in the balance of influence was in the opposite direction, against the Conservative influence of the Grenvilles. ' "Corn" had achieved what his [Chandos's] faggot voters could not do – broken down the party who called themselves Reformers. "Catholics" were to finish the job.'[9] In Lincolnshire, too, Richard Olney has found that after 1832 'it is possible to describe the politics of most if not all the . . . gentry in terms of national party labels' and, more interesting still, that, despite the low frequency of contested elections, there is no evidence that a compromise was agreed between the parties at any election between 1832 and 1885.[10]

Historians are generally agreed that landed influence was usually rooted in the social deference of the agricultural community, not in intimidation and coercion. Some of them believe that the distinction makes no practical difference, that deference, as much as coercion, excluded political choice.[11] They are, as Richard Davis pointed out, using the word 'deference' in a different sense from Bagehot and the word 'influence' in a different sense from the Whig authors of the Reform Act.[12] Bagehot and the Whigs distinguished between influence and public opinion: both operated at the same time. Deference to social superiority (and the high cost of elections) meant that the House of Commons continued to be filled by men of substantial property; public opinion had a say in which particular men of property filled it. The more intensely an opinion was held, the less landed influence meant landed control. The Whig, Lord Lansdowne, complained in 1837 that the farmers of Wiltshire were 'completely in the dependence of the squires who are nineteen out of twenty against us, and at present in close alliance with the church, so that every country parish is organized against us'.[13] No doubt it was the squires' allegiance which parties needed to win in the counties, but they could be influenced from below as well as from above. Lord Chandos became the 'Farmers' Friend' because he listened to, and cultivated, the opinions of Buckinghamshire farmers.[14] If influence had blotted out opinion as completely as some historians have suggested Palmerston could not have said, of his unexpected defeat at Devonshire South in 1835, that he was beaten by the cry of the Church in danger, by Althorp's increase in the spirits duty, and by the Tory farmers who, being in arrear and hoping for rent abatements, were 'more than usually dependent on landlords'.[15]

It is, indeed, impossible to make sense of election results between the first two Reform Acts if the role of opinion is brushed aside or relegated to footnotes. The statistics of split-voting in two-member constituencies (that is an elector's dividing his two votes between candidates of rival parties) give some indication of the importance which voters attached to the party affiliation and the opinions of candidates: split-voting declined when the parties at Westminster were sharply divided and rose when they were not. Thus in 1835, when the lines between Whig, Liberal Conservative, 'moderate reformer', and Conservative were blurred, 18 per cent of a representative sample of the English borough electorate split their votes. As the party lines hardened in the House of Commons, the number of split votes fell, to 15.1 per cent in 1837 and to 8.6 per cent in 1841, the lowest percentages at any elections before 1868. When, by 1847, the two-party alignment of the previous decade had been broken by the Conservative split over the repeal of the Corn Laws, split-voting rose again to 26.3 per cent, the highest percentage before 1868.[16] Such variation cannot be explained by local factors or by influence; it is the reflection of a genuine party struggle. The same may be said of the variations in the Conservative share of the vote in the English boroughs from 1832 to 1841. It was greatest in the large two-member boroughs, where influence was least important; in the small one-member boroughs, where opinion was most easily bribed and controlled, it actually declined.[17] It is, furthermore, precisely in accordance with a gradual movement of opinion, not the erratic and unsystematic jerks attributable to local causes, that the Conservative share of the vote should have risen *steadily* at each of the three elections after 1832.

The findings of recent research are therefore in accordance with the views of politicians in the 1830s. They believed that the Conservatives succeeded in winning the mind of the country. 'Our measures were proposed honestly,' Francis Baring reflected on the morrow of the Whigs' overthrow in 1841. 'The country is against them. . . . The country is tired of the old hands and wants to try a new doctor.'[18]

What was the meaning of the Conservative victory in 1841? Certainly it was a triumph for Peel. His contribution was essential. His reputation for fair-mindedness, administrative efficiency, and patriotism had gained him a standing in the country higher than that of any other politician since the younger Pitt. Already in 1841, by umpiring the conflicts between the Whig government and the Conservative House of Lords, he seemed to have raised himself above the indignities of party warfare. Croker was right to observe as the curiosity of the 1841 elections that 'all turns on the name of Sir Robert Peel' and that nearly every Conservative candidate declared himself to be 'Peel's man'.[19] What mattered, however, was what those candidates, and the electors who gave them their votes, believed that Peel represented. Peel, himself, may have believed that the Conservative party 'stood in the first place for strong executive government as the rock on which all else must stand';[20] throughout his second premiership he was to appeal to his followers' loyalty to men, not measures. And posterity, which has looked at the measures as well as the men, may be right to praise Peel as the architect of the mid-Victorian compromise, the reconciler of class antagonisms, the high priest at the wedding of agriculture and manufacturing. 'Sir Robert's ultimate object', Thomas Kebbel wrote in 1886, 'was to build up a great middle-class barrier, combining popular progress with constitutional principles, against the Radical revolution which seemed imminent; and in this . . . he entirely succeeded.'[21] But Peel and the Conservative party were not the same thing. Peel's greatest achievement, the repeal of the Corn Laws, was a disaster for the Conservative party. Leader and party did not, as it turned out, stand on the same rock. To look at the Conservative party through Peel's eyes is distorting; Peel was always more interested in what he thought the party ought to be than in what it was. It was, of course, important that by 1835 Peel should have disentangled himself from the Ultras and that they, for their part, should have learned to live with him.[22] There is an element of truth in the view that the victory of 1841 was the fruit of Peel's 'efforts to make the Conservative party attractive to the commercial and industrial classes'.[23] In 1841 the Conservative share of the poll in the large two-member boroughs with an electorate of more than 1,000 was 46 per cent, a large jump from the 31 per cent in 1832 and the 38 per cent in 1835.[24] On the other hand, the Conservatives' share of the forty-five seats for the major manufacturing towns remained constant at thirteen at each of the elections of 1835, 1837, and 1841.[25] The view, therefore, that commerce and industry propelled Peel into office in 1841 is far too one-sided. It accords neither with the principal grounds of the Conservatives' appeal to the electorate nor with the constituency which, in 1841, the Conservatives represented.

Conservatism in the 1830s rested on the determination to uphold the monarchical, aristocratic, Anglican constitution. In that it was scarcely to be distinguished from Whiggery, and by 1841 even the Radicals had, for the time being at least, abandoned the frontal attack on the constitution. But the Conservative party was more than a constitutional party: it was a religious and predominantly landed party. From 1835 to 1841 Conservative candidates, with varying degrees of emphasis, identified themselves with hostility to the claims of Dissenters and Irish Catholics and with a deep attachment to the landed interest and its supposed mainstay, the protective tariffs on grain.

As early as 1831 Mrs Arbuthnot, reporting on the by-election at Cambridgeshire, noted that the farmers were disconcerted by the language of the Radicals, who, they feared, would make the repeal of the Corn Laws one of the first acts of the reformed parliament.[26] The reformed House of Commons turned out to be much less radical, as Lord Grey had intended, than many Tories had expected. In the immediate post-reform years attention was distracted from the Corn Laws by high employment and good wages in the manufacturing districts and by depressed wheat prices, produced by three successive full harvests from 1832 to 1834. In many counties, nevertheless, the 1835 elections revealed the farmers' determination to tie Conservative candidates to agricultural protection and, the more immediate issue of that year, the repeal of the malt tax. For voters in the English counties, the defence and relief of the agricultural interest was at the very heart of the Conservative party.[27] By 1841 the Corn Laws had become a leading issue between the Liberals and the Conservatives. In 1838 the Anti-Corn Law League had been started in Manchester. For the next three years bread prices rose while the Lancashire cotton industry fell steadily deeper into unemployment. At the same time, the Chancellor of the Exchequer, Spring Rice, attempted in vain (inhibited partly by Conservative opposition to an income tax, for the introduction of which in 1842 Peel has been lavishly praised) to eliminate the annual budgetary deficit. In 1841 the Whig government, therefore, seized upon two conclusions of the Select Committee on Import Duties – that a lower rate of duty would, by increasing consumption, yield higher revenues and, by encouraging food imports, stimulate the export of languishing manufactures – and proposed to replace the sliding scale of corn duties by a fixed duty of 8s per quarter.

In that year's elections, the Corn Laws were almost the only issue in the agricultural counties and the northern towns. Lord John Russell told the Queen that the towns of Lancashire, Cheshire, and the West Riding were 'roused to strong excitement by the prospet of a reduction of the duty on corn'.[28] At Preston the people were 'perfectly wild in favour of the Cheap Bread cry, which has to a great extent restored their confidence in Ministers'.[29] The Conservative leaders looked with favour on the electoral advantages to be won from the Corn Law issue.

> In E. Cumberland [Graham wrote to Bonham in 1839] the Yeomen, who opposed me at the last Election, are in the field and active in getting up Petitions to both Houses against any Change whatever in the existing tariff law. I have advised the Conservatives, when our Opponents are well committed to this Petition, cordially to adopt it, and to act in perfect concert on this Subject without reference to past differences. *Here* at last I think we may turn the Anti-Corn Law Movement to a good account. I am afraid in the Towns, where manufactures are carried on, it will tell against us: in towns connected with rural Districts it should operate in our favour: and at present in the purely manufacturing Towns we have not much to lose.[30]

Graham's confidence was well placed. In 1841 the *Bucks Herald* declared that 'the great struggle of the General Election will arise from the question, of whether the Agriculturalists of the Empire shall or shall not retain that protection which is virtually necessary to their existence as land owners, farmers, and labourers'. The Conservatives won the three Buckinghamshire county seats and both Aylesbury and Buckingham, where the Corn Law issue forced the Liberal candidates to retire before the poll.[31] At the small borough of Horsham, in Sussex, there was a startling result. For the first time since the Reform Act the Conservatives put up a candidate, Robert Scarlett. He raised the Corn Law issue and forced the sitting Radical member, Robert Hurst, who had beaten the Whig candidate at three successive elections, to withdraw from the contest.[32] That the Corn Laws had become a clear party issue was demonstrated in south-east Wales, which returned nine Conservative protectionists and three Liberal free traders,[33] and also at Lincolnshire North. There protectionist associations had been active since 1833. At the 1835 elections the associations contained both Whigs and Conservatives. By 1841 the number of farmers who plumped for the Conservative candidate, the arch-Protectionist, Robert Christopher, showed that they were now 'willing to accept the party of Sir Robert Peel as the political friend of agriculture'.[34] The prominence of the tariff issue at the 1841 elections may, even so, have kept down the Conservative majority. By then agricultural opinion was firmly Conservative. The free-trade scare could bring the Conservative party few new county seats. The Liberal Whip, Edward Ellice, believed, on the contrary, that by taking up the fixed duty Russell stemmed the Conservative tide and saved the Liberals about thirty-five borough seats.[35]

The parliamentary Liberal party was drawn almost as heavily from the landed interest as the Conservatives.[36] But in 1841 it was not the party of the land. It was also, like the Conservatives, composed almost entirely of Anglicans. But in 1841 it was not the party of the Church. Religion appears to have been the most consistent determinant of voting behaviour in the nineteenth century, at least before 1880. 'The sort of political consciousness manifested in Victorian elections was more obviously religious than economic in origin.'[37] In the 1830s Church-and-King Conservatism was the bulwark against the Dissenting (excluding the conservative Wesleyan Methodists) and Irish Catholic allies of the Whigs. Dissenters were displeased by the slow pace of Liberal legislation in their favour, particularly on Church rates and the Church's control of education and marriage services, but they were not wooed by the olive branch which Peel extended to them in the Tamworth Manifesto. The *Eclectic Review* called Peel's promise to abolish Church rates and the Church's monopoly of marriage a trick to cajole the Dissenters and divide them at the elections. At a large meeting early in 1835 the Dissenting deputies resolved that 'this deputation cannot but record its total want of reliance on the granting of any effectual relief to Dissenters by a political party which has ever been opposed to affording to that ... body their just and equal rights'.[38] Their distrust was reasonable. Although Peel was willing to relieve the Dissenters of irritating civil disabilities, he wished the Church to remain the moral tutor of the state by continuing to have a monopoly of education.

Education is the great question to which the public attention should be called [he wrote to Croker in 1837]. We are to have agitation on that now. It was tried on Church Rates – that failed. It was tried on appropriation of Church Revenue – that failed. One is absolutely abandoned, the other sent to sleep in a Select Committee. Now the trial is to be made with education . . . if there is to be a national system of education, excluding the direct intervention of the National Church . . . there is an end of the Church, and probably an end of any religious feeling at all ultimately.

But, secondly, there is no ground on which the members of the Church, if united (lay and clerical) can so confidently and successfully defy agitation. They have it in their power to act independently of Sovereigns, Ministers, and Parliaments; to institute a system of education, based on instruction in the doctrines of the Church, which, if worked out with moderation and discretion, shall command much more of public confidence than any Government system founded on a different principle.[39]

The Dissenting deputies were, apparently, right to doubt the sincerity of Peel's promise to abolish Church rates.

At the elections of 1835 and 1837 Conservative candidates everywhere raised the cry of 'the Church in danger', particularly Church rates, and after the 1837 elections Lord Melbourne, talking of the Whig losses to John Hobhouse, 'evinced no despondency, but remarked that the Church had been too much for us'.[40] By 1837 the great force of Anglican discontent was directed, not so much against the Dissenters, as against the Irish Catholics, whose seventy-odd representatives, the Irish Brigade led by O'Connell, were the indispensable buttress of Whig governments from 1835 to 1841. Francis Baring placed O'Connell at the centre of the 1837 elections.

The elections have run queerly – not unexpectedly to me. I certainly thought it possible that the new reign might have given rise to a little enthusiasm; but as soon as it was clear that there was nothing of the kind and that it would be a regular tug of principle between the two parties, I did not expect much difference. We have gained everywhere excepting in the English counties; there we have been beaten handsomely, partly owing to bad management, over confidence, and suchlike things, but principally because squires and clergy are dead against us, and the county voters are under the sway of the 'Church in danger' cry . . . we may talk of intimidation, small causes, etc., the real truth is that the great body of the *English* people have been, and are, against anything like liberal government in Ireland. Everything which I should call liberal, and even you call liberal, in Ireland has always been done against the feeling of the mass of the people in England proper, whether Tories or Whigs; and O'Connell and the 'Church in danger' have been the cause of our being beaten in England.[41]

Conservatives agreed. 'Our great force has been Protestantism,' wrote Lord Ashley in 1841; 'we began the re-action with it; every step of success has been founded on it.[42] Ashley was a fanatical, evangelical bigot. Sir James Graham was not. But he was willing to use Protestant fervour to beat the Liberals.

Protestantism is the only weapon with which we can encounter Republicanism: and we have the Staff in our hand and we must lay about us, wielding the Church

both in Scotland and in England against O'Connell and his Tail: and as in London
he is the strength of the Government, so here we must make him their Bane.[43]

Peel, too, acknowledged after the 1841 elections that the Irish issue
was a major cause of the Liberals' downfall.[44]

In the constituencies there were calls for the repeal of Catholic emancipation
and for an end to the parliamentary grant to the Catholic seminary at
Maynooth, described by one provincial Conservative newspaper as 'that
infamous nest of Bigotry, Superstition, and Intolerance'.[45] The party leadership
was disturbed by the scurrilous anti-Catholic propaganda which emanated
from the Conservatives' only evening London newspaper, the *Standard*,[46] but
the language used by Croker in the *Quarterly Review*, the organ of intellectual
Conservatism, was not refined. Croker advanced the feeble argument that it
was not, as the Irish Radicals, the Irish Poor Law Commissioners, and other
less radical observers believed, the system of land tenure and the absence of
manufacturing which were accountable for Ireland's economic and social
distress. It was the Catholic faith, now 'soured into superstition'.[47] *The Times*
took the more respectable line that the Church in Ireland was the only bond
between the two nations, the only guarantee of imperial unity, then
threatened by O'Connell's campaign for the repeal of the Union.[48] It took no
notice that by the Lichfield Compact of 1835 O'Connell called off his repeal
campaign in return for Whig assurances of fair government in Ireland.

The geography of the Conservative majority in 1841 was in keeping with
Conservative opinions. Peel's party drew its strength from England, not
Scotland or Ireland, and from the agricultural counties and smaller boroughs,
not the centres of dense population and manufacturing. Fremantle gave the
Conservatives 367 seats after the 1841 elections, the opposition 289, making a
Conservative majority of seventy-eight.[49] That majority came from England
and Wales, where the Conservatives won 302 seats to the Liberals' 196. In
Scotland the Conservatives were in a minority of nine, in Ireland, for obvious
reasons,[50] a minority of nineteen. That English bias of Conservatism had
already been shown by the fact that fifty-four of the fifty-eight Liberals who
had crossed the floor of the Commons in the 1830s sat for English seats.[51]
More specifically, the Conservative majority came from the English and
Welsh counties, in which the Conservative advantage was 137 seats to 22; all
but five of the county seats in the agricultural section of the country south of
the Trent were won by Conservatives. In Scotland the Conservatives held
twenty of the thirty county seats. Only in Ireland, where the votes of the
Catholic freeholders could not be overcome, did the Conservatives have a
minority of the county representation.

Conservatives could therefore be thankful that the Reform Act had not
distributed representation according to population. Had it done so, England's
share of seats, on the basis of the 1841 census, would have been reduced from
500 to 392, while Scotland's would have been raised from fifty-three to fifty-
nine and Ireland's from 105 to 207. It is an obvious, but seldom remarked, fact

that the Conservative victory in 1841 rested on a system in which an English member represented 32,000 persons, a Scottish member, 48,000 and an Irish member, 81,000. The Conservatives drew further benefit from the same imbalance between large and small boroughs. England returned 323 borough members, but only thirty-three of them sat for the sixteen largest boroughs which contained half of the country's borough population. Conservatives won only seven of those seats.

In the boroughs Conservative strength lay largely in the small rural towns, especially in the South and West, whose electorates were smaller than 1,000. They were the 'controlled' boroughs, most of which, so Joseph Parkes claimed, the Liberal managers left 'entirely to the Tories'.[52] It is true that in 1841 there were forty-four Conservatives returned from the larger boroughs, so that in a narrow sense 'urban Conservatism was necessary to give landed Toryism its parliamentary majority'.[53] Even so, the Conservatives' appeal lay more in the older, settled, commercial centres like the City of London, Westminster, Bristol, Hull, and Liverpool (where the 'Orange' vote was important) than in the industrial towns. Both Whig and Conservative spokesmen agreed that the majority of the commercial and professional classes, especially bankers and lawyers, were Conservative and had been for some time.[54] Professor Vincent has suggested that fragmentary evidence yields the conclusion that the business classes tended to Conservatism in the established provincial capitals, to Liberalism in the market towns and new industrial centres. And he puts forward as a possible explanation of that variation that businessmen in places like Bristol and Liverpool were less conscious of being in conflict with the great landowners of the surrounding countryside than were lace manufacturers in Nottingham or cotton manufacturers in Manchester.[55] Whatever the explanation, of the forty-five major manufacturing seats, the Conservatives, even in 1841, won only thirteen, the same number as in 1835. That result varied only very slightly over the period from 1835 to 1865. Peel's alleged middle-class leanings reaped no greater reward in the manufacturing towns than the more aristocratic Conservatism of Lord Derby in the 1850s and 1860s.[56] In 1835, when Peel pointed to Conservative gains at Bristol, Exeter, Hull, Leeds, Liverpool, Northampton, Norwich and Yarmouth as evidence of popular urban support, he conveniently overlooked the fact that all those places, except Leeds, were notorious for their corrupt freemen.[57] The elections at Newcastle upon Tyne in 1836 and 1837 show how the freeman franchise – which the Tories fought hard to retain in 1831–32 – could benefit the Conservatives.[58]

Percentage of votes cast at Newcastle, 1836 and 1837

	1836			1837		
	Con	Lib	Rad	Con	Lib	Rad
Freemen	69	31	–	65	30	5
Ten-pounders	37	63	–	31	65	4

The freemen's votes were expensive. In 1847 the retiring Conservative member for Newcastle, John Hodgson Hinde, said that it would have required £10,000 to unseat him.[59] Without the freemen's support, the Conservatives could not have wrested Newcastle from liberalism's grip on the north-east. There was, it may be said, an element of rough justice in the Conservatives' exploitation of the freeman vote. It was not decisive everywhere,[60] but where it was it helped to redress the imbalance of the reform act in giving 69 per cent of the seats to the boroughs, even though they made up only 44 per cent of the population, an imbalance not entirely offset by the rural nature of many small boroughs.

Conservatism suffered in the towns from the decided Liberal bent of the £10 householders. There was no more solidly Liberal group than the tailors, drapers, and shoemakers, the artisan elite of the working class, who are perhaps better described, in the language of R. S. Neale, as part of the 'middling classes'. In some places their Liberalism may have reflected the influence wielded by the leading manufacturers, as it has been suggested happened at Gateshead, where William Hutt, the unopposed Liberal member from 1841 to 1874, was the town's leading coalowner and where the other large employers in various industries were uniformly Liberal.[61] There is no way of demonstrating that influence returned Hutt. Rochdale, the majority of whose large employers were Conservative,[62] was a Liberal stronghold.

The Conservatism of the wealthy urban 'aristocracy' may, indeed, have hurt the Conservative party electorally. Memory and history worked on the Liberal side, as J. T. Brash wrote of the Scottish boroughs, in which the Conservatives won only two seats in 1841.

> The strength of support for the Whigs in the early 1830s was derived partly from the widespread desire for municipal and parliamentary reform, and partly from opposition to the old Tory cliques in the burghs and their landed allies and patrons. The main cause of opposition to Conservative candidates after 1832 was that they were nominees of those families which had been most closely associated with the old system of burgh politics. . . . A vote in 1837 for the Whig candidate [at Haddington Boroughs], Robert Steuart, may have been a vote for Lord Melbourne and his administration; it was certainly a vote against the Lauderdale interest and all that it stood for past and present.[63]

The Reform Act and municipal reform breathed new life into town politics by releasing the civic energies of shopkeepers and small businessmen who were eager to improve their towns' amenities and who expected no encouragement from the Tories, who had stifled their activities and ignored their abilities.[64] The Municipal Reform Act of 1835 marked the beginning, not the end, of the middle-class challenge to oligarchic town politics. Moreover, in those towns not immediately affected by the Act, reformers began at once to agitate for incorporation. Thus, at places like Manchester and Sheffield, which were not incorporated until 1838 and 1843 respectively, Liberalism derived strength from the reformers' fight to win control of town government. The traditional Conservative interest, lodged in the surrounding countryside or, if living in the town, allied by trade with rural Conservatives, was remote from popular, improving local politics. Conservatives in Rochdale were the 'pillars of pre-1832 society, still impressive, but in a backwater from the main life of the town'.[65] At Oldham, the small citadel of seventy wealthy families, including coalowners and hatters whose business interests promoted close ties with the county gentry, has been described as 'sealed off by their economic function and concomitant capital from the petty bourgeoisie and the population as a whole'.[66] The same is true of Wales, where the dissenting chapels became the centres of Liberal organization against what was viewed as an hostile landowning Conservatism.[67] That popular basis of town Liberalism, which, it is worth noticing, does not fit neatly into a Liberal/free trade, Conservative/protection framework, was undoubtedly reinforced by expressions of Conservative hostility to middle-class aspirations. In 1834, for example, *Blackwood's* lamented that Peel and Wellington had not tried to defuse the parliamentary reform agitation in the late 1820s by enfranchising the wealthy tip of the manufacturing interest, the owners of houses rated at £50 annually.

> It is a remarkable, but well-ascertained fact, that the Conservative party is nowhere so strong as in the higher classes of the great manufacturing towns. It is more powerful in that description of persons at Glasgow, Manchester, Liverpool, and Birmingham, than either in London, Dublin, or Edinburgh. The reason is, that the richer and more opulent classes in these great commercial districts are more immediately brought in contact with the working classes of the community; the terrible dangers of democratic ascendancy are more forcibly brought before their eyes.[68]

Conservatism, then, even under the moderate leadership of Peel, was handicapped in the large boroughs by its historic and still prevailing association with the Church of England and the landed interest, and with indifference to and ignorance of the life of manufacturing. The geographical divide between Conservatives and Liberals, leaving Ireland aside, was the Trent, neither a broad nor a deep river, and one often crossed by both parties. The social divide was more impassable. It lay, again leaving Ireland aside, between the Church of England and Protestant nonconformity. The Conservatives' greatest electoral weakness (although, of course, it is but the other side of their greatest strength) was Dissent's impressive loyalty to Liberalism, especially its Radical side. Whether a Dissenting shoemaker was a Liberal because he was a shoemaker or because he was a Dissenter, whether indeed the question even makes sense, are matters too complicated to be disentangled here. What happens to be so is that Dissent flourished, as it always had, in the towns; that it was the religion of a majority of those £10 householders to whom the political world was opened in 1832; and that the evidence for Dissent's support of Liberalism is clearer than the evidence for the party affiliation of any economic group.

In the wake of the 1832 elections, the Duke of Wellington singled out the Dissenters as Conservatism's most active adversaries.

I have compared notes with others, and I think that all agree in the same story. The revolution is made, that is to say, that power is transferred from one class of society, the gentlemen of England, professing the faith of the Church of England, to another class of society, the shopkeepers, being dissenters from the Church, many of them Socinians, others atheists . . .

. . . a new democratic influence has been introduced into elections, the copy-holders and free-holders and leaseholders residing in towns which do not themselves return members to Parliament. These are all dissenters from the Church, and are everywhere a formidably active party against the aristocratic influence of the Landed Gentry. But this is not all. There are dissenters in every village in the country; they are the blacksmith, the carpenter, the mason, etc., etc.[69]

The Duke's view was exaggerated. The agricultural interest was not swamped in the counties. By 1841 it had returned, almost completely, to the Conservative party. But the Duke was not wrong about Dissent. The table below gives a religious breakdown of the vote at three borough elections in the 1830s.[70]

Religion and party at three boroughs, 1832–37

		Dissenters	Anglicans
Leicester,	C	93	811
general election, 1832	L	1,024	125
Devizes,	C	13	144
by-election, 1835	L	110	35
Christchurch,	C	8	108
general election, 1837	L	61	44

That striking correlation between religion and party occurs also in Professor Vincent's tabulation of the behaviour of Dissenting ministers in twenty-eight constituencies at various elections between 1830 and 1847: they cast 362 Liberal votes against only 21 for Conservative candidates.[71] Surprisingly, even the Wesleyan Methodists, presumably goaded by the agitation against Church rates, appear to have overcome their tradition of political quietism, their antipathy to Roman Catholicism, and the Conservative injunctions of their Conference leader, Jabez Bunting, to vote heavily Liberal in 1841.[72]

In many English constituencies Dissenters were the force behind Liberal victories.[73] In Scotland the alliance of Dissent, the £10 franchise, and Liberalism produced what one Scottish Conservative, Alexander Pringle, called 'a complete revolution in the Government'.[74] The upper classes in Scotland were overwhelmingly Conservative, the lairds increasingly isolated from the social life and reformist ferment in the country after 1832. The Conservative hold on the Scottish counties was dented by the £10 occupant-owner and leaseholder franchise introduced into the counties by the Scottish Reform Act. (The Melville interest was quick to exploit the weaknesses in the act by buying up property to create faggot votes, but the Whigs were soon just as greedily fraudulent.)[75] From Perthshire, Ayrshire, Edinburgh-shire (Midlothian) and Fifeshire, Peel received explanations of Conservative defeats, all of them put down to the swamping of the county constituencies by £10 Dissenters.[76] By the late 1830s Conservative fortunes were wrapped up in the Church patronage question, or the Veto controversy, a kind of Scottish mutation of the Oxford Movement's anti-erastianism, but far stronger, rooted in the populace and, unlike the Oxford Movement, led by the Evangelical wing of the Presbyterian Kirk.

In 1834 the General Assembly of the Kirk passed a Veto Act, which transferred the power of vetoing the nomination of ministers from the presbytery to the male heads of congregations. Four years later, after a series of legal wrangles, the Act was overruled by the House of Lords. The 'Scotch seceders', as they were known even before their final break with the state Kirk in 1843, were anti-intellectual in their theology and popular in their Church politics. Neither the Scottish aristocracy nor the Conservative leadership in England sympathized with their aims. As Graham wrote in 1839, the lower classes were flushed to make common cause with the seceders, while the aristocracy and a large majority of the gentry were ready to resist the encroachments of ecclesiastical democracy.

> This secession from the Establishment will be union with the Voluntaries; from thence to Chartism there is but one step; and history reminds us of the fatal effects of the combination of such combustible materials as Scotch dissent and Scotch republicanism . . . if no accommodation of this unhappy difference be possible, Scotland will be torn asunder by a religious strife . . . and as relates to the Conservative Party in Scotland, this quarrel, if protracted, will be fatal. The controversy has now assumed so angry an aspect, that I have little hope of any reasonable adjustment.[77]

Lord Aberdeen's attempt to settle the dispute in 1840 failed. His Bill did not, at any rate, recognise the principle of the popular veto. The Kirk was the Scottish equivalent of the Established Church. It was impossible for Conservatives to sanction what was, in effect, a separation of Church and State. Peel's rebuff of a deputation of seceders in June 1841 was, according to Sir Thomas Cochrane, the Conservative candidate at Greenock, 'playing the devil here and in Renfrew, and will do the same in all parts of Scotland, it being a tool in the hands of the Radicals'.[78] Cochrane attributed his defeat at Greenock to the veto controversy; but his was the best Conservative showing there at any election between the first and second Reform Acts. The Scottish boroughs were beyond Conservative hopes. At the 1841 elections in Scotland the Conservatives made a net gain of three seats. The veto question may have, as Graham had predicted, counteracted the Conservative advantage to be won from the Whig government's refusal to grant money for Church extension, but there is no basis for Arbuthnot's calculation that, in combination with Catholic intimidation in Ireland, it cost the Conservatives a majority of 100.[79] What the veto controversy did accomplish, not only for the 1841 elections, but for the future as well, was to apply fresh cement to the alliance between Dissent and Liberalism in Scotland.

Tory Radicalism

The representation of the Conservative party in the 1830s would be incomplete if it left out the movement which went by the name of Tory Radicalism. It was a movement remote from the concerns of Peel and the party leadership and negligible in its contribution to the Conservative revival after 1832. Yet it was, in a partial manner, expressive of the historic Conservative claim to be a national party, operating at the behest of no sectional interest. In 1975, just before his bid to retain the leadership of the Conservative party ended in defeat, Edward Heath published a statement of his political creed, a statement which laid primary stress on the pursuit of social harmony and the balancing of competing interests.

> The historic role of the Conservative party is to use the leverage of its political and diplomatic skills to create a fresh balance between the different elements within the state at those times, when, for one reason or another, their imbalance threatens to disrupt the orderly development of society.[80]

In the early nineteenth century the greatest apparent obstacle to the progress of the nation was the conflict between town and countryside, between agriculture and manufacturing. Conservative principle, the desire to reconcile conflicting elements of society, informed Lord Grey's Reform Bill in 1831 and Peel's repeal of the Corn Laws in 1846. To others, however, it appeared that the critical imbalance was between capital and labour, or between the employed and the employing. Some Conservatives attempted to direct Conservatism to the redress of working-class grievances.

In the first half of the nineteenth century the interaction of the industrial and agricultural revolutions, the rapid increase in population, and the *laissez-faire* injunctions of the political economists, whatever lasting benefits it may have brought, produced pockets of extreme poverty and dislocated traditional patterns of living.[81] The result was a great protest movement, beginning in 1831 as a campaign to secure a statutory ten-hour day for the cotton operatives, shifting in the mid-thirties to an agitation against the Whigs' Poor Law of 1834, and swelling, as the 'Hungry Forties' began in 1838, into the radical movement for the Charter. None of those campaigns achieved a parliamentary success (until the Factory Act of 1847). But what parliamentary support they did receive came more from the Conservatives than from the Whigs or the Radicals. The table below gives the anti-Poor Law vote in four divisions between 1838 and 1841.[82]

Party breakdown of anti-Poor Law votes in the House of Commons

	Total in favour	Con	Lib and Rad
Repeal of the Poor Law, 20 February 1838	19	13	6
Extension of outdoor relief, 29 July 1839	49	30	19
Abolition of commissioners' legislative powers, 25 March 1841	77	53	24
Opposition to five-year renewal of the Poor Law, 22 March 1841	137	101	36

A few Conservatives also voted for one of the most radical proposals of the decade, John Maxwell's motion to enact a minimum wage for the handloom weavers, to whom the competition of the power loom had brought severe distress. Maxwell's motion was debated twice, gaining eighteen Conservative votes in 1835 and twenty-six in 1837. On the second occasion Conservative votes accounted for two-thirds of the minority in favour, including three party managers, Granville Somerset, Charles Ross, and Frederick Shaw.

Outside parliament Tory Radicalism was a larger movement. The Conservative press, in London and in the north, was overwhelmingly against the Poor Law, and the national leadership of both the Ten-Hours and the anti-Poor Law campaigns drew heavily on the passionate oratory of Tory Evangelicals like Richard Oastler, 'Parson' Bull, Michael Sadler, and Joseph Stephens. Religion fired their passion, but Professor Kitson Clark gave insufficient weight to the attraction of humanitarian, paternalist Toryism for Evangelicals when he described Oastler and his companions as Evangelicals who *happened* to be Tories.[83] Evangelicalism sprang naturally from within the Established Church, with its national curacy of the souls of the poor, and its natural political home was therefore Toryism.

Tory Radicalism was nevertheless a small and discordant element of Peelite Conservatism. In the House of Commons there were more Conservative than Liberal opponents of the Poor Law; they were still very few. Tories dominated the national leadership of the Ten-Hours and anti-Poor Law movements, but at the regional and local levels they were far less prominent.[84] In the constituencies the prevailing Conservative attitude to the working classes found its expression in the hundreds of Operative Conservative Associations which were started throughout the country, especially the West Midlands and the North, in the years 1835 to 1837. They had no connection with Tory Radicalism. They were established to counteract Radical propaganda by appealing to the constitutional and religious conservatism of the politically illiterate. The three objectives of the Stockport association, listed by the chairman in his inaugural address, were the standard ones of constitutional Conservatism: the defence of the Church, the Crown, and the House of Lords. Neither industrial questions nor the Poor Law was mentioned.[85] The Blackburn association was formed, in the words of its secretary, 'to give the working classes an opportunity of learning the incomparable fitness of the Constitution in Church and State to insure the spiritual and secular welfare of all grades of the community'.[86] Most of the societies had reading rooms, stocked with Conservative newspapers and high Tory journals like *Blackwood's* and *Fraser's Magazine*. In his history of the Operative Societies, published in 1838, N. Paul listed a number of advantages which Conservatism offered to the operatives; the maintenance of the constitution, the reduction of taxes and government salaries, and the resistance to the wages-lowering anti-Corn Law League. Only once did he refer to the Poor Law or factory reform, and then obliquely, in an attack on the Whigs.

> As Overseers [of the poor] ... they exercise their power in most hard-hearted and cruel manner and trample upon those common sympathies which adorn and elevate the human character. And, as Masters, they are almost proverbial for their *total* and *entire* disregard of the happiness and comfort of those under their care.[87]

That was the tone of Tory Radicalism. But Paul made no specific link between Conservatism and the practical demands of the workers.

Tory Radicalism had roots deep in the paternalist traditions of landed society, with its concern to protect the poor and its belief in the moral economy of the 'just price'. It was Tory county magistrates who, at the end of the eighteenth century, had developed the Speenhamland system of making up labourers' wages, according to the price of bread and the size of a man's family, out of the county rate. It was a Tory Chief Justice, Lord Kenyon, who, in the famine year of 1795, the year when the Speenhamland system was introduced, reminded county magistrates that, although most of the acts against forestalling and regrating had been repealed, they remained offences at common law. And it was Tory magistrates who connived at bread riots, not riots really, but organized takeovers of markets from the regraters in order to sell grain at the customary and just price.[88] In the 1830s the county magistrates and the landed circles from which they were drawn were still the heart of the Conservative party. Why, then, did Tory Radicalism evoke so tepid a response in the party? The answer lies in several directions. Tory Radicalism ran against the economic orthodoxy of the day, it involved Conservatives in cooperation with unpalatable allies, and it promised no electoral return. And in the specific instance of the Poor Law it ran against the economic interest of the Conservative party's agriculturalist supporters.

By the 1830s the *laissez-faire* notions of the political economists had seeped into the minds of the administrative class, including the front benches of both political parties. Economic liberalism had been the creed of Pitt and during the first three decades of the nineteenth century it made substantial inroads on the Tory party. Tory governments and Tory parliaments presided over the destruction of the last remnants of the moral economy in the years before Waterloo. Protective legislation in crafts and industry was repealed and the common law enforcement of a minimum wage faded away. Then in the 1820s liberal Toryism took its first steps towards free trade and repealed the Spitalfields Acts and the Combination Acts. If in the 1830s Peel and the bulk of his party were unwilling to look backward to a 'golden past' or forward to centralized control of manufacturing, it was not because they lacked imagination or sympathy. Peel had succumbed to the argument that the increase of the country's wealth depended on freeing industry from the shackles which constrained it. It must be remembered that in doing so he, and his followers, were taking up *Radical* arguments, listening to the advice of men like Bentham and Francis Place. In opposing the factory reformers and upholding the Poor Law, they were not behaving as reactionaries; they were proving their liberalism. Tory Radicalism appeared to beckon them to turn back on the progress that had been made in turning the old Tory party, excessively attentive to the views of hierarchical, agricultural society, into a modern Conservative party, alive to the needs of industry. For Peel the danger to social harmony came principally from the division, electoral, emotional, and commercial, between town and country, between cotton factory and wheat field. In the 1830s he was not yet contemplating sacrificing the Corn Laws (at least there is no evidence that he was); but neither was he prepared to jeopardize the expansion of industrial production by regulating workers' hours and wages. Peel was not, it needs to be remarked, thereby exhibiting a want either of sympathy with the working classes or of concern for their standard of living. He was arguing for what has ever since been an important contention of capitalist apologists and Conservatives: that the surest method of raising the standard of living of all classes is to allow industry the freedom to expand.[89] The free-market nostrums of the political economists may have been misguided – there were handloom weavers and woollen croppers advancing an under-consumption explanation of capitalist crisis[90] – but to side with the economic experts of the time was not to be stubborn; it was to be progressive.

Factory reform challenged the free market orthodoxy directly. The anti-Poor Law movement did so less obviously and it had more appeal for Conservatives. The revolutionary structure of elected Poor Law boards and central commissioners struck at the traditional authority of the landed gentry and the justices of the peace. The new Poor Law not only reduced the level and availability of poor relief and forced the break-up of families sent to sexually segregated workhouses; it also threatened the deferential structure of rural society and the practical autonomy of parish administration. The supporters of the Poor Law accepted innovation in response to the pressure of social change. Tory opposition to the new law had a genuinely and profoundly conservative basis. It was rooted in a preference for the historic role of local self-government and it was expressed in language evocative of the past. It took its stand on the higher morality and utility of power exercised within and by small communities over power exercised by central organs of the state. The social ideals of the anti-Poor Law Tories (and also some Liberals), with their emphasis on preserving closely-knit communities and utilising parish officials' intimate knowledge and humane understanding of the lives of the poor, have recently been described as 'the ideals of a pre-industrial culture in which the political structure is dominated by upper-class leadership and in which social tensions are resolved by upper-class paternalism'.[91]

Yet in the Conservative-dominated rural south the anti-Poor Law movement never came to life. The explanation may be economic self-interest. Since 1785 the poor rate, with a slight downward turn in the 1820s, had risen sharply. And although the contribution of the Speenhamland, or allowance, system to the rising cost of poor relief and the mounting surplus of agricultural labour has been questioned by modern scholars,[92] Peel and most politicians of the 1830s believed that the system had encouraged pauperism and created an artificial labour surplus, for which evils the new Poor Law was a harsh, but necessary, remedy. Landowners might have been willing to maintain an expensive form of poor relief if it had brought social stability, but that was a conclusion difficult to sustain in the wake of the agricultural riots of 1830. Captain Swing doomed the old Poor Law. By the latter 1830s landowners, although they might object to some features of the new law, were gratified to see that it seemed to be accomplishing its purposes of reducing the poor rate and raising agricultural wages. For that reason alone it would have been impossible for a party which depended upon the support of the agricultural interest to attach itself to a campaign to repeal the new Poor Law.

It was in the north that the anti-Poor Law movement caught fire. Designed to eradicate an 'artificial' rural pauperism, the new law was ill-suited to cope with the cyclical unemployment of an industrial economy. The winter of 1837–38, when the new law was taken into the north, was the high point of Tory Radicalism. Conservatives, including members of parliament, attended protest meetings in great numbers and joined in the harassment of Alfred Power, the assistant commissioner sent to prepare the way for the introduction of the new system in the north.[93] But Conservative enthusiasm soon waned. The 1837 elections to the boards of guardians responsible for administering the Poor Law revealed that anti-Poor Law sentiment was not powerful enough to break down traditional political loyalties. Only at Huddersfield was there effective cooperation between Tories and Radicals. Elsewhere the voting followed the national pattern: Liberal candidates polled heavily in the towns and were massively supported by Dissent, while Conservative candidates drew most of their support from rural districts and the Established Church.[94] On that evidence it was apparent that Tory Radicalism would not strengthen urban Conservatism at parliamentary elections. Then, as the movement gathered force, the Radicals began to disobey the law, refusing to implement the Registration Act of 1836 (a subsidiary activity charged to the Poor Law guardians for reasons of administrative convenience)[95] and encouraging the non-payment of rates. It was difficult for Conservatives to consort with a movement which in 1837–38 produced riots at Bradford, Oldham, Rochdale, Todmorden, and Hudders-field. By the end of the decade the anti-Poor Law campaign had become submerged in the radical demand for the Charter. Conservative support drifted away. The initial premise of the Tory Radicals, that the landed gentry were the natural allies of the working man against the factory owner and against the central state, was too narrow to sustain Chartism, with its demand for manhood suffrage, backed by mumbled threats of physical force.

It was the franchise question which exposed the inherent weakness of Tory Radicalism. Either a working-class alliance had to be cemented by Conservative approval of franchise reform or else Tory Radicalism had to remain a movement of no electoral significance. There was, it is true, some evidence that by 'exclusive dealing' (that is the boycotting of shopkeepers who voted the wrong way) the unfranchised could influence parliamentary elections.[96] But exclusive dealing was too spasmodic and too unpredictable to enter seriously into Conservative calculations, and where it had been effective in 1835 and 1837, it had been directed against Conservative candidates.[97] It made much better sense to attend to the views of the manufacturers and tradesmen. The bulk of the working-class Conservative vote came from the freemen, who were a steadily declining section of the electorate, since most of them were men to whom the 1832 Reform Act had extended the franchise merely for the duration of their lives.[98]

The Conservative party, of course, had no intention of widening the franchise and no motive to do so. There were instances of Chartist support for Conservative candidates at the 1841 elections, fostered by Chartist suspicions of the anti-Corn Law League's covert desire to reduce wages.[99] But Chartist backing did not guarantee Conservative candidates the working-class vote. At Northampton the Tory-Chartist candidate received only 40 of the 400 shoemakers' votes; one of the most notorious sweated trades remained solidly Liberal.[100] At Bath the two Conservative members who had been let in by Whig–Radical dissension in 1837 were ousted in 1841 by a Liberal–Chartist alliance.[101] And at the Sunderland by-election of 1841 the Conservative candidate, despite his opposition to the Poor Law and his protectionist attacks on the advanced free-trade opinions of his Liberal opponent, Lord Howick, did not attempt to gain Chartist favour. Instead, he tried to bribe a Chartist into standing in order to split the Liberal vote.[102]

Tory Radicalism, then, however appealing it was to the humanitarian, anti-capitalist, and anti-centralist strain in early Conservatism, came up against electoral realities. In certain constituencies popular feeling, especially where it took the form of Radical disenchantment with the Whigs, provided a temporary inducement to Tory–Radical cooperation. But a middle-class limit to the electorate made nonsense of a lasting Tory alliance with the working class.

Tory Radicalism was never an organized section of the parliamentary party. Nor did it rest on a coherent political or social philosophy able to meet the requirements of contemporary society. Humanitarian sentiment helped to feed the Ten Hours movement, but the principal Tory objection to the new Poor Law was its threatened destruction of parish administration. If humanitarianism had been the source of the objection, it ought to have produced Tory support for the Public Health Bill of 1848. Lord Ashley, indeed, recognized that public health was 'essentially a working man's question', affecting 'his capacity to eat and sleep in comfort, to go abroad, and to gain a livelihood'.[103] Yet while 88 per cent of the free-trade Peelites voted for the Public Health Bill, 56 per cent of the Protectionists voted against it, opposing its centralizing features, as many of them had the Poor Law's, 'by a kind of historical arcadianism, which used legal, constitutional and historical arguments to establish the legitimacy of institutions of local government by relating them to the ancient Anglo-Saxon constitution and the Common Law tradition'.[104] The common strand in Tory/Protectionist attitudes to factory reform, poor relief, and public health was, despite the significance of Ten Hours legislation for the future, the apprehension felt by defenders of a rural society under siege. As a distinct movement Tory Radicalism was a spent force by 1841, apart from the transient appearance of it effete offspring, Disraeli's 'Young England' coterie, in the early 1840s. The attitudes and emotions which gave rise to the movement, however, continued to exercise a divisive influence on the Conservative backbenches after 1841. They reinforced the anti-manufacturing bias of agricultural Conservatism, which, together with Protestant anti-Irish sentiment, was to undermine Peel's effort to make the nationalist, Anglican and predominantly rural majority which placed him in office in 1841 an efficient and reliable instrument of his brand of Conservative government.

Notes and References

Opinion and the Conservative majority of 1841

1 Walter to Sir James [Scarlett], 10 Dec, 1834: Peel MSS, Add. MSS 40505, ff. 24–5.
2 R. Williams to Peel, Jan, 1835: *ibid*, Add. MSS 40411, ff. 1–2.
3 Pringle to Peel, 19 Jan, 1835: *ibid*, Add. MSS 40410, ff. 269–72.
4 H. J. Hanham, for example, wrote in 1968 that 'county politics were relatively uninteresting before 1885, because the result depended so much on the existence of an organization capable of bringing very large numbers of voters to the polls' and that 'the chief sphere of political conflict in the country was in the boroughs' (Hanham, *Reformed Electoral System*, 14).
5 Wood to F. Baring, 22 July 1841: Baring, *Journals and Correspondence*, i, 181; See also Lord Sydenham to Lord Fitzharris, 13 July 1841: 'Of course *you* will get all the counties, we all the great towns, and the small boroughs will be anybody's money' (Malmesbury, *Memoirs of an Ex-Minister*, i, 134–5).
6 Vincent, *The Formation of the Liberal Party, 1857–1868*, xxv.
7 Seymour, *Electoral Reform in England and Wales*, 78–9.
8 Close, 'Elections of 1835 and 1837', 134–5.
9 Davis, *Political Change and Continuity*, 126.
10 Olney, *Lincolnshire Politics*, 236–7.
11 Dr Clarke, for instance, agrees that 'in England evictions for political reasons were rare'; but he sees no difference between deference and landlord control: 'Thus there was no effective challenge to deferential politics in the English countryside before the Third Reform Act 1884; but with the enfranchisement of the agricultural labourers, the old style of landlord control broke down.' (Clarke, 'Electoral sociology of modern Britain', *History*, Feb, 1972, 38–9.)
12 Davis, 'The Whigs and the idea of electoral deference: some further thoughts on the great Reform Act', *Durham University Journal*, Dec, 1974, 79–91.
13 Prest, *Russell*, 118.
14 Spring, 'Chandos and the farmers', *passim*.
15 Davis, 'Whigs and . . . electoral deference', 85.
16 Nossiter, 'Aspects of electoral behaviour in English constituencies, 1832–1868', in *Mass Politics*, ed. Allard and Rokkan, 165.
17 The figures for the Conservative share of the poll are given by Nossiter (*ibid*, 181: percentages): one-member boroughs, 48.5 in 1832, 47.8 in 1841; two-member medium boroughs (under 1,000 voters), 36 in 1832, 48.8 in 1841; two-member large boroughs, 31 in 1832, 46 in 1841.
18 Diary entry, 23 July 1841: Baring, *Journals and Correspondence*, i, 179–80.

19 Croker to Peel, 20 July 1841: Parker, *Peel*, ii, 475.
20 Gash, *Reaction and Reconstruction*, 130.
21 Kebbel, *History of Toryism from 1783 to 1881*, 262.
22 It was believed by several Conservatives that the party would have fared better even than it did at the 1835 elections if those elections had taken place a few months later, by which time the public reaction against Wellington's temporary premiership would have been dissipated by the evidence that Peel meant to govern in the spirit of the Tamworth Manifesto. When Peel took over from Wellington, electoral arrangements for an early dissolution were already begun. (Gladstone memoranda, 8 April and 25 July [1835], and 6 Feb, and 25 Oct, [1836]: *Memoranda*, 47–9, 52, 66–7, 73–5; Wellington to Peel, 15 Nov, 1834: Peel, *Memoirs*, ii, 18–20; Kitson Clark, *Peel and the Conservative Party*, 198.)
23 Lindsay and Harrington, *The Conservative Party, 1918–1970*, 7.
24 Nossiter, 'Electoral sociology', 181.
25 See Appendix 8.
26 Mrs Arbuthnot, *Journal*, 23 Oct, 1831, ii, 432–3.
27 See Davis, *Political Change and Continuity*, 120–6; Olney, *Lincolnshire Politics*, 103–8; Close, 'Elections of 1835 and 1837', 71; Kent, 'Staffordshire politics', chapter 2. In his *Reaction and Reconstruction in English politics* (p. 131) Professor Gash called the Conservative party 'a constitutional and religious party, not a social and economic party'; his views had changed, wrongly I think, from the time when, in *Politics in the Age of Peel* (p. 276), he had described Thomas Duffield, the member for Abingdon, as 'an ordinary tory county member, more stirred by agricultural topics than anything else'.
28 Russell to Queen Victoria, 16 July 1841: Victoria, *Letters*, i, 277–8.
29 G. Jeeson to Stanley, 28 June 1841: Derby MSS, 3/3. See also Dobson, *History of the Parliamentary Representation of Preston*, 70–1. E. Bradyll informed Stanley that he expected a large Whig majority at Bolton on 'intimidation, bribery & the Corn Law cry' Bradyll to Stanley, 30 June 1841: Derby MSS, 3/3. At Bradford the Liberals made the total repeal of the Corn Laws their main election argument (Wright, 'A radical borough: parliamentary politics in Bradford, 1832–41', *Northern History*, 1969, 146).
30 Graham to Bonham, 27 Jan, 1839: Peel MSS, Add. MSS 40616, ff. 58–9.
31 Davis, *Political Change and Continuity*, 146–7.
32 Albery, *A Parliamentary History of Horsham*, 321.
33 David, 'Political activity in south-east Wales', 152–9.
34 Olney, *Lincolnshire Politics*, 104–6, 111.
35 Prest, *Russell*, 184.
36 The Conservative parliamentary party was only slightly more aristocratic than the Liberals. The 1841 House of Commons contained 127 Irish peers, and sons, nephews, and brothers of peers. Of those, 52 were Liberals and 75 Conservatives, not a large difference proportionately (Fremantle MSS, 110/9).
37 Clarke, 'Electoral sociology', 44; Dr Clarke's conclusion is supported by the research of many scholars. See Vincent, *Liberal Party*, 96–118; Fraser, 'The fruits of Reform: Leeds politics in the eighteen-thirties', *Northern History*, 1972, 89–111; Nossiter, 'Voting behaviour, 1832–1872', *Political Studies*, xviii, 1970, 385.
38 Cowherd, *Politics of Dissent*, 90.

39 Peel to Croker, 12 Nov, 1837: Croker, *Correspondence and Diaries*, ii, 320–1.
40 Broughton, *Recollections*, 10 Aug, 1837, v, 93.
41 Baring to J. L. Mallet, 16 Aug, 1837: Baring, *Journals and Correspondence*, i, 127–8.
42 7th Earl of Shaftesbury, *Diary*, 16 March 1841: Broadlands MSS, SHA/PD/2.
43 Graham to Bonham, Jan, 1839: Peel MSS, Add. MSS 40616, ff. 43–6.
44 Peel, *Speech at Tamworth, July 28, 1841*, 10.
45 *Leicester Conservative Standard*, May 1835. See also the March and April issues, and the *Morning Post*, 13 March 1835, for calls to repeal Catholic emancipation. For candidates' views, see the *Parliamentary Touchstone, passim*, but especially the speech of Sir Francis Burdett, the lifelong Radical turned Conservative, at Westminster: 'England now stands in a position between her foes and her friends . . . domestic foes, whose exertions against her best interests are unwearied and unceasing. She has now to defend herself against Irish priests – against the bigoted, ignorant, and insane Irish papists, guided and governed by the great hired agitator of Ireland, Mr Daniel O'Connell. I object to the return of members who are sent into Parliament to support the administration which is not ashamed to depend for its existence upon the aid of Mr. Daniel O'Connell.' (*Parliamentary Touchstone*, 18–19.)
46 See Fremantle's correspondence with Bonham and Lord Redesdale, Aug. to Nov, 1840: Fremantle MSS, 80/5 and 80/13.
47 *Quarterly Review*, December 1840, 120–3.
48 See *The Times*, 26 Feb, 1836.
49 See Appendix 1.
50 In addition to paying for their anti-Catholicism at the Irish elections, Conservative candidates complained that they suffered from the Irish registration law, which differed from the English in a number of ways. There was no annual revision of the register, there was no appeal against improper additions or against improper rejections by the revising barristers, and there was no public officer appointed to prepare and check the list of claimants. J. D. Larkin claimed that at the Cork election of 1837 'between 100 & 200 dead men were personated on the part of the Radical Candidates, & a still greater number of men who had parted with their lands in respect of which they had been registered, were admitted to the poll' (Larkin to Peel, 28 Sept, 1837: Peel MSS, Add. MSS 40424, ff. 173–9). Emerson Tennent, defeated at Belfast, made the same complaint: 'What chiefly defeated us was the accursed system of imperfect registration involved in the Irish Reform Bill. Although there are not more than 1800 voters entitled to poll nearly 4000 remain upon the face of the registry since 1832, affording the most facile materials for the manufacture of faggot voters. . . . If we cannot get an amended Registration Act for Ireland immediately, no man in his senses will be found to contest a borough against a popish constituency. But with a *bona fide* £10 constituency annually registered no radical could presume to contest Belfast.' (Tennant to Peel, 9 Aug, 1837: *ibid*, ff. 51–3.)
51 The other four were split between Scotland and Ireland, the two Irish converts being members for Belfast, the most English and Protestant of the Irish boroughs.
52 Close, 'Elections of 1835 and 1837', 388.
53 Gash, *Reaction and Reconstruction*, 136.
54 Wellington to Croker, 30 Sept, 1833: Croker, *Correspondence and Diaries*, ii, 216–20; Broughton, *Recollections*, 8 May 1835, v, 36; *Blackwood's*, Feb, 1833, 269

and April 1834, 536.

55 Vincent, *Pollbooks*, 20–3.

56 See Appendix 9.

57 Close, 'Elections of 1835 and 1837', 136–7.

58 This table is from Nossiter, 'Elections and political behaviour', 150.

59 *Ibid*, 151.

60 At Preston, for example, two Liberals were returned in 1841, even though the register had a majority of freemen (Dobson, *History of Parliamentary Representation of Preston*, 63–4).

61 McCord, 'Gateshead politics in the age of Reform', *Northern History*, 1969, 167–83.

62 Vincent, *Liberal Party*, 115n.

63 Brash, 'The Conservatives in the Haddington District of Burghs, 1832–1852', *Trans. East Lothian Antiquarian and Field Naturalists'Society*, 1968, 44–5.

64 The radicalism of the Scottish burghs owes something to the system by which town councils were appointed by a 'superior'. The Duke of Hamilton, the Duke of Gordon, and Lord Douglas were Conservative landowners and respectively superiors for Strathaven, Kirriemuir, and Hundly, neglected towns in which the inhabitants were exposed to bad housing and disease, and in which there was no effective control over the management of burgh property or council money. (Saunders, *Scottish Democracy*, 145–57.

65 Vincent, *Liberal Party*, 112.

66 Foster, *Class Struggle and the Industrial Revolution*, 183.

67 See the work of I. G. Jones listed in the bibliography.

68 *Blackwood's*, April 1834, 536–7.

69 Wellington to Croker, 6 March 1833: Croker, *Correspondence and Diaries*, ii, 205–7.

70 This table is from Close, 'Elections of 1835 and 1837', 141.

71 Vincent, *Pollbooks*, 67–8; Dr Vincent gives no corresponding tables for Anglican ministers, but a table of church organists' voting for the years 1852 to 1872 shows their preference for Conservative candidates by a margin of 44 votes to 6, and one for sextons in the same period shows their Conservative preference by a margin of 24 votes to 4 (*ibid*, 57–8).

72 An excerpt from the *Weslyan Chronicle*, [1841], gave the votes of Methodists in twenty-nine boroughs and seven counties as Liberal, 1,370, and Conservative, 308, with 41 votes split (*ibid*, 69–70). In Lincolnshire, however, while Church rates drew Methodists into Liberalism in the 1830s and 1860s, Methodist Liberals in local Church rate contests appear to have voted Conservative in 1841. 'In parish politics the Church of England might be the enemy, but in national politics the Wesleyan, like the low Churchman, seems to have been more concerned to oppose the Church of Rome' (Olney, *Lincolnshire Politics*, 59–61).

73 See, as examples, Harrison and Trinder, *Drink and Sobriety in an Early Victorian Country Town* Wright, 'A Radical borough', 152–8; Thompson, 'Whigs and Liberals in the West Riding, 1830–1860', *EHR* April 1959, 226–7; Vincent, 'The electoral sociology of Rochdale', *EHR*, Aug, 1963, 31–55. Henry Liddell, the only Conservative returned for a Durham county seat in 1837, was not surprised by the energetic Liberalism of Dissent: 'You are aware that Dissent prevails to a great extent in the North Division of Durham & that . . . simply from the enormous increase of population in the immediate neighbour-

hood of the Collieries, so that districts which a few years back were firmly rural are now covered with a dense population. It is natural that in such localities which the efforts of the Dissenters have contributed to rescue from Heathenism, the population should have become attached to the doctrines of their teachers, natural also that among such a population there should be a strong feeling against Church Rates – a feeling which in many instances has been most temperately & sensibly expressed to me during my Canvas.' (Liddell to Peel, 25 June 1837: Peel MSS, Add. MSS 40423, ff. 282–4.)

74 Pringle to Peel, 19 Jan, 1835: *ibid*, Add. MSS 40410, ff. 269–72. Peel himself doubted 'whether there was a country in which a more complete revolution has ever taken place within two years than that which has taken place in Scotland' (Peel to Goulburn, 24 June 1833: Parker, *Peel*, ii, 222–4). For evidence that, in practice, the reform act failed to work a revolution in Scottish politics, see Ferguson, 'The Reform Act (Scotland) of 1832: intention and effect', *Scottish Historical Review*, xlv, 1966, 105–16.

75 *Ibid*, 109–11.

76 Clerk to Peel, 13 Aug, 1837: Peel MSS, Add. MSS 40424, ff. 65–8; Lord Ailsa to Peel, 16 July 1837, *ibid*, Add. MSS, 40423, ff. 338–41; see also A. Pringle to Peel, 6 Feb, 1833; *ibid*, Add. MSS 40403, ff. 174–6.

77 Graham to Arbuthnot, 13 Dec, 1839: C. Arbuthnot, *Correspondence*, 212–14.

78 Cochrane to Bonham, 21 June 1841: Parker, *Peel*, ii, 469.

79 Graham to Bonham, 16 Oct, 1838: Peel MSS, Add. MSS 40616, ff. 17–20; Arbuthnot to Bonham, 23 July 1841: *ibid*, Add. MSS 40617, f. 101.

Tory Radicalism

80 *Daily Telegraph*, 3 Feb, 1975.

81 The best, although also the most controversial, discussion of that social upheaval is Thompson, *The Making of the English Working Class*.

82 These figures are a summary of more detailed statistics in Close, 'Elections of 1835 and 1837', 422, they include tellers.

83 Kitson Clark, *Peel and the Conservative Party*, 140.

84 Edsall, *The Anti-Poor Law Movement, 1833–44*, 61–4, 74, 87.

85 *The Conservative*, 1 Aug, 1836.

86 Paul, *A History of the Origin and Progress of Operative Conservative Societies*, 28.

87 *Ibid*, 24–5.

88 Thompson, *English Working Class*, 63–8.

89 See Lubenow, *The Politics of Government Growth*, 156–60.

90 Thompson, *English Working Class*, 206, 297–8.

91 Lubenow, *The Politics of Government Growth*, 52.

92 Blaug, 'The myth of the old Poor Law and the making of the new', *J. Econ. Hist.*, xxiii, 1963, 151–84; Baugh, 'The cost of poor relief in south-east England, 1790–1834', *Econ. HR*, Feb, 1975, 50–68.

93 Edsall, *The Anti-Poor Law Movement*, 77, see also Thomis, *Politics in Nottingham*, 246–8.

94 Edsall, 76–89.

95 The 1836 Act provided for the civil registration of Dissenters' births, marriages, and deaths. Dissenting support for Liberal defenders of the Poor Law at the boards of guardians elections may have been fostered partly by the desire to place responsibility for the registration in friendly hands. If so,

the registration issue drove a wedge between anti-Poor Law Dissenting Radicals and Tory Radicals.

96 See the discussion of Oldham politics in Foster, *Class Struggle*, 52–6.

97 Close, 'Elections of 1835 and 1837', 169.

98 Dr Vincent's table of the labourers' votes (which does not include the major industrial towns) shows a marked tendency for labourers to vote Conservative. The table covers the years from 1830 to 1872, and what is remarkable is the decline of the Conservative share of the working-class vote as the years went by. The most probable explanation is the dying off of the freeman voters. (The table is in *Pollbooks*, 59–60.)

99 Chartist-backed Conservatives won at Bradford, Leeds, and Nottingham. (Wright, 'A Radical borough', 145–6; Diary, 7th Earl of Shaftesbury, 23 June and 3 Sept, 1841: Broadlands MSS, SHA/PD/2; Thomis, *Politics in Nottingham*, 249). At Coventry the Conservative candidate, Thomas Weir, was defeated, but 'about 100 Chartists' ignored the Whig candidate and either plumped for the Radical or split between the Radical and Weir (E. Ellice to Lord Holland [1841]: Holland House MSS, Add. MSS 51587, f. 94).

100 Foster, *Class Struggle*, 104.

101 Neale, *Class and Ideology*, 54–7.

102 Heesom, 'Sunderland by-election', 68–72.

103 Lubenow, *Politics of Government Growth*, 70.

104 *Ibid*, 85.

Chapter 9

Conservatism in office

The economy and the 1842 budget

Peel took office in September 1841, at the head of the first government in English history to rest on the support of a single-party majority. The victory of 1841 was a party victory. Yet just two weeks after kissing hands, in a celebrated phrase which bears repeating, Peel said in the House of Commons that 'no considerations of mere political support' would induce him to hold office 'by a servile tenure, which would compel me to be the instrument of carrying other men's opinions into effect'.[1] The great question facing the Conservative party in 1841, recognized by many observers at the time, was whether its dogmas would prove elastic enough to bear the strains placed on them by the practical requirements of office, whether the impressive unity which it had achieved in opposition could be sustained once the incentive to replace an objectionable ministry had been removed. Every incoming government faces the same test. It was a weakness of the Conservative position that the rallying cry of the party in the mid-1830s, when the foundation of its victory had been laid, had by 1841 lost its immediate force. The threat to the constitution had, for the moment at least, subsided. In its place had arisen the attack on the Corn Laws. As the Radical member for Leeds, Sir William Molesworth, put it, having failed to break down the constitution, the Radicals had 'fallen back on the inquiry, what can be done to improve the material condition of the people – the answer is the application of the principles of free trade'.[2]

Had the free-trade argument gained prominence simply, as Molesworth seemed to imply, because the Radicals were fishing for an issue, Peel might easily have ignored it. The reason lay deeper. The national economy was in difficulty. The Industrial Revolution had accentuated the fluctuations of the trade cycle and subjected the country to severe and frequent alternations of slump and boom, for one major reason: that the dominant cotton industry was dependent upon a highly elastic demand market, both at home and abroad. The sharp fluctuations of the economy exposed the weakness of the country's banking system, which lacked central direction and control and left hundreds of county banks precariously dependent on the regional fortunes of particular trades and *vice versa*. At the same time it was evident that the taxation structure of the country wanted repair. It had proved incapable of providing the means to pay the old wartime debt (at the inflated wartime prices) while also balancing the budget. And taxes, levied almost entirely in the form of customs and excise duties, bore unfairly on the poor.

The severe unemployment and trade recession of the years 1838–42 inaugurated a new era in British politics. Financial questions achieved a political importance far greater than ever before. The issues which had commanded the attention of parliament just a few years earlier lost their primacy. The critical matter requiring Peel's attention in the autumn of 1841 was the manifest instability and insecurity, for employer and employee alike, of the new industrial society. It was not, of course, simply that conditions had changed. So had men's attitudes. Economic instability, unemployment, and industrial unrest had been just as evident in the years 1816–22. The difference lay in Peel's conviction, foreign to Lord Liverpool, that economic management was a primary function of government and that fiscal policy could be a regulator of social harmony. Peel did not hide from himself the fact that the nation's economy had become dependent on manufacturing and that manufacturing was in crisis.

> Something effectual must be done to revive the languishing commerce and manufacturing industry of this country [he told Croker in 1842]. Look at the congregation of manufacturing masses, the amount of our debt, the rapid increase of poor rates within the last four years . . . and then judge whether we can with safety retrograde in manufactures.[3]

By making the prosperity of a manufacturing economy the central preoccupation of a Conservative government, Peel was asking the Conservative party to shift its ground. In the end he failed. And although the split in the party over the repeal of the Corn Laws in 1846 was the result of a number of factors, among them Peel's reluctance to cultivate the affections of his backbenchers, it is difficult to see how he could have succeeded. For, despite the solidity of the party during the first two sessions of Peel's administration, there was from the beginning a divide in the party between those, like Peel and his ministerial colleagues, Graham, Ripon and Gladstone, who believed that the duty of a Conservative government was to foster the welfare of all classes in society and to adapt laws and institutions to changing circumstances, and those who believed that it was to defend the special place of the landed interest in the state. As early as 1834, after the debate on Joseph Hume's motion to repeal the Corn Laws, Peel confided to Croker that, although he defended the farmers' need for some protection, he was disquieted by the agriculturalists' 'invidious and startling argument' that 'the landed interest as the most important ought to be a favoured class, for the benefit of which the rest of the community may properly be taxed'.[4] Four years earlier he had been a decided advocate of a property and income tax because 'it was expedient to reconcile the lower with the higher classes and to diminish the burthen of taxation on the poor men'.[5]

During the years of opposition that side of Peel's politics had not been much on display. His opinions, however, had not changed, and when he came into office the circumstances of an accumulating annual deficit, averaging £1.5 million over the previous five years, and the worst industrial slump since the war provided a splendid, if daunting, opportunity for bold financial reconstruction. Peel had both the imagination and the resolve to seize it. He had also the advantage of an opposition too discredited by a series of ineffectual budgets to offer powerful resistance. The result was the budget of 1842. It was one of the great achievements of Peel's career, less dramatic than the repeal of the Corn Laws four years later, but a more comprehensive tribute to his political gifts. It was both the response to an immediate budgetary requirement, the need to overcome the deficit, and the initiation of a policy to deal with a far greater difficulty, the 'condition of England'.

The budget had three main parts. It reintroduced an income tax for the first time since 1816, it lowered the protection given to imported grain by a revision of the 1828 sliding scale of corn duties, and it continued the dismantling of the general tariff wall which Robinson had begun in the 1820s. The income tax was levied at sevenpence in the pound and calculated to yield a revenue of £3,700,000. Other items, principally the increased duty on stamps and spirits in Ireland (exempted, as before, from the income tax) and an extended duty on coal exports, were expected to raise the total revenue from new sources to £4 million. That eliminated the deficit, covered the anticipated fall in revenue from the new corn duties, and still left a surplus of £500,000 by which to justify general tariff reductions. The new sliding scale of wheat duties lowered the maximum duty from 50s 8d when the home price was 36s or less to 20s when the home price was 50s or less. Other duties were adjusted to meet new criteria: no duty on a raw material was henceforth to exceed 5 per cent, on a partly manufactured article, 12 per cent, nor on a manufactured article, 20 per cent. Sugar was the only major commodity left untouched, for the good reason that the Whigs' fall had been precipitated by their proposal, in May 1841, to reduce the tariff differential between imported slave-grown and free-grown sugar. In framing the budget Peel made some notable miscalculations. The expected surplus turned into a deficit of £2,200,000 by 1843, partly because the fall in the customs revenue had been underestimated, partly because the increased duties in Ireland had failed in the opposite direction, but above all because Peel had overlooked the fact that the second instalment of the income tax, collected twice a year, would not arrive until after the end of the financial year. It was, therefore, as Stafford Northcote wrote late, 'no slight evidence of the confidence which Sir Robert Peel had inspired, that his reputation as a financier did not suffer from the exhibition of his mistakes'.[6]

Within a year, critics would have been silenced. In 1844, after the deficit was supplied, the surplus was £1,200,000. The interest of the budget lay, at any rate, not in its details, but in the broad ground which it staked out. By reintroducing the income tax and relaxing the restrictions on free trade Peel laid the foundations of Victorian finance. The income tax, it is true, was proposed as a temporary measure to enable the government to meet the demands on the exchequer only until the rise in imports should offset the effect of lower duties. The customs revision, too, stopped far short of free trade. Peel, giving hostages to fortune, told the Commons that abolishing the Corn Laws would not relieve industrial distress, but simply add to it rural poverty.[7] It is also true that the budget was shaped by practical necessities. The financial year 1840–41 had revealed that the failure in the revenue had occurred principally in that part from which four-fifths of the whole came, the customs and excise. Francis Baring had added 5 per cent to the customs duties with little effect. Peel, Graham, Ripon, Gladstone and Herries were all agreed that recourse to an income tax was unavoidable. As Peel said in his budget speech, the country had 'arrived at the limits of taxation on articles of consumption'.[8] Having settled for an income tax, Peel decided that it would be a mistake to establish the cumbersome machinery necessary to collect it for a paltry revenue. Hence the surplus. And hence the reduction of tariffs.

Yet it is evident that Peel was doing more than meeting necessity by unwelcome measures. The 1842 budget did not make the repeal of the Corn Laws inevitable; but it set the tone of the administration. Peel had kept his distance from Tory Radicalism; he was nevertheless convinced that something had to be done to raise wages by increased manufacturing production and to reduce the cost of living by lightening the burden of taxation on the poor and lowering the price of consumer goods, including food. The new taxes bore heavily on the landed class. Pitt had placed the level of exemption from his wartime income tax at £60. Peel raised it to £150. Even then he gave as a reason for using the surplus to reduce tariffs his desire to make the new tax acceptable to 'the working class at least'. Peel may have come into office convinced only that an income tax was necessary to balance the budget. By the end of his first year in office he was taking the broader view that a shift from indirect to direct taxation offered the best remedy for poverty and social dislocation. As Professor Gash has shown, in one of the best sections of his biography, the severe hunger and unrest of the summer of 1842 wrought upon Peel's mind. The government did not shrink from putting down riots and prosecuting Chartists, but when agriculturalists complained of falling prices, Peel wondered at their myopia. Fremantle passed on to him the grumblings of Sir Charles Burrell, the member for Shoreham, and received a sharp reply.

> If Sir Charles had such cases before him as I have before me of thousands and tens of thousands in want of food and employment, at Greenock, Paisley, Edinburgh, and a dozen large towns in the manufacturing districts, he would not expect me to rend my garments in despair if 'some excellent jerked beef from South America' should get into the English market, and bring down meat from 7½d or 8d a pound.[9]

Peel was not the cold political calculus which some have portrayed him, though he rarely gave his emotions public airing. By the end of the summer of 1842, perhaps the most distressed year of the whole century, he had decided that consumption had to be raised by increasing the purchasing power of the population. 'The danger,' he told Croker in October, 'is not low price from the tariff, but low price from inability to consume.'[10] Not surprisingly, he began to doubt the value of the Corn Laws. In May he told Gladstone that he would have difficulty in ever again defending them in principle,[11] and from there it was a short step to agreeing with Graham's prediction at the end of the year that repeal was only a matter of time: 'The next change in the Corn Laws must be to an open trade.'[12]

Peel carried his party with him in 1842. Despite the fact that the income tax had always been regarded as an emergency measure, justifiable only by a national crisis like the French wars, only two Conservatives voted against it. The new sliding scale was opposed by only nine Conservatives. The expendable Duke of Buckingham, the 'farmer's friend', resigned the Privy Seal in protest, but the other agriculturalist in the cabinet, Sir Edward Knatchbull, though angered by the cabinet's decision to reduce the duty on imported apples without consulting him (he represented Kent) remained. The income tax, at 3 per cent, was not nearly so severe as the 10 per cent tax imposed by Lord Henry Petty in 1806. The new Corn Law had not reduced duties as much as Peel and officials at the Board of Trade had wished. After consultations with Robert Christopher, the member for Lincolnshire, it was fixed at a level designed to guarantee the farmer a stable and fair price of between 54s and 58s a quarter. There was, therefore, insufficient reason for backbenchers to harass a government newly placed in office after more than a decade of opposition. The prevailing mood of the agriculturalists, who knew nothing of the private direction of Peel's and Graham's thoughts, was perhaps expressed by a leading article in the *Maidstone Journal* in April.

> Injurious as we fear it is likely to prove in certain districts, inadequate as we apprehend to be the protection, which at particular points of the new scale is afforded to occupants of poor wheat lands, and generally the growers of barley and oats . . . it is far better for the agriculturalists to accept with the best grace they can, a measure prepared by a friendly government, avowedly desirous of affording them the utmost possible extent of protection consistent with a due regard to the general interests of the empire, rather than to trust to the tender mercies of those who repudiate the very principle of protection.[13]

Suspicions had nevertheless been aroused. Greville looked only at the division lists when he remarked upon Peel's 'complete mastery' over his followers, who had 'surrendered at discretion' and were 'as well disciplined and as obedient as the crew of a man-of-war'.[14] Murmurs of discontent came from many quarters. Philip Pusey, disturbed by Peel's description of the revised sliding scale as an experiment, warned Gladstone that the farmers had gone with Peel 'to the very utmost point they could with respect to corn'.[15] And when Peel claimed in the Commons 'that on the general principle of free trade there is now no great difference of opinion, and that all agree in the general rule that we should purchase in the cheapest market and sell in the dearest', Stanley, after Graham the most important of Peel's cabinet colleagues, remarked that 'Peel laid that down a great deal too broadly'.[16] In April Knatchbull recorded in his diary his belief 'that the Government has lost the good opinion of a large portion of the agriculturalists' and in the autumn Arbuthnot advised Peel that 'many of our Ultra friends are dissatisfied with the measures of last session'.[17]

In the country the chief sources of displeasure were the decision to remove the prohibition on the import of cattle, a measure against which eighty-five Conservatives voted in the House of Commons, and the reduction of the duty on seed crops. Reports from the constituencies, however, emphasized the dispirited morale of the opposition and the Conservative farmers' grudging acceptance of Peel's policies. 'The farmers here grumble,' a squire wrote to Fremantle, 'but that is their natural language – however I believe the majority of sensible people . . . think the country is now in the best hands.'[18] For the next three years agricultural questions lost some of their prominence, thanks largely to the revival of trade and an upward swing in agricultural prices, which left the government free to give the 1842 arrangements their promised 'fair trial'. In 1843, advised by Fremantle that to do otherwise would jolt the squires' confidence,[19] the cabinet decided to oppose a Radical motion for an inquiry into the burdens on land, supposedly onerous enough to justify agricultural protection. The session of 1843 was, by comparison with the one before, a dull one, barren of important legislation except for Stanley's Bill to extend imperial preference to Canada by lowering the duty on Canadian wheat.

Yet two influential Conservatives, Knatchbull from inside the cabinet and Lord Ashley from without (he had declined the offer of a household appointment in order to retain the freedom to promote the causes of factory reform and Protestant ascendancy),[20] were impressed by the diminished standing of the government after two years in office. Knatchbull put the responsibility on Peel's manner.

> I am satisfied that we are now in office only because it is not easy or possible to form another Government. I never in my time saw a Minister who possessed more absolute power in the House of Commons than Peel. His influence and power is most extraordinary – in the House he is everything, but there his power ceases – if he was the same in Council and in all his intercourse with mankind he would exceed everything this Country or perhaps any other ever had . . . by his power in the House of Commons alone does he keep his party together, out of the House his conduct is well calculated to destroy it. Cold and uncourteous to everyone, even to his colleagues in office, who appear to me to be afraid to differ from him – at times in manner almost insolent – it will be found when he dies, that no Minister ever possessed fewer friends, or would be personally less lamented.[21]

Ashley's analysis went deeper, although he, too, found fault with Peel's personal leadership.

How, and by what means, from what Cause, or what influence have the Ministry so declined in public and private estimation? that it is so is shown by the papers . . . by the joy of the Opposition, by the dejection of friends; by the looks, they say, and the language of the Government themselves – their numbers are undiminished, and yet they carry nothing; they have committed no leading & palpable folly; and yet no one confides in their wisdom; no great and manifest crime; and yet who animates himself by conviction of their honesty? all is doubt, uncertainty, vain wishes and disappointed hopes; much anger and discontent, personally and collectively, with present men, & yet an unwillingness to change them. I speak of the House & the Clubs, for among the middling and other classes, they seem increasingly raised; it wd not be easy for them to assign a definite reason; but they all *feel* displeasure which would neither ask nor admit argument at a general Election.

Compare the state of moral and political power they possessed in 1841 with what they possess in 1843; and it is as Lord Bacon to a Baby!

Among secondary causes, a very principal one is the high expectation formed of the mighty contrast the Tories were to exhibit in comparison with the Whigs – now the contrast they have exhibited, and it is a beneficial one, is far less in what they have done, than in what they have not done; they have produced and carried but few things; but they have introduced no mischievous legislation, & made no wicked appointments . . .

Peel has committed great and grievous mistakes in omitting to call his friends frequently together to state his desires & rouse their zeal. A few minutes and a few words would have sufficed; energy & fellowship would have been infused; men would have felt they were companions in arms; they now have the sentiment of being followers in a drill.[22]

Ashley's criticisms were undoubtedly coloured by personal disappointment, since the government had just abandoned its Factory Bill in the face of the outcry from Dissent at the proposal to place factory education under Anglican control. But the harsh judgement of Peel was echoed in many quarters over the next two-and-a-half years. And it was significant that the government found disfavour with the only *bona fide* agriculturalist in the cabinet and the most powerful spokesman for Evangelical Protestantism in parliament.

It would be idle to imagine that the Conservative party was already in danger of splitting. When the Bill to lower the duty on Canadian corn came up, seventy rural members met at the Carlton and resolved to vote against it, even at the risk of bringing down the government. In the event the revolt turned out to be 'much cry and no wool . . . despite the meetings, the Chairmanships, the resolutions etc. etc., Stanley carried his vote by a majority of 83!'[23] The meeting itself, however, is an indication that the backbenchers' concern at the drift of events in 1843 was something more than mid-term restlessness. Outside parliament the Irish repeal movement and the campaign of the Anti-Corn Law League were gathering momentum. The Irish Arms Bill of 1843, which merely required the registration of all firearms, was thought by many Conservatives to be a pusillanimous response to the repeal campaign, which held large outdoor meetings of the Catholic peasantry, indulged in revolutionary language verging on the seditious, and collected funds derided by its opponents as 'the O'Connell rent'. At the same time the Anti-Corn Law League's successes at by-elections were cause for disquiet. John Bright's victory at Durham in July deprived the Conservatives of the share of the representation which they had enjoyed since 1835, and a League candidate also won at London, a seat which Bonham and Fremantle had expected to gain.[24] In October, for the first time, the League put all its formidable machinery, including the oratory of Bright and Cobden, into the Liberal campaign at a rural town, Salisbury. The Conservative candidate won the election, but the Liberal, an outspoken free-trader, gained 45 per cent of the vote, an impressive tally in a southern cathedral town.[25]

The Anti-Corn Law League was a double thorn in Peel's side. By its vitriolic denunciations of the rapine greed and selfishness of the landed proprietors it stiffened the protectionist resolve of the agriculturalists and gave point to their argument that the debate on the Corn Laws touched issues far broader than economics, thus making it all the more difficult for the government to conduct a gradual relaxation of tariffs. In 1843 the League's intense activities also stayed Peel's hand in Ireland. The similarities between O'Connell's campaign and the free-trade agitation made it impossible to act against the one and ignore the other. The cabinet reasonably decided that it must tolerate both, but in doing so it exposed itself to Ashley's taunt that the great victory of 1841 had been in vain. 'Extreme and perpetual caution', Ashley wrote, 'is not true and constant wisdom – free men will not, & cannot, be ruled by it.'[26]

It was Ireland which, in 1843, brought into public view the quartet of romantic visionaries known as 'Young England': George Smythe, Lord John Manners, Henry Baillie-Cochrane and their mentor, Disraeli.[27] Inspired by a common antipathy to erastian liberalism in religion and utilitarian, middle-class liberalism in politics and economics, the four young Tories had in 1842 decided to act and vote together. Their old-fashioned Church-and-King Toryism, with its heavy overtones of the seventeenth century, led them to oppose the Irish Arms Bill and so drew attention to themselves as a potentially disrupting ginger group within the Conservative party. But, although their call for a revivified monarchy and a reawakened aristocracy, thwarting the middle classes by a benevolent rule of the people, undoubtedly struck a responsive chord in some backbenchers, there was little practical sense in their accusing Peel of behaving like Cromwell in Ireland when he should have been modelling himself on Strafford and Charles I.

In 1842 Disraeli informed his wife, with obvious relish, that he found himself 'without effort the leader of a party chiefly of the youth and new members' and in the same year he hinted at gathering around himself '40 or 50 agricultural malcontents'.[28] No doubt Disraeli knew that such speculation was fanciful. A handful of members fluttered for a session or two on the fringes of the group, but it never amounted to anything. Young England was justly described by George Eliot as 'the aristocratic dilettantism which attempts to restore the "good old times" by a sort of idyllic masquerading, and to grow feudal fidelity and veneration as we grow turnips, by an artificial system of manure'.[29] Robert Blake has recently called it 'the reaction of a defeated class to a sense of its own defeat'.[30] Young England was too idiosyncratic, not just in the flamboyance of its individual members, to attract a following from among even those Conservatives who might have been its allies. Ashley, who shared their paternalist outlook, was put off by the 'papistical' leanings of Manners's and Smythe's High-Church Tractarianism.[31] And the Protestant sensibilities of those backbenchers who were flattered by Young England's elevation of an aristocratic ideal were bound to be offended by Disraeli's recommendation of a generous and comprehensive social reform of Irish institutions. Young England was never more than a local expression of the as yet largely unarticulated distrust which Peel's muted liberalism was sowing on the Conservative backbenches. Its days as a semi-formal body ended when the original four split on the vote on the Maynooth grant in 1845.

By then Disraeli's ambitions were outgrowing the faintly comical dress of Young England. It had nevertheless suited him well enough for a time; indeed the main significance of the movement was the emergence of Disraeli as a parliamentarian of the first rank. Unreasonably piqued at Peel's refusal to gratify his presumptuous request for office in 1841 (he had been in the Commons for only four years), Disraeli spent the next three years uncertain whether to cast his lot with Peel or whether to strike a semi-independent line. Young England gave him his first taste of political 'leadership' and encouraged him to adopt a tone of language markedly distinct from official Conservatism. He also experienced the publicity granted to a party dissident, as when, after his first really noteworthy parliamentary speech in 1844, a thorough examination of the Irish question – 'a starving population, an absentee aristocracy, and an alien Church, and in addition, the weakest executive in the world'[32] – he was praised by Peel in the Commons for having delivered 'a very able speech . . . not the less to be admired because it departed from the ordinary routine of Parliamentary eloquence and touched on more comprehensive and general views'.[33] It is unlikely that Peel's remark, which pinpointed the difference in the two men's parliamentary styles, erased the effect on Disraeli of not having received the Whips' circular at the beginning of the session. That quarrel (caused by Disraeli's attacks in 1843 on the government's foreign and Irish policy) was soon repaired, but Disraeli, along with others, had noticed how brittle Peel could be in the face of criticism. An early example of Peel's vulnerability had occurred in 1843 when, with ill-natured bad grace, he had taunted George Smythe with the advice to vote against the government's Irish Arms Bill. Disraeli's full-blooded assault on Peel in 1845, remarkable for its effrontery and self-confidence, came after two years in which he observed Peel and the party carefully and gradually tested his own strength and abilities.

Backbench revolts

It was in the nature of early Victorian politics that on occasions Peel's government should be opposed by substantial numbers of its regular supporters. Despite the growth of party feeling in the 1830s, the habit of independence remained. It was neither surprising nor very alarming that eighty-five Conservatives should vote against the new duty on imported cattle in 1842, nor that more than sixty of them should vote against the Ecclesiastical Courts Bill and the Canada Corn Bill in 1843. It was, indeed, noticeable that agricultural and religious questions drew out opposition to the government, but on none of those votes was the government in danger of being overthrown. The same might be said of the two well-known Conservative 'revolts' in 1844, on the government's factory legislation in March and on its revision of the sugar duty in June. Neither revolt was intended to turn the government out and on each occasion the government overcame an embarrassing defeat in the House of Commons by successfully appealing to the House to reverse its vote against the ministerial proposals.

Yet for several reasons the two episodes bore a more serious aspect than previous shows of backbench independence.[34] They did not, of course, suddenly change the complexion of the Conservative party. Nor did they fundamentally alter the relationship between the government and its backbench supporters. They did, however, bring more into the open light conflicting strands of opinion in the party; they exacerbated the strained relationship which existed between Peel and some of his followers, and in doing so they exposed the unreliability of party in its infancy as the bedrock of ministerial stability.

Both disputes touched on Peel's attempt gradually to ally the Conservative party with a liberal economic policy. Sir James Graham's Factory Bill made no concession to the advocates of a ten-hour day for textile workers. Lord Ashley, who had kept a distance from Peel's government partly in order to retain his freedom of action on social questions, therefore introduced an amendment to reduce the hours for women and young persons from twelve to ten. The amendment was passed with the support of ninety-five Conservatives, but four nights later the House of Commons recinded its vote and restored the twelve-hour day. In June the government's proposal to lower the duty on free-grown foreign sugar from 63s per hundredweight to 34s (leaving the duty on slave-grown sugar at the existing level) represented to some people's minds an unwarrantable inroad on the structure of colonial preferential tariffs. In particular it was seen as a breach of faith with the West Indian sugar producers who had been promised a clear market advantage over their foreign rivals when parliament had raised their labour costs by abolishing slavery in 1833. Philip Miles, Conservative member for the port of Bristol, therefore moved an amendment to lower the duty on colonial sugar from 24s to 20s. It passed with the support of sixty-two Conservatives. Then, as in March, the government succeeded in getting the House of Commons to reverse its vote three nights later.

Both disputes were settled in the government's favour after Peel let it be known that he would resign if the House of Commons persisted in its opposition. Peel thus demonstrated his strength when the Commons was presented with the choice between a Conservative government and a Whig government. Even so, the large number of Conservatives who were willing to vote against official government policy on major issues of economic policy testified to the strength of feeling within the parliamentary party against the textile manufacturers and against any tampering with the special trading status granted to the colonies. Miles' amendment, moreover, was drafted in collaboration with the Whigs,[35] and in calling for a reduction in the colonial duty, not, as might have been expected from a Conservative opponent of free trade, for a higher duty on foreign sugar, it revealed how determined he and his Conservative supporters were to attract Liberal votes and defeat Peel's proposal. Few of the dissidents had come to Disraeli's conclusion that 'Peel had completely failed to hold together his party, and must go, if not now, at least very speedily',[36] but nor were the bulk of them prepared to come to heel at Peel's command. Peel's threat of resignation in March induced only two Conservative supporters of the ten-hours amendment to change their votes, although a strong government whip persuaded seventeen of them to abstain and brought twenty new Conservatives, absent for the first vote, to the government's defence.[37] In June the threat succeeded in changing only four Conservative votes. Once again the government was rescued by the action of ten of Miles' supporters who stayed away for the second division and by the votes of forty-three government supporters who had been absent for the first division.[38]

The resolution of the two crises illustrated that, in the short term, Peel's government was not in danger and that the Whips' office exercised considerable authority. Bonham told Peel that there were at most twenty backbenchers '*now* almost inimical to the government'.[39] The long-term effects are more difficult to assess. There were probably few Conservatives like William Ferrand and William Blackstone, who voted against Peel in June 'for the express purpose of throwing him out'.[40] The intention of the majority of the dissidents, nevertheless, to maintain the government in office while dictating policy to it, gave rise to a fertile debate about the role of party in the post-reform political world. And Peel's intransigent adherence to the government's proposals revived criticism of his aloof style of leadership.

Peel's passion in politics was for administration, for getting things done. In the House of Commons the depth and range of his knowledge and the evident seriousness of his purpose, so markedly in contrast to the style of his predecessor, Lord Melbourne, gave him an unrivalled authority. His parliamentary statements were direct, logical, comprehensive and grave. Disraeli looked back on him in 1852 as 'the greatest Member of Parliament that ever lived'.[41] But whether from shyness or from arrogance, if indeed they be different things, he was reluctant to play the part of an affable party leader. When he needed rest from the routine of office he retired to the seclusion of Drayton Manor to enjoy the domestic comforts of his wife and children. He made little effort to establish links of friendship and mutual confidence with his supporters. In his shortcomings Peel was not, of course, exceptional as a party leader, but aloofness from the rank and file – he was rarely seen at the Carlton – was especially damaging to a man whose opinions, ever since his conversion to Catholic emancipation, were suspected by many members of his party. It was unfortunate, too, that his two most important cabinet collegues were men of similar outward manner. One was Sir James Graham, responsible for the 1844 Factory Bill, a man of ability who, Gladstone said, 'knew more of economic and trade matters . . . than the rest of the Cabinet of 1841 all put together',[42] but a man, also, who was disliked by the gentlemen of his neighbourhood in Cumberland for being 'sneering and supercilious in his general manner'.[43] As Home Secretary, Graham was more frequently in communication with members of parliament than any other minister, and in the conduct of his office, according to Ashley (not, it is true, the most even-tempered or impartial of witnesses), he 'contrived to render himself so thoroughly odious that I cannot find the human being who will speak a word on his behalf'.[44] The other was Lord Stanley, not, like Peel and Graham, all work and no play, but rather given somewhat immoderately to the pleasures of the race course and the hunting field. His almost Olympian detachment from his parliamentary fellows flowed from assumptions of aristocratic pride and was later, when he had succeeded Peel to the leadership of the party, to encourage criticism of his leadership similar to, but less hostile than, that laid against Peel.

In 1844 it was Graham and Stanley who were the most resolute opponents of compromise on the sugar and factory questions in the cabinet. What angered many Conservatives was that despite good reasons for their expecting Peel at least to listen to their opinions – it was well known that many manufacturers were ready to accept an eleven-hour day and the sugar question was precisely the issue on which Melbourne's government had been forced to accept defeat and ask for a dissolution in 1841 – Peel showed singular disinterest in doing so. In the debate on the Factory Bill he referred to his readiness to resist 'the temptation of obtaining party support' by agreeing to a proposition which he believed injurious to the country's welfare.[45] The posture had merit. The language was graceless. In the middle of both crises he called a meeting of the party, not, however, to discuss the disagreements, but simply to announce his decision to resign if beaten again. His appeal was coldly to the malcontents' dread of a Whig government, not to their attachment to a Conservative one. Even before the 1844 session, a Conservative backbencher had complained of the party's being governed by 'Fremantle and a little clique'.[46] At its end, Richard Monckton Milnes, the liberal Conservative member for Pontefract who was to be a Peelite after 1846, found Peel's methods of leadership 'absolutely indefensible'.

> He is asking from his party all the blind confidence the country gentlemen placed in Mr. Pitt, all the affectionate devotion Mr. Canning won from his friends, and all the adherence Lord John and the Whigs get from their 'family compact' without himself fulfilling any of the engagements on his side.[47]

Behind the clash of personalities and the superficial criticism of Peel's style stood the more substantial quarrel about the function of party. Put simply, it was a quarrel between those, like Peel and Graham, who looked to party primarily as the obedient instrument of ministerial decisions and those, like Disraeli and Ashley, who looked to party primarily as the source of government policy. The issue was not, of course, so sharply drawn. There was ground for the backbenchers' irritation at Peel's seeming disregard for their opinions; there was also force to Peel's argument that ministers had a right to expect their supporters to forego opinions on specific questions rather than risk the life of a government in whom they placed a general confidence. What was lacking was the elaborate paraphernalia of modern parties – manifestoes, party conferences, and powerful constituency organizations – which serves, in ordinary circumstances, to allow party to operate as both the source and the instrument of ministerial authority.[48]

Even the modern structure of party might not have been proof against the shock given to the Conservative party in 1845 by Peel's proposal to increase and make permanent the annual parliamentary grant voted for the support of the Roman Catholic seminary at Maynooth in county Kildare. The 'Irish question', a wonderfully simple tag for the complex difficulties, social, economic, religious and racial, with which the Irish people and their English governors had to contend, contributed in one way or another to the demise of almost every nineteenth-century government. Melbourne's government paid a heavy price for its cooperation with the Irish Radicals, although it was able, at least, by appointing Catholics to the Irish administration and by carrying some useful reforms, to provide Ireland with six years of quiet government. The advent of a Conservative government in 1841 was the signal for O'Connell to renew his peasant movement for the repeal of the union with Great Britain. Overshadowed at first by the industrial depression in England, the Irish question came more and more to press its claims on Peel's government. The Maynooth Bill thus came at the end of Peel's three-year search to find a Conservative method of governing Ireland, one which should do justice to Ireland without subverting the position of the Irish Church or the Union and without alienating those of his supporters who cherished deep Anglican sympathies.

The search ended in failure when half of the Conservative party in the House of Commons refused to support the Maynooth Bill. Their decision was the fruit of several years of mounting frustration at the apparent unwillingness of a Conservative government either to prosper the Anglican

Church or to arrest the growth of Irish Catholic nationalism. The Maynooth Bill revived bitter memories of an Anglican parliament's capitulation to the Dissenters in 1828 and to the Roman Catholics in 1829. It also marked another stage in the decline of the Established Church's special relationship with the state. For some years the political strength of Dissent had acted as a check on the enjoyment of that exclusive care of parliament to which the Established Church had long accustomed itself to feel entitled. Not since 1824 had parliament voted money for Church extension, despite the urgent need for the Church to provide for the expanding population in the manufacturing towns of the North. Peel had no desire to revive the practice. His position, clearly expressed when he established the Ecclesiastical Commission in 1835, was that the Church should redistribute its existing income to make it serve new requirements.[49] He worked closely with Bishop Blomfield to maintain the influence of the Church in national life,[50] but he turned a deaf ear to those Churchmen on the Conservative backbenches who asked for state aid to Church extension. In 1843, too, the government yielded to the protests of the Dissenters and abandoned its scheme to place the education of factory children in Anglican hands. Then, a year later, the Church party suffered two defeats, on Lord Powis's motion to save a condemned Welsh bishopric and on the Bishop of Exeter's Bill to provide chaplains for workhouses out of parliamentary funds.

In Ireland the erosion of the Church's position had cut much deeper, directly by the suppression of ten bishoprics and the abolition of the cess in 1833, indirectly by Acts like the Irish Poor Law of 1838, which provided for the election of Poor Law guardians by a rate-paying suffrage and so transferred the control of an important local institution from the Protestant landowners to the priest-led Catholic tenantry. Conservatives who looked to Peel's government to reverse the tide were soon disappointed. Gratified at first by the appointment of Earl de Grey as Lord-Lieutenant, who persistently ignored Peel's instructions and removed Catholics from the Irish magistracy,[51] they were made nervous by the cautious wait-and-see attitude which the government adopted towards O'Connell's growing repeal campaign. The Irish Arms Act of 1843, which simply renewed the requirement that all firearms be registered, was dismissed by Protestant Tories as 'the merest drivelling'[52] and the debate on the third reading of the Bill was marked by 'the bitterness and insolence of his [Peel's] *soi-disant* friends'.[53] In the summer of 1843 O'Connell's increasingly provocative language and the series of 'monster' outdoor meetings which he organized finally gave Peel the opportunity to act. O'Connell was arrested in October and convicted by a packed jury of inciting to treason. In September 1844 he was acquitted on appeal by the law lords.

It was then that Peel, in Disraeli's version, decided to outbid the Liberals by sending 'messages of peace' to Ireland: the Charitable Bequests Act of 1844, which replaced the Protestant board in charge of Irish charities by a crown-appointed board of Protestants and Catholics and relaxed the Statute of Mortmain to enable gifts of real property to be made to the Catholic Church, and the Maynooth Bill.[54] Disraeli was wrong. In 1843 Peel had already established the Devon Commission to investigate the vexed question of land tenure in Ireland and in a series of cabinet papers early in 1844, months before O'Connell's acquittal, he had outlined his policy for Ireland, described by Professor Gash as 'an exercise in rigorous logic'.

> As long as Ireland remained disaffected, the United Kingdom was embarrassed in its foreign relations and vulnerable in time of war. Ireland would remain a source of danger until it was efficiently governed. It could not be efficiently governed as long as Irish courts and juries were useless to provide the foundation of law and order. They would continue to be useless until the professional middle classes in Ireland identified themselves with the state. They would not so identify themselves until they and their Church were given political and cultural as well as legal equality. This full equality could only come if professionally, eductionally, and socially they were given the same opportunities as Protestants. To achieve this, after centuries of inferiority, parliament and the taxpayer must come to the assistance of the Irish Catholics both lay and clerical.[55]

Peel's analysis almost entirely overlooked the economic roots of Ireland's discontent. Even so, it brought to Irish affairs a spirit of fairness and justice which underlay the Maynooth Bill. The Bill had three main objects: to increase the parliamentary grant from £9,000 to £26,360 and to make it permanent, not annual; to provide a specific grant for one year only of £30,000 for new buildings; and by incorporating the college trustees to empower them to take and hold land to the value of £3,000 annually.

As a practical contribution to solving the Irish question the Maynooth Bill meant little. As a gesture it signified far more. In 1843 Ashley had found a speech of Peel's in defence of the Irish Church wanting in ardour.

> I question whether Russell's attack on the Irish Church would be more formidable than Peel's defence of it. He asserted no principles, appealed to no feelings, stirred no sympathies – his argument which was for the House and his own party must have been pitiful for the Country . . . he urged, and with ability, various inconveniences that must result from the abolition of the Church; but, if the matter turn on inconveniences, might it not be proved that the inconvenience of upholding it is quite a great as the inconvenience of destroying it? – unless the Irish Church can be defended on the ground of solemn principle, it is altogether indefensible.[56]

There was the nub of England's relation with Ireland. The outcry against the Maynooth proposals within the Conservative party was raised against a background of fear, not just for the future of the Irish Church, but with it the future of the Union. Peel knew what forces were opposed to him. In January 1845 he allowed to Gladstone, in a remark revealing how little importance he by then attached to preserving the Conservative party, that he was determined to bring forward his proposals knowing that they would 'very probably be fatal to the Government'.[57]

The Bill was opposed by 147 Conservatives on the second reading and 149 on the third reading, when only 148 voted for it. The Conservative opponents of Peel's Irish policy had their own rigorous logic. They were not moved by bigotry alone. The national Established Church was the keystone of their Conservatism, and the solution to the Irish question, in its religious aspect, was therefore either that Ireland should remain Catholic and leave the nation or remain in the nation and accept the Irish Church. Believing that the Church in Ireland had a mission, they naturally preferred the second choice. Maynooth appeared to be a stepping-stone to the first. They were, of course, powerless to prevent the Bill's passing. Peel was unmoved by the vigorous agitation of the Central Anti-Maynooth Committee in the country and by the petitions which rained upon parliament, because he knew that the temporary alliance of Dissenting voluntarists and Conservative Anglicans against the Bill was of no permanent electoral significance. He knew, too, that the Anglican opposition came chiefly from the evangelical Low Church and that he was supported by numerous Broad and High Churchmen.[58] Inside parliament, Gladstone's decision to overthrow his youthful notion of the state's duty to propagate the true faith and support the Bill left the 'Protestants' leaderless. With the solid support of the Whigs, the Bill became law.

In the process, however, severe damage had been done to the Conservative party. After the second reading of the Bill, Graham recorded that 'our party is shivered and angry and we have lost the slight hold which we ever possessed over the hearts and kind feelings of our followers'.[59] It was galling to anti-Maynooth Conservatives to have to accept defeat in parliament when, just as in 1829, they appeared to represent the overwhelming preponderance of opinion in the country. Between the beginning of February and the end of May, the House of Commons had received 10,204 petitions containing 1,284,296 signatures against the Bill and only ninety petitions containing 17,482 signatures in its favour.[60] Peel was right that the outcry represented 'mainly the opposition of Dissent'[61] and therefore came from outside the Conservative party's natural constituency. At seventeen by-elections held between April and October the Conservatives lost only one of thirteen Conservative-held seats and gained one of the four opposition seats.[62] There were, nevertheless, signs of strong feeling against the Bill in Conservative strongholds. At the West Kent by-election in April Lord Holmesdale, the popular son of the Earl of Amherst, was selected by a majority of Conservative gentlemen as their candidate at a meeting of the local association. A minority of the gentlemen present, however, distressed by his pro-Maynooth views, succeeded in bringing forward Colonel Austen, the president of the West Kent Protection Society and an anti-Catholic, and Holmesdale withdrew. Colonel Austen was then returned unopposed.[63] At Woodstock the pro-Maynooth member, Lord Blandford, resigned in deference to his father's views, and an anti-Catholic was returned in his place.[64] Not surprisingly, therefore, preparations to reverse the House of Commons' decision were begun as soon as the Bill became law. On 17 June Lord Winchilsea and Lord Kenyon, unable, as Peel had realized, to cooperate with the Dissenters of the Central Anti-Maynooth Committee, presided over the first meeting of the National Club, formed 'in support of the Protestant principles of the Constitution'.[65] Eighteen Conservative members of parliament sat on its committee. Circulars were sent to every incumbent Anglican clergyman and meetings were organized to denounce the Maynooth grant and prepair for a Protestant offensive at the next elections.

Ashley had misgivings about the prospects of the National Club's campaign.

> Heard [he recorded in his diary] . . . that this Club will go forward. I am indisposed exceedingly to join it; first, because I see but scanty materials for such a combination; and a *public* effort should not be manifestly a weak one; secondly the materials I do see are not such as fill me with confidence; some of them are well-intentioned men, but scarcely any have a spark of judgement or self-control . . .
>
> It is difficult to say what extremes they may not demand of their associates; I saw a printed paper circulated *confidentially* to call a meeting to form a union the members of which should bind themselves by an engagement to oppose all and everything that might be said or done by the present Ministry! . . .
>
> The operation of it, say what they will, must be political; it must be directed to divisions and Elections; very legitimate, no doubt, but at present without much hope of fruit. You will displace Peel, if you can, very legitimate again, to bring in Russell; but then you must proceed to displace Russell to bring back Peel, causing thereby perpetual confusion & hazard without a prospect of success. Were the Protestants strong enough to form a Government of their own, the case would be widely different; but they are many degrees from such a position.[66]

It required a larger issue than Maynooth for the Conservative right wing to direct its energies to 'divisions and Elections'. The formation of the National Club caused scarcely a ripple on the political waters. Gladstone remarked that the session of 1845 closed 'like the calmest of summer sunsets' and that 'the numerical and on the whole the moral strength of the party was still entire'.[67] Yet many Conservatives were disturbed by the liberal drift of Peel's government. Disraeli, in a famous satirical attack on Peel during the Maynooth debate, had charged Peel with plundering the Whigs' policies and had called upon the House of Commons to overturn his 'dynasty of deception'.[68] J. C. Colquhon, in the same debate, had accused Peel of reducing the word 'Conservative' to 'a mere name, a name, too, without a notion'.[69] There was no organized opposition to Peel within the party in 1845. But of the 162 Conservative opponents of the Maynooth Bill, only twenty were to vote for the repeal of the Corn Laws a year later, whereas 133 of them were to vote against it. The ten-hours crisis, too, had had no immediate repercussions, but the eighty-five Conservative supporters of ten hours who voted on repeal in 1846 divided by fifty-nine to twenty-six to retain the Corn Laws. It would be impossible to show that a single Conservative vote in 1846 was tipped into the anti-repeal scale by an accumulated sense of grievance against Peel's government. On the other hand, it is not simply imagination to suggest that it might have been so. The opposition to the Maynooth grant coincided with renewed apprehension for the Corn Laws felt by the agriculturalists in the light of the substantial free-trade provisions included in the 1845 budget. When Ashley, disturbed by the suggestion that Peel's government ought to be overthrown, advised Colquhon that anti-Catholicism was too frail a foundation to support the political ends of the extremists in the National Club, Colquhon replied, 'Oh yes, that is very true; but we must eke it out with high agricultural protection, & those in some of *your* questions'.[70] At the very least, by the autumn of 1845, Peel wanted, as Neville Chamberlain did in May 1940, what is most valuable to a party leader, the fund of trust and affection on which to draw when, in a crisis, he needs to appeal from men's convictions to their loyalties.

Notes and References

The economy and the 1842 budget

1 17 Sept, 1841, *Hansard*, 3rd series, lix, 555.
2 Molesworth to Gladstone, 4 June 1841: Gladstone MSS, Add. MSS 44777, ff. 77–81.
3 Peel to Croker, 27 July 1842: Parker, *Peel*, ii, 528–30.
4 Peel to Croker, 24 March, 1834: Croker, *Correspondence and Diaries*, ii, 231–3.
5 Ellenborough, *Political Diary*, 14 March 1830, ii, 211–14. In June 1841 Ripon told Graham that the success of Peel's administration would depend upon its taking 'an enlarged view of what the actual condition of society demands' (Peel MSS, Add. MSS 40446, f. 5).
6 S. H. Northcote, *Twenty Years of Financial Policy*, 47.
7 9 Feb, 1842, *Hansard*, 3rd series, lx, 204.
8 Northcote, *Financial Policy*, 15–16.
9 Gash, *Sir Robert Peel*, 361.
10 *Ibid*, 360.
11 Morley, *Gladstone*, i, 260.
12 Graham to Peel, 30 Dec, 1842: Parker *Peel*, ii, 551. Gladstone kept notes of a conversation with Peel in August, 1843, during which Peel spoke 'very freely': 'Trade etc. That if he were not hampered by party considerations he should wish to propose a Corn Law with a duty of 10/– from 50/– to 60/–, to cease altogether at 65/– and with a maximum of 14/– uniting the fixed with the sliding principle. That the revenue of the country showed so little elasticity, that unless there should be improvement during the coming autumn, some further great operation would be necessary next session. That the income tax must be extended to five years instead of three . . . and he hinted that it would be a very great good if they would raise it to 5 per cent. That the cotton, wool and sugar duties must at all events be dealt with next year – and also silk. And that some further effort to relieve trade might be necessary: that if an increase in the income tax were found requisite it must be combined with relief to the consumer.' (Gladstone memorandum, 29 August 1843: Gladstone, *Memoranda*, 220–2).
13 *Maidstone Journal*, 12 April 1842.
14 Greville, *Memoirs*, 13 March 1842: v, 15–16.
15 Gladstone memorandum, 5 Dec, 1842: Gladstone, *Memoranda*, 184–6.
16 10 May 1842, *Hansard*, 3rd series, lxiii, 382; Morley, *Gladstone*, i, 263.
17 Knatchbull-Hugessen, *Kentish Family*, 242–3; Arbuthnot to Peel, 30 Oct, 1842: Parker, *Peel*, ii, 532–3.
18 J. Osborne to Fremantle, Oct, 1842. Fremantle MSS, 81/2. 'We are all disappointed,' H. W. Tancred, the Liberal member for Banbury, wrote to his agent, 'that you in the country take the Income Tax so quietly, & the Tories

laugh at us. If there is any steam in the country we neither for love nor money can get it up, & must allow our triumphant enemies to ride over us' (Trinder, *A Victorian M.P. . . . the Correspondence of H. W. Tancred, 1841–1859*, 7). Edward Sterling reported to Fremantle in October that 'the Whig-radical spirit languishes throughout west Cornwall – so much so that at the last (recent) registrations for Falmouth etc., there was no Whig agent to look after them' (Fremantle MSS, 81/2).

19 Gladstone memorandum, 15 March 1843: Gladstone, *Memoranda*, 190–1.
20 7th Earl of Shaftesbury, Diary, 1, 2, and 3 Sept, 1841: Broadlands MSS, SHA/PD/2. Shaftesbury was offended by the offer of only a minor government position, which he called 'a plain, cruel, unnecessary insult'.
21 Knatchbull, Diary, 18 Aug, 1843: Knatchbull-Hugessen, *Kentish Family*, 251–2.
22 7th Earl of Shaftesbury, Diary, 8 June 1843: Broadlands MSS, SHA/PD/3.
23 *Ibid*, 27 May 1843: Broadlands MSS, SHA/PD/3.
24 Gash, *Sir Robert Peel*, 385.
25 For details of the Salisbury by-election, see Cobden's letters to his wife in November 1843 (Cobden MSS, Add. MSS 50748) and reports in the *Salisbury and Wiltshire Herald*.
26 7th Earl of Shaftesbury, Diary, 8 June 1843: Broadlands MSS, SHA/PD/3.
27 For the activities of Young England, see Monypenny and Buckle, *The Life of Benjamin Disraeli*, ii, 162–96, and Blake, *Disraeli*, 161–76.
28 Monypenny and Buckle, *Disraeli*, ii, 166, 411.
29 'The natural history of German Life', *Westminster Review*, July 1856, 55. It may be worth noting that George Eliot was equally astringent in her comments on those who believed 'that all social questions are merged in economical science, and that the relations of men to their neighbours may be settled by algebraic equations'.
30 Blake, *Disraeli*, 165.
31 7th Earl of Shaftesbury, Diary, 13 July 1843: Broadlands MSS, SHA/PD/3.
32 16 Feb, 1844, *Hansard*, 3rd series, lxxii, 1007–17.
33 Monypenny and Buckle, *Disraeli*, ii, 192.

Backbench revolts
34 I have discussed these crises in detail in 'The ten hours and sugar crises of 1844: government and the House of Commons in the age of reform'. *Hist. J.*, xii, 1, 1969, 35–57, and more cursorily in *The Politics of Protection*, 16–22. My interpretation of the effect of the two episodes on the Conservative party has been questioned by D. R. Fisher, 'Peel and the Conservative Party: the sugar crisis of 1844 reconsidered', *Hist. J.*, xviii, II (1975), 279–302. Dr Fisher disputes my statement that by the end of the 1844 session Peel's 'hold over a large section of his party was at an end', partly, I believe, because he attaches to the word 'hold' a weaker meaning than I do. I was undoubtedly wrong to imply that a party leader ever did, in those days, have a hold over his followers' votes. But Dr Fisher, strangely, finds a divergence between my view and the statement of Professor Gash that 'a silent change had come over the relationship' between Peel and the Conservative party. I have nowhere suggested, as Dr Fisher implies, that a 'majority' of the party was 'permanently alienated' from Peel's leadership by the end of 1844, merely that from a section of the party Peel would henceforth find it more difficult than before to command assent. Dr Fisher seems to wish to treat each division in the 1841 parliament as an insulated event. I prefer to see in the

events of 1844 and 1845 part of the explanation of what happened to the Conservative party in 1846. I agree with Professor Conacher that 'explosions such as that which occurred in the Conservative party in 1846 do not come completely out of the blue' (Conacher, *The Peelites and the Party System,* 11).

35 Buckingham to Bonham, 16 June 1844: Peel MSS, Add. MSS 40547, f. 4.

36 Broughton, *Recollections,* vi, 146. Disraeli's remark was addressed to Hobhouse at a Whig dinner party at which Disraeli sounded out leading members of the opposition on a possible alliance against Peel of Whigs and Tory malcontents.

37 Fisher, 'The opposition to Sir Robert Peel in the Conservative party, 1841–1846', unpublished thesis, 263n.

38 Fisher, 'Peel and the Conservative Party', 290.

39 Bonham to Peel, [June 1844]: Peel MSS, Add. MSS 40547, ff. 1–2.

40 Fragment: *ibid,* Add. MSS 40547, f. 7.

41 B. Disraeli, *Lord George Bentinck: A Political Biography,* London, 1852, 320.

42 Gladstone memorandum, 3 June 1897: Gladstone, *Autobiographica,* 53–6.

43 William Sterling to Fremantle, 4 Sept, 1841: 'Graham is not very popular with the Gentlemen of this county – and the excuse is to be found . . . more, I suspect, in his personal character, than in his political history & proceedings. In the neighbourhood of Netherby he is but little liked – sneering and supercilious in his general manner, & harsh and unkindly towards the poor. He has never had many cordial friends in Society, nor any enthusiastic support upon the Hustings. To a certain point, nevertheless, he is a man of talent. . . . But he has in his field of vision neither breadth nor distance.' (Fremantle MSS, 110/5.) Edward Stanley recorded a similar impression in 1854: 'It is singular that Graham, who is even unpopular with the multitude on account of his supposed cold and calculating temperament, who is regarded as eminently an intriguer, as skilful and unscrupulous in using other men for his tools, himself remaining safe and irresponsible – should be one of the most impudent speakers now in Parlt.' (Stanley MSS. Diary, 11 March 1854.)

44 7th Earl of Shaftesbury, Diary, 8 June 1843: Broadlands MSS, SHA/PD/3.

45 18 March 1844, *Hansard,* 3rd series, lxxiii, 1241.

46 Morley, *Gladstone,* i, 266.

47 Reid, *The Life, Letters, and Friendships of Richard Monckton Milnes,* i, 331.

48 For a lengthier discussion of this quarrel, see Stewart, 'The ten hours and sugar crises', 44–57.

49 See Kitson Clark, *Churchmen and the Condition of England, 1832–1885,* 94–5.

50 See Welch, 'Blomfield and Peel: a study in cooperation between Church and State, 1841–1846', *J. Eccles. Hist.,* April 1961, 71–84, and Brose, *Church and Parliament, passim.*

51 Gash, *Sir Robert Peel,* 394–400.

52 *Fraser's Magazine,* July 1843, 124.

53 Greville, *Memoirs,* 11 August 1843, v, 126–8.

54 Disraeli, *Bentinck,* 133–4.

55 Gash, *Sir Robert Peel,* 420–1.

56 7th Earl of Shaftesbury, Diary, 15 July 1843: Broadlands MSS, SHA/PD/3.

57 Gladstone memorandum, 14 Jan, 1845: Gladstone MSS, Add. MSS 44777, ff. 212–15.

58 See the numerous letters from Anglican clergymen which Peel received in support of his policy in Peel MSS, Add. MSS 40564 and 40565.

59 Graham to Hardinge, 23 April 1845 (copy): Graham MSS, microfilm 120/88.

60 Machin, 'The Maynooth Grant, the Dissenters and Disestablishment, 1845–1847', *EHR*, Jan, 1967, 64n.

61 Peel to Croker, 22 April 1845: Croker, *Correspondence and Diaries*, iii, 32.

62 Ashley lamented, not quite accurately, that 'the ministry of Peel enjoys the continuance of public favour far more than I anticipated for him after his Maynooth policy – many elections have taken place, and he has carried every one – how is this?' (7th Earl of Shaftesbury, Diary, 18 Aug, 1845. Broadlands MSS, SHA/PD/4). The Conservative loss occurred at Dartmouth, which the Liberals had represented since 1832 until a by-election in November 1844. The Conservatives gained the shipping town of Sunderland, where, it is worth noting, the protectionist railway 'king', George Hudson, made his entry into parliamentary politics. They held Abingdon, Belfast, Cambridge, Down, Midlothian, Exeter, Kent West, Leominster, Linlithgowshire, Suffolk West, Wigan and Woodstock.

63 Andrews, 'Political issues in the county of Kent, 1820–1846', unpublished thesis.

64 *The Times*, 28 April and 2 May 1845.

65 *The Times*, 23 June 1845.

66 7th Earl of Shaftesbury, Diary, 21 June 1845: Broadlands MSS, SHA/PD/4.

67 Gladstone MSS, Add. MSS 44745, ff. 181–2.

68 11 April 1845, *Hansard*, 3rd series, lxxix, 565–9.

69 *Ibid*, 501–2.

70 7th Earl of Shaftesbury, Diary, 20 June 1845: Broadlands MSS, SHA/PD/4.

Chapter 10

The great divide

Free trade versus protection

The story of the repeal of the Corn Laws is one of the most dramatic and best known in the history of modern English politics. For the Conservative party repeal was a watershed. Ever since 1815 the party had suffered spasms of hostility between its 'ultra' and 'liberal' wings. In 1846 the downfall of Peel's government led to the permanent separation of the two wings and the rebuilding of the Conservative party under a new leadership. From 1846 the history of the Conservative party proceeds to the present without a break. That a party which had survived the divisions of the 1820s, the disruption of Catholic emancipation, and the crisis of the Reform Bill should finally come to the parting of the ways in 1846 requires explanation. Of course, by becoming more highly organized, the party had also become more brittle. At least it was harder to put the broken pieces together again. It has been suggested in the last chapter that Peel's decision to repeal the Corn Laws came at a time when elements in his party were already disgruntled and that his government was therefore in a weaker position on the eve of repeal than has often been supposed. The free trade issue was ideally suited to bring matters to the pitch. Not only did it give rise to a wide-ranging debate about the economic, social and political, and constitutional responsibilities of a Conservative government. It also fixed attention on the relationship between members of parliament and their constituencies. The issue itself may well have been sufficient to account for the decision of two-thirds of the Conservative party in the Commons to reject the legislation of their government. Without the pressure from the agricultural counties to sustain them, however, it is doubtful whether their action would have led to the division of the party into two distinct rival groups, Peelites and Protectionists.

Peel's decision to repeal the Corn Laws when he did was a response to the news which reached England in the early autumn of 1845 that Ireland, whose potato crop was devastated by blight, faced a year and more of famine. Despite the fact that the Irish peasantry was too poor to buy wheat, Peel was probably right to believe that famine presented the Anti-Corn Law League with an irresistible, if illogical, argument for opening the ports to the free import of wheat and so providing the country with cheap bread. Had it not been for the potato failure, Peel, or so at least he claimed, intended to dissolve parliament at the end of the 1846 session and go to the country with the promise that a new Conservative government would repeal the Corn Laws.[1] The Irish calamity merely determined Peel's timing. He had already been persuaded both that the Corn Laws acted as as brake upon the growth of manufacturing industry and the increase of national prosperity and that, as a source of class antagonism, they endangered the social fabric of the nation and the existence of a territorial aristocracy.

For nearly forty years after the publication in 1932 of C. R. Fay's *The Corn Laws and Social England* it was orthodox historical opinion that the heated post-1815 controversy about the economic consequences of protection was based on the false assumption that the Corn Laws kept up the price of grain, whereas in reality postwar deflation and increased arable production combined to keep prices well below the level at which the Corn Laws came into operation. It was also widely accepted that in the two decades *after* repeal, the so-called Golden Age of English farming, production continued to increase, so that the farmers' fears of free trade were demonstrated to be groundless. Recent re-examination of the question, however, has pointed to the fact that in years of scarcity the Corn Laws did protect the home grower and, furthermore, that after 1846 rising imports were accompanied by a decline in home production.[2] There is little doubt that the low wheat prices which marked the years from 1849 to 1852 were possible only because free trade brought an increase in imports from countries which produced wheat at considerably less cost than England.[3]

There was an economic case for the protectionists, although as a purely economic case it was in the defence of a minority landowning class. The purely economic argument for free trade had a much broader appeal. The Anti-Corn Law League had risen to national prominence and political importance during years of crisis for early industrial capitalism, a crisis of growth marked by poor harvests and high bread prices, heavy unemployment and a fall in the profits from manufactures.[4] The crisis may have been overcome, to a large extent, by the railway boom of the mid-1840s, but in 1845 that could not be perceived. What did become increasingly evident to Peel was that a rising population made agricultural self-sufficiency a thing of the past and that to feed the nation cheaply it was necessary to remove the virtual ban imposed by the Corn Laws on imports from the distant lands of Russia and America which, owing to a contraction of western European grain production, were henceforth to be major sources of Britain's wheat.[5] He also came to believe that free trade, by lowering the price of bread and therefore improving the home market for industrial goods and, more important, by stimulating the growth of the international textile trade, was an essential prerequisite of industrial expansion. It was, his colleague, Gladstone, wrote at the end of his career, from learning 'the cause of the different trades out of the mouths of the deputations' which arrived in Whitehall in the black year of 1842, that his 'faith in Protection except as a system of transition crumbled rapidly away'.[6] For Peel and Gladstone, the economic facts of the matter made the free-trade argument unanswerable. 'Whenever it should be established as a *rule*,' Gladstone remarked in 1842, in attempting to justify to Philip Pusey Peel's description of the 1842 sliding scale as an experiment, 'that the growth of the country was less than its consumption, then the graduated scale . . . meant prohibition up to the point of the minimum duty: that was not yet established, but it had seemed to be upon the verge of being established. *When* that was clear, it would be impossible to maintain the law.'[7] It angered Peel that the opponents of repeal in 1846 were men who passed their days 'in hunting and shooting and eating and drinking' and could not know the motives of official men, 'who have access to the best information, and have no other object under Heaven but to provide against danger, and consult the general interests of all classes'.[8] Susan Fairlie, adopting the same point of view, believes that had the figures showing the failure of wheat production to match rising consumption been generally available, the Corn Law controversy would have been impossible, since the free traders would have won the debate almost before it started.[9]

That belief rests on the assumption that the protectionists would have sacrificed what they believed to be the economic interest of the landed class in the economic interest of the nation. Moreover, even if they had been convinced of the economic 'facts', they might not have looked at the whole question of repeal through Peel's eyes. At bottom, what separated Peel and the protectionists was the importance which each side attached to the Corn Laws, not simply in their effect on the profits to be made from wheat-growing, but in their relation to the political and social position of the landed community.

Peel represented the case for free trade as a necessary concession to new interests in society, a concession which would save the aristocracy from an outright radical assault. Repeal was 'true Conservative policy', proposed by a Conservative government so that 'the voice of disaffection should be no longer heard, and that the thought of the dissolution of our institutions should be forgotten in the midst of physical enjoyment'.[10] Peel stood on the same ground that he had occupied in the 1830s. The fundamental duty of a Conservative government was to defend the constitution and the landed aristocracy. Conditions having changed, so had the manner of the defence. 'The worst ground on which we can *now* fight the battle for institutions,' he wrote to a Conservative backbencher in January 1846, 'for the just privileges of Monarchy and Landed Aristocracy – is on a question of food.'[11] Peel's attitude flowed logically from two of his beliefs. The first was that repeal was inevitable, that the Anti-Corn Law League must sometime win the day; it was therefore prudent and conservative for constituted authorities to pre-empt 'a disgraceful struggle' which they were bound to lose,[12] or, as

Aberdeen put it to Queen Victoria, to grant as a boon what they would be forced to yield.[13] The second was that repeal was in the economic interest of the landed class, as he explained to the House of Commons in May 1846.

> I believe it to be of the utmost importance that a territorial aristocracy should be maintained. I believe that in no country is it more important than in this, with its ancient constitution, ancient habits and mixed form of government. . . . The question only is – what in a certain state of public opinion, and in a certain position of society, is the most effectual way of maintaining the legitimate influence and authority of a territorial aristocracy. . . . I said long ago that I thought agricultural prosperity was interwoven with manufacturing prosperity; and depended more on it than on the Corn Laws. . . . I believe the interests direct and indirect of manufacturing and agricultural classes to be the same.[14]

Men who did not share Peel's belief that repeal was inevitable and that it was to the economic advantage of the farmers naturally disagreed also that it was constitutionally and socially desirable. Croker turned Peel's argument around.

> I look farther, much, [he wrote to Brougham in 1843] than the mere questions of prices of corn and rates of wages, which are what, to a logician, I may venture to call mere *accidents*; the *substance* is the existence of a landed gentry, which has made England what she has been and is; without which no representative government can last; without which there can be no steady mean between democracy and despotism . . . *no duty at all* will be the overthrow of the existing social and political system of our country. There's a corn law lecture for you.[15]

Sir Charles Burrell expected from the introduction of free trade, not only poverty and distress, but 'anarchy, confusion, and the rending in tatters Kingly Government and the long-envied constitution of the realm'.[16] Since Cobden himself admitted that the Anti-Corn Law League conducted its operations in 'the belief that we had some distinct class-interest in the question',[17] it is not surprising that the Duke of Richmond should see in repeal, not the socially conservative solution to an economic problem, but a large step towards democrcy.

> I will ask you, if the Anti-Corn Law League succeed in ruining the Agricultural interest – I will ask you whether they will stop there. Did you ever know success produce moderation upon any political party? It is the first step; they feel that it is the yeomanry of England that stand between them and the democratic principles which they wish to carry out.[18]

In the eyes of the protectionists, Peel's capitulation to the Anti-Corn Law League vindicated the methods of mass extra-parliamentary agitation and pointed the way to democratic republicanism.

The repeal issue exposed the extent of the disagreement, at its root psychological, between those Conservatives who wished to freeze social relationships in their existing mould and those who wished to adapt forms to meet changing circumstances. Repeal, that is, exposed in acute form the tension which always exists in a conservative, or preservative, party. With it goes always the constitutional question, whether a party, or rather the government drawn from that party, is justified in carrying into effect changes which it has previously resisted. In 1846 the view that Peel was betraying his party and those voters who had placed him in office in 1841 lodged itself in the minds of the three men who were to come forward as the leaders of the protectionist Conservatives: Disraeli, Lord George Bentinck, and Lord Stanley. Disraeli argued against Peel, as he had over the Maynooth grant in 1845, that by stealing the Whigs' clothing he was depriving the constitution and the electorate of a legitimate opposition. Opposition from Conservative protectionists was the necessary corrective to such 'tyranny'.

> I advise . . . that we all, whatever may be our opinions about free trade, oppose the introduction of free politics. . . . Above all, maintain the line of demarcation between parties; for it is only by maintaining the independence of party that you can maintain the integrity of public men, and the power and influence of Parliament itself.[19]

Lord George Bentinck emerged from the shadows of the back benches because, however much repeal might lower the costs of running his extensive stud farms, he would not be sold.[20] The somewhat tortuous path which Stanley travelled in 1846 requires careful attention: but at the bottom of it lay the conviction, which he gave as one of his reasons for resigning from Peel's government, that 'our support of the Corn Laws has been the main inducement to others to give us the support which placed us, and has kept us, in Office'.[21]

The animus which protectionist Conservatives felt for Peel was fed by suspicions that he had not recently changed his mind, but had all along deceived them by hiding his belief in the inevitability of free trade. In Croker's language, the Irish famine served as the 'practical excuse and opportunity for executing this secret design'.[22] Lord Eglinton, who was to serve as a protectionist whip in the Lords after 1846, said that 'nothing but indignation with Peel's treachery' would have induced him to take up an active career in politics.[23] Although the notion that Peel had, in 1842, hatched a long-term plot of deception is nonsense, there was something disturbing in Peel's attitude towards the 1842 sliding scale. Gladstone, by 1845 a firm free-trader, remained in the government, but even he was troubled by the suspicion that 'nothing could have been more base than to propose the law in 1842 for the chance of a run of good harvests and with the intention of withdrawing it upon the first notion, not even the experience, of a bad one'.[24] Peel cast doubts upon his integrity by arguing in 1842 that the Corn Laws did not cause industrial distress, while claiming three years later that the 1842 tariff reductions had ushered in prosperity. He also attributed his government's success in turning a deficit into a surplus to the increased imports which flowed from the 1842 revision of the tariff, whereas, as Gladstone showed in a pamphlet published in 1845, the income tax made up for the decrease in revenue from articles affected by the revision.[25]

Why, then, in view of the difficulties he faced, did Peel not take Stanley's advice and try to hold his party together by suspending the Corn Laws as a temporary measure of relief, while leaving the larger question to be settled once the immediate crisis had passed? It must at once be recalled that Peel resigned, when Stanley and the Duke of Buccleuch announced that they could not remain in a cabinet committed to repeal, and that he came back into office only because the Whigs did not choose to form a government. He was therefore left to deal with the matter and it was foreign to his nature to conduct a government on principles in which he did not believe. Moreover, just as party had not succeeded in obliterating the habit of independence on the back benches, nor had it entirely overcome the view that a minister's first service was owed to the Crown. By the autumn of 1845 Peel was as weary of his party as some of his followers were distrustful of him. Fitzroy Kelly, who joined the government in 1845, remarked that 'Peel's contempt for his party was very apparent to all who came into office with him'[26] and Graham told Croker in the middle of the 1845 session that 'the country gentlemen cannot be more ready to give us the death-blow than we are to receive it'.[27] Governments, like people, grow old, and though such a state of mind does not explain Peel's action, it helps us to understand it. Peel had spent a long and successful career on the liberal side of the Tory and Conservative party, without courting the Ultras and often without pleasing them. The party had suffered revolts before. No one expected that, although Peel's government might fall, repeal would do irreparable damage to the party he led. The attempt to organize the Ultras in 1829–30 had failed. In 1845 the Maynooth dispute did not even give rise to the attempt. It is therefore not quite right to say that in 1846 repeal was more important to Peel than the Conservative party. The issue did not present itself so starkly to men's minds until after the event. Gladstone, looking back after fifty years, put the matter best: 'From the language he held to me in December 1845 I think he expected to carry the repeal of the Corn Law without breaking up his party. But meant at all hazards to carry it.'[28]

The split in the party

Peel's expectation that the agriculturalists were too weak by themselves to inflict lasting damage on the party was widely shared.

> I am much disposed to agree with you [Thomas Baring wrote to his brother in December 1845] that the agriculturalists will not gain much by fighting Peel.... The misfortune is that we see a great interest in the country with a Ministry in which it has no confidence, without the power of forming another, and with a body of men arranged against them who have shown by their language and acts such a bitter rancour as to savour much of personal hostility. Concession is not,

therefore, merely a sacrifice of interest, but one of pride, influence, power and existence, and I fear we must expect much passion as well as the folly of speech.[29]

That the passion and the folly passed into the organization of a Protectionist party was an astonishing event, unparalleled in English history. It was the mark of how deeply party had worked its way into men's political consciousness that the Conservative protectionists were not content simply to fight repeal to the end, nor even to revenge themselves on the government by throwing it out of office, but that they set about to organize themselves, without any of the party's leaders except Lord Stanley and without the aid of the whips or the party's electoral staff, into a separate party. Of course, they were angry.

> When the great disruption of the Tory party under Sir Robert Peel took place in 1846 [the Earl of Malmesbury wrote], I for the first time took a strong part in politics – not for any liking of that stormy life, which I had always shunned – but from a sincere conviction that the abolition of the Corn Laws, proposed by Peel, would be the ruin of all who depended directly or indirectly upon land. The gallant Duke of Richmond, Lord George Bentinck, and I were among the first to rally our partisans in and out of Parliament by all the means which political hostility allows.[30]

But anger will not sustain a party. Behind the parliamentary party stood the constituencies. In 1846 constituency opinion, in some places even organization, counted for much more than it had in 1829. Peel, who never in his career represented a popular constituency and who only once, at the Oxford by-election of 1829, had to suffer a contest, may not have appreciated the pressure which was exerted upon Conservative members to hold fast to the Corn Laws. It is, indeed, misleading to speak of the creation of a new party in 1846. So it appeared. But it makes more sense to say that the Conservative party, not only the two-thirds of the parliamentary party who voted against repeal, but also the party in the country, threw over the leadership and the minority which supported it and then began to reorganize itself.

The first steps to organize agricultural opinion in defence of the Corn Laws began in 1843–44, just at the time, that is, when the Anti-Corn Law League was extending its activities into the counties in an attempt to win over the tenant farmers to free trade. On the eve of the 1844 session of parliament, Sir John Tyrell, Conservative member for Essex, advised Fremantle that he might find it necessary to move an amendment to the Address, if it did not contain a statement of the government's resolve to oppose the activities of the Anti-Corn Law League.

> I feel strongly with regard to the manner in which the League have been permitted to gain strength in consequence of the absence of any opposition from the Govt. The agricultural body have now determined to act in themselves. If the Govt support them they will be a most powerful engine on their behalf, on the other hand if no assurance is given them of the permanency of the existing measures.[31]

The beginnings of what became popularly known as the 'Anti-League' took place in Essex on the initiative of a tenant farmer, Robert Baker, who, at a meeting attended by the Duke of Richmond, established an Essex Protection Society in April 1843.[32] It was Baker's association which lay behind Tyrell's anxiety at the beginning of 1844. Constituency pressure on county members was not new. In the 1820s the Agricultural Association, consisting principally of tenant farmers and small squires, had pressed members of parliament to vote for a reduction in taxes and the repeal of Peel's 1819 Currency Act.[33] But although English history afforded precedents for large-scale radical movements outside parliament, never before had there been such a large campaign for a conservative object as that mounted by the agriculturalists from 1844 to 1846.

In the first few months of 1844 there was established a network of county protection societies. Where, as in Gloucestershire, the Conservative leaders were reluctant to involve themselves in grass-roots activities which might smack of democracy, others had to move.

> In East Gloucestershire [Innes Lyon wrote to Fremantle in January 1844], we are peculiarly circumstanced. Both our Conservative Members are, and have been, absent. Lord Bathurst, whom I have seen several times, has been timid to move. Lord Ducie is very active, and decidedly hostile. Lord Fitz Hardinge and the Whigs are for fixed duty – in short, for any measure to embarrass the Government.
>
> It became necessary for some one to move the Farmers – and, faute de mieux, I have been actively engaged for the last month in doing so thro' the medium of Peter Mathews, an influential Cotswold Farmer, who looks after my Farms and property there – and himself holds a farm at £1,000 a year.
>
> We are to have a public meeting. They have written to me to propose Resolutions. These can easily be done, but it is wished to go a step further – to present petitions from every Parish against any further alteration of the Corn Laws. Upon this latter point, I wished to have solicited your *personal* advice.[34]

In Kent, where many Conservatives, especially among the gentry, were inhibited for constitutional reasons from adopting the tactics of the League, the tenant farmers formed their own protection society.[35] The founding meeting of the Buckingham Agricultural Protection Society, held in January 1844, was organized exclusively by, and in its language implicitly for, tenant farmers. It was resolved at that meeting 'that although this Society has emanated from the Tenants and Cultivators of the Soil as being the most deeply interested yet they invite all persons concerned with the prosperity of Agriculture to join with them'. It was also resolved to apply to the landed proprietors of the neighbourhood to subscribe to a fund to meet the expenses of meetings, advertisements, petitions to parliament, and publications. The Duke of Buckingham and John Hall, who was to be elected to parliament at the Buckingham by-election of December 1845, each contributed £50.[36] In South Lancashire the Conservative member, John Wilson Patten, who sat for the northern division of the county, was drawn into the organization of Conservative resistance to the League. He sent an account of the arrangements to Stanley, who had represented North Lancashire until his elevation to the Lords in September 1844.

> When I last saw you I told you that Blackburn & myself had summoned a Meeting of 'Delegates' from the various Polling Districts of South Lancashire, for the purpose of ascertaining the state of political feeling in the Division & adopting such measures as might be thought most requisite for withstanding the present onslaught on the Register by the 'League'. We met on Friday last, & I think you may perhaps like to hear the result . . .
>
> There was . . . some difference of opinion as to the best mode of mending matters, & I am sorry to say that in all the Districts there appeared to be a feeling that the Landed Proprietors did not come forward sufficiently, either in the way of attending meetings, which they themselves originated, or in their assistance to the Registration . . .
>
> After considering a variety of suggestions, it was at last agreed to establish, or rather to re-establish two Registration funds; a central one for maintaining a working staff, & a District one to prepare & organize matters in each Polling District for the Central Staff. A temporary Central Committee was formed, & one gentleman from each Polling District undertook to furnish to this Committee the name & address of each principal landowner in his District. The Central Committee are forthwith to write to the Gentlemen urging them to support the respective funds. In the meantime the delegates on their return home were to stir up their Districts with a view to increasing the Register, & both the Central Committee & the Delegates are to report the result of these proceedings to an adjourned meeting on the 14th.
>
> It was pretty clear that Blackburn & myself, who were the only Landed 'Squires' present, were looked to to perform the first duty of the Central Committee. We have therefore divided the work as well a we could & are now engaged in performing it. . . . We propose to ourselves about £800 per an. for the Central Fund, & the District requirements vary from £50 the lowest (Ormskirk) to £200 the highest (I think Bolton).[37]

Patten was describing what had become standard methods of party organization, not the formation of a new protection society. But what is striking is that the South Lancashire Conservative association was revived in response to the challenge presented by the Anti-Corn Law League and that its operation depended upon the protectionist enthusiasm in the lower reaches of the agricultural hierarchy. The apprehensions of the tenant farmers gave birth to a newspaper called *The Agricultural Advertiser and Tenant Farmers' Advocate* in January 1844. On its provisional committee sat secretaries of local protection societies, including Robert Baker. Its motto was 'Measures and Not Men' and its purpose was to defend the Corn Laws.[38]

In February 1844 the local protection societies were, at the instigation of Baker and the Essex society,[39] brought together under the Central Agricultural Protection Society, with the Duke of Richmond as president and the Duke of Buckingham (Chandos, 'the farmers' friend') as vice-president. Its committee was composed of eighteen Conservative members of parliament and twenty tenant farmers.[40] It was supported by funds from the local branches: Essex sent £500 and Buckingham sent £200.[41] The society adopted rules which forbade it to participate in party politics. Direct interference in elections was prescribed, despite the concern caused by the Anti-Corn Law League's systematic assault upon the electoral register. The committee of the society explained that

> if not the letter of the law, at any rate . . . the spirit of the constitution regards the electors of every county and town fully able to choose and control their own representatives in the House of Commons, and whenever strangers interfere, no matter with how much industry, or with how much money, we are of opinion that the constituencies of this great and enlightened country will, in the vast majority of instances, look upon such interference as an impertinence and an insult.[42]

The society intended to restrict itself to making agricultural opinion, of whatever party, known to parliament by the ancient method of petitioning.

The rules reflected the caution of the parliamentary members of the committee. By 1845 the tenant farmers were becoming impatient. The 1845 budget, which renewed the income tax and made further inroads on the tariff wall, provoked Richmond to lead a deputation of twenty-two tenant farmers, accompanied by a handful of members of parliament, to Downing Street to entreat Peel to reduce the burden of taxes on the land. The deputation failed in its object; and only one Conservative, the proudly independent William Blackstone, voted against the renewal of the income tax. After the next, rancorous meeting of the Central Protection Society, on 17 February, the secretary of the society, Henry Byron, wrote to Richmond that the farmers were bent on a more decidedly political course.

> It is sincerely to be wished that this carping spirit among the farmers (the natural result, however, of their depressed condition) may be allayed – but I much fear from all I hear, that it is more likely to spread than to decrease. There cannot be a doubt that the position of the Agricultural Members of Parliament at the present time is a most unpleasant, difficult and critical one, for it is clear that to a *parliamentary* course the tenant farmers point to a man.[43]

The farmers succeeded in getting the Protection Society to exercise its influence on behalf of Philip Miles' amendment to the Income Tax Bill to enable farmers to appeal against the assessment of their rent. The society sent circulars to the local branches urging them to rouse their members to vote for the amendment. The amendment was defeated, but sixty-two Conservatives, forty-two of them county members, voted for it.[44]

When the repeal crisis arrived, then, it was probable that at least some members would find it difficult to withstand the strength of protectionist sentiment in their constituencies. As Arbuthnot said to Peel in 1842, some county members were 'more clamorous on account of their constituents, than from any apprehension for their own pockets';[45] and a year later, when the Canada Corn Bill came up, Peel was informed that 'all the *Cons. want* . . . to vote with the Govt., but they are afraid of offending their constituents'.[46] Not all county members objected to the pressure placed upon them. When the

1842 budget was before the House of Commons, Philip Pusey, in calling upon Conservatives to look at measures, not men, said that 'I certainly think the County Members are bound to obtain the best terms they can, since it is not our own property we are dealing with, but that of our constituents'.[47]

At a meeting in the first week of December 1845 the Central Protection Society rescinded its non-political rule.[48] In January it established an election committee and distributed a circular to local societies advising them of the tactics to employ against the government.

> It is recommended to the County and Local Protection Societies, that they do immediately form Committees, of not more than Twelve Gentlemen, to wait upon the Members in their several districts who were elected on Protective principles, and press them either to reject the proposal of Sir Robert Peel, or at once to resign their Seats, and appeal to their different constituencies for a sanction of the change in their political opinions.[49]

The local societies were informed in that circular that a committee of tenant farmers had been appointed 'to attend in London during the debate on Protection of Native Industry, for the purpose of affording practical information to the friends of Protection (Members of Parliament) which they may require'.

Some Conservatives, of course, refused to act as mere delegates and commit themselves to a course of action in parliament. Sir Thomas Fremantle, no longer the Chief Whip, but still a loyal government supporter, lectured Henry Smith, the secretary of the Buckingham protection society, on the constitutional independence of members of parliament.

> I have to acknowledge the receipt of your letter, written by direction of the Members who attended a general meeting of the Buckingham Agricultural Protection Society on the 3rd Inst., in which you call upon me for an early answer whether I will be prepared to advocate and support the views of that Society, embodied in a resolution, a copy of which had been forwarded to me.
>
> Altho' you have not favored me with the names of the gentlemen who composed the meeting referred to, I conclude that many of them are among the number of my friends and constituents. I should be sorry, therefore, to make a reply to their enquiry, which they might deem uncourteous, but I must request upon you to inform them, that I decline most respectfully to enter into any engagement with reference to my conduct in a future Session of Parliament.
>
> If the Constituency which I have the honor to represent shall have reason to be dissatisfied with my conduct as their representative, they will be entitled to demand an explanation from me, and I shall receive with deference and attention any representations which they may think fit to address to me, but I must for my own part claim the right to exercise my own judgement as to the course, which I ought to pursue and to act in conformity with my own sense of public duty.
>
> I should betray the great trust which has been reposed in me, and forfeit at the same time the good opinion of my Constituents, were I to bind myself to advocate and support the views, and to obey the instructions of any self-constituted society, however deserving of my respect and regard the gentlemen who compose that society may individually be.[50]

The protection societies were singularly unsuccessful in persuading free-trade Conservatives to offer themselves for re-election. All but a handful of them dismissed the suggestion, for the reasons which Caledon DuPre, the member for Buckinghamshire and himself a protectionist, gave to Smith.

> Having been out of town this morning engaged in the business of my petty Session, I found on my return your letter and was informed that a deputation of gentlemen had called on me. I much regret that those gentlemen had this unnecessary trouble. . . . I must beg of you to state to them, what I am very sorry not to have had an opportunity of doing in person, that it is my intention to offer to the ministerial measure every opposition in my power . . . but I must beg respectfully but most decidedly to differ from them in the view they take of their right to call on a county member to resign his Seat; I beg to remind you and them that I was elected by the county at large, and do not feel myself responsible to a body which though most respectable is merely a local association assembled for local purposes. To a majority of my constituents, legally convened, I should bow with submission, but I cannot do so to any one of the societies which are established in different parts of the county. This is no unimportant distinction and one involving a great constitutional principle, which I shall be prepared to defend in any place or at any time.[51]

Nevertheless, at meeting after meeting in December and January Conservative members responded to constituency feeling by promising to vote against total repeal.[52] The Times's leader writer was not looking very hard when he reported that 'wherever we turn our eyes, whether to Gloucestershire, Shropshire or Cambridgeshire, we find the same symptoms – disorganization and dissension among some country gentlemen, indifference on the part of others, whilst the great body of the tenant farmers appear wholly unconcerned, or very lukewarm in the Protection cause'.[53] Of course the level of interest was not uniform throughout the country. Richard Olney found that the 1846 session passed with 'very little agitation among the Lincolnshire farmers', for reasons both political and economic: against the united front of Peel, Russell, and the Anti-Corn Law League opposition was futile; and since, despite a fall in prices, Lincolnshire farmers were still doing well, 'their feeling was for settling the question and allowing the markets a time of quiet in which to adjust themselves'.[54] It was natural that livestock farmers should care less about the Corn Laws than arable farmers,[55] but the difference was not felt everywhere. In Buckinghamshire, where livestock farming was important, the cry for protection was loud, helped, perhaps, by Chandos's success over the years in making the Corn Laws a symbol of the rural community and its values.[56]

Even if, what may be thought improbable, the protection societies actually turned few members' votes, they provided a counterweight to the pull of government authority. They kept Conservative members who might otherwise have wavered up to protectionist the mark. The central offices in Old Bond Street, moreover, provided an alternative headquarters to the Carlton for those Conservatives who were eager to rally the party against the government.

'The Agricultural Constituencies seem to be riding in every direction,' Lord George Bentinck wrote in the first week of January, 'and the cry of "No Surrender" seems very general.'[57] The few free-trade Conservatives who fought by-elections early in 1846 found the combination of the farmers' anger and the Central Protection Society's funds too formidable to overcome. At Nottinghamshire South, Lord Lincoln, standing for re-election after taking a seat in the cabinet, was defeated by Thomas Hildyard, who was sent an agent and £2,000 by the Bond Street election committee.[58] Lord Ashley, who surprisingly decided to vote for repeal, offered himself for re-election to the Dorsetshire electors. His colleague, Henry Sturt, did the same. They paid for their constitutional scruples.

> Messrs Floyer and Ker Seymer [Ashley entered in his diary] put up by large body of Gentry for the county; subscription made, their expenses to be paid! How can I stand against this? They have already canvassed the County by means of the Farmers and paid agents. . . . There are many Gentlemen favourable to us; but they do not combine or even move . . . all the stirring men are on the other side . . . had I a responsible committee, or ten thousand pounds in the Banker's hands, I might sustain a successful fight; but I cannot begin with less security.
>
> Quite clear that Dorsetshire is hopeless – the hostility is very great; canvasses ask the votes *against* me personally & by name.[59]

Both Ashley and Sturt declined to go to a poll and the protectionists, Floyer and Ker Seymer, were elected without a contest.

At Westminster the parliamentary opposition to the government began to marshal its forces early in January. The task in front of them was daunting. When Peel returned to office on 20 December, after Lord John Russell's failure to form a government, he brought with him all the members of his last cabinet except Stanley. At least three of them – Graham, Aberdeen, and Sidney Herbert – were free-traders. The others, who in early November had withheld their assent to repeal, were moved primarily by the consideration that no other government but Peel's could stand and that the Crown had, therefore, a claim on their services. They did not think that the Corn Laws were worth a constitutional crisis.[60] Stanley, isolated by his colleagues' decisions, publicly owned that he neither desired a protectionist government nor thought one possible. So personal were the motives for his resignation that he advised Gladstone to join a government which he felt compelled to leave and made no attempt to dissuade the Duke of Buccleuch, who had originally decided to resign with him, from remaining in it.[61]

The split in the party in 1846 followed approximately the line which divided the official 'men of business' from the backbenchers. When the Protectionists formed a government in 1852, only two of the forty-five office-holders, other than Stanley, had held office under Peel.[62] In addition the Chief Whip, Sir John Young, who had succeeded Fremantle in 1844, and the election manager, Francis Bonham, sided with Peel. The onus of leading the rearguard protectionist action in the House of Commons therefore fell upon men unaccustomed to political leadership or political management, above all upon one of the most extraordinary characters in English political history, Lord George Bentinck.

Bentinck was a woefully poor speaker whose thin, cracking voice had seldom been heard in the House of Commons. Since his election to the House in 1826, his parliamentary career had been passed in obscurity. He was known to the public, if at all, as the ruthless opponent of skulduggery in the world of horse-racing. At the beginning of 1846 he had no thought of leading a party. He did not expect, either, that repeal could be defeated. But he looked upon Peel and his accomplices as 'no better than Common Cheats'[63] who were giving a shock to the political system by their 'wholesale examples of political lying and pledge-breaking'.[64] Come what might, it was necessary that 'for the sake of Political Morals and the Characters of Public Men . . . a salutary lesson should in all cases be taught to the delinquent Politicians'.[65] Repeal acted upon Bentinck as ship money did upon Hampden. And of Bentinck it may be said, as Clarendon said of Hampden, that when he drew his sword, he threw away the scabbard. Not until he had succeeded in driving Peel from office did Bentinck relax his efforts. It was a six-month long labour, and at the end of it the Conservative party was broken.

Early in January 1846 Bentinck got in touch with the Duke of Richmond, and at meetings at the Protection Society's offices they planned their parliamentary strategy. Bentinck and Richmond were assisted by a small group of Conservative backbenchers, including Charles Newdegate, William Beresford, Philip Miles, George Bankes, and Stafford O'Brien, the chairman of the Protection Society's publications committee. Their work quickly bore fruit. On 14 January Bentinck reported that his lists contained 180 anti-Peel Conservatives.[66] Two weeks later, at a meeting held the day before the meeting of parliament, Philip Miles was chosen to act as leader of the protectionists and Newdegate was made his assistant. When the first night of the repeal debate came on, Lord John Russell was surprised to find the protectionists 'a very strong and compact party, from 220 to 240 in the House of Commons, and no one knows how many in the Lords'.[67] Since the entire Whig opposition supported repeal, those numbers gave the protectionists no hope of defeating the government on the Corn Bill in the House of Commons. Nevertheless, at Bentinck's insistence, it was agreed to prolong the struggle in the Commons for as long as possible, so that the voice of the country should have time to make itself heard before the Bill reached the Lords.

In drawing out the Bill's passage through the Commons the protectionists were successful, and as the weeks passed what had begun as a temporary arrangement for getting up the vote on a specific issue acquired a more lasting character. On 31 March, at a meeting summoned by Stafford O'Brien, a committee was formed for 'considering and deciding upon the course to be

adopted by the Party in Parliament on all important occasions'.[68] Until then
the protectionists had been led by a group of men: Miles, Bentinck, O'Brien,
Bankes, and Disraeli. For a party which intended to broaden its activities it
was desirable to settle the leadership question. There was no doubt who
should be the leader. Though subsequently pre-eminent, and in 1845 and 1846
the most oratorically brilliant of Peel's adversaries, Disraeli was not in the
running. He needed time to demonstrate to the country gentlemen that,
flamboyant, literary, Jewish-born and unlanded though he might be, he was
the best leader they could have. They appreciated the effect of Disraeli's
wounding thrusts at Peel; but they did not warm to the manner of them.
Bentinck, the very type of a country member, had earned their gratitude and
their respect. Every night he had attended the debates from beginning to end.
From a state of economic ignorance he had, in the hours when parliament was
not sitting, made himself familiar with the statistics of trade and production.
It was his energy and persistence which raised the protectionist opposition to
the government from a protest into a rebellion.

There was, however, one drawback. Bentinck had never disguised his
unflinching attachment to religious toleration. He had none of the Anglican
prejudices of those Conservatives who had stridently denounced the religious
liberalism of successive governments. In April he reluctantly accepted the
leadership for which he knew he was not fitted, on the understanding that he
would fill the post only until a more suitable permanent appointment could
be made and that he was free to pursue his own course on religious
questions.[69] At the same time, Stanley was drafted into the leadership of the
party in the Lords, although it was not until after the 1846 session that Stanley
acknowledged the position. At a meeting at Richmond's house from which
Stanley was conspicuously absent, the protectionist peers decided 'to look
upon Stanley as the leader of the party, and to do nothing without consulting
him'.[70] Lord Malmesbury was appointed protectionist Whip in the Lords and
Lord Eglinton his assistant.

The installation of Bentinck as the official leader in the Commons of what
must now be called the Protectionist party had one great consequence: it
meant that even after repeal had passed, the government would be driven to
its defeat. The Protectionists tried to overthrow the government on several
minor issues before the Corn Bill became law. In that they failed. And an
attempt to reach a compromise in the Lords on a small fixed duty was nipped
in the bud by Lord John Russell.[71] But on the day that the Corn Bill passed its
third reading in the House of Lords, the Commons was debating another in
the long series of nineteenth-century Coercion Bills for Ireland. The Whig
opposition had tabled an amendment to have the Bill read that day six
months. On 8 June the Protectionists met at the house of George Bankes to
decide whether to support the opposition amendment. Irish coercion was not
the most suitable issue by which the Protectionists might slake their
vengeance on Peel. Their ranks included most of the anti-Catholic section of

the Conservative party. But it was the first issue which came to hand and it was clear that it was not Ireland, but Peel's government, which was at stake. The Protectionist leaders decided to oppose the Bill. On 25 June sixty-nine Protectionists joined with the Whigs to defeat the government. Peel resigned at once and a new chapter in the history of the Conservative party began.

For the repeal of the Corn Laws Peel had the support of 119 Conservatives. Against him were the remaining two-thirds of the party. A matter of interest to historians for some time, as it was so passionately to men living in the 1840s, has been whether a connection existed between the social and economic status of members of parliament and their votes on the repeal of the Corn Laws. In a pioneer study of the question forty years ago, J. A. Thomas came to the conclusion that the business and manufacturing classes tended to favour repeal and the landed class to oppose it.[72] Thomas thus corroborated the contemporary interpretation of things. Recently, however, his findings have been disputed by Professor Aydelotte, who is concerned to remove class from the interpretation of the Corn Law debate. He has argued that 'Thomas's conclusions are in fact incorrect' and that, inside the House of Commons, 'the country gentlemen, qua country gentlemen, cannot be associated in any distinctive sense . . . with the opposition to the repeal of the Corn Laws'.[73] Thomas analysed the votes of the whole of the House of Commons and found a higher proportion of pro-repeal votes among non-landed members than among landed. Professor Aydelotte does not disagree with the figures; he takes issue with Thomas' interpretation of them, because he finds fault with Thomas' method.

> Thomas failed to hold the party variable constant while testing for other correlations. In other words, he committed the elementary statistical error of failing to take into account all possibly relevant variables. As a result his conclusions were distorted. Businessmen and men unrelated to the landed class were proportionately more numerous on the Liberal side of the House, which supported repeal almost unanimously, and hence figures for parliament as a whole do show . . . some relationship between men's personal backgrounds and their votes on the Corn Law Bill. However, findings for the whole House shed no light whatsoever on whether votes were related to personal background, since this test does not take into account two other matters which have repeatedly been shown to be to some degree relevant to votes: party and constituency. When these two variables are controlled, the class correlations virtually disappear.

Professor Aydelotte does not mince words. Yet the question is more subtle than he allows.[74] He has, indeed, shown that within the Conservative party the landed and non-landed sections split almost identically on repeal (though, even so, slightly in the direction of Thomas' argument) and he therefore makes the reasonable suggestion that the most probable explanation of a member's votes, beyond the irreducible one that men have minds, is to be sought in the party to which he belonged and the type of constituency he represented. Finding the explanation there, however, does not take the argument away from class.

Professor Aydelotte's own breakdown of the voting by constituency is conclusive. The landed section of the Conservative parliamentary party was not proportionately more opposed to repeal than the non-landed. But the section which *represented* the land was markedly so: 86 per cent of the members who sat for county and university constituencies voted against repeal, 63 per cent of those who sat for rural boroughs with an electorate of less than 500, and 50 per cent of those who represented boroughs with an electorate of more than 500. Those figures suggest that contemporaries who interpreted the repeal issue in class terms may not have been, as Professor Aydelotte claims that they were, 'seriously mistaken concerning the general course of events'.

Then there is the role of party. Professor Aydelotte concludes that the reason the Whig businessmen voted for free trade was that they were Whigs. It may be so (although such a degree of party authority must have made the Conservative split almost impossible). Or it may be the other way around. Party often determines opinion. Opinion also determines a man's choice of party. What Professor Aydelotte does not consider is the whole context of political behaviour. He does not consider that men's personal backgrounds may have helped to shape their opinions and therefore their choice of party, so that the reason why the Whigs had more businessmen than the Conservatives may have been that businessmen tended to hold Whiggish opinions. Non-landed politicians may have found their way into the Whig party because of their general outlook, an outlook which was likely to lead them to vote for free trade. If so, then an analysis of the repeal divisions within the whole of the House of Commons is a better guide than an analysis of the Conservative members only. Thomas, it may be supposed, took that for granted.

Removing the class element from the crisis of 1846 makes nonsense of the feelings of those Conservatives who bitterly resented Peel's 'betrayal' of the Conservative party. That the landed and non-landed individuals of the parliamentary party voted so similarly matters not nearly so much as the fact that the landed class supplied a higher proportion of the Conservative party than of the Whigs and that Conservatives who sat for agricultural constituencies voted overwhelmingly in what they assumed to be the interest of the class which they represented. It is surely not accidental that for a generation after 1846 the Conservative party was, and suffered electorally for being, firmly tied to the agricultural community.

Notes and References

Free trade versus protection
1 Prince Albert memorandum, 25 Dec, 1845: 'He [Peel] said he had been determined not to go to a general election with the fetters the last election had imposed upon him, and he had meant at the end of the next Session to call the whole Conservative Party together and to declare this to them. . . . This had been defeated by events coming too suddenly upon him, and he had no alternative but to deal with the Corn Laws before a national calamity would *force* it on.' (Victoria, ii, 76–9.)
2 Fairlie, 'The Corn Laws and British wheat production, 1829–76', *Econ. HR*, April 1969, 88–116.
3 *Ibid*, 92–3, 103; Tooke and Newmarch, *A History of Prices and of the State of Circulation from 1792 to 1856*, v, 57.
4 For a discussion of 'the crisis of the first phase of British capitalism', see Hobsbawm, *Industry and Empire*, 54–9 and 88–97.
5 Fairlie, 'The nineteenth-century Corn Law reconsidered', *Econ. HR*, Dec, 1965, 562–73.
6 Gladstone memorandum, 12 July 1894: Gladstone, *Autobiographica*, 72–6.
7 Gladstone memorandum, 8 Dec, 1842: *Memoranda*, 184–6.
8 Peel to his wife, 16 Dec, 1845: Peel, *Private Letters*, 273.
9 Fairlie, 'Corn Laws and wheat production', 96.
10 *Hansard*, 3rd series, lxxxiii, 95.
11 Peel to B. Denison, 7 Jan, 1846: Peel MSS, Add. MSS 40532, ff. 89–90.
12 Peel to Hardinge, 24 Sept, 1846: Parker, *Peel*, iii, 473.
13 Queen Victoria to the King of the Belgians, 7 July 1846: Victoria, *Letters*, ii, 103–4.
14 4 May 1846, *Hansard*, 3rd series, lxxxvi, 53–70.
15 Croker to Brougham, 19 Feb, 1843: Croker, *Correspondence and Diaries*, iii, 13.
16 Burrell to the Duke of Richmond, 27 Dec, 1843: Goodwood MSS, 1651, f. 295.
17 Morley, *The Life of Richard Cobden*, i, 140–1.
18 Speech at the meeting of Central Agricultural Protection Society, 12 Jan, 1846: *Morning Herald*, 13 Jan, 1846.
19 22 Jan, 1846, *Hansard*, 3rd series, lxxxiii, 122–3.
20 Monypenny and Buckle, *Disraeli*, ii, 360.
21 Stanley memorandum for the cabinet, 3 Nov, 1845: Derby MSS, 27/5. The memorandum is printed in Appendix 10.
22 *Quarterly Review*, June 1847, 294–5.
23 Eglinton to Stanley, 12 Oct, 1848: Derby MSS, 148/2.
24 Gladstone memorandum, 6 Dec, 1845: Gladstone MSS, Add. MSS 44777, ff. 233–6.

25 Peel, *Memoirs*, ii, 102–6; Gladstone, *Remarks Upon Recent Commercial Legis-lation*, 7–12.
26 Stanley Diary, 20 March 1853.
27 Graham to Croker, 22 March 1845: Parker, *Peel*, iii, 172.
28 Gladstone memorandum, 12 July 1894: Gladstone, *Autobiographica*, 72–6, Kelley gave his opinion to Edward Stanley that Peel 'took it for granted that wherever he went they would follow. On the Corn Law question he expected a few hard words, a little murmuring, and then that all would go on as before. This belief he retained even during the spring of '46: and his disappointment was proportionate when compelled to resign' (Stanley Diary, 20 March 1853.) Once the debate had begun in the Commons, however, and the strength of the protectionist opposition to the government revealed, Peel informed the Queen that he did not expect the Conservative party to survive (Peel to Queen Victoria, 11 Feb, 1846: Parker, *Peel*, iii, 339).

The split in the party
29 Baring, *Journals and Correspondence*, i, 230.
30 Malmesbury, *Memoirs of an Ex-Minister*, i, 41.
31 Tyrell to Fremantle, 21 Jan, 1844: Fremantle MSS, 81/8.
32 For the origins and organization of the Anti-League, see Lawson-Tancred, 'The Anti-League and the Corn Law crisis of 1846', *Hist. J*, iii, 2, 1960, 162–83.
33 Spring and Crosby, 'George Webb Hall and the Agricultural Association', *J. Brit. Stud*, ii, 1, 1962, 115–31.
34 Lyon to Fremantle, 27 Jan, 1844: Fremantle MSS, 81/8.
35 Andrews, 'Political issues in the county of Kent, 1820–1846', unpublished thesis, 250–67.
36 Volume of Minutes of the Buckingham Agricultural Protection Society: Archdeacon MSS, D/AR/6/unnumbered.
37 Patten to Stanley, 28 Dec, 1844: Derby MSS, 147/6. 'Blackburn' is J. I. Blackburne, the Conservative member for Warrington from 1832 to 1847.
38 See the printed circular announcing the new newspaper, Archdeacon MSS, D/AR/6/unnumbered.
39 At a meeting of the Buckingham Agricultural Protection Society on 17 Feb, 1844 there was read a circular letter from the chairman of the Essex society inviting Buckingham to send delegates to London on 20 February to the meeting to establish a central society (volume of 'Minutes of the Buckingham Agricultural Protection Society', Archdeacon MSS, D/AR/6/unnumbered).
40 Cayley, *Reasons for the Formation of the Agricultural Protection Society*, London, 1844.
41 H. T. Biddell to H. Smith, 27 April 1844; C. Greaves to H. Smith, 19 April 1844: Archdeacon MSS, D/AR/6/26.
42 Report of the General Committee of the Agricultural Protection Society for Great Britain and Ireland, Dec, 1844: *ibid*, D/AR/6/32.
43 Byron to Richmond, 23 Feb, 1845: Goodwood MSS, 1669, f. 194.
44 The amendment was opposed by 151 Conservatives, including 67 county members (Fisher, 'The opposition to Sir Robert Peel in the Conservative Party, 1841–1846', unpublished thesis, 202).
45 Arbuthnot to Peel, 9 April 1842: Peel MSS, Add. MSS 40484, ff. 105–6.
46 W. Y. Peel to Peel, [May 1843]: *ibid*, Add. MSS 40529, f. 39.
47 Pusey to Richmond, 10 April 1842: Goodwood MSS, 1644, f. 1441–2.

48 *Standard*, 11 Dec, 1845.
49 Circular letter from Henry Byron, 29 Jan, 1846: Archdeacon MSS, D/AR/6/unnumbered.
50 Fremantle to Smith, 7 Jan, 1846: *ibid*, D/AR/6/28. Smith's appeals to Buckinghamshire members to support Miles' motion of March, 1845, had elicited similar responses. Rice Clayton replied guardedly that he should 'lose no opportunity of supporting any measure or motion . . . which I may consider likely in any way to promote the real interest of the Tenant Farmers or of agriculturalists in general' (Clayton to Smith, 12 March 1845: *ibid*, D/AR/6/27). Christopher Tower, Caledon DuPre, and William Fitzmaurice also refused to pledge themselves before hearing the debate in the House, although Tower and Fitzmaurice avowed their intention to vote with Miles (Tower to Smith, 16 March 1845; DuPre to Smith, [9] March 1845; Fitzmaurice to Smith, 14 March 1845: *ibid*). Only Sir John Chetwode evinced a strong desire to act in close liaison with the protection society, and even he took care to inform Smith that he voted with Miles before receiving Smith's request that he do so (Chetwode to Smith, 11 and 12 March 1845: *ibid*).
51 DuPre to Smith, 2 Feb, 1846: *ibid*, D/AR/6/28.
52 See the daily reports in the *Standard* and *John Bull*.
53 *The Times*, 11 Feb, 1846.
54 Olney, *Lincolnshire Politics*, 118–19.
55 'In 1846 when the Duke of Buccleuch received a report on the attitude of his tenants in Roxburghshire to the abolition of the Corn Laws, it appeared that only a few of the arable farmers were at all concerned over the question; those with sheep and cattle interests "don't seem to care *one farthing* about it".' (Brash, 'Conservatives in the Haddington district of Burghs', *Trans. E. Lothian Antiquarian . . . Society*, 1968, 62).
56 Spring, 'Chandos and the Farmers', 278.
57 Bentinck to Portland, 2 Jan, 1846: Portland MSS, PWH/193.
58 Bentinck to Portland, 11 and 13 Feb, 1846: *ibid*, PWH/ 203, 205.
59 7th Earl of Shaftesbury, Diary, 9 and 12 Feb, 1846: Broadlands MSS, SHA/PD/4. Although he complained of his lack of funds, Ashley turned down Bonham's offer of £2,000, because, in his maverick fashion, he wished not to compromise his 'independence of thought and action': (*ibid*, 6 Feb, 1846).
60 Wellington to Croker, 6 Jan, 1846: Croker, *Correspondence and Diaries,* iii, 52–5; Buccleuch to Peel, 22 Dec, 1845: Peel, *Memoirs*, ii, 254–7; Lyndhurst to Peel, 2 Dec, 1845; Peel MSS, Add. MSS 40442, ff. 305–6.
61 Peel, *Memoirs*, ii, 229–32; Stanley to Peel, 22 Dec, 1845: Parker, *Peel*, ii, 287; Peel to Prince Albert, 23 Dec, 1845: Victoria, *Letters*, ii, 76.
62 Sir Frederick Thesiger and Fitzroy Kelley, the Attorney-General and Solicitor General respectively, both in 1846 and 1852. Wellington was the commander-in-chief in 1852, but he held the commission on non-political grounds.
63 Bentinck to Stanley, 7 Jan, 1846: Derby MSS, 132/13.
64 Bentinck to Stanley, 20 Jan, 1846: *ibid*.
65 Bentinck to Portland, 10 Feb, 1846: Portland MSS, PWH/202.
66 Bentinck to Portland, 14 Jan, 1846: *ibid*, PWH/196.
67 Russell to his wife, 16 Feb, 1846: MacCarthy and Russell, *Lady John Russell*, 81.
68 O'Brien to Disraeli, 28 March 1846: Hughenden MSS, B/XXI/S/452.
69 Disraeli, *Bentinck*, 179.
70 Malmesbury, *Memoirs*, i, 169.

71 For details of the parliamentary battle of 1846 see Stewart, *Politics of Protection*, 60–76.

72 Thomas, 'The repeal of the Corn Laws, 1846', *Economica*, April 1929, 53–60, and 'The House of Commons, 1832–67', *ibid*, Oct, 1929, 49–61.

73 Aydelotte, 'The country gentlemen and the repeal of the Corn Laws', *EHR*, Jan, 1967, 52, 59. The quotations from Professor Aydelotte which follow are all taken from this article.

74 It does not inspire confidence in Professor Aydelotte's judgement that he counters Disraeli's famous metaphorical description of the 'men of metal' who marched into the lobbies against Peel by pointing out that the eight metal manufacturers in the Conservative party split their votes in roughly the same proportion as the rest of the party (*ibid*, 55–6).

Part III

The age of Derby

Chapter 11

The Protectionist years I: 1846–50

The new leaders: Stanley and Bentinck

For a generation after the repeal of the Corn Laws the Conservative party ceased to be a governing party. Not until 1874 did it again win a majority at the polls. The initiative in politics passed to the Liberals. Various causes contributed to the party's long season of dormancy. As it had in the early 1830s, so for many years after 1846 the party suffered from its identification with an issue in politics that had been settled. The party fell back on its bedrock support in the agricultural counties, and the electoral imbalance of the 1832 system made it extremely difficult for a predominantly landed party to gain power. In 1831–32 the Conservatives were not interested in creating equal electoral districts. The very phrase smacked of 'scientific' radicalism. Yet the Whig-Liberal hegemony from 1832 to 1874 owed a great deal to the circumstance that a county member represented many more people than a borough member. In 1841 the Conservatives overcame that handicap because they appeared to be a more effective antidote than the Whigs to the radicalism of the 1830s. They took office against a background of aggressive extra-parliamentary agitation and severe economic dislocation. The circumstances after 1846 were very different. The 1850s and 1860s were the peak years of Victorian prosperity and political stability. Chartism collapsed at Kennington Common in 1848 and for the next twenty years the most persistent radical activity, the Liberation Society's campaign against Church rates and established religion, was conducted, for the most part, discreetly within the Liberal party. For two decades Liberalism, led cautiously by Lord John Russell and blandly by Viscount Palmerston, offered little scope for a Conservative reaction. There was no evident reason why the electorate should prefer to be governed conservatively by the Conservatives rather than the Whigs.

Those circumstances might not, even so, have operated to keep the Conservatives in a permanent minority had the two wings of the party made their peace after the rupture of 1846. From 1846 to 1852 the progress of the Protectionist party was bedevilled by the irreconcilable conflict between the desire to reunite the Conservative party and the desire to return to some kind of protectionist policy. Had the Protectionists come quickly to accept free trade as a *fait accomli*, the split in the party might not have become permanent. As it was, protection was not officially abandoned until after the 1852 elections, and by then it was too late to repair the damage. No Peelite served in the Protectionist government formed in 1852. When it fell after ten months in office, six leading Peelites joined in a coalition government with the Whigs. It was the Protectionists who became the bearers of the Conservative tradition. But they did so shorn of the best political talents in the party. In 1846 all the coming men on the Conservative side of politics – men like Gladstone, Lord Lincoln, Sidney Herbert, Edward Cardwell, and Lord Dalhousie – had cast their lot with the free-traders. Without them the Protectionist, and eventually once more the Conservative, party suffered from the disadvantage that none of its members, except Stanley and, less obviously, Disraeli, was of acknowledged ministerial calibre.

From 1846 to 1868 the party was led by Stanley (after his father's death in 1851, Lord Derby), at once the longest serving and the least known of Conservative leaders. His relative obscurity is the result of his having led the party in its leanest years and also of his own personality and style of leadership. After 1846 his public career was veiled in reticence. His ambition was sapped by a species of fatalism. No doubt he was justified in feeling that the current of the age ran against the Conservative party, and that his duty was to be the faithful custodian of a creed out of fashion. Certainly his career after 1846 exhibits a curious passivity, in which were joined the feeling that office was scarcely a prize to be sought and the apprehension that in office the Conservatives had little that was distinctive to offer the nation. Before 1846 Stanley was, had been perhaps for too long, the rising star of politics. In 1844, weary of the House of Commons, he retreated to the House of Lords. Thereafter he carried about him the resigned air of a man conscious that he would never achieve the commanding power for which he had once seemed so evidently destined.

Nothing in Stanley's career before 1846 suggested that he would one day find himself at the head of the right wing of the Conservative party. All his experience, as a Canningite, reformer, and minister in Peel's government, had been in the political centre. Early on in Peel's administration he had expressed misgivings about the direction of Peel's thought in commercial matters, but he had supported the Maynooth grant wholeheartedly and during the two crises of 1844 had taken a hard line in cabinet against Gladstone's suggestion that Peel should find a compromise with the rebels. Stanley's resignation in 1845 was not, therefore, the culmination of a slowly maturing separation from the government. He cut himself off from his political friendships without having made new ones to replace them. He acted without illusions and without any immediately practical political intent. 'Though it is difficult to foresee the future, my own opinion is that my official life is over, and I am well content that it should be so. The political current seems steadily setting in a direction which leaves me high and dry on the beach.'[1] Stanley did not leave Peel's government because he was a protectionist. In the long memorandum which he prepared for the cabinet in the first week of November 1845 he argued only that repeal was irrelevant to the Irish famine and that the government had, therefore, no case to introduce it on a plea of necessity.[2] Stanley resigned to preserve his reputation for political consistency, not to fight for the Corn Laws against a Conservative government. He explained to Ellenborough that he could not honestly have recommended as a minister 'measures in which, as an individual peer, I can honestly advise acquiesence'.[3] He meant, at the beginning of 1846, to vote for free trade, believing that the notion of forming a Conservative government 'upon any other system and composed of any other materials' was a delusion.[4] Stanley's object was to preserve the Conservative party 'as a safeguard against the innovating spirit of the present day in matters even more essential than the maintenance of the Corn Laws'.[5] That was precisely Wellington's reason for remaining in the government. It made less sense as a reason for leaving it.

As the session of 1846 unfolded, Stanley's precious position became increasingly difficult to maintain. The size of the protectionist opposition to Peel rendered it impossible that a future Conservative government should be formed without their support. The violence of the protectionists' attacks on Peel made it impossible that they should ever again be led by him. Thus Stanley's hope that the Conservative party should survive the 1846 session intact vanished. His position therefore changed. By March he had decided to speak and vote against repeal. Two days after he had informed the Duke of Rutland of that change,[6] the protectionist peers decided to look upon him as their leader. Their decision had no marked effect upon Stanley. In January he had resisted Bentinck's pleas that he assist in the organization of the protectionist opposition to repeal. Throughout March and April, as the Corn Bill made its way through the Commons, he continued to deprecate the idea of a formally organized Protectionist party. As late as the first week of May he held to his opinion that 'the attempt to form any party except so far as relates to an united effort to reject or greatly modify the measures now contemplated would be premature'.[7] But by the beginning of June, after making an impassioned speech in defence of the landed aristocracy, in which he referred to the repeal of the Corn Laws as a 'great delusion' and a 'hazardous and fearful experiment',[8] Stanley was no longer able to resist the pressure of events. He approved of the decision to overthrow Peel on the Coercion Bill, because he realized that Conservative reunion could not take place under Peel. It was therefore important to get the dissolution out of Peel's hands.[9] Although there is no date on which Stanley explicitly or publicly acknowledged his position as leader of the Protectionist party, he attended the dinner given to the party by the Duke of Richmond on 8 July, when Lord George Bentinck hailed him as the leader of the party in both Houses.[10]

Down to 1846 the careers of Stanley and Bentinck had run parallel. Both were sons of famous and powerful Whig families. Both had been Canningites in the late 1820s and reformers in the early 1830s. Bentinck had been a member of the Derby Dilly and had followed Stanley into the Conservative party. In 1846 they found themselves the leaders of a new party. Yet each took a quite different view of the function of the Protectionist party. Bentinck recoiled from the thought of ever again cooperating with the free-trade apostates. Stanley wished to use his leadership to smooth the way to reconciliation with them. What were the prospects for reunion? Before the Protectionist dinner of 8 July was held, two attempts to keep the party together had already failed. Ellenborough's suggestion, made on 29 May, that Peel should resign to allow someone else (presumably Stanley) to lead a united Conservative government, was smartly rejected by Peel as an infringement of the royal prerogative and, more to the point, as a practical impossibility: 'a Conservative Government to be formed on the retirement of the present Government must be I presume a Government formed on the principle of Protection to domestic Industry – or some analogous principle.'[11] A month later Brougham and Lyndhurst attempted to bring Protectionists and Peelites together in opposition to the new Whig government's sugar legislation, which destroyed the tariff distinction between free-grown and slave-grown sugar. As a further instalment of free trade, even one which abandoned the long-defended Conservative preference to colonial over foreign sugar, the measure was welcome to the Peelites, but what really counted was their refusal to defeat the Whig government when there was no prospect of their being able to form one in its place. Brougham's plan to bring Goulburn and Gladstone together with the Protectionists as the 'New Conservative' party was impractical, since the other leading Peelites, especially Herbert and Lincoln, were not included.[12] The Sugar Bill was supported by forty-seven Peelites and opposed by none.

Those two abortive schemes for reunion originated in the House of Lords. From the outset of Russell's government, the Conservative free-traders, Brougham and Ellenborough, took their places in the House beside Buckingham and Richmond as a sign 'that the quarrel was a bygone quarrel'.[13] There was no Peelite peer – the name of Peelite could not properly be applied to Wellington, who occupied the politically neutral post of Commander-in-Chief and who ever since urging Stanley to take command of the Conservative party in February 1846 had looked upon him as its leader[14] – who could rival Stanley in authority, certainly not the retiring Duke of Buccleuch, who acted as the Peelite peers' spokesman. Having taken such a minor part in the repeal debates, Stanley had no difficulty in maintaining friendly links with the Peelite peers. Of course there were some Protectionists who wished to perpetuate the division. In August the Assistant Whip, Lord Eglinton, raised the question of what should be done about the elections to the Scottish representative peerage at the next dissolution. The incumbent sixteen representative peers included ten Protectionists and four Peelites; Eglinton did 'not see why the four black sheep . . . should not be replaced by better men, if we can manage it', although he was willing to spare Lord Home 'from his relationship to Buccleuch'.[15] Mansfield went further in recommending that 'there must be no compromise whatever, but that we must fight the Peelites indiscriminately'.[16] In December, however, Eglinton reported to Stanley that the general feeling was against meddling,[17] and the 1847 elections left the balance as it had been, on the understanding that future vacancies would be filled by Protectionist nominees. Croker was wrong to say that 'in the Lords there is almost unanimity – that is, they are all rallied under Stanley – Peelites and Protectionists',[18] but the two sections maintained their separate identities with generous mutual forbearance.

In the Commons, where the debate on the Corn Laws had been attended by bitter personal recriminations, and where members were mindful of the passions which the issue had raised in their constituencies, the task of reconciliation was formidable. Reunion would have to be the child of time. Goulburn replied to Lyndhurst's suggestion that he should lead the 'New Conservatives' in the Commons by saying that a hasty reunion would appear 'factious'.[19] Peel renounced party connection and office for ever and Graham, who resigned his membership of the Carlton, resolved never again to act with the Conservatives who had turned Peel out of office. Peel's explanation of his decision was more than a statement of his intentions for the future. It was a comment on his experience as the Conservatives' leader.

> I intend to keep aloof from party combinations. So far as a man can be justified in forming such a resolution, I am determined not again to take office . . .
>
> I will take care too not again to burn my fingers by organizing a party. There is too much truth in the saying 'The head of a party must be directed by the tail'.[20]

Apart from Peel and Graham, the Peelite leaders looked forward to the eventual reconstruction of the Conservative party. Dalhousie, Lincoln and Herbert turned down Russell's invitation to join his government. As Gladstone put it, the Peelites were bound to give the Whig government a fair trial; but 'if so much confidence is due to them, how much more is due towards friends from whom we have differed on the single question of free trade'.[21]

For the rest of the 1841 parliament's life, until the elections of 1847, the Peelites and the Protectionists acted apart. Before the assembling of parliament in 1847, Beresford and Stanley sent the usual party circulars only to those whom Eglinton called 'our own people',[22] not so much from motives of sectarian jealousy, as from the fear of offending the Peelites and driving some of them 'who might be doubting into a decided part against us'.[23] Stanley's strategy was to make no overt moves towards reunion until after the 1847 elections. The appeal to the electorate would settle the tariff question in one way or the other and the party could then come together on the basis of accepting the popular verdict.[24] How that strategy was to succeed was far from clear. It depended upon a free-trade result at the next elections, since the Peelites would not return to a Conservative party pledged to restore protection. Yet all the Protectionists, including Stanley, looked on reunion as the result of Peelite repentance. A meeting of Protectionist peers in December agreed on the merit of being 'conciliatory to the repentant Peelites';[25] Stanley talked of building 'a *pont d'or* for the penitent';[26] and at the beginning of Russell's government, when Peel took up his post on the opposition front benches, the Protectionists remained on the government side of the House so that the Peelites would have to move to them in 'an overt act of submission on their part'.[27] (It was, of course, impossible for Whigs and Protectionists all to crowd together on one side of the House, and at the beginning of 1847 the Protectionists sensibly moved to the opposition benches, their leaders sitting from the gangway to the red box, the Peelite leaders from the red box to the Speaker's chair.) Stanley's strategy was muddled. If he looked forward to reunion with the Peelites after the elections had compelled the Protectionists to come to terms with free trade, then his patronizing attitude towards them in the year before the elections made little sense. Lord Ellenborough found it distasteful that the Peelites were expected to crawl back to the party on their knees. 'They have nothing to repent – they did what was right – and they should evince a consciousness that they did so, and a proper self-respect, while they are willing to co-operate on new ground with those who differed from them last year.'[28] On the other hand, if the elections were to settle the question in favour of protection, then the electorate needed to be given a fair choice. Yet Stanley worked successfully to prevent Protectionists from standing against Peelites and he advised the party, in the months before the elections, that the prevailing high corn prices made it impolitic to raise the issue of protection.[29]

Stanley was, so it appears, playing for time, in the hope that a year of ceasefire would be followed by the reunion of the party in the new parliament. He was thwarted by Bentinck's intemperance and the continued strength of protectionist feeling in the agricultural constituencies. After a tour of those constituencies in September, 1846, Disraeli reported that the Conservative rancour against Peel ran 'in all its primal virulence'.[30] Bentinck, too, found that the farmers looked on him as their own 'Pet'.[31] Bonham concluded that 'the bitterness of a *select* but most active portion of the Protectionists' in the constituencies put Conservative cooperation at the next elections out of the question.[32] In December Bentinck tried to revive the agitation to abolish the malt tax. He was angry with Stanley for using his influence to block the scheme. Stanley accepted the Treasury's argument for the malt tax, but he also discovered that the agriculturalists in the party were almost all opposed to Bentinck, for the simple reason that taking the lower ground of malt-tax repeal smacked of compromise on protection.[33]

That argument suited Stanley's purpose. A pledge to abolish the malt tax would keep off the Peelites just as much as a commitment to restore protection. For the Peelites Bentinck felt only contempt.

> My heart sickens at the thought of . . . early reconciliation with those who have been either principals or Aids and Abettors in the Conspiracy against the Constituencies of the Empire – and I feel confident that we shall lose caste in the Country and with that portion especially of the Country in which our strength lies if we do anything of the kind. My inclination is to rouse the Country to make a clean sweep of them from the face of the Earth, and with the exception of Peel alone, I believe that this may easily be done, indeed it will not be easy to prevent it.[34]

Beresford 'failed utterly' to persuade Bentinck that fraternization with the lesser Peelites at least could do no harm.[35] Bentinck's hot temper led him to make the rash and unsustainable charge that Peel, by refusing to serve in Canning's government despite having privately become a convert to Catholic emancipation, had harried Canning to his death. He also laid against the late ministers the equally false accusation that they, in particular Ripon and Gladstone, had been guilty of a 'profligate avidity for patronage'.[36] 'The vile and blackguard attack of Lord George Bentinck', Arbuthnot wrote to Peel, 'has done good. Everybody, save the most rabid portions of the Protectionists, is disgusted.'[37]

Bentinck's outbursts, though they occurred in the immediate aftermath of repeal, were not quickly forgotten by the Peelites. Nor did Bentinck's anger soften with the passing of time. Aided by Beresford, he and the Tory press, over Stanley's protests, lent their support to the radical John Bright, in his contest at the Manchester by-election of January 1847, against Lord Lincoln, to whom some Conservatives looked as the future leader in the Commons of a reunited party. In the Commons Bentinck's erratic behaviour was a continual cause of embarrassment to the Protectionists. The Peelite Whip, John Young, left a memorable portrait of Bentinck's parliamentary style, written after a debate in March 1847:

> Lord George Bentinck made a furious onslaught on the Government . . . his voice was raised to a screaming pitch – his eyes gleamed like a wild animal at feeding time, and his whole deportment was so excited that no man out of Bedlam ever came near it. The Government people laughed, and cried oh, oh – his own people, now a select band, sat silent and downcast – and Newdigate, his own secretary to the Treasury and chosen confidant – repudiated his sentiments and apologized for him. This will I think close his career as a party leader – at any rate he will have no party to lead.[38]

Bentinck was not only a stumbling block in the way of Peelite-Protectionist cooperation, but also increasingly a source of weakness for the Protectionist party itself. His freedom from Protestant prejudice brought him into clashes with his own backbenchers and the Tory press. And even on the major Protectionist initiative of the 1847 session, his Bill to help relieve Irish distress by a government programme of railway building, more than 100

Protectionists abstained from voting. The party was made to look silly by Bentinck's inability to argue the case for his Bill in detail; and in his inexperience he had neglected to discover before introducing the Bill that the Irish Protectionists were against it. In April George Hope told Stanley that 'organised and directed by George Bentinck the bulk of the party will not suffer themselves to be',[39] and when, in the same month, Bentinck made an unexpected and violent attack on the Irish Secretary, Henry Labouchere, Greville reported that he was hooted by his own party.[40] Bentinck was aware of the antipathies which he aroused, but he did not offer to resign, and Stanley, unwilling to take the risk of splitting the party in the Commons and offending the diehards in the country on the eve of the elections, did not consider replacing him.

The elections of the summer of 1847 returned a solid majority of free-traders, Peelite and Liberal. Although the disruption of the previous year made the Conservative members elected difficult to classify (Gladstone counted fewer than 60 Peelites, Bentinck 85 of them, and Beresford 120), the returns were roughly 336 Liberals, 85–90 Peelites, and 225–30 Protectionists.[41] Whatever the precise mixture, the combined Conservative loss was about fifty seats. By all Stanley's arguments in the foregoing months, the Protectionists might have been expected to concede defeat and announce that they were ready to cooperate with the Peelites. Instead, the Protectionists, with Stanley's consent, chose not to interpret the result as a valid expression of the popular will. They argued that the Protectionist argument had been unable to make any headway against that summer's artificially high agricultural prices (in May wheat fetched the old wartime price of 114s) and that had the elections been delayed a few months, until after the sharp fall in prices in the autumn and the severe financial crash which that fall in prices produced, the result would have been different. There was, however, a flaw in the argument. Even without low prices the Protectionists had swept the southern agricultural constituencies. There was no reason to suppose that in any circumstances they could have made inroads into Liberal territory. The most that could be said was that low prices might have induced more Protectionists to stand against Peelites – there were only ten seats where the two sections faced each other, eight of them won by Peelites[42] – but even victories in those contests would not have given the Protectionists a majority. With the length of a full parliament before him, Stanley might have borne the immediate recriminations to which the abandonment of protection would give rise. As the only Protectionist of national stature, he was in a powerful position, as nearly indispensable as a party leader may be. The difficulty was that the autumn of 1847, when the credit structure of the national financial system was in collapse and gold was being drained out of the country to pay for food imports, was a peculiarly inopportune moment to convince the party, then in full cry against Peel's currency legislation and tarriff policy, of the practical necessity of conceding defeat to the free-traders. Thus the moment to seek the reunion of the party was passed by and the question deferred until the next elections should take place.

Stanley was undoubtedly concerned not to repeat Peel's error, as he saw it, of paying too little attention to his followers' opinions. That error, he remarked to Bentinck in November 1847, had been 'the rock on which, mainly, Peel split'.[43] Sometime later he was consulted by a backbencher who was undecided whether to vote for the admission of the Jews to parliament. 'Don't go against your party,' Stanley advised him, 'unless your conviction is very strong indeed; if there is any doubt in your mind give them the benefit of it; hear what they have to say with an inclination to think them right.'[44] In the years after 1846 Stanley's fundamental political object was to maintain a strong Conservative party as a bulwark against the advance of radical democracy. Since radicalism was quiescent, the cry of the constitution in danger was neither electorally persuasive nor urgent enough to act as the bond of the parliamentary party. Agricultural protection and militant Protestantism were emotionally more powerful agents for keeping the party together, and as the dream of reunion faded, Stanley became increasingly willing to depend on them. It was not certain, in the autumn of 1847, that by dropping protection, the Protectionists would gain the Peelites, who were reminded of the other main ground of Conservative quarrels by the 'No Popery' cry which many Protectionist candidates had raised on the hustings. Although Stanley did not share Croker's view, published in the *Quarterly Review* in September 1847, that the schism was now irreversible,[45] reunion did not seem any closer, and in the meantime it was necessary that the Whig government should be opposed by a firmly united, better organized Protectionist party.

The end of Bentinck

In 1855 Gladstone wrote in the *Quarterly Review* of the ineffectiveness of the Protectionist opposition to Russell's government.

> The Government of Lord John Russell was scarcely confronted by an opposition at all. There were occasional rallies under Lord George Bentinck and Mr. Disraeli, to take a vote on the subject of protection; but there was no organised staff of statesmen watching with a jealous eye and habitually criticising the operations of Government, as occasion offered, in each of its departments.[46]

The criticism was broadly true (although it overlooked some notable Protectionist successes, such as their combining with the Radicals in 1848 to prevent the government from doubling the income tax). But Gladstone did not give enough consideration to the reasons for the Protectionists' listlessness. For the first three years of Russell's government the most urgent questions before parliament were the government's proposals for dealing with the Irish famine, and on those questions the Protectionists agreed to a moratorium in the party warfare. It was not easy for the Whips to persuade country gentlemen to be at Westminster for the whole session,[47] and to attend debates late at night, when they knew that on any important question involving free trade or the existence of the government, the Peelites were bound to give the government a majority. The Protectionists fought against the repeal of the Navigation Laws, a logical corollary to free trade, and succeeded in postponing their demise from 1848 to 1849. But they could not save the old system and they knew it. Stanley, far from lamenting the Protectionists' apparent supineness, was happy to restrain them. He did not see 'on public grounds any justification of an *active* opposition to the Government'[48] until either the Protectionists were powerful enough to govern on their own or the Conservative party were reunited. He intervened to prevent Russell's defeat in 1848 on Sir John Pakington's amendment to the government's Bill to reduce the sugar duties, by persuading Philip Miles, a thorough protectionist, to argue the case for allowing the free-trade policy three more years of fair trial. Bentinck sneered at the 'downright Peelism' of his 'pusillanimous House of Lords leader',[49] but Stanley's tactics made sense. The Protectionists could not govern on the basis of the House of Commons returned in 1847 and a dissolution so soon after the last elections was out of the question. As late as 1851, when the Queen asked Stanley to form a government, she would not promise him a dissolution, which was one of the reasons he declined to take office.

The 1847 elections solved one matter for the Protectionists: what to do about Bentinck. Lionel Rothschild's return for the City of London raised, not for the first time, the question whether Jews, by swearing a special oath omitting the words 'on the true faith of a Christian', ought to be allowed to sit in parliament. Bentinck, a lifelong supporter of 'Jewish emancipation', was already at odds with the party for its exploitation of anti-Catholic feeling at the elections. High agricultural prices having prevented the Protectionists from making much capital of the tariff issue, the 'No Popery' cry, whipped up by Beresford and the high Tory press, especially the *Morning Herald*, had figured as the most prominent mark of many Protectionist candidates. Backed by the exertions made by the National Club, many of them pledged themselves to vote for the abolition of the Maynooth grant. Although anti-Catholicism seems to have gained few seats for the Protectionists,[50] extreme Protestants in the party were in no mood in the autumn of 1847 to tolerate Bentinck's religious Whiggism. Nor was Bentinck, described by Lord John Manners as the 'Strafford of the 19th century',[51] capable of bending with them to remove. When the vote on Rothschild came on in December, he ignored Stanley's advice merely to record a silent pro-Jewish vote[52] and treated the Commons to a full-blooded assault on religious bigotry.

That speech ended his leadership. Beresford sent him a note saying that he no longer commanded the allegiance of the party and Bentinck, without a moment's hesitation, gave in his resignation to George Bankes, who had acted as unofficial leader at the beginning of 1846. Bentinck was resentful of the way in which the Protestants had turned on him, but he was happy to be relieved of a responsibility which from the beginning had been beyond his abilities and his ambition.

> Appointed on account of my uncompromising spirit, I am dismissed for the same reason. . . . In April, 1846, they would have me, *nolens volens*, for their leader. I in vain warned them that my religious differences from them, as well as my want of capacity to lead a party, alike disqualified me for the office. I foretold all that has come to pass – all in vain . . .
>
> However, the great Protectionist party having degenerated into a 'No Popery', 'No Jew' party, I am still more unfit than I was in 1846 to lead it. . . . Beresford, Newdegate, and Mr. Phillips of the *Morning Herald* have raised all this artificial zeal in the cause of religion. . . . I am necessarily the first victim.[53]

Without Bentinck's unflagging parliamentary stint in 1846, the Protectionist party might not have been organized. Thereafter his leadership was not only an embarrassment to the party, it was scarcely exercised. The consciousness of his shortcomings had inhibited Bentinck from attempting to manage the Protectionist party in the Commons. In the Lords Stanley himself sent out circulars and notices; in the Commons, while Bentinck was leader, they always went out under the names of the Whips. For the same reason, Stanley had been obliged to hold meetings of the party in both Houses.[54] Nor had Bentinck taken much interest in the electoral organization of the party. After the 1847 elections, which the Protectionists had fought without any headquarters separate from the Carlton Club (except for the Protection Society's central offices), Beresford complained to Stanley that his attempt to establish a party registration office in London with county branches was looked upon by Bentinck as 'old woman's work'.[55] Bentinck was also 'with all persons the main stumbling block' to Conservative reunion.[56] Stanley asked for (and did not receive) a list of the Protectionists who, Beresford claimed, had complained of Bentinck's leadership; but he made no attempt to persuade Bentinck to continue. He contented himself with expressing to Bentinck his irritation at Beresford's independent action and congratulating the 'Wild Bird' on regaining the liberty 'to wing his way rather more than of late to Newmarket'.[57] The saddest aspect of the affair was that only a year before Bentinck had sold his prize stud in order to devote himself to political leadership.

Finding a replacement for Bentinck proved to be a far more difficult business than getting rid of him. None of the principals in the early days of the party's organization – George Bankes, Stafford O'Brien, or Philip Miles – was considered to be of sufficient stature for the job; J. C. Herries, who had last held office under Lord Goderich, was a supporter of the Jews and rightly felt himself to be too old; and Disraeli, who had been so effective an adversary of Peel, was not at first even considered. Disraeli was handicapped by more than his Jewish birth, literary proclivities, and landless position, much as they counted against him. His parliamentary style, relentlessly sarcastic, had not endeared him to the House of Commons. In the 1830s he had tried to enter parliament as a Radical and a Whig, before successfully contesting Maidstone as a Conservative in 1837. Then, during Peel's administration he had separated himself from the 'brute force' of Conservative backbenchers by acting as the leader of Young England. In short, his sense of party loyalty had still to be demonstrated. He was, moreover, neither a 'Protestant' nor, really, a protectionist. He had voted with Bentinck to admit Jews to parliament and his defence of the Corn Laws in 1846 had principally been that they ought not to be repealed by Peel's government. When, in a conversation in 1849, Palmerston called him a protectionist, Disraeli was reported to have replied, 'Search my speeches through, and you will not find one word of Protection in them'.[58] Finally, by the venom of his attacks upon Peel in 1845 and 1846, he had made himself as distasteful to the Peelites as ever Bentinck was.

By 1849, nevertheless, Disraeli had assumed the leadership of the party in the Commons and the Bentinck family was providing the money to set him up as a landed gentleman at Hughenden. The leadership fell to him for want of competition. In 1848 the party had no Commons' leader; the weekly party meetings which had taken place in 1846 and 1847 were discontinued; the party was directed by Beresford and Newdegate, with the result, Bentinck said, that there was 'no longer any cohesion among the Old Party except on the Jew Bill'.[59] The party needed a leader. No other Protectionist could match Disraeli's parliamentary skills, a fact which Stanley had implicitly acknowledged by asking him to sum up the 1848 session for the Protectionists in the Commons. He did so in a speech which even Beresford, who was implacably opposed to making Disraeli the leader, praised as 'very able and forceful'.[60] Bentinck's death in September released his supporters to become Disraeli's advocates. They included influential men like Miles, Bankes, Robert Christopher, and 'King' Hudson, but since they did not speak for the majority of the party, Stanley, at the beginning of 1849, suggested that the leadership be shared by three men – Herries, the Marquis of Granby (who had turned it down in 1848), and Disraeli. Disraeli felt keenly the slight implied in the offer, but, as Stanley's son recorded, his ambition conquered his pride.

> I returned from America. Found my Father, by his own accord, ready to take office. He however feared that Ministers would resign, in order to force him into power prematurely. He wished for delay, as tending to heal fresh wounds and reunite the party.
>
> He repeated a conversation between himself and Mr. Disraeli on the subject of the leadership. He proposed the triumvirate . . . D. refused. My Father reminded

him of his offer to act with Lord George under Granby. 'It is quite true,' D. said, 'that I acceded to such an arrangement when acting in unison, and on terms of equality, with Ld George Bentinck: but I am Disraeli the adventurer and I will not acquiesce in a position which will enable the party to make use of me in debate, and then throw me aside.' My Father replied that the lead of the Commons was a question to be decided by the party in that House, and not by him; they had raised strong objections to Mr. D. being sole leader, and he could not in such a matter attempt to coerce them.

Mr. D. then declined all interference in party arrangement and said that he should be happy to give an independent support, but that he would speak only when it suited him, as a private member. He wished to retire and devote at least part of his time to literature.

'All this is very well,' my Father answered, 'but the position is one which you cannot hold. Peel has tried it and you see how his influence is gone. Your proposal, if it means anything, means that we are to lose you altogether.'

Mr. D. thanked Lord S. for speaking so frankly, but said his mind was made up. My Father determined, as he told me, to try once more. He represented that Mr. D. must be himself aware of the impossibility of acting alone. 'I would not apply to you any such terms as you have applied to yourself: but this I will say, that certain feelings exist, call them prejudices if you will, that will make many of our friends desire, in the man who is to lead them, a degree of station and influence which circumstances have not as yet enabled you to acquire: and if I were speaking to an ambitious man, and speaking for your interest alone, I tell you fairly, I could suggest no proposal which I think you would gain more by accepting. You escape the envy which attaches to a post of solitary and supreme command; you are associated with two men, neither of whom in point of abilities can stand in your way for a moment . . .'

Mr. D. took his leave with many expressions of gratitude for the tone in which Lord S. had spoken, but repeated that his determination remained unchanged. At the first meeting, however, to which Herries and Granby were summoned, my Father thought it well to send him an invitation also. He came, sat down, discussed the address, and without any formal acceptance has ever since continued to act as one of the three.[61]

Stanley was not merely giving other men's views when he referred to Disraeli's lack of station and influence; he agreed with Beresford that superior ability in the House did not by itself entitle a man to leadership; a leader needed social standing and personal influence 'and in this respect Disraeli labours under disadvantages which I do not think he can overcome'.[62] Stanley's main objection to Disraeli was that he was 'the most powerful *repellent* we could offer to any repentant or hesitating Peelites'.[63]

Nevertheless all the objections to Disraeli yielded to the argument, as the aging Ultra, the Duke of Newcastle, put it, 'that we must of necessity choose the cleverest man that we possess'.[64] Neither Granby nor Herries, as Stanley had impressed upon Disraeli, had the will or the ability to put themselves forward as real leaders. The triumvirate existed in name only. Only a few weeks after the arrangement had been completed, when Stanley was projecting a Protectionist cabinet in case the Lords should force Russell's resignation by rejecting the repeal of the Navigation Acts, Herries agreed to step down in favour of Disraeli whenever the party should come into office.[65]

Protection reaffirmed

After just twelve years in the House of Commons, Disraeli, who had done more than any other man to undermine Peel's authority over the Conservative party, had risen to leadership. He meant to use it. He was convinced that it was essential for the progress of the party that it should free itself from the deadweight of protection, not because he cared very much about regaining the Peelites, but because he believed that it was impossible to gain a majority for protection at a general election. In the autumn of 1849 he therefore set about attempting to convert the party in parliament and the farmers in the country to a scheme for raising and equalizing the land tax and establishing a sinking fund from the increased revenue thereby provided. He argued that the sinking fund would assist the farmers by acting on the price of funds and by enabling them to borrow money at a low rate of interest. It was a half-baked scheme, open to many objections. But what mattered was that, in a series of public speeches, Disraeli was attempting to woo the party away from indirect taxation towards direct taxation, to move the party in the direction of Cobden's Financial Reform Association. For Disraeli, the abandonment of protection was the price to be paid for securing the true conservative interests of the nation. It was Peel's argument of 1846 in a slightly new guise.

> The political situation appears to be this: unless the agricultural constituencies (county and borough) are prevented from running amuck against the financial system of this country, which, out of suffering and sheer spite and vexation, it is not unnatural that they should do, it is all over with England as a great monarchy; and it must become not only, in its imitation of the United States, a second-rate Republic, but a second-rate and manufacturing Republic.[66]

Disraeli's proposals came at an inopportune time. From 1849 until the spring of 1852 English agriculture passed through its most depressed season since 1815. The price of wheat fell from 56s10d at the end of 1848 to 36s11d by the summer of 1850. And since those years were marked by the unusual coincidence of poor English harvests and abundant European ones, it was easy to draw the conclusion that the culprit was free trade. In 1850–51 the volume of wheat imports was eight times what it had been in 1845–46 and 1846–47[67] For three years the farmers had to sell reduced crops at low European prices.

The result was a revival of protectionist enthusiasm in the country and a stiffening of the party's attachment to the Corn Laws. In 1848 and 1849 the Protectionists won a series of startling by-election triumphs: at Cirencester and Kidderminster, which they had not even bothered to contest in 1847, at Reading, where they had been soundly beaten, and at Staffordshire South, Hampshire North, and Cork. Cork was a quite remarkable success, since it had been held by the Liberals at every election since 1832. George Hamilton, who was to be one of the party's election managers for Ireland in the 1850s, assured Stanley that it was not an isolated, freak result.

> So many persons of various parties in this Country have spoken to me recently with reference to the expediency of a movement in support of the principle of protection . . .
>   My position in this Country and various circumstances happen to bring me into very frequent and friendly communication with men of almost every shade of opinion, political and religious; and I can venture to assure your Lordship that the support given to Colonel Chatterton at the Cork Election conveys no exaggerated representation of the State of feeling and opinion now from one end of Ireland to the other.[68]

Isaac Butt, too, the foremost Irish Protectionist, was confirmed in his belief of 'the possibility of reclaiming from priests and agitation the popular mind of this country to a moderate and national Conservative Protectionist party'; if a general election were held, the majority of Irish constituencies would return Protectionists.[69]

In England the signs of reaction led to the launching, in May 1849, of the National Association for the Protection of British Industry and Capital. The National Association, which merged with the Central Protection Society at the end of 1849,[70] was scarcely distinguishable from the Protectionist party. The Duke of Richmond was its president; Lord Malmesbury, the Protectionist Chief Whip in the Lords, was one of its trustees; and fifty-five Protectionist members of parliament, including Beresford, Newdegate, Herries, and Granby, were among its founding members.[71] It is not clear what part, if any, Stanley and Disraeli played in the new organization. Their names appear in the list of members of the provisional committee, but they do not appear in a list of contributors printed in 1851.[72] The chairman and moving spirit of the association was George Frederick Young, the owner of extensive shipyards in Limehouse, who compensated for his political obscurity (he had attracted little notice as the Liberal member for Tynemouth from 1832 to 1837, although, curiously, he was a member of the Derby Dilly) by an unadulterated devotion to protection and a flair for popular agitation. In October 1849 his association, backed by local protection societies, called for the dissolution of parliament and passed a resolution condemning Disraeli's sinking fund.[73] Disraeli did battle with Young and lost. On 31 October, in deference to the views of Stanley, he recanted in a speech at Aylesbury in which he reaffirmed his adherence to protection.

Stanley's views were recorded by his son in May 1849.

> Some conversation with my Father on the question of Protection. He does not think it hopeless to restore a moderate fixed duty: and proposes to combine this

with a sliding scale, to commence when the price of corn is very low: the two extremes of said scale being (say) 35s per quarter and 60s. Between these the duty to remain fixed: to decrease at 60s and increase when the price fell below 35s.[74]

To what extent Stanley's opinions were drawn from his followers cannot be known. Certainly they had undergone a change. In 1846 he had allowed Russell's sugar legislation to pass without a fight on the argument that the free-trade policy must be played out logically. In 1849 he opposed the repeal of Navigation Acts and came within ten votes of defeating the government in the House of Lords because he did not accept the inference that free trade had become the settled policy of the country.[75] From all sections of the party Stanley was informed that the Protectionist reaction was genuine and growing. His closest colleague, Lord Malmesbury, who was not given to rash excitement, told him that 'our principles are gaining favour with thousands who were carried away with the free trade cry in 1846';[76] Beresford reported that 'decidedly the feeling in favour of restoring Protection is getting very strong';[77] and even Disraeli's great friend, Lord John Manners, who in the immediate aftermath of the repeal struggle had earnestly advised the party to learn to live with free trade, now believed that 'to change our flag' would destroy the party in the country.[78]

The reaction in the country was not so firmly based as the Protectionists liked to believe. None of the by-election victories came in a major urban constituency, none in Scotland or Wales. With the exception of Cork they all took place in small boroughs of the south and west of England and in English counties. Moreover, as the young Stanley remarked of the success at the Boston by-election in 1851 of a candidate with 'little to recommend him except his Protectionist opinions', a few more signs of such reaction might 'force on the new Reform Bill'.[79] In Ireland, one by-election was far from demonstrating that Catholic Protectionists, even if they were growing in number, would vote in a general election for the Protestant party of Beresford and Sir Robert Inglis. Nevertheless, Stanley could not ignore the upsurge in protectionist enthusiasm among the faithful. Asked by Young to adjudicate the dispute between the mass of the party and Disraeli, Stanley wrote a letter to Disraeli in which he made it plain that the party must not be seen to be weakening on protection.

> I confess that what gives me most uneasiness . . . is the indication which I fear I see . . . of your not only considering a return to Protection hopeless, but of wishing to impress on our friends the conviction that it is so. Events alone can show whether at any time, and if so within what time, a return to that principle may be practicable: but of this I am firmly convinced, that the public mind is beginning to be impressed with the conviction that Free Trade has proved a delusion; and at the point at which we now stand, our clear policy is to seek to encourage this conviction. Our hold on the public mind is our adherence to the principles for which we have contended; and I think we commit a great error, and insure the loss of nine-tenths of the support we have, if we abandon the cause as hopeless, before our friends are prepared to consider it.[80]

While the Protectionists were thus turning their backs to the Peelites, the Peelites themselves were showing the strains which the British tendency towards a two-party system has ever since 1832 placed upon third parties. They had fared well at the 1847 elections. Of the 119 Conservatives who had voted for repeal in 1846, eighty-eight stood for re-election and seventy-eight were returned (although two of them thereupon announced that they had become Liberals and three more were subsequently unseated by petitions). In addition there were 'potential Peelites' in the thirty-five newly elected 'free-trade' Conservatives.[81] Without Peel's leadership the Peelites were a somewhat incoherent collection. Young's issue of a circular at the beginning of the 1847 session was the only formal sign of Peelite organization before Peel's death in 1850.[82] Goulburn described them as a party of observation,[83] sustaining the Whigs in power for so long as the Protectionists constituted a threat to free trade, but looking eventually to reunion. But a party of observation is not really a party at all, as Brougham observed to Ellenborough when he sent him his calculation that the new parliament contained eighty-five Peelites.

> But then what right have we to call them Peelites – except some dozen or so? . . . as leadership & still more place is now out of the question with him [Peel] there can be no *party* of Peelites and in that sense of men to take office by turning out the Govt Peel has nothing like a party – and yet in no other sense can any party be said to exist.[84]

Brougham's observation was born out by events. Although the eminent among them worked in close and regular consultation, the Peelites did not vote as a solid bloc in the House of Commons during the life of the 1847 parliament. By the time parliament was dissolved in the summer of 1852, the 120 Peelites and potential Peelites listed by Professor Conacher could be divided, by their votes in divisions, into 48 Peelites, 32 Derbyites, and 40 doubtfuls.[85]

But while there was a gradual thinning of the ranks, marked by the sliding of eighteen Conservatives who had voted for repeal in 1846 into the Protectionist camp, none of the leading Peelites had moved perceptibly closer to the Protectionists. The distinction between the Peelite 'front bench' and the rank-and-file was sharpest on religious issues. The leaders supported Jewish emancipation in 1848, but the Peelites as a whole opposed it by forty-one votes to twenty-nine. Again, in 1851, the leaders voted against the Ecclesiastical Titles Bill, but the group as a whole voted by seventy-one to twenty in its favour. Among the thirty-two Peelites who were Derbyites by 1852, the distinction was even more marked. They opposed Jewish emancipation by thirteen votes to two, and supported the Titles Bill by twenty-four to two. From 1848 to 1850 there were several overtures made to Gladstone, Goulburn, and Graham to take the lead of the Protectionists in the Commons, but none of them was backed by the authority of Stanley or

Disraeli and they aroused little interest. Issues kept cropping up – the operation of Peel's 1844 Bank Act, Jewish emancipation, the sugar duties, and the Navigation Acts – to remind the Peelite leaders that reunion would create as many difficulties as it would solve. On the other hand, none of them, except for Graham, evinced any desire to ally themselves with the Whigs. Even Graham kept his distance. In 1849 he told Sir John Pakington that he was closer to the government than to the 'implacable Protectionists', and Pakington concluded that the Peelites were lost for ever.[86] Yet just a few weeks before, Graham had declined to join Russell's government, though it was significant that the reason he gave was his objection to the influence of the conservative Whigs, especially Palmerston at the Foreign Office.[87] The one occasion when the Peelites voted solidly against the government was on the Protectionist motion of censure upon Palmerston for his high-handed conduct in the defence of Don Pacifico.

By 1849 Gladstone, who with Goulburn was thought to be the Peelite nearest in sympathy to the Protectionists, was disenchanted with Peel's view that it was necessary to sustain the Whigs in power in order to prevent a Protectionist government from restoring the Corn Laws. He believed that a Protectionist government would, far from risk the future of free trade, finally expose the impotence of Stanley and his followers to re-impose food duties.[88] Gladstone was not alone in becoming restless. In February 1850 he was joined by thirty-four Peelites in supporting Disraeli's motion calling upon parliament to relieve agricultural distress by lowering the charges placed on the land by the poor law. After the division, which Russell's government survived by only twenty-one votes, John Young described the Peelites' state of mind in a letter to Peel.

> They will stand by Free Trade; they are the men who carried the repeal of the Corn and Navigation Laws, and will steadily maintain that policy. But they have no sympathies with and no confidence in the present Government . . . they will not make sacrifices, and risk their seats night after night, and year after year, for those whom they cannot help regarding as political opponents.[89]

The Peelites' discontent was fed by the consciousness that the decline of the constitutional authority of the Crown and the rise of party had sharply reduced the usefulness of small groups or parties in politics. The Peelites were free traders, but not Liberals, Conservatives, but not protectionists. They represented no particular opinion or constituency in politics. The most obvious difference between them and the Protectionists was that they held only six seats in the English and Welsh counties. Yet only one Peelite, Edward Cardwell, sat for a large city, and that city was Liverpool, not so much a manufacturing town as a commercial centre with a deep Orange tradition. Despite their votes in 1846, the Peelites were not distinguished by close ties with commerce and manufacturing. They sat, for the most part, for middling and small boroughs, uniformly scattered over the country. Only in

Ireland, where religion divided men, broadly speaking, into Catholic Liberals and Protestant Protectionists, were they under-represented. From 1847 to 1851 the Peelites drifted. Greville and Lord Clarendon, the Whig Foreign Secretary, were both mildly puzzled by the Peelites' behaviour in neither joining the Protectionists nor facilitating a junction with the Whigs.[90] What the Peelites needed to make up their minds was a shake-up in the political world. That was provided for them by the ministerial crisis which followed the defeat of Russell's government in February 1851, and the experience of a Protectionist government in 1852.

Notes and References

The new leaders: Stanley and Bentinck

1 Stanley to Ellenborough, 27 Dec, 1845: Ellenborough MSS, PRO 30, 12/21/9.
2 The memorandum is printed in Appendix 10.
3 Stanley to Ellenborough, 27 Dec, 1845: Ellenborough MSS, PRO 30, 12/21/9.
4 Stanley to Bentinck, 14 Jan, 1846 (copy): Derby MSS, 176/2.
5 Stanley to Colquhon, 17 Jan, 1846 (copy): *ibid*, 176/2.
6 Stanley to Rutland, 7 March 1846 (copy): *ibid*. 176/2.
7 Stanley to Newcastle, 6 May 1846 (copy): *ibid*. 176/2.
8 25 May 1846, *Hansard*, 3rd series, lxxxvi, 1175–6.
9 Bentinck to Portland, 9 June 1846: Portland MSS, PWH/220.
10 Stanley to Lyndhurst, 9 July 1846 (copy): Derby MSS, 177/1; Bentinck to Stanley, 10 July 1846: *ibid*, 132/13. Stanley's assumption of the leadership was so informal that even Bonham was not certain until the end of the year of Stanley's position. 'There are the young [circular] letters and also the one of Stanley and Beresford to their respective Houes,' he wrote to Lord Mahon on 30 Dec, [1846]. 'I did not think that S. was prepared to commit himself so entirely to that alliance. However he ought to be the best judge of his own course.' (Chevening MSS, 489.)
11 Peel to Ellenborough, 29 May 1846: Ellenborough MSS, PRO 30, 12/21/1.
12 Campbell, *Lives of Lord Lyndhurst and Lord Brougham*, 163–4; Bentinck to Stanley, 10 July 1846: Derby MSS, 132/13.
13 Gladstone memorandum, 9 July 1846: Gladstone MSS, Add. MSS 44777, ff. 242–52.
14 In October 1847 Arbuthnot assured Stanley that Wellington had played no part, despite rumours to the contrary, in persuading the Peelite, Lord Dalhousie, to Accept Russell's offer to go to India as governor-general. Wellington retained his 'undeviating attachment to the Conservative party' and it was his 'continued desire that you should be at the head of it' (Arbuthnot to Stanley, 12 Oct, 1847: Derby MSS, 116/5). A week later, Arbuthnot told Stanley that Wellington had had no communication with Peel since the fall of Peel's government. He bore Peel no ill will, 'but feeling that the dissolution of our great Conservative Party was the work of Peel, he has thought it better to abstain from communication which could not be satisfactory to either of them' (Arbuthnot to Stanley, 19 Oct, 1847: *ibid*). Dalhousie took the Indian post on the explicit understanding that it implied no party connection with the Whigs.
15 Eglinton to Stanley, 23 Aug, 1846: Derby MSS, 148/2.
16 Eglinton to Stanley, 4 Oct, 1846: *ibid*, 148/2.
17 Eglinton to Stanley, 2 Dec, 1846: *ibid*, 148/2.
18 Croker to Hardinge, 10 July 1846: Croker, *Correspondence and Diaries*, iii, 72.

19 Gladstone memorandum, 24 July 1846: Gladstone MSS, Add. MSS 44777, ff. 261–8.
20 Peel to Hardinge, 24 Sept, 1846: Parker, *Peel*, iii, 474.
21 Morley, *Gladstone*, i, 294.
22 Eglinton to Stanley, 1 and 27 Dec, 1846: Derby MSS, 148/2. The Peelites were more adventurous. John Young sent circulars to 240 Conservatives in the Commons and received 90 'cordial' replies (Lincoln to Peel, 1 Jan, 1847: Peel MSS, Add MSS 40445, ff. 386–7).
23 Eglinton to Stanley, 2 Dec, 1846: Derby MSS 148/2.
24 Stanley to Bentinck, 12 July 1846 (copy): *ibid*, 177/1.
25 Eglinton to Stanley, 2 Dec, 1846: *ibid*, 148/2.
26 Stanley to Bentinck, 24 Jan, 1847 (copy): *ibid*, 177/1.
27 Stanley to Bentinck, 12 July 1846 (copy): *ibid*, 177/1.
28 Ellenborough to Lincoln, 3 Jan, 1847: Ellenborough MSS, PRO 30, 12/21/3.
29 Stanley to Newdegate, 10 Dec, 1846 (copy): Derby MSS, 177/1.
30 Disraeli to Lady Londonderry, 1 Sept, 1846 (draft): Hughenden MSS, B/II/7.
31 Bentinck to Stanley, 28 Sept, 1846: Derby MSS, 132/13.
32 Bonham to Gladstone, 14 Aug, 1846: Gladstone MSS, Add. MSS 44110, ff. 187–8.
33 Stanley to Lord Ashburton, 16 Jan, 1847 (copy): Derby MSS, 177/1; Salisbury to Stanley, 7 Jan, 1847: *ibid*, 134/6.
34 Bentinck to Stanley, 10 July 1846: *ibid*, 132/13.
35 Beresford to Stanley, undated: *ibid*, 149/1.
36 See Stewart, *The Politics of Protection*, 81, 89.
37 Arbuthnot to Peel, 10 July 1846: Parker, *Peel*, iii, 361.
38 Conacher, *The Peelites and the Party System, 1846–52*, 21.
39 Hope to Stanley, 5 April 1847: Derby MSS, 134/1.
40 Greville, *Memoirs*, 31 March 1847, v, 435–7.
41 Tufnell, the Liberal Whip, and Dod both gave these figures. For details of the various classifications made, see Stewart, *The Politics of Protection*, 111–12.
42 One of those contests was at Monmouthshire, where the sitting members, Lord Granville Somerset, a Peelite, and Charles Morgan, a Protectionist, were returned. Granville Somerset's brother, the Duke of Beaufort, put up a second Protectionist candidate, his cousin, Captain Edward Somerset, and spent £20,000 on his behalf. But the Peelite-Protectionist division was so marked, that Lord Granville was re-elected on the strength of 1,821 plumpers' votes cast for him, against only 180 for his cousin and 85 for Morgan. Had the Protectionists been able to persuade even 2.6 per cent of the supporters of Lord Granville to split their votes, two Protectionists would have been returned. (David, 'Political and electioneering activity in south-east Wales, 1820–1852', unpublished thesis, 163–7).
43 Stanley to Bentinck, 2 Nov, 1847 (copy): Derby MSS, 177/2.
44 Stanley MSS: Diary, 19 April 1849.
45 'Parliamentary prospects', *Quarterly Review*, Sept, 1847, 541–78.

The end of Bentinck

46 'The declining efficiency of parliament', *Quarterly Review*, Sept, 1856, 532. In 1850 a Conservative journalist had made the same point: 'The Protectionists, as a body, and especially their leader, have many and great disadvantages almost peculiar to their party. . . . They are not yet a *working party*, nor have they ever been a well-organised Opposition' ('Prospects and policy of the United Party of Con-

servative-Protectionists', *The Conservative Magazine*, Aug, 1850, 2).

47 The Whips themselves did not always set an example. 'I have received a letter from Eglinton,' Malmesbury wrote to Stanley on 19 Nov, 1848, 'containing his decided resignation & telling me I must find a substitute *"forthwith"* . . . as Eglinton was appointed at his own earnest request to me, I am rather surprised at his giving up. He puts it upon the inconvenience of coming up *early* in the year.' (Derby MSS, 144/1.) When no one could be persuaded to replace him, Eglinton agreed to 'help an amateur during the middle of the Session, but he can't stand the beginning & the end' (Malmesbury to Stanley, 31 December, 1848, *ibid*). At the beginning of 1850 Lord Nelson reluctantly agreed to replace Eglinton, while Eglinton consented to whip the Scottish peers. (Malmesbury to Stanley, 25 Nov, 1849, and 11 Jan, 1850: *ibid*).

48 Stanley to G. Hope, 7 April 1847 (copy): Derby MSS, 177/2.

49 Bentinck to Disraeli, 12 March 1848: Hughenden MSS, B/XX/Be/52.

50 See Stewart, *The Politics of Protection*, 109–11.

51 Manners to Disraeli, 12 Oct, 1847: Hughenden MSS, B/XX/M/67.

52 Bentinck to Disraeli, 3 Nov, 1847: *ibid*, B/XX/Be/40.

53 Bentinck to Croker, 26 Dec, 1847: Croker, *Correspondence and Diaries*, iii, 158–60. 'You spoke to me so kindly coming out of the House on Friday night about my speech on the Jew Question', Bentinck wrote to Sir William Jolliffe, 'that I cannot refrain from writing to tell you what has resulted. I got a letter from Beresford on Monday which to be brief conveyed a notice from Several Sections (I have not enquired who constitutes those Sections) of the Party that by my speech and vote on the Jew Bill I had disappointed the just expectations of the Party, forfeited their confidence, & entailed upon myself the loss of my position as Leader. I need not tell you that I am much too proud to wait to be cashiered. . . . I therefore after writing a reply and receiving a rejoinder inclosed the correspondence to Bankes gracefully "resigning without requiring or waiting to be cashiered the trust which had been reposed in me". I have not a word of complaint to make. I think I ought never to have been the leader of the Party – I was a most unnatural Leader for a high Protestant Party.' (Bentinck to Jolliffe, 24 Dec, 1847: Hylton MSS, DD/MY/C/2165.)

54 Stanley to Bentinck, 27 Oct, 1847 (copy): Derby MSS, 177/2.

55 Beresford to Stanley, undated: *ibid*, 149/1.

56 Arbuthnot to Stanley, 19 Oct, 1847: *ibid*, 116/5.

57 Stanley to Bentinck, 26 Dec, 1847 (copy): *ibid*, 177/2. In a letter to Stanley of two days earlier, Bentinck had written that he felt like 'a caged bird escaped from his wired prison' (Bentinck to Stanley, 24 Dec, 1847. *ibid*, 132/13).

58 Stanley MSS. Diary, 19 May 1849. 'This last saying,' Stanley added, 'whether genuine or fictitious, is near the truth. His great displays on the Corn question have been all attacks on opponents, not assertions of a principle. He is now anxious to drop the subject of a protective duty altogether: but this the party will not allow.'

59 Bentinck to C. Michele, 16 April 1848: Lucas, *Lord Glenesk and the 'Morning Post'*, 31.

60 Beesford to Stanley, undated: Derby MSS, 149/2.

61 Stanley MSS: Diary, 20 March 1849.

62 Stanley to Beresford, 2 Sept, 1848 (copy): Derby MSS, 178/1.

63 Stanley to Christopher, 8 Jan, 1849 (copy): *ibid*.

64 Newcastle to Stanley, 7 Jan, 1849: *ibid*, 147/14.

65 Stanley MSS: Diary, 23 March 1849; Disraeli to his sister, 26 March 1849: Disraeli, *Lord Beaconsfield's Correspondence with his Sister*, 222-3.

Protection reaffirmed

66 This extract is from a printed letter which Disraeli sent to George Frederick Young (Monypenny and Buckle, *Disraeli*, iii, 221-2). He expressed similar sentiments to young Stanley in June 1849: 'Called on Disraeli with facts and figures for his speech. He expressed himself strongly on the necessity of making an effort next year, and making it on new principles. He seemed to intimate that we, the Conservative party, were engaged in a losing cause; but said if we became more democratic, what could England be except an inferior copy of America?' (Stanley MSS: Diary, 17 June 1849.)

67 See Tooke and Newmarch, *History of Prices*, v, 9-34.

68 Hamilton to Stanley, 26 Nov, 1849: Derby MSS, 150/9. Two months later, Hamilton reported that his requisition for a Dublin county meeting had been 'signed by persons of all Classes and Parties . . . the tone of the answers I have received to the Circular is very satisfactory, and convinces me that the time is approaching when in Ireland every question will give way to that of a moderate protection to the produce of the land' (Hamilton to Stanley, 28 Dec, 1849: *ibid*). For a similar assessment, see Lord Downshire to Stanley, 10 Jan, 1850: *ibid*, 124/6.

69 Butt to Disraeli, 22 Oct, 1849: Hughenden MSS, B/III/35.

70 H. Byron to Richmond, 21 July 1849: Goodwood MSS, 171, ff. 247-8; Newdegate to G. F. Young, 14 Dec, 1849 and Young to Newdegate, 17 Dec, 1849, enclosed in Byron to Richmond, 19 Dec, 1849: *ibid*, 1726, ff. 1380-1.

71 *National Association for the Protection of British Industry and Capital. Report of the Provisional Committee, 26 June, 1849,* London, 1849.

72 *Ibid*, 1744, f. 78.

73 Lord Stanhope to Young, 24 and 29 May, 3 June 1849: Young MSS, Add. MSS 46712/3, packet 15; *Illustrated London News*, 20 Oct, 1849.

74 Stanley MSS: Diary, 20 May 1849.

75 Stanley to Phillips, 9 Jan, 1848 (copy): Derby MSS, 177/2.

76 Malmesbury to Stanley, 3 Dec, 1848: *ibid*, 148/1.

77 Beresford to Stanley, 4 Dec, 1849: *ibid*, 149/2.

78 Manners to Disraeli, 24 Oct, 1850: Hughendon MSS, B/XX/M/68.

79 Stanley MSS: Diary, 24 April 1851.

80 Monypenny and Buckle,*Disraeli*, iii, 223-6.

81 Conacher, *Peelites and the Party System*, 30.

82 *Ibid*, 26.

83 Goulburn to Peel, 19 Dec, 1846: Peel MSS, Add. MSS 40445, ff. 386-7.

84 Brougham to Ellenborough, 23 Sept, 1847: quoted in Conacher, *Peelites and the Party System*, 32.

85 The large number of doubtfuls was in the nature of things, as may be illustrated by the vacillations in the career of John Benbow. Benbow sat for Dudley, a proprietary borough in the hands of Lord Ward, the largest landowner in the Black Country. At Ward's direction he voted for repeal in 1846. At the 1852 election he pledged his support for Church rates and declared himself a friend of Lord Derby's government. Professor Conacher has therefore rightly classified him as a Derbyite. Benbow voted for Disraeli's budget in November, 1852, in the division which brought down Derby's government. When the Peelites joined

with the Whigs to form the coalition government of Lord Aberdeen, however, he followed Lord Ward's wishes and supported them. He voted for Gladstone's 1853 budget, including the legacy duty, which was bitterly resented by the Conservatives.

36 Conacher, *Peelites and the Party System*, 32.

37 Graham to Peel, 16 Jan, 1849: Peel MSS, Add. MSS 40452, ff. 515–20.

38 Gladstone memorandum, 12 Dec, 1848: Gladstone MSS, Add. MSS 44777, ff. 278–80.

39 Young to Peel, 22 Feb, 1850: Parker, *Peel*, iii, 532–3.

40 Greville, *Memoirs*, 5 July 1848, vi, 87–9; Clarendon to G. Cornewall Lewis, 2 July 1848: Maxwell, *The Life and Letters of George William Frederick, Fourth Earl of Clarendon*, i, 291.

Chapter 12

The Protectionist years II: 1851–52

The ministerial crisis of 1851

When parliament assembled in February 1851 the future course of parties hung on the answers to two questions. The first was how long Russell's government, made vulnerable by the disruptive presence of Lord Palmerston at the Foreign Office and by its dependence on the Radicals and the Peelites in the House of Commons, could survive. The second was how long the Peelites would continue to eschew formal connection with either the Whigs or the Protectionists. The two questions were not distinct. It was the Court's ambition to see in office a Whig ministry which excluded Palmerston and included the leading Peelites. Palmerston's habit of conducting his business without consulting or even informing the Crown and his readiness to applaud the careers of European revolutionary nationalists had become increasingly irritating to the Queen and embarrassing to Russell. But in June 1850, in the famous Don Pacifico debate, Palmerston had made himself virtually irremovable by winning public acclaim for his '*Civis Britannicus sum*' speech, in which he presented his seemingly extravagant use of the navy to back up Don Pacifico's claims for damages against a Greek mob which had ransacked his house as the just and proper defence of British subjects throughout the world. In the same debate, the Peelites, by voting with the Protectionists against Palmerston, had blocked their entry into the Whig cabinet for so long as Palmerston remained at the Foreign Office. Then, at the beginning of 1851, they placed themselves even further from the Whigs by opposing the Ecclesiastical Titles Bill, the government's concession to the Protestant fervour which swept the country in reaction to the supposed 'papal aggression' implied by Cardinal Wiseman's adoption of the title 'Archbishop of Westminster' in the previous October.

The Ecclesiastical Titles Bill, which forbade Roman Catholic prelates to assume territorial titles, was as innocuous as it was popular in the country. But although it received a majority of 395 to 63 on its first reading, it dislodged one of the props under Russell's government. Twenty Irish radicals showed their displeasure with Russell's capitulation to Protestant opinion by voting for Disraeli's motion for agricultural relief in the third week of February. That vote revealed how shaky the government's foundations had become. The Protectionists came within fourteen votes of defeating the government. On 22 February their work was done for them. In a sparsely attended House, the Radicals, undeterred by Russell's promise that the government would bring in a franchise reform bill in the following session, succeeded in carrying Locke King's motion to equalize the borough and county franchises. Russell, weary of being caught in the middle of the quarrel between Palmerston and the Queen and stymied by the conservative Whigs in his ambition to broaden the franchise and reform the structure of landholding in Ireland, took the opportunity to resign.

When Russell delivered up the seals of office to the Queen, he advised her to send for Stanley. There followed a week of complicated negotiations, during which, as *Punch* put it, 'everybody went to call upon everybody',[1] and at the end of which Russell's government returned to office unchanged. That was, perhaps, the logical outcome of Russell's almost gratuitous resignation. Yet, inconclusive though it was, the ministerial crisis was important for the Conservative party. The Peelites, by refusing to serve under Stanley, increased the distance between themselves and the Protectionists. By refusing also to serve under Russell, they placed themselves in a painfully isolated position and exposed themselves to the charge of being the obstacle to ministerial stability. When the opportunity to join the Whigs offered itself once more in 1852, they were the more ready to take it.

Twice in the 1850s, in 1851 and 1855, Stanley returned the royal commission to form a government. Those failures have been cited as evidence that Stanley wanted serious political purpose, that, as Graham put it, 'he followed politics as an amusement, as a means of excitement, as another would gaming or any other very excitable occupation'.[2] Graham, and others like him, were influenced by Stanley's uninhibited delight in sport; but Lord Malmesbury, who was closer to Stanley than any other politician after 1846, did not think that sport interfered with his political business.

> He himself [Stanley] was the keenest sportsman I ever met; whilst he was in the field his whole attention was in his present pursuit, and woe to him who attempted to divert him to politics at the time. When over, he could divest his mind completely of the sport and sit down at once to write the longest and most important paper straight off, in a delicate hand and without a single erasure – so completely could he in a few moments arrange his subject in his mind. I have often witnessed this *tour de force* both in and out of the Cabinet.[3]

It was, perhaps, because Stanley gave his instinct for fun healthy outlet in the proper places that he did not look upon politics as a game and that he conducted his political affairs with a calm dispassion. After the Protectionists had declined office in 1851, Greville met Stanley at Newmarket. In his diary he reflected upon the two sides to Stanley's nature.

> At Newmarket on Sunday. . . . It was worth while to be there to see Stanley. A few weeks ago he was on the point of being Prime Minister, which only depended on himself. Then he stood up in the H. of Lords, and delivered an oration full of

gravity and dignity, such as became the man who had just undertaken to form an administration. A few days ago he was feasted in Merchant Taylors' Hall, amidst a vast assembly of Lords and Commoners, who all acknowledged him as their Chief. He was complimented amidst thunders of applause upon his great and Statesmanlike qualities, and he again delivered an oration, serious as befitted the lofty capacity in which he there appeared. If any of his vociferous disciples and admirers, if some grave Members of either H. of Parliament, or any distinguished foreigner who knew nothing of Lord Stanley but what he saw, heard, or read of him could have suddenly found themselves in the betting room at Newmarket on Tuesday evening and seen Stanley there, I think they would have been in a pretty state of astonishment. There he was in the midst of a crowd of blacklegs, betters, and loose characters of every description, in uproarious spirits, chaffing, rowing, and shouting with laughter and joking. His amusement was to lay Ld. Glasgow a wager that he did not sneeze in a given time, for which purpose he took pinch after pinch of snuff, while Stanley jeered him and quizzed him with such noise that he drew the whole mob around him to partake of the coarse merriment he excited. It really was a sight and a wonder to see any man playing such different parts, and I don't suppose there is any other man who would act so naturally, and obey all his impulses in such a way, utterly regardless of appearances, and not caring what anybody might think of the Minister and the Statesman as long as he could have his fun.[4]

More to the point during the ministerial crisis of 1851 than Stanley's supposed political levity was his despondency about the prospects for the Conservative party. He told Croker in August 1850 that he put little faith in the ability of 'the *gentlemen* of the country', who had been made apathetic by 'desertions and defeats', to halt the progress towards republicanism and the lowering of the weight, in the social scale, of the proprietors of the soil. 'I have never before', he confessed, 'taken so gloomy a view of our position.'[5]

At his first audience with the Queen, on 23 February, Stanley told her that since the Protectionists had not been the instruments of Russell's downfall, they were not obliged to come to the Crown's rescue by replacing his government.[6] Since his party was in a substantial minority in the House of Commons, he would be able to form a government only if she promised him a dissolution or the Peelites agreed to serve in his cabinet.[7] When the Queen refused to promise him a dissolution, he advised her to look for a Whig – Peelite government. It was only when that search ended in failure that Stanley agreed to negotiate with the Peelites.

Those negotiations, which lasted for three days, constituted the first formal attempt to reunite the Conservative party. It was hopeless from the start. Lincoln, who had gone to the Lords as the Duke of Newcastle on his father's death in January, grandly instructed his colleagues that 'self-denial and a generous abnegation of all considerations but honour and patriotism are the great and distinguished duties which now devolve upon us'.[8] Gladstone and Aberdeen took the lower ground that they could not join an administration which proposed, as Stanley explained to them during the negotiations, to place a fixed duty of 5s or 6s on imported wheat. Aberdeen's refusal left Stanley 'more despondent and depressed' than his son remembered ever to have seen him. Although the two men had failed, after protracted consultations, to reach agreement on an amendment to the Irish Franchise Bill in 1850, they had been on friendly terms ever since 1846. Aberdeen was regarded as one of the more conservative Peelites. He distrusted Palmerston's meddling in European affairs and just two weeks before Russell's resignation he admitted to Stanley that free trade had not produced its anticipated benefits.[9] He clung to free trade, as he frankly said, from piety to Peel's memory.[10] Edward Stanley left an engaging portrait of his father's reaction to Aberdeen's decision.

> During the day [25 February], which was one of unceasing occupation, my Father's spirits sustained him: but at night they failed utterly: after dinner, a note from the Queen being brought him, he answered it rapidly and in few words: then, leaning his elbows on the table, and resting his head in his hands, he sat in that posture without speaking or moving during at least a quarter of an hour. Yet in all this agitation, he has not once missed giving my brother (a boy of 10) his usual lesson in the morning: and when we went into the drawing room he called for his chessboard and played two games in succession, in which he became so entirely absorbed as if no such things as Courts or Cabinets existed.[11]

Having failed to catch the Peelites, Stanley held a meeting of the leading Protectionists to consider whether they would form a government by themselves. Only Disraeli, who was impatient for office, and Malmesbury, who believed that the party would cut a worse figure by refusing power than by failing in the attempt to exercise it, were in favour of it. Spencer Walpole and Joseph Henley, two of the leading candidates for high office, had apparently decided (although they did not say so at the meeting) not to join a government pledged to restore protection.[12] But the real reason for deciding not to come in was that Stanley and the majority of his colleagues felt, from the want of ability and official experience among themselves, unequal to the task of governing without a majority in the Commons, in circumstances in which the necessity for some government other than a Whig one had not been demonstrated.[13]

On 28 February Stanley informed the Queen of his failure. Disraeli was despondent at the outcome and accused Stanley of being indifferent to power;[14] Malmesbury grumbled that Stanley's 'failure of nerve' had made the party the laughing stock of the country;[15] and there was some discontent on the back benches,[16] not surprisingly, in view of Stanley's disarmingly frank statement in the Lords that he had declined to take office because his party, 'though it no doubt comprises men of talent and intellect, yet contains within itself, I will not say no single individual, but hardly more than one individual of political experience and versed in political business'.[17] To compensate for the failure there was the relief felt in some quarters at having escaped reunion with the Peelites. When Disraeli gave his blessing to Stanley's invitation to Gladstone, and avowed his willingness to surrender the Commons' leadership to him, young Stanley warned of the effect which such an arrangement would have on the party.

> At 11 this morning [25 February], my Father received a note summoning him again to attend at the Palace. He did so, and immediately afterwards called on Disraeli, whom I saw in the afternoon. The subject chiefly discussed was the constitution of the new Cabinet. . . . D. expressed his willingness to serve under Gladstone if the latter could be brought over. . . . I told D. also, as I well thought, that Gladstone as a leader would be equally obnoxious to Protestants and Protectionists: that the farmers never could be brought to understand that his, D.'s, supersession had been his own act: they regarded him as their representative and would take it ill that those who had borne the burden and heat of the day should be set aside to make way for allies who only at that moment ceased to be enemies.[18]

Eglinton congratulated Stanley on having placed himself 'in the highest position which an honest politician can hold' and having 'done more to elevate and consolidate our Party than any coalition could have effected'.[19] At least the party's commitment to protection had survived the crisis. And when Stanley undertook the delicate task of explaining to his followers his reasons for refusing office at a party meeting two weeks later, 'though silent and ill-pleased, they acquiesced, and applauded to the very echo when he appealed to them to say "whether he still possessed their confidence or not?" '.[20] The most balanced defence of Stanley came, surprisingly, from Greville, who once referred to Stanley as 'of all men the one to whom I have felt the greatest political repugnance',[21] and whose diary is punctuated by sarcastic swipes at Stanley's frivolity and irresponsibility.

> His conduct seems obnoxious to no reproach, and he did what he was bound to do with reference to the Queen and his party. They would have been intolerably disgusted if he had left untried any means of forming a Government, and though there will be some grumbling and disappointment amongst them, they have no cause for complaint. He tried everything and everybody, as I believe, without either the desire or the expectation of succeeding. Nothing surprises me more than that anybody should think he could form a Government, as many very acute people did. What happened was almost sure to happen – the fear and reluctance of many of his own people to undertake a task for which they were conscious they were unfit.[22]

Greville's account was, in one detail, inaccurate. Stanley had not tried everybody. Ever since 1846 there had been suggestions that the conservative Whigs and the Protectionists should make common cause against the Radicals. No doubt there was logic in the view that the great Whig landowners had more in common with Stanley and the protection societies than with Cobden and the freehold land societies. But habit was stronger than logic; the notion of a Whig–Protectionist alliance existed outside the bounds of practical politics. Palmerston's uneasy position in the Whig government, however, had given rise to the speculation that he might throw in his lot with Stanley. A week before Russell's resignation, Disraeli described Palmerston as 'a man who bore no malice, who liked office, whose tendencies were Conservative, and who would find no difficulty in throwing over former colleagues'.[23] Disraeli thought that Palmerston could be caught, but since it was only eight months since the Protectionists had censured his conduct over Don Pacifice, Stanley displayed no interest in approaching him.

Palmerston had become the key to ministerial stability. Without him the Whigs could not sustain a government. With him the Protectionists would suddenly take on the appearance of a governing party. It was to Palmerston, as much as to the Peelites, that the Protectionists now began to look. Gladstone and Aberdeen had made protection the ground of their refusal to join Stanley, but there were signs that the Peelites were moving generally in the direction of liberalism. The ground between Aberdeen and the Protectionists had opened up in the previous spring, when he and Stanley had failed to reach agreement on the Irish Franchise Bill. Stanley objected to the lowering of the franchise to extend to occupiers of land rated to the poor law at £8 and to freeholders rated at £5, because it meant giving 'the whole preponderance to mere numbers over property, intelligence, and independence, to Roman Catholic numbers over Protestant property'.[24] It would therefore, he believed, create an Irish constituency which would render a future Conservative government impossible.[25] Stanley began to doubt the usefulness of the Peelites in the fight against democracy. In February 1851 Aberdeen told the Queen that he felt no difficulty about Russell's pledge to introduce a new Reform Bill, for 'he felt a good deal of the Radical in him sometimes'.[26] Prince Albert noted that from the remarks of Russell, Graham, and Aberdeen, 'it is clear that all parties are relieved by the failure of their attempt to form a Coalition Government, but determined to form a positive junction, which will be most salutary to the country'.[27] Russell predicted a Whig–Peelite coalition once the Ecclesiastical Titles Bill were out of the way, and even Herbert and Newcastle, the most persistent advocates of Peelite independence, agreed that 'upon the first proposition of a Stanley Government the junction of parties would be completed, and there would be only *one* strong opposition'.[28] It was, a year later, the experience of a Protectionist government which finally drove the Peelites into the arms of the Whigs.

Whatever the implications of the 1851 ministerial crisis for the future, its resolution, the reinstatement of the Russell ministry, left matters as they had been. Disraeli was eager to profit from the lesson that every man of note had declined to work with Stanley because of protection. Walpole agreed with him. They wanted the party to announce that it now accepted the impossiblity of forming a protectionist government.[29] But in his statement to the Lords on 28 February, Stanley made it clear that a small fixed duty on wheat remained party policy and promised that the Protectionists would (as it had been agreed at a party meeting)[30] resist with all their strength the continuation of the income tax in that year's budget. In his budget speech, just before the government's resignation, Charles Wood had carried the argument for direct taxation on property as opposed to indirect taxation on consumption farther than any previous Chancellor of the Exchequer had done. Disraeli wished to swim with that current, but Stanley, as he told the Lords, held it to be 'an object not only of vital importance, but one to which the faith of successive Ministries has been pledged, that the Income Tax should not be permitted to degenerate into a permanent tax'.[31] Stanley came out of the negotiations with the Peelites a changed man. Until 1851, although he had striven to gratify the protectionism of the party, his ruling idea had been that only a reunited Conservative party could successfully resist the movement towards industrial democracy. He had repeatedly, although diffidently, quarrelled with the high Protestant line taken by Beresford and the Tory press. Now Russell was pledged to a new Reform Bill, wheat prices were still languishing below 40s, and the Peelites appeared destined to merge with the Whigs. Stanley, therefore, as Lord Lonsdale noted with delight, 'recast his parts'.[32] It became his object to consolidate the Protectionists and rouse them to the struggle against radicalism, even at the price of giving the Protestant zealots in the party free rein.

> If I can consolidate with them the now awakened spirit of Protestantism, and at the same time keep the latter within reasonable bounds, [he wrote to Croker on 22 March] I can go to the country with a strong war-cry, with which, indeed, *The Times* furnished me the other day, 'Protestantism, Protection, and down with the Income Tax'. But let our watchwords be what they may, the real struggle, the real battle of the Constitution which has to be fought is whether the preponderance, in the legislative power, is to rest with the land and those connected with it, or with the manufacturing interests of the country. If the former, the Throne is safe; if the latter, in my deliberate judgment, it is gone. How are we then to bring the masses of the electors to the support of the former rather than the latter alternative?
>
> In my mind, among all its evils and all its dangers, the evocation of the Protestant spirit, which has been aroused, is not without its use. Even the most Radical towns . . . are so furiously anti-Papal, that that feeling will neutralise the cheap bread cry.[33]

The restoration of the Whig government left Palmerston in his accustomed place at the Foreign Office. Relations between him and some of his colleagues remained strained and when, in December, Napoleon III took control of the French government by a *coup d'état*, Palmerston gave Russell cause to dismiss him. The cabinet decided to adopt a neutral stance towards events in France, but Palmerston, already in hot water for having championed the cause of the Hungarian nationalist, Lajos Kossuth, privately congratulated the French ambassador on Napoleon's success. Unable to get from Palmerston a satisfactory explanation of his behaviour, Russell dismissed him, knowing when he did that he was almost certainly giving the administration its death notice. When the 1852 session of parliament began, the Whig government had just enough time to introduce its Reform Bill, to extend the franchise to £6 householders in the boroughs and £10 occupiers in the counties, before Palmerston got his revenge. His amendment to the government's Militia Bill was carried by 136 votes to 125 and on the next day the cabinet unanimously agreed to resign.

On 21 February the Queen asked Stanley, now, since his father's death in June, the Earl of Derby, to form a government. This time there was no question of his refusing. There was, however, no indication that the protectionist reaction had spread beyond the agricultural constituencies, nor that the Peelites were any closer to the Protectionists than they had been a year earlier. The Protectionists owed their good fortune to the disarray of the Liberal party. They came into office in 1852 only because a Whig government had been shown, as it had not been shown in 1851, to be impossible.

Derby's first government

The first of Derby's three short ministries was necessarily undistinguished. Disraeli, with no practical experience of finance, combined the Chancellorship of the Exchequer with the leadership of the Commons; Malmesbury, whose knowledge of international affairs was, as he admitted, restricted to what he had gleaned from editing his grandfather's diplomatic correspondence,[34] went to the Foreign Office; and Spencer Walpole, one of the party's few competent debaters, but apprehensive that he had been placed too high,[35] became Home Secretary. The cabinet bore, also necessarily, a somewhat high Tory aspect, with the Earl of Lonsdale as President of the Council, Salisbury as Privy Seal, the Duke of Northumberland as First Lord of the Admiralty, and the Earl of Hardwicke as Postmaster-General. Disraeli described it as a cabinet with 'six Dukes of Buckingham',[36] and Derby answered a complaint that it was exclusively Protestant by pointing out that the government had no Roman Catholic supporters.[37] 'Great and not *very* pleasant events' was how Queen Victoria described the change of ministries; she prepared to 'take the trial as patiently as I can',[38] consoling herself with the knowledge that a Protectionist government would end the existing confusion of parties.

> One thing is pretty *certain* – that *out* of the *present state* of confusion and discordance, a *sound state* of *Parties* will be obtained, and *two Parties*, as of old, will again exist, without which it is *impossible* to have a *strong* Government. *How* these Parties will be formed it is impossible to say at present.[39]

Everything hinged on the core of forty Peelites, who sat on the opposition benches, but below the gangway, and the sixty or seventy Irish Radicals, who were estranged from Russell by the Ecclesiastical Titles Bill and who, especially if the reports of the protectionist recovery in Ireland were true, might be induced to come to an understanding with the Derbyites.

Derby took office on the understanding that parliament would be dissolved as soon as the essential parliamentary business, chiefly the voting of supplies, but extended to include a Bill granting New Zealand its own constitution, a Militia Bill, and a useful procedural reform of the chancery courts, was passed. The elections were to settle once and for all the free-trade controversy. In fact the Protectionists took office knowing in their hearts that they had lost the battle. In the Lords Derby announced that the party would place its recommendation of small fixed duty before the electorate, but he made it plain that the main ground on which it would seek the voters' confidence was the need to defend the Protestant institutions of the country and to supply 'some barrier against the current of that continually increasing and encroaching democratic influence in this nation'.[40] Agricultural prices had for some months been showing a steady rise and protectionism was on the wane. When Lord Stanley, as Derby's heir now was, returned to England from India in May, the first thing he learned was that

> practically, though not quite avowedly, Protection had been abandoned. The farmers and country gentlemen generally appeared satisfied that nothing more could be done for them: at least no complaint was heard from them, nor did any unreasonable expectation seem to be excited: a few M.P.s expressed suspicion, but they were very few.[41]

As Malmesbury put it, the party was reduced to 'playing out the cause of Protection consistently until a General Election'.[42]

By the time that parliament was dissolved in July, even the element of consistency had vanished. In his provisional financial statement in April – the budget was postponed until after the elections – Disraeli had disclosed his intention to embrace direct taxation wholeheartedly and remodel its structure so that its burden did not fall principally on the landed class.[43] In the Lords in May, Derby stated publicly what he had earlier confided to the Queen, that he remained a protectionist without expecting that a protectionist majority would be returned at the elections.[44] The Protectionists thus went to the polls in July 1852, not with a policy, but in search of one. If they gained a majority they might turn out to be protectionists after all; if they did not, they would certainly be free traders. The *Edinburgh Review* remarked justly that 'an abstract entity was formed called Derbyism' and that 'the persons initiated into the mysteries and hidden doctrines to it were called Derbyites'.[45] The majority of Protectionist candidates, although they muttered phrases about relief to the agricultural interest, stood on the declaration either that they opposed the re-imposition of a corn duty or that they recognized its impracticability.

The Protectionists were nevertheless the only party to gain seats at the elections, although not enough of them to produce a Protectionist majority.

Estimates of the returns varied widely,[46] but most accounts agreed that the Protectionists had raised their numbers from 280 to about 300 and that the Peelites remained at about forty. The elections thus produced only a minor change in the balance of parties. In two other respects they were important. They put paid to the possibility of Conservative reunion or of a Protectionist bargain with the Irish Radicals.

In Ireland, whence Lord Eglinton, the Lord-Lieutenant, reported in May that the country was quiet, Ribbonism in abeyance, the crops thriving, and land selling at improved prices,[47] the Protectionists gained only four seats, a far cry from the breakthrough predicted in 1849–50 and three fewer than the Irish Secretary, Lord Naas, had predicted just before the elections.[48] The protectionist reaction had not taken place, as James Emerson Tennent, who was returned for Lisburn, had informed Derby in December.

> I owe it to you & to the party, to put you in possession of some facts, regarding the state of feeling in the North of Ireland. . . . I spent last summer there, chiefly in the Co. Antrim, Co. Down, and Fermanagh; and in Belfast, & the neighbourhood of Lisburn. I thus saw much of the feeling of the Conservative party, both agricultural and in the towns; and while they are eagerly your supporters on every other question, there is much difference of opinion as to Protection; and the views of those most favourable to it are singularly moderate. Observe I speak of *Conservatives*, the Whigs of course are Free Trade advocates – though *some* of them are also for moderate protection, but these are few.[49]

Naas did not put his disappointment down to the slackness of Protectionist organization; on the contrary, 'every gentleman in Ireland of our side went into the struggle with a will'.[50] What overcame the Protectionists was the power of the priests and the newly organized Tenant Right League.

The Protectionists were bitter at the influence wielded by the Catholic clergy, who, according to Naas, harangued the tenant farmers into a state of religious fury. The farmers were 'made to believe that if they voted against the priests' nominee they were certain to be damned in the next world and they had most unmistakeable intimations of the probability of their being sent there very soon'.[51] Eglinton reported that the priests were 'working harder & more unscrupulously than they ever did before' (acidly explaining that as partly a reaction to the thinning of their flocks and the emptying of their pockets by famine and emigration) and recommended that in future they be banned from the vicinity of the polling booth.[52] It is true that clerical electoral activity in Ireland reached its peak in 1852,[53] but the Protectionists, too, were better organized and richer there than in any other part of the country.[54] The 1852 elections, lacklustre in England and Scotland, drew heat in Ireland from religious friction. However disturbing the turning of the clerical screw might be to the Protectionists, they could scarcely have expected to win the trust of Irish Catholics. The apprehensions which had attended Eglinton's appointment as Lord-Lieutenant proved justified: only one Catholic was appointed to the Irish administration and Catholic Crown prosecutors were replaced by Protestants on some circuits. In May Richard Spooner, a Protectionist backbencher who made an unrelenting assault on the Maynooth grant his special parliamentary province, succeeded in drawing from Walpole a hedged assent to the establishment of a committe to inquire into the grant's operation. Walpole opposed the grant in principle, believed, nevertheless, that it ought to be left alone unless 'clearly abused', but knew that the majority of the Protectionists were eager to stir the question because they soon had to face their constituents.[55] Although Protectionist candidates in Ireland prudently canvassed in support of the Maynooth grant,[56] they could not escape the consequences of the Protestant sentiment which was whipped up in the English constituencies. Nor were they helped by the government's proclamation of mid-June reminding Catholics that it was against the law for them publicly to exercise their religion by holding outdoor processions. The proclamation was carefully time to appeal to the protestant electorate in England.[57] It was followed, two weeks later, by the Stockport riots, in which twenty-four Irish labourers' houses were sacked and two Catholic chapels wrecked. Those two events, the proclamation and the riot, cost the Protectionists probably seven Irish seats.[58]

The Protectionists had hoped to profit in Ireland from the Catholics' disgust at the Whigs' Ecclesiastical Titles Bill. The Whigs were, indeed, the big losers in Ireland: their representation fell from twenty-one seats to five.[59] But the void created by the collapse of O'Connell's repeal movement was filled by the more radical Tenant Right, or Irish Independent, party, which, in alliance with the Catholic Defence Association returned fifty-three members pledged to independence of both Whigs and Conservatives unless one of those parties promised to introduce legislation to protect tenant farmers and compensate them for improvements made to their tenancies. It was the return of those fifty-three Independent members which was the significant feature of the Irish elections. In December Disraeli's atempt to bargain for the Irish Radicals' support foundered on Derby's unwillingness to take up radical land reform in Ireland.

In England, where the Protectionists gained about fifteen seats, there was no clear issue to raise the elections above the normal placid mid-Victorian level. Each election contained its own mixture of local and national ingredients, although there is some evidence that, despite the elasticity of party ties at Westminster, cross-party voting remained low.[60] The Peelites and the Protectionists fought the elections as separate parties; neither side made an effort to reach an electoral pact. Indeed, the Protectionists made a spirited assault on several leading Peelites: Gladstone at Oxford University, Cardwell at Liverpool, Roundell Palmer at Plymouth, Sidney Herbert at Wiltshire, and Sir George Clerk at Dover. The virtual abandonment of protection and the ineffectiveness in the quiet summer of 1852 of the appeal against democracy left Protestantism as the distinguishing mark of the Protectionists. Where Protectionists opposed Peelites, they did so chiefly by demanding an inquiry into, or the abolition of, the Maynooth grant. On that issue, although Gladstone and Herbert survived, Cardwell, Roundell Palmer, and Sir George Clerk lost their seats.

The Protectionists' resort to the Protestant cry, along with their fudging of the tariff issue and Beresford's alleged involvement in bribery,[61] sealed the split in the Conservative party. At the beginning of Derby's government in February, Gladstone, Herbert and Newcastle were uncertain about which party they should eventually join. Gladstone, whose decision was the most important, not only because of his own rising reputation (it was not until he presented his 1853 budget that Gladstone began to acquire a national stature), but because his example was likely to be followed by Newcastle and Herbert, held to the opinion that 'a Liberal policy would be worked out with the greatest security to the country through the medium of the Conservative party'.[62] In a later, memorable phrase, Gladstone recalled that in 1852 his opinions leaned one way, his lingering sympathies the other. It was of some importance that Gladstone's high-Church sympathies, like those of Herbert and Newcastle, jarred with the latitudinarian indifference of Whiggery to the Established Church. It was not easy to set aside the memory of a decade in which Conservatism had rallied itself in opposition to the 'destructive' religious views of Russell and the radical element in the Liberal party. On the other hand, Gladstone had taken a giant step towards liberalism when he supported the Maynooth grant in 1845; and by 1852 the anti-Catholicism of the low-Church party among the Protectionists was as great an obstacle to union with them as Russell's liberalism was to a junction with the Whigs. Gladstone had already, although he discreetly tucked the matter away in the back of his mind, been visited by the dream of Irish disestablishment. He had also, in 1851, discovered in the fate of political prisoners in Naples the cause of liberal nationalism, and by publishing an attack on Austria's rule in Italy in two letters to Lord Aberdeen had dissociated himself from the Conservative principle of legitimacy.

When the 1852 elections had finished, Gladstone was the only leading Peelite who, on the surface at least, remained open to the suggestion of Conservative reunion. Graham thought that the extensive bribery practised by the Protectionists, which was much castigated by the Liberal press, must demonstrate to the Peelites that reunion was out of the question.[63] Newcastle and Aberdeen agreed that they could not act with the Protectionists without a feeling of degradation.[64] Aberdeen saw in the Derby government's shuffling on protection and exploitation of anti-Catholicism evidence that the Protectionists would sacrifice any principle in order to retain power. 'The only test proposed at the elections', he wrote to Newcastle late in July, 'involved a principle of religious bigotry pregnant with mischief for the future and more objectionable to me than Protection itself. Altogether the conduct of the Government is quite unprecedented, and their whole proceeding is the most dishonest I have ever witnessed.'[65]

The attitude of his colleagues left Gladstone, who even after the elections continued to look on the 'sober-minded portion' of the Protectionists 'as the most valuable raw material of political party in the country',[66] isolated. Since he would not return to the Conservative party alone, his future was being decided for him. In the months between the elections and the recall of parliament to receive Disraeli's budget in November, Peelites and Whigs corresponded daily in an attempt to lay the foundation for a ministry to replace Derby's government. Russell was reluctantly brought to accept that, having alienating the Irish and Palmerstonian elements in the Liberal party, he was no longer able to lead it. The door was thus opened for Aberdeen to enter into the leadership of what may be called the centre-left of British politics.

The Peelites and the Whigs came together in opposition to Disraeli's budget. Gladstone was able, on a narrow interpretation of the word, to counter Disraeli's accusation that his budget was defeated by a coalition. It is doubtful, however, whether any budget would have satisfied the Peelites. In July Gladstone told Aberdeen that he could not accept Disraeli's 'quackish' financial opinions,[67] and all the other Peelite leaders were bent on throwing out the government. It was nevertheless satisfactory to the Peelites that they were able to find in Disraeli's proposals ample justification for their behaviour, in an age when to eject a government from office simply because it had failed to win a majority at the polls was still tinged with 'faction'.

At the beginning of the session the Protectionists acknowledged in a resolution passed by the House of Commons that they accepted the finality of free trade. Disraeli therefore drew up his budget in accordance with the country's preference for direct to indirect taxation. The political world waited with great anticipation to see how he would be able to square the agriculturalists' expectations of compensation for the loss of protetion with the necessity of pleasing the free-trade majority in the House of Commons. It was not disappointed. Disraeli failed, in the eyes of his opponents, to square that circle. But his budget was a great curiosity, a bold scheme to reorganize the financial structure of the country. It had two principal objects: to relieve the landed classes and to remodel the framework of taxation on the principle that direct taxation ought to be levied nearly as universally as indirect taxation.

At first glance the budget appeared to be a fair-minded capitulation to free trade and a recognition that agriculture had lost its special position in the national economy. It provided for the progressive reduction of the tea duty from $2s2\frac{1}{4}d$ in the pound to $1s$ and there was little to cheer traditionally Tory interests in the specific proposals made on their behalf. The reduction of the malt duty by one-half, presented partly as a boon to the consumer, was small compensation for the loss of the Corn Laws; the West Indian sugar growers, who had suffered a gradual whittling away of the preference given to their imports over foreign sugar, were granted only the trifling compensation of being allowed to refine sugar in bond; and the shipping interest, which had lost the protection of the Navigation Laws in 1849, had to be content with minor reductions in tolls and light dues. Greville's immediate reaction was that the budget was 'of a Free Trade character altogether' and that it would 'make the Government safe'.[68]

Disraeli's opponents did not take so charitable a view of the reduction in the malt duty and their appetite for office was whetted by the other main provisions of the budget, those concerning the income tax and the house tax. Disraeli extended the income tax to profits from Irish investment and salaries (but not from land) and, in England, he lowered the exemption level on industrial incomes from £150 to £100, on incomes from property from £100 to £50. For farmers the exemption level was raised from one-third of their rent to one-half. The tax on houses and shops was to be doubled. The increased revenue from the house tax was designed to supply the loss entailed by the reduction of the malt tax, and Macaulay expressed the dissatisfaction of the free-traders when he described the budget as 'nothing more than taking money out of the pockets of the people in towns and putting it into the pockets of growers of malt'.[69] The same objection was raised by Gladstone, when he pointed out that one section of the population – the middle-class householders and shopkeepers whose incomes exceeded £100 – bore the weight of Disraeli's new taxation.

Yet the gravest objection to the budget, felt especially keenly by Gladstone, was not that it was too conservative in its solicitude for the agricultural interest, but that it was too radical in its innovations.[70] Disraeli offended against two canons of the classical school of finance which ran from Pitt to Peel. In somewhat blindly groping his way towards a notion of deficit financing, he broke the rule that the first object of a Chancellor of the Exchequer was to secure a large surplus, by dint of which he might then remit taxes. And in distinguishing between permanent incomes (derived from land and funded property) and precarious incomes (derived from farming, trades, and the professions), the former to remain taxable at 7*d* in the pound, the latter at the reduced rate of only 5¼*d*, he broke the rule that all varieties of income should be taxed at the same rate. The Peelites objected to Disraeli's creating his own deficit by halving the malt tax and then supplying it by new taxation and by the unorthodox expedient of abolishing the Public Works Loans Board and applying its balance of £360,000 to the national revenue.[71] They objected even more strongly to the breach of faith with the public creditor which, they argued, was implied in the tax distinction between precarious, or what today is called earned, incomes and permanent, or unearned, incomes. The *Edinburgh Review*, noting that the principle of a 'graduated income tax' was welcomed by a large section of the public, isolated it as the one item in the budget which Derby's government would bequeath to the future.[72] The graduated income tax was favoured by liberal economists, and Gladstone believed that Disraeli introduced it in 'a most daring bid for the support of the Liberal majority'. But not a single Radical voted for the budget, while the remodelling of the income tax appalled the Peelites more than any other of Disraeli's proposals. Gladstone called it 'the flagrantly vicious element' in the budget, despite the fact that it left income from landed property to be taxed at the higher rate.[73] In the end, Gladstone concluded that the budget was the least conservative he had ever known.[74]

The venom of the Peelites' assault on the budget doomed Derby's government. Three days before the debate began, Disraeli and Walpole, without consulting Derby, had bargained for the support of the Irish Radicals by promising that the government would accept a recommendation from the select committee then sitting in favour of Sharman Crawford's Bill to legalize the free sale of land in Ireland and to secure fair rents by impartial valuation. It is inconceivable that Disraeli would have been able to persuade the Conservatives to honour that pledge had the Irish members kept the government in power. When Naas and Lord Napier, the Irish Under-Secretary, got wind of the affair, they threatened to resign, and Derby, to prevent a revolt against Disraeli in the party, announced in the Lords on the eve of the budget debate that his government would not contemplate enacting Sharman Crawford's Bill. No Irish Radical voted for Disraeli's budget and Disraeli claimed that he had been thwarted by Derby.[75] But the extension of the income tax to Ireland would probably have cost him most of the Irish Radicals' votes, especially since, what he did not know at the time, the Whigs had given the Irish members a secret guarantee that they would not apply it to Ireland.[76]

On 16 December Disraeli's budget was defeated by a vote of 305 to 286. Every leading Peelite voted against it. Gladstone's figures for the thirty-eight members of the Peelite 'core' who voted in the division were thirty-three against the government and five for it. In addition, five doubtfuls and ten new Peelites opposed the budget.[77] For various reasons the formal entry of the Peelites into the Liberal party was delayed until the famous Willis's tea-room meeting of 1859. Lord Aberdeen's government, which succeeded Derby's government immediately after the budget defeat, was avowedly a coalition, not a fusion, of Whigs and Peelites. For the next seven years Conservative supporters of the coalition tended to call themselves liberal Conservatives, not Liberals. Derby's language to describe the implication of the coalition for the Conservative party was cautious. 'The Break', he wrote to Lord Londonderry, 'is now, I fear, wider than ever.'[78] It is clear in retrospect, however, that, except for a few Peelites who were still to limp back to the Conservatives, it was final. Of the fifteen Peelite members of Aberdeen's government – including the six cabinet ministers, Gladstone, Graham, Newcastle, Herbert, Argyll, and the Prime Minister – none was ever again to join a Conservative administration. The passing of the years had taught the Peelites to look upon the bulk of the Derbyites as reactionaries. '*Peelism* – if I must still use the word,' Newcastle wrote in April 1853, 'is really the most advanced form of Liberal opinion, cleared of that demagogic Liberalism which characterised the Liberalism of twenty years ago and, on the other hand, of that oligarchic tendency of the old Whigs.[79] To be a Peelite, or a Liberal Conservative, in 1853 meant more than being eager to extend the frontiers of free trade and religious tolerance. It meant a willingness to tackle parliamentary reform with Lord John Russell and to take up competitive examinations for the civil service with the Liberals.

It meant also, since it is unwise to leave personality out of politics, an unwillingness to act with Disraeli, in whom the *Edinburgh Review* at the beginning of 1853 saw only 'meretricious glitter, overwhelming presumption, open disregard of principle, innate vulgarity . . . and utter absence of earnestness and truth'.[80] In 1852 the antipathy between Disraeli and the Peelites swelled to a new peak. Derby believed that the Peelites' decision to act with the Whigs was 'mainly to be attributed to the jealousy & hatred (the word is not too strong) felt by the Peelite party in the House of Commons towards Disraeli',[81] and Graham, from the other side, claimed that Derby could have had all the Peelites if he had shaken off Disraeli.[82] In his final speech, just before the budget division, Disraeli mixed coarse humour with mocking jibes at the Peelites. So enraged was Gladstone that, in breach of the convention which accords the Chancellor of the Exchequer the last word, he jumped up, at 1 o'clock in the morning, to deliver an impassioned rejoinder. Holding his ground against the catcalls of the Protectionists, he lectured Disraeli on the qualities which were expected of a statesman.

> I must tell the right hon. gentleman that whatever he has learned – and he has learned much – he has not yet learned the limits of discretion, of moderation, and forbearance, that ought to restrain the conduct and language of every member of this House, the disregard of which is an offence in the meanest among us, but is of tenfold weight when committed by the Leader of the House of Commons.[83]

Gladstone then proceeded to subject the budget to a painstaking dissection, ending with the judgement that it was 'the most subversive in its tendencies' of all the budgets he had known. Robert Blake has rightly remarked that Gladstone's speech, coming as it did from one who was still regarded (even by himself) as an impeccable Conservative, more than any other single event ended the possibility of a reconciliation between the Peelites and the Derbyites.[84] Both sides were roused to anger.

> Gladstone's look when he rose to reply [Stanley wrote in his diary] will never be forgotten by me: his usually calm features were livid and distorted with passion, his voice stark, and those who watched him feared an outbreak incompatible with Parliamentary rules. So stormy a scene I never witnessed. I went to the Carlton after the division: the language held was unmeasured: those who had voted with Gladstone prudently kept away: they could not have escaped insult.[85]

During the next week the Carlton was the scene of acrimonious quarrels. Some of the Derbyites proposed 'to break it up, and substitute a club purely Conservative, in the commonly understood sense of the word'.[86] Three nights after the budget division, Gladstone went to the Carlton, where Beresford and a score of Protectionists were getting drunk at a private party. Finding Gladstone in the mess-room after dinner, they insulted him so broadly that he was compelled to retire. Derby's attempts to recapture Gladstone did not cease until 1859. Historians have usually concentrated their attention on Gladstone's reasons for frustrating them. What has been overlooked is the determination of a large number of Conservative backbenchers not to have him.

One other personal relationship, the partnership of Derby and Disraeli, deserves remark. Given a creditable alternative, Derby would not have chosen Disraeli as his lieutenant. Temperamentally they were poles apart. Disraeli wondered at Derby's extraordinary patience and resource in adversity, while Derby sneered at Disraeli's 'tendency to extremes of alternate excitement & depression'.[87] Derby's chief disappointment in 1851–52 arose from the defection of the Peelites to the Whigs, Disraeli's from the frustration, first of not gaining and then of failing to retain, office. When, in a desperate bid to save his budget and the government, Disraeli tried to seduce the Radical, John Bright, with visions of a Radical–Conservative administration, Derby told him sharply that it was better to be 'defeated honestly in a fairly-fought field than escape under a cloud' and that if the Conservatives were to be the government, they must be it 'by our own friends, and in spite of combinations, and not by purchasing a short-lived existence upon the forbearance of the Radical party'.[88] But Derby had also come to admire Disraeli's perserverance in leading the party, almost single-handed, night after night in the House of Commons. He was impressed by Disraeli's repeated offers to give up the leadership to any recruit, whether Graham, Gladstone, or Palmerston, who might strengthen the party. In February 1852 he told Disraeli that he would never forget his 'generous self-sacrifice' in urging that Palmerston be invited to lead the government in the House of Commons.[89] Nine months later he was warm in his praise of Disraeli's speech introducing the budget.

> I cannot resist congratulating you in writing . . . on your masterly performance of last night. I had the satisfaction of hearing the whole of it, except the first half-hour; and I can truly say that I listened to the whole exposition with entire satisfaction, and admiration of the clearness and breadth with which you stated your views, and the skill with which you introduced the various topics and trod over very difficult ground.[90]

Derby and Disraeli never became close friends. The tastes of the huntsman and classical scholar did not coincide with those of the fashionable novelist and flirt. Disraeli was not invited to Knowsley until 1853 (and when he got there he found it 'furnished like a second-rate lodging house . . . from sheer want of taste');[91] Derby never condescended to stay at Hughenden. Periods of mutual coolness, especially in the mid-1850s, marred their relationship and unsettled the party. Derby was now and then visited by suspicions that

Disraeli was restless to supplant him and Disraeli never was able to reconcile himself to Derby's *andante* political tempo. Yet their alliance lasted from 1852 to 1868 unblemished by any serious rift.

Notes and References

The ministerial crisis of 1851

1 *Punch*, 8 March 1851.
2 Quoted in J. K. Glynn, 'The private Member of Parliament, 1833–1868,' unpublished thesis, p. 7.
3 Malmesbury, *Memoirs*, i, 42. Malmesbury had good reason to defend Stanley's addition to shooting. Each autumn he and Spencer Walpole received generous gifts of pheasant and grouse from Knowsley.
4 Greville, *Memoirs*, 10 April 1851, vi, 290–1.
5 Stanley to Croker, 18 Aug, 1850: Croker, *Correspondence and Diaries*, iii, 219–21.
6 Stanley was not being entirely accurate, since the Conservatives had purposely stayed away from the division on Locke King's motion. The Whigs could, on their own, have outnumbered the 100 Radicals who voted for the motion, and the Conservatives were naturally 'indignant at the evident intention of the Cabinet to throw on them the burden and unpopularity of resistance' (Stanley MSS, Diary, 20 Feb, 1851).
7 Whether Stanley would have been pleased by the promise of a dissolution is open to doubt. The public was still gripped by the 'papal agression' mania, and Stanley told his son that he 'would have run any risk rather than dissolve while all the country was still under the influence of violent religious excitement' (*ibid*, 1 March 1851).
8 Newcastle to Graham, 23 Feb, 1851: Parker, *Graham*, ii, 129.
9 Stanley MSS, Diary, 6 Feb, 1851. Aberdeen was the only Peelite whom Stanley, projecting him for the Foreign Office, his post in Peel's government, had included in his prospective cabinet list of 1849.
10 Prince Albert memorandum, 23 Feb, 1851: Victoria, *Letters*, ii, 352–6.
11 Stanley MSS, Diary, 25 Feb, 1851.
12 Grenville, *Memoirs*, 23 Feb, 1851, vi, 271. According to Greville, Walpole repeated this sentiment twice to Viscount Jocelyn, a Peelite who had moved into the Protectionist camp. Henley had for two years been urging the party to let down protection and had angered many Protectionists by more than once recommending publicly that the salaries of civil servants be reduced in line with the lower prices prevailing since the introduction of free trade, a line of argument which implied that he accepted the permanence of free trade. Nevertheless, both Henley and Jocelyn joined Derby's government in 1852.
13 For Disraeli's humorous account of the meeting, see Monypenny and Buckle, *Disraeli*, iii, 291–5.
14 Stanley MSS, Diary, 15 April 1851.
15 Malmesbury, *Memoirs*, i, 278–9.
16 Greville, *Memoirs*, 27 Feb, 1851, vi, 271: 'His rabble are very violent, and abuse

him for not at once taking the Government.'

17 28 February 1851, *Hansard*, 3rd series, cxiv, 1008. Disraeli's discontent was undoubtedly aggravated by the reference to only one man of political experience, since everyone knew that Stanley was referring to Herries, Chancellor of the Exchequer in 1828.

18 Stanley MSS, Diary, 25 Feb, 1851.

19 Eglinton to Stanley, 2 March 1851: Derby MSS, 148/2.

20 Stanley MSS, Diary, 14 March 1851.

21 Greville, *Memoirs*, 20 March 1858, vi, 352–4.

22 *Ibid*, 2 March, 1851, vi, 275–8.

23 Stanley MSS, Diary, 16 Feb, 1851.

24 Stanley to Aberdeen, 16 May 1850: Aberdeen MSS, Add. MSS 43072, ff. 146–54.

25 Stanley to Aberdeen, 21 May 1850: *ibid*, Add. MSS 43072, ff. 162–3.

26 Prince Albert memorandum, 23 Feb, 1851: Victoria, *Letters*, ii, 352–6.

27 *Ibid*, 25 Feb, 1851: *Letters*, ii, 361–3.

28 *Ibid*.

29 Stanley MSS, Diary, 23 Feb, 1851.

30 *Ibid*, Diary, 21 Feb, 1851.

31 28 Feb, 1851, *Hansard*, 3rd series, cxiv, 1003–26.

32 Lonsdale to Croker, 23 March 1851: Croker, *Correspondence and Diaries*, iii, 23–40.

33 Stanley to Croker, 22 March 1851: *ibid*, iii, 235–7. Disraeli, too, apparently became reconciled to the necessity of playing the Protestant card. 'I saw Dizzy today,' Malmesbury wrote to Derby on 25 Nov, 1851, '& I think he sees the policy of playing out the cause of Protection consistently until a General Election. He is very *Protestant*' (Derby MSS, 144/1).

Derby's first government

34 Malmesbury, *Memoirs*, i, 41.

35 Stanley MSS, Diary, 19 March 1851.

36 Gladstone memorandum, 12 March 1852: Gladstone MSS, Add. MSS 44778, ff. 1–4.

37 Derby to H. Lambert, 25 March 1852 (copy): Derby MSS, 180/1.

38 Queen Victoria to the King of the Belgians, 24 Feb, 1852: Victoria, *Letters*, ii, 450–1.

39 Queen Victoria to the King of the Belgians, 17 March 1852: *ibid*, ii, 463–4.

40 15 March 1852, *Hansard*, 3rd series, cxix, 1010.

41 Stanley MSS, Diary, June 1852.

42 Malmesbury to Derby, 25 Nov, 1851: Derby MSS, 144/1.

43 30 April 1852, *Hansard*, 3rd series, cxxi, 9–36.

44 Derby to Queen Victoria, 25 May 1852 (copy): Derby MSS, 180/2.

45 *Edinburgh Review*, Oct, 1852, 530. There was a parallel to this extraordinary behaviour in October 1974, when Edward Heath asked the electors to vote for a national government by returning Conservative candidates, while also making it plain that a Conservative *majority* would obviate the need for national government.

46 For an exhaustive display of that variety, see Conacher, *Peelites and the Party System*, 115–20.

47 Eglinton to Derby, 30 May 1852: Derby MSS, 148/2.

48 Naas to Derby, 31 July 1852: *ibid*, 155/1.

49 Tennent to Derby, 5 Dec, 1851: *ibid*, 131/7. Isaac Butt, the foremost Protectionist spokesman in Ireland, failed to get the nomination at Lisburn because of his extreme views on the question. He was returned, however, for Youghal, where he defeated the Radical candidate by only two votes.

50 Naas to Derby, 31 July 1852: Derby MSS, 155/1.

51 *Ibid*.

52 Eglinton to Derby, 1 June, 22 July, and 7 Oct, 1852: *ibid*, 148/2.

53 Whyte, 'The influence of the Catholic clergy on elections in nineteenth-century Ireland', *EHR*, April 1960, 239–59.

54 Whyte, *The Independent Irish Party, 1850–9*, 54–7.

55 Walpole to Derby, 29 Dec, 1851: Derby MSS, 153/1.

56 See 'The Government and the elections', *Fraser's Magazine*, July 1852, 112–26.

57 'I had a curious letter from Disraeli, in which he repeats the expression of his alarm concerning the elections, and ascribes the loss of several seats to our taking up with the "Protestant cry". I don't differ from this view: but who allowed that cry to be raised?' (Stanley MSS, Diary, 19 July 1852.) 'Saw Disraeli, who spoke despondingly of the elections, laying all the blame of what he called our failure on the proclamation respecting R. Catholic processions, which has created great exasperation and alienated many moderate men, even on our side. But this proclamation was carefully framed, with his approval, with a view to its effect upon the Protestant voters!' (*Ibid*, Diary, 21 July 1852.)

58 That is the calculation of Whyte, *Independent Irish Party*, 61. Naas claimed that they accounted for his prediction of 7 gains in Ireland not being fulfilled (Naas to Derby, 31 July 1852: Derby MSS, 155/1).

59 *Ibid*.

60 At the election for the northern division of Northumberland, the Whig candidate, George Grey, standing against two Protectionists, had 829 plumpers among his 1,300 votes. In the southern division of the county, the lone Protectionist candidate, H. G. Liddell, standing against a Whig and a Radical, was elected with 1,627 plumpers among his 2,132 votes. The parties maintained their line of demarcation despite the Protectionist candidates' avowals that they did not seek to restore the Corn Laws. (The figures are from Carrick, 'Three Northumberland constituencies in the general election of 1852: North and South Northumberland and Tynemouth', unpublished thesis, 32, 53.)

61 Beresford instructed a Protectionist agent named Frail to send down to Derby a 'good and safe' man. The man sent there was caught in the act of bribery, with a bag of gold and Beresford's letter to Frail in his possession (*The Times*, 23 July 1852; Stanley MSS, Diary, 25 July 1852). For a year Beresford was in disgrace, and the threat of prosecution in Queen's Bench hung over him. At the beginning of 1854 the threatened prosecution was abandoned for lack of evidence. The Peelites' professions of horror at Beresford's imprudence were somewhat out of keeping with the standards of the age. Wilson Patten told Stanley at the beginning of 1853 that only 35 of the 120 petitions brought to the elections committee would be proceeded with: 'all the rest were compromised; the law, as it stands, respecting bribery was so strict, and the observance of it so lax, that, he said, not 1/10th of the entire House was legally elected. . . . All bribery cases break down on one point – the proof of agency' (Stanley MSS, Diary, 16 Feb, 1853).

62 Morley, *Gladstone*, i, 419.

63 Graham to Bonham, 18 July, 1852: Peel MSS, Add. MSS 40616, ff. 342–5.

64 Newcastle to Aberdeen, 2 Aug, 1852: Aberdeen MSS, Add. MSS 43917, f. 11.
65 Quoted in Conacher, *Peelites and the Party System*, 127–8.
66 *Ibid*, 130.
67 Gladstone to Aberdeen, 30 July 1852 (copy): Gladstone MSS, Add. MSS 44088, ff. 133–7.
68 Greville, *Memoirs*, 6 dec, 1852, vi, 375–6.
69 Trevelyan, *Life and Letters of Lord Macaulay*, ii, 579.
70 The best discussion of this aspect of the budget is in Blake, *Disraeli*, 317–21.
71 See the speeches of Gladstone and Goulburn, *Hansard*, 3rd series, cxxiii, 1660, 1681.
72 'The fall of the Derby Ministery', *Edinburgh Review*, Jan, 1853, 265–6.
73 Gladstone memorandum, 14 Sept, 1897: Gladstone, *Autobiographica*, 76–80.
74 Morley, *Gladstone*, i, 437.
75 Greville, *Memoirs*, 29 Jan, 1853, vi, 393–6.
76 *Annual Register*, 1853, 78–9; Disraeli to Derby, 24 April 1853: Derby MSS, 145/3.
77 Conacher, *Peelites and the Party System*, 168.
78 Derby to Londonderry, 21 Dec, 1852 (copy): Derby MSS, 182/1.
79 Newcastle to Lord Granville, 18 April 1853. Fitzmaurice, *The Life of Granville George Leveson Gower, Second Earl of Granville*, i, 79–80.
80 *Edinburgh Review*, Jan, 1853, 421.
81 Derby to Londonderry, 21 Dec, 1852 (copy): Derby MSS, 182/1.
82 Greville, *Memoirs*, 22 May 1853, vi, 423–4.
83 16 December 1852, *Hansard*, 3rd series, cxxiii, 1666–94.
84 Blake, *Disraeli*, 332.
85 Stanley MSS, Diary, 16 Dec, 1852.
86 *Ibid*, Diary, 17 Dec, 1852.
87 *Ibid*, Diary, June 1852.
88 Derby to Disraeli, [15 December 1852]: Monypenny and Buckle, *Disraeli*, iii, 440–1.
89 Derby to Disraeli, 21 Feb, 1852: *ibid*, 342–3.
90 Derby to Disraeli, [4 December], 1852: *ibid*, iii, 434.
91 Hughenden MSS, A/X/A/66.

Chapter 13

Conservatism at mid-century

The party under Beresford

At the end of 1852 the Conservative party was not simply discredited and demoralized. It was also, at least by comparison with the days of Bonham and Fremantle, decrepit. After 1846 most of the agents who had been recruited by Bonham and his staff remained loyal to the Peelites. From 1846 to 1852 the Protectionists had no equivalent to Bonham. On Beresford and the Whips alone fell the double duty of managing the party in parliament and supervising the party's electoral business. How far Beresford's organization reached into the constituencies is, on the paltry evidence available, difficult to determine. Beresford had the assistance of a Mr. W. Brown, apparently a paid full-time agent, whom young Stanley described as 'a shrewd Parliamentary practitioner',[1] but the terms and date of whose appointment are not known. There was also a solicitor called Frail, who was the man who sent down to the borough of Derby the agent caught in the act of bribery in 1852.[2] Frail went about the country attending to Protectionist electoral activity, but if Samuel Phillips, the editor of the *Standard*, is to be believed, he was inefficient. In 1849 Phillips complained to Disraeli that 'if Beresford did not send Frail down into the country every three months or so to do nothing and then to turn in his report, the cause of Protection would be at a standstill. There never was such mismanagement or rather there never has been anything but such mismanagement.'[3] It was not easy, after the events of 1846, to find constituency workers. 'The conduct of Peel & his myrmidons', Malmesbury wrote, 'has certainly created a great deal of apathy in the middle class of our party, & numbers who rode their breeches off for us five years ago are confounded & discouraged at, to them, such unintelligible treachery.'[4] Malmesbury was writing in the autumn of 1846. By 1849, when the revival was on the upswing, the local protection societies were hard at work. They were, indeed, what amounted to the party's organization in the country. But, as Newdegate pointed out in 1852, when he sent to the Duke of Richmond a copy of a circular put out by G. F. Young's National Association, advising electors to vote for Derbyite candidates, the Association had 'never interfered directly with any election'.[5]

At the Carlton Club there was an election committee, at least from 1851, composed of Malmesbury, Salisbury, Forbes MacKenzie, Colonel Forrester, young Stanley, and others. According to Stanley, its functions were 'ill-performed', principally, it seems, because it lacked sufficient information from the localities. The committee was 'grossly practised upon' in its choice of agents, fifteen of whom, acting for the National Association, but paid by the central party, were discovered to be 'notoriously strong Liberals'. Stanley was surprised to find as many boroughs applying to the committee for candidates as there were candidates seeking boroughs, and even more surprised to discover that 'the idea of choosing men personally and locally known seemed scarcely to occur to anyone'.[6] Such lack of coordination between the Carlton and the constituencies sometimes produced comical results. A Banbury Conservative reported that at the 1852 elections the party was 'progressing fairly until the Carlton sent down Alderman Sidney . . . who talked such radicalism that the Rads laughed at us and said he was just the man for them' and that 'from that moment the Party was broken up'.[7]

There was also an election fund for the 1852 election, administered by Lord Colville, one of Malmesbury's assistants in the House of Lords. Like its predecessors, it was unable to attract much money away from the constituencies. Even the leaders of the party were reluctant to contribute to it. Lord Eglinton, who expected that the contest for the Ayrshire district of burghs would cost him £1,000, agreed to donate £300 to the central fund only if there were no contest for the county.[8] Disraeli informed Lord Derby that his contribution would be devoted to the Buckinghamshire election, which had assumed 'a serious aspect'.[9] Registration seems to have been neglected. There was nothing exceptional, of course, in the central party's unwillingness to provide money for registration. As Derby explained to a Cork Conservative in 1854, he was 'not aware of any fund at the disposal of the Carlton Club, or of any other body, for such purposes as establishing a Registration Machiney', especially for a county as wealthy as Cork, which 'if unwilling to make the necessary efforts for its own emancipation . . . must submit to have the Conservative interest unrepresented as at present'.[10] Derby was, it is true, peculiarly uninterested in electoral management. He took no part in the arrangements of the election committee and claimed even not to know who were its members.[11] Reports of the Protectionists' neglect of the register came, however, from all over the country, from Bath, where the party was described as *'supine, inert, indolent'*,[12] from Staffordshire South, where, Lord Lewisham reported, no one would attend to it 'in spite of all I can do',[13] and from Abingdon, where the Conservatives lost for the first time since 1832.[14] In Scotland, carefully managed by Graham in the late 1830s, the decline was particularly noticeable.

> The registration of Voters in Scotland [a Conservative wrote to Disraeli in 1855] has hitherto been very much neglected, so much so that at the last general Election it was found that in several Burghs not one half of the constituency were in a position to vote . . . and, in general, the state of the Registration Roll for the

counties was very incomplete and imperfect. . . . It is a matter of notoriety that in several instances the result of the last general Election might have been different had the Roll presented the true state of the Constituency.[15]

Such reports must be treated with caution. When Malmesbury, in urging upon Disraeli at the beginning of 1853 'the absolute necessity of reforming our personnel and getting matters into an administrative form', claimed that the Protectionists had lost the 1852 elections from bad management,[16] he was in danger of ignoring, for the moment at least, the connection between ideas and organization. The Protectionist organization at Bath was weak partly because even strong organization was likely to achieve little for the party in one of the most Radical boroughs in the country.[17] The same might be said of Scotland, where ever since 1832 the burghs had been unchallengeably Liberal. So, too, the difficulty which the party experienced in recruiting candidates – 'I see few, if any, young men coming forward, or taking an interest in public affairs, imbued with Conservative principles,' Stanley told Croker in 1850 –[18] reflected upon the unfashionable appeal of protection and Protestantism. In 1852 four young journalists, whom Lord Henry Lennox had been trying to engage for the *Morning Herald*, refused to write for so violently anti-Catholic a newspaper.[19]

Managing the press was always a touchy business. Conservative leaders had for some time shyed away from either contributing money to, or purchasing outright as commercial ventures, newspapers over which they should have no editorial control. In 1840, when the party, against the wishes of Bonham, declined to involve itself directly in the management of the *Courier*, despite the objections which it made to the Ultra-Tory line taken by the only Conservative evening newspaper then published in London, the *Standard*, Lord Redesdale, the Chief Whip in the Lords, noted that 'there is less willingness to support papers by gifts of money, than any other conservative interest. Our party does not take kindly to them. We seem to think that they ought to support themselves.'[20]

In 1847 the opportunity arose for the party to buy the *Morning Post*, which since 1833 had been stout in its defence of the agricultural interest.[21] In 1842 its editor and part-owner, C. Eastland Michele, had taken out a mortgage in order to buy out his fellow-owners, who wished to use the *Post* to advocate free trade. Five years later, unable to pay off the mortgage, Michele appealed to the Protectionist party to save the newspaper. Bentinck failed to persuade his father to put up the required £25,000. A year later, Disraeli took the matter in hand, setting up a committee to provide writers for the paper in an attempt to revive its languishing circulation and, if that effort were successful, to purchase it. The plan fell through. Only young Stanley contributed articles to the paper and the committee soon ceased to meet. Only the Duke of Richmond among the Protectionist peers evinced any readiness to subscribe to a fund to purchase the newspaper.[22] The result was that in 1849 the *Post* passed into the hands of the mortgager, T. B. Crampton, and a Palmerstonian editor, Peter Borthwick. The Protectionists had lost their most valuable editorial support, just at the time, too, when the Peelites, who already enjoyed the advocacy of *The Times*, gained control of the *Morning Chronicle*, a traditionally Whig paper which Disraeli had shown some interest in buying.[23] In the same year Beresford and Disraeli quarrelled with the editor of the *Morning Herald*, Samuel Phillips, and lost their influence with the only remaining London morning newspaper on the Protectionist side.[24] The Protectionists were thus left, apart from the histrionic, ultra-Protestant evening *Standard* and weekly *John Bull*,[25] with only the *Quarterly Review* as a reliable mouthpiece. But even the *Quarterly* was failing to keep its best writers,[26] and quarterly publications were, at any rate, being superseded in influence by the growing circulation of the daily press, both national and local. That influence was distinctly anti-Conservative. Dod's figures for newspaper circulation in England and Scotland in 1852 were almost two to one in favour of the Liberals: 167 Liberal newspapers with 531,961 readers, 122 Conservative newspapers with 230,841 readers, and 82 neutral newspapers with 182,589 readers.[27]

It was not simply from stinginess that the Protectionists withheld financial support from the press. Nor was it simply from the unwillingness, reasonable in itself, to take on the responsiblity of ownership or to trust its funds with other people. It was also that gentlemen felt contempt for the trade of journalism. Throughout his life Derby, like Peel and Wellington before him, would not soil his hands by direct dealing with journalists. Lord Mandeville believed that 'all authors or rather all men litterary [sic] by profession are dreadfully conceited'[28] (a belief which Disraeli's behaviour may have done little to discourage). Young Stanley commented that the Conservatives regarded all journalists as hacks,[29] and after close involvement in the efforts to improve the party's standing in the press in the late 1840s, he came to share the view.

> The party in general seemed to regard the newspaper interest as their natural enemy, and any attempt to turn it into their friend as mere waste of time: my Father sympathised in this view. Disraeli thought nothing could be done with existing journals, and that our only hope lay in founding a new one. I find journalists a difficult class to deal with. They have the irritable vanity of authors, and add to it a sensitity on the score of social position which as far as I know is peculiar to them. Having in reality a most secret influence – rating this above its true worth, and seeing that it gives them no recognised status in society, they stand up for the dignity of their occupation with a degree of jealousy I never saw among the members of any other profession. Moreover as from the anonymous nature of their writing the separate work of each can never be distinguished, they consider their individual reputation as involved in that of the paper to which they contribute: and refuse accordingly to act except with colleagues whose abilities they recognise. The actual state of Conservative journalism is as low as it well can be.[30]

In 1852 there was a curious arrangement designed to help counteract the hostility of the press towards the Protectionist government. Each member of the cabinet consented, just before the elections, to contribute two per cent of his official salary to a fund for the support of Conservative writers. The writers, however, were never found and the money was mostly returned.[31] The scheme, at any rate, was launched too late and promised too little to prevent Derby from regretting, in the face of the editorial onslaught against his government, that he had not previously recognized 'the possible powers of the press in a crisis'.[32]

The nadir of Conservatism

It is a habit of politicians, on the morrow of defeat, to look upon the future as closed to them. In December 1852, and for some time thereafter, the air around Westminster was thick with prophecies that Conservatism was dead. The formation of the Aberdeen coalition, by bringing together all the anti-Conservative sections (including even two renegades from Irish Independency, John Sadlier and William Keough), seemed to reduce the fact that the Conservatives were the largest single party in the House of Commons – Forbes MacKenzie, Beresford's successor as Chief Whip in 1852, put them at 300, Malmesbury, with keener judgement, at 292[33] – to an empty statistic. 'I think the game is up as regards the Conservative party (so called),' the Earl of Hardwicke wrote to Croker. 'It is clear to me that the union of Whigs and Peelites, with the side-door open to the Radicals, leads to these consequences – that while our party will be thinned, so slow and moderate will be the democratic downward tendency, that as a party we shall be deprived of a link strong enough to hold us together.' The opposition to Disraeli's adjustments of the house tax and income tax had, in Hardwicke's opinion, demonstrated the power of the £10 householders to resist any proposal to tax themselves and in that power was foreshadowed the future impossibility of a Conservative government. 'It is now . . . clear that the power and preponderance are in the hands of, and turn to, the trade, moneyed, and manufacturing classes, that the land will be governed by them, and obliged to submit to a state of things that will enhance the value of trade.'[34] Walpole, too, believed that the doubling of the house tax had been fatal and that Conservatism had been dragged down by Disraeli's budget. 'Where it will all end, Heaven only knows! I tremble for the future.'[35] There was, in the circumstances predictably, criticism of Disraeli. By his unorthodox budget he had suffered the Conservatives to be defeated without providing them with the satisfaction of going out on a clearly Conservative principle.

But underneath the ordinary recriminations in defeat there was the more deeply-felt conviction that Conservative principles themselves had become impotent. Protection was buried, Protestantism was generally admitted to have lost the party as many seats as it had gained it at the last elections, and, as Stanley remarked at the end of 1853 of the Conservative appeal against democracy around the corner, it was 'hardly credible that while entire apathy prevails on this question among the masses, the Conservative class has worked itself into a paroxysm of alarm, and talks everywhere of revolution as impending'.[36] Mid-Victorians were, of course, thoroughly mindful of, and frequently disturbed by, the constitutional and social change being wrought in their lifetimes. Bertrand Russell told the story of his grandfather, Lord Stanley of Alderley, who, 'while wandering in his mind during his last illness [in 1869], heard a loud noise in the street and thought it was the revolution breaking out, showing that, at least sub-consciously, the thought of revolution had remained with him throughout long prosperous years'.[37] On the other hand, as memories of the French Revolution receded, so did the fear of its contagion. Lady Charlemont probably spoke for many people when she told Tocqueville in 1835 that she had heard it said every year that there was going to be a revolution 'and at the end of the year we always found ourselves in the same place'.[38] It was difficult to make political capital, especially in the 1850s, from a 'revolution' which never did break out, but which made headway only gradually.

Before the defeat on the budget, although after the elections had failed to return a Protectionist majority, Croker had outlined to Derby a dreary future for the Conservative party.

> You have an awful part to play, and you will play it honourably, and to the greatest possible degree successfully. You may postpone the catastrophe, and save us from immediate revolution, but you cannot save us from the ultimate and irresistible effects of the Reform Bill. Your own personal character, the homogeneity of the great Church-and-King party, the gravitation towards the soil, the innate aristocracy of all classes, may enable you to resist – if you will resist – for a while; and the harder we die the easier will be the resurrection; but depend upon it, die this constitution must. . . . The Queen is already a puppet. The House of Commons is King, as the first attempt of any opposition to his popular Majesty will show. Our sole hope now is the, not *'dolce'*, but *'difficile far niente'*. You can stand, perhaps; but if you attempt to manoeuvre, either by retreat or advance, we are all lost.[39]

Like Croker, Derby was vulnerable to bouts of political fatalism. 'I have known as long ago as 1845,' he told Stanley two weeks after leaving office, 'that I was playing a losing game: I said so than: I thought I was left high and dry for ever: the tide has risen once, high enough to float me again, which was more than I expected: it will never do so again: the game is lost, but I think it ought to be played and I will play it out to the last.'[40] Three months later he repeated his conviction that he would never again hold office, and added that the Aberdeen government, with its great strength and prestige, could, by adopting conservative measures, destroy the Conservative party within two years.[41] Derby rarely analysed, at least for public consumption, his objections to democratic politics. It is not clear whether, like John Stuart Mill, he feared that democracy might mean mediocrity in government, or, like Matthew Arnold, that it might led to the tyranny of the majority. His presentation of the argument against democracy took always the narrow constitutional ground; if his real fears were of a social revolution in property relations, he did not give them utterance. In his conversation with Stanley, however, he revealed how deeply he disliked the interference of public opinion in government.

> My Father repeated more than once a conviction which he said had been forced upon him early in life – that real political power was not to be had in England: at best you could only a little advance or retard the progress of an inevitable movement. Even in America, a President could do much by his own will: an English Minister had more responsibility, more labour, and less authority, than the ruler of any people on earth.[42]

That remark helps to explain one of Derby's characteristics, remarkable in a man who held the leadership of his party for twenty-two years: his comparative lack of interest in gaining power. What lent great force to the Conservative party in the 1830s was Peel's evident desire for power and the buoyant confidence of Conservatives that, sooner or later, he would get it. Under Derby's leadership the Conservatives carried the air of defeat about them for a generation. For that Thomas Kebbel laid the blame on Derby. Kebbel allowed that Derby's personal qualifications for the Conservative leadership were impeccable. 'In his high rank, his spotless character and his great wealth he was a second Lord Rockingham' and 'in his intellectual force, his fervid eloquence, and his happy wit, he was a second Fox'. Such a combination of gifts ought to have triumphed over all obstacles. They did not, because Derby was not 'actuated by the ordinary motives of English politicians'.

> In politics, as in war, it is by combination and calculation, by patience and perseverance, and the long and careful study of all the problems of the age, that permanent triumphs are attained; and for these the late Lord Derby had little or no inclination. In the then temper of the public mind, a Conservative Government should properly have been in office. Yet the Tories were obliged to look on while the Liberals occupied their place, and carried out their principles in disguise. . . . It was just as easy for the Tories to have governed England from 1855 to 1865 as for the Liberals; and the only thing that prevented it was that Lord Palmerston possessed just those qualities in which Lord Derby was deficient.[43]

One of the reasons why the Conservatives, after years of standing as the party opposed to democracy, accepted radical reform from Disraeli in 1867, was that he showed them, at least, a healthy appetite for office.

Yet it would be foolish to place great stress on Derby's personality as a major cause of the Conservative party's distress from 1852 to 1866. There was, after all, during all those years, no indication that the party, or even a single influential one among them, wished to be rid of him. The explanation for what Robert Blake has aptly called the 'years of frustration' lay elsewhere, in the political consequences of the Peelites' decision to work with the Liberals and in the electoral consequences of the Conservative party's being a party of the landed interest and, what it has rarely been in its history, a really *conservative* party.

When Lord Aberdeen undertook to lead the Whig–Peelite coalition in 1852, he was careful to have it understood that he had not given himself over to advanced liberalism. No government, his famous phrase ran, could be too liberal for him, provided that it did not abandon its conservative character. Liberal Conservatism became a catchword of the age. In Palmerston it found its representative. It was not Palmerston himself, so much as the opinion which he represented, that the Conservatives needed to capture. Twice in 1852 Derby invited Palmerston to join his government. Palmerston declined, giving as his courteous and sensible reason that, having acted for twenty-two years with the Whigs, it would not answer nor be agreeable to him to 'go slap over to the opposite camp'.[44] It was her husband's opinion, Lady Palmerston said, that 'in England change of principle was more easily forgiven than change of party'.[45] It was, of course, to the advantage of conservative interests that the liberal forces between 1852 and 1865 should be led by a man so temperamentally indifferent to change as Palmerston, just as it was that the acquisition of the Peelites should relieve Whiggery of some of its dependence upon the rdicals. It was to their advantage that radicalism should provide so ineffective a challenge to the conservative leadership of Liberalism that Dissent, while it unobtrusively manured the grass roots of Liberal politics, should be unable to abolish Church rates or the jurisdiction of the ecclesiastical courts and that the freehold land societies which sprang into existence in the late 1840s should fail in their aim to overthrow the aristocratic control of county politics by invading the countryside with radical small-property owners.[46] 'It is astonishing', Cobden wrote in 1857, 'that the people at large are so tacit in their submission to the perpetuation of the feudal system as it affects the property in land long after it has been shattered to pieces in every other country except Russia.[47]

The liberal–conservative temper of the age was thus welcome to Conservatives, but obstructive to their progress as a party. Darius Clayhanger's political hero was Sir Robert Peel. 'Darius had known England before and after the repeal of the Corn Laws, and the difference between the two Englands was so strikingly dramatic to him that he desired no further change. He had only one date – 1846. His cup had been filled then.'[48] But Darius, who revered the memory of Peel and who desired no change, was a Liberal. Not until the 1880s, stirred by the issue of Irish Home Rule, did he become a Conservative. The mid-Victorian Conservative party was, as Eric Hobsbawm has described it, the 'organ of all that was out of sympathy with industrial Britain . . . a permanent political minority lacking an ideology or a programme'.[49] What else was it to be? To be a liberal Conservative, prepared to abolish Church rates, or give up the clergy reserves in Canada, or reform the ancient universities, or get rid of the taxes on newspapers, was to become a Peelite, to partake in the destruction of the Conservative party.

When the Conservatives next won a parliamentary majority, at the elections of 1874, they did so after the country had experienced a rush of reformist legislation from Gladstone's first ministry. And when, at the end of the century, they held power, with one brief interruption, from 1886 to 1905, they had become a different party, the party, not only of the land, but of capital and Unionism, the antidote to the Home Rulers and the threat of powerful trade unionism. As Churchill put it, early in the twentieth century, the Conservative party had changed (although the change was not so stark as he liked to present it) from one 'of religious convictions and constitutional principles' to 'a new party, rich, material and secular'.[50] The Conservative party in the 1865 parliament was composed of nearly 200 landowners and 112 members whose background was chiefly industrial or commercial. By 1892 the ratio was almost directly reversed: 163 landowners and 298 industrialists and financiers.[51] To say, as it is often said, that the Conservative party is remarkable 'because it is fairly rare for an avowedly conservative party so to flourish that it can, over many generations, continue to provide . . . the government of a constitutional country'[52] is to overlook the difference between the mid-Victorian party, which sought to *defend* the Church and the land, and its successors, which have sought to prosper the *progressive* interests of capital.

In 1849 Croker wrote in the *Quarterly Review* that the great question in politics was not the struggle 'between Democracy and Monarchy, not between Democracy and Aristocracy, but between Democracy and PROPERTY' and he went on to say that 'Landed Property is the foundation of all property'.[53] The Conservative party in 1852, as the division on Disraeli's budget makes plain, faithfully reflected that view.

Analysis of the budget division, 16 December 1852

	Majority	Minority
County members		
England and Wales	29	113
Scotland	14	12
Ireland	35	24
	78	149
Borough members		
England and Wales	187	119
Scotland	21	1
Ireland	21	19
	229	139
Combined total	307	288

(These figures include the tellers)

In 1833 the ratio of landed members to 'business' members in the Liberal party was six to two, in the Conservative party, eight to one. In 1865 it was six to five in the Liberal party, nine to two in the Conservative party.[54] The Liberals adjusted themselves much more quickly to the changing economic and social structure of the country. The Conservatives were bound to suffer from their narrow base. In 1850 the part of the working population employed in agriculture in America was 65 per cent, in France 52 per cent, in Belgium 50 per cent. In Great Britain (excluding Ireland) it was only 22 per cent. Even in the Netherlands, next to Great Britain the least agricultural nation, the figure was 44 per cent.[55] In 1851, too, the census disclosed that for the first time more Englishmen lived in towns than in the country.

Not only was the Conservative party hemmed in by the encompassing conservatism of mid-Victorian Liberalism and its own narrow social base, it also found it difficult to make headway in the relatively placid atmosphere of political debate which characterized the period. The old view that the 1850s and 1860s were barren of constructive legislation has long ago been put to rest, above all by W. L. Burn's suavely reticent book, *The Age of Equipoise*, published in 1964. There was great deal of social legislation passed every year. It was not, however, of the kind which stimulated public interest in the philosophical contentions between parties. The fundamental question which had agitated politicians in the 1830s and 1840s, the question whether the state ought to meddle in social matters, had been answered by such legislation as the Mines Act of 1842, the Factory Act of 1847, and the Public Health Act of 1848. Debate continued about whether social legislation ought to be compulsive or permissive, but in the 1850s and 1860s the impetus to social reform was administrative, not political, and debates on it were poorly attended. Writing in the *Oxford Essays* for 1858, Lord Robert Cecil, the future Lord Salisbury and Conservative Prime Minister, bemoaned the 'tacit unanimity with which this generation has laid aside the ingenious network of political first principles which the industry of three centuries of theorists had woven'.[56] What Gladstone, in 1856, called the 'general abatement of extreme views and an abandonment of impracticable purposes'[57] produced a relaxation of party discipline in the House of Commons. Governments were compelled, the Liberal member of parliament, Robert Lowe, wrote in 1857, 'to put upon those mystic words, the confidence of the House of Commons, a much looser construction than formerly'.

> Men treat Parliament more as a debating club, and less as a deliberative assembly. They are apt to look at every question upon its abstract merits, without sufficiently reflecting that a vote of the House of Commons is something more than a mere affirmative or negative proposition; that it is a practical step, which ought to be based upon practical considerations, and must be followed by immediate practical results.[58]

To explain the change from the strict party voting of the 1830s and early 1840s Lowe cited, not only the want of major issues of principle to divide parties, but also the prevailing prosperity of both agriculture and manufacturing industry and the influence of public opinion on parliamentary proceedings.

> The circle within which mere party differences are allowable or possible is greatly contracted by the enlarged political judgment of the nation. . . . No sooner is a question distinctly raised in Parliament, than it is thoroughly ventilated and discussed by the press; opinion is formed, and against that opinion no party leader in the House of Commons is bold enough to make a resolute stand.[59]

Despite the weakening of party *discipline* in the House of Commons, which must not automatically be taken as a sign of weakening party *attachments*, it was remarkable that the organization of parties in the constituencies remained, as Gladstone perceived with satisfaction, 'in its old and simple form of dualism'.

> This division of local parties may indeed be at present almost as much animal as intellectual, but it is dignified by traditional recollections, and it is probably the best or only way, in which the communication of ideas between representatives and constituents can be practically maintained. We also find in it the basis upon which, in an altered posture of public affairs, we may again see the old parties once more arrayed face to face, and in something like their old condition . . . the constituencies . . . do not appear to feel, as the representatives have felt, the debilitating and disorganising influences so patent within the walls of Parliament. Whether they have or have not distinctive opinions – whether they do seek or do not seek separate and opposite ends – whether the antagonist candidates can or cannot succeed in imparting to their respective speeches and addresses a decent amount of difference – it is beyond all doubt that, as the constituencies have been so they mean to continue, divided as Conservative and Liberal respectively; and none of the wizards of Peelism, or of Palmerstonism, or of Manchesterism, or of Administrative Reform, or of Voluntaryism, or of any other personal, intermediate, sectional, or hybrid creed, will at least in our day, dislodge them from the impregnable stronghold of their set electioneering habits and ideas.[60]

Gladstone's remarks point to an important, but overlooked, aspect of the age of Palmerston, that the two-party system remained an essential part of British politics. Party did not die, after a premature birth in the earlier part of the century, to be re-fathered by the Reform Act of 1867. The history of the Conservative party in the years between 1852 and 1866 is not very interesting for the ideas which it contributed to national affairs, nor for the impact which it made on the legislation of the period. The interest lies in the simple event that in difficult times it survived as a large and well-organized party.

It was, indeed, given the state of the party at the end of 1852, something more than survival. It was a rehabilitation. For that Disraeli deserves much credit. Almost alone among the Conservative leaders, he looked forward, at the beginning of 1853, to opposing the Aberdeen coalition wholeheartedly and to rebuilding the Conservative party. It was his appointments, of Sir William Jolliffe as Chief Whip and Philip Rose as election manager, which secured for the party as firm a foundation as that which it had enjoyed under Peel.

Laying the new foundations

When Disraeli came to consider the reorganization of the party in 1853, two things were clear. One was that the party needed a new Chief Whip in the House of Commons; the other was that it was desirable to separate the management of the party inside parliament from its electoral management outside. The two jobs required two men, even though it was obvious that the two men should work closely together.

In 1852, when Beresford had been appointed Secretary at War, Forbes MacKenzie had been made the Chief Whip. He had not given satisfaction[61] and had been unseated for bribery at Liverpool; Beresford was not considered for his old post, not only because of the cloud of corruption which hung over him, but also because he had never got on with Disraeli, who did not disguise his objections to Beresford's ultra-Protestantism, and because he had often, by his rough speech and partisan temper, embarrassed the party.[62] Another candidate, Augustus Stafford, was precluded by a parliamentary committee's exposure of his misconduct at the Admiralty in 1852. In the circumstances it told rather for than against Jolliffe that he was, as Henry Drummond put it to Disraeli, 'too delicate to know how to bribe half the Irish and the press'.[63] Jolliffe was appointed by Disraeli after full consultation with Derby, who told Disraeli that he looked forward to 'very useful results from his popularity and tact' and that he expected Jolliffe to 'do much towards reuniting the disjecta membra of our body politic'.[64] Like Fremantle, Jolliffe was a Chief Whip typical of the age, a landed gentleman of no ministerial ambition, well connected with the network of Conservative families and therefore able to exercise powerful influence over the backbenchers and move easily in the complex tangle of local influences which determined the character of constituency politics. Like Fremantle, too, he was not restricted to mere whipping. He was responsible for the overall supervision of the party's affairs, as appears from the agenda of duties which he drew up on his appointment.[65]

1 Procure Books with 'Electoral Facts' leaving several pages to each County District and Borough . . .
2 Transfer information already obtained to the respective places in private Book where such as is desirable may be transferred for general reference.
3 Correct 'Electoral Facts' so far as is necessary by the proceedings in Committee this session.
4 When opportunity occurs ascertain and note in working Book all useful intelligence
    1 As to men of influence in the Place
    2 What description of candidate most likely to succeed

3 Particulars of former elections
4 Number of freemen
5 Number of houses and rental
6 Population last census
7 Registered Electors (last Register)
5 Make list of Counties Cities and Boroughs where no Conservative agent
6 Investigate the case of all places where no Conservative Members
    1st by enquiring of any neighbouring influential supporters
    2nd by widespread enquiries made as may be always prudent
    3rd Ascertain who are the influential people on the other side and whether
       the non-success is caused by supineness or otherwise
7 Obtain Election cases for reference
8 Get Parliamentary report of election proceedings of this session and analyse.

Jolliffe was responsible for electoral management, but the day-to-day running of electoral affairs was entrusted to Philip Rose, Disraeli's solicitor, and his legal assistant in the firm of Baxter, Rose, Norton and Co., Markham Spofforth. Rose declined to take a paid position, apparently because he felt that it would lower his reputation in the legal world. In a letter to Disraeli setting forth the terms of his firm's relations with the party,[66] Rose explained that he 'could not afford to be looked upon in the light of a paid political agent' and that he therefore had agreed to act as 'a confidential medium and to share in the deliberations and responsibility of those appointed to manage the Election affairs and to take a general supervision of affairs'. Spofforth was therefore 'the ostensible political agent of the party' (the title was not officially used until 1871), salaried at £300 annually and responsible for maintaining an office at Westminster 'for the use of parties seeking information on Election matters'. He was, in addition, to be reimbursed for incidental expenses, expected to amount to about £100, arising from postage and the lithographing of circulars.

> His duties are to collect and keep records of the most accurate voters lists of every Borough & County in the United Kingdom, to open communications with our friends and establish friendly relations in every place. To record all information available for the objects of this and to make himself acquainted with the names of parties and the alterations effected at each Registration he will of course be in daily communication with me and will watch and report also every opening which occurs.

Between Spofforth and the parliamentary party there was established a linking committee or 'council of advice', headed by Jolliffe, Rose, and George Hamilton. In order to reduce the risk of the parliamentary party's becoming directly associated with any corrupt dealings by its agents, it was agreed that Spofforth should communicate personally with the committee only in exceptional circumstances, otherwise through Rose.

As it must obviously be impraticable to avoid all direct communications between Mr. Spofforth and the . . . members of the Committee, he has been made to understand that he is not retained by them nor are they answerable for his acts and that he is not to consider them under any pecuniary liability to him for his salary or otherwise. In fact he does not know, nor is it necessary that he should know from what source his salary is to be paid. He is content to believe that it will be paid him by or thro me. The cautious nature of these arrangements was prompted by the timidity of our friends who compose the Committee who, with the disclosures of last session fresh in their recollection, were unwilling to trust themselves in the hands of an untried agent. I look to much of this timidity disappearing as we proceed and as the party discovers the real value of the man whose services have been secured, for I am satisfied he will prove himself an efficient agent, but in any case, I think the double arrangement has its advantages. By it the party has secured the twofold object of a confidential medium, who may as occasion requires be in direct personal communication with the leaders of the party and in the execution of their wishes may adopt their suggestions as his own and they also have at command an arrived political agent who is concentrating his attention upon the machinery necessary for the future success of our plans and as to whom the leaders of the party need not be in any direct communication and for whose acts they cannot individually be held accountable.

Rose ended his letter to Disraeli, written some months after Spofforth's appointment, by saying that the records passed on by Beresford's staff were scanty and useless, but that Spofforth had been busily gathering information and that he was happy to work 'with an entirely new staff untrammeled by the associations of the past'. And in a postscript, he added that, like all solicitors who had worked for party organizations as agents, Spofforth looked for reward to being engaged to handle election petitions. He understood, however, that 'although the Committee will, where a fair opportunity offers, endeavour to procure his employment by the friends of the party, they will not engage to do so indiscriminately but they will rather discourage the notion of the necessity of employing the agent of the party in *all* cases'.

That last cautionary note was probably intended to allay apprehensions that Spofforth might interfere, uninvited, in the autonomous relationship of a private member with his own agent or solicitor. Some other points of interest appear from the new arrangements. It is evident that the formal institutions of party organization were still sufficiently suspect for Rose to wish not to sully his reputation by an official appointment as political agent. That was so partly because, as the shielding of Spofforth suggests, it was assumed that no agent could conduct his business efficiently without contravening the laws against bribery and corruption.[67] But, however gingerly and secretively the party behaved in employing Rose and Spofforth, the significant aspect of the new arrangements was that neither of them had any parliamentary connection with the party. Bonham had been a member of parliament. His headquarters had been the Carlton Club. Neither Rose nor Spofforth ever sat in parliament. Their offices were in Victoria Street. Compared to Bonham, they were outsiders. Their appointment may therefore be regarded as a step towards a more 'professional' organization of the party, towards the creation of Central Office in 1867.

Important as the reorganization of the party's machinery was for the long-term interests of the party, its action in reviving Conservative fortunes would necessarily be slow. Disraeli was eager to harass the Aberdeen coalition from the start and to discredit it in the minds of the public. He therefore turned his attention once more to the debilitated condition of the Conservative press. In March 1853 he established his own newspaper, called the *Press*, to counteract what he believed to be the baneful influence of the *Standard* and the *Morning Herald*. After the failure to purchase one of the existing newspapers in 1848–49, Disraeli, Malmesbury and young Stanley had been impressed with the need to found a newspaper of their own.

> It seems [Disraeli said in the printed circular announcing the launching of the *Press* and soliciting funds to support it] that the whole ability of the country is arrayed against us, and the rising generation is half ashamed of a cause which would seem to have neither wit nor reason to sustain and adorn it. Experience has shown that propping up obsolete organs is a mere waste of energy and capital. We require something which will produce as striking and as rapid an effect on opinion as the *Anti-Jacobin* when it was started by Mr. Canning, or the *Edinburgh Review* when it first rose.[68]

The reference to Canning was an indication that Disraeli intended to use the *Press* to propagate his own, distinctive brand of Conservatism, aggressive, sharp-edged, and willing to comprehend new ideas and embrace new allies in the search for power. He had the keen support of Stanley and Malmesbury. 'The Captain does not care for office,' Stanley wrote from Knowsley in January, 'but wishes to keep things as they are, and impede "Progress" . . . Don't let us plunge into a reactionary course of opposition and suffer political martyrdom for a cause in which we neither of us believe.' From Heron Court in Hampshire, Malmesbury sent similar encouragement. 'I agree entirely with you,' he wrote, 'that our party is repugnant to the urban taste, and that we should try something to recover the towns' interest, but no operation can be compared in difficulty to it. . . . I trust to your genius to give us a standard and a war-cry.'[69]

At the beginning of the 1853 session Malmesbury and Stanley advised Disraeli that the attacks delivered on Louis Napoleon by some cabinet ministers, in particular Charles Wood and Sir James Graham, threatened to undo the friendship of France and England which had been the principal achievement of Malmesbury's tenure of the Foreign Office. By officially recognizing the Emperor's government, Malmesbury had linked France with England against the three northern, absolutist powers. Disraeli therefore began his assault on the Aberdeen coalition, in the second week of the new session, with a long speech on foreign affairs. With the Crimean war just over a year away, but not yet foreseen, Disraeli charged the government with being indifferent to the friendship of France. Then he broadened the attack, in words reminiscent of his argument in 1845, that Peel, by stealing the Whigs' clothing, was destroying the action of a constitutional opposition.

> We have at the present moment a Conservative Ministry and a Conservative Opposition. Where the great Liberal party is I pretend not to know. . . . We have now got a Ministry of Progress, and everyone stands still. We never hear the word 'reform' now; it is no longer a Ministry of Reform; it is a Ministry of Progress, every member of which agrees to do nothing. All difficult questions are suspended. All questions which cannot be agreed upon are open questions. Now, I do not want to be unreasonable, but I think there ought to be some limit to this system of open questions . . . at least let your answer for me to-night prove that among your open questions you are not going to make an open question of the peace of Europe.[70]

It was a prescient speech, delivered with great gusto. The ministry had been in office less than two months, but Disraeli had put his finger on its great weakness, which was to become more apparent as the months went by, its inability to resolve its internal disputes about how to proceed with parliamentary reform at home and how to deal with the threat of Russian aggrandisement in the Balkans. It was also a speech calculated to infuriate his opponents, described by Greville, a supporter of the coalition, as a speech 'of devilish malignity, quite reckless and shamelessly profligate', marked by 'a liberal infusion of that sarcastic vituperation which is his great forte'.[71] The opposition press was united in denouncing Disraeli's descent into 'faction', and it was those attacks, Stanley believed, which finally drove Disraeli to revive 'the long suspended project of setting up an organ for himself'.[72]

In March the circular announcing the *Press* went out to those Conservatives who Disraeli judged would be sympathetic and a staff was assembled. Samuel Lucas, a former writer for *The Times*, was appointed editor, and a core of contributors was enlisted, including Stanley, Bulwer Lytton, the former Young Englander, George Smythe, and George Bentinck. Derby poured cold water on the scheme, not simply for the customary reason that the party would find itself compromised by opinions published in its name but without its sanction, but, more immediately, because he feared that the *Press*, if it took an advanced or progressive line, would divide the Conservatives into warring sections. He prevailed upon the Duke of Northumberland to withdraw his offer of £2,000, but he was unable to quench Disraeli's enthusiasm.

> D's ardour [Stanley wrote in his diary], great from the first, rose higher and higher as the plan assumed definite form. He talked of a circulation of from 10,000 to 15,000: of driving all other weekly journals out of the field: even of shaking the power of the Times. I have never seen him so much excited on any subject, except once in a conversation at Hughendon in 1851.[73]

Enough money was found for the *Press* to make its appearance on 7 May 1853. By the end of July it had gained a circulation of 2,000; the party had contributed £2,500 and Disraeli had matched that amount from his own pocket.[74] By 1854 the circulation may have reached a figure over 3,000,[75] respectable enough, but too low for a weekly journal to have much impact on public opinion. In 1858 Disraeli sold the *Press* and in 1866 it ceased operations.

Disraeli claimed, in a circular letter printed in March 1854, that the *Press*, 'launched at a moment when the party was disorganised and depressed', had helped to rally the Conservative cause in parliament and in the country.[76] Whatever its action in the country, it had upon the parliamentary party rather, as Derby had feared, a disjointing influence. It served as a vehicle for Disraeli and Stanley, restlessly seeking a new path for the Conservative party to follow, now that protection was dead, to promote unorthodox, occasionally radical, causes in the name of Conservatism; and it therefore served, also, as an argument against Disraeli for less adventurous members of the party. It played an important part, although more symbolic than original, in the dissensions and quarrels which disturbed the Conservative opposition during the life of the Aberdeen government.

Notes and References

The party under Beresford

1   Stanley MSS, Diary, 15 march 1851 (1855 note). In 1853 Philip Rose told Disraeli that he did not wish 'to be looked upon in the light of a paid political agent, much less as the successor to W. Browne' and that Markham Spofforth 'who has succeeded to Browne's office will be the ostensible political agent of the party' (Rose to Disraeli, 17 Nov, 1853. The letter is in the possession of the present Sir Philip Rose. I am grateful to Sir Philip for permission to quote from it and to Mr Bernard Gill for a copy of his transcription of it.)

2   Stanley MSS, Diary, 25 July 1852. Frail continued to assist the party after 1852. In 1854, the ex-Whip, Charles Newdegate, who, like Frail and Beresford, was relieved of official responsibility for party management in 1853, passed on to Jolliffe information which he had received from Frail about Liberal electoral activity in the counties. 'Frail's information is from a safe source,' Newdegate told Jolliffe. '*Don't forget that man* – but do not use his name' (Newdegate to Jolliffe, 29 July 1854: Hylton MSS, DD/HY/Box 24/7).

3   Phillips to Disraeli, 6 Sept, 1849:. Hughenden MSS, B/XXI/P/224.

4   Malmesbury to Stanley, 13 Sept, 1846: Derby MSS, 144/1.

5   Newdegate to Richmond, 3 June 1852: Goodwood MSS, 1762, f. 1283.

6   Stanley MSS, Diary, 15 March 1851 (1855 note).

7   Sidney North to Colonel Taylor, 7 Dec, 1855: Hylton MSS, DD/HY/Box 24/9. Colonel Edward Taylor was made an Assistant Whip in 1853.

8   Eglinton to Derby, 1 June 1852: Derby MSS, 148/2. 'I have heard from Colville', Eglinton wrote, 'that the subscriptions for the General Election fund are not progressing favourably, in consequence of so many people having Elections of their own to look after.'

9   Disraeli to Derby, 12 July 1852: *ibid*, 145/2.

10   Derby to J. M. Sloane, 3 Nov, 1854 (copy): *ibid*, 183/1.

11   Derby to C. Lemprierre, 1 July 1853 (copy): *ibid*, 182/2.

12   [Illegible] to Sir William Jolliffe, 11 May 1855: Hylton MSS, DD/HY/Box 24/9. Jolliffe was made Chief Whip in 1853.

13   Lewisham to Jolliffe, 8 Aug, 1853: *ibid*, DD/HY/Box 18/8.

14   M. Spofforth to Jolliffe, 19 Oct, 1854: *ibid*, DD/HY/Box 24/8.

15   J. Wallace to Disraeli, 17 May 1855: *ibid*, DD/HY/Box 24/9.

16   Malmesbury to Disraeli, 12 Jan, 1853: Hughenden MSS, B/XX/Hs/29.

17   For a discussion of electoral politics in Bath, see Neale, *Class and Ideology in the Nineteenth Century*, 41–60.

18   Stanley to Croker, 18 Aug, 1850: Croker, *Correspondence and Diaries*, iii, 221.

19   Lennox to Disraeli, 7 Aug, 1852: Hughenden MSS, B/XX/Lx/8.

20   Redesdale to Fremantle, 21 Nov, 1840: Fremantle MSS, 80/13. For the

negotiations with the *Courier* see Stewart, 'The Conservative party and the 'Courier' newspaper, 1840', *EHR*, April 1976, 346–50.

21 See Lucas, *Glenesk and the 'Morning Post'*, 29–40 and Hindle, *The Morning Post, 1772–1937*, 177ff.

22 Stanley MSS, Diary, 19 and 25 May 1849; Malmesbury to Stanley, 12 and 25 Nov, 1849: Derby MSS, 144/1.

23 Stanley MSS, Diary, 15 June 1849.

24 Beresford to Disraeli, March 1849: Hughenden MSS, B/XX/Bd/9. The specific ground of the quarrel between Disraeli and Phillips is not known, but they took opposite views of the Jew question and protection, Phillips being a diehard. In January 1852 Disraeli wrote to Derby about Phillips: 'I have no communication of any kind with Mr. Phillips. I saw him, rather frequently, about three years ago at the instance of a section of our friends, but between reserve on my part & illness on his, wh. removed him from town, &, as I understand altogether from his political pursuits, I never saw him again until last session, when he requested an interview with me that he might develope [sic] a scheme for the organization of the provincial press, in order to advocate the views of the 'Protection Society'. . . . This, I believe, was the last time, that I had the honour of seeing Mr. Phillips & I concluded that he was an uncompromising Protectionist.' (Disraeli to Derby, 20 Jan, 1852: Derby MSS, 145/2.)

25 In July 1849 the editor and part-owner of *John Bull* asked the Protectionists for a loan to prevent the paper from falling into hostile hands. Young Stanley, to whom Newdegate had referred him, 'absolutely declined', but subscribed £100 personally (Stanley MSS, Diary, 24 July 1849).

26 *Ibid*, Diary, June 1852. Stanley got his information from the *Quarterly's* editor, J. G. Lockhart.

27 Dod, *Electoral Facts*, 109, 278, 322.

28 Mandeville to Derby, 6 Nov, 1855: Derby MSS, 156/9.

29 Stanley MSS, Diary, 21 March 1851 (1855 note).

30 *Ibid*. Diary, 8 April 1851 (1855 note).

31 *Ibid*. Diary, June 1852.

32 Derby to Disraeli, 1852: Hughenden MSS, B/XX/S/105.

The nadir of Conservatism

33 Stanley MSS, Diary, 17 Dec, 1852; Malmesbury, *Memoirs*, i, 375.

34 Hardwicke to Croker, 30 Dec, 1852: Croker, *Correspondence and Diaries*, iii, 259–60.

35 Walpole to Croker, 13 Jan, 1853: *ibid*, iii, 261.

36 Stanley MSS, Diary, 14 Dec, 1853.

37 Russell, BBC radio talks, published as *Ideas and Beliefs of the Victorians, 20.*

38 Quoted in Watson, *The English Ideology*, 42.

39 Croker to Derby, 11 Aug, 1852: Croker, *Correspondence and Diaries*, iii, 256.

40 Stanley MSS, Diary, 28 Dec, 1852.

41 *Ibid:* Diary, 24 March 1853.

42 *Ibid*. Stanley agreed, saying that 'the only posts of power which appeared to remain were the Governor-Generalship of India and the editorship of the Times'.

43 Kebbel, *History of Toryism*, 316, 303–4.

44 Palmerston to W. Temple, 30 April 1852: Ashley, *The Life of . . . Palmerston: 1846–1865*, i, 336–41.

45 Stanley MSS, Diary, 25 July 1852.

46 See Martin, 'Land reform', in Hollis, ed., *Pressure From Without*, 150–2.
47 Morley, *Cobden*, ii, 215.
48 Bennett, *Clayhanger*, Book 2, Chapter 2.
49 Hobsbawm, *Industry and Empire*, 98.
50 Quoted in Southgate *The Conservative Leadership, 1832–1932*, 1.
51 Lindsay and Harrington, *The Conservative Party, 1918–1970*, 19.
52 Southgate, *Conservative Leadership*, 2.
53 *Quarterly Review*, Dec, 1849, 292.
54 Glynn, 'The private member of Parliament, 1833–1868', unpublished thesis, 40.
55 These figures are from the table in Cipolla, *The Economic History of World Population*, 30–1. The table gives no figure for Germany in 1850, but in 1900 the German figure was still 35 per cent, by which time the figure for Great Britain had fallen to 5 per cent.
56 'The theories of parliamentary reform', *Oxford Essays*, 1858, 52–79.
57 *Quarterly Review*, Sept, 1856, 563.
58 'The past session and the new parliament', *Edinburgh Review*, April 1857, 557. The article appeared, of course, anonymously; It has been attributed to Lowe by Clive, 'The *Edinburgh Review*: the Life and Death of a Periodical', in *Essays in the History of Publishing, ed. Briggs, 130*.
59 *Edinburgh Review*, April 1857, 558. Lowe's view of the power of the press was widely held in the mid-1850s, drawing force from the widespread conviction that the press, heavily pro-Turk and anti-Russian, had driven the Aberdeen government reluctantly into the Crimea. Croker, after citing the 1832 Reform Act, called the power of the newspapers 'the second cause of the weakness of the Government'. 'Mechanical improvements, extension of education and of business, of literary taste and commercial intercourse, have developed the powers of the press to an enormous influence – an influence the greater because it has become so subtle that we breathe it as we breathe the air, without being conscious of the minuter particles that enter into its composition. . . . The Reform Bill has made seats, and therefore the profession of public life, so precarious that no man can venture to brave the press, and what with the audacity of censure, or the exaggeration of flattery with which it visits individuals, there has grown up, and is still growing, an influence over the conduct of members so imperious that the Speaker, instead of demanding from the Sovereign freedom of speech, had much better ask it from the *Times*.' (Croker to Brougham, 21 July 1854: Croker, *Correspondence and Diaries*, iii, 338–9.) An example of how the press could influence members comes from Leicestershire in 1855. When Roebuck's censure motion on the government for its conduct of the Crimean war came up in January – the motion on which the Aberdeen government fell from office – the *Leicester Advertiser*, disappointed that many Conservatives had stayed away from the division on the Foreign Enlistment Bill in December, called on them all to be in the places. It was that article, C. H. Frewen, Conservative member for Sussex East, believed, that 'brought all the Leicestershire M.P.s to the scratch' to vote with Roebuck (Frewen to Jolliffe, undated: Hylton MSS, DD/HY/Box 18/10).
60 *Quarterly Review*, Sept, 1856, 560, 567.

Laying the new foundations

61 Stanley MSS, Diary, 9 Feb, 1853.
62 'B. is not without average ability, but his temper the worst I ever knew,' wrote Stanley. 'I have heard him curse men to their faces on very slight provocation, and

his conversation is one perpetual reviling of the opposite party. He appears to be always arguing. His constitution is very gouty, and his blood Irish. Being hooted lately on the hustings at Braintree, he told the people 'they were the vilest rabble he had ever seen, and he despised them from his heart'. Language like this from a Minister is sure to provoke comments, and the matter is made worse by an unlucky imputation of bribery at Derby, resting on doubtful authority, but plausible enough to gain credit.' (*Ibid*, Diary, 21 July 1852.)

63　Drummond to Disraeli, 5 March 1852. I apologize for having lost record of the source of this letter.
64　Derby to Disraeli, 14 Nov, 1853 (copy): Derby MSS, 182/1.
65　'Agenda, 1853': Hylton MSS, DD/HY/Box 24.
66　Rose to Disraeli, 17 Nov, 1853: see n.1 of this chapter.
67　For details of the widespread practice of electoral corruption between 1852 and 1867, see Gwyn, *Democracy and the Cost of Politics in Britain*, 61–92.
68　Monypenny and Buckle, *Disraeli*, iii, 492.
69　*Ibid*, iii, 483.
70　18 Feb, 1853, *Hansard*, 3rd series, cxxiv, 245–82.
71　Greville, *Memoirs*, 19 Feb 1853, vi, 402–3.
72　Stanley MSS, Diary, 16 Feb, 1853 (1855 note).
73　*Ibid*, Diary, 14 March 1853.
74　*Ibid*, Diary, 30 June 1853.
75　Monypenny and Buckle, *Disraeli*, iii, 505.
76　*Ibid*, iii, 503.

Chapter 14

Conservatism and the Aberdeen coalition: 1853–55

Disraeli, Derby, and the role of opposition

The years of the Aberdeen coalition, which lasted from 1853 to the beginning of 1855, were marked, on the Conservative side, by a running quarrel between Derby and Disraeli about the proper tactics of a Conservative opposition. It was characteristic of Lord Derby that, after a tiring and difficult year in office, when the inexperience of his cabinet colleagues had placed a heavy personal burden on him, he should take the line of least resistance. 'The great difficulty', he wrote in January 1853, 'will be to keep the Conservative party together without the excitement of a systematic opposition which we must avoid as far as possible. The chance for Conservatism is the disruption of the Cabinet from internal differences.'[1] In the same month, having inferred from some language used by Stanley that Disraeli was casting about for new allies, he advised Disraeli that a majority could not be gained by a union of the Conservatives with either the Whigs or the Radicals.

> We shall have a difficult game to play. We must to a certain extent keep up the spirits of our party; but we must exercise, and get them to exercise, great patience and forbearance, if we do not wish, by an active and bitter opposition on our part, to consolidate the present combination between those who have no real bond of union, and who must, I think, fall to pieces before long, if left to themselves.[2]

For the first three months of 1853 Derby remained in the country, 'in almost entire seclusion, seeing few of his former colleagues and attending debates in the Lords only on a few great occasions'.[3] He would not call a meeting of the party and 'generally thought it best to leave Ministers alone'.[3] His absence from London gave rise to rumours that he had become indifferent to politics and was contemplating resigning from the Conservative leadership. Greville had seemingly been correct to predict that, his government having been broken up, Derby

> would not be very likely to place himself again in such a situation, and to encounter the endless difficulties, dangers and mortifications attendant upon the lead of such a party, and above all the necessity of trusting entirely to such a colleague as Disraeli in the House of Commons without one other man of a grain

of capacity besides. As it is, he will probably betake himself to the enjoyment of his pleasures and pursuits, till he is recalled to political life by some fresh excitement and interest that time and circumstances may throw in his way.[4]

For the next three years the Conservative party was deprived of a constant, invigorating lead from its commander. Disraeli was not alone in complaining of Derby's inertia; and there were, as an entry in Malmesbury's diary for April 1855 illustrates, some grounds for complaint.

> Lord Derby returned today from Newmarket, so full of his racing that he could think and talk of nothing else, and knew nothing of the last week's events; and when I alluded to our propositions at the Vienna Conference having been rejected by Russia, he asked, 'What propositions?' – evidently not having looked at a newspaper for the whole week. Such is the character of this remarkable man, who has the habit and power of concentrating his whole mind upon the subject which occupies him at the moment, and dismissing it totally, with equal facility.[5]

Disraeli grumbled in September 1853 that the only despatches he received from Knowsley were haunches of venison,[6] but since he himself suffered from mild visitations of the gout, he might have been more tolerant of Derby, who was subject to far more virulent and frequent attacks of the disease. In 1853 and 1854 Derby passed long periods, sometimes extending over many weeks, in bed, and Malmesbury believed that the exessive pain which he endured shook his nerve and 'robbed him of much of his former courage and energy'.[7]

Illness no doubt reinforced Derby's languor, but far more important was his assessment of the political situation. He took the reasonable view that a party which had just demonstrated its inability to sustain a government ought not immediately to set its sights on ousting its successors from office. Nothing permanent would be achieved by defeating the Aberdeen government. On the other hand, if, as Derby expected, the coalition were to break down from its own instability, then the question of Conservative reunion would arise once more. Against that day it was prudent to refrain from persistent attacks on Peelite ministers. Derby knew, moreover, that the majority of the party would not tolerate a factious alliance with incompatible allies, temporarily constructed for the narrow object of bringing down the government. Conservatism retained its fondness for the Queen's ministers. Just as Peel and Wellington, in the 1830s, had foresworn indiscriminate opposition to Melbourne's government, so in the 1850s Walpole argued that the honourable course for the Conservatives was to maintain their own principles when that meant differing from the government, but otherwise 'to support the Executive Government, because it is the Executive Government, wherever they can'.[8]

It was because Disraeli appeared so resolutely to turn his back on that kind of Conservatism that Henry Drummond, comparing him to Walpole and Newdegate, who understood 'the abstract principles on which monarchy is founded', described him as 'the most reckless man in the country . . . who is himself the model of a destructive'.[9] That side of Disraeli ought not to be exaggerated, but it was the side that showed most prominently in the early 1850s. In February 1853 Stanley recorded that Disraeli was in frequent intercourse with Milner Gibson and the Manchester Radicals – 'but secretly, fearing the effect on Lord Derby and the party if these confidences were known'.[10] He was also corresponding with the editor of the Catholic newspaper, the *Tablet*, in an effort to reach an understanding with the Irish radicals,[11] despite the fact that the terms of such an understanding, tenant right and either Catholic endowment or Anglican disendowment, were certain to be unacceptable to the Conservative backbenchers. In 1854, ready to beat the government with any stick, he sought and obtained a meeting with David Urquhart, a paranoiac eccentric (he believed that Palmerston was a Russian spy in the pay of the Tsar) who had sat as a Tory for Stafford from 1847 to 1852, and who had since leaving the Commons established 'foreign affairs committees' throughout the country to combat the infiltration of Russian agents in English government.[12] Part of the attraction which Urquhart held briefly for Disraeli lay in the growth of his 'National League' in those northern towns where Conservatism was weak: Newcastle, Sheffield, and Birmingham in particular. Urquhart's movement combined Russophobia with visionary dreams of restoring to the monarchy the powers which it had exercised before the rise of cabinet and party government. It attracted some Conservative support in the north, but it was idle to suppose that Urquhart had anything substantial to offer the party.

None of that, perhaps, was taken very seriously, even by Disraeli. More serious was the independent line taken by Stanley and Disraeli in the *Press*, which had been established, Stanley said, to be 'the organ of moderate Conservative opinions' and to counter the influence which 'the least enlightened part' of the party had on the public through the *Morning Herald* and the *Standard*.[13] The founding of the *Press* provoked the editor of *John Bull* to send a memorandum to Conservative members of parliament.

An endeavour is being made to set up a paper describing itself as a 'new weekly Conservative journal, intended to fill an obvious void in journalism', the announcement of which bears a semblance of authority calculated to mislead the public into a belief that the journal in question is to be henceforth the recognised organ of the Conservative party.

Under these circumstances the Editor of the *John Bull*, the old-established weekly organ of the Conservative party, thinks it due alike to the interests of that journal, and to the cause to which its columns are devoted, that he should appeal to the sense of justice of the Members of the party, claiming their support against an attempt to supplant an existing and tried organ by a new publication without definite principles, whose object evidently is to promote a new and spurius kind of Conservatism, which would ignore the Church, admit the Jew to Parliament, and abandon the Protestant character and safeguards of the British Constitution. The Editor of the *John Bull* ventures to think that he is warranted in making this appeal, by the steady and faithful support which his journal has, for upwards of thirty years, given to the Conservative cause.[14]

The sharpest offence given by the *Press* came later, after the formation of Palmerston's government in 1855, when it advocated peace in opposition to the government's continued prosecution of the Crimean war. But right from the start it provoked criticism by its fierce attack on the Aberdeen coalition, its advocacy of franchise reform, and its general argument for an alliance of Whigs and Conservatives. And the editor of *John Bull* was right to put his finger on the suspect 'Protestantism' of the *Press*. Disraeli continued to vote for Jewish emancipation and in 1854 Stanley voted to abolish Church rates.

Disraeli's parliamentary performance did little to reassure Conservatives. The waspish sarcasm of his opening attack on the Aberdeen coalition's alleged indifference to the friendship of France dismayed those Conservatives whom Greville called 'the more sensible men of the party', one of whom, Thomas Baring, was on the point of getting up to disavow Disraeli.[15] A few weeks later, when Joseph Hume moved a resolution to abolish certain protective duties, a resolution which even Gladstone opposed, Disraeli suddenly gave Hume his support and 'tried to steal a division'.[16] Conservatives went into the lobby against Hume and Disraeli and the motion was easily beaten. But Stanley commented that Disraeli's unexpected behaviour was 'the commencement of a practice afterwards indulged in by the opposition leader, and which to some extent damaged his position among members of his own party: I mean the practice of effecting a sudden coalition with some discontented section of the Liberals, and by their aid, and taking advantage of a surprise, securing an unexpected victory'.[17] In April, Conservative backbenchers were unhappy when Disraeli voted with the Manchester Radicals to abolish the advertisement duty on newspapers: 'They disliked it as coming from the Radical side of the House; as being given in favour of the press; and because the opposite had been taken last year when we were in office.'[18]

The most damaging episode occurred in June on the government's Bill to reform the administration of India. The Bill did not end the dual control of the Indian government exercised by the Board of Control and the East India Company. Disraeli thought that supreme authority should be vested in a cabinet minister. Unfortunately, so did the Radicals, whose opposition to the Bill guaranteed strong Conservative support for it. At Disraeli's suggestion, nevertheless, Stanley put down an amendment against the Bill, and the party was made to look silly when it split 110 against the Bill and 87 for it.[19] Derby sent to Disraeli a long letter of remonstrance.

> I should not do my duty by you and by the party if I did not frankly express to you my opinion that a considerable portion of the dissatisfaction which has shown itself is attributable to an uneasy feeling among our Conservative friends as to a supposed understanding, and to a certain extent combination, between yourself and the Manchester school . . . they are unwilling, apparently, to unite with men of whose intentions they entertain no favourable view, for the purpose of overthrowing the Government. I confess that I share this latter feeling, and should be sorry to see the Administration displaced by a vote produced by a junction of the most conflicting elements, when the means of forming a new Government are

not very obvious, and when the country is involved in very serious external difficulties.

Disraeli had raised eyebrows earlier in the session by his withdrawal from the House before the vote on the secret ballot and by his absence on the vote on Gladstone's succession duty on landed property, which Croker denounced as 'a more serious derangement of the old constitution than Catholic Emancipation or even the Reform Bill'.[20] It was with such episodes in mind that Derby concluded his letter.

> In short, I cannot conceal it from you that there is reported to me to be a growing fear, and the Government Press does its utmost to keep up the opinion, that you are gradually withdrawing yourself more and more from the Conservative portion of our supporters, and seeking alliances in quarters with which neither they nor I can recognise any bond of union. And I think it is to this feeling more than anything else that is to be attributed the division which at present prevails.[21]

It may seem strange that Disraeli should have behaved in such maverick fashion when it was known to everyone that he commanded little personal following in the Conservative party. Derby told the Prince Consort in 1852 that 'Mr. Disraeli knew that he [Derby] possessed the confidence of three hundred of his supporters whilst Mr. Disraeli, if he separated himself from him, would very likely not carry five with him',[22] and as late as 1859, after ten years of leadership, his position was far from secure. In that year a Conservative who was alarmed by rumours that Derby was about to retire asked Jolliffe to prevail upon him to remain, rather than hand the party over to Disraeli, 'whom the party *never heartily trust*, and whom half the country gentlemen secretly look upon as an adventurer and a charlatan to this day'.[23] Lord Lonsdale attributed Disraeli's behaviour to his 'extraordinary confidence in his powers of speech. He thinks always he is going to put the question and he will carry the whole House with him. He has been deceived so often that he ought to be wiser. As a party leader he will be encouraged, but I doubt if there is a single man that would be his follower.' But Lonsdale added that, although it was difficult to discipline troops led by Disraeli, he was 'our best man'.[24] It was partly the knowledge that, however much they might distrust him, the party had no one to replace him, which allowed Disraeli so much freedom of action. In 1853 and 1854 the only man mentioned as a possible replacement was Sir John Pakington, Colonial Secretary in the 1852 government, whose sole claim to consideration was his approximation to the stolid respectability of a Conservative country gentleman.

There is, however, more to the matter. It was all very well for Walpole to talk of the duty of upholding the Crown's executive ministers, but in the days when that doctrine had commanded allegiance, the institutions of party and a loyal opposition were in their infancy. Disraeli's course was erratic in the mid-1850s, not only because he was moved by impatient ambition, but also because he believed that an opposition party would disintegrate if it were left to lie dormant. As Robert Blake has written, Disraeli was 'the first statesman systematically to uphold the doctrine that it is the duty of the Opposition to oppose'.[25] Why, then, in 1853, for all that he harassed the government, did he show so little interest in consolidating the Conservative opposition under his leadership? The answer may lie in his ambivalent feelings about the country gentlemen. Although he championed the cause of the country gentlemen in 1846 and praised them in his biography of Lord George Bentinck, published in 1851, as 'men of honour, breeding and refinement, high and generous character, great weight and station in the country',[26] he had no natural sympathy with them and in his darker moods looked upon them with contempt. At the beginning of 1853, when the years of frustration in coaxing the party away from protection had ended in the bitterness of defeat, he treated Stanley to a rounded denunciation of the Conservative backbenchers.

> They could not be got to attend to business while the hunting season lasted; a sharp frost would make a difference of 20 men. They had good natural ability . . . but wanted culture: they never read: their leisure was passed in field sports; the wretched school and university system was at fault: they learnt nothing useful, and did not understand the ideas of their own time.[27]

What is difficult to explain is why Disraeli, of Jewish-Italian descent and of urban literary tastes, should have devoted his political career to the defence of the territorial aristocracy from which the country gentlemen were drawn. Robert Blake has suggested that the explanation may lie in Disraeli's romantic veneration of the past and his thorough dislike of state centralism.[28] Disraeli said in the House of Commons in 1848 that there could be no government which was not based on 'traditionary influences and large properties round which men may rally'; they were 'the only security for liberty and property'.[29] Whatever the answer, there is no doubt that when Disraeli told Derby in 1848 that the office of a Conservative leader was 'to uphold the aristocratic settlement of this country' and that that was 'the only question at stake however manifold may be the forms which it assumes in public discussion, and however various the knowledge and the labour which it requires',[30] he meant what he said. What the year 1853 serves to illustrate is that the ease with which Disraeli separated means from ends often obscured the Conservatism of his politics.[31] Disraeli understood, better than Derby or Peel, the truth in Augustine Birrell's remark that the House of Commons likes leaders 'who can make business go, who will show sport, and lead their hounds across a good line of country'.[32] His mistake was sometimes to choose the wrong country.

The tug-of-war between Derby and Disraeli heightened the feeling among Conservatives that the political current had left them adrift. Although Gladstone's 1853 budget contained something for every party or interest except the landed Conservatives – the succession duty and the abolition of the advertisement duty for the Liberals, the remission of debt for the Irish, and cheaper tea and soap for the working class – the Conservatives were unable to rally a united party against it. The official opposition amendment against the budget was defeated by 323 votes to 252, the majority including not only forty-three Peelites, or regular Liberal-Conservative supporters of the coalition, but also thirty-nine Derbyites. Disraeli brought only 228 Conservatives into the opposition lobby with him.[33] In March, the Bill to place the clergy reserves (land set apart to provide revenue for the Church in Canada) at the disposal of the colonial legislature was resolutely denounced by Derby in the Lords, but only after it had passed easily through the Commons with the support of forty Peelites and twenty-two Conservatives.[34] On one important clause the government was saved by the votes of ninety-four Conservatives. 'You promised the present Govt. more generous indulgence than they showed towards the late Govt.,' George Hamilton, an Assistant Whip, wrote to Derby, 'and they have received it.'[35] At the end of the 1853 session, Malmesbury reckoned the number of dependable Conservative supporters at only 150.[36] That figure did not, of course, represent the true strength of the Conservative party. An independent member and a lax party member were not the same animal. Stanley estimated the number of 'real' independents in the 1852 parliament at less than forty,[37] far more than fifteen years earlier, but far less than would justify the tag, 'the golden age of the independent member', which is often given to the 1850s. As Hamilton remarked to Jolliffe, Conservative divisions in 1853 were not cause for alarm, since 'in opposition the bonds of party have always a tendency to become slackened ... but I don't think the allegiance of any of his party to Lord Derby, if called forth by his personal influence, would be found wanting'.[38]

The party's impotence in the Commons was not redressed by a Conservative majority in the House of Lords. The Peelite and independent peers gave Aberdeen's government a majority on every important question – the clergy reserves, the legacy duties, the Oxford University Bill – except one, Jewish emancipation, which, in 1854, was rejected even by the Commons. It was a mark of how little control the Conservative peers exercised that Derby's amendent to the clergy reserves Bill in 1853, to save from confiscation those proceeds from reserves invested for the benefit of both Established and Nonconformist Churches, was rejected in a full House by forty votes. Nine bishops voted in the majority. 'It is remarkable,' Greville wrote towards the close of the 1854 session, in which the government had had to abandon Bills dealing with public health, education, and religion,

> that the Government are unquestionably stronger in the House of Lords than in the House of Commons, as has been clearly proved by the result of the Oxford University Bill. Derby endeavoured to alter it, and was completely defeated. There were several divisions, in all of which the Government obtained large majorities, and at last Derby said it was evidently useless to propose alterations, as the Government could do what they pleased in that House.[39]

Even the most famous victory of the Lords in the 1850s, their vote on

Palmerston's nomination of Sir James Parke to what would have been the first life peerage in 1856, was not, as it has sometimes been represented, won by the Conservative party alone, but by a rare union of Conservatives, Peelites, independents, and 'old Whigs'.[40]

During the recess before the 1854 session, the Conservative leaders and Whips took steps to improve the party's performance in the Commons. Since it is usually Derby who is accused of having been indifferent to the state of the party, it is worth noting that in November 1853 he prodded Disraeli to attend more to the management of the backbenchers, and to build 'a strong foundation of personal confidence, which must be maintained by constant attention and even by some indulgence of the personal prejudices of those whom we lead'.[41] In mid-December, Disraeli, Malmesbury, and the Earl of Hardwicke went to Knowsley, where they combined a few days' sport with a 'Cabinet Council' on the state of the party. There it was agreed to adopt Jolliffe's suggestion that Disraeli should hold meetings of the party every Saturday morning during the parliamentary session and that at Derby's annual pre-session meeting the leaders' views on major questions should be made clear to the party. Derby sent a report of the Knowsley discussions to Jolliffe.

> When Disraeli was down here, we had of course some conversation on the mode of carrying on the business of the party; and I told him that I entirely approved of the suggestion of appointing frequent meetings of the members of the H. of Commons at his house; and also of appointing fixed times at which the principal members of our party might have an opportunity of conferring with him. I have often urged on him before the necessity of more frequent intercourse of this kind between himself and our friends; and also of his occasionally seeing the whole party at *his* house; for though I am very willing to interfere when I can do so usefully, there is much that must be managed by the leader of the House of Commons; and I cannot but think that much of the disorganisation which has prevailed has been owing to the want of unrestricted intercourse of this kind. I hope and believe that Disraeli is himself convinced of this: and also of the necessity for the maintenance of his position, of taking a really Conservative line in and out of the House.[42]

Derby himself agreed to be in London some days before the 1854 session was to begin 'for the purpose of having the party well in hand . . . and, by personal conferences with individuals, of ensuring beforehand, so far as possible, complete unity of action upon all the great questions'.[43]

Disraeli's new leaf took on an orange colour. When, in November, Derby had advised Disraeli to pay regard to his followers' prejudices, he had had particularly in mind the anti-Catholic views of the National Club, which he described as a mischievous body 'whose extreme pretensions and views must not be encouraged', but whose members must be kept 'in good humour by civility'.[44] Anti-Catholicism still burned bright in many constituencies. Joseph Napier, Conservative member for Dublin University, claimed that Protestant issues, the defence of Anglican education and opposition to the

Maynooth grant, were 'the only questions which are of real interest to the country',[45] and Walpole believed that the chief source of the party's malaise was the want of a 'stronger manifestation of Church & Protestant principles'.[46] That was the background to Disraeli's impassioned defence of the Protestant constitution in May, during the debate on Spooner's annual motion for an inquiry into the Maynooth grant, a speech so strong that Stanley reminded Disraeli of the electoral damage which, they had agreed, anti-Catholicism had done in 1852 and warned him against burning his fingers with 'that infernal Protestantism'.[47]

Disraeli's speech marked his first deliberate attempt to cultivate the friendship of the 'Protestants' in the party. As a way of fostering party unity it came at a bad time. Two months earlier parliamentary politics had been transformed by the government's declaration of war on Russia. Even Walpole was alarmed that Disraeli should, in those circumstances, exploit Protestant feeling as a means of 'making differences or disunion among the people, when there ought to be nothing but concord and harmony'.[48] Walpole's attitude was symptomatic of the block which the Crimean war placed in the path of Conservative revival, just at the time when Conservative spirits were showing signs of recovering from the defeat of 1852. The war put domestic issues in the shade. The Aberdeen government abandoned its Reform Bill, thus eliminating for a time the most probable agent of a renewed division of parties on clear lines of principle. After ten months of war it was also compelled to abandon office. Derby's prediction that the coalition would fall apart came true. But it was war, not a quarrel between radical and conservative members of the cabinet, which brought down the government. And it was Palmerston who reaped the reward of Aberdeen's fall. For the Conservatives, the war meant the frustration of their hopes that the stricter attention to management adopted at the beginning of 1854 would produce a united party behaving as a well-drilled opposition.

The 1855 ministerial crisis

'The administrative miscarriages of the war in the Crimea during the winter of 1854-55 destroyed the coalition government.' So wrote John Morley.[49] The origins of those miscarriages and the sufferings to which they exposed the British army have no place in this book. On 23 January 1855, the opening night of the parliamentary session, Arthur Roebuck, a Radical, gave notice of a motion for a committee to inquire into the management of the war. Lord John Russell, after two years of fitful bickering with his colleagues, decided that he could not defend the government against the implications of Roebuck's motion and resigned. Six nights later Roebuck's motion was passed by the astonishing margin of 305 votes to 148, whereupon ministers resigned.

Lord Derby then took one of the most controversial decisions in the history of the Conservative party. Summoned by the Queen, he invited Palmerston and two leading Peelite members of the defeated government, Gladstone and Sidney Herbert, to join a Conservative administration and, on their declining his invitation, decided not to try a purely Conservative government.

From the day when his first government fell, it had been Derby's tactic to await the day when the Aberdeen coalition should fall apart. The day had come. But it had never been Derby's intention to stage a re-run of the 1852 government. He had looked forward to the collapse of the coalition because he expected it to lead to renewed negotiations for a Conservative alliance, with the Peelites, with Palmerston, or with both. In 1851 the formation of a Protectionist government had hung on the attitude of the Peelites. It did so again in 1855, but by then it was Palmerston who mattered, for reasons which Stanley had outlined to Disraeli in November 1853.

> Supposing resignations, Palmerston becomes master of the situation; will he be content to play a secondary part? Will he lead the Commons under my father? And in that event, you cooperating with him as joint leader, what becomes of Gladstone? G. and his follower, S. Herbert, are to all appearance very strongly bound by personal ties to Palmerston. Can that connection be broken? Or, supposing P. to take the command in person, what will be our position? It is evident to me that few of our friends would oppose *him*, consequently that our *role* as an Opposition will speedily become absurd.[50]

There were contained all the elements of the 1855 ministerial crisis. It turned out that Palmerston was not prepared to play a secondary part, that he would act only in concert with Gladstone and Herbert, and that his succession to the premiership left the Conservative opposition, if not absurd, at least stranded.

Palmerston had not been a partisan in the free-trade controversy and he therefore felt none of the Peelites' qualms about acting with 'reactionaries'. He had no enthusiasm for reform. At the end of 1853 he had resigned, for ten days, from Aberdeen's cabinet in protest against Russell's Bill to disfranchise sixty-two small boroughs and lower the franchise to £6 in the boroughs and £10 in the counties. As a Whig put it then, Palmerston did not want to lose his constituency of Tiverton and 'would rather bombard Sebastopol than the small Boroughs'.[51] In his political views, although not in his antecedents, Palmerston was closer than the Peelites to the Conservatives, and in the autumn of 1852, despite Palmerston's rejection of Derby's overtures, Greville and Graham had predicted that it would end in his going over to them.[52] But by the end of Aberdeen's first year in office, Greville had changed his tune. He noted that the Conservatives flattered Palmerston and looked forward to having them as their leader in the Commons, but he believed that the chance had come and gone. 'Palmerston is sixty-nine years old,' he wrote, 'and it is too late for him to look out for fresh political combinations and other connexions, nor would any object of ambition repay him for the dissolution of all his personal and social ties.'[53]

In January 1855 Palmerston was in a powerful position. In a military crisis, his years of experience as a redoubtable, and much critized, Foreign Secretary took on a new significance. Russell had waived his claim to the Liberal leadership by abandoning his colleagues under fire, while Palmerston, having been placed by Aberdeen at the Home Office, was not departmentally incriminated by the disasters in the Crimea. The press was loud for him. The court accepted that, in the last resort, it could not proscribe him. Palmerston knew, therefore, that so long as Derby did not become Prime Minister, he would.

When, therefore, Derby made his first act in carrying out the Queen's commission to form a government the invitation to Palmerston to take the lead of the House of Commons, Palmerston readily assented to Derby's suggestion that his answer should depend upon his bringing Gladstone and Herbert into the cabinet with him. Palmerston knew what reaction to expect from that quarter, but for good measure he insisted that Clarendon also come in as Foreign Secretary. Derby could scarcely yield so much – as Malmesbury remarked, Palmerston, supported by Gladstone, Herbert, *and* Clarendon would be omnipotent in the cabinet and 'the real Premier'[54] – and Clarendon showed no interest in the proposal. The Peelites, too, scarcely gave the matter a second thought. With the exception of Russell, it was not the old Whigs, but they, who had been the progressive element in Aberdeen's government, the strongest supporters, for instance, of Russell's Reform Bill.[55] Gladstone, moreover, made the impossible stipulation that he retain the Chancellorship of the Exchequer, which Disraeli, having already consented to give up the leadership of the Commons to Palmerston, could not with honour surrender, especially since, as Stanley said, he and Gladstone had for three years 'been so directly and personally opposed on questions of finance'.[56] Even had Gladstone wished to rejoin the Conservatives, there was a large obstacle in his way.

> Had Gladstone . . . jumped from Lord Aberdeen's Cabinet into Lord Derby's [Goulburn wrote], separating himself from colleagues who in spite of temptation to the contrary had manfully resisted with him the attack upon the Government, and uniting himself with those by whom the attack had been mainly supported, I do not see what explanation could have been made by him to allay the suspicion which such conduct would have excited.[57]

Palmerston and Herbert sent polite notes to Derby, saying only that they believed that they could not render his government a useful service by joining it, and offering support to any government formed to carry the war to a satisfactory peace. Gladstone went further. He told Derby that he was disposed on public grounds 'to believe that the formation of a government from among your own political friends would offer many facilities at this moment, which other alternatives within view would not present'.[58] The advice was genuine. Gladstone did not believe that Palmerston would be able to make a majority in the Commons between the two extremes of the

Conservative party on the one side and the jealous faction of Russell Whigs on the other.[59] A purely Conservative government therefore offered the best prospect of a stable and enduring administration.

Derby did not take up Gladstone's hint. In 1851 he had called the Protectionist front-benchers together to discuss whether to form a purely Protectionist government. This time he did not bother. On receiving Gladstone's refusal, he informed the Queen that, although his followers made the 'most compact' party in the Commons, without additional strength he was unable to form a creditable government.

> He had no men capable of governing the House of Commons, and he should not be able to present an Administration that would be accepted by the country unless it was strengthened by other combinations; he knew that the whole country cried out for Lord Palmerston as the only man fit for carrying on the war with success, and he owned the necessity of having him in the Government, were it even only to satisfy the French Government, the confidence of which was at this moment of the greatest importance.[60]

Many years later, Gladstone described Derby's decision as a 'palpable and even gross' error and attributed it to Derby's want of 'strong parliamentary courage'.[61] Disraeli, for once, found himself in agreement with Gladstone. Yet it is evident that Derby had no doubts about the course which he took. He began and ended his attempt to form a government on the same day. He made no effort to persuade Palmerston or Gladstone to change their minds. He did not attempt to bring in Palmerston or the Peelites alone. He did not even see Gladstone and Herbert personally, but was content to use Palmerston as his emissary. And in the end he declined to form a purely Conservative government without formally consulting any of his colleagues. Was Gladstone's judgement right? Did Derby, in the words of Morley, fling away 'a golden chance of bringing a consolidated party into the possession of real power'?[62] For the next ten years, interrupted only by the short-lived Conservative government of 1858-59, Palmerston was to remain Prime Minister. If Gladstone was right, Derby consigned the Conservatives to long years of needless opposition.

One small matter may be disposed of immediately. Disraeli later suggested, in a note among his papers, that Derby acted in the belief that Palmerston would not succeed in forming a government and that the Conservatives could then come into office made powerful by the public knowledge of Palmerston's failure.[63] There is no evidence, in Derby's language to the Queen, to parliament, or to his colleagues, that he looked forward to such a result.

There are a number of things to be said in Derby's defence. It is worth noting, at the outset, Palmerston's cautionary advice, given during the Roebuck debate, to those Conservatives who were crowing over the fall of Aberdeen as the fulfilment of their prediction that coalition government was bound to fail.

I warn you against giving encouragement to vulgar clamour against a coalition, because I will venture to say that in the present state of politial parties in this country, you will never be able to form a Government, strong enough to carry on its affairs with the support of Parliament, that is not founded more or less upon the principle of coalition.[64]

Gladstone's argument, in reality, was that a purely Conservative government should rest on the support of an informal coalition of members of the House of Commons. It was not unreasonable of Derby to suspect men who would not give public expression to their good will by joining his government. It is also worth noting Stanley's evidence that Derby was not alone in dismissing the idea of a purely Conservative government. Two days before Derby saw the Queen, Malmesbury, Walpole, and Stanley agreed that the experiment was hopeless.[65]

They may have been wrong, but it is fancy to assume that a Conservative government would have brought the war to a successful conclusion and then, basking in public favour, have gained a majority, either from the permanent adhesion of other sections than its own backbenchers or from the votes of the electorate at a subsequent election. That Palmerston made a triumphant appeal to the country as a war hero in 1857 does not mean that Derby would have done. Nor is there any reason to suppose that the men who would not assist Derby in the midst of a national crisis would have come to his aid once the crisis was passed. In short, the prospect before Derby in January 1855 was simply another minority government, in circumstances, moreover, less favourable even than those of 1852. The crisis of 1855 was an administrative crisis. The House of Commons had brought down the most experienced cabinet since the days of Liverpool because it had lost confidence in that government's ability to manage the war. Was it to be supposed that it would give its confidence to a government of almost no practical experience, especially in foreign and military affairs? Both in 1851 and 1855 Derby justified his behaviour on the grounds of his colleagues' inexperience. The justification was far more telling in 1855 than in 1851. A Conservative government, on trial before a House of Commons and a press who knew that the Prime Minister the country wanted was sitting opposite from them, might have lasted only a few weeks.

There is one other important consideration. In 1852 the Protectionists, divided as they were over the very question of protection and resigned as many of them were to the near certainty that the Corn Laws could not be restored, were nevertheless eager for office. In 1855 the Conservatives were not, in their minds, prepared to exploit the disaster which overcame Aberdeen's government. There are few moments more propitious for an opposition than the moment when public opinion turns against a government at war. Yet when such a moment came, in December 1854, when even *The Times* turned in fury on the Aberdeen government, the Conservative response was hesitant and divided.

When the Aberdeen government declared war on Russia in February 1854 there were many Conservatives who believed, with some cause, that a united cabinet would have avoided war, either by compelling Turkey to accept the Tsar's conciliatory proposals at Olmütz in October 1853, or by leaving Russia in no doubt of England's determination to fight, if necessary, to defend Turkey's stake in Europe.

> On the Conservative side [Stanley wrote] the war is not popular, at least not to the extent that the newspapers, and our acquiescence, would lead a looker-on to suppose. . . . Of the country gentlemen, some joined the war-cry out of mere thoughtlessness, some out of fear of Russia, some in order to annoy the Gov't, some to stave off reform; a few because they liked the prospect of popularity, which was to cost them nothing in the way of a sacrifice of class-interests: but there remained a large number who dislike prospective disturbance in Europe, who object to fight when England has nothing to gain: and who in their hearts agree with Cobden.[66]

There was, however, a difference between wishing that war had not been declared and refusing to support the government once it had, especially since at the beginning the government professed the limited objective of containing Russia, of defending Constantinople in order to preserve the European balance of power. 'Russia is quite wrong,' Derby wrote to Walpole in the summer of 1853, '& we must maintain the integrity & independence of Turkey – but "securitus in modo – fortiter in re".'[67] On 20 February 1854 Disraeli announced in the House of Commons that the Conservatives would abstain from factious opposition for the duration of the war. Then, in September, the fateful decision to invade the Crimea with the object of capturing Sebastopol was put into operation. The sequel is well known. The expedition failed. And the army, short of supplies, food, medical facilities, and proper shelter, faced the severities of the Crimean winter trapped in a small enclave of the Black Sea coast.

The Aberdeen government called a special ten-day meeting of parliament on 12 December to gain assent to two measures of emergency legislation: a Militia Bill, to enable militia regiments to be sent abroad, and a Foreign Enlistment Bill, to enable 15,000 troops to be recruited abroad, trained in England, and despatched to the Crimea. Both Bills went across the grain of national tradition. The Conservatives had therefore to decide whether to seize the opportunity to try to bring down the government. Lord Claud Hamilton wanted the party to mount an all-out assault on the ministry.

> I confess to the feeling of great impatience [he wrote to Jolliffe] if good opportunities are not well cultivated & favourable sentiments in the public mind are not turned to account. . . . The blunders which excited the anathema of Bright should be constantly stirred, & the [illegible] expedient of the enlistment of foreigners kept well before the public eye – these matters all fly in full face whilst the daily accounts from the east prove such a total want of foresight, of ministerial ability and common organisation. We surely ought not to remain silent or to

exhibit such courteous forbearance as to enable them to extricate themselves from their present position, & to seek for renewed popularity by radical reforms or organic innovations. . . . I do hope our leaders will blow the trumpet with no uncertain sound, so that all may prepare themselves for battle.[68]

Edward Baldock, the member for Shrewsbury, was 'quite charmed to think you are going to oppose the Foreign Enlistment Bill, the people of all grades down here are up in arms about it'.[69] Colonel Taylor, however, informed Jolliffe that '*Miles* & a section of our people whom he may be supposed to represent have declared that they will support Government through thick & thin as regards the war' and recommended that a meeting of the party be called for the morning of 12 December 'to decide what our line of conduct as a party should be – & to resolve on unanimity – for we cannot with out reduced members afford any split'.[70]

The meeting was not held and the split occurred. Derby began the Conservative offensive by upbraiding the government for its ineptitude and shortsightedness,[71] and in the Commons the Conservative front-benchers, led by Disraeli, Pakington, Stanley, and Bulwer Lytton, spoke against the Foreign Enlistment Bill. They thus placed themselves in the embarrassing company of the Radical 'peace party', twenty-one Liberals, led by Cobden, Bright, Miall, Baines, and Milner Gibson, who were to vote against the Bill. Only two of those Liberals, Cobden (the West Riding) and Thomas Alcock (Surrey East), represented a county; half of them sat for large industrial towns in the north.[72] The opposition to the Bill did not, therefore, consist of men able to act together in the support of a future government, a consideration which may have weighed with some of the Conservative backbenchers. There was already some concern in the party at the peace line being taken by the *Press*. George Hamilton agreed with the *Press* that the extension of the war beyond its original defensive object was a mistake; nevertheless, 'the War should be prosecuted & with the utmost vigour until Turkey is safe & we advocate no peace inconsistent with the permanent security of Turkey'.[73] J. W. Freshfield voted for the Foreign Enlistment Bill because it was his 'general feeling . . . that every thing that could be done for our brave fellow subjects & allies in the Crimea should be done & that Government measures should be supported so far as they appeared to me to have that tendency'.[74]

The Foreign Enlistment Bill passed its second reading by 241 votes to 202, the third reading by 173 to 135. The Militia Bill was allowed to pass without a division. The second reading of the Foreign Enlistment Bill was supported by fourteen Conservatives and a further eighty stayed away without pairing. Jolliffe and his staff did their best to bring the whole party to the divisions and Disraeli described the whipping as 'admirable'.[75] The high number of absentees therefore evinced Conservative uneasiness about bringing down the government.

It is certainly provoking [George Hamilton wrote to Jolliffe] that so many of our men and they not the *doubtfuls* should have been absent. . . . Still it won't do to complain or to scold them.

I attribute their absence to an impression, derived perhaps from Derby's language on the first night of the Session, that it was not intended to make any serious attack upon the Ministry before Xmas – and also to an indisposition to refuse any demand for aid made upon the responsibility of ministers . . .

No blame can possibly attach to yourself or Taylor – because you did all that was possible for any men to do.[76]

Colonel Taylor advised 'remonstrance in some shape, otherwise . . . our whipping labours are completely thrown away'; but he warned Jolliffe 'not to affront, & so alienate completely, those who declined voting'.[77] Against such a large-scale defection the Whips were powerless. They had no answer to, indeed they shared, the opinion of men like Freshfield, who, although he regretted differing from his leaders, defended his vote for the Enlistment Bill as 'open to an independent Member & not discreditable as it respects party'.[78]

Disraeli attributed the abstentions to backbench fears of a change of government and another weak Derby ministry,[79] and George Hamilton drew from them the conclusion that a reconstruction of Aberdeen's government (as Palmerston's government proved to be) was preferable to a complete change of ministers.[80] Disraeli seldom remained downcast for long. By the middle of January he was urging Jolliffe 'to assemble our troops, & collect our forces, for a general engagement within the first fortnight of our re-assembly'.[81] Jolliffe, however, thought Disraeli's enthusiasm wrong-headed[82] and Derby was firmly against attack.

> Our Irish friends, & very likely some of our English ones too, are as impatient that we should make a general attack on the Govt., as the latter are said to be that Lord Raglan should make an immediate assault on Sebastopol. Lord R. seems to think that there would be more probability of his knocking the heads of his army against stone walls, than of achieving a great success; & accordingly proceeds in a more methodical, though perhaps less striking, course; & I am very much more inclined to think that we should follow his example, & not risk an assault leading to a great action, in which we should probably be beaten, & in which, if not, our success would be very embarrassing to ourselves & still more to the Country. Our own strength is not sufficient to form a Govt . . . & it is obvious that if we succeeded in carrying a vote of censure on the whole management of the war, such a vote would render it impossible for us to obtain a reinforcement from any part of the present Administration; & with Bright & his friends we can have no sympathy, & no possibility of combination.[83]

When Roebuck's motion came on, the Conservatives mustered 220 votes in its support, but after Walpole's statement to the Commons, extraordinary in such grave circumstances, that the Conservatives were voting simply for an inquiry and for a cabinet reconstruction, not for the overthrow of the government,[84] the meaning of those votes was not clear. When the result was announced the Conservatives, under instructions from their leaders, abstained, as Palmerston told the Queen, 'from giving the cheer of triumph which usually issues from a majority after a vote upon an important occasion'.[85]

Aberdeen's government fell, not because it was too weak to withstand the force of the Conservative opposition, but because it was unable to prevent the desertion of eighty-five of its usual supporters. There was no collaboration between the Conservatives and the Liberal deserters. In those circumstances, Derby was able to tell the Queen that, although 'his followers could not help voting when Lord John Russell told them on authority that there was the most ample cause for enquiry', they were not the instruments of Aberdeen's downfall and bore no obligation to form a government.[86]

Buckle, looking at events through Disraeli's eyes, wrote that 'the party generally was profoundly disappointed' by Derby's refusal to take office.[87] He cited Henry Lennox's report to Disraeli that the Carlton was 'frenzied with rage';[88] but Lennox was a member of Disraeli's inner circle and habitually unreliable in his opinions. Stronger support came from Lord Malmesbury, who said that Derby's decision gave 'great offence to his party'.[89] Disraeli himself was dismayed that his chief had again bolted, and no doubt, as he pointed out, the party smarted under Derby's confession of their incompetence and resented being brought up to vote only to see the prize of victory turned down. Lord Arthur Hervey snarled that the Conservatives had become a *'Great Obstructive Incompetency'*.[90] But much of the party's discontent was not with the failure to take office, but with the approach which Derby had made to Gladstone, so that the feelings of disappointment were assuaged by the relief, felt in almost every quarter of the party, that junction with the renegade had been avoided. Gladstone's high-Churchmanship, tinged, as many thought, with Puseyism, his habit of bewildering the House of Commons with veiled allusions and logical discourses which Robert Lowe dubbed 'the metaphysics of finance',[91] and the decidedly liberal direction in which he was pointed, combined to make him dreadful to the Conservative backbenchers. Lord Mandeville told Jolliffe that an alliance with Gladstone would have destroyed the party,[92] and his opinion was shared by Robert Christopher, Walter Long (who cited the intense anti-Gladstone feeling of the sixty members of parliament, mostly Conservatives, who were members of the National Club), George Hamilton, and Colonel Taylor.[93] In the end Derby was thankful that Gladstone had said no.

> Gladstone's refusal [he wrote to Lord Ellenborough] has saved us from imminent disaster, for such is the intensity of feeling among the best of my supporters against him, partly on account of his religious tendencies, partly in consequence of the bearing of his financial measures, that had he joined me, I should not only have had to encounter great dissatisfaction, but possibly the loss of fifty or sixty votes, & some of them men whom I had destined for Office.[94]

Derby's authority seems not to have been undermined by the events of January 1855, despite Disraeli's remark that 'any party-leader professedly pretending to the Premiership ought to be ready to take office with the help of his own followers alone' or else 'resign his claims to be First Minister'.[95] At a meeting of the party on 20 February, attended by 170 commoners and 50 peers, Derby defended his conduct in a speech of much 'frankness and dexterity'[96] which Colonel Taylor said satisfied all the grumblers.[97] Even Disraeli, in a letter to his wife, said, as politicians repeatedly do, that he had never heard a finer speech than Derby's and that every man was content, even enthusiastic.[98] Derby was incapable of mean or coy behaviour. He deserved the loyalty and affection which the party, whenever he appealed to them personally, unfailingly gave him, as they did even in February 1855, when, after two years in opposition, they were in a weaker position than they had been even in December 1852, having confessed their inability to govern, having turned their back on Gladstone, and having opened the door to a Prime Minister with whom they would gladly have joined hands and against whom they were in no mood to look forward to opposition.

Notes and References

Disraeli, Derby and the role of opposition
1 Derby to H. Lambert, 4 Jan, 1853 (copy): Derby MSS, 182/1.
2 Monypenny and Buckle, *Disraeli*, iii, 483.
3 Stanley MSS, Diary, 14 March 1853.
4 Greville, *Memoirs*, 29 Jan, 1853, vi, 393–6.
5 Malmesbury, *Memoirs*, ii, 21.
6 Blake, *Disraeli*, 343.
7 Malmesbury, *Memoirs*, ii, 7–8.
8 Walpole to Croker, 28 March 1854: Croker, *Correspondence and Diaries*, iii, 334–5.
9 Drummond to Croker, 19 Dec, 1853: *ibid*, iii, 268–9.
10 Stanley MSS, Diary, 9 Feb, 1853.
11 *Ibid*, 1 March 1853.
12 See Shannon, 'David Urquhart and the Foreign Affairs Committees', in Hollis, *Pressure From Without*, 239–61.
13 Stanley MSS, Diary, 14 March 1853.
14 Hylton MSS, DD/HY/Box 24/6; the memorandum is dated 12 July 1853.
15 Greville, *Memoirs*, 20 Feb. 1853, 403–4.
16 Stanley MSS, Diary, 3 March 1853 (1855 note).
17 *Ibid*.
18 *Ibid*, 14 April 1853. The Conservative backbenchers did not know that the first draft of Disraeli's 1852 budget had included the removal of the advertisement duty, one of the items which Disraeli had been forced to abandon in the face of the Court's insistence on increased naval estimates to meet the alleged threat to the country's security implied by Louis Napoleon's ascendancy in French politics.
19 Conacher, *The Aberdeen Coalition, 1852–1855*, 93.
20 Croker to Herries, 31 July 1855: Herries MSS, NRA/67.
21 Derby to Disraeli, 20 June 1853: Monypenny and Buckle, *Disraeli*, iii, 511–12.
22 Eyck, *The Prince Consort*, 197.
23 'A Conservative – ex M.P.', to Jolliffe, 22 November, 1859: Hylton MSS, DD/HY/Box 24. Jolliffe's correspondent ended his letter by saying that he was 'speaking the sentiments of a large number of the Conservative party'.
24 Lonsdale to Croker, 22 Aug, 1852: Croker, *Correspondence and Diaries*, iii, 257.
25 Blake, *Disraeli*, 340–1.
26 Disraeli, *Bentinck*, 299–300.
27 Stanley MSS, Diary, 4 Feb, 1853.
28 Blake, *Disraeli*, 267–73.
29 Corry, ed., *Parliamentary Reform. A series of speeches . . . by the Right Hon. B. Disraeli, 1848–1866*, 21.
30 Monypenny and Buckle, *Disraeli*, iii, 125.

31 For an interesting treatment of this large subject, see Lewis, 'Theory and expediency in Disraeli's policy', *Victorian Studies*, March 1961, 237–58. Even Gladstone, in his speech in the Commons marking Disraeli's death in 1881, praised Disraeli's 'long sighted consistency of purpose' (Blake, *Disraeli*, 716).

32 Birrell, 'The House of Commons', in *Selected Essays, 1884–1907*, 316.

33 Conacher, *Aberdeen Coalition*, 73.

34 *Ibid*, 101.

35 G. A. Hamilton to Derby, 21 March 1853: Derby MSS, 150/9.

36 Malmesbury to Disraeli, 18 Sept, 1853: Monypenny and Buckle, *Disraeli*, iii, 515.

37 Stanley MSS, Diary, 4 Feb, 1851 (1855 note).

38 G. A. Hamilton to Jolliffe, undated: Hylton MSS, DD/HY/Box 24/7.

39 Greville, *Memoirs*, 9 July 1854, vii, 45–6.

40 Anderson, 'The Wensleydale peerage case and the position of the House of Lords in the mid-nineteenth century', *EHR*, July 1967, 486–502.

41 Derby to Disraeli, 14 Nov, 1853 (copy): Derby MSS, 183/1.

42 Derby to Jolliffe, 6 Jan, 1854: Hylton MSS, DD/HY/Box 18/1.

43 Derby to Lonsdale, 20 Dec, 1853 (copy): Derby MSS, 182/2.

44 Derby to Disraeli, 14 Nov, 1853 (copy): *ibid*, 183/1.

45 Napier to Jolliffe, undated: Hylton MSS, DD/HY/Box 18/15.

46 Walpole to Derby, 10 Dec, 1853: Derby MSS, 153/1.

47 Monypenny and Buckle, *Disraeli*, iii, 544.

48 *Ibid*, iii, 544–5.

The 1855 ministerial crisis

49 Morley, *Gladstone*, i, 521.

50 Monypenny and Buckle, *Disraeli*, iii, 527.

51 J. Parker to F. T. Baring, 9 Jan, 1854: Baring, *Journals and Correspondence*, ii, 19–20.

52 Greville, *Memoirs*, 31 Aug, 1852, vi, 359–60. Greville recorded this opinion on his return from a visit to Broadlands, Palmerston's country residence.

53 *Ibid*, 17 Dec, 1853, vi, 470–1.

54 Malmesbury, *Memoirs*, ii, 9.

55 See the letters from Aberdeen, Herbert, and Argyll to Russell, printed in Russell, *The Later Correspondence*, ii, 128–35.

56 Stanley MSS, Diary, 31 Jan, 1855.

57 Goulburn to Ellenborough, 1 Feb, 1855, printed in Jones, 'The Conservatives and Gladstone in 1855', *EHR*, Jan, 1962, 97.

58 Gladstone to Derby, 31 Jan, 1855: Derby MSS, 135/9.

59 Morley, *Gladstone*, i, 526–7.

60 Queen Victoria memorandum, 31 Jan, 1855.
   In a curious note, for the argument of which I have no confirming evidence, Malmesbury wrote that he had 'positive proof that the French Ambassador, Walewski, throughout the late events, has been most active in the intrigue which has placed and kept Lord Palmerston in office, both as against Lord John and Lord Derby. The Emperor has a great admiration for him, and told me once, "Avec Palmerston, on peut faire des [sic] grandes choses",' (Malmesbury, *Memoirs*, ii, 12). Walewski, however busy he might have been, had no influence on Derby's behaviour.

61 Morley, *Gladstone*, i, 527.

62 *Ibid*, 528.

63 Monypenny and Buckle, *Disraeli*, iii, 560.

64 *Hansard*, 3rd series, cxxxvi, 1222–6.
65 Stanley MSS, Diary, 22–30 Jan, 1855.
66 *Ibid*, Diary, 20 Feb, 1854.
67 Derby to Walpole, 7 July 1853 (copy): Derby MSS, 182/2.
68 C. Hamilton to Jolliffe, undated: Hylton MSS, DD/HY/Box 24/9.
69 Baldock to Jolliffe, 17 Dec, 1854: *ibid*, DD/HY/Box 18/13.
70 Taylor to Jolliffe, undated: *ibid*, DD/HY/Box 24.
71 12 Dec, 1854, *Hansard*, 3rd series, cxxxvi, 1–3.
72 Conacher, *Aberdeen Coalition*, 514, n8.
73 G. A. Hamlton to Jolliffe, 29 Oct, [1854]: Hylton MSS, DD/HY/Box 24/7.
74 Freshfield to Jolliffe, 21 April 1855: *ibid*, DD/HY/Box 24/9.
75 Disraeli to Jolliffe, 20 April, 9 Jan, 1855: *ibid*, DD/HY/6/2165.
76 G. A. Hamilton to Jolliffe, 6 Jan, 1855: *ibid*, DD/HY/Box 24/9.
77 Taylor to Jolliffe, undated: *ibid*, DD/HY/Box 24.
78 Freshfield to Jolliffe, 20 April 1855: *ibid*, DD/HY/Box 24/9.
79 Disraeli to Jolliffe, 9 Jan, 1855: *ibid*, DD/HY/6/2165.
80 G. A. Hamilton to Jolliffe, 6 Jan, 1855: *ibid*, DD/HY/Box 24/9.
81 Disraeli to Jolliffe, 15 Jan, 1855: *ibid*, DD/HY/c/2165.
82 Jolliffe to Derby, 16 Jan, 1855: Derby MSS, 158/10.
83 Derby to Jolliffe, 14 Jan, 1855 (copy): *ibid*, 183/1.
84 *Hansard*, 3rd series, cxxxvi, 1055–6.
85 Palmerston to Queen Victoria, 30 Jan, 1855: Victoria, *Letters*, iii, 99–100.
86 Queen Victoria memorandum, 31 Jan, 1855: *ibid*, 102–4.
87 Monypenny and Buckle, *Disraeli*, iii, 567.
88 *Ibid*.
89 Malmesbury, *Memoirs*, ii, 7.
90 Hervey to Jolliffe, undated: Hylton MSS, DD/HY/Box 24/9.
91 *Edinburgh Review*, April 1857, 561.
92 Mandeville to Jolliffe, undated: Hylton MSS, DD/HY/Box 24/9.
93 Christopher to Jolliffe, 23 Jan, 1855; Long to Jolliffe, 12 March 1855; G. A. Hamilton to Jolliffe, undated: *ibid*; Stanley MSS, Diary, 31 Jan, 1855. Stanley's diary contains the following entry: 'When events were doubtful, Jolliffe called upon me with a letter from Taylor, containing a strong remonstrance against the admission of Gladstone. He said the "Protestant party" would leave us to a man, especially the Irish part of it: Napier and Whiteside, by forming such an alliance, would lose their seats: that we should not know whose support to count upon etc. in short that the union would be to us a source not of strength but weakness. From other conversations, and reports that reached me from various sources, I have no doubt but that this representation was in the main just.' James Whiteside, one of the party's Irish election managers, sat for Enniskillen, in Fermanagh. Joseph Napier shared the representation of Dublin University with George Hamilton.
94 Derby to Ellenborough, 3 Feb, 1855 (copy): Derby MSS, 183/1.
95 Stanley MSS, Diary, 5 Feb, 1855.
96 G. A. Hamilton to Jolliffe, undated: Hylton MSS, DD/HY/Box 24/9.
97 Taylor to Jolliffe, undated: *ibid*.
98 Monypenny and Buckle, *Disraeli*, iii, 568.

Chapter 15

The heyday of Palmerston I: Inside parliament

The 'truce of parties'

Palmerston became Prime Minister forty-six years after his first official appointment. He was nearing his seventieth birthday. Office represented to him the culmination of a career; it did not represent the opportunity to fulfil a political purpose great or small. Few people expected him to last very long, although only Disraeli could have described him as 'really an imposter, utterly exhausted, and at the best only ginger-beer, and not champagne' and dismissed him as 'now an old painted pantaloon, very deaf, very blind, and with false teeth, which would fall out of his mouth when speaking, if he did not hesitate and halt so in his talk'.[1] Yet, for all his years and sterile political imagination, Palmerston survived until his death in 1865 and for a decade the Conservative party reposed in his shade. At three elections, held in 1857, 1859, and 1865, the Conservatives failed to win a majority. For sixteen months, from February 1858 to June 1859, they formed a government, but critics of Derby's alleged timidity in 1855 discovered that, just as in 1852, the chief effect of a minority Conservative government was to infuse a greater sense of purpose and a renewed spirit of cooperation into the several strands of the Liberal opposition. Seldom in its long history has the Conservative party been less powerful than it was during the decade of Palmerston's ascendancy. But then, since Palmerston was a Liberal by habit, not by creed, it has never had less reason to lament its impotence. Conservatives had little cause for complaint in a decade in which the measure which, more than any other, excited parliamentary passions was Gladstone's proposal, rejected by the Lords in 1860 and finally passed as part of the budget in the following year, to abolish the excise duty on paper and so prosper the work of the popular press. Palmerston earned Salisbury's praise for leading parliament to do 'that which it is most difficult and most salutary for a parliament to do – nothing'.[2]

Derby accepted a secondary role with bland equanimity. On the eve of the 1857 meeting of parliament, when the fractiousness of the government party was encouraging predictions of Palmerston's fall, he sent to Malmesbury his appraisal of the position and prospects of the Conservative party.

> That it is in a certain state of disorganisation is not to be denied, nor, I think, to be wondered at; indeed, I am disposed to be rather surprised to find how mere fidelity to party ties, and some personal feeling, has for so long a time kept together so large a body of men, under most adverse circumstances, and in the absence of any cry or leading question, to serve as a broad line of demarcation between the two sides of the House . . . since Palmerston came into office, he has adroitly played his cards, so as to avoid, with one or two exceptions, making any attacks upon our institutions, or affording much ground for censure from a Conservative Opposition. In short, he has been a Conservative minister working with Radical tools, and keeping up a show of Liberalism in his foreign policy, which nine in ten of the House of Commons care nothing about. That a Conservative party should have held together at all under such circumstances is rather to be wondered at, than that there should be apathy and indifference when there is nothing to be fought for by the bulk of the party . . . For myself, I *never* was *ambitious* of office, and am not likely to become more so as I grow older; but I am now, as I have been, ready to accept the responsibility of it if I see a chance not only of taking but of keeping it.[3]

Derby's passivity was the subject of some criticism in Conservative circles. Colonel Taylor found great merit in the accusation of the *Herald* and the *Standard* that the party was weak from its want of a distinctive policy,[4] and Sotheron Estcourt, one of the more 'independent' Conservatives, told Jolliffe at the beginning of 1856 that it was scarcely worth his while to continue whipping 'unless you can really advance some intelligible cause, on some distinct principle'. He advised Jolliffe to resign his office if he were unable to draw from the party's leaders 'some Plan, which will provide a Government'.[5] The weakness of Estcourt's case was his inability to offer any practical guide to the party.

> Whig & Tory, I am persuaded are the only Distinctions that Englishmen will accept, because like a Domino at a Masquerade, they mean nothing and cover anything. A party has now to be constructed *de novo*: Protestantism is too dangerous a Bond for Practical Men, who look to form a government: Toryism is the only Banner that will rally people, and the Task before our leaders ought to be to shew that Toryism is not necessarily antagonistic to Progress.[6]

Estcourt was not alone in his discontent. After two years of Palmerston's government, Malmesbury found it 'impossible to conceal from ourselves that the *animus* of our Party is very unsatisfactory'. He told Derby that his opinion was confirmed by reports from the best men in the party, in reply to which his counsel was patience. 'My answer has always been that the Conservative party can never be an active one except in Office, or in Opposition against a Minister who attacks our Institutions, & that we are now without either of these stimulants and therefore dormant.'[7] Walpole, too, took Derby's view of things, especially after Palmerston's landslide victory at the 1857 elections. 'There is only one way to redeem lost ground,' he wrote to Jolliffe in the spring of 1857, '& that is to give up . . . all mere struggles for place & power, & act upon those Conservative Principles of which we are or ought to be the exponents, & to bide our time when Palmerston is unable to go on, & the liberals quarrel with each other.'[8]

Derby was thus strengthened by the sympathetic support of the two most respected members, other than himself, of his past and future cabinets; he retained his virtual freehold of the Conservative leadership. Gathorne Hardy, newly elected at a by-election at Leominster early in 1856, accepted Derby's policy of watching and waiting as 'of course the only mode in which we can safely act'.[9] And when, in February 1857, Derby addressed a meeting of 160 members of the Commons' party, he was received with affection and approval. The meeting was called after the government's majority on the budget had risen to eighty, helped by the votes of about two dozen Conservatives who, it was said, had wished to record their displeasure at Derby's revived interest in approaching Gladstone, who was a severe critic of the budget. Derby declared 'in the most emphatic manner' that he should regard any member who attempted to dictate the course he should take as no longer attached to the party, and the declaration was received 'with long-continued cheering, and the greatest enthusiasm and the most complete confidence in Lord Derby were expressed'.[10]

It was late in Derby's career to expect him to change his habits of leadership. He continued to abstain from direct involvement in the management of the Commons' party, although Jolliffe and Taylor regularly sought his advice and kept him informed. Taylor, especially, wished that Derby would meet the backbenchers regularly. After the session of 1856, in which Pakington separated himself from his colleagues by his sustained advocacy of national, secular education and in which he and Walpole invited the reproach that 'from the front bench they were not speaking the sentiments of the party' by speaking against Spooner's motion for an inquiry into the operation of the Maynooth grant,[11] Taylor concluded that if Derby 'continues to hold aloof, does nothing, & communicates with nobody, it is only natural that many of our best men should complain, & finding no redress, & receiving no explanation, should ride off on their own hobbies'.[12] Disraeli, too, was criticized by Jolliffe for leading a life of seclusion, associating only with his intimate friends and his small circle of Buckinghamshire Conservatives.[13] In short, Pakington complained, the party was constructed on 'the peculiar principle of nobody ever communicating with anybody'.[14]

Yet, although the absence of clear direction produced occasional episodes of Conservative disunity in the House of Commons, there was not a serious decline in the party's lobby strength. The major Conservative offensive of 1855 was Disraeli's motion in May censuring the government for its wavering between a policy of peace and a policy of war, between Palmerston's refusal to accept peace without a Russian guarantee of the neutrality of the Black Sea and Russell's advice to the Vienna peace conference, which had just broken down in failure, to conclude a peace without insisting on that guarantee. When the motion was lost by 298 votes to 208, Derby sent to Ellenborough an analysis of the division, in which he included as Conservatives none of the Peelites, but only those members who received notes from Jolliffe and who would 'support a Conservative *Government*, though they may not always go with a Conservative opposition'.[15]

For Disraeli's motion		Against Disraeli's motion	
Conservatives	208	Liberals	298
Do. Paired	21	Do. Paired	21
Do. Tellers	2	Do. Tellers	2
Liberals	11	Conservatives	21

Strength of parties in the House of Commons

Conservatives present	210	Liberals present	300
paired	21	paired	21
voted with Govt.	21	voted with Opn.	11
absent	40	absent	27
	292		359

The Conservative turnout, including pairs and tellers, of 231 members, or 79 per cent of the party's maximum strength as assessed by Derby, compares favourably with the Liberal turnout of 89 per cent in view of Disraeli's unpopularity with the party and the natural inclination not to disturb a government embroiled in war, especially only three months after the Conservatives had declined to enter into office. The same may be said of the division on Cobden's Canton censure motion of March 1857. The bombardment of Canton, after the Chinese authorities had refused to apologize for the arrest of the Chinese crew of a British ship trading illegally in the closed port, provided a rare opportunity for a grand assault on Palmerston, although it also gave Palmerston a platform from which to appeal to the John Bull spirit which he had so successfully exploited in the Don Pacifico debate seven years earlier. Palmerston was defeated, and forced to dissolve, by the votes of sixty-three Liberals and Peelites and 202 Conservatives. He was supported by twenty-four 'Self-called Conservatives'; and fifteen Conservatives were absent without cause.[16] By modern standards the size of the Conservative defection was alarming, but Derby, knowing how partial many Conservatives were to Palmerston and how offensive cooperation with Cobden and Gladstone was to them, congratulated Jolliffe on bringing the bulk of the party to the post.[17] Jolliffe put the number,of regular Conservative supporters of Palmerston at eleven, Derby at only five. As Pakington remarked, the solidity of the Conservative bloc in untoward circumstances was 'a remarkable proof of the influence of English politics & the strength of party ties'.[18]

That the Crimean War became an issue of party politics at all, so soon after Palmerston's rise to power, was the work of Disraeli, who tried, without success, to rally the party in the autumn of 1855 by attacking the government for its failure to make peace, chiefly on the argument, as Jolliffe reported to Derby, that it was 'impossible for a party to exist without a policy, and still less possible for an opposition to be of the same policy as the Government'.[19] Conservative opinion ran against him. Disraeli argued that by failing to take office in February the Conservatives had confessed their unwillingness to continue the war. It was a silly argument and it drew from Derby a measured statement of his intention not to treat the war as a party issue.

> I cannot admit that we shrunk from *conducting the war*. On the contrary, the existence of the war, and its general popularity with the country, would have given us our best chance of carrying on the Government. Whether we ought to have undertaken it, it is now too late to inquire; but having been, in common with the country at large, parties to entering into it, and having blamed previous Governments for want of vigour in carrying it on, we cannot with honour, or even with regard to party interests, constitute ourselves a peace Opposition, merely because we have a war Ministry, and I will never consent to weaken an Administration to which I am opposed, by increasing their difficulties in carrying the country through what has become an inevitable war. . . . If the Conservative party cannot be kept together on any other grounds, it is time that it should fall to pieces, or at least that I should retire from the scene.[20]

Disraeli had the backing of Stanley, who floated the notion of a Conservative 'peace party' in articles published by the *Press*, but Conservatives generally shared Palmerston's determination to prosecute the war until Russia should be compelled to accept the neutrality of the Black Sea. Disraeli was placing himself, moreover, in the company of the Radical and Peelite opponents of the war. With high spirits he looked forward to scaring the government 'by holding up the bugbear of an understanding with Gladstone and Bright',[21] but Stanley, his pacifist leanings notwithstanding, understood the futility of working to a Conservative purpose with such instruments.[22]

It ought not to be supposed that Conservative support for the war was inevitable, especially since the war entailed the doubling of the rate of income tax. Conservatives, of course, found it more difficult than Radicals to oppose the Queen's ministers on such an issue, but Disraeli contended against more than the constitutional and patriotic scruples of his followers. Colonel Taylor found the backbenchers dismayed by press reports of a 'junction of planets & the mooted triumvirate of Disraeli, Gladstone & Bright' and concluded that 'so long as war lasts, & is made a national question, politics and party will be secondary considerations'.[23] Members of parliament knew, and the fate of the Manchester Radicals at the 1857 elections showed them to have been right, that opinion in the country was against an early peace. In the agricultural constituencies the war spirit was especially strong,[24] sustained partly, as Claud Hamilton remarked, by war-extended cultivation and war-inflated prices.[25] Conservatives therefore feared for their seats if the opposition should give Palmerston the opportunity to dissolve on a war cry.[26]

I am glad [Derby wrote to Jolliffe at the end of 1855] that your Agents are awake and keeping themselves prepared for the possibility of a Dissolution, but I confess I agree with Disraeli in thinking it most improbable. The only event which in my opinion would induce Palmerston to have recourse to it, or hold out to him a prospect of advantage from it, would be the manifestation of a strong peace party in the House of Commons, especially if it bore anything of the aspect of a combination. Depend upon it that Taylor and his informant, Stanhope, are right as to the feeling of the Country, which is altogether in favour of the prosecution of the War. I should be sorry to say or do anything to influence this feeling; but it would be very bad policy on our part to run counter to it.[27]

Beyond the tactical and patriotic motives which inhibited the Conservative opposition to Palmerston until the war came to an end in January 1856, there lay a more lasting source of Conservative weakness, the admiration, namely, which many Conservatives felt for Palmerston, combined with the awareness that Palmerston in office was the surest brake on forward-driving liberalism. In 1856 Hugh Cairns, the Conservative member for Belfast and Solicitor General for Ireland in the 1858–59 government, whom George Hamilton commended as 'a man of no ordinary intelligence' who had 'a large opportunity of collecting opinion', reported that the disposition of the country was eminently conservative, but that 'the conservative feeling is tending rather towards Palmerston than to us', helped in that direction by the popular impression that Derby had grown indifferent to politics.[28] That feeling necessarily communicated itself to the Conservative benches in parliament, especially after Palmerston's electoral triumph of 1857. Townshend Mainwaring, who sat for Denbigh district as a Conservative from 1841 to 1847 and re-entered parliament under the same colours in 1857, voted with Palmerston in the Conspiracy Bill division of February 1858. which brought down Palmerston's government and installed the Conservatives in office. Mainwaring wrote to Jolliffe that, although his inclination was to give Derby a steady support, he wished to hold himself at liberty to act as a 'free supporter of all administrations'.

As a principle I do support whoever [sic] Her Majesty calls to her Councils. It has ever been my great pride to have supported that great Minister Sir Robert Peel: & with scarcely less satisfaction Lord Palmerston, to whom I yet feel the Country owes a large debt of gratitude for his wise Administration during the perils of the Russian War.[29]

Mainwaring's attitude, though a throwback to earlier days, was not eccentric. At the beginning of the new parliament elected in 1857, Jolliffe received notice from at least seven, perhaps more, Conservatives that they no longer wished to receive the Conservative whip. One of them, the Marquess of Blandford, never a reliable supporter of the party in opposition, had, even before the dissolution, 'determined not to be a party to any endeavour which might be made on the conservative side of the House to displace Palmerston';[30] another, Nicholas Kendall, the member for Cornwall East, told Jolliffe that, although he believed he was as strong a Conservative as any other member of the House of Commons, he could not identify himself with opposition to Palmerston.

> I, in common with many others, have felt that our Leaders have been indefinite in their Policies, injudicious in their Tactics & exhibiting for a long time a strong leaning towards Mr. Gladstone & his friends & I confess I should, in the present state of Parties, view with alarm any probably successful attempt to remove Lord Palmerston from office & besides this I admired his conduct in the Russian war & thought him justified in the course he adopted as regards that with China, & tho' I should again & again find myself in the same Lobby with yourself, I still think I may so far call myself a supporter of the Gov. at the present moment that I ought not to receive your circulars, as being one of the opposition party.[31]

Derby regretted the decision of those Conservatives who resigned the whip, but he was unable to quarrel with it. 'My *hope*', he told the Earl of Harrington at the beginning of the new parliament, 'is that Lord Palmerston may have the firmness, instead of bidding against Lord John Russell for the support of the Ultra Liberal Party, to resist their pretensions, in which case I should feel it to be my duty not only to embarrass him, but to give him any aid in my power.'[32]

The Conservative gravitation towards Palmerston manifested itself most markedly in the vote on the Conspiracy Bill. After it was discovered that Orsini's plot to assassinate the French emperor had been hatched in England, and the grenades to be used for the murder manufactured there, Palmerston, in response to French pressure, introduced a Bill changing conspiracy to murder from a misdemeanour to a felony punishable by imprisonment for life. The Bill was reasonable enough, but public opinion resented the government's yielding to French demands, and the government was beaten on the amendment of the Radical, Milner Gibson, by a vote of 234 to 215. Palmerston was already in some difficulty over his appointment as Lord Privy Seal of Lord Clanricarde, who was widely condemned as a reprobate, and there was doubt whether he would survive a motion then tabled to abolish the office.[33] Nevertheless, his defeat on the Conspiracy Bill surprised nearly everyone. The Conservatives had voted by three to one to give the government leave to introduce the Bill and they had not joined in the consultations of Milner Gibson with Lord John Russell and Sir James Graham in framing the amendment. Nor did the Conservative leaders act to rally the party in support of the amendment. 'I am anxious that you should be fully aware', Derby wrote to Clarendon, 'that no measures were taken on our side of the House to obtain an attendance hostile to the Government – no meeting was held – no 'whip' was out; & the division, such as it was, was, with my friends, the result of spontaneous conviction that that amendment could not honestly be resisted.[34] What influence Derby exerted personally was to advise Conservatives to support Palmerston, although it was characteristic of him that he chose not to make his views widely known. When a backbencher informed Derby that he would have voted to give the government leave to bring in the Bill had he known Derby's opinion, Derby replied, in language that Lord Liverpool might have used, that he was 'very far from wishing that you, or any of our friends, in deference to my opinion, should take a line opposed to their own conscientious convictions'.[35] Left to their own lights, the Conservatives split on the Bill: 146 of them, including Disraeli,[36] joined with the Peelites and the Russell Liberals to defeat the government; but on a division which it was obvious might, and as it turned out did, lead to a Conservative government, 112 Conservatives voted with Palmerston.

The Conservative government which was formed in 1858 proved to be but an interlude in Palmerston's ascendancy. Back in office from 1859 to 1865, Palmerston discovered that he could once again rely upon Conservative good will. The Conservatives' recovery at the 1859 elections was insufficient to keep Derby in office, but it left the party very powerful, in numbers at least, and when Derby took his leave of office, the Queen, 'urging the great objections there were to eternal changes',[37] entreated him not to use his power against Palmerston. Derby readily assented, and for the next six years cooperation between Palmerston and the Conservatives was steady enough for the *Quarterly Review* to hail the rise of a new model Whig system, in which 'the Whigs should furnish the placemen, the Radicals should furnish the votes, and the Conservatives should furnish the policy'.[38] Conservatives were reassured by the composition of Palmerston's cabinet, which included three dukes, the brother of a fourth, five other peers or sons of peers, and three baronets of landed property.

'We now live in anti-reforming times, [Gladstone wrote to Graham in 1860]. 'All improvements have to be urged in apologetic, almost in supplicatory tones. I sometimes reflect how much less liberal, as to domestic policy, in any true sense of the word, is this Government than Sir Robert Peel's; and how much the tone of ultra-Toryism prevails among a large portion of the Liberal party.[39]

In the 1860 session Palmerston was happy to use the Conservatives to defeat the abolition of Church rates, parliamentary reform, and Gladstone's abolition of the paper duty. After the last had been thrown out by the House of Lords, Robert Cecil wrote in the *Quarterly Review* that the proceedings in parliament manifested unmistakable signs of a Conservative reaction against the liberalism of Gladstone, Bright, and the Dissenters. He did not, however, recommend that the Conservatives should seek to exploit that reaction in a partisan manner. He applauded the speech in the Lords in which Derby had said that, in throwing out the Paper Duty Bill, the Conservative peers had no desire to disturb or overthrow the government. 'There is no reason to fear', Cecil wrote, 'that any factious trickery will shorten Lord Palmerston's tenure of power. Every Conservative owes a debt to him . . . which it would be ingratitude, for mere party motives, to forget.'[40]

In the same spirit, Robert Ward, a Conservative journalist from Maidenhead, wished the party to uphold Palmerston, since the real political battle brought Liberals and Conservatives on to the same side against the Manchester Radicals.[41] Derby was therefore acting on behalf of more than a circle of his close colleagues when, at the beginning of 1860, he sent Malmesbury to Palmerston with the messsage that if the government were to break up from internal dissensions, 'the Conservative Party would support during the . . . ensuing Session any administration which Viscount Palmerston might be able provisionally to make',[42] which assurance enabled Palmerston to use his weight in cabinet against Gladstone in the fight with the Lords over the Paper Duty Bill. Even Disraeli had come, by the end of 1860, to see that it was expedient to leave Palmerston in power,[43] and in January 1861 Malmesbury once more gave an official pledge to Palmerston that, so long as his government did not touch parliamentary reform nor take part in a war against Austria on behalf of the Italian nationalists, the pact of 1860 was to continue.[44] Not until Palmerston's death in 1865 suddenly changed the direction of official Liberal policy by placing it in the hands of Russell and Gladstone did the Conservatives again set their sights on office.

Derby's second government

Buttressing Palmerston's government commended itself to those Conservatives who believed, as Wellington had in the 1830s, that Liberalism was less dangerous in office than in opposition, because the Liberals' desire to gain power acted as an incentive to the development of radical policies and the Conservatives' desire to retain it softened their spirit of resistance. In 1864 J. Wilson Patten, an ex-Peelite and one of the party's senior backbenchers, deprecated an attack on the government because 'the conservative party is ten times more powerful for good on the opposition benches, then it would be in office, unless with a majority large enough to make it thoroughly master of the position'.[45] One of the reasons for the Conservatives' placid acquiescence in Palmerston's second government was the experience of a Conservative minority government in 1858-59. Derby's explanation to the Lords of his refusal to take office in 1855 had included a powerful statement of his dislike of governing without the support of a party majority.

> To hold that high and responsible situation dependent for support from day to day upon precarious and uncertain majorities, compelled to cut down this measure and

to pare off that; to consider with regard to each measure not what was for the real welfare of the country, but what would conciliate some half-dozen men here, or obviate the objections of some half-dozen there; to regard it as a great scramble through the session of Parliament and boast of having met with few and insignificant defeats: I say this is a state of things which cannot be satisfactory to any minister and which cannot be of advantage to the Crown or to the people of the Country.[46]

The prospects in 1858, when Palmerston resigned after the defeat of his government on the Conspiracy Bill, were even worse than they had been in 1855. The 1857 elections had reduced the Conservative party to about only 260 seats, their lowest point since the early 1830s. Derby nevertheless resolved to take office, since, as he explained to the Earl of Northumberland, the failure to accept the Queen's commission 'would have been the signal for the utter & final dissolution of the party' and the failure to accomplish it would have been 'almost, if not quite, as disastrous'.[47]

Derby's second government presided over the passing of some useful legislation. Indeed, the removal of the property qualification for members of parliament (attended by scarcely any notice being taken of the logical contradiction entailed in requiring electors to be wealthier than the elected) and the admission, at long last, of Jews to parliament by a Conservative government illustrated a point for which the nineteenth century affords ample evidence, that it is sometimes easier for a Conservative government to pass reforming legislation than it is for a Liberal one hindered by a Conservative opposition. There was also the India Act of 1858, which, while altered in details, simply enacted the Liberal proposal, born of the Mutiny, to end the power of the East India Company directors and vest authority for the government of India entirely in the Crown.[48] Acts to facilitate the drainage of the Thames (in 1858 the Commons rose earlier than usual to escape the summer stench), to extend the sphere of municipal government, and to confer self-governing status on British Columbia were also passed, but as Disraeli remarked to Derby, 'everyone knows that all that we did would really have been done by our predeccessors'.[49]

The significance of the 1858–59 government in Conservative history is that it failed to provide the basis for a recovery of the party in the way that Peel's minority government of 1834–35 had. Instead it acted as the impetus to Liberal consolidation. When Derby was forming his government, Stanley listed among reasons why a Conservative ministry was not likely to stand that 'it is, and since 1853 has been (I write from personal knowledge, not from hearsay) the earnest wish of the more advanced Liberals to see a Derby Ministry formed . . . the effect of such a step being to unite every section of the Liberal party in opposition'.[50] For the Conservatives to turn office to the permanent advantage of the party required a junction with Gladstone and with a section of the Whigs. Greville believed that the body of Liberal-Conservatives elected to support Palmerston in 1857 would see that their wisest course was to align with the Conservatives against radicalism.[51]

Matters, however, were rather complicated. Gladstone, on whom much depended, had convinced himself that Palmerston was 'by far the worst Minister the country has had during our time',[52] and he had voted against the Conspiracy Bill. He had no desire to displace the Derby government. On the other hand, he was by now the chief object, with Bright, of Conservative anti-radical propaganda and, carrying few votes with him (at least not by personal allegiances), was likely by his presence in a Conservative cabinet to weaken, not strengthen, the party. For that reason, and also for the reason that the Whigs, however conservative their politics, would find it difficult to stifle their pride and act under Derby, Stanley concluded that the Conservatives' attempt to govern would prove hopeless.[53]

So it turned out, even though the government lasted until June 1859. Derby invited Lord Grey, a Conservative Whig whose importance derived from the alliance of a distinguished name with ministerial experience, to join his government. He told Grey that he wished 'to step out of the ancient limits of parties & to avail myself of the services of independent men'.[54] He made a similar appeal to the Duke of Newcastle, to whom he wrote that he wished to enlist 'eminent men of Liberal–Conservative opinions, who are not at this moment fettered by engagements'.[55] But like every previous effort to overcome the Conservatives' electoral failure by a parliamentary coalition, Derby's overtures bore no fruit. Grey for the Whigs, and Newcastle, Gladstone and Herbert for the Peelites, all turned him down. The 1858 cabinet therefore bore the same narrow aspect as the cabinet of 1852, although it was strengthened by two recruits, Stanley at the Colonial Office and General Peel at the War Office.

The notion of a Whig–Conservative alliance had been in the air ever since 1846. It was never taken very seriously, certainly not by the Whigs, and in 1858 there was no issue large enough to force a shake-up of parties. Gladstone's objections to Palmerston – a meddlesome foreign policy involving the maintenance of large military and naval establishments and thus of the income tax, a consistent preference for low-church bishops, and an habitual dislike of legislation – were not the sort to drive lifelong Liberals into the Conservative party. Even on Gladstone they did not act powerfully. For two years it had been widely predicted that he would at last rejoin the Conservatives, and in 1857 Derby had described him to Jolliffe as 'expecting to hear from me and very hungry';[56] But the feelings of Conservative backbenchers and the consideration due to Disraeli prevented Derby from offering to Gladstone the only position which might have secured him, the leadership of the House of Commons.[57] Gladstone was, at any rate, pulled in the other direction by the desire of his Peelite colleagues to act with Russell. Amid all the fluctuations of Gladstone's thoughts and sympathies in 1858, on one matter he was resolute: he would not join Derby alone, powerless, as he later put it, to give to Conservatism a liberal bias.[58] In May he had no hesitation in refusing Derby's invitation to replace Ellenborough at the Board of Control.

An air of unreality hung about Derby's attempt to broaden the party's appeal by bringing Grey and Gladstone into the cabinet. Grey was a poor substitute for Palmerston. A Whig–Conservative merger depended on the willingness of either Palmerston or Derby to yield leadership to the other. The 'distribution of power', as Graham said, was 'the only real difficulty between them'.[59] Once Palmerston had rejected the Conservatives in 1852, and had established himself as the leader of liberal-conservative opinion, Derby had little room for manoeuvre. The Aberdeen coalition had failed to produce a fusion of Whigs, Peelites and Radicals, but in 1859 the parts were put together again. Impelled by two issues – parliamentary reform and the Italian war of national independence from Austria – the various sections of the opposition were able to melt their differences in pursuit of the overthrow of the Conservative government. The Conservative Reform Bill of that session,[60] too conservative to appeal to either the country or parliament, was rejected by 330 votes to 291. At the subsequent elections the Conservatives recovered their losses of 1857, but once more failed to win a majority. When the new parliament assembled, the Italian struggle against Austria had become, not least in the minds of Gladstone and Russell, the dominating issue of English politics. Suspicions that Derby and Malmesbury were preparing to throw the weight of England on the Austrian side were unfounded, but widespread, and by failing to publish the correspondence of the Foreign Office with the French and Italian governments, Derby let slip the opportunity of dispelling them. Whether, as Malmesbury believed, its publication would have saved the government,[61] is conjecture. On 6 June a historic meeting of Peelites, Radicals, Russell Liberals and Palmerston Liberals laid the foundations of the Victorian Liberal party of Gladstone and plotted the downfall of Derby's government. Russell agreed to act under Palmerston and it was resolved to move a vote of no confidence in the government. Six days later ministers were beaten by 323 votes to 310, a large Conservative muster, but not large enough to prevent the second attempt at minority Conservative government from ending in failure.

Notes and References

The 'truce of parties'

1 Disraeli to lady Londonderry, 2 Feb, 1855: Monypenny and Buckle, *Disraeli*, iii, 566–7.
2 M.Pinto-Duschinsky, *The Political Thought of Lord Salisbury, 1854–68*, 92.
3 Derby to Malmesbury, 15 Dec, 1856: Malmesbury, *Memoirs*, ii, 53–4.
4 Taylor to Jolliffe, 20 Aug, 1855: Hylton MSS, DD/HY/Box 24.
5 Estcourt to Jolliffe, 1 Jan, 1856: *ibid*, DD/HY/Box 24/11.
6 *Ibid*.
7 Malmesbury to Derby, 7 Dec, 1856: Derby MSS, 144/1.
8 Walpole to Jolliffe, 26 April 1857. Hylton MSS,DD/HY/Box 18/8.
9 Gathorne-Hardy, ed., *Gathorne Hardy, First Earl of Cranbrook, a Memoir*, i, 110.
10 Malmesbury, *Memoirs*, ii, 61–2.
11 G. A. Hamilton to Jolliffe, undated: Hylton MSS, DD/HY/Box 24/11.
12 Taylor to Jolliffe, 25 Nov, [1856]: *ibid*, DD/HY/Box 24.
13 Jolliffe to Derby, 23 Oct, 1855: Derby MSS, 158/10. In November 1861 Disraeli wrote to Jolliffe that he and his wife had been at Hughenden for three months, 'quite alone this whole season', and in the following August, once more at Hughenden, he reminded Jolliffe of 'the extreme seclusion in wh. we live with very few companions except books & trees' (Disraeli to Jolliffe, 4 Nov, 1861 and 8 Aug, 1862: Hylton MSS, DD/HY/c/2165).
14 Pakington to Jolliffe, 11 Nov, 1855: *ibid*, DD/HY/Box 18/11.
15 Derby to Ellenborough, 30 May 1855 (copy): Derby MSS, 183/1.
16 Jolliffe to Derby, 4 March 1857: *ibid*, 158/10.
17 Derby to Jolliffe, 4 March 1857: Hylton MSS, DD/HY/Box 18/2.
18 Pakington to Jolliffe, 11 Nov, 1855: *ibid*, DD/HY/Box 18/11.
19 Jolliffe to Derby, 23 Oct, 1855: Derby MSS, 158/10.
20 Derby to Disraeli, 25 Oct, 1855: Monypenny and Buckle, *Disraeli*, iv, 21–2.
21 *Ibid*, iv, 18. The phrase was spoken to Count Vitzthum, the Saxon legate at St James's.
22 Stanley MSS, Diary, Nov, 1855.
23 Taylor to Jolliffe, 14 Oct, 1855: Hylton MSS, DD/HY/Box 24.
24 Taylor to Jolliffe, 29 Nov, [1855]: *ibid*,
25 Hamilton to Jolliffe, 3 Jan, 1856: *ibid*, DD/HY/Box 18/8.
26 Viscount Chelsea to Jolliffe, 27 Nov, 1855: *ibid*, DD/HY/Box 24; Taylor to Jolliffe, [Nov, 1855]: *ibid*.
27 Derby to Jolliffe, 20 Nov, 1855: *ibid*, DD/HY/Box 18/1.
28 Hamilton to Jolliffe, [Dec, 1856]. *ibid*, DD/HY/Box 24/11.
29 Mainwaring to Jolliffe, 12 March [1858]: *ibid*, DD/HY/Box 18/14.

30 Blandford to Jolliffe, 9 March 1857: *ibid*, DD/HY/Box 18/13.
31 Kendall to Jolliffe, 19 May 1857: *ibid*, DD/HY/Box 18/13.
32 Derby to Harrington, 28 April 1857 (copy): Derby MSS, 183/2.
33 Greville believed that Clanricarde's appointment was 'the real cause of the downfall of the Government' (*Memoirs*, 2 March 1858, vii, 334), and a pamphleteer commented that the House of Commons, already irritated by Palmerston's insouciant manner, was offended by an appointment 'characteristic of Palmerstonian effrontery' (Anonymous, 'The late crisis', *Academica: An Occasional Journal*, Cambridge, 1858).
34 Derby to Clarendon, 20 Feb, 1858 (copy): Derby MSS, 184/1. Feuchtwanger has written that Colonel Taylor 'was said to have been instrumental in bringing down Palmerston in 1858 by bringing Tories at the last moment on Lord Derby's instructions to vote against the Government'. (*Disraeli, Democracy, and the Tory Party*, 242–3). Palmerston seems to have believed something of the sort. He told the Queen that 'Lord Derby had caught at an opportunity of putting the Government in a minority': (Palmerston to Queen Victoria, 19 Feb, 1855: Victoria, *Letters*, iii, 134–5). I have found no evidence which counters Derby's statement to Clarendon.
35 Derby to S. Warren, 12 Feb, 1858 (copy): Derby MSS, 184/1.
36 Malmesbury wrote that when the vote was announced 'Disraeli's face was worth anything – a mixture of triumph and sarcasm that he could not suppress' (Malmesbury, *Memoirs*, ii, 96).
37 Greville, *Memoirs*, 27 Jan, 1860, vii, 455–8.
38 *Quarterly Review,* April 1965, 543.
39 Gladstone to Graham, 27 Nov, 1860: Parker, *Graham*, ii, 403.
40 'The Conservative Reaction', *Quarterly Review*, July 1860, 300.
41 Ward to Stanley, 4 June 1860: Hylton MSS, DD/HY/Box 24/6.
42 Palmerston to Queen Victoria, 1 Jan, 1861: Victoria, *Letters*, iii, 539–40).
43 Disraeli to Derby, 8 Dec, 1860: Derby MSS, 146/1.
44 Malmesbury to Palmerston, 29 Jan, 1861: Broadlands MSS, GC/MA/196. 'I think that in your communications with Palmerston,' Derby wrote to Malmesbury on 26 December 1860, 'you cannot be too explicit. He is a gentleman, and will know that you and I are dealing with him *de bonne foi*, and will not suspect a 'dodge', if we make any exception to our promise of support. I should, however, be quite ready to assure him that, though we might, in debate, object to some of the 'sayings and doings' of the Foreign Office (and chiefly the *sayings*, or rather, *writings*), we would not countenance any movement on the subject of foreign policy calculated to defeat the Government, unless it were on the impossible supposition that they should desire us to take an active part in an attack by Sardinia and France on Venetia. I cannot believe that the Government will be so mad as to sanction such a policy; but an exception made in such a case from our promise of support will rather serve to strengthen than to shake a belief in the sincerity of our general profession' (Malmesbury, *Memoirs*, ii, 243–4). I do not know why Derby chose not to deal directly with Palmerston, unless it was because ever since 1852, when Palmerston had given generous assistance to Malmesbury at the Foreign Office, the two men had remained on very friendly terms.

Derby's second government
45 Patten to Derby, 28 June 1864: Derby MSS, 147/6a.

46 1 Feb, 1855, *Hansard*, 3rd series, cxxxvi, 1254–60.

47 Derby to Northumberland, 22 Feb, (copy): Derby MSS, 184/1.

48 I am not suggesting that the Conservatives' India Act was simply a concession to a hostile majority. In a long letter on Indian affairs written to Jolliffe in Nov, 1857, Derby said that it was clear that 'we must abolish the distinction between the Queen's & the Company's service' (Derby to Jollife, 25 Nov, 1857 (copy): *ibid*, 183/2).

49 Disraeli to Derby, 3 April 1859: *ibid*, 145/6.

50 Stanley MSS, Diary, 21 Feb, 1858.

51 Greville, *Memoirs*, 16 June 1858, vii, 371–3.

52 Gladstone to Graham, 14 Feb, 1858: Parker, *Graham*, ii, 338.

53 Stanley MSS, Diary 21 Feb, 1858.

54 Derby to Grey, 21 Feb, 1858 (copy): Derby MSS, 184/1. In his autobiography, the eminent Conservative journalist, Sir Archibald Alison, wrote that in 1860 the majority of the Conservative party, lacking confidence in Disraeli, 'inclined to Earl Grey as their future leader' in the event of Derby's retirement (Alison, *Autobiography*, ii, 449–50.

55 Derby to Newcastle, 21 Feb, 1858 (copy): Derby MSS, 184/1.

56 Derby to Jolliffe, 11 Jan, 1857: Hylton MSS, DD/HY/Box 18/1.

57 That is not to say that the offer of the leadership *would* have secured him, although Malmesbury recorded Lord Grey's opinion that Gladstone would have accepted it (Malmesbury, *Memoirs*, ii, 99–100).

58 Gladstone memorandum, 1897: Gladstone, *Autobiographica*, 80–3.

59 Graham to Russell, 9 May 1859: Parker, *Graham*, ii, 382.

60 The Bill is discussed in the last chapter of this book.

61 Malmesbury, *Memoirs*, ii, 188–9.

Chapter 16

The heyday of Palmerston II: Outside parliament

The party under Jolliffe

On the eve of the 1859 elections Greville asked Disraeli for his estimate of the Conservatives' prospects at the polls and Disraeli answered that 'there was so much luck in these matters that it was difficult to speak positively'. He then went on to predict a gain of forty seats to the Conservatives: 'from the day of their taking office they had looked forward to a dissolution . . . their organisation was excellent, they had plenty of candidates and of money.'[1] Historians have tended to write of the mid-Victorian years as if party organization barely existed. Professor Vincent is not alone in claiming that 'the national parties themselves . . . had no regional organizations whatever at this time',[2] although it is not evident what shades of meaning he intends by the words, 'national', 'themselves', and 'regional'. Nor is the judgement entirely wrong. There were constituencies where formal party organization, whether central or local, would have been superfluous, where Conservative candidates prospered without it. There were, too, constituencies in which the registration was poorly attended, in which there was no regular party agent, and for which, at times, neither money nor candidates could be found. In Merionethshire the Conservative party was so well served by the traditional methods of landlord influence that it 'could afford to be without an organization',[3] and in Cardiganshire, as late as the 1868 elections, the Conservatives had 'no public organization whatsoever, no registration society', but 'relied throughout upon an unofficial organization of their voting power by traditional means, that is to say by recruiting all the available lawyers in the country, and employing estate agents as party managers in the localities'.[4] The view, nevertheless, that organized party simply did not exist contains a bias towards present-day standards and forms of organization and pays too little regard to the efforts of the central party managers, not, indeed, to control party activity in the constituencies, but to oversee it and, where necessary and possible, to assist it. Party organization, at least on the Conservative side, suffered no decline in the 1850s and 1860s.

The Conservatives accepted Palmerston's ascendancy and upheld his authority because they were in a minority in the House of Commons. They would rather have replaced him in power by gaining a majority, and to that end they worked hard. In 1859 Derby roused himself to make personal appeals to many Conservatives to expend all the money and time which they could spare on the elections. 'We stake the last Conservative card on the issue of the forthcoming Election,' he wrote to a former member of parliament, urging him to persuade his son to stand, '& we want every man we can get.'[5] The Conservatives suffered from certain electoral handicaps. They had no platform orators to compete with men like Bright, Cobden, and Edward Miall. But then they did not wish to encourage, nor themselves have reason to employ, missionary politics. Derby refused to address the Huddersfield Conservative Association in 1859, because 'it would obviously be impossible for the Leader of the Conservative Party to imitate the example of Mr. Bright, & hold meetings in various places, under whatever name, for the purpose of promulgating their [the Conservatives'] views'.[6] Another difficulty was that, being chiefly a party of the counties, the Conservatives found the mechanics of organization more difficult than the Liberals. 'Their strength lies in the towns & manufacturing villages, & therefore concentrated,' a West Riding Conservative pointed out in 1854, 'ours in the rural districts, where prompt unity of action is difficult.'[7] Great expense and preparation were needed to bring the scattered Conservative electorate to the polls. But then, also, the Conservatives were not eager to import the Radical passions of the towns into the counties. The Conservative hold on the counties was maintained partly because the county voters remained, in a sense, politically quiescent, resistant to the attempts of the Radicals to turn grievances arising from the game laws and the terms of land tenure into issues of national party politics.

The organization of the party under Jolliffe, Rose and Spofforth was not, nor was it intended to be, encompassing in its scope or uniform in its agency. As in the days of Bonham, political organization remained highly personal. Everything depended on the knowledge which the party managers acquired of local habits and the tact with which they used it. Much might, for example, be accomplished by a just dispensation of patronage. In 1854 Derby recommended Lord Portarlington for a vacancy in the Irish representative peerage in order to reward him for having 'practically returned our Candidate for the Boroughs of Portarlington' and in order also to purchase his support at the next election.[8] In 1857 Portarlington contributed £100 to the election fund.[9] Two years later, Eglinton congratulated Derby on having made Edward Grogan, the member for Dublin city, a baronet, 'for it will put our supporters here in spirits'; after the election, Eglinton claimed that the baronetcy alone had saved the borough's two seats for the Conservatives.[10] Persons of varying social degree had to be placated and cajoled. Thus Rose informed Jolliffe in 1856 of the state of Westminster politics and the possibility of returning a Conservative for that traditionally Liberal constituency.

Apropos of Westminster which we were discussing yesterday I agree with you that the thing is feasible and I don't think the organization would be so difficult as we at first supposed. But there is one obstacle which I will mention and you can consider whether it can be removed. There is in Westminster a Brewer, Mr. Joseph Charles Wood, who exercises considerable influence among the lower class of voters and from having a majority of the public houses in the low part of the City is of course a most important man to secure. He is staunch in his politics and if he exerted himself could do us immense service, being a really good speaker as well as a bustling active man. But he has been lukewarm at the last Elections and is still in dudgeon in consequence of his not having been put in the Commission of the peace for the County, which he considers his position entitles him to. I understand he is reputed to be a man of wealth. . . . The objection to his being in the Commission is that he is a Brewer, but this has been looked over in recent instances – and upon my sending to him to ask if he will help us to organize a Conservative Committee preparatory to the next election, he related his grievances to me . . .

Do you think anything can be done to put Wood who is really an influential man into good humour? There may perhaps be reasons . . . for not wishing to put him into the Commission extra those stated, & if so there is nothing more to be said, but if it is only on the ground of his trade seeing that some exceptions are made it would be of great advantage to us, especially with a view to Westminster, if the difficulty could be overcome.[11]

Rose was here acting in the manner appropriate to the electoral realities of the age: informing himself of the opinions and mood of an important local man, talking to him in person, and in that way carefully laying the ground before organizing a Conservative committee. It was the kind of work which he and Spofforth did daily. It would be wrong to conclude that everywhere where there was no Conservative agent, no Conservative committee, nor a Conservative candidate at an election, the organization of the party showed itself to be deficient. It was part of the job expected of Rose and Spofforth that they should, by preliminary soundings, discover where it would be wasteful, unnecessary, or impracticable, to spend precious funds on a constituency. When a vacancy occurred at King's Lynn in 1854, a constituency whose representation had been shared by a Peelite and a Conservative since 1846, the Peelite section in the town put up a Liberal banker from Norwich, John Gurney, to succeed their former member, Viscount Jocelyn. The opportunity of a Conservative gain seemed to have presented itself, but Gurney was rich, had strong local connections, and espoused moderate opinions which even the Radicals accepted. Jolliffe therefore heeded Stanley's advice that 'sending down a stranger would be a mere waste of money and trouble'[12] and the Conservatives did not contest the by-election. In an age which cared nothing for such things as a party's percentage of the total national vote, there was no harm in leaving hopeless constituencies alone; to do so was often safer than to meddle.

The division of labour among the party managers ran in this way. Jolliffe took general competence and expected to be kept informed of all the activities of Rose and Spofforth. He also undertook extensive correspondence with the constituencies himself and was the chief link between Rose and Derby. Beyond the routine of collecting information and endeavouring to find suitable agents and reliable contacts in the constituencies, Rose and Spofforth did nothing without first securing Jolliffe's assent. They neither gave their blessing to a prospective candidate nor promised money for a contest without Jolliffe's approval. Electoral funds were controlled by the Chief Whip, Jolliffe until 1859 and thereafter Colonel Taylor. Derby described Jolliffe's transfer of the party fund to Colonel Taylor in 1860 as 'the formal act of your resignation of your arduous office'.[13] 'Elections I find are not to my taste,' Taylor once said, '& they do not prosper when I intefere.'[14] But there was no strict line drawn between the functions of whipping and electoral management, and Taylor and George Hamilton did both as Assistant Whips. Nor was there a clear distinction between the activities of Rose and Spofforth, who both went about the country to assist local parties, took part in the selection of candidates, worried about the state of the registration, and advised Jolliffe on the appropriation of money.[15] The parliamentary leaders themselves rarely interfered directly in the work of the electoral staff, although during a general election, when a special enlarged committee was formed, Disraeli would attend its meetings, and Derby was, now and then, called on to lend his name and authority to negotiations which seemed to require them. Thus in 1859, when a row threatened to develop between the sitting Conservative member for Midhurst and a rival Conservative aspirant for the seat, it was Derby who wrote to the Duke of Richmond to ask him to arbitrate the quarrel.[16] In the same year he conducted negotiations with Lord Bathurst, whose support was essential for the success of a second Conservative candidate at Cirencester, and with the Duke of Hamilton, whose influence prevailed in Lanarkshire.[17]

There is no doubt that the party managers performed their duties conscientiously and thoroughly. It is more difficult to measure their real influence on the constituencies and election results. At the end of 1856, Malmesbury gave his opinion that they had achieved little.

> If Palmerston knew our unprepared & I may say our *destitute* condition he ought to dissolve immediately. The miserable £500 a year that Colville & I have collected from 20 Peers, has enabled Mr. Rose (who works *gratis!*) to nearly complete an analysis of the English *Boroughs*, but Scotland & Ireland are, as far as I know, ignored, & the counties everywhere left to themselves.[18]

Malmesbury was wrong about Ireland, where a notable advance was made in

1853 by the establishment of a separate Irish office of the party; and it was reasonable that, financially restricted as they were, Rose and Spofforth should pay little attention to the Liberal stronghold of Scotland. (Archibald Alison, who as sheriff was responsible for supervising the registration court at Glasgow, noted that afer 1853 there was a sharp decline in the number of claims and objections which he had to adjudicate 'in consequence of the decline of interest in the votes, from the great and increasing preponderance of the Liberal party'.[19]) In England, the counties were much less in need, and more jealous, of interference than the boroughs, not only because the counties were already predominantly Conservative, but also because the Conservative gentry had habitually lent its assistance to the prestigious county elections and neglected the rural boroughs. During his years as 'principal agent' Rose rightly focused his attention on the small and middling boroughs.

Malmesbury's opinion, moreover, was given at a time when the party was still in the middle of rebuilding. In March 1855 Rose sent to Jolliffe an appraisal of what had been accomplished since 1853 and of what it was necessary to do in the future.[20] He began by saying that as much had been done as could be done with the means at hand. A dossier on every borough and county was being compiled and communication had been established with 'confidential parties', or what may be called semi-official agents, in 114 boroughs. 'There is every reason to be satisfied with the progress made,' he wrote. 'Still with all this I cannot help feeling that we are far from doing all that might be done with advantage to the party and that our present organization is by no means sufficient to compete with the activity displayed in the other side.' The chief weakness was the want of preparation in the constituencies before vacancies arose. And behind that lay the want of adequate funds. In order to ensure that constituencies were ready with candidates and organization for an election at any time, two things were needed: more money and a couple of full-time roving agents. Spofforth's salary of £300 was not enough even to cover the cost of simply collecting information. Rose therefore suggested that two separate accounts be established: one for the yearly expenses of maintaining the organization and one for election expenditure itself.

Rose appears to have been jealous of Spofforth's influence or, at any rate, eager that Spofforth should not forget that, just as he was a junior assistant in the law firm, so he was in the Conservative organization. In 1855 he complained to Jolliffe that the agreement that Spofforth should not communicate directly with the Whips and party leaders was not being observed,[21] and in his 1855 review of the party's position, he remarked that Spofforth was 'not available for conducting elections nor is he quite suited to the task of collecting the previous information in the boroughs and preparing the way for our Candidates'. His 'proper vocation' was to be the chief assistant to Rose in London. It was quite out of keeping with the 1853 arrangements that Spofforth should be reduced to a mere clerk, but Rose may not have been moved only by jealousy. Spofforth seems to have been somewhat heavy-handed. In a letter of 1875 Disraeli praised him for serving the party for many years with honour and industry 'if not always with perfect judgement'.[22] There was, too, another reason for hiring permanent central agents. The Corrupt Practices Act of 1854 required that a candidate's agent be formally appointed and that election expenses be declared by the agent. Solicitors would therefore probably find the business of managing elections less alluring than before. Rose had already employed one man as a temporary roving agent, and had sent him to Northampton, Montrose, Oxford and Barnstaple. He wished to employ him, and one other agent, permanently, at a salary of £400 each. He was careful to point out to Jolliffe that the role of such agents would be merely to complement, not supersede, the activities of local Conservatives.

Rose's recommendations were distributed among the Whips for discussion. Taylor and Hamilton gave them only a meagre approval. They agreed that a couple of agents should be hired to visit the most critical boroughs, but thought that a special fund of £100 would be sufficient for the purpose. They discounted the need for an election fund before a dissolution and expressed doubts about the value of such a fund even then.

> I very much doubt [Hamilton wrote] whether we did not lose more than we gained thro' the Election fund, at the last General Election. The moment a fund is raised every Candidate, or would-be Candidate, smells it, and it is like the distribution of patronage. You affront 5 for 1 you please.[23]

Whether Rose was able to persuade the party to hire full-time agents is not clear. Probably he was not. Spofforth continued to spend time visiting constituencies,[24] and Rose's correspondence with Jolliffe makes no mention of any other permanent agents based in London.

But there was really no question of discontinuing the practice of subsidising candidates in important contests. A note of Taylor's mentions Derby's 'sanction to a general Election fund',[25] and it is possible that something more than the traditional fund, raised at the time of an election and then dissolved, was intended. In 1860 Derby agreed with Jolliffe that it was 'essential to keep up a permanent supervision of all Election matters, which cannot be done without a permanent fund to rely upon'.[26] In 1856, moreover, when there was little talk of a dissolution, twelve Conservative peers subscribed £9,000,[27] far more than can be accounted for by the special subscription raised to defray the expenses of Walpole's defence against petition of the seat he won at that year's by-election at Cambridge University. That a permanent fund had been established may also be inferred from the £45 which John Yarde Buller, the member for Devonshire South, sent to Jolliffe in 1856, £25 for the

Cambridge petition and £20 for his 'former promised subscription'.[28] The £9,000 subscribed by the peers was not, of course, very much. It is true that election expenses decreased slightly in the 1850s, although not by so much as Rose's remark that the 'proper and legitimate' expenses at Reigate could not exceed £400[29] might suggest. Hard-fought elections, like Walpole's at Cambridge, in the first week of which £940 was spent on advertising alone,[30] cost far more, and county elections were rarely won for less outlay than £3,000[31] What Rose called the 'sinews of war' were insufficient to enable the party to subsidise more than a few candidates. 'I only write to assure you that we are doing all we can,' Jolliffe told Derby in the middle of the 1857 elections, 'and I believe all that can be done, unless we went to work quite regardless of expense, and with an unlimited Sum of Money to give to candidates.'[32]

Yet the party was certainly not poor. The 1859 elections produced the most concerted Conservative electoral effort of the Palmerston years. Greville noted that 'the Derbyites are making great efforts, and have collected a very large sum of money'.[33] Derby may have contributed as much as £20,000 and his donation was matched by the Duke of Northumberland, who was, over a period of twenty years, by far the most generous subscriber to the party.[34] Each cabinet minister gave at least £500.[35] 'Pat' Talbot, Derby's private secretary, who used his aristocratic connections to raise money for the party, put the amount raised independently of the cabinet at £28,000.[36] Some ambiguous lists in Rose's 1859 election notebook suggest that as much as £50,000 may have been paid out of the central fund to assist candidates in about three dozen English boroughs and three counties.[37] In addition, at least £6,000 was spent by Colonel Taylor in Ireland.[38] There was, also, money left over after the elections to help pay for petitions.[39]

If Jolliffe had, indeed, more than £50,000 to spend on the 1859 elections, it was an exceptionally large amount. Disraeli asked for £100,000 in 1868, but there is no evidence that he got it. The Liberal fund in 1868 was only £15,000 and in 1874 it dropped to £10,000.[40] The Conservatives, as Professor Vincent has remarked, were much better supported by the rich men than were the Liberals.[41] What was true of the party's central coffers may also, if the Preston by-election of 1862 was typical, have been true of money subscribed locally. At that election the Liberal candidate, George Melly, was backed by the town's principal cotton manufacturers (just then, of course, suffering from the dislocation of trade with the United States), but nevertheless lost to the Conservative, Sir Thomas Hesketh. The Liberals spent £4,000, yet were unable to compete against the £12,000 which, according to a member of the Liberal committee, the Conservatives spent on the voters alone.[42] In the mid-Victorian years the Conservative party, although its resources were meagre by later standards, was richer than its opponents and more generously supported than it had been in the days of Peel. There was more than self-congratulation to Rose's statement in 1864 that the party had never been in better shape.

> I believe there never was a time in the history of the Conservative party when it was so thoroughly organized as at present. The effect of the continous communication kept up during the last few years with our local represent- atives through the Kingdom is now being realized and we never were so well prepared for a General Election, come when it may. These effects are mainly due to the unity of management which has prevailed ever since our re- organization commenced. There has been only one recognized Head. The scattered threads have been drawn together and have been pulled from one centre and by no other system could we have accomplished what has been done.[43]

An important addition to the party's electoral machinery was the Central Conservative Society of Ireland, founded at Dublin in 1853. Ireland was thus well in advance of Scotland, where, although lip-service was paid to the idea of regional offices by the foundation of the Scottish National Constitutional Association in 1867, effective organization had to await the establishment of the National Union of Scottish Con- servative Associations in 1882.[44] Scottish Conservatism remained what it had been since 1832, a discredited creed. Ireland was different. Even in 1857, when the Conservatives lost ground in Scotland, England and Wales, they gained five seats in Ireland. The mid-century political lull did not extend to Ireland, where the activity of the priests and the tenant right party acted as a spur to the Conservatives. The new society was the Conservative response to the intense electioneering of their opponents. It used the existing network of solicitors who served as Conservative agents, but it provided them with funds and general guidance, and was able, in some places, to establish registration societies where none had previously existed.[45] In its report of January 1859 the society announced its great satisfaction with the improvements which had been effected.

> There has not been, since the formation of this Society six years ago, a revision so favourable to the Conservative party as the one recently closed . . . where Conservative Registration Societies exist, or where the Registry is attended to by competent agents, an improved registration has invariably been the result. This is not the consequence of any apathy or want of attention to their interests on the part of the Radicals or so-called Liberals. For wherever there was a prospect of improving their position, or wherever even a hope of doing so existed, their agents were at work as actively as ever. . . . Your Sub-Committee ascribe the success of the Conservative party at the Registries chiefly to the fact that a more perfect organization has been successfully established . . .
>
> Your Sub-Committee have afforded the usual assistance to the agents, and your Secretary went as a deputation, during the Revision Sessions, to Newry and Bandon, end was able to render considerable assistance to the local agents in those places.[46]

The report analysed the progress which had been made in forty-six constituencies returning seventy-four of Ireland's 105 members. In fourteen of them the Conservative share of the register had increased; in only two had it declined. The remaining constituencies were so decidedly fixed in their behaviour that registration contests could produce no change at an election. Of them, twenty-two were safe Conservative seats, seven were safe Liberal seats, and one was a seat whose representation had been shared for many years.

In England, although Rose, occasionally sent agents to the boroughs, registration remained the occupation of local solicitors, hired by candidates themselves. After each revision in October Jolliffe sent out printed forms to the local agents, asking them to return details of the claims and objections made and the revised state of the register, but there is no record of his having sent money to places where more efficient registration was wanted. It is impossible to discover the general level of local activity throughout the country except by an exhaustive study of the local press, which might reveal how many Conservative associations formed in the 1830s were still thriving and how many new ones came into being after 1846. It would not show stagnation and decline, at least not everywhere. In 1863, for example, the Buckinghamshire association was still operating in all parts of the county, as may be shown by a letter which Henry Smith, still the secretary of the borough association at Buckingham, received from William Powell, the chief agent of the county association.

> With a view to ascertain the strength of the Conservative party throughout the County, it is considered desirable that a Committee should be formed in each Agent's district and that such Committee should be divided into Sub Committees comprising one active supporter at least resident in each parish and who would be willing to canvas the Electors and return the result of such Canvass to the agent for the district, by this means the whole of the County may be canvassed within a very short time and at a small expense to the Candidate.[47]

There were also new associations, notably at Liberal-held Manchester and Leeds. The Leeds association was founded in July 1852, and began immediately to direct its attention to the state of the register and the recruiting of candidates, both for the borough and for the West Riding, reporting in one year a gain of fifty voters on the register for each constituency.[48] The Manchester association was formed in 1858. Its secretary was John Ludlow, who had been the registration agent of the party in Lancashire South since 1852. Ludlow pointed out that, although the association knew it could not return a Conservative for Manchester, it hoped to exert enough influence in the borough to promote the return of moderate Liberals.[49] Like the Leeds association, the Manchester association also served the surrounding county. A Conservative registration society was formed in each polling district of Lancashire South, collecting its own subscriptions and also contributing to the general fund in Manchester.[50]

The Manchester and Leeds associations were both formed solely on the initiative of local Conservatives. It was in the selection and provision of candidates that the central party managers, especially Jolliffe, rendered their chief service. Just as Bonham before him, Jolliffe had to tread warily for fear of giving offence to established relations in the constituencies. When Rose suggested to H. Butler-Johnstone, the sitting member for Canterbury, that a second Conservative candidate stand with him at the 1859 elections, Butler-Johnstone objected that to put up two candidates would jeopardize the return of even one Conservative (presumably because the Liberals would also put up a second man). Butler-Johnstone was in a powerful position to argue his case, since he had himself paid all the expenses of registration since 1853 and had conducted his own campaigns. 'I am', he stressed to Jolliffe, 'under no obligation either pecuniary or political to the Conservative party for my return. I have always given a consistent and uncompromising support to Lord Derby and his party, and therefore feel I have a right to ask that no one should be forced upon me in any way at the next election.'[51] Candidates continued to fear the consequences of too close an association with the central party. When William Miles' agent chose Jolliffe's son to stand at the Wells by-election of 1855, Jolliffe told Miles that his son must appear 'as representing the Conservative families of the neighbourhood, in fact the Man of the Place, and not of the Party or of the Carlton Club'.[52]

The writ of the Carlton might stop at the door of a powerful Conservative landowner. In 1856 even Lord Derby shrank from suggesting to Lord Egmont, 'who is rather touchy on such matters', that he would like Forbes Mackenzie to stand at the Midhurst by-election.[53] Still, there were many constituencies which looked to Jolliffe to help them find candidates. Some selections from Rose's 1859 election notebook give an idea of the range of knowledge which Jolliffe had at his disposal.

Abingdon

Visited in 1856 & 1857. A split in the Conservative party. Cons. Intr. neglected. Corrupt.

Communicate with Mr. Graham Esq. Sol. but not the active Agent. Acting agent. Brownley Chaloner Esq. Sol. Abingdon.

Not hopeless if well fought – alacrity of great moment – See Mr. J William's letter of 19 March.

17 March, 1859 – Mr. Wm. Graham states "a very good man may do something at Abingdon – there is no one in the neighbourhood – if such a man can be found, no time should be lost".

Note – he will have to conciliate Graham by the promise of a place for a son or nephew.

Mr. Lefroy says, I find it is admitted on all hands that without the hearty co-operation of Mr. Graham a contest would be hopeless.

28 March – Mr. Graham writes – Is Abingdon a good chance for William Napier Lord N's Brother – he is anxious to procure a seat.

29 March – Mr. Graham writes – not the slightest hope – what is wanted is a Country gentleman spending his own income amongst the electors – no such person – Can get a meeting with a few leading Conservatives.

Mr. Lefroy asks has Lord Overstone or Lord Coventry been induced to interfere with Mr. Morland or has Mr. Earle communicated with Major Lindsay. Mr. Graham writes that Mr. Theobald will not come forward & is evidently disposed for further negociations.

Berwick

Candidates. Capt. C. W. Gordon
             Ralph C. Earle
Visited in 1855. 56.
See Capt. Gordon.
Communicate with the Revd. G. Hamilton Vicar.
Legal agents. R B Weatherhead
             J Rowland doubtful
Chairman of Conservative Committee. J A Dunlop Esq.
Chairman of Freemen. Mr. James Ellison.
The Revd. G. H. Hamilton writes that Captn. Gordon places himself in his hands and that if Mr. Earle comes, he Mr. Earle must win. Gordon is safe, but second Candidate necessary – must be so introduced as to keep Rd. Hodgson off – second Candidate has an excellent opening – in arranging for second Candidate Captn. Gordon should not be put to much further expense – if Hodgson were to come as a third it would endanger the second Seat but not Gordon's. (20 march, 1859).

(See also Mr. Hamilton's letter of 22d. March). Everything is already locally arranged for your introduction (second Candidate, Mr. Earle) even the Circulars are written with blanks for the date – neither of present members are popular – Mr. Stapleton has lost caste in the Queen's Bench & Mr. Marjoribanks has offended the Conserves. There is a probability of a third ultra Radl. Candidate coming forward – an arrangement ought to be made immediately.

24th March – Wrote to Mr. J. R. Dunlop Chairman of Conservative Committee as to Mr. Earle becoming a candidate.

24th March – Wrote to Revd. Mr. Hamilton that Mr. Earle should think of Berwick only and would issue an address on his acceptance by the Constituents.

Bridgewater

Candidate. W. D. Lewis Esq.
Visited in 1856. 57. 58. Registration attended.
Communicate with Richard Smith Esq.
             John Trevor Esq. Sols
A workingman's Committee exists here who have obtained a Candidate thro' Mr. Crosse. Care must be taken not to widen the breach with Mess. Smith & Trevor.

March 21. Mr. W. D. Lewis writes he is willing to be one of the Candidates – he will not in any case go beyond £1500 – the arrangements of the party at B. appear extremely loose & do not beget confidence in their safety – if not here another place will do.

Mr. R. Smith asks for an interview on Wednesday Evening or Thursday Morning with Captn. Ives & Coll. Astell to arrange terms.

March 24/59, Mr. W. D. Lewis writes, the failure of negociation has nothing to do with the misunderstanding between the Club & the Lawyers there – it is a money question – he explained why he must issue an address – perhaps the impending death of Coll. Tynte may alter the question.

28th March – Mr. Richard Smith writes he is ready to meet the two Candidates at any time – a day's notice necessary – friends here getting impatient to have the engagement completed.

23d. March – wrote to Mr. Lewis regretting the termination there and as to doing what is possible in other quarters and inviting him to meet Committee.

25th. March – Mr. Lewis writes you need not fear I will do harm to the Cause – but I must set the Public right.

Lyme Regis

Communicate with Captn. Hussey. Fairfield. Lyme Regis.

H. Marder Esq. Surgeon.

March, 1859. Captn. Hussey states that the party is in a deserted state while Coll. Pinney's Electioneering Machinery is perfect. Should it be attempted to unseat him a *confidential* Agent should be sent down at once with full powers. Captn. Hussey's address is, Fairfield, Lyme Regis.

Plymouth

Communicate with Mr. Alderman Mennie.

18 March. Mr. Cochrane writes that a Mercantile man especially a Ship Builder or Owner would have a fair chance.

March, 1859. Mr. Alderman Mennie states "Nothing in the shape of Local Candidates" – wants men in the Shipping interest or a Director of the South Western Rlwy Coy. – He gives the followg. list of City Shipowners but knows nothing of their politics. Ascertain if any of them are Conservative and will stand. List is appended.

23 March. Mr. Spofforth writes – Aldn. Mennie strongly of opinion that with a first class Shipowner like Green & anor. man like MacKenzie of Totnes both seats may be won – that he suggests it should be ascertained if Mr. Green or other Shipowner (See List) can be got to stand & then will immediately put matters in train. He will delay his reply to Mr. MacKenzie till Saturday.

24 March/59. Should be attended to without delay as the Sitting Members have always the best chance.

29th March – Mr. Triscott writes if Lord Valletort stands his success is certain.

4 April – Mr. Triscott writes favorable opinions at Plymouth.

Rose's notebook has little to say about the counties. But wherever there was a borough without an established 'patron' or group of Conservative families to dominate its politics, it was usual for the association or agents there to work closely with the party managers in London. In 1855 the Leeds association resolved to take no step towards selecting a candidate until the party leaders had been consulted and a list of prospective candidates was sent to Jolliffe with the request that he advise them which names he found most suitable.[54] Jolliffe was likewise informed by the secretary of the Weymouth Conservative Association, formed in 1857, that at its first meeting the members had resolved 'that a deputation should be sent to the Carlton Club and the Great Western Railway and request them to name two fitting Conservatives for the representation of Weymouth and that the Clubs [of the Weymouth association] should pledge themselves to support any persons you might mention'.[55] Local managers also inquired of Jolliffe on occasion whether a member's parliamentary performance satisfied the party leaders in order to help them decide whether he ought to be retained.[56]

Rose concentrated on the boroughs because it was there that the Liberal majority might be overcome. By the mid-1860s, nevertheless, some Conservatives began to take alarm at the progress which the Liberal Registration Association was making in the counties, particularly in supervising the tangled legal negotiations necessary to get the county out-voters in the boroughs on to the register. In 1863 a group of Conservatives, headed by the Earl of Shrewsbury and Viscount Ingestre, took matters into their own hands and decided to form a Conservative society on the Liberal model. Without the assistance or sanction of Rose and Jolliffe, they launched their National Conservative Registration Association and appointed Henry Smith, for twenty years a prominent Conservative organizer in Buckinghamshire, as its secretary. The association failed to gain the approval of the official party managers. Less than a year after it had been formed, Rose complained to Derby that it was doing more harm than good. He was, no doubt, eager to keep his firm in control of the party's management, but he also made the reasonable point that the new association interfered with Colonel Taylor's authority and produced unfair accusations from the constituencies of meddling by the official party.[57]

Without the blessing of party headquarters, Shrewsbury's association was doomed. It played no part in the 1865 elections. But those elections once again failed to restore the Conservatives' county representation to the 1852 level, and a year later Colonel Taylor and his assistant, Viscount Nevill (later Lord Abergavenny), revived the abortive scheme of 1863 and established the first official Conservative national registration association. Taylor announced the formation of the new association in a circular letter dated 18 June 1866:

> At the last General Election the Conservative Party had in many instances to regret the want of an Efficient County Registration Organisation. Several seats were jeopardised and many lost on account of their being no Central Association attending to that department so very important especially to voters resident in London and its neighbourhood.

The Liberal Party have had for some years an Organisation of this description which is admitted by both Parties to have been of the greatest service to their Cause. It is proposed immediately to imitate the example of our opponents and form an Efficient Association in London appointing a Secretary whose whole and sole duty will be to give information and assistance in Registration to County Agents free of charge, to keep ledgers of all non-resident votes, and have a network of communication throughout the Kingdom properly established.[58]

The centralization of county registration was the first of a number of new departures taken in the late 1860s, including the reorganization of the party headquarters under the name of Central Office and the founding of the National Union of Conservative and Constitutional Associations. Their history belongs to the story of the Conservative party after the passing of the 1867 Reform Act, when Disraeli succeeded to the leadership of the party and, within two years, severed the Conservatives' connection with the firm of Rose and Baxter and entrusted the organization of the party to John Gorst.

The year 1867 has always held a special place in Conservative history as the year in which a Conservative government gave the country a democratic constitution and the Conservative party, in order to meet the new challenge of mass politics, gave itself the institutional foundations of a modern centralized party. The notion which Disraeli so artfully propagated after the event, that he had foreseen the harvest which the Conservatives could reap from a working-class electorate and so had deliberately set out to educate his party by espousing a radical Reform Bill, has long since been exposed for the nonsense it was. But the notion that 1867 marks a clear break in the history of the party's organization has remained, partly because the Conservatives' landslide victory at the 1874 elections appeared to give it credence, but more because so little was known of the party's organization between 1852 and 1867. Feuchtwanger, noting that Gorst had a list of constituencies in 1874 containing 'a wealth of information on local Conservative associations, clubs, registration societies, and their secretaries' and that he was 'assiduous in making local contacts', concluded that 'developments since the days of Spofforth had been swift'.[59] But that description of Gorst's work could, without alteration, be applied to the work of Jolliffe, Rose, and Spofforth before him. Gorst played a major part in the 1874 victory. But his symbolic significance has been greatly exaggerated. He was not the architect of the modern Conservative party. The foundation had been well laid by his predecessors.

Yet it is not simply ignorance of the work of Gorst's predecessors that has led historians to regard it as pre-modern. More important is the false distinction which is drawn between the so-called 'disciplined' parties of today and the 'undisciplined' parties which existed before 1867. The principal difference between party organization in the mid-nineteenth century and now is that then the influence of the central party failed to reach many constituencies, which is one way of saying that mid-Victorian voters were more interested in choosing their own representatives and somewhat less interested in choosing a government. The difference is not a mechanical one. Much silliness has been written about the power of party discipline in the twentieth century, as if party discipline were a matter of rules and punishments. Party can exercise discipline only over men's minds. However much displeasure a member may give to his leaders, he is immune from their punishment so long as his local party and, ultimately, his electorate continue to support him. Of course, a member who wishes to advance his career does well not to lose favour with his leaders, but that was as true of the nineteenth or any other century as now. Party unity is stronger now than it was a century ago because the *idea* of party has gradually seeped deeper into the political thought of the nation, because it has been more unquestioningly accepted that government works best through the party system. A constituency has come to feel that its representation is diminished if it returns an independent member to Westminster. It was not so in the mid-nineteenth century. The pull of party, although it was steadily increasing, was balanced by the pull of local independence. Even so, in the 1850s and 1860s, the central organization of the Conservative party, despite the even temper of political debate and the consequent decline in importance of national issues in the constituencies, operated as thoroughly and efficiently as it had in the days of Bonham. In a few significant ways, such as the establishment of the Dublin office in 1853 and the national registration associations in 1863, it strove to extend itself. Organization alone was unable to produce a Conservative majority. But the institution of party did not, as the textbooks would have it, rise after 1832, fall away after 1846, and advance again after 1867. It followed a path of steady growth, albeit at an uneven pace, throughout the century.

The elections of 1857, 1859 and 1865

The results of the elections of 1857 and 1859, as calculated by the Conservative party managers, are given in the tables which follow.[60] The 1865 elections, for which no Whips' tabulations have been discovered, marked a Conservative decline from the recovery of 1859, although not one so sharp as to return the party to the low-water mark of 1857. By McCalmont's unreliable classifications, the Conservatives lost eleven seats in 1865; Malmesbury put the number of losses at fifteen

Election returns, 1857

	Cons	Others	Con gains	Con losses	Net gains and losses
English counties	91	53			
boroughs	96	223			
universities	4	0			
Total	191	276	30	51	—21
Welsh counties	10	5			
boroughs	2	12			
Total	12	17	1	2	—1
Scottish counties	12	18			
boroughs	1	22			
Total	13	40	1	4	—3
Irish counties	28	36			
boroughs	14	25			
universities	2	0			
Total	44	61	9	4	5
National totals	260	394	41	61	—20

Election returns, 1859

	Cons	Others	Con gains	Con losses	Net gains and losses
English counties	99	45	11	3	8
boroughs	117	203	27	12	15
universities	4	0	0	0	0
Total	220	248	38	15	23
Welsh counties	10	5	0	0	0
boroughs	6	8	1	0	1
Total	16	13	1	0	1
Scottish counties	15	15	1	1	0
boroughs	0	23	0	0	0
Total	15	38	1	1	0
Irish counties	34	30	7	1	6
boroughs	19	20	3	2	1
universities	2	0	0	0	0
Total	55	50	10	3	7
National totals	306	348	50	19	31

seats, leaving the Conservatives at about 290 members.[61] That was about the same number as in 1852. It would have been slightly higher had the forty-four Peelites in the 1852 parliament identified by Professor Conacher returned to the Conservative fold. None of them did. Of these forty-four there were twenty-seven returned in 1857 as Peelites or Liberals, twenty-three in 1859, and eighteen in 1865. By 1865 they had shaken free of their Peelite past and were simply Liberals.

The most striking feature of the returns is that in 1857 the Conservatives suffered a net loss of twenty-three *county* seats and that their recovery in 1859 occurred principally in the smaller boroughs. Two remarks may be made about the county results. In the first place, the losses of 1857 cut most deeply into the fringe of the party. Rose gave the 'Conservatives' a gain of four in 1857, assigning to the 'Liberal-Cons or Half-government men' a loss of thirty-seven seats.[62] The curiosity, in an election dominated by Palmerston, that a larger part of those Conservatives who had voted against Palmerston on the China division were returned than of those who had voted with him, may be explained by their representing safe Conservative seats. Where the Liberal challenge was strong, Palmerston's appeal may have tipped the scales. Thus Disraeli, while he admitted that the elections left the party in 'a most delicate position', remarked that 'its essential strength has carried it thro' the late trial with marvellous fair fortune'.[63] In the second place, the county results reflect little on the central party's management. The counties were largely beyond the reach of Rose and Jolliffe. Despite the fact that the Conservative county members were the core of the party's reliable support in the division lobbies, they remained independent of central interference in their elections. The pull of Palmerston was therefore greater in the counties than it was in the boroughs, where Rose and Jolliffe worked to keep up party feeling. Most county elections continued to pass uncontested: of the sixty-eight county constituencies, forty-three went uncontested in 1857, fifty-four in 1859, and forty-four in 1865. One of the reasons for the mild Conservative recovery in 1859 was the falling-off of Liberal challenges.

In the boroughs the work of Rose and Jolliffe and the money spent on selected constituencies seems to have been rewarded. There were twenty-six boroughs which can be identified as having probably been subsidized out of the central fund in 1859.[64] In them the Conservatives gained seven members and lost only one (although one of the seven was subsequently unseated by petition); and when, in 1865, the Conservatives lost their borough gains of the previous election, Spofforth explained to Derby that half of the losses 'were unexpected and ought not to have occurred', had he not foolishly relied upon 'the assurance of the sitting Members & their principal agents that they were safe and required no interference'.[65] What formal organization might achieve in the boroughs was shown at Weymouth, where a Conservative association was formed in 1858 and where in 1859 two Conservatives were returned for the first time. Weymouth Conservatives, in addition to organizing themselves, received help from London. 'Our friends here have worked hard,' the Conservative agent told Jolliffe, 'and I must tell you that the assistance the Government have given the town in the appointment of Magistrates & other matters of the like Kind has contributed to the result.'[66]

The Conservatives also reaped some reward from their improved organization in Ireland, where the majority which they gained in 1859

bore evidence of Irish Catholic disenchantment with the Whigs, a disenchantment dating from Russell's 'Protestant aggression' in 1850 and
sustained by apprehensions that Palmerston would abet the cause of
Irish nationalism, which threatened the temporal power of the Vatican.
Since the Irish Independent party had disintegrated, some Irish Catholics
and some of their representatives in parliament, flattered by the court
which Disraeli was eager to pay them, began to look in the Conservatives'
direction.'[67] From Derby's 1858–59 government they received some minor
concessions, such as their own military and prison chaplains, and the
vague hint of a Tenant-right Bill. About fifteen non-Conservative Irish
members gave the Derby government a steady support and a majority of
Irish members voted for the 1859 Reform Bill. Cardinal Wiseman and
Archbishop McHale of Tuam called on Catholics to support Conservative candidates at the elections. Those elections yielded a Conservative majority in Ireland for the only time since 1830. It was,
however, a temporary triumph, born of assiduous electioneering and
transient political circumstances. The Conservatives exploited the Liberals'
fall from favour in Ireland, but in matters of education and land
tenure they showed no serious interest in risking the permanent support
of Irish Protestants, especially in the north, by devising a thorough plan
of reform on behalf of the Catholic population. In 1865 the gains made in
1859 were wiped out and three years later, when Gladstone took up the
Irish question in earnest, the first major English politician to do so since
Russell in the 1830s, the Conservatives fell back to their pre-1857 norm
of forty Irish seats.

The important fact of the elections, of course, was that, as in 1847 and
1852, the Conservatives failed to break the Liberal-led majority in
parliament. In the prevailing electoral conditions, when peculiarities of
place counted for so much, it may be futile to look for general
explanations of the Conservatives' failure. A bit more bribery here or a
more efficient agent there might have done the trick. Certainly there was
no great issue at stake between the parties. Yet it may be that certain
conditions, not least the absence of major issues, favoured the party
which already had a majority.[68] There was, for one thing, the rising
prosperity of the country. Britain's standard of living was the highest in
the world and improving. The spread of industrialization abroad, which
by the late 1870s was to appear as a serious threat to Britain's manufacturing supremacy, in the years between 1840 and 1865 provided an
expanding market for British capital goods. Exports in 1856 valued
£115,890,000, a figure far higher than that of any previous year.[69] Greville
noted that the year 1857 began strangely: 'After three years of expensive
war the balance-sheet exhibited such a state of wealth and prosperity as
may well make us "the envy of surrounding nations".'[70] By the end of the
1850s industrial expansion was drawing off sufficient numbers of the

rural population to allow the conditions of farm workers to improve, according to Professor Hobsbawm, dramatically.[71]

The issues of social distress and poverty which had figured so prominently in parliament's proceedings in the 1840s gave way to questions of foreign affairs. Debates about foreign affairs – the supposed imperial ambitions of Napoleon III, the Crimea and the Eastern Question, the *risorgimento* and the rule of Austria in northern Italy, the Schleswig-Holstein question – took up far more time than they had in the 1830s and 1840s. They made little impression on the constituencies, but what influence they did have rebounded to the advantage of Palmerston. The Liberals drew handsomely on Palmerston's personal popularity in 1857 as a successful war minister and the upright defender of British trading interests in China. The pacifist-inclined Manchester Radicals were defeated in large numbers and Conservative candidates were wary of separating themselves too sharply from Palmerston's government. Greville scorned the 'egregious folly' of the electorate in making Palmerston an idol, and he was provoked to see 'Conservatives endeavouring to bolster up their pretensions by saying they would have supported Palmerston on the China question, if they had been in Parliament, or promising to support him if they are elected'.[72] Part of the Conservative fondness for Palmerston in the constituencies seems to have stemmed from the distaste which many Conservatives felt for the rapprochement which Derby and Gladstone were rumoured to be effecting, especially since the Peelites had voted against Palmerston on the China motion. 'I have had very unsatisfactory letters about the elections,' Malmesbury wrote in his diary. 'The report of the coalition with the Peelites has done us irreparable mischief, but Palmerston's personal popularity is the real cause of his successes.'[73]

Even in Buckinghamshire, one of the most Conservative counties, Conservative candidates paid their respects to Palmerston. John Hall, a staunch Protestant and in former days a steadfast protectionist, told the Buckingham electors that, although he lamented the origin of the China war, 'I shall feel it my duty to give the Government of Lord Palmerston my best support in adopting such measures as may be necessary to bring it to a speedy and honorable conclusion, as I did on the recent occasion of the Crimean War'.[74] His fellow Conservative candidate, Philip Box, the chairman of the Buckinghamshire Protection Society in the 1840s, pledged himself 'to uphold that Government which maintains the honor and dignity of the Country'.[75] Neither Hall nor Box mentioned any other issue in his address. From Hampshire North an agent reported that the farmers were so 'alarmingly Palmerstonian in their ideas' that he was compelled 'to assert, in the name of the Conservatives, that Lord P. would meet certainly with forbearance at their hands, and with support, if he chooses to bid for it against the radicals'.[76] Such Conservative declarations were commonplaces at the 1857 elections. Claud Hamilton advised the party not to put up Walpole for the Speakership at the beginning of the new parliament, because 'so many new men have pledged themselves to support Palmerston and would not like on the first occasion to run counter to his wishes'.[77] Taylor and the rest of the Whips took the same view,[78] and Walpole, much put out, was not nominated. There was sense to Disraeli's comment after the 1857 elections, even if he put the argument too bluntly, that 'the people of England have not forgiven, & probably never will forgive, the shrinking from responsibility in the spring of 1855'.[79]

It is evident that the Conservative alliance with Palmerston which emerged into full light in 1860 had its roots in the constituencies. It was not a deal hatched in the corridors of Westminster. Conservative opinion found itself without a rallying cry once what Robert Lowe tendentiously called 'the artificial connection established by the Corn Laws between the Tory party and the agricultural interest'[80] had been removed. The high agricultural prices fostered by the Crimean War made it easy for the agriculturalists to accept the verdict of the 1852 elections. Thereafter, a protectionist past became, in some places, a handicap. At Ashburton what was wanted was a Conservative candidate 'whose antecedents respecting the Corn Laws should not be objectionable';[81] at Kidderminster, a leading Conservative told Jolliffe, 'it would be better, perhaps, if *it could be arranged, not* to have a candidate who has been mixed up with the questions of Protection'.[82] Reports of the apathy of the Conservative gentry were more frequent than ever in 1857 and 1859. In 1841 the Conservatives held 137 of the 159 English and Welsh county seats; in 1857 they held only 101, and in 1859 only 109. Many counties returned to the 'peace' which the Corn Law issue had broken. In 1861 Pakington explained why a Conservative meeting had resolved unanimously not to oppose the Liberal candidate, H. F. Vernon, at the Worcestershire East by-election.

> We received an authorised statement on Mr. Vernon's behalf, that when he met the Liberal Party some time since, with a view to his standing, he refused to vote for the abolition of Church Rates, or to pledge himself on any other subject, & would only express willingness to support the Ministry of Lord Palmerston. He has since married into a Conservative family (Lord Haddington's) & is surrounded by Conservative connections, so he is not likely to have become more liberal, & personally he is, by position & fortune, a most fit man. On the other hand, we have no candidate! So we thought it the wisest course to conciliate so eligible a man by not showing our teeth in vain.[83]

Religious questions did not lose their importance in the 1850s and 1860s. After a half-century of religious revival, England was publicly a more religious nation in 1855 than it had been in 1815. Public fast days, proclaimed in 1832 for the cholera outbreak, in 1847 for the Irish famine, in 1855 for the opening of the Crimean War, and in 1857 for the Indian mutiny, were gravely observed by the mass of the people.[84] When Sir Benjamin Hall started Sunday concerts by military bands in London's parks in 1856, parliament found itself involved in the Sabbatarian controversy. Palmerston welcomed the new entertainments at first, but under pressure from the agitation of the Sabbatarians, who were said to be building an organization capable of carrying elections, the cabinet gave way and the concerts stopped.[85] The Maynooth grant, too, continued to irritate Conservative backbenchers, and in 1855 Walter Long, the member for Wiltshire North, informed Jolliffe that strong feeling was again welling up on the question 'and the National Club, which includes upwards of 60 Members of Parliament, are instigating Electors not to vote for any Candidate who will not support their views'.[86] There is, however, no evidence that the fundless National Club played much part in the 1857 elections. Disraeli made Protestant noises in 1855 and Maynooth retained a subliminal influence in some Conservative sections of the country in the mid-1850s more because there was a vacuum to be filled than because anti-Catholics had a real expectation that the grant might be discontinued.[87] Derby's fastidious detachment from Spooner's annual attempts to persuade parliament to re-open the Maynooth issue helped to prevent its becoming an important element in the party battle. The Conservative leaders did not wish to imperil the electoral gains which they confidently expected to make in Ireland by exalting a stale issue which, however deeply it may have moved some Conservatives, was incapable of attracting new voters to the party. Nor, should he come into office, did Derby wish to be saddled with anti-Maynooth pledges, since, as he said, any attempt to modify the 1845 Act would have 'the usual effect of displeasing all parties and overthrowing the Government which should attempt it'.[88]

More important, politically, than Sabbatarianism or anti-Catholicism, was the Dissenters' ancient grievance against the universally levied Church rates. In the late 1850s, the Liberation Society mounted a systematic and well-financed campaign of propaganda to abolish them, yet with what electoral effect it is difficult to assess. The society had an electoral sub-committee and the *Liberator* claimed that its activities were responsible for the Liberal gains in twenty counties in 1857, but the society had scarcely any money to spend on electioneering itself and Professor Vincent has concluded that the connection between the Liberal victory of 1857 and the 'uniquely vigorous electoral campaign by the Dissenters' must remain an open question.[89] In Nonconformist Wales, fertile ground for the Liberation Society, the Conservative-held counties were not effectively challenged by the society until the mid-1860s.[90] The Liberation Society was, moreover, so much more interested in exacting abolitionist pledges from Liberal candidates than in defeating Conservatives that in 1865 it claimed success in six constituencies in which Conservatives had beaten 'negligent' Liberals.[91] Like Maynooth, the defence of Church rates was not an issue which could help the Conservatives to break through in those places, like the large towns and Scotland, where the Liberals' overwhelming superiority denied them a majority. In 1859, in an attempt to find a compromise which would prevent the issue from *costing* the party seats, Derby's government introduced a bill which, in effect, would have allowed objectors to the rate to be exempted from its payment. Although Disraeli claimed in 1861 that 'in internal politics there is only one question now, the maintenance of the Church',[92] Conservatives did not bring to the defence of the Church the zeal which had fired them in the 1830s. As Cecil remarked, sadly, in the *Quarterly Review* in 1861, 'Churchmen were passive and helpless, without leaders and without union – more occupied in discovering that one brother Churchman was Romanizing or another Calvinizing, than in taking heed of the advance of the common enemy'.[93] In the words of the *Annual Register,* the 1865 elections took place 'under circumstances of as little excitement as can perhaps ever be expected to attend the choosing by a great nation of its representative body . . . for there was no prominent question or pending controversy which the voters were called upon to decide'.[94] Church rates came to an uncontroversial end in 1868, when Gladstone, the Dissenters, and Conservative ministers cooperated on abolishing them.[95] As much as any other issue, the Church rates question revealed that organized parties had won so secure a place in national politics that they could be sustained by their traditions, even when, as in the years from 1852 to 1865, they were divided by no major disagreement on contemporary issues.

Notes and References

The party under Jolliffe

1 *Greville, Memoirs*, 20 April 1859, vii, 412–14.
2 Vincent, *Formation of the Liberal Party*, 71.
3 I. G. Jones, 'Merioneth politics in mid-nineteenth century', *Journal of the Merioneth Historical and Record Society*, 1968, 325. In Merionethshire Nonconformist tenants of the Conservative landlord, R. W. Price, who voted for the Liberal candidate in 1859 were evicted. But political evictions were as rare as Price's outspokenness in saying that, in return for helping his tenants and building comfortable houses for them, he 'expected that they would allow me one *small* favour that I asked of them' (*ibid,* 308).
4 I. G. Jones, 'Cardiganshire politics in the mid-nineteenth century. A study of the elections of 1865 and 1868', *Ceredigion,* 1964, 31.
5 Derby to R. Bateson, 5 April 1859 (copy): Derby MSS, 186/2.
6 Derby to I. W. Jacombe, 22 Oct, 1859 (copy): *ibid.*
7 A. Duncombe to Jolliffe, 25 July 1854: Hylton MSS, DD/HY/Box 24/7.
8 Derby to Viscount Doneraile, 24 Nov, 1854 (copy): Derby MSS, 183/1; Derby to Lord Jersey, 25 Nov, 1854 (copy): *ibid.*
9 Eglinton to Jolliffe, 20 March 1857: Hylton MSS, DD/HY/Box 18/8.
10 Eglinton to Derby, 27 March and 3 May 1859: Derby MSS, 148/3. Derby described Grogan to the Queen, in a letter containing a list of recommended peerages, as a man whose 'large property and local interests return not only himself but his colleagues'. (Derby to Queen Victoria, 22 March, 1859 (copy): *ibid,* 187/2). Patronage could not, of course, work miracles. Lord Seafield was raised to a peerage in 1858 in the hope that he might exert himself to return Conservatives for Banffshire at the next election (Derby to the Earl of March, 24 August, 1858 (copy): *ibid,* 185/1), but Banffshire continued its tradition of returning two Liberals unopposed. Failure to reward ambitious men could deprive the party of a candidate. There is a hint in Derby's letter to Earl Howe that that is what happened at Aylesbury in 1859. 'I am very glad to hear', Derby told Howe, ' . . . that we shall have so good a candidate to fight the battle of Aylesbury as Col. Curzon. Of course, anything that we can do to support him we will. As a Govt. I do not know that we can do anything' (Derby to Howe, 5 March 1859 (copy): *ibid,* 187/2). Curzon did not, in the event, stand.
11 Rose to Jolliffe, 12 March 1856: Hylton MSS, DD/HY/Box 24.
12 Stanley to Jolliffe, 18 Aug, 1854: *ibid,* DD/HY/Box 18/5.
13 Derby to Jolliffe, 9 Sept, 1860: *ibid,* DD/HY/Box 18/3.
14 Taylor to Jolliffe, [Aug, 1854]: *ibid,* DD/HY/Box 24.

15 The letters of Rose and Spofforth in the Hylton MSS provide ample evidence that Professor Hanham drew too sharp a distinction, when he wrote that Spofforth attended to the business of recruiting agents and Rose to that of interviewing candidates and advising constituency parties, although it is true that, as the senior partner, Rose delegated most of the routine work to Spofforth (Hanham, *Elections and Party Management* 357).

16 Derby to Richmond, 12 April 1859 (copy): Derby MSS, 186/2. Derby accepted the responsibility of keeping up to date with the state of the party's organization with a kind of begrudging good humour. 'I have received a *volume* this morning from Rose,' he wrote to Disraeli on 6 Jan, 1859, 'to which I will give immediate attention' (*ibid*, 187/1). The volume was Rose's notebook containing information about all the constituencies.

17 Derby to Bathurst, 21 April 1859 (copy), to Colville, 7 April 1859 (copy), and to Hamilton, 11 April 1859 (copy): *ibid*, 187/2.

18 Malmesbury to Derby, 7 Dec, 1856: *ibid*, 144/1.

19 Alison *Autobiography*, ii, 85.

20 Rose to Jolliffe, March 1855 (copy). The letter is in the possession of Sir Philip Rose. A transcript of it was given to me by Bernard Gill.

21 Fragment in Rose's hand, dated 1855: Hylton MSS, DD/HY/Box 24.

22 Feuchtwanger, *Disraeli and the Tory Party*, 106–7.

23 Hamilton to Jolliffe, 17 March 1855: Hylton MSS, DD/HY/Box 24/9.

24 Rose to Jolliffe, 7 July 1855: 'I prevailed on Mr. Spofforth to go down with Lord Grey de Wilton, tho' he will not interfere in the management of his Election. He will however advise him on the remit of his canvass & see that his arrangements are put upon a proper footing in case it is determined that he should perserve in going to the Poll. This is a great relief to me as Lord Wilton expressed his senses so strongly to me that his Son should not make a false step on his first start and seemed quite satisfied with the plan of sending Mr. Spofforth down to take care of him & prevent his being bested' (Hylton MSS, DD/HY/Box 24): Jolliffe to Derby, 30 Oct, 1857: 'We have a number of Candidates who would gladly spend their money at Harwich, with a good chance, and . . . Mr. Spofforth, *Mr. Rose's Lieutenant*, went down there to see what could be done, & found a local man Canvassing' (Derby MSS, 158/10). See also Spofforth's account of his 1857 election expenses in Appendix 12.

25 Taylor to Jolliffe, 27 Dec, [1855]: *ibid*, DD/HY/Box 24.

26 Derby to Jolliffe, 9 Sept, 1860: *ibid*, DD/HY/Box 18/3.

27 Hanham, 'British party finance, 1868–1880', *Bull. Inst. Hist. Res.*, May 1954, 83.

28 Buller to Jolliffe, 10 March 1856: Hylton MSS, DD/HY/Box 24/10.

29 Rose to Jolliffe, 11 Oct, 1855: *ibid*, DD/HY/Box 24. In 1853 Richard Hodgson, the member for Berwick from 1837 to 1847, said that he had spent between £2,000 and £3,000 on each of his contests, 'but that was in the palmy days of unrestricted expenditure. Less than the former amount would carry the seat' (Hodgson to Jolliffe, 8 Aug, 1853: *ibid*, DD/HY/Box 24/6). Of course, the change was neither dramatic nor uniform. 'Shrewsbury will not suit Sir John with his views and determination to spend nothing in illegal practices,' Rose wrote to Taylor in 1856. 'No one has a chance there who is careful as to cost or the mode in which his money is spent' (*ibid:*, DD/HY/Box 24).

30 Rose to Jolliffe, 26 Jan, 1856: *ibid*, DD/HY/Box 24.
31 In 1859 a Conservative agent boasted that the contest for Lancashire South, which brought two Conservative gains, cost only £5,300, whereas he knew from the Liberal agent that the Liberals had spent £8,000 (T. Bold to Jolliffe, 9 June 1859: *ibid*, DD/HY/Box 24).
32 Jolliffe to Derby, [March 1857]: Derby MSS, 158/10.
33 Greville, *Memoirs*, 15 April 1859, vii, 412.
34 He could afford to be. The House of Northumberland was one of the richest in the kingdom. In 1876 Bateman's *Great Landowners* gave the annual rental from Northumberland's 183,397 acres as £176,048, second only to the £217,163 which the Duke of Buccleuch's 460,108 acres yielded. Derby's acreage did not place him among the top dozen landowners, but the annual income of the 15th Earl was estimated in 1876 to be £163,713, which placed him third behind Buccleuch and Northumberland.
35 Malmesbury to Derby, 27 Oct, 1864: Derby MSS, 144/2a.
36 Talbot to Jolliffe, 25 and 26 April 1859: Hylton MSS, DD/HY/Box 24. Talbot was the brother of the Earl of Shrewsbury, he married Derby's daughter, Emma, in 1860.
37 See Appendix 11.
38 Taylor to Jolliffe, 25 April 1859; Rose to Jolliffe, 26 April 1859: Hylton MSS, DD/HY/Box 24.
39 In July 1859 Rose sent £500 to Maidstone, £250 to Norwich, £300 to Gloucester, and £200 to Cheltenham for petition expenses. He told Jolliffe that he was 'called upon for hundreds every day for witnesses' (Rose to Jolliffe, 29 July 1859: *ibid*, DD/HY/Box 24).
40 Hanham, *Elections and Party Management*, 372.
41 Vincent, *Formation of the Liberal Party*, 9.
42 Taylor, 'Politics in famine-stricken Preston: an examination of Liberal party management, 1861–65', *Trans. Hist. Soc. Lancashire and Cheshire*, 1955, 123–30.
43 Rose to Derby, 20 May 1864: Derby MSS, 113/R.
44 Urwin, 'The development of the Conservative party organization in Scotland until 1912', *Scottish Historical Review*, Oct, 1965, 96–7.
45 G. A. Hamilton to Derby, 26 June 1855: Derby MSS, 150/9.
46 *Central Conservative Society of Ireland. Report of the Sub-Committee*, Dublin, 1859.
47 Powell to Smith, 24 Nov, 1863: Archdeacon MSS, D/AR/6/9. Three weeks later Powell again wrote to Smith: 'I forward you a list of the Parishes within each agent's District in the County that you may know to whom to communicate in cases where a Voter has a Parish within your district and is resident in a Parish in some other district within the County' (Powell to Smith, 18 Dec, 1863: *ibid*). The tracking down of county out-voters was the most important job of registration societies.
48 Printed document, headed 'Leeds Conservative Association', undated: Hylton MSS, DD/HY/Box 24.
49 Ludlow to Jolliffe, 23 June 1858: *ibid*, DD/HY/Box 24/13.
50 Printed document, headed 'South Lancashire Registration', May 1859: *ibid*, DD/HY/Box 24.
51 Butler-Johnstone to Jolliffe, 19 March 1859: *ibid*, DD/HY/Box 24.
52 Jolliffe to Derby, 23 Oct, 1855: Derby MSS, 158/10.
53 Derby to Jolliffe, 17 Jan, 1856 (copy): *ibid*, 183/2.
54 H. Lampen to Jolliffe, 22 Feb, 1855: Hylton MSS, DD/HY/Box 24/9.

55 W. Mourproves to Jolliffe, 19 Aug, 1857: *ibid*, DD/HY/Box 18/8.

56 For example, Grantley Berkeley to Jolliffe, 6 May 1858: 'Are *you satisfied with the support* that Carden gives to our Government? I mean the member for Gloucester? In short do you wish him to retain his Seat for that City at the next Election?' (*ibid*, DD/HY/Box 18/6). A similar question, although it did not refer to a sitting member, was put to Jolliffe by the agent, John Cox, in 1854: 'I am applied to by all sections of the Conservative party. . . . My object in writing to you now is . . . to ascertain whether Mr. B. Moore will be acceptable as a candidate at Maldon to Conservative Party at Headquarters. If I have a letter from you in the affirmative, as I expect, I shall go immediately to Maldon' (Cox to Jolliffe, 17 June 1854: *ibid*, DD/HY/Box 24/7).

57 Rose to Derby, 20 May 1864: Derby MSS, 113/R.

58 The copy of the circular sent to Derby is in the Derby MSS, 112/T.

59 Feuchtwanger, *Disraeli and the Tory Party*, 122.

The elections of 1857, 1859 and 1865

60 The 1857 figures are taken from a fragment in Jolliffe's hand, headed 'General Election Returns 1857' (*ibid*, DD/HY/Box 24/11); the 1859 figures are taken from a printed circular, signed by Rose's assistant, Edmonstone Hendrick, headed 'General Election, 1859' (*ibid*, DD/HY/Box 24). The discrepancies between the 1857 returns and the 1859 totals of gains and losses arise from changes at by-elections and from the difficulty in classifying some self-styled Liberal Conservatives, with strong Palmerstonian leanings, as Derbyites or other.

61 Malmesbury, *Memoirs*, ii, 339–40. The *Annual Register* also gave the Conservatives 290 members, although, from a different classification of the dissolved parliament, it calculated that they had lost twenty-four seats (*Annual Register*, 1865, 159).

62 Fragment in Rose's hand headed 'House of Commons, Saturday 21st March, 1857': Hylton MSS, DD/HY/Box 24/11.

63 Disraeli to Jolliffe, 29 April [1857]: *ibid*, DD/HY/c/2165.

64 See Appendix II.

65 Spofforth to Derby, 2 Aug, 1865: Derby MSS, 113/S.

66 W. Thompson to Jolliffe, 30 April 1859: Hylton MSS, DD/HY/Box 24.

67 The best treatment of this subject is Hoppen, 'Tories, Catholics, and the general election of 1859', *Hist. J.*, xiii 1. 1970, 48–67.

68 Philip Rose might have disagreed. 'I am happy to say that I have very good news of the Registration thus far,' he wrote to Jolliffe on 30 Sept, 1856. 'It is not so much that parties are influenced by strong political feeling as they are sick & tired of their present members and are anxious for a change' (Hylton MSS, DD/HY/Box 24).

69 Northcote, *Twenty Years of Financial Policy*, 296.

70 Greville, *Memoirs*, 9 Jan, 1837, vii, 254–6.

71 Hobsbawm, *Industry and Empire*, 88–97.

72 Greville, *Memoirs*, 28 March 1857, vii, 279–80.

73 Malmesbury, *Memoirs*, ii, 64. On 6 March, just before the elections began, Malmesbury recorded the following entry: 'Dr. Fergusson called. He says the China question is an unfavourable one for our party . . . also that a coalition with the Peelites is denounced. I fear he is right, for nobody is a better judge of public feeling than a doctor who is constantly seeing all kinds of people'

(*ibid*, ii, 63–4). In December 1855 a Conservative wrote to Jolliffe of public feeling in Oxfordshire: 'I take for granted that the rumour about Dizzy and Gladstone was a Weak invention of the Enemy otherwise there will be a precious smash in our Party' (S. North to Jolliffe, 7 Dec, 1855: Hylton MSS, DD/HY/Box 24/9).

74 Election address, 17 March 1857: Archdeacon MSS, D/AR/6/19.

75 Election address, 21 March 1857: *ibid*.

76 G. Sclater to Jolliffe, 6 April 1857: Hylton MSS, DD/HY/Box 18/5.

77 Hamilton to Jolliffe, 23 April 1857: *ibid*.

78 Taylor to Jolliffe, undated: *ibid*, DD/HY/Box 18/8.

79 Disraeli to Jolliffe, 29 April [1857]. *ibid*, DD/HY/c/2165.

80 *Edinburgh Review*, April 1857, 574.

81 S. Triscott to Jolliffe, 22 Nov, 1855: Hylton MSS, DD/HY/Box 24/9.

82 J. M. Chellingworth to Jolliffe, 14 March 1855: *ibid*.

83 Pakington to Derby, 18 Nov, 1861: Derby MSS, 141/10a

84 Anderson, "The reaction of Church and Dissent towards the Crimean War", *J. Eccles. Hist.*, Oct, 1965, 209–20. Mrs. Anderson argues that the doctrine of an active Providence was more widespread in 1855 than it had been at the beginning of the century and quotes the Evangelical *Record's* rebuke of Palmerston for being 'behind the age' in attributing the cholera to human filth, not divine retribution. 'He forgets that fifty years have elapsed since he sat at the feet of the *Edinburgh Review*, and laughed at the doctrine of Providence, as fit only for Methodists and missionaries' (215).

85 Greville, *Memoirs*, 14 May 1856, vii, 227–9.

86 Long to Jolliffe, 12 March 1855: Hylton MSS, DD/HY/Box 24/9.

87 'I am much obliged to you', J. M. Sumner wrote to Jolliffe, 'for informing me that you have presented the petition forwarded from Petersfield against the Maynooth grant. I believe that the feelings of the country are very strong upon the subject, although I fear that there is little likelihood that they will influence the House in their decision' (Sumner to Jolliffe, 5 May 1855; *ibid*, DD/HY/Box 24/9).

88 Derby to H. Lambert, 5 Jan, 1856 (copy): Derby MSS, 183/2.

89 Vincent, *Formation of the Liberal Party*, 73.

90 See the articles by I. G. Jones listed in the bibliography.

91 Thompson, 'The Liberation Society, 1844–68', in Hollis, *Pressure From Without*, 223.

92 Disraeli to Malmesbury, 22 Feb, 1861: Malmesbury, *Memoirs*, ii, 247.

93 'Church-rates', *Quarterly Review*, Oct, 1861, 549.

94 *Annual Register*, 1865, 153.

95 See Anderson's excellent delineation of this dénouement to a long-standing quarrel, 'Gladstone's abolition of compulsory Church rates: a minor political myth and its historiographical career', *J. Eccles. Hist.*, April 1974, 185–98.

Chapter 17

1867: The end of an era

The Conservatives and reform before 1867

The Liberal triumph at the elections of July 1865 left Lord Derby content to continue in a supporting role in politics. 'Our game must be purely defensive,' he wrote to Disraeli in the last week of July, 'and we must be ready to support the moderate portion of the Cabinet, and watch for every opportunity of widening the breach between them and the Rads.'[1] In the last session of the 1859 parliament Conservative backbenchers had shown signs of impatience with their leaders' 'timid political creed',[2] but Derby believed that the only practical policy was to endeavour to keep a disappointed party together in order 'to avail ourselves of any contigency which may arise, or any serious breach in our opponents' ranks in the event of Palmerston's death, however little we may expect it even then'.[3] Two months later Palmerston was dead. 'The truce of parties is over,' Disraeli exulted. 'I foresee tempestuous times, and great vicissitudes in public life.'[4] Disraeli was right. Palmerston's death opened the way to one of the most remarkable reversals in modern English politics. Within two years his successors, the Liberal ministry of Lord John Russell, had been ousted from office for attempting to effect a moderate, 'safe' extension of the franchise, and a Conservative government, led for the third time by Lord Derby, had guided through parliament a radical Reform Bill, a Bill which was, as the *Edinburgh Review* described it, 'more democratic in its character than any of those which it was the creed of the Tory party to denounce, and containing within it every element of fancied danger which has warmed their rhetoric and inspired their political action for the last thirty years'.[5] In 1867 male household suffrage came to Great Britain. 'Really,' wrote Alfred Russell Wallace, the co-founder of the theory of natural selection, 'what with the Tories passing Radical Reform Bills and the Church periodicals advocating Darwinism, the millenium must be at hand.'[6]

The final shape of the 1867 Reform Act owed little to the Conservatives' political assumptions and much to their calculations of party advantage. That the Conservatives should have been responsible for the Act was largely accidental. It owed nothing to latent Conservative impulses; it was not the fruit of a slow-maturing sentiment in the party that radical reform had become a necessity. Radical reform created a new political world in which the Conservative party had afterwards to act; but it was not the testament to what Conservatives had learned from the past. For the historian of the party of Derby, there are two questions about it which matter: how did the Conservative party come, as a body, to give its assent to such a Bill and to what extent did the Act bear a Conservative imprint? The party did not, it is true, give its assent quite as a body. Three cabinet ministers resigned. Yet in comparison with the storms which accompanied the emancipation of the Catholics and the repeal of the Corn Laws, those resignations were but a murmur. Somewhat surprisingly, at least on the surface of things, the Conservative party survived the year 1867 intact.

From the day in 1848 when Lord John Russell abandoned the official Whig position that the 1832 Reform Act had provided a final settlement of the parliamentary franchise and thereby reintroduced the question of parliamentary reform to cabinet discussions, the Conservative leaders had been careful not to occupy the old Tory ground of inflexible resistance to it. Despite the failure of the Radicals to generate a sustained public demand for reform, both Liberals and Conservatives came to profess their readiness, although not their enthusiasm, for a moderate measure of reform, one which, while falling short of manhood or household suffrage, should extend the franchise to a section of the working class. Liberal governments introduced Reform Bills in 1854 and 1860; Derby's government introduced one in 1859. The country received the defeat, or abandonment, of those Bills with indifference. None of them went very far in the direction of democracy. The Liberals adopted as their standard a £6 franchise in the towns; the Conservative Bill of 1859 left the borough franchise at £10.

The Conservative view of reform in the 1850s and 1860s rested on the assumption that the electorate would continue to behave in the future as it had behaved in the past, that the Liberals' strength would continue to lie in the towns and the Dissenting chapels, the Conservatives' in the shires and the Anglican churches. That division of the electoral spoils had produced a Conservative minority at five successive elections between 1847 and 1865. Yet Derby and Disraeli did not seek a fundamental alteration of the system; rather, they sought to amend the system in order to make it work to the Conservatives' advantage. As soon as the 1857 elections were over, Disraeli asked Derby to consider 'whether a juster apportionment of M.P.s may not be the question on wh. a powerful & enduring party may be established' and suggested that the Conservatives should begin a fresh discussion of parliamentary reform.[7] Disraeli had two changes in mind: to add fifty members to the county representation by reducing the smallest two-member boroughs to one seat and to increase the influence of the land in county elections by transferring the votes of £10 householders in the counties to the boroughs. 'Consider', he wrote, 'whether a reform in such a spirit wd. not be extremely beneficial to the Conservative party, as the present arrangement, wh. leaves the balance of power in small Boro's, wh. are ruled by cliques of Dissenters, seems fatal to the maintenance of the present aristocratic & ecclesiastical institutions.' Derby ignored Disraeli's suggestion. In his view, the Conservative cause was better upheld by supporting Palmerston against the Radicals than by tampering with the electoral system. But Disraeli's scheme contained the premise which underlay the Conservative attitude to reform down to 1867: that the distinction between the counties and the boroughs should be not only maintained, but sharpened. As Disraeli put it in 1853, Conservatives 'drew a distinction between measures for purifying, & for reforming, parliament'. They were resolved to maintain without further compromise 'the aristocratic principle in our constitution as the keystone of the arch'.[8] Disraeli was not looking for ways of making more voters vote Conservative. He was looking for ways of making the votes of Conservative voters count for more.

The Conservative Reform Bill of 1859 betrayed the same strategy. To justify the Conservatives' taking the initiative in reform at all, Derby explained to the Queen that, although the Conservatives were not responsible for the revival of the reform controversy, they could not ignore the precedent of two Bills having been laid on the table in 1852 and 1854, nor could they disregard Palmerston's promise that a Liberal government would introduce another when it regained office.[9] Derby and Disraeli had decided that the Conservatives' best hope of becoming the majority party and remaining in office lay in spiking their opponents' guns by settling the reform question themselves. The 1859 Bill had four main provisions: it maintained the borough franchise at £10 and lowered the county franchise to that level; by a number of 'fancy franchises' it extended the vote laterally to the possessors of £60 savings or £10 annual income from the funds and to university graduates; it disfranchised fifteen small boroughs, giving eight of the seats thus released to the counties; and it transferred the votes of urban freeholders from the counties to the boroughs. So mild a Bill, and one displaying so marked a Conservative bias, necessarily attracted the opposition of the Liberal and Radical majority in the Commons, where it was defeated by 330 votes to 291.

The most striking aspect of the Bill was the abandonment of the distinction between the borough and county franchises, a break with the Conservative past sufficient to provoke the resignation of two senior cabinet ministers, Spencer Walpole and Joseph Henley. In 1854, when the Liberals were about to bring forward their reform measures, Derby's opinion had been that '*the* thing to be resisted is the assimilation of the

County and Borough Franchises, by swamping the County Constituency with Ten Pounders',[10] and at that time, too, Disraeli told Stanley that what he most dreaded was the blow which equalisation would deal to the territorial influence. It would let in the principle of equal electoral districts and provide no resting-point for reform to stop short of the absolute sovereignty of the people.[11] Sir James Graham, writing in 1857, called the distinction between the two franchises 'the touchstone of adherence to the Derby party'.[12] But when, in 1859, Walpole contended that it was essential for the maintenance of the aristocratic element in the constitution to uphold the distinction between votes conferred upon property (the county franchise) and votes conferred upon residence (the borough franchise), Derby answered that the principle had been abandoned when the tenants-at-will had been admitted to the county lists in 1832. He also argued that to equalize the franchises was to give to the settlement an appearance of finality which would enable the whole constituency to unite against further reform.[13]

The argument transcended constitutional niceties. John Bright had frequently declared that reform would be useless unless it produced a change in the country's fiscal system, by which he meant an acceleration of the gradual process by which indirect taxation was being replaced by direct taxation. Walpole was concerned not to give to 'temporary & fluctuating occupations a preponderating Influence over Property & Intelligence', because it was that section of the community which was 'almost exempt from direct taxation, and therefore interested in forcing their Representatives to fix that taxation permanently on others'.[14] The quarrel between free traders and protectionists was over, but the spirit which had infused it lived on to animate political debate. In 1860, when Gladstone proposed to abolish the paper duty and add an extra penny to the income tax, Lord Robert Cecil, writing in the *Quarterly Review,* took up Walpole's theme.

> Inasmuch as all classes alike pay indirect taxation, while only those who do not receive weekly wages pay the income-tax, this change is a direct and simple transfer of taxes from one class of the community to another. . . . This question of the incidence of taxation is in truth the vital question of modern politics. It is the field upon which the contending classes of this generation will do battle. . . . The struggle between the English constitution on the one hand, and the democratic forces that are labouring to subvert it on the other, is now, in reality . . . a struggle between those who have, to keep what they have got, and those who have not, to get it.[15]

Cecil's objection to the 1859 Reform Bill was that it moved the Conservative party towards the side of the have-nots. The leaders of the party could scarcely publish views so blatantly self-interested; nor, after the experience of the previous twenty-five years, were they willing to make indirect taxation the touchstone of Conservatism. It was impossible, moreover once Locke King's motion to assimilate the county and borough franchises had been passed against the government by a large majority in 1858, to frame a Bill acceptable to the Commons which did not incorporate that recorded judgment of the House.[16] There was, at any rate, to console Conservatives, some reason to believe that the £10 county occupiers were a more Conservative group than their betters. Malmesbury's inquiries in Dorset villages satisfied him on that point, and even George Bentinck, who attempted to lead a backbench revolt against any Conservative Reform Bill, believed that £10 was as safe as any higher limit.[17] As the Conservative agent in Cambridgeshire explained it, the £10 occupiers were 'tradesmen all under the thumb of the Agriculturalists in Parishes who are mostly Conservatives', whereas the £20 occupier,was 'an *independent man* not to be biassed, and caring not for the Farmer, the Squire or my Lord'.[18] When, therefore, the cabinet, which had originally wished to place a £20 limit on the county franchise, adopted instead the borough qualification, it was in the hope that the change would strengthen the Conservatives in the counties. They were not offering a sop to the urban electorate.

The 1859 Reform Bill gave no hint that the Conservatives wished to break out of their minority status by wooing the townsfolk. Rather they sought to widen the gulf between the Liberal boroughs and the Conservative counties, to shore up their position in the counties by removing the votes of borough freeholders from the county to the borough registers in order to expunge an urban element from the rural electorate. Conservative agents had pressed the necessity of such a clause upon Disraeli and Derby as a counterweight against the admission to the vote of the £10 occupiers. Derby believed that the urban freeholders of Southampton gave Hampshire South to the Liberals, and that Brighton did the same for Sussex, the metropolitan boroughs for Middlesex, Southwark and Lambeth for Surrey East, and Manchester for Lancashire South.[19] The returns from the English counties at the 1865 elections showed him to be right.[20]

Urban freeholders and county voting in England, 1865

	% of urban freeholders	Average %	Number of seats	Conservative % of seats won
I	53–32	39%	28	46%
II	29–17	23%	25	68%
III	16–0	6%	91	71%

Transferring the votes of the urban freeholders was, Derby believed, the only way to enlist the support of the bulk of the county members on the Conservative backbenches for reform.[21] There was a more obvious, more direct, way of exploiting the county bias of Conservatism. That was to increase the number of county seats. There was a logical case for re-

distribution on a large scale. In 1866 the counties, with a population of
11½ million, returned 162 members; the boroughs, with a population of
8½ million, returned 334 members. There was, that is, only one county
member for every 70,000 inhabitants, but one borough member for every
26,000.[22] Disraeli had on several occasions in the 1850s seemed eager to
propose a redistribution in favour of the counties,[23] but the 1859 Bill
produced only eight new county seats. That was because redistribution
had several serious drawbacks. The imbalance in the representation may
have hurt the Conservatives, although many of the borough members sat
for small towns whose electorate was more rural and agricultural in its
outlook and habits than industrial and urban. To alter it might hurt the
party even more. For one thing, the imbalance was most unfairly
weighted against the industrial county divisions, like Kent West, Durham
North and Glamorgan, not against their neighbouring farming divisions,
Sussex West, Westmorland, and Radnorshire.[24] Redistribution on an
arithmetic rule would bring only a small increase of members to the
agriculture county divisions, certainly not enough to persuade the
Conservatives to adopt the democratic principle of 'one man, one vote'.
Representation by population would also entail a massive increase in the
number of seats allotted to the sixteen largest cities in the country and to
Ireland and Scotland.[25] So long as the Conservative strategy was limited to
bolstering their preponderance in the English counties, to increase the
county representation by an argument from numbers was therefore
impossible. It would merely open the way to the destruction of the small
boroughs in favour of the Liberal strongholds of Ireland, Scotland and the
industrial towns.

The 1859 Bill did so little to reform real abuses in the existing system,
while attempting to squeeze the utmost Conservative advantage from it,
that it excited only a feeble protest from the Conservative backbenches.
On 16 March, Beresford, Newdegate, and Bentinck – senior backbenchers
of the type who today serve on the 1922 committee – held a meeting of
about forty members in an attempt to put pressure on the government to
drop the Bill.[26] But after Disraeli had introduced it a full meeting was
held at Derby's house, at which everyone declared his readiness to
support the Bill as a necessity.[27] Only a handful of Conservatives failed to
vote for the second reading. Despite the conservative character of the
Bill, its introduction set a precedent. It showed that that a Conservative
government was prepared to take up reform and that the party was
willing to support it in an attempt to dish the Liberals. It was that
precedent which Lord Robert Cecil, in an article on the Liberals' 1860
Bill, found to be the lamentable and irrevocable contribution of the
1858–59 government to English politics.

The aversion to Reform, common to both Conservatives and Whigs, has been
paralysed and struck dumb by this fatal precedent. It was impossible, when

the Conservatives had proposed a ten-pound county franchise, for the Whigs to refuse to go as far. When the Conservatives had consented to begin the disfranchisement of the boroughs, it was no longer open for Lord John Russell to do as he had done in 1852, and omit the schedules altogether. . . . It has been no longer possible to resist the 1860 Bill on the second reading on the ground that Reform is needless, for the necessity of Reform has been admitted. . . . It is no longer easy to struggle against the ten-pound franchise in the counties, for the ten-pound franchise has been admitted. There remains nothing to which we have not committed ourselves, except the lowered franchise in the boroughs.[28]

The Conservative surrender

Cecil's last citadel, the £10 household franchise in the boroughs, fell at the hands of Conservative assailants in 1867. And just as there was nothing in the Conservative past, so there was nothing in the circumstances attending the Conservatives' return to office in 1866, to foretell the event. Disraeli said that the radical Reform Act of 1867 was passed 'to destroy the present agitation and extinguish Gladstone and Co'.[29] Historians have usually taken Disraeli's cue and ascribed the Conservatives' willingness to take what Derby frankly confessed to be a 'leap in the dark'[30] to their desire, after twenty-five years of shallows and miseries, to dish the Liberals at any price or to the fears implanted in them by the swelling of the public demand for reform, expressed especially in the misnamed Hyde Park 'riots' of July 1866. Disraeli also claimed, after the event, that he had intended to educate his party, and one scholar has recently argued that the Reform Act represented a deliberate attempt to build a Tory democracy from an alliance of the Conservative landed interest and the working class.[31]

Both the argument that the Conservatives were coerced by extra-parliamentary agitation and the argument that they were moved by a vision of a Tory-democratic future are difficult to sustain. Neither argument can answer the facts, that the cabinet was slow to convince itself of the necessity of taking up reform at all and that, when it did so, it produced for the consideration of parliament a distinctly moderate Bill designed to exclude the working class from effective political power. It was, no doubt, impossible, as the cabinet came to see, to set aside the precedent of 1859 and ignore the popular protest which followed the defeat of the Liberal government's 1866 Bill and remain in office. Derby admitted as much in his first ministerial speech, in July 1866, when he announced that nothing would give him 'greater pleasure than to see a very considerable portion of the class now excluded admitted to the franchise'.[32] But acknowledging the force of public opinion and succumbing to threat are different things. A broken park railing and a trampled bed of tulips were not the stuff to frighten a government into radical reform.[33] The agitation of the Reform League was a help to the Conservative leaders, not a threat. It lent credence to the plea of necessity and substance to the party manoeuvring inside parliament.

The feeling that the working classes were rootedly conservative had been some time growing. Greville remarked upon it in 1858.

> Among the events of last week one of the most interesting was the Queen's visit to Birmingham, where she was received by the whole of that enormous population with an enthusiasm which is said to have exceeded all that was ever displayed in her former receptions at Manchester or elsewhere. It is impossible not to regard such manifestations as both significant and important. They evince a disposition in those masses of the population in which, if anywhere, the seeds of Radicalism are supposed to lurk, most favourable to the Conservative cause, by which I mean not to this or that party, but to the Monarchy and the Constitution. . . . This great fact lends some force to the notion entertained by many political thinkers, that there is more danger in conferring political power on the middle classes than in extending it far beneath them, and in point of fact that there is so little to be apprehended from the extension of the suffrage, that universal suffrage itself would be innocuous.[34]

Ever since 1832 the few working-class voters, mostly freemen, whom the first Reform Act had not disfranchised had shown a marked Conservative inclination. Their behaviour at five Newcastle elections may serve as an example.[35]

Votes of freemen and £10 householders at Newcastle elections, 1832–59

		Con	Lib	Rad
1832	Freemen	39	42	19
	£10	30	44	26
1836	Freemen	69	31	–
	£10	37	63	–
1837	Freemen	65	30	5
	£10	31	65	4
1859 by-election	Freemen	49	51	–
	£10	27	73	–
1859	Freemen	47	43	10
	£10	46	47	7

Newcastle was not exceptional. John Cox, the Conservative agent in Essex, wrote to Jolliffe in the 1850s that 'the great Majority of the Freemen about the town of Maldon are Conservative, and as they are many of them labouring men it is essential that they should be put on the register'.[36] Professor Vincent's study of the pollbooks at sixty-one borough elections revealed a distinct Conservative preference among working-class voters. At forty-one of those elections there were more workers' votes for the leading Conservative than for the leading Liberal.[37] Since the freemen were notoriously corruptible, those figures might simply indicate Conservative skill at bribery. In addition, the Conservative share of the labourers' vote declined during the period between the two Reform Acts.[38] Still, some Conservatives, like Stanley, who worked in the 1850s to give Conservatism a more liberal face, were impressed by the potential Conservative loyalties of the working class. Stanley's visit to Bury in 1853 persuaded him that the mill-workers 'seemed to have (except in Church matters) many Conservative tendencies, but are kept aloof by the mingled timidity and pride of the country gentlemen'. The discovery fixed in Stanley the purpose of 'shaping my political course so as not to lose their support'.[39]

Stanley's views, however, were eccentric. The liberal attitudes which he adopted in the 1850s – he was one of the first Conservative converts to the abolition of Church rates – made him the object of suspicion among his party colleagues. The notion that the winning of household suffrage was the outcome of the Conservatives' conscious bid to erect a Tory-democratic majority against the Liberals is fanciful. It does not fit the facts. After twenty-five Liberals joined with the Conservatives to defeat Edward Baines's motion for reform in the spring of 1865, Disraeli recommended that Derby make use of his confidential connections with the great Whig families to prepare the ground for the formation of 'an anti-revolutionary party on a broad basis'.[40] Such a realignment of parties might have followed logically from the years of cooperation between Derby and Palmerston. But a year later, Derby's invitation to the leaders of the Adullamites, the forty-odd Liberals who had combined with the opposition to overthrow Russell's government by defeating its Reform Bill, to join his government was turned down. Derby was unwilling to yield the premiership to his son, Stanley, or to sacrifice Disraeli to make way for a Liberal leader in the House of Commons, since those changes must necessarily have given the Conservative party a liberal facelift. For their part, the Whigs and the Liberal anti-reformers were not prepared to lose their identity in the Conservative party.[41] Fusion awaited the Irish Home Rule crisis of 1885–86. Derby and Disraeli kept their places.

In the end, the failure to achieve a Whig-Conservative coalition advanced the cause of radical reform. It raised to office once more a minority Conservative government susceptible to putting places above principles. But the failure did not immediately turn the government's mind to the necessity of a Conservative Reform Bill. In August Disraeli clutched at the straw of Admiralty maladministration as an issue which had 'struck deep into the public mind' and which, if taken up earnestly, would divert the country's interest from parliamentary reform.[42] As late as mid-September, when Derby, mindful of the enthusiastic receptions then being given to John Bright's reform tour, wrote to Disraeli that he was coming 'reluctantly to the conclusion that we shall have to deal with the question of Reform',[43] Disraeli replied that 'observation and reflection have not yet brought me to yr conclusion'.[44] Nor can it be said that the Conservatives, however reluctantly they came to reform, embraced it wholeheartedly when they did. The Bill which they finally presented to parliament adopted the strikingly democratic slogan of rated household suffrage. Gladstone's 1866 Bill had deliberately stopped short of making the working classes the majority of the electorate by placing a £7 rental limit on the franchise. The Conservatives removed the limit and went beyond even John Bright's demand for a £6 rated franchise. (In fact, between Bright's franchise and the Conservatives' there was little to choose, since there were few houses rated below £6.) But the omission of a lodger franchise, the provision for dual votes to the propertied, and the qualifications attached to the householder's vote itself – personal payment of rates and two-year residence – made the Bill less sweeping even than Gladstone's. Personal payment of rates, required of the £10 householders under the 1832 Act, was the crucial safeguard, because a majority of householders preferred to compound with their landlords to pay the rate for them. What the Conservatives wished to do in 1867 was to give the working classes the vote with one hand and take it away with the other.

Dr Himmelfarb, who puts the argument for Tory democracy, has discovered in a supposed difference between Liberal utilitarian doctrine and Conservative anti-philosophical historicism the explanation of the Conservatives' radicalism. In her view, the Liberals, believing as they did in a society composed of rational individuals seeking their self-interest, were preoccupied with numbers. They presumed that each individual exercised 'the maximum amount of power available to him so as to achieve the maximum satisfaction of his interests'. It followed that reform, by enfranchising a class of voters with interests distinct from the interests of those classes already in possession of political power, was capable of producing a fundamental alteration of the social order. Liberals had therefore to calculate their numbers with great care.[45] Conservatives, on the other hand, who believed 'that the social hierarchy was independent of ephemeral arrangements, that national character was more important than particular laws', could blandly conduct bold political experiments and 'take liberties with the constitution'.[46] In sharp contrast to the Liberal enumerators, then, the Conservatives could eschew calculations and adopt the cavalier attitude of 'in for a penny, in for a pound'. It may at once be said again that the Conservatives did not betray such adventurous spirits in the Bill which they presented to parliament.

Dr Himmelfarb's argument rests on the evidence, not of the Conservative party as a whole, but of Disraeli. Disraeli, indeed, carried throughout his career a murky romantic conception of a national community in which the workers and the aristocracy should be united against the radical representatives of the mercantile and industrial sections of the community. It was rhetoric to sting the Liberals. But whatever moved Disraeli (and in the autumn of 1866 romantic notions of national Tory democracy did not move him at all), there is no reason to suppose that it also moved the Conservative backbenchers or his cabinet colleagues. It is not true that the Conservatives were careless of numbers. Lord Malmesbury, in despair at the way in which the government's Bill was being transformed by a series of radical amendments in the Commons, complained that 'the Conservative members seem disposed to adopt anything and to think that it is "in for a penny, in for a pound" '.[47] Dr Himmelfarb takes literally Malmesbury's metaphor. But the Conservative leaders were as well and as regularly supplied with statistics as their opponents. It was one of the rewards of the party's reorganization in the 1850s that during the decade before 1867 Rose and Baxter had the means of collecting a mass of electoral information from all parts of the country. Derby pored over the returns which they sent to him concerning the probable consequences of various schemes of reform. As Rose remarked after a three-hour interview with Derby on the subject of reform in 1859, 'no one ought to venture to talk to Lord Derby who does not thoroughly understand his subject'.[48] It was because they had studied the figures that Derby and Disraeli hedged household suffrage round with safeguards. And it was the same careful scrutiny which persuaded three cabinet ministers, Lord Cranborne (previously Cecil), Lord Carnarvon and General Peel, to resign, safeguards or no safeguards, rather than support the government's Bill.

> Household suffrage [Carnarvon wrote to the Duke of Richmond] will produce a state of things in many boroughs the results of which I defy any one to predict. In Leeds for example the present number of electors are about 8500. With household suffrage they will become about 35,000. Is there any one who dares to say what will be the character & tendency of that constituency. It may be good or bad: but it is a revolution.[49]

The 1867 Reform Act did not spring from hidden sources of Tory democracy in the Conservative party. It mattered, nevertheless, that by 1867 the Conservatives were no longer frightened by the phrase 'household suffrage'. Gladstone's Bill had put the franchise at £7 rental precisely because any lower limit would make the working-class voters a majority of the electorate. The Conservative leaders shared Gladstone's fears. After the 1867 Bill had been introduced in the Commons, Disraeli wrote to Derby that he would take the line in debate that, although the government wished to be guided by the opinion of the House, it regarded personal rating and adequate residence as fundamental principles: 'all we desire is to secure a general representation without preponderance of class'.[50] But Derby needed to frame a Bill different from Gladstone's. He needed to justify the defeat of the Liberal government's moderate Bill. The answer lay in the slogan 'household suffrage'.

It might have been expected that the three resigning ministers should become the leaders of a powerful anti-reform group of the party. It did not happen. The force of the resignations was blunted by Derby's good fortune in persuading the heads of two of the most distinguished Tory families, the Duke of Marlborough and the Duke of Richmond, to fill the vacant places along with Henry Corry. Carnarvon told Richmond, ten days after his resignation, that he did not wish 'to make mischief or even to give way to the bitterness which I can hardly help feeling'.[51] The materials for a rearguard action seem not to have existed. By the time Cranborne and his fellow discontents resigned, in the first week of March, there was a strikingly common resolve among Conservative backbenchers that they ought to seize the chance to settle the reform issue with a comprehensive Bill based on safeguarded household suffrage. In the last week of February the cabinet decided to plump for a Bill based on £6 rating in the boroughs and £20 rating in the counties in order to keep the cabinet united. But by that time the pressure from the backbenches for household suffrage was becoming powerful. On 25 February, the day on which Cranborne, Carnarvon and Peel gave their £6 ultimatum to the cabinet, a group of Conservatives, after discussing the matter at the Carlton, sent a deputation to Disraeli to inform him that household suffrage must be the basis of the Bill. When Disraeli replied that the cabinet had resolved to stick at £6, he was told by Samuel Greaves, the member for Liverpool, that 'the feeling was so strong it would find vent in some embarrassing way'.[52] On the same day Disraeli learned that the Conservative member for Cheltenham, Charles Schreiber, had given notice of a question for the next night, the object of which was to demonstrate that a rated franchise, with personal payment of the rate, was quite conservative enough without further checks. 'All I hear and observe', Disraeli wrote to Derby, 'more and more convinces me that the bold line is the safer one, & moreover, that it will be successful.'[53]

Disraeli had now decided that, rather than 'die in a ditch', the government should let the dissentient cabinet ministers go. He informed Derby that a meeting of backbenchers was being got up at the Carlton to sign a memorial to Cranborne, Peel, and Carnarvon 'to show them that they have completely misapprehended the feeling & spirit of the party'.[54] The meeting, attended by about 150 members of parliament, was held on 28 February. No resolutions were passed, but there was 'a general disposition evinced in favour of rated residential household suffrage' and 'an anxious desire expressed that we should fix upon the franchise we thought best and then stick to it, declining to carry our opponents' measures'.[55] The meeting made it clear that what the Conservatives on the back benches wanted was a successful Conservative Bill to beat Gladstone and also to provide a barrier against manhood suffrage and democracy. Their prescription was household suffrage protected by personal payment of rates. The backbenchers were not yet leaping in the dark. They had done their homework, as James Emerson Tennent, a leading light in the Irish organization of the party, pointed out in a memorandum to Derby's secretary, 'Pat' Talbot.

> Edw. Ellice MP regards Household Suffrage, even without dual voting, as a Conservative measure – & illustrates it by the cases of Coventry, where a franchise equivalent to it already exists. Nothing but his late Father's personal influence kept Coventry for the liberals – & on his death it returns & will return 2 Conservatives.
>
> Mr Moncrieff late Lord Advocate of Scotland concurs with Mr Ellice & tells me that of the Scotch Boroughs there are Six which he knows, in which the Whig MP is certain to lose his seat; & of these two within his own knowledge will return two Conservatives, instead of the present liberals.
>
> The Rural districts surrounding Boroughs is very likely to provide Conservative electors under teritorial influence.
>
> In Belfast, a careful return has already been made of the numbers which Household Suffrage will add to the present constituency. It amounts to 1600; & after apportioning this according to individual politics, 300 will be added to the existing Conservative majority.[56]

'The convergence of the views of Ministers and backbenchers on household suffrage', F. B. Smith has written, 'unified the party. The squires had at least a policy to fight for and a leader who seemed sympathetic to their views and competent for all emergencies.'[57] By working with the backbenchers to press household suffrage on the cabinet, Disraeli had gained, in a measure which he had not previously enjoyed, their confidence. That confidence gave Disraeli his calm strength, his unruffled authority, in the parliamentary debates which followed. In 1829 and 1846 the opponents of Catholic emancipation and free trade were moved by antipathy to their leaders and by passions beyond the adulterating influence of political manoeuvring. They opposed the changes root and branch. In 1867 Cranborne had no root-and-branchers to call upon. Having got the party to support the introduction of its Bill, the government had surmounted its major hurdle. Thereafter all other considerations yielded to the party's determination to settle reform themselves and beat Gladstone and company. In the next two months a series of radical amendments, stripping household suffrage of all the safeguards surrounding it, were passed by the House of Commons with scarcely a murmur from the Conservative back benches. The government opposed the reduction of the residence qualification from two years to one, but when it was beaten by eighty-one votes, Disraeli simply announced that the government accepted the change.

The other two principal amendments – the admission of lodgers to the franchise and the abolition of the distinction between personal and compounding rate payment – were accepted without a division.

Hodgkinson's amendment, which abolished compounding, destroyed the government's original Bill. It added at least 500,000 and perhaps as many as a million householders to the electorate.[58] Yet Disraeli told the House that the amendment was not contrary to the principles of the Conservatives' Bill. On the contrary, it would 'enforce the policy which we recommend, give strength to the principles which we have been impressing upon the House'.[59] Disraeli was trapped. He had paraded personal payment as the test of a man's fitness to exercise the franchise, a mark of civic consciousness and personal responsibility. His real motive was to keep the majority of householders, who were compounders, off the electoral rolls. Hodgkinson neatly ruined the Conservatives' ploy by proposing, not that compounders be enfranchised, but that compounding be abolished. Every ratepayer was made to meet Disraeli's test.

It was the measure of members' weariness of the subject of reform, of their feeling that some Bill or other must be passed that session, and also of their ignorance of the vexedly intricate question of rates, that Hodgkinson's amendment was casually incorporated in the Bill. Robert Lowe explained further that, once the hare of household suffrage had been started, members feared to stop its course lest they offend their future constituents.[60] Whatever happened to the Conservatives' Bill, no one doubted any longer that they *were* future constituents. As Dudley Baxter pointed out in a memorandum for Lord Derby in March, even if the Conservatives succeeded in retaining the essential safeguards of personal payment and two-year residence, they could not long maintain them against the hostility of Gladstone and the Radicals.[61] By resisting the radical amendments, the Conservatives would not be holding back democracy. They might save their souls, but they would eventually be outbid by Bright and Gladstone. That, Cranborne argued, was the decisive consideration.

> From the moment that a household suffrage was promised from the Conservative Treasury Bench it became certain that a Reform Bill and a strong Reform Bill would be passed. The hopes of deriving any advantage from further rsistance were consequently much weakened; while the danger of quarrelling with the new constituency, whose advent to power was assured, grew into alarming proportions. Many thought the position hopeless, and submitted in silence to a disaster which seemed inevitable.[62]

If the disaster of democracy could not be avoided, after all, there was another disaster which might: handing over to Gladstone power and the credit for having brought democracy to pass. Derby frankly owned to the House of Lords that his ruling passion had been to smash the Liberals.

> My Lords, I have upon former occasions, unfortunately, occupied the position of a Minister on sufferance . . . and upon both occasions I have failed

. . . I did not intend for a third time to be made a mere stop-gap until it should suit the convenience of the Liberal party to forget their dissensions, and bring forward a measure which should oust us from office and replace them there; and I determined that I would take such a course as would convert, if possible, an existing majority into a practical minority.[63]

Yet the 1867 Reform Act was not entirely a surrender to radical demands. By keeping reform in its own hands, the Conservative government kept control of the redistribution of seats and the redrawing of constituency boundaries. It was thus that, having yielded to Radicalism in the boroughs, the Conservatives were able to get their way in the counties. They also got their way in Scotland. The Redistribution Bill gave twenty-five new seats to the counties, nineteen to the boroughs (only four to the industrial cities of the north and two to the metropolis), and one to London University. The boundary commissioners carried out their instructions to bring within the borough constituencies those built-up areas surrounding them which otherwise would have constituted an urban element in the county electorates. In addition, by setting the county occupation franchise at £12 (a compromise between the Bill's original £15 limit and Locke King's attempt to make it £10), the Act preserved the exclusive character of the county electorate. In England at the 1868 elections, the ratio of electors to population in the boroughs was one to eight; in the counties it was one to fifteen. In Scotland the difference was even more marked. The borough ratio there was one to nine, the county one to twenty-seven.[64] Scotland received only seven new seats, and three of those went to the counties, two to the universities.

So, in the end, the Act upheld one fundamental Conservative principle: the necessity of maintaining the distinction between the borough and county electorates. Had the Conservatives correctly divined the future, they might not have cared much for the principle. In 1884, agricultural labourers were admitted to the franchise. Equalization of the borough and county franchises was at last brought to pass. And as the century ran its course the assumption that the national pattern of voting would remain unchanged was disproved. The Liberals made dramatic inroads into the counties, and the Conservatives found unexpected strength in the cities. The Conservatives succeeded in giving to reform in 1867 a distinctive Conservative stamp, but they did so in ways that showed that they were inspired, not by a vision of the future, but by their interpretation of the past.

The end of an era

Throughout the parliamentary session of 1867 Lord Derby had been in more or less constant pain, for the most part unable to attend the House of Lords. In February 1868 he at last succumbed to the ravages of the gout and retired. The premiership and the leadership of the Conservative party passed to Disraeli. The change came at an appropriate time. Derby's long tenure of the Conservative leadership had been distinguished by his habitual, one might almost say temperamental, disposition to put principles above place. Disraeli, on the other hand, was conspicuously susceptible to bartering for office, and there were many observers who saw that the new age of party politics would be more suited to men of his stamp than to men like Derby. It is a truism to remark that the 1867 Reform Act ushered in the age of mass politics, and that parties were therefore compelled to develop mass organizations. But it was as much the manner of the act's passing as what it contained that worried men like the Earl of Northumberland. 'Lord Derby and Disraeli . . . have let in the mob upon us,' he wrote to Jolliffe, now Lord Hylton, 'and will, of course, give way whenever they find themselves hard pressed.'[65] Leaders, Cranborne concluded, must henceforth be followers:

> As the wind blows, so will they point. Any minister who takes it as his first principle that he will not be 'ousted', renounces all pretensions to independence. He becomes the slave of the majority of the House of Commons. He is a leader in no other sense but that in which the first horse in a team is called a leader: he is the first to be driven.[66]

In 1829 Wellington bowed to necessity. In 1846 Peel responded to the dictates of rational conviction. In 1867 Disraeli paid service to ambition. No one drew the moral more pointedly than Robert Lowe, speaking in the final debate on the Reform Bill.

> We have inaugurated a new era in English politics this session, and depend upon it, the new fashion will henceforth be the rule and not the exception. This session we have not had what we before possessed – a party of attack and a party of resistance. We have instead two parties of competition who, like Cleon and the Suasage-seller of Aristophanes, are both bidding for the support of Demos.[67]

The winning of household suffrage was part of the process, no doubt already well advanced, by which society came to resolve its conflicts more and more by political action, less by judicial. It was no accident that the Industrial Revolution and democratic institutions made their progress side by side. A society whose relationships are static, or at least which believes that they are static, is relatively uninterested in politics. It regulates its behaviour by judicial process. But a society which is constantly changing, and which expects and seeks to change, needs constantly to remake its rules by a political process. So Peel, taking note of the changes in the structure of the national economy, sought in 1846 to abolish what he considered to be an outdated and obstructive economic rule. Those Conservatives who clung to a static view of society opposed him.

In the last quarter of the nineteenth century the Conservative party gradually changed its character. It became the party of capital, the representative of a progressive element in society. The change was marked by the increasing numbers of merchants and industrialists in the parliamentary party.[68] It was also marked by the sections of society which began for the first time to give it their support. The railway interest, for example, was predominantly Liberal down to 1868; thereafter it shifted its allegiance to the Conservative party.[69] The change was reflected in its leaders, no longer, by the twentieth century, a Bentinck, a Derby or a Salisbury, but a Canadian iron-merchant, Bonar Law, and two Midland industrialists, Baldwin and Neville Chamberlain. Before 1867 the party was the representative of the land. Peel was opposed by two-thirds of his party, because they expected the party to be a genuinely conservative party, the party of resistance. The protectionist inheritors of the Conservative party represented a narrow class, but they did not look upon politics as the arena of class conflict. They defended the wealth of the agricultural class because they wished to perpetuate a closed society. They wished to preserve the traditional institutions of society. Landed estates were not so much commercial ventures for the making of profits as trusts to be passed on intact from generation to generation. To men who looked upon the land in that way it was no answer to their protectionism to encourage scientific methods of farming and the breaking-up of encumbered estates by modifications in the law of primogeniture or entail. The land was not simply a form of capital; it was the basis of social stability, the natural environment of traditional values. Landed society was a world ruled by gentlemen, who expected politics to be a gentlemen's pursuit. As late as the 1860s, even the Liberal party remained 'the expression of personal rivalries and political differences within the aristocracy broadly defined'.[70] It was Peel's ungentlemanly conduct in 1846 that Mr Thorne, in *Barchester Towers,* was unable to forgive.

> In politics, Mr. Thorne was an unflinching conservative. . . . When that terrible crisis of free trade had arrived, when the repeal of the corn laws was carried by those very men whom Mr. Thorne had hitherto regarded as the only possible saviours of his country, he was for a time paralysed . . . now all trust of human faith must for ever be at an end. Not only must ruin come, but it must come through the apostasy of those who had been regarded as the truest of true believers. Politics in England, as a pursuit for gentlemen, must be at an end.[71]

Peel's behaviour in 1846 was apologetic. In 1867 Disraeli was aggressive. Under his leadership the Conservatives did what for the previous twenty-five years Derby had scorned to do: they competed in the open market-place. They were thus, however consciously, adjusting themselves to an age which was opening up the civil service to competitive examination and the minds of men to the action of a popular press. It was not bad luck that the Conservatives had remained a minority party under Lord Derby. For a generation they had looked on their function as being purely defensive. That was an attitude which sometimes led them into the unnecessary defence of institutions of no essential Conservative bearing. The admission of a few Jews to parliament, for example, offered no threat to the Established Church. Jewish emancipation was opposed, not because of itself, but because the Church and its parliamentary bulwark felt themselves, in mid-Victorian England, to be under siege. It was also an attitude which condemned them to opposition.

Professor Vincent has argued that mid-Victorian parties 'simply did not know, quantitively and analytically, why they and not the other side were in power' and that they were therefore unable and did not try 'to relate policy to the structure of their majorities'.[72] That may be true of the Liberal party, which was a far more heterogeneous group than the Conservatives and contained within itself a far wider spectrum of opinion. Derby's difficulty in the 1850s and 1860s was not his ignorance of where his support lay. He knew perfectly well, for example, that Disraeli's flirtations with the Irish Radicals would founder on the anti-Catholic antipathies of the Conservative electors. His difficulty lay in finding a way to expand the party's base without alienating its bedrock supporters in the English counties. He took command of the party in circumstances that made it his first priority to see that the party did not fall apart. He led, after all, the largest single party in the House of Commons. It was the effect of the mid-Victorian electoral system, pernicious for the long-term progress of the party after 1846, that the counties and small boroughs always returned a large enough Conservative bloc to Westminster for the party to avoid looking elsewhere for new support. Had the party, after 1846, been reduced to the dire condition in which it had found itself in 1832, it might have been forced to reappraise itself and make a fresh start. As it was, to have made a bid for the votes of the towns, especially of the Dissenters on issues like Church rates or education, was to risk forfeiting the allegiance of its natural supporters and weakening the most powerful instrument of resistance in the state. The boroughs were Liberal, not simply because the shopkeepers and the Dissenters were uninterested in the Conservatives, but also because the Conservatives were uninterested in them. It was not the business of a genuinely conservative party to suggest new programmes to lure new voters.

The party's defensive preoccupations condemned it to opposition. But at least they also made the opposition benches seem comfortable. Derby was noticeably untempted by office because Conservative principles, as he saw them, might be as well, or better, served in opposition. Once the Conservative party had become the party of capital and private enterprise and had inherited the mid-Victorian Liberals' cry of freedom, it was able to seek power in the knowledge that there were victories to be won. In its defensive stage, the party was justly suspicious of bidding for office. In office, its greatest 'victories' – 1829, 1846, and 1867 – were necessarily defeats.

Notes and References

The Conservatives and reform before 1867

1 Derby to Disraeli, 24 July 1865: Hughenden MSS, 14 Derby.
2 J. Whiteside to Derby, 6 June 1865: Derby MSS, 154/6a James Whiteside, member for Dublin University, was an Assistant Whip and a leading organizer of the party in Ireland.
3 Derby to Disraeli, 12 Aug, 1865: Hughendon MSS, 14 Derby.
4 Monypenny and Buckle, *Disraeli*, iv, 424.
5 *Edinburgh Review*, Oct, 1868 539.
6 Himmelfarb, *Darwin and the Darwinian Revolution*, 307.
7 Disraeli to Derby, 21 April 1857: Derby MSS, 145/3.
8 Disraeli to Derby, 13 Dec, 1853: *ibid.*
9 Derby to Queen Victoria, [7 Dec,] 1858 (copy): *ibid*, 186/1.
10 Derby to Jolliffe, 6 Jan, 1854: Hylton MSS, DD/HY/Box 18/1.
11 Stanley MSS, Diary, 22 Dec, 1853.
12 Graham to Mounsey. 6 March 1857: Parker, *Graham*, ii, 303–4.
13 Derby to Queen Victoria, 18 Feb, 1859 (copy): Derby MSS, 186/2.
14 Walpole to Derby, 27 Jan, 1859: *ibid*, 153/3.
15 *Quarterly Review*, April 1860, 523.
16 Derby to C. D. Griffiths, 2 March 1859 (copy): Derby MSS, 187/2. Griffith was the Conservative member for Devizes.
17 Malmesbury to Derby, 26 Dec, 1858: *ibid*, 144/2; Disraeli to Derby, 1 Jan, 1859: *ibid*, 145/6.
18 F. B. Smith, *The making of the second Reform Bill*, 40–1.
19 Derby to Queen Victoria, 18 Feb, 1859 (copy): Derby MSS, 186/2.
20 This table is taken from Nossiter, 'Elections' (unpublished thesis), 428.
21 Derby to J. B. Stanhope, 13 March 1859 (copy): Derby MSS, 187/2.
22 Seymour, *Electoral Reform*, 320n.
23 See, for examples, Disraeli to Derby, 13 Dec, 1853, and 21 April,1857: Derby MSS, 145/3.
24 The ratio of members to inhabitants in the industrial counties were as follows: Kent West, 1 to 138,000; Durham North, 1 to 84,000; Glamorgan, 1 to 71,000. The farming divisions were much nearer the national mean: Sussex West, 1 to 26,000; Westmorland, 1 to 24,000; Radnor, 1 to 18,000 (Seymour, *Electoral Reform*, 323n).
25 The sixteen largest towns were Birmingham, Bristol, Finsbury, Greenwich, Lambeth, Leeds, Liverpool, London, Manchester, Marylebone, Salford, Sheffield, Southwark, Tower Hamlets, Westminster, and Wolverhampton. Their population was half that of the total population of the parliamentary

boroughs, but they sent only thirty-three of England's 323 borough members to Westminster (Mackay, *Electoral Districts;* pamphlet 1848).

26 Disraeli to Derby, 23 Feb, 1859: Derby MSS, 145/6; Northbrook, *Baring Journals and Correspondence,* ii, 107.
27 Colchester, *Memoranda of My Life,* 317.
28 *Quarterly Review,* April 1860, 550–1.

The Conservative surrender
29 Wright, *Democracy and Reform, 1815–1885,* 74.
30 This famous phrase was first used by Philip Rose, in a letter to Lord Derby, to describe the moderate Liberal Reform Bill of 1860: ' I shall at once prepare our leading Correspondents in the Country, whose standing and intelligence are such as to do justice to our cause, to be ready to give evidence to a Lords committee on the franchise. . . . We shall be able completely to smash the government's returns & shew what a reckless leap in the dark they have taken in their bill' (Rose to Derby, 2 April 1860: Derby MSS, 113/R).
31 Himmelfarb, 'The politics of democracy: the English Reform Act of 1867', *Brit. Stud.,* May 1966, 97–138.
32 9 July 1866, *Hansard,* 3rd series, clxxxiv, 726–44.
33 The most forthright interpretation of the decisive effect of public agitation on parliament is Harrison, 'The tenth April of Spencer Walpole: the problem of revolution in relation to reform, 1865–67', in his *Before the Socialists,* 78–136.
34 Greville.
35 This table is taken from Nossiter, 'Elections', 150.
36 Cox to Jolliffe, 14 July [185–]: Hylton MSS, DD/HY/Box 18/8.
37 Vincent, *Pollbooks,* 17, 58–60.
38 Professor Vincent's table (*Pollbooks,* 58–60) shows that in the eight towns where enough elections are included to make comparisons possible, the Conservative share of the working-class vote had fallen considerably from the level of the 1830s by the 1850s and 1860s.
39 Stanley MSS, Diary, 22 Nov, 1853 (1855 note).
40 Disraeli to Derby, 6 Aug, 1865: Derby MSS, 146/2.
41 For detailed treatment of this subject, see Cowling, 'Disraeli, Derby and fusion, October 1865 to July 1866', *Hist,* viii 1, 1965, 31–71, and Winter, 'The Cave of Adullam and parliamentary reform', *EHR,* Jan, 1966, 38–55.
42 Disraeli to Derby, 20 Aug, 1866: Derby MSS, 146/2.
43 Smith, *Second Reform Bill,* 134.
44 Disraeli to Derby, 24 Sept, 1866: Derby MSS, 146/2.
45 Himmelfarb, 'Politics of Democracy', 116.
46 *ibid,* 111.
47 Malmesbury, *Memoirs,* ii, 369–70.
48 Monypenny and Buckle, *Disraeli,* iv, 182.
49 Carnarvon to Richmond, 11 March 1867: Goodwood MSS.
50 Disraeli to Derby, 24 March 1867: Derby MSS, 146/3.
51 Carnarvon to Richmond, 11 March 1867: Goodwood MSS.
52 Smith, *Second Reform Bill,* 158–9.
53 Disraeli to Derby, 25 Feb, 1867: Derby MSS, 146/3.
54 Disraeli to Derby, 26 Feb, 1867: *ibid.*
55 Lord J. Manners to Malmesbury, 28 Feb, 1867: Malmesbury, *Memoirs,* ii, 367–8.

56 Tennent memorandum, sent to Lord Derby by Col. Talbot, 23 March 1867: Derby MSS, 52/7.
57 Smith, *Second Reform Bill*, 164.
58 *Ibid*, 202–4.
59 17 May 1867, *Hansard*, 3rd series, clxxxvii, 723.
60 20 May 1867, *ibid*, 735.
61 Baxter memorandum on the loss of the dual vote, 22 March 1867: Derby MSS, 52/7.
62 *Quarterly Review*, Oct, 1867, 541.
63 Quoted *ibid*, 547.
64 Smith, *Second Reform Bill*, 239.

The end of an era
65 Northumberland to Hylton, 4 Nov, 1868: Hylton MSS, DD/HY/c/2165.
66 *Quarterly Review*, Oct, 1867, 549.
67 Quoted in Himmelfarb, 'Politics of democracy', 137.
68 Thomas, *The House of Commons, 1832–1901*, 14–15, 158.
69 Alderman, *The Railway Interest*, 1973.
70 Vincent, *Formation of the Liberal Party*, xxxiii.
71 Trollope, *Barchester Towers*, chapter XXII.
72 Vincent, *Formation of the Liberal Party*, 50.

Appendix 1

A = Aye   N = no   a = absent   – = no longer in the House of Commons.

Sources. The party classification of those Ultras in the 1833 parliament is based on the classifications given in Dod, *Electoral Facts*, McCalmont, *The Parliamentary Poll Book*, and Buckingham, *The Parliamentary Review and Family Magazine*. Those members about whose status all three sources agree are given as C (Conservative) or L (Liberal). Those members about whom the sources disagree are given as d (doubtful).

Appendices

Appendix 1 The behaviour of the Ultras, 1830–1833

Planta's moderate Ultras	Parnell's motion	Reform Bill, 22 March 1831	Party, 1833
J. J. Buxton	N	N	–
H. Burton	a	A	L
R. Bateson	A	N	C
W. Bankes	a	N	C
T. T. Drake	a	N	–
W. T. Drake	a	N	–
T. Estcourt	a	N	C
W. O. Gore	N	N	–
R. Handcock	a	N	–
T. Jones	a	N	C
Viscount Ingestre	a	N	C
E. Kerrison	A	N	C
J. D. King	a	N	–
G. Keek	A	A	–
G. Lennox	A	A	L
A. Lefroy	A	N	–
T. Lefroy	A	N	C
T. Legh	A	a	–
N. Malcolm	A	N	–
Lord Mandeville	A	N	C
P. Miles	a	N	–
W. Miles	a	N	–
Lord Newark	A	A	d
S. G. Price	N	N	–
W. Patten	A	A	C
J. Pollen	N	N	–
L. Palk	N	N	–
G. Rose	N	N	–
Captain Rose	a	N	–
G. Rochefort	A	N	–
H. Sumner	A	N	–
T. A. Smith	a	N	C
E. T. Shirley	N	N	–
Lord Tullamore	A	N	C
R. Vaughan	a	N	C
H. Willoughby	A	a	d
Captain Wemyss	a	A	d

Planta's moderate Ultras	Parnell's motion	Reform Bill, 22 March 1831	Party, 1833
General Archdall	a	N	C
L. Buck	A	A	–
W. Duncombe	A	N	C
A. Duncombe	A	N	–
Q. Dick	A	N	C
Lord Encombe	A	N	–
General Gascoyne	a	N	–
R. Gresley	N	N	–
W. Heathcote	A	N	–
R. Inglis	a	N	C
Lord Kenyon	A	N	–
H. King	A	A	–
E. Knatchbull	A	N	C
H. Maxwell	A	N	C
General O'Neill	a	A	–
N. W. Peach	a	N	–
M. T. Sadler	A	N	–
Lord Stormont	A	N	C
C. W. Sibthorp	A	N	–
A. Trevor	N	–	–
B. Vyvyan	A	N	C
Lord Uxbridge	a	A	–
C. Wetherell	a	N	–

Appendix 2   Conservative gains inside the House of Commons, 1832–1837

Reformers who were Conservatives by the elections of 1832

J. E. Baillie (Bristol)
R. Bethell (Yorkshire E)
Sir John Owen (Pembrokeshire)
Hugh Owen Owen (Pembroke District)
R. Palmer (Berkshire)

J. W. Patten (Lancashire N)
Viscount Sandon (Liverpool)
Colonel Wood (Brecknockshire)
C. W. W. Wynn (Montgomeryshire)
W. W. Wynn (Denbighshire)

Reformers who became Conservatives, 1833–37
(*a*) The twenty from Dod's *Electoral Facts*

Lord George Bentinck (King's Lynn)
Sir Francis Burdett (Wiltshire N)
J. C. Colquhon (Kilmarnock District)
Alderman Copeland (Stoke)
W. Feilden (Blackburn)
S. Glynne (Flintshire)
R. Godson (Kidderminster)
Sir J. Graham (Cumberland E)
G. Granville Harcourt (Oxfordshire)
W. Hughes Hughes (Oxford)

J. V. B Johnstone (Scarborough)
W. Long (Wiltshire N)[1]
R. Lopes (Westbury)
J. Pemberton Plumptre (Kent E)
T. Sheppard (Frome)
G. Sinclair (Caithness-shire)
S. Spry (Bodmin)
Lord Stanley (Lancashire N)
G. Harcourt Vernon (Retford)
R. Williams (Dorchester)

(*b*) The additional eleven

W. Bingham Baring (Staffordshire N)[2]
C. Burrell (Shoreham)[3]
Lord A. Chichester (Belfast)
J. Davenport (Stoke)[4]
C. S. Forster (Walsall)[5]
J. J. H. Johnstone (Dumfriesshire)

J. Hodgson (Newcastle-upon-Tyne)
General O'Neill (Antrim)
C. Russell (Reading)[6]
J. E. Tennent (Belfast)[7]
R. Weyland (Oxfordshire)

1. The *Spectator* included Long among its sixteen doubtfuls returned at the 1837 elections, but really was in no doubt. 'Our contemporaries are quarrelling about Mr. Walter Long; but we never can consent to reckon among the Liberals a man who not only avows that he owes his return to the Tories and was deserted by the Reformers, but that he deems it an honour to be the colleague of Sir Francis Burdett – that most offensive specimen of a political traitor' (*Spectator*, 19 Aug, 1837). Burdett had become a Conservative after representing Westminster for a number of years as an extreme Radical with a national reputation.
2. Baring voted for the repeal of the Test Acts, for Catholic emancipation, and for the Reform Bill. His Whig opponent at the 1837 elections chastised him for standing as a Conservative, since he had been 'a disciple of Lord Grey's school'. Baring had moved over to the Conservatives on the issue of Church reform. (Kent, 'Party politics in Staffordshire', unpublished thesis, 4.)
3. In 1836 the *Assembled Commons*, which was wary of too readily marking a reformer's change of colours, called Burrell a Conservative. The *Parliamentary Touchstone* of 1838 agreed and gave an example of Burrell's opinions from his election speech of 29 July 1837: 'The present Government did not advocate the moderate and safe principles of Lord Grey, whom he had supported. He would continue to act on the same principles he had always advocated – the great principles of the Constitution.'
4. In the 1833 parliament Davenport voted for Hume's motion into public distress, for the repeal of the Corn Laws, and for shorter parliaments. But after 1835 he was 'An exemplary follower of Sir Robert Peel' (Wedgwood, *Staffordshire Parliamentary History*, 83.)
5. Forster was elected as a liberal reformer in 1832 and had a liberal voting record in 1833–34. But in 1834 he announced that 'the present ministry's alliances are alarming' and at the elections of 1835 he drew heavily on Conservative support. By 1836 the *Staffordshire Advertiser* was paying tribute to his stand against Radicalism and calling him one of the mainstays of the Conservative cause at Walsall (Kent, 'Party Politics in Staffordshire', ch. 5). In 1836 the *Assembled Commons* called him a Conservative.
6. Russell was a West India proprietor and chairman of the Great Western Railway who was returned as a reformer in 1831 and 1832. But in 1832 he received considerable support from Conservative elements in Shoreham and was welcomed by the Tory *Berkshire Chronicle* as a Conservative. By 1835 he was clearly a Conservative and provoked a Radical candidature against him at that year's elections (Gash, *Politics in the Age of Peel*, 283–6).
7. Dod's *Pocket Paliamentary Companion* for 1835 says of Tennent: 'In 1832 he was elected as a Reformer; opposed to the repeal of the Union, in favour of free-trade, the abolition of all monopolies, the reduction of the duty on advertisements, and an efficient reform in the Church; favourable to the principle of the ballot. In 1835 he was returned as a Conservative.' The ballot, free trade, and the removal of 'taxes on knowledge' were favourite radical demands. Tennent, from Dod's statement of his opinions, apparently left the reformers on Irish and Church issues.

Appendix 3   Stanley's list of members of the Derby Dilly, 23 February 1835

	Vote on Russell's Irish Church, motion, 3 April,1835	Party classification by Fremantle's lists, 1839–40
Sir A. Agnew (Wigtonshire)	N	–
D. Barclay (Sunderland)	a	–
Lord George Bentinck (King's Lynn)	N	C
Sir R. Bulkeley (Anglesea)	N	–
E. Buller (Staffordshire N)	A	W
S. Canning (King's Lynn)	N	C
Alderman Copeland (Coleraine)	A	C
P. C. H. Durham (Devizes)	N	–
J. M. Fector (Dover)	N	C
Sir Robert Ferguson (Londonderry)	N	W
P. H. Fleetwood (Preston)	N	W
C. S. Forster (Walsall)	N	C
Sir J. Graham (Cumberland E)	N	C
J. Hardy (Bradford)	N	–
R. Ingham (South Shields)	a	C
J. J. H. Johnstone (Dumfriesshire)	N	C
J. V. B. Johnstone (Scarborough)	N	C
J. J. Knox (Dungannon)	a	C
Sir R. Lopes (Westbury)	N	C
Thomas Marsland (Stockport)	N	C
J. Martin (Sligo)	N	W
Sir O. Moseley (Staffordshire N)	N	–
Colonel Jones Parry (Caernarvon District)	N	–
G. R. Pechell (Brighton)	A	W
M. Phillips (Manchester)	A	W
J. Pemberton Plumptre (Kent E)	N	C
G. R. Robinson (Worcester)	A	–
Sir E. Dolman Scott (Lichfield)	a	–
T. Sheppard (Frome)	N	C
J. E. Tennent (Belfast)	N	C
W. Turner (Blackburn)	a	W
Sir Harry Verney (Buckingham)	a	W
R. Walker (Bury)	A	W
R. Weyland (Oxfordshire)	N	C
Henry Wilson (Suffolk W)	a	–
G. F. Young (Tynemouth)	a	C
Lord Stanley (Lancashire N)	N	C
[one illegible]		

A=aye   N=no   a=absent   –=no longer in the House of Commons.

Knox gave up his seat in June 1838, and therefore does not appear in Fremantle's lists of 1839 and 1840. The *Spectator* included him among the Conservatives elected in 1837 and Fremantle did not quarrel with that classification in his corrected copy of the *Spectator's* list.

Appendix 4

Members of the Derby Dilly, not included in Appendix 2, who became Conservatives, 1835–41 (with the date of their first election to the reformed parliament)

S. Canning (King's Lynn) 1835
J. M. Fector (Dover) 1835
J. Hardy (Bradford) 1832[1]
H. Gally Knight (Nottinghamshire N)
    1835[2]
J. J. Knox (Dungannon) 1832
T. Marsland (Stockport) 1832
G. F. Young (Tynemouth) 1832

Non-Conservatives who voted for Manners Sutton, not included in Appendix 2, who Became Conservatives, 1835–41
Sir George Crewe (Derbyshire S) 1835
J. Cripps (Cirencester) 1835
T. G. Greene (Lancaster) 1832
J. Halse (St Ives) 1832[3]
R. Ingham (South Shields) 1832
Sir G. Noel (Rutlandshire) 1832[4]
W. Rickford (Aylesbury) 1832
Alderman Thompson (Sunderland) 1833
J. E. Vivian (Truro) 1835
Sir E. Wilmot (Warwickshire N) 1832

1. Hardy stood for Bradford, with E. C. Lister, as a reformer in 1832. Both were elected. In 1835 Bradford Radicals, disappointed by Hardy's conservative voting record, nominated another Radical to stand with Lister. The Conservatives then adopted Hardy as their candidate and he topped the poll on the cry of 'the Church in danger'. He was defeated in 1837 and therefore does not appear in Fremantle's lists. In 1841 he was re-elected as a Conservative. (See Wright, 'A Radical borough: parliamentary politics in Bradford, 1832–41', *Northern History*, 1969, 138–41).
2. Gally Knight was a prominent adherent of Stanley and a member of the Dilly. He does not appear in Stanley's list because he did not enter the House of Commons until a by-election in March. In 1835 he stood 'on the grounds of absolute independence of party', in 1837 as a Conservative (see Gally Knight to Peel, 19 Aug, 1837: Peel MSS, Add. MSS 40424, ff. 87–8).
3, 4 Halse died in May 1838 and does not appear in Fremantle's lists of 1839–40. But Fremantle included him as a Conservative in his corrected copy of the *Spectator*'s list of returns at the 1837 elections. Noel died in March 1838 and is included for the same reason.

Appendix 5 Fremantle's analysis of divisions, House of Commons, 1838–1840

(Fremantle MSS, 80/1)

		Molesworth's motion, 6 March 1838	Eliot's motion (Spain), 27 March 1838	Irish tithes, 14 May 1838	Irish corporations, 11 May 1838	Lords' amendment, Irish corporations, 2 Aug. 1838	Address, 5 Feb, 1839	Russell's motion of confidence, 19 April 1839	Speakership, 27 May 1839	Jamaica Bill, 19 June 1839	Stanley's motion (education), 20 June 1839	Education, 24 June 1839	Liddell's motion, 27 Feb, 1840	Irish Registration, 26 March 1840	Graham's motion (China), 7 April 1840
Cons	present	289	279	300	268	156	274	298	301	259	277	277	242	252	262
	absent	14	–	4	15	19	17	7	8	15	8	7	22	18	7
	paired	11	21	7	28	137	22	10	8	39	34	39	60	47	45
		314	–	311	311	312	313	315	317	313	319	323	324	317	314
Whigs	present	316	313	319	288	171	289	320	319	269	282	275	214	236	275
	absent	11	–	12	23	33	26	9	12	34	20	17	54	52	19
	paired	11	21	7	28	137	22	10	8	39	34	39	60	47	45
		338	–	338	339	341	337	339	339	342	336	331	328	335	339
Doubtful	present	2	–	0	0	0	0	0	0	0	0	0	0	0	0
	absent	2	–	3	2	0	0	0	0	0	0	0	0	0	0
		4	–	3	2	0	0	0	0	0	0	0	0	0	0
Vacant		1	3	2	5	1	7	3	2	2	2	2	5	5	4
Speaker		1	1	1	1	1	1	1	0	1	1	1	1	1	1
	Total	658		655*	658	654*	658	658	658	658	658	657*	658	658	658

* The discrepancies in the total for the 1838 divisions are explained by the absence of members who were on the Durham mission to Canada. For the missing member on the 1839 vote there is no explanation.

Appendix 6 Staffordshire Conservative Association: receipts and expenses from its formation, March 1835 to May 1837

1835

Rooms and meetings	11.15. 0
Printing, stationery etc.	47.15. 2
Professional agents	193.13. 5
	£253. 3. 7

Messrs Briscoe, Horden and Smith's expenses to and from London previous to Sir Francis Goodricke's election	48.12. 0
	£ 48.12. 0

Claims, objections, attendance at Barristers' Courts during 1835

Claimants' shillings paid	38. 8. 0
Rooms	17. 7. 8
Advertising, printing, stationery	83.12. 1
Professional agents	750. 6. 5
Agents, non-professional	18. 8. 0
Witnesses' expenses	37.12. 0
	£946. 4. 2

Business of the Association 20th June 1835 to 20th June 1836

Rooms	6.11. 6
Advertising, printing, stationery	76. 1. 3
Professional agents	122.12. 1
	£205. 5. 3

Claims, objections, attendance at Barristers' Courts, 1836

Rooms	2.17. 6
Advertising, printing, stationery	4. 2. 0
Claimants' shillings paid	3.15. 0
Professional agents	343.17. 0
Witnesses' expenses	7.14.10
	£362. 6. 4

General business 20th June 1836 to 20th June 1837

Rooms	3.11. 6
Advertising, printing, stationery	42.14. 6
Professional agents	132. 2. 3
	£178. 8. 3

Messrs Briscoe, Horden and Smith's expenses to and from London	54.10. 0
	£54.10. 0

Cash paid by Mr Briscoe for collecting subscriptions	10. 6

	Liabilities	£2049. 0. 1
	Receipts	1099.10. 4
	Minus	949. 9. 9

Receipts in detail
The Association –

subscriptions	609. 9. 0
donations	114. 2. 6
	723.11. 6

Registration Fund –

donations		375.18.10
	Total received	£1,099.10. 4

Paid to stationers and others on account	£550. 6.11
Retained by agents on account	236. 5.10
In treasurer's hands	312.17. 7

Source. This statement appears in Kent, 'Party politics in the county of Staffordshire during the years 1830 to 1847', unpublished thesis, App. A. It is taken from the Harrowby MSS.

Appendix 7   Conservative expenses at the 1837 election for Staffordshire North

Cheedle

Innkeepers	50. 5. 0
Printer	3. 1. 4
Solicitor	60. 9. 0
	£113.15. 4

Abbot's Bromley

Innkeepers	66.19. 1
Canvassers, constables, messengers	10. 5. 6
Printers	12. 3. 0
To Benjamin Cape, check clerk	2. 2. 0
To W. T. Smith } Professional Bills	26. 5. 0
W. Robinson	19.12. 0
	£132. 1. 7

Stone

Innkeepers	398. 5. 1
Canvassers, messengers, constables	14. 3.
Printing	9.16. 9
Music, band	3.15. 0
Check clerks	22. 1. 3
Professional bills – solicitors	48. 4. 0
	£496. 5. 1

Stafford

Innkeepers	357.10. 7
Canvassers, messengers, constables	40. 6. 0
Printers	41.17. 2
Music – Weston band	8. 0. 0
Flag carriers	1.10. 0
Garland carrier	15. 0
Ringers etc. – nomination day	4. 4. 0
– polling day	2. 2. 0
Check clerks	17. 6. 6
Professional bills	60.11. 6
	£527.17. 9

Burton[1]

Expenses at Lichfield committee	24. 0. 0
Innkeepers	138. 1. 3
Canvassers, messengers, constables, expresses	5. 2. 0
Printing etc	16. 4. 0
Check and writing clerks	7.16. 6
Professional bills	73.10. 6
	£240.14. 6

Tunstall

Public houses	26.18. 5
Canvassers	3. 6
Music – Tunstall Band	12. 0. 0
Professional bills	26.15. 0
	£65.16.11

Eccleshall

Public houses, refreshment tickets for voters, hire of carriages, waiter, Servants, hostlers etc.	171.19. 5
Canvassers, messengers, constables, expresses	7.11. 6
Printing etc.	5.18. 0
Music	3. 7. 6
Ribbons	16. 1. 3
Check clerks	14.14. 0
Professional bills	71.15. 0
	£291. 6. 8

Leek

Public house bills	578.17. 6½
Canvassers, messengers, constables, expresses	9. 0. 6
Printing etc.	33. 4. 0
Check and writing clerks	26. 5. 0
Ribbons	3. 4. 0
Professional bills	158.19.10
	£809.10.10½

Newcastle

Public house – refreshment tickets	302. 9. 9½
Canvassers, messengers	25.13.10
Printing	69.11. 5
Check and writing clerks	20.14.10
Ringers	3. 0. 0
Professional bills (solicitors)	66. 3. 8½
	£487.12. 9

Burslem

Public houses	132.17. 6
Canvassers, messengers	17. 6. 6
Printing	35. 5. 0
Music	25.14. 0
Ringers	2.10. 0
Ribbons, flags etc.	4. 6. 1½
Professional bills	66.19. 8
	£274.18. 9½

Hanley and Shelton

Public houses	81.19. 3
Canvassers etc.	2. 0. 0
Printing	6. 3. 6
Music	6. 0. 0
Professional bills	49. 2. 0
	£145. 4. 9

Stoke, Penkhull Tenton etc.

Public houses	25. 7. 0
Canvassers etc.	1. 5. 0
Printers	5. 5. 0
Professional bills	26. 5. 0
	£58. 2. 8

General Election charges

Undersheriff for booths, returns	171.15. 9
Chair, dressers	8. 0. 0
Silver for distribution on chairing day	10. 0. 0
Stafford ringers	10. 0. 0
56 copies of register (10s each)	28. 0. 0
Postage	4.16.10
To John Walter, gilding letters for chair	2. 6
	£222.15. 1

Total election expenses

Public houses etc.	2,463.11. 4
Canvassers	133.18. 7
Printing	247.18. 8
Music, flags etc.	80.12.10½
Ringers	9.15. 0
Check clerks	110.19. 3
Professional bills	787. 7. 2½
Other charges	222.15. 1
	13.16. 0
	1. 5. 0
	£4,071. 9. 0

Source. This statement appears in Kent, 'Party politics in Staffordshire', Appendix B. It is taken from the Harrowby MSS.

[1] Something went awry with the Burton account.

Appendix 8   Election results at the leading manufacturing towns, 1832–1865[1]

	1832	1835	1837	1841	1847	1852	1857	1859	1865	*Totals* L	C(P)
Halifax	L L	L C	L L	L L	L P	L L	L L	L L	L L	16	2(1)
Kidderminster	L	L	C	C	P	L	L	L	C	5	4(1)
Warrington	L	C	C	C	C	C	C	C	C	1	8
Rochdale	L	C	L	L	L	L	C	L	L	7	2
Dudley	L	C	C	C	C	C	L	L	L	4	5
Bradford	L L	L C	L C	L C	L L	L C	L C	L C	L C	11	7
Sunderland	L L	L C	L C	L C	L C	L C	L C	L L	L L	12	6
South Shields	L	L	L	L	L	L	L	L	L	9	0
Tynemouth	L	L	L	L	L	L	L	C	L	8	1
Leeds	L L	L C	L L	L C	L C	L L	L C	L C	L C	12	6
Oldham	L L	L L	L L	L L	L P	L P	L L	L L	L L	16	2(2)
Wolverhampton	L L	L L	L L	L L	L L	L L	L L	L L	L L	18	0
Sheffield	L L	L L	L L	L L	L L	L L	L L	L L	L L	18	0
Stockport	L C	L C	L C	L L	L P	L L	L L	L L	L L	14	4(1)
Ashton	L	L	L	L	L	L	L	L	L	9	0
Huddersfield	L	L	L	L	L	L	L	L	L	9	0
Bury	L	L	L	L	L	L	L	L	L	9	0
Gateshead	L	L	L	L	L	L	L	L	L	9	0
Wakefield	L	L	C	L	C	C	C	L	L	5	4
Birmingham	L L	L L	L L	L L	L L	L L	L L	L L	L L	18	0
Wigan	L L	L C	L L	C C	L P	L C	L C	L C	L C	10	8(1)
Blackburn	L L	L L	L C	C C	L C	L L	L C	L C	C C	10	8
Salford	L	L	L	L	L	L	L	L	L	9	0
Newcastle	L C	L L	L C	L C	L L	L L	L L	L L	L L	15	3
Bolton	L C	L C	L C	L L	L P	L L	L C	L C	L C	11	7(1)
Walsall	C	C	L	L	L	L	L	L	L	7	2
Liverpool	L C	L C	C C	C C	L P	C C	L C	L C	C C	5	13(1)
Manchester	L L	L L	L L	L L	L L	L L	L L	L L	L L	18	0
Preston	L C	L C	L C	L L	L L	L C	L C	L C	C C	10	8
Totals L	39	32	32	32	32	35	34	36	33	305	
Totals C(P)	6	13	13	13	13(7)	10(1)	11	9	12		100(8)

C = Conservative   P = Peelite   L = Liberal

[1] This list is taken from the 1851 census list of twenty-nine towns lying within the 'chief manufacturing districts'.

The towns are listed according to the religious denomination of their inhabitants:

More than 50% Anglican		*More than 50% Non-conformist*		*More than 50% Nonconformist and Catholic*
Halifax	56.5%	Rochdale	74.4%	Wakefield
Kidderminster	55.4	Dudley	68.6	Birmingham
Warrington	54.5	Bradford	68.0	Wigan
		Sunderland	67.7	Blackburn
		South Shields	64.5	Salford
		Tynemouth	61.1	Newcastle
		Leeds	59.4	Bolton
		Oldham	58.2	Walsall
		Wolverhampton	56.8	Liverpool
		Sheffield	56.5	Manchester
		Stockport	55.3	Preston
		Ashton	53.0	
		Huddersfield	52.8	
		Bury	52.4	
		Gateshead	51.7	

Appendix 9   Fremantle's tabulation of the 1841 election results
(Fremantle MSS, 110/9)

Losses and gains

	Gains	Losses	Net gains
English boroughs	39	31	8
English counties	24	1	23
Scotch boroughs	2	1	1
Scotch counties	5	3	2
Irish boroughs	5	1	4
Irish counties	5	1	4
Total	80	38	42

Breakdown of Seats

	English boroughs (341)		English counties (159)		English total (500)		Con. majority
	C	L	C	L	C	L	
1840	157	184	114	45	271	229	42
1841	165	174	137	22	302	196	106

	Scotch boroughs (23)		Scotch counties (30)		Scotch total (53)		
	C	L	C	L	C	L	
1840	1	22	18	12	19	34	−15
1841	2	21	20	10	22	31	− 9

	Irish Boroughs (41)		Irish counties (64)		Irish total (105)		
	C	L	C	L	C	L	
1840	14	27	21	43	35	70	−35
1841	18	23	25	39	43	62	−19

Appendix 10 Stanley's Memorandum for the Cabinet on the Corn Laws, 3 November 1845

We are called upon to deliberate as to the measures to be adopted in consequence of the extensive failure of the Potato Crop, principally, though not exclusively, in Ireland. It is proposed, not as the sole remedy, but as an essential first step, to suspend (and it is avowed that in this case to suspend means to repeal) the Corn Laws. I endeavour to look at this question apart from all personal feeling: and if I were convinced that the abolition of these laws was necessary, I hope that I could unite in recommending it, leaving it to others to carry the recommendation into effect. But I am not so convinced. The evil which we have to entertain is not a general scarcity of provisions in the aggregate, at home, accompanied by a superabundant supply abroad. Were that the case, although even then I should be disposed not hastily to abandon my belief in the selfacting principle on which we proposed and have vindicated the existing Corn Laws, the remedy proposed would at least meet the nature of the evil. But our position is widely different. The Potato Crop has very generally failed: but Wheat is a fair average Crop; Barley, though some of it may not be of the first quality, is abundant in quantity; and Oats are far above an average both in quantity and quality. It must be remembered also that admitting that even half the Potato Crop is destroyed, it is the half of such a Crop as hardly ever was known, especially in Ireland. I lay no stress on the fact that the price of Potatoes has not materially risen, because the alarm which has been created has had the effect of freeing large quantities prematurely into the market, and has thus affected the present price, possibly at the expense of the future. But this same panic has caused great speculation in Oats – the description of grain on which, if able to obtain them, the Potato-fed population would naturally fall back. Yet in spite of the probable great demand for Oats, and the operations of the speculators, the last accounts from Ireland represent the price of Oats as again falling; a certain indication of an abundant supply of that description of grain. I more than doubt therefore the fact of there being, in the Country at large, an alarming deficiency in the whole amount of provision for the food of the people; though it is unquestionable that in certain districts there is a lamentable deficiency of that which is the ordinary food of the great mass of the people. But if we have a short supply at home, it is quite certain that our foreign means of supply are very limited. Most of the countries from which we are accustomed to draw our supplies have no surplus to spare, and have closed their ports against exportation. We must look mainly to the Mediterranean and to North America. Now with regard to the latter, as the Eastern states do not supply a sufficiency of grain for their own consumption, our supplies are drawn exclusively from the West; the markets of Montreal and New York check each other; and the produce of the Western States reaches us practically at a duty of 4s the quarter of Wheat. The effect, as far as America is concerned, of opening the ports would be to give to the New York carrying trade the bonus of 3s which is now enjoyed by Canada: and this would be the whole possible reduction, if the consumer were to derive the whole benefit. We do not know what supplies may be expected from the Mediterranean; but we have no reason to anticipate that they will be unusually large. But whatever they may be, the present state of the market is exactly that which would invite foreign speculators. The prices are good (and from the inferiority of a great portion of the English Wheat they are far higher for good Foreign than the average would indicate) with a tendency to rise; precisely the state to induce the transmission of grain to be bonded, and to await still higher prices. We have already in bond above 600,000 quarters. Now what will be the effect of opening the Ports? Not only these 600,000 quarters will at once be thrown upon the market; but the alarm excited by such a measure will induce every Farmer to hurry into the market in order to anticipate the flood of foreign Corn which he will expect shortly to arrive. Prices will fall rapidly and largely. Consumption will be stimulated. Your scanty home supply, far from being economised, your available source in bond will be exhausted; and what is then to be the consequence, six months hence, of a failure in your expected foreign supply? If we have a short crop at home, my firm belief is that opening the ports will ultimately aggravate the danger; while rising prices will at once check consumption, and invite foreign supplies, to await the hour of our greatest necessity.

What then is to be done? Is the Government to remain passive, and with the knowledge which it has of the extent and magnitude of the evil, to take no precautions, and to devise no means of relief. Very far from it. If England were alone concerned, I think such would be the wisest course. In England, if prices are high, most providentially employment is universal, and wages are higher than they were ever known to be. There never was a time at which the labouring population would suffer less from a high price of the necessaries of life. In England also, the different classes will support each other; and if the farmers suffer from the loss of a portion of their crops, they are in some degree indemnified by the price of other parts of their produce, and they may rely on the forbearance, and assistance, of their Landlords. But in Ireland the case is very different. With many of the small farmers and tillers of the soil, the question is not that of loss of profit, but loss of subsistence. They depend on their produce for food, and if it fails, they have no money to buy elsewhere. There is no doubt but that vast numbers of the Irish Peasantry must be supported for a considerable period of this year by charity, or must die of famine. But it does not follow that it must be supported by the Government; and the Government which should attempt such a system would involve itself in incalculable expense and lamentably fail in its object. Even in Ireland, all districts are not, and will not be, equally distressed. In Ireland, as in England, providentially there is at this time more employment and at higher wages than at any former period. In the neighbourhood of great public works, the distress will be very much mitigated; and where the bulk of the population of a district are employed, I would be very cautious in giving Government aid for the relief of individual distress. Such interference tends to check the exercise of private charity, in which the lower class of Irish especially are never deficient. If I were to suggest the course to be taken by the Irish Government, I should say, require every Lord Lieut. of a County to repair to his post. Place yourselves in unreserved communication with them. Among them are men of all parties, who on such an occasion will cooperate with you heartily, and give you valuable assistance. Let them see, each for his own County, and check, the reports of your Constabulary Officers. Where you can confide in them, invite them to associate with themselves such of the leading gentry, or Deputy Lieutenants as they may recommend. Compel them to know the actual state of their own neighbourhoods from week to week; and let the country know that they do know it. Appoint Commissioners, one of whom should be the Chairman of the Board of Works, and the others men well acquainted with Ireland, to advise with the Lieutenants as to works to be undertaken, either of a public or a private nature – facilitate the latter, if necessary, by advances by way of loan – require, if possible, local contributions towards the former. Confine as far as possible Government works to the districts in which there are few resident Landlords with sufficient means to provide for the exigencies of their own neighbourhoods. Let works of whatever description be superintended by men who will neither be bullied nor cheated; pay mainly in food, and only very partially in money. And for this purpose, and also for that of averting absolute famine in districts where all are alike poor and distressed (and such districts there will be) have as accurate information as can be gained from time to time of the amount of provision available in each separate locality and of its price, bearing in mind that from the bulk of food, and from the imperfections of the means of communication, one district may enjoy comparative abundance and cheapness, while another may be suffering famine prices. I think the Government, in such an emergency, ought to go farther. I think that trustworthy Commissioned Officers should be employed, whose duty it should be to check the markets, as was done partially in 1831, by the purchase of provisions where they may be abundant, and transporting them to districts in which exorbitant prices may indicate either absolute scarcity, or artificial scarcity caused by locking up supplies. I am aware that this is an unusual interference of the Government with the ordinary course of supply and demand; but the circumstances are such as to call for unusual interference, and the prevention of famine is a justification of a temporary departure from ordinary rules. I would go farther. If our confidential reports, on the price in the markets, gave us the least reason to suppose that the Oats crop would be insufficient to meet the increased demand upon it consequent on the failure of potatoes, I would, by Order in Council if Parliament were not sitting, and by application to Parliament if it were, take off the duty on Indian Corn, which is applicable to all the same purposes as Oats, and can be imported considerably cheaper. Your supply of that description of food which is most applicable to the particular case for which you have to provide would thus be largely increased. Even if the people were reluctant to use it, its consumption by cattle would set free an equal amount of Oats or other grain. It could be readily obtained, and in large quantities, from every state in the Union, including those on the Atlantic coast. It is the article of which the United States have the greatest abundance, and which they are most desirous of introducing into our Markets. It is said that this proposition has been damaged by its being supported as in the interest of Agriculture. I am so far from seeing the objection, that if you can, with the concurrence of the Agricultural Body, introduce an article which shall, at a time of possible dearth, increase the available supply of cheap and wholesome food, I think it is a great additional recommendation to the proposal. I fling aside at once in such a case all mere party considerations: I endeavour to put by all considerations of our character for capacity, foresight and public consistency; but I must bear in mind that our support of the Corn Laws has been our main inducement to others to give us the support which placed us, and has kept us, in Office; and it must not be forgotten that, come what may, if general distress prevails, we shall have to depend in great measure on the cooperation of the Landed Proprietors in England and in Ireland. Will not the abolition of the Corn Laws, at our suggestion, deprive (not *us*, but) the Government, of that cooperation? Many of the Irish Landlords will already be severe sufferers by the loss of rent, arising out of that very distress which we are about to call on them to assist in mitigating. We are calling on them to make exertions to the utmost of their powers; is it wise, or just, at that very moment to inflict on them increased pecuniary injury, permanently as they will believe & as I believe; but at all events temporarily, from the panic which will be created among all classes of Tenants? The effect of the abandonment of the Corn Laws at this time will not be that of deliberate conviction, but of hasty flight from our position, in consequence of clamour, aided by most unfortunate, but temporary circumstances. I well know that if the Leaders of all parties, and especially the Head of the Government, declare against them, their doom is fixed. Were I satisfied of the necessity of the measure, I would not shrink from the responsibility or the obloquy attending it, nor from the praises which it will receive from our most violent opponents; but I am not so satisfied by anything I have yet heard; and much as I regret differing from Colleagues whose opinions and judgment I respect, for whom I have the highest personal regard, and from one of whom I have never differed on any public question for above twenty years, I cannot bring myself to concur in, and must enter my protest against, advising Her Majesty that the Corn Laws ought to be abandoned.

Stanley   Nov. 3. 1845

Derby Mss, 27/5

Appendix 11 Payments from the central fund to the Constituencies, 1859 elections

Rose's 1859 election notebook contains, on pages 23 to 30, some lists, both of persons and places, with amounts of money attached to them. There has been a deliberate, but careless, attempt to erase the lists (which were written in pencil), perhaps as a precaution against their falling into the hands of the parliamentary commissioners after the statutory requirement of 1854 that agents declare all their expenses. '*For goodness sake be careful about money – & open no account whatever,*' Lord Colville, an Assistant Whip in the House of Lords, wrote to Jolliffe. '*If there was any suspicion your bankers books could be produced. Get all your cheques cashed as you require money*' (Colville to Jolliffe, undated: Hylton Mss, DD/HY/Box 24).

The lists seem most probably to refer to money spent by the party out of its central fund in 1859, but they might be simply amounts requested, not necessarily granted. Or they might be agents' advice of how much money was required. They might, even, be a record of amounts which candidates were prepared to put up on their own account. Since the lists are so selective, however, by far the greatest probability is that they record payments made by Rose and Jolliffe.

The lists are not necessarily complete. Also, the entry of a name more than once may be simply repetition or it may indicate successive payments to the same place or person. The sums which are legible amount to £47,100. Putting each illegible payment at £300 raises the total to £52,500.

It has been possible to identify only some of the names of persons. H. J. Selwin was the Conservative candidate at Ipswich in 1859, R. Benson at Reading, J. Bramley Moore at Lymington, Sir Harry Leeke at Dover, Ralph Earle at Berwick, and Sir J. D. Elphinstone at Portsmouth.

Page 23					
Reading	500	Portsmouth	1,000	Thornton	200
Berwick?	700	Sandwich	1,000	Cooke (Peterboro)	100
Hull?	200	Bedfordshire	200	illegible	500
Selwin	300?	Sir Harry Leeke	300	illegible	150
Chatham	300?	Worcester	300	Bridman?	300
Portsmouth	100?	Taunton	500	Elphinstone	400
Lewes?	500?		£7000		
Bedford	300?	Bristol	500		
Taunton	500?	Bridport	500	*Page 26*	
Bristol?	500?	Winchester	200	There are six illegible entries,	
illegible	100?	Salisbury	200	one of them with the amount	
Winchester	300?		£7050	1,500. A line is drawn	
Salisbury?	200?	B Moore & Greene?	500	underneath those entries,	
Rochdale	500?	London	150	beneath which is the figure	
illegible	500	Newcastle	300	£4,000.	
Dover	300	illegible	7,800?		
illegible	300	Rochdale	200		
Devonport	500	illegible	250	*Page 27*	
Norwich	500	Leicester?	200	Forde	400
		illegible	500	Wayfield?	200
Page 24		Norwich	500		
Banbury	200	Lewes	?		
Benson	500	Taunton	500	*Page 28*	
illegible	700	Chester	250	Kydd	500
illegible	500	Berkshire	500	illegible	200
B Moore	500			Greene?	500
Kydd	200	*Page 25*		Dilbury	100?
illegible	200	There are thirteen illegible		Cooke	100?
H Bull?	200	entries, followed by		Wells	300?
Selwin	400	Forde?	400	illegible	100
Chatham	300	Earle	700	illegible	200

Page 29		
Kydd	200	
illegible	200	
Yelverton?	300 to	
	500	
Mr Benson	500	
B Moore	500	
R Earle?	700	
Newcastle?	500	
Reading	500	
illegible	300?	
illegible	400?	
Selwin	300 to	
	500	
Chatham	300	
illegible	500	
illegible	1,500	
illegible	?	
illegible	300	
illegible	1,000	
illegible	?	
illegible	?	
illegible	300 to	
	500	
Page 30		
Forde?	400	
Worcester	300 to	
	500	
Chatham	300	
Taunton	500	

Appendix 12 Spofforth's account of expenses, 1857 elections

This account was submitted to Jolliffe (Hylton MSS, DD/HY/Box 24/11).

1857	*General Election*	*Mr. Spofforth's Account*	
March 9	Journey to Marlborough to arrange for the support of Messrs. Merriman, the principal Conservatives there, to a Conservative Candidate.	*Paid Railway and other expenses*	1.17.0
10	Journey from Marlbro' to Bath near Chippenham and Devises to arrange Conservative opposition according to instructions engaged till late at night.	*Paid expenses*	1.15.5
11	Journey from Bath to Tewkesbury to arrange for the retirement of Mr. Cox and endeavouring to heal the split in the Conservative Interest Mr. Cox having agreed to abide by the decision of a Conservative Agent as to whether it was the Interest of the Party that he should retire engaged till late at night, Journey from thence to Worcester to see the Conservative supporters there and ascertain their intention with regard to the Election.	*Paid travelling and other expenses*	2. 9.4
12	Journey from Worcester to Stafford to ascertain the State of the Registry and report if any Conservative Candidate would have a good chance to be returned. Attending all day going through Register and conferring with various supporters of the Interest at Stafford and in the Neighbourhood when I was concluded that Lord Ingestre and no other Candidate would be successful writing Report to Mr. Rose accordingly.	*Paid Travelling and other expenses*	2. 2.3
13	Journey late at Night to Chelford in North Cheshire engaged all next day at Knutsford and other Place to see several Gentlemen and ascertain whether Mr. Langford Brooke would be accepted as a Candidate or whether anyone else could successfully oppose the late Members.	*Paid travelling and other expenses*	4. 0.0
14	Journey from Knutsford and to Mr. Traffords and thence to Lichfield travelling all night. Journey from Lichfield to Coventry to see Mr. Wilmot arranging for Conservative opposition to Messrs. Ellis and Paxton engaged all day.	*Paid travelling and other expenses*	1. 8.0
15	Returning to town.	*Paid travelling and other expenses*	2. 1.6
			15.13.6

Time Engaged – night and day – from 9th to 15th March equals 12 days   52.10.0

£68. 3.6

Bibliography

Manuscript sources

Aberdeen MSS (British Museum)
Archdeacon MSS (Buckinghamshire Record Office)
Broadlands MSS (National Register of Archives)
Chevening MSS (Kent Archives Office)
Derby·MSS (Knowsley, Lancashire)
Ellenborough MSS (Public Record Office)
Fremantle MSS (Buckinghamshire Record Office)
Gladstone MSS (British Museum)
Goodwood MSS (West Sussex Record Office)
Goulburn MSS (Surrey Record Office)
Graham MSS (Bodleian Library, Oxford)
Hughenden MSS (Hughenden, High Wycombe)
Hylton MSS (Somerset Record Office)
Peel MSS (British Museum)
Portland MSS (Nottingham University Library)
Stanley MSS (Liverpool Record Office)

Newspapers and journals

Annual Register
Blackwood's Edinburgh Magazine
British Quarterly Review
Chambers' Historical Newspaper (Edinburgh), 1832–35
Companion to the Newspaper; and Journal of Facts in Politics, Statistics, and Public Economy, 1833–36
The Conservative, 1836–37
Conservative Magazine, 1850
Edinburgh Review
Fraser's Magazine
John Bull
Leicester Conservative Standard, 1835–37
Morning Herald
Parliamentary Review and Family Magazine, 1833–34
Standard
The Times
Quarterly Review
Westminster Review

Contemporary pamphlets

(See also the list of pamphlets in R. Stewart, *The Politics of Protection*, Cambridge 1971.)

Address of the Delegates from the Agriculturalists Assembled in London, together with an Address to the Delegates from the Committee of the National Association for the Protection of Industry and Capital throughout the British Empire, London 1850.

Address of the Right Honourable Sir R. Peel, to the Electors of the Borough of Tamworth on the Close of the Poll, July, 25, 1837, Tamworth, 1837.

Analysis of the British House of Commons as at Present Constituted, London, 1823.

The Assembled Commons; or Parliamentary Biographer, London, 1838.

The Assembled Commons, 1836. An Account of Each Member of Parliament, London, 1836.

The Cabinets Compared; or, an Enquiry into the Late and Present Administrations, London, 1828.

A Correct Report of the Addresses of the Right Honourable Sir Robert Peel, Bart., to the Electors of Tamworth, July 24, 1837, and August 7, 1837, Tamworth, 1837.

The Duke of Wellington and the Whigs, London, 1830.

'The Late Crisis', *Academica. An Occasional Journal*, Cambridge, 1858.

A. MACKAY, *Electoral Districts; or the apportionment of the representation of the country on the basis of its population, being an inquiry into the working of the Reform Bill*, London, 1848.

National Association for the Protection of British Industry and Capital. Report of the Provisional Committee, London, 1849.

Observations of Two Pamphlets (Lately Published) Attributed to Mr. Brougham, London, 1830.

The Parliamentary Indicator: containing a list of the Members returned to the Commons' House of Parliament at the general election in January, 1835, London, 1835.

Parliamentary Manual for the Year 1836, London, 1836.

Parliamentary Manual for the Year 1838, London, 1838.

A PARLIAMENTARY REPORTER, *Memoirs, Political and Personal, of the New Ministry*, London, 1852.

The Parliamentary Touchstone, a Political Guide to the House of Commons, London, 1838.

Parties and Factions in England at the Accession of William IV, London, 1830.

Review of the Long Cabinet, in its Decline and Fall, London, 1827.

Speech of H. Gally Knight, Esq., Delivered at the Moot Hall, Mansfield, at the Nomination of Candidates to Serve in Parliament for the Northern division of Nottingham, July 31, 1837, Nottingham, 1837.

Supplement to the Black Book; or, Corruption Unmasked, London, 1823.

Books

ALBERY, W. *A Parliamentary History of Horsham, 1295-1885*, London, 1927.

ALDERMAN, G. *The Railway Interest*, Leicester, 1973.

ALLARD, E. and ROKKAN, S. *Mass Politics*, New York, 1970.

ALISON, SIR ARCHIBALD. *Some Account of My Life and Writings: an autobiography by the late Sir Archibald Alison*, ed. Lady Alison, 2 vols, Edinburgh, 1883.

ALTICK, R. D. *Victorian People and Ideas*, London, 1974.

ANDERSON, O. *A Liberal State at War. English politics and economics during the Crimean War*, London, 1967.

APPLEMAN, P., MADDEN, W. A. and WOLFF, M. eds. *1859: Entering an Age of Crisis*, Bloomington, Indiana, 1959.

ARBUTHNOT, CHARLES. *The Correspondence of Charles Arbuthnot*, ed. A. Aspinall, London, 1941.

ARBUTHNOT, Mrs. *The Journal of Mrs Arbuthnot, 1820-1832*, ed. F. Bamford and the Duke of Wellington, 2 vols, London, 1950.

ARGYLL, GEORGE DOUGLAS. 8th Duke of, *Autobiography and Memoirs*, ed. the Dowager Duchess of Argyll, 2 vols, London, 1906.

ASPINALL, A. *Lord Brougham and the Whig Party*, Manchester, 1927.

ASPINALL, A. *Politics and the Press c. 1780-1850*, London, 1949.

ASPINALL, A. *The Formation of Canning's Ministry, February to August, 1827*, London, 1937.

ASPINALL, A. ed., *Three Early Nineteenth Century Diaries*, London, 1952 (cited as *Three Diaries*).

ASPINALL, A. and SMITH, E. A. eds., see *English Historical Documents*.

BALFOUR, LADY FRANCES. *The Life of George, Fourth Earl of Aberdeen*, London, 1922.

BARING, F. T. 1st Baron Northbrook. *Journals and Correspondence of Francis Thornhill Baring, Lord Northbrook*, ed. the Earl of Northbrook, 2 vols, London, 1902.

BARTLETT, C. J. *Castlereagh*, London, 1966.

BAXTER, M. *In Memoriam R. Dudley Baxter, M.A.*, privately printed, 1878.

BEALES, D. E. D. *England and Italy, 1859-60*, London, 1961.

BEAN, W. W. *The Parliamentary Representation of the Six Northern Counties of England*, Hull, 1890.

BELL, H. C. F. *Lord Palmerston*, 2 vols, London, 1936.

BENNETT, A. *Clayhanger*, London, 1910.

BLAKE, Lord. *Disraeli*, London, 1966.

BLAKE, Lord. *The Conservative Party from Peel to Churchill*, London, 1970.

BLOCK, G. D. M. *A Source Book of Conservatism*, London, 1964.

BRADY, A. *William Huskisson and Liberal Reform*, London, 1928.

BRIGGS, A. ed. *Essays in the History of Publishing, in celebration of the 250th anniversary of the House of Longman, 1724-1974*, London, 1974.

BROCK, M. *The Great Reform Act*, London, 1973.

BROCK, W. R. *Lord Liverpool and Liberal Toryism*, Cambridge, 1941.

BROSE, O. J. *Church and Parliament. The reshaping of the Church of England, 1828-1860*, Stanford, 1959.

BROUGHTON, Lord. *Recollections of a Long Life*, (ed. Lady Dorchester), 6 vols, London, 1909-11.

BROWN, L. *The Board of Trade and the Free-Trade Movement*, Oxford, 1958.

BUCKINGHAM AND CHANDOS, Duke of. *Memoirs of the court of George IV, 1820-1830*, 2 vols, London, 1850.

BUCKINGHAM AND CHANDOS, Duke of. *Memoirs of the Courts and Cabinets of William IV and*

Victoria, 2 vols, London, 1861.

BUCKINGHAM AND CHANDOS, Duke of. *The Private Diary of Richard, Duke of Buckingham and Chandos*, vol. 1, London, 1862.

BUCKINGHAM, J. S. ed. *The Parliamentary Review and Family Magazine.*

BUDGE, I. and URWIN, D. W. *Scottish Political Behaviour*, London, 1966.

BULMER-THOMAS, I. *The Growth of the British Party System*, vol. 1, London, 1965.

BURGHESH, Lord. *see* Westmorland, 11th Earl of.

BURN, W. L. *The Age of Equipoise. A study of the Mid-Victorian generation*, Norton edition, New York, 1965.

BUTT, J. and CLARKE, I. F. ed. *The Victorians and Social Protest*, Newton Abbot, 1973.

BUTTERFIELD, H. *George III and the Historians*, London, 1957.

CAMPBELL, Lord. *Lives of Lord Lyndhurst and Lord Brougham*, London, 1869.

CANNING, GEORGE. *Some Official Correspondence of George Canning*, ed. E. J. Stapleton, 2 vols, London, 1887.

CANNON, J. *Parliamentary Reform, 1640–1832*, Cambridge, 1972.

CAYLEY, E. S. *Reasons for the Formation of the Agricultural Protection Society*, London, 1844.

CHADWICK, O. *The Victorian Church: Part I, 1829–1860*, London, 1967.

CIPOLLA, C. M. *The Economic History of World Population*, rev. edn, Penguin, 1970.

COCKBURN, H. *Journal of Henry Cockburn, being a continuation of the memorials of his time, 1831–54*, 2 vols, Edinburgh, 1874.

COCKBURN, H. *Letters Chiefly Connected with the Affairs of Scotland from Henry Cockburn to Thomas Francis Kennedy, M.P., 1818–1852*, London, 1874.

COLCHESTER, CHARLES ABBOT, Lord. *The Diary and Correspondence of Charles Abbot, Lord Colchester*, 3 vols, London, 1861.

COLCHESTER, CHARLES ABBOT, Lord. *Memoranda of My Life from 1798 to 1859 Inclusive*, London, 1909.

CONACHER, J. B. *The Aberdeen Coalition, 1852–1855. A study in mid-nineteenth-century party politics*, Cambridge, 1968.

CONACHER, J. B. *The Peelites and the Party System*, Newton Abbot, 1972.

COWHERD, R. G. *The Politics of English Dissent*, New York, 1956.

COWLING, M, *1867: Disraeli, Gladstone, and Revolution. The Passing of the Second Reform Bill*, Cambridge, 1967.

COX, H. *A History of the Reform Bills of 1866 and 1867*, London, 1868.

COX, H. *Whig and Tory Administrations During the Last Thirteen Years*, London, 1868.

CREEVEY, THOMAS. *The Creevey Papers. A selection from the Correspondence and Diaries of the late Thomas Creevey, M.P.*, ed. H. Maxwell, 2 vols, London, 1903.

CROKER, JOHN WILSON. *The Correspondence and Diaries of the Late Right Honourable John Wilson Croker*, ed. L. J. Jennings, London, 1885.

DAVIS, R. W. *Political Change and Continuity, 1760–1885: A Buckinghamshire study*, Newton Abbot. 1972.

DISRAELI, BENJAMIN. 1st Earl of Beaconsfield, *Parliamentary Reform. A series of speeches on that subject delivered in the House of Commons by the Right Hon. B. Disraeli, 1848–1866*, ed. M. Corry, London, 1867.

DISRAELI, B. 1st Earl of Beaconsfield, *Lord George Bentinck: a political biography*, London, 1852.

DISRAELI, BENJAMIN. 1st Earl of Beaconsfield, *Whigs and Whiggism: political writings by Benjamin Disraeli*, ed. W. Hutcheon, London, 1931.

DISRAELI, BENJAMIN. 1st Earl of Beaconsfield. *Lord Beaconsfield's Correspondence with his Sister, 1832–1852*, ed. R. Disraeli, London, 1886.

DISRAELI, BENJAMIN. 1st Earl of Beaconsfield, *Letters from Benjamin Disraeli to Frances*

Anne, Marchioness of Londonderry, 1837–61, ed. the Marchioness of Londonderry, London, 1938.

DOBSON, W. *History of the Parliamentary Representation of Preston During the Last Hundred Years*, Preston, 1856.

DOD, C. R. *The Pocket Parliamentary Companion*, London, 1833 *et seq.*

DOD, C. R. *Electoral Facts from 1832 to 1853 Impartially Stated*, Harvester edition, ed. H. J. Hanham, Brighton, 1972.

DUDLEY, 1ST EARL OF. *Letters to 'Ivy' from the First Earl of Dudley*, ed. S. H. Romilly, London, 1905.

EDSALL, N. C. *The Anti-Poor Law Movement, 1833–44*, Manchester, 1971.

ELLENBOROUGH, Lord. *A Political Diary, 1828–1830*, ed. Lord Colchester, 2 vols, London, 1881.

English Historical Documents, 1714–1783, ed. D. B. Horn and M. Ransome, London, 1957; *1783–1852*, ed. A. Aspinall and E. A. Smith, London, 1959.

ERICKSON, A. B. *The Public Career of Sir James Graham*, Oxford, 1952.

FABER, R. *Beaconsfield and Bolingbroke*, London, 1961.

FAIRLIE, H. *The Life of Politics*, London, 1968.

FAY, C. R. *The Corn Laws and Social England*, Cambridge, 1932.

FAY, C. R. *The Corn Laws and Social England*, Cambridge, 1932.

FAY, C. R. *Huskisson and his Age*, London, 1951.

FEILING, K. G. *The Second Tory Party, 1714–1832*, London, 1938.

FERGUSON, R. S. *Cumberland and Westmorland M.P.s from the Restoration to the Reform Bill of 1867*, London, 1871.

FEUCHTWANGER, E. J. *Disraeli, Democracy, and the Tory Party*, Oxford, 1968.

FOORD, A. S. *His Majesty's Opposition, 1714–1830*, Oxford, 1964.

FORRESTER, E. G. *Northamptonshire County Elections and Electioneering, 1695–1832*, Oxford, 1941.

FOSTER, J. *Class Struggle and the Industrial Revolution*, London, 1974.

FRASER, D. *The Evolution of the British Welfare State. A History of Social Policy Since the Industrial Revolution*, London, 1973.

GASH, NORMAN. *Politics in the Age of Peel*, London, 1953.

GASH, NORMAN. *Reaction and Reconstruction in English Politics*, Oxford, 1965.

GASH, NORMAN. *Mr Secretary Peel*, London, 1961.

GASH, NORMAN. *Sir Robert Peel*, London, 1972.

GATHORNE-HARDY, A. E. ed., *Gathorne Hardy, First Earl of Cranbrook, a Memoir*, vol. 1, London, 1910.

GILL, J. C. *Parson Bull of Byerley*, London, 1963.

GLADSTONE, W. E. *Gladstone to his Wife*, ed. A. T. Bassett, London, 1936.

GLADSTONE, W. E. *The Prime Minister's Papers. W. E. Gladstone. 1. Autobiographica; 2. Autobiographical Memoranda* (cited as *Memoranda*), ed. J. Brooke and M. Sorenson. London, 1971–72.

GUTTRIDGE, G. H. *English Whiggism and the American Revolution*, California, 1963 edn.

GUTTSMAN, W. L. *The British Political Elite*, London, 1965.

GUTTSMAN, W. L. ed. *A Plea for Democracy: an edited selection from the 1867 Essays on Reform and Questions for a Reformed Parliament*, London, 1967.

GREVILLE, CHARLES CAVENDISH FULKE. *The Greville Memoirs, 1814–1860*, ed. L. Strachey and R. Fulford, 8 vols, London, 1938.

GWYN, W. B. *Democracy and the Cost of Politics in Britain*, London, 1962.

HANHAM, H. J. *Elections and Party Management: politics in the time of Disraeli and Gladstone*, London, 1959.

HARE, T. *A Treatise on the Election of Representatives Parliamentary and Municipal*, London, 1859.

HARRISON, B. and TRINDER, B. *Drink and Sobriety in an Early Victorian Country Town: Banbury, 1830–1860*, Supplement 4 of *English Historical Review*, 1969.

HARRISON, R. *Before the Socialists: Studies in Labour and Politics, 1861 to 1881*, London, 1965.

HERRIES, E. *Memoir of the Public Life of the Right Hon. John Charles Herries*, 2 vols, London, 1880.

HILL, R. L. *Toryism and the People, 18320–46*, London, 1929.

HIRST, F.W. *Gladstone as Financier and Economist*, London, 1931.

HOBSBAWM, E. J. *Industry and Empire: an economic history of Britain since 1750*, London 1968.

HOBHOUSE, HENRY. *The diary of Henry Hobhouse*, ed. A. Aspinall, London, 1947.

HOLLIS, P. ed. *Pressure from Without in Early Victorian England*, London, 1974.

HORN, D. B. and RANSOME M. eds. *see English Historical Documents*.

HUSKISSON, WILLIAM. *The Huskisson Papers*, ed. L. Melville, London, 1931.

JENNINGS, W. I. *Party Politics: I, Appeal to the People; II, The Growth of Parties; III, The Stuff of Politics*, 3 vols, Cambridge, 1962.

JONES, W. D. *Lord Derby and Victorian Conservatism*, Oxford, 1956.

JONES, W. D. *Prosperity' Robinson. The Life of Viscount Goderich, 1782–1859*, London, 1967.

KEBBEL, T. E. *History of Toryism from 1783 to 1881*, London, 1886.

KEBBEL, T. E. *The Life of the Earl of Derby*, London, 1892.

KEMP, B. *King and Commons, 1660–1832*, London, 1957.

KIRK, R. *The Conservative Mind*, London, 1954.

KITSON CLARK, G. *Peel and the Conservative Party*, London, 1929.

KITSON CLARK, G. *The Making of Victorian England*, London, 1962.

KITSON CLARK, G. *An Expanding Society: Britain, 1830–1900*, London, 1967.

KITSON CLARK, G. *Churchmen and the Condition of England, 1832–1885*, London, 1973.

KNATCHBULL-HUGESSEN, H. *Kentish Family*, London, 1960.

LANG, A. *Life, Letters and Diaries of Sir Stafford Northcote, First Earl of Iddesleigh*, 2 vols, London, 1890.

LEWIS, SIR GEORGE CORNEWALL, Bart. *Letters of the Right Honourable Sir George Cornewall Lewis, Bart., to Various Friends*, ed. G. F. Lewis, London, 1870.

LINDSAY, T. F. and HARRINGTON, M. *The Conservative Party, 1918–1970*, London 1974.

LUBENOW, W. C. *The Politics of Government Growth: Early Victorian Attitudes Toward State Intervention, 1833–1848*, Newton Abbot, 1971.

LUCAS, R. *Lord Glenesk and 'The Morning Post'*, London, 1910.

LUDOVICI, A. M. *A Defence of Conservatism*, London, 1927.

MACHIN, G. I. T. *The Catholic Question in English Politics, 1820–1830*, Oxford, 1964.

MAGNUS, P. *Gladstone*, 2nd edition, London, 1963.

MALMESBURY, EARL OF. *Memoirs of an Ex-Minister*, 2 vols, London, 1884.

MARSHALL, J. D. *The Old Poor Law, 1795–1834* (Economic History Society pamphlet), London, 1968.

MARTINEAU, J. *The Life of Henry Pelham, Fifth Duke of Newcastle*, London, 1908.

McCALMONT, F. H. *The Parliamentary Poll Book*, Nottingham, 1880.

McDOWELL, R. B. *British Conservatism, 1832–1914*, London, 1959.

MELBOURNE, WILLIAM LAMB. 2nd Viscount. *Memoirs of Viscount Melbourne*, ed. W. M. Torrens, London, 1890.

MITCHELL, A. *The Whigs in Opposition, 1815–1830*, Oxford, 1967.

MONYPENNY, W. F. and BUCKLE, G. E. *The Life of Benjamin Disraeli, Earl of Beaconsfield*, 6 vols, London, 1910–20.

MORLEY, J. *The Life of William Ewart Gladstone,* London, 1903, vols

MORLEY, J. *The Life of Richard Cobden,* 2 vols, London, 1908.

NAMIER, L. B. *Crossroads of Power,* London, 1962.

NEALE, R. S. *Class and Ideology in the Nineteenth Century,* London, 1972.

NORMAN, E. R. *Anti-Catholicism in Victorian England,* London, 1968.

NORMAN, E. R. *The Catholic Church and Ireland in the Age of Rebellion, 1859–1873,* London, 1965.

NORMAN, E. R. *A History of Modern Ireland,* London, 1971.

NORTHAM, R. *Conservatism the Only Way,* London, 1939.

NORTHBROOK, 1st Baron. see Baring, F.T.

NORTHCOTE, S. H. *Twenty Years of Financial Policy: a summary of the chief financial measures passed between 1842 and 1861,* London, 1862.

NORTHCOTE, SIR STAFFORD. *Life, Letters and Diaries of Sir Stafford Northcote, first Earl of Iddesleigh; see* Lang, A., ed.

NOWLAN, K. B. *The Politics of Repeal,* London, 1965.

O'GORMAN, F. *The Whig Party and the French Revolution,* London, 1967.

OLNEY, R. J. *Lincolnshire Politics, 1832–1885,* Oxford, 1973.

PARES, R. *King George III and the Politicians,* Oxford, 1953.

PARKER, C. S. *Sir Robert Peel from his Private Papers,* 3 vols, London, 1899.

PARKER, C. S. *The Life and Letters of Sir James Graham,* 2 vols, London, 1907.

PAUL, W. *A History of the Origins and Progress of Operative Conservative Societies,* Leeds, 1838.

PEEL, SIR ROBERT. *Memoirs by the Right Honourable Sir Robert Peel,* 2 vols, ed. the Earl of Stanhope and E. Cardwell, 2 vols, London, 1858.

PEEL, SIR ROBERT. *The Private Letters of Sir Robert Peel,* ed. G. Peel London, 1920.

PERKINS, H. *The Origins of Modern English Society, 1780–1880,* London, 1969.

PHIPPS, E. ed. *Memoirs of the Political and Literary Life of Robert Plumer Ward,* 2 vols, London, 1850.

PINTE-DUSCHINSKY, M. *The Political Thought of Lord Salisbury, 1854–68,* London, 1967.

POPPER, K. *The Poverty of Historicism* (1957), 3rd edn, New York, Harper Torchbook, 1964.

PREST, J. *Lord John Russell,* London, 1972.

PRYDE, G. S. *Scotland from 1630 to the Present Day,* London, 1962.

RAIKES, THOMAS. *Private Correspondence of Thomas Raikes with the Duke of Wellington and Other Distinguished Contemporaries,* ed. H. Raikes London, 1861.

RAIKES, THOMAS. *A Portion of the Journal Kept by Thomas Raikes, Esq., from 1831 to 1847* 4 vols, London, 1857.

READ, D. *Press and People, 1790–1850: opinion in three English cities,* London, 1961.

READ, D. *Cobden and Bright: a Victorian political partnership,* London, 1967.

ROBSON, R. ed. *Ideas and Institution of Victorian Britain,* London 1967.

ROLE, P. J. V. *George Canning: Three Biographical Studies,* London, 1965.

RESTOW, W. W. *British Economy of the Nineteenth Century,* Oxford, 1948.

RUSSELL, B. *Ideas and Beliefs of the Victorians,* New York, paperback, 1968.

RUSSELL, LORD JOHN. *The Later Correspondence of Lord John Russell,* ed. G. P. Gooch, 2 vols, London, 1925.

ROWE, D. J. ed. *London Radicalism, 1830–1843: a selection from the letters of Francis Place,* London, 1970.

SAINTSBURY, G. *The Earl of Derby,* London, 1892.

SAUNDERS, L. J. *Scottish Democracy, 1815–1840: the social and intellectual background,*

Edinburgh, 1950.

SEYMOUR, C. *Electoral Reform in England and Wales*, reprint, Newton Abbot, 1970.

SMITH, F. B. *The Making of the Second Reform Bill*, Cambridge, 1966.

SMITH, H. S. *The Parliaments of England from George I to the Present Time*, 3 vols, London, 1844–50.

SOUTHGATE, D. *The Passing of the Whigs, 1832–1886*, London, 1962.

SOUTHGATE, D. *'The Most English Minister . . .': the policies and politics of Palmerston*, London, 1966.

SOUTHGATE, D. ed. *The Conservative Leadership, 1832–1932*, London, 1974.

STANMORE, Lord. *The Earl of Aberdeen*, London, 1893.

STANMORE, Lord. *Sidney Herbert, Lord Herbert of Lea*, 2 vols, London, 1906.

STEWART, R. *The Politics of Protection. Lord Derby and the Protectionist Party, 1845–1852*, Cambridge, 1971.

TAYLOR, E. R. *Methodism and Politics, 1791–1851*, Cambridge, 1935.

THOMAS, J. A. *The House of Commons, 1832–1901*, Cardiff, 1939.

THOMIS, M. I. *Politics and Society in Nottingham, 1785–1835*, Oxford, 1969.

THOMPSON, F. M. L. *English Landed Society in the Nineteenth Century*, London, 1963.

TOOKE, T. and NEWMARCH, W. *A History of Prices and of the State of Circulation from 1792 to 1856*, 6 vols, London, 1928 edition.

TROLLOPE, A. *Barchester Towers*, Chapter 18.

TRINDER, B. S. *A Victorian M.P. and his Constituents: the correspondence of H. W. Tancred, 1841–1859*, ed. B. S. Trinder, Banbury Historical Society, vol. 8 for 1967, 1969.

TURBERVILLE, A. S. *The House of Lords in the Age of Reform, 1784–1837*, London, 1958.

VICTORIA, Queen. *The Letters of Queen Victoria*, ed. A. C. Benson, and the Viscount Esher, vols 1–4, London, 1907.

VINCENT, J. R. *The Formation of the Liberal Party, 1857–1868*, London, 1966.

VINCENT, J. R. *Pollbooks: how Victorians voted*, Cambridge, 1967.

WALKER-SMITH, D. *The Protectionist Case in the 1840s*, Oxford, 1933.

WALPOLE, S. *The Life of Lord John Russell*, 2 vols, London, 1889.

WARD, J. T. and WILSON, R. G. ed. *Land and Industry: the landed estate and the Industrial Revolution*, Newton Abbot, 1971.

WATSON, G. *The English Ideology: studies in the language of Victorian politics*, London, 1973.

WEDGWOOD, J. C. *Staffordshire Parliamentary History from the Earliest Times to the Present Day*, in *Collections for a History of Staffordshire*, 1933, vol. iii, *1780–1841*.

The Wellesley Papers. The Life and Correspondence of Richard Colley Wellesley, Marquess Wellesley, 1760–1842, 2 vols, London, 1914.

WELLINGTON, ARTHUR WELLESLEY. 1st Duke of, *Despatches, Correspondence, and Memoranda of Field Marshal Arthur, Duke of Wellington (in Continuation of the Former Series)*, ed. 2nd Duke of Wellington, 8 vols, London, 1867–80.

WHIBLEY, C. *Lord John Manners and his Friends*, 2 vols, London, 1925.

WHITE, R. J. ed. *The Conservative Tradition*, London, 1950.

WHYTE, J. H. *The Independent Irish Party, 1850–9*, Oxford, 1958.

WILKINSON, W. J. *Tory Democracy*, New York, 1925.

WILSON, R. *Canning's Administration: narrative of formation*, ed. H. Randolph, London, 1872.

WILSON, R. G. *Gentlemen Merchants: the merchant community in Leeds, 1700–1830*, Manchester, 1971.

WOODS, M. *A History of the Tory Party*, London, 1924.

YONGE, C. D. *The Life and Administration of Robert Banks, Second Earl of Liverpool*, 3 vols, London, 1868.

YOUNG, G. M. *Victorian England. Portrait of an Age*, 2nd edition, London, 1953.

ZIEGLER, P. *Addington*, London, 1965.

WESTMORLAND, 11th Earl of. *Correspondence of Lord Burghesh, afterwards eleventh Earl of Westmorland, 1808–1840*, ed. R. Weighall, London, 1912.

Unpublished theses

ALDRICH, R. E. 'Education and the political parties, 1830–1870', M.Phil. thesis, University of London, 1967.

ANDREWS, J. H. 'Political issues in the County of Kent, 1820–1846', M.Phil thesis, University of London, 1967.

BICKERSTAFFE, D.'Politics and party organisation in Oldham, 1832–1914', M.A. thesis Durham University, 1964.

BREWER, R. C. 'An investigation into the effects of the 1832 Reform Act on the general elections of 1832, 1835, and 1837 in Ireland', M.Sc. thesis, University of London, 1965.

BYLSMA, J. R. 'Political issues and party unity in the House of Commons, 1852–1857: a scalogram analysis', Ph.D. thesis, University of Iowa, 1968.

CARRICK, A. E. 'Three Northumberland constituencies in the general election of 1852: North and South Northumberland and Tynemouth', M.A. thesis, Durham University, 1965.

CLOSE, D. H. 'The elections of 1835 and 1837 in England and Wales', D. Phil. thesis, Oxford University, 1967.

DAVID, I. W. R. 'Political and electioneering activity in South-East Wales, 1820–1852', M.A. thesis, University of Wales, 1959.

FISHER, D. R. 'The opposition to Sir Robert Peel in the Conservative Party, 1841–1846', Ph.D. thesis, Cambridge University, 1969.

FRASER, P. 'The conduct of public business in the House of Commons, 1812–1827', Ph.D. thesis, University of London, 1957.

GLYNN, J. K. 'The private Member of Parliament, 1833–1868', Ph.D. thesis, University of London, 1949.

JONES, L. 'An edition of the correspondence of the First Marquis of Anglesey relative to the general elections of 1830, 1831, and 1832', M.A. thesis, University of Liverpool, 1956.

KENT, G. B. 'Party politics in the county of Staffordshire during the years 1830 to 1847', M.A. thesis, University of Birmingham, 1959.

NOSSITER, J. T. 'Elections and political behaviour in County Durham and Newcastle, 1832–74', D.Phil. thesis, Oxford University, 1968.

TUNSIRI, V.'Party politics of the Black Country and neighbourhood, 1833–1867', M.A. thesis, University of Birmingham, 1964.

Articles

ALTHOLZ, J. L. 'The political behaviour of the English Catholics, 1850–1867', *J. Brit. Stud.*, November 1964, 89–103.

ANDERSON, O. 'The reactions of Church and Dissent towards the Crimean War', *J. Eccles. Hist.,* Oct. 1965, 209–20.

ANDERSON, O. 'The Wensleydale peerage case and the position of the House of Lords in the mid-nineteenth century', *EHR*, July 1967, 486–502.

ANDERSON, O. 'Gladstone's abolition of compulsory Church rates: a minor political myth and its historiographical career', *J. Eccles. Hist.,* April 1974, 185–98.

ASPINALL, A. 'The Canningite party', *Trans. Roy. Hist. Soc.,* 4th series, 1934, 177–226.

ASPINALL, A. 'The last of the Canningites', *EHR*, 1935, 639–69.

AYDELOTTE, W. O. 'A statistical analysis of the Parliament of 1841: some problems of method', *Bull. Inst. Historical Research,* Nov. 1954, 141–55.

AYDELOTTE, W. O. 'The House of Commons in the 1840s', *History*, Oct. 1954, 249–62.

AYDELOTTE, W. O. 'Parties and issues in early Victorian England', *J. Brit. Stud.,* May 1966, 95–114.

AYDELOTTE, W. O. 'The country gentlemen and the repeal of the Corn Laws', *EHR*, Jan. 1967, 47–60.

BAUGH, D. A. 'The cost of poor relief in south-east England, 1790–1834', *Econ. Hr*, Feb. 1975, 50–68.

BEALES, D. E. D. 'Parliamentary parties and the "independent" member, 1810–1860', in Robson ed. *Ideas and Institutions of Victorian Britain*, 1–19.

BEALES, D. E. D. 'Peel, Russell and reform', *Hist. J.,* 4 (1974), 873–82.

BERRINGTON, H. 'Partisanship and dissidence in the nineteenth-century House of Commons', *Parliamentary Affairs*, Autumn 1968, 338–73.

BEST, G. F. A. 'The Protestant constitution and its supporters, 1800–1829', *Trans. Roy. Hist. Soc.,* 5th series, 1958, 105–27.

BLAKE, LORD. 'The Fourteenth Earl of Derby', *History Today*, December 1955, 850–9.

BLAKE, LORD. 'The rise of Disraeli', in *Essays in British History Presented to Sir Keith Feiling*, ed. H. R. Trevor-Roper, London, 1964, 219–46.

BLAUG, M. 'The myth of the old Poor Law and the making of the new', *Journal of Economic History*, xxiii, 1963, 151–84.

BRADFIELD, B. T. 'Sir Richard Vyvyan and the fall of Wellington's government', *University of Birmingham Historical Journal*, xi, 2 (1968), 141–56.

BRADFIELD, B. T. 'Sir Richard Vyvyan and the country gentlemen, 1830–1834', *EHR*, Oct. 1968, 729–43.

BRASH, J. I. 'The Conservatives in the Haddington district of Burghs, 1832–1852', *Trans. E. Lothian Antiquarian and Field Naturalists' Society*, 1968, 37–70.

BRIGGS, A. 'Middle-class consciousness in English politics, 1780–1846', *Past and Present*, April 1956, 65–72.

BRIGGS, A. 'The language of class in early nineteenth-century England', in *Essays in Labour History*, ed. A. Briggs and J. Saville, London, 1960, 43–73.

CAHILL, G. A. 'Irish Catholicism and English Toryism', *Review of Politics*, Jan. 1957, 62–76.

CAHILL, G. A. 'The Protestant Association and the anti-Maynooth agitation of 1845', *Catholic Historical Review*, October 1957, 273–308.

CLARKE, P. F. 'Electoral sociology of modern Britain', *History*, February 1972, 31–65.

CLINE, C. L. 'Disraeli and Peel's 1841 Cabinet', *JMH*, Dec, 1939, 509–12.

CLIVE, J. 'The *Edinburgh Review*: the life and death of a periodical', in Briggs ed., *Essays in the History of Publishing*, 114–40.

CLOSE, D. H. 'The formation of a two-party alignment in the House of Commons between 1832 and 1841', *EHR*, April 1969, 257–77.

CONACHER, J. B. 'The British party system between the Reform Acts of 1832 and 1867', *Canadian Historical Association Report*, 1955, 69–78.

CONACHER, J. B. 'Peel and the Peelites, 1846–50', *EHR*, July 1958, 431–52.

CONACHER, J. B. 'The politics of the "Papal aggression" crisis, 1850–51', *Canadian Catholic Historical Association Report*, 1959, 13–27.

CONDON, M. D. 'The Irish Church and the reform ministries', *J. Brit. Stud.*, May 1964, 120–42.

COWLING, M. 'Disraeli, Derby and fusion, October 1865 to July 1866', *Hist. J.*, viii, 1 (1965), 31–71.

CROMWELL, V. 'The losing of the initiative by the House of Commons, 1780–1914', *Trans. Roy. Hist. Soc.*, 5th series, 1968, 1–23.

CUNNINGHAM, T. P. 'The 1852 general election in County Cavan', *Briefne*, 1966, 108–35.

CUNNINGHAM, T. P. 'The Burrows-Hughes by-election', *Breifne*, 1967, 175–212.

DAVIS, R. W. 'The Whigs and the idea of electoral reform: some further thoughts on the great Reform Act', *Durham University Journal*, December 1974, 79–91.

DREYER, F. A. 'The Whigs and the political crisis of 1845', *EHR*, July 1965, 514–37.

FAIRLIE, S. 'The nineteenth-century Corn Law reconsidered', *Econ. HR*, Dec. 1965, 562–73.

FAIRLIE, S. 'The Corn Laws and British wheat production, 1829–76', *Econ. HR*, April 1969, 88–116.

FERGUSON, W. 'The Reform Act (Scotland) of 1832: intention and effect', *Scottish Historical Review*, xlv, 1966, 105–16.

FINLAYSON, G. B. A. M. 'Joseph Parkes of Birmingham, 1796–1865: a study in philosophic radicalism', *Bull. Inst. Hist. Res.*, 1973, 186–201.

FISHER, D. R. 'Peel and the Conservative Party: the sugar crisis of 1844 reconsidered', *Hist. J.*, xviii, 2 (1975), 279–302.

FRASER, D. 'The fruits of reform: Leeds politics in the eighteen-thirties', *Northern History*, 1972, 89–111.

FRASER, D. 'Areas of urban politics: Leeds, 1830–1880', in *The Victorian City: images and realities*, ed. H. J. Dyos and M. Wolff, London, 1973, ii, 763–88.

FLICK, C. 'The fall of Wellington's government', *JMH*, March 1965, 62–71.

GASH, N. 'Ashley and the Conservative Party in 1842', *EHR*, Oct. 1938, 679–81.

GASH, N. 'F. R. Bonham: Conservative "Political Secretary", 1832–47', *EHR*, Oct, 1948, 502–22.

GASH, N. 'Peel and the party system, 1830–50', *Trans. Roy. Hist. Soc.*, 5th series, 1950, 47–69.

GLICKMAN, H. 'The Toryness of English conservatism', *J. Brit. Stud.*, Nov. 1961.

GOLBY, J. 'A great electioneer and his motives: the fourth Duke of Newcastle', *Hist. J.*, viii, 2 (1965), 201–18.

GUNN, J. A. W. 'Influence, parties and the constitution: changing attitudes, 1783–1832', *Hist. J.*, xvii, 2 (1974), 301–28.

GUTTSMAN, W. L. 'The general election of 1859 in the cities of Yorkshire', *International Review of Social History*, ii, 1957, 231–58.

HANHAM, H. J. 'British party finance, 1868–1880', *Bull. Inst. Hist. Res.*, May 1954,

69–90.

HANHAM, H. J. 'Ashburton as a parliamentary borough, 1640–1868', *Trans. Devonshire Association*, 1966, 206–56.

HEESOM, A. J. 'The Sunderland by-election, September, 1841', *Northern History*, ix, 1974, 62–78.

HENNOCK, E. P. 'The sociological premises of the first Reform Act: a critical note', *Victorian Studies*, March 1971, 321–7.

HILL, B. W. 'Executive monarchy and the challenge of parties, 1689–1832: two concepts of government and two historiographical interpretations', *Hist. J.*, xii, 3 (1970), 379–401.

HIMMELFARB, G. 'The politics of democracy: the English Reform Act of 1867', *J. Brit. Stud.*, May 1966, 97–138.

HOPPEN, K. T. 'Tories, Catholics, and the general election of 1859', *Hist. J.*, xiii, 1 (1970), 48–67.

INGLIS, K. S. 'Patterns of religious worship in 1851', *J. Eccles. History*, April 1960, 74–86.

JOHNSON, D. W. J. 'Sir James Graham and the "Derby Dilly"', *University of Birmingham Historical Journal*, iv, 1 (1953), 66–80.

JONES, I. G. 'Franchise reform and Glamorgan politics in the mid-nineteenth century', *Morgannwg*, 1958, 47–64.

JONES, I. G. 'The Liberation Society and Welsh politics, 1844 to 1868', *Welsh history Review*, i, 1961, 193–224.

JONES, I. G. 'Cardiganshire politics in the mid-nineteenth century: a study of the elections of 1865 and 1868', *Ceredigion*, 1964, 14–41.

JONES, I. G. 'Merioneth politics in mid-nineteenth century', *Journal of the Merioneth Historical and Record Society*, 1968, 273–334.

JONES, I. G. 'Politics in Merthyr Tydfil', *Glamorgan Historian*, x, 1974, 50–64.

JONES, J. R. 'The Conservatives and Gladstone in 1855', *EHR*, Jan. 1962, 95–8.

KEMP, B. 'The general election of 1841', *History*, June 1952, 146–57.

KEMP, B. 'Reflections on the repeal of the Corn Laws', *Victorian Studies*, March 1962, 189–204.

KENT, G. B. 'The beginnings of party political organisations in Staffordshire, 1832–41', *North Staffordshire Journal of Field Studies*, 1961, 86–100.

KITSON CLARK, G. 'The repeal of the Corn Laws and the politics of the forties', *EHR*, Aug. 1951, 1–13.

KITSON CLARK, G. 'The electorate and the repeal of the Corn Laws', *Trans. Roy. Hist. Soc.*, 5th series, 1951, 109–26.

KITSON CLARK, G. 'Hunger and politics in 1842', *JMH*, December 1953, 355–74.

KRIEGEL, A. D. 'The politics of the Whigs in opposition, 1834–1835', *EHR*, May 1968, 65–91.

LARGE, D. 'The decline of the "Party of the Crown" and the rise of parties in the House of Lords, 1783–1837', *EHR*, Oct. 1963, 669–95.

LAWSON-TANCRED, M. 'The Anti-League and the Corn Law crisis of 1846', *Hist. J.*, iii, 2 (1960), 162–83.

LEWIS, C. J. 'Theory and expediency in Disraeli's policy', *Victorian Studies*, March 1961, 237–58.

LINDSAY, E. C. B. 'Electioneering in East Lothian, 1836–37', *Trans. E. Lothian Antiquarian and Field Naturalists' Society*, 1960, 46–60.

MACAULAY, T. B. 'Gladstone on Church and State', in *Critical and Historical Essays*, ed. A. J. Grieve (Everyman's Library), London, 1967, 3 vols.

MACHIN, G. I. T. 'The Duke of Wellington and Catholic emancipation', *J. Eccles. Hist.*, Oct. 1963, 190–208.

MACHIN, G. I. T. 'The Maynooth grant, the Dissenters and disestablishment, 1845–47', *EHR*, Jan. 1967, 61–85.

MACHIN, G. I. T. 'Gladstone and nonconformity in the 1860s: the formation of an alliance', *Hist. J.*, xvii, 2 (1974), 347–64.

MARSHALL, J. D. 'Corrupt practices at the Lancaster election of 1865', *Trans. Lancashire and Cheshire Antiquarian Society*, 1952–3, 117–30.

McCORD, N. 'Gateshead politics in the age of reform', *Northern History*, 1969, 167–83.

McCORD, N. 'Some aspects of north-east England in the nineteenth century', *Northern History*, 1972, 73–88.

McCORD, N. and CARRICK, A. E. 'Northumberland in the general election of 1852', *Northern History*, 1966, 92–108.

MOORE, D. C. 'The other face of reform', *Victorian Studies*, Sept. 1961, 7–34.

MOORE, D. C. 'Concession or cure: the sociological premises of the first Reform Act', *Hist. J.*, ix, 1, 1966, 39–59.

MOORE, D. C. 'Social structure, political structure, and public opinion in mid-Victorian England', in Robson, *Ideas of Victorian Britain*, 20–57.

MOORE, D. C. 'The Corn Laws and high farming', *Econ. HR*, Dec. 1965, 544–61.

MOORE, D. C. 'Political morality in mid-nineteenth century England: concepts, norms, violations', *Victorian Studies*, Sept. 1969, 5–36.

MOSSE, G. L. 'The Anti-League: 1844–46', *Econ. HR*, Dec. 1947, 134–42.

NOSSITER, T. J. 'Recent work on English elections, 1832–1935', *Political Studies*, Dec. 1970, 525–8.

NOSSITER, T. J. 'Aspects of electoral behaviour in English constituencies, 1832–1868', in *Mass Politics*, ed. Allard and Rokkan, 160–89.

PERKIN, H. J. 'Land reform and class conflict in Victorian Britain', in *The Victorians and Social Protest*, ed. Butt, 173–239.

ROSE, M. E. 'The Anti-Poor Law movement in the North of England', *Northern History*, 1966, 70–91.

SAINTY, J. C. 'The evolution of the parliamentary and financial secretaryships of the Treasury', *EHR*, July 1976, 566–84.

SALTER, F. R. 'Political nonconformity in the eighteen-thirties', *Trans. Roy. Hist. Soc.*, 5th series, 1953, 125–43.

SMITH, E. A. 'The Yorkshire elections of 1806 and 1807: a study in electoral management', *Northern History*, 1967, 60–90.

SMITH, E. A., 'The election agent in English politics, 1734–1832', *EHR*, 1969, 12–35.

SPRING, D. 'The English landed estate in the age of coal and iron: 1830–1880', *J. Econ. Hist.*, Winter 1951, 3–24.

SPRING, D. 'Earl Fitzwilliam and the Corn Laws', *American Historical review*, Jan. 1954, 287–304.

SPRING, D. 'English land ownership in the nineteenth century: a critical note', *Econ. HR*, April 1957, 472–84.

SPRING, D. 'Lord Chandos and the farmers, 1818–1846', *Huntingdon Library Quarterly*, May 1970, 257–81.

SPRING, D. and CROSBY, T. L. 'George Webb Hall and the Agricultural Association', *J. Brit. Stud.*, ii, 1, 1962, 115–31.

STEWART, R. 'The ten hours and sugar crises of 1844: government and the House of Commons in the age of reform', *Hist. J.*, xii, 1 (1969), 35–57.

STEWART, R. 'Understanding English conservatism with apologies to Joyce Cary', *Canadian Journal of History*, Autumn 1971, 153–69.

STEWART, R. 'The Conservative Party and the "Courier" newspaper, 1840', *EHR*, April, 1976, 346–50.

STUART, C. H. 'The formation of the coalition cabinet of 1852', *Trans. Roy. Hist. Soc.*, 5th series, 1954, 45–68.

TAYLOR, H. A. 'Politics in famine-stricken Preston: an examination of Liberal Party management, 1861–65', *Trans. Historic Society of Lancashire and Cheshire*, 1955, 121–39.

THOMAS, J. A. 'The House of Commons, 1832–67', *Economica*, April 1929, 49–61.

THOMAS, J. A. 'The repeal of the Corn Laws', *Economica*, April 1929, 53–60.

THOMAS, J. A. 'The system of registration and the development of party organisation, 1832–70', *History*, February 1950, 81–98.

THOMPSON, F. M. L. 'English landownership: the Ailesbury Trust, 1832–56', *Econ. HR*, August 1958, 121–32.

THOMPSON, F. M. L. 'Whigs and Liberals in the West Riding, 1830–1860', *EHR*, April 1959, 214–39.

THOMPSON, F. M. L. 'Land and politics in England in the nineteenth century', *Trans. Roy. Hist. Soc.*, 5th series, 1965, 23–44.

URWIN, D. W. 'The development of the Conservative Party organisation in Scotland until 1912', *Scottish Historical Review*, Oct. 1965, 89–111.

VINCENT, J. R. 'The electoral sociology of Rochdale', *Econ. HR*, Aug. 1963, 76–90.

WARD, J. T. 'West Riding landowners and the Corn Laws', *EHR*, April 1966, 256–72.

WARD-PERKINS, C. N. 'The commercial crisis of 1847', *Oxford Economic Papers*, 1950, 74–94.

WELCH, P. J. 'Blomfield and Peel: a study in cooperation between Church and State, 1841–1846', *J. Eccles. Hist.*, April 1961, 71–84.

WHITTINGTON-JONES, B. 'Liverpool's political clubs, 1812–1830', *Trans. Historic Society of Lancashire and Cheshire*, 1955, 117–38.

WHYTE, J. H. 'The influence of the Catholic clergy on elections in nineteenth-century Ireland', *EHR*, April 1960, 239–59.

WHYTE, J. H. 'Landlord influence at elections in Ireland, 1760–1885', *EHR*, Oct. 1965, 740–60.

WILLIAMS, D. 'The Pembrokeshire elections of 1831', *Welsh History Review*, 1960, 37–64.

WILLIAMS, G. A. 'The making of radical Merthyr, 1800–1836', *Welsh History Review*, 1961, 161–87.

WINTER, J. 'The Cave of Adullam and parliamentary reform', *EHR*, Jan. 1966, 38–55.

WOOLLEY, S. 'The personnel of the Parliament of 1833', *EHR*, 1938, 240–62.

WRIGHT, D. G. 'A radical borough: parliamentary politics in Bradford, 1832–41', *Northern History*, 1969, 132–66.

WRIGHT, D. G. 'Leeds politics and the American Civil War', *Northern History*, 1974, 96–122.

Illustrations

1. The first House of Commons elected after the Reform Act of 1832, from the painting by Sir G. Hayter.

2. 'Evidently not content'   *A John Doyle cartoon of 1830 shows the Ultra-Tory Lords (from left) Stanhope, Eldon, Cumberland and Newcastle, who had helped to turn out Wellington's government, alarmed at the prospect of radical Whig reform.*

3. 'Old attitudes in new positions'   *A Doyle cartoon of 1837 shows the former Whig cabinet ministers, Lord Stanley (left) and Sir James Graham, flanking their new leader, Sir Robert Peel, on the opposition front bench.*

4. Sir Henry Hardinge, the unofficial 'Treasurer' of the Conservative organization in the 1830s, from the painting by Sir F. Grant.

5. Sir Thomas Fremantle, the Conservative Chief Whip in the House of Commons, 1837–44, from the painting by E. U. Eddis.

To the Worthy and Independent Electors

OF THE

Borough of Buckingham,

And the adjoining Parishes,

GENTLEMEN,

In the expectation that Parliament will be Dissolved within a very brief period, I hasten to inform you that it is my intention to present myself before you at the approaching Election, as a Candidate for the honour of again representing your ancient and loyal Borough in the great Council of the Nation.

This distinguished honour you have been pleased to confer upon me in six successive Parliaments, and I venture to hope that my public conduct has been such as to entitle me to a continuance of your confidence.

I have endeavoured by zeal and industry in the discharge of my Parliamentary duties, to promote your local interests, and the general welfare of my Country, and to carry into practical effect those principles of Conservative Policy, the advocacy of which first recommended me to your notice, and still continues to be the best passport to your favor.

Among the various important questions which now agitate the public mind, there is one which more immediately affects your interests, dependent as they are on the cultivation of the soil,—I mean the alteration of the Corn Laws proposed by Her Majesty's Ministers. To the substitution of a fixed duty on the importation of Foreign Grain for the present graduated scale, I cannot give my assent, because I am satisfied that no fixed duty could be practically enforced; and that the result of such an experiment would eventually be the entire withdrawal of Legislative Protection from British Agriculture,—a result, which in the complicated and artificial state of property in this country, with the prevailing high prices which are caused by the amount of taxation necessary for the payment of our Public Debt and Establishments, and with the local burdens which press on the Land, would, in my opinion, be ruinous to all those who depend on Agriculture for their support; and which would ultimately prove injurious to the other great interests of the community.

And I am prepared to defend the policy of the present Corn Law, not only on the ground that it affords reasonable protection to the British Farmer, (to which in common with all other producers and manufacturers he is justly entitled,) but because I believe that under its provisions the consumer has obtained, and will obtain, a more steady supply of food at a moderate price, than could be afforded him by an unrestricted trade in corn; for if British agricultural produce were once exposed to free competition with that of other countries, a large portion of our own lands could no longer be cultivated with profit—the labourer in husbandry would be thrown out of employment,—and the vast population of this Empire would be rendered dependent for the means of subsistence, almost exclusively on Foreign nations,—a resource which may at any moment be cut off from us, by the accident of a bad harvest, the hostility of rival states, or the casual interruption of our commercial intercourse with them.

Such is the position in which Her Majesty's present advisers seek to place the people of England by their new Corn Law. It is for you, Gentlemen, and the other great constituencies of the empire, to declare by your votes at the forthcoming Election, whether you will retain at the head of affairs, Ministers who advocate such measures,—who possess the semblance of authority, but without the power or influence of an Administration,—whom the present House of Commons has, by a solemn resolution, pronounced to be unworthy of its confidence,—and who, if I mistake not, will soon be removed by the honest verdict of their countrymen, from the offices which they now hold in violation of the spirit of the Constitution.

I have the honour to be,

GENTLEMEN,

With feelings of gratitude and regard,

Most faithfully

Your obedient humble Servant,

Thos. F. Fremantle.

Swanbourne,
June 11, 1841.

RICHARD CHANDLER, PRINTER, BUCKINGHAM.

6. *The 1841 election address of Sir Thomas Fremantle, Conservative member for Buckinghamshire, is devoted to one issue, the defence of the Corn Laws.*

SWELL MOB AT THE OPENING OF PARLIAMENT.

PUNCH (A.D.), "NOW THEN! WHAT'S YOUR LITTLE GAME?"
D—R—Y. "OUR LITTLE GAME! NOTHIN'—WE'RE ONLY 'WAITING FOR A PARTY.'"

8. *Derby and Disraeli in a Punch cartoon of 1857. 'Swell mob' was the contemporary slang for the upper crust of well-dressed pickpockets who preyed upon 'swell' victims.*

THE MAN WOT PLAYS SEVERAL INSTRUMENTS AT ONCE.

7. *A Punch cartoon of 1845. Lord John Russell looks on dismayed as Peel dons the Whig hat of 'Free Trade', and beats the drum for concessions to Ireland.*

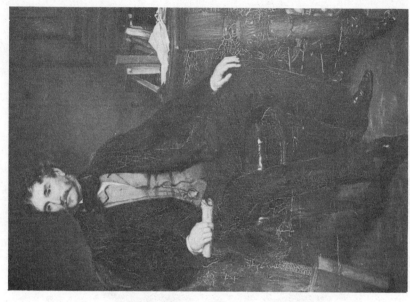

10. *Sir William Joliffe, 1st Baron Hylton, the Conservative Chief Whip in the House of Commons, 1853–59.*

9. *Edward Stanley, 14th Earl of Derby, leader of the Conservative Party 1846–68, from the painting by F. R. Say.*

THE POLITICAL EGG-DANCE.

12. Disraeli in a Punch cartoon of 1867, nimbly making his way through the reform battlefield without breaking any eggs.

THE HONEST POTBOY.

Derby (aside) "DON'T FROTH IT UP THIS TIME, BEN. GOOD 'MEASURE—THE INSPECTORS HAVE THEIR EYE ON US"

11. Disraeli and Derby in a Punch cartoon of 1867, bowing to circumstances and drawing up unadulterated reform.

13. Stratfield Saye, the Berkshire manor house bought for the Duke of Wellington by the nation in 1817.

14. Drayton Manor, Sir Robert Peel's country house in Staffordshire.

15. *Knowsley Hall, the Lancashire Seat of the Derby family since the fifteenth century.*

16. *Hughenden Manor, Buckinghamshire, the Queen Anne house bought by Disraeli with the help of Lord George Bentinck in 1848.*

Index